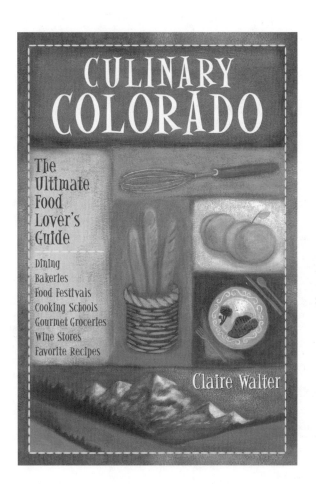

CULINARY
COLORADO

The
Ultimate
Food
Lover's
Guide

Dining
Bakeries
Food Festivals
Cooking Schools
Gourmet Groceries
Wine Stores
Favorite Recipes

Claire Walter

FULCRUM PUBLISHING

Golden, Colorado

This book is dedicated to the dedicated—

to the bakers, butchers, cheese makers, chefs,

culinary instructors, farmers, ranchers, restaurateurs, retailers,

wine makers, and other visionaries who are committed to

putting fine food and wine on Colorado's tables.

Text copyright © 2003 Claire Walter
Illustrations copyright © 2003 Fulcrum Publishing, Inc.

The information in *Culinary Colorado* is accurate as of May 2003. Prices, hours of operation, addresses, phone numbers, websites, and other items change rapidly. If something in the book is incorrect, please write to the author in care of Fulcrum Publishing, 16100 Table Mountain Parkway, Suite 300, Golden, Colorado 80403.

Library of Congress Cataloging-in-Publication Data

Walter, Claire.
  Culinary Colorado : the ultimate food lover's guide / Claire Walter.
    p. cm.
  ISBN 1-55591-455-1 (Paperback : alk. paper)
  1. Food—Guidebooks. 2. Grocery trade—Colorado—Guidebooks. 3.
Cookery—Colorado. I. Title.
TX354.5.W517 2003
641.3'1'025788—dc21
                        2002151211

Editorial: Marlene Blessing, Daniel Forrest-Bank, Michelle Asakawa
Design: Elizabeth Watson
Cover image and interior illustrations: Mindy Dwyer

Printed in the United States of America
0 9 8 7 6 5 4 3 2 1

Fulcrum Publishing
16100 Table Mountain Parkway, Suite 300
Golden, Colorado 80403
(800) 992-2908 • (303) 277-1623
www.fulcrum-books.com

Contents

Introduction

Had I tried to write this book when I first moved to Colorado in late 1988, it would have been very slim, and the research would have been easy. In those days, only a modest number of really fine restaurants were scattered throughout Colorado. Even ambitious chefs seeking to extend their creative reach had a hard time finding purveyors who could guarantee the reliable delivery of the fresh or nontraditional ingredients that imaginative cuisine requires—and a hard time finding customers willing to try cutting-edge foods. Things are different now. Colorado chefs can get almost anything they need—and so can home cooks. Coloradans' knowledge of and appetite for fine food, and wines to go with it, have exploded, paving the way for a book aimed at those who love to eat well. Colorado chefs have begun to receive national recognition. Food festivals, once largely confined to the Food & Wine Classic at Aspen, plus some chili cook-offs, pie-baking contests, and the like, now abound throughout the state and around the calendar. The wine industry, which was just getting underway in 1988, is booming.

Culinary Colorado is a celebration of the present state of dining and home cooking in this state. In addition to listing the best places to eat out in Colorado, I've written this book for people who like to cook and are eager to learn how to cook better. I scouted out food festivals, cooking schools, purveyors of cookware and kitchen utensils, wine specialty shops, and gourmet food stores. Since fresh produce is key to so much good food, Colorado's many excellent seasonal farmers' markets appear in Appendix C (see page 463) and Western Slope farmstands are found in the Grand Junction and the Grand Valley chapter (see page 336). For the home cook, I've also scouted good butchers and retail stores that sell gourmet lines of pastas, spices, herbs, preserves, marinades, sauces, and other gourmet ingredients. And, for those times when a quality take-out meal is called for, I've looked for stores that prepare such items with the same care that any good cook—talented amateur or gifted pro—would be proud to serve.

For updated information and Colorado food news, please visit www.culinary-colorado.com

What You Will Find in This Book

Bakeries

Colorado author Pam Houston once compiled an anthology of her short stories and called it *Cowboys Are My Weakness.* I could write a book called *Good Bread Is My Weakness.* I can't escape the seductiveness of a chewy, crusty, flavorful, lovely loaf, fresh from the oven if possible. A hearty slab, slathered with sweet butter, makes a satisfying breakfast. Two slices of great Italian, rustic, or rye bread bracketing good filling reminds me why the Earl of Sandwich is revered today, not for his military prowess but for the food named after him.

A baker who turns out quality bread and rolls or quality desserts is in the same league. Delectable sweets—whether in the form of a cake, a pie, a continental torte, or a tray of continental-style pastries—get my vote. In summer and fall, when Colorado farms and orchards produce excellent and abundant fruits, bakers and pastry chefs have a field day. Whatever the time of year, good pastries, perhaps accompanied by a silky dessert wine or a foamy cappuccino, make a perfect end to a dinner.

Colorado's storied quality of life improved for me when I finally experienced really good baguettes and flaky croissants. Many bakeries that produce these also have cafés as part of their operations. They serve above-par breakfasts and often make delicious sandwiches, from-scratch soups, quiches, and salads to consume in in-store cafés or take out. These don't qualify as haute cuisine in either the classical or contemporary sense, but they use fresh, quality ingredients and make everything with care. I figure that anything I can do to steer readers away from fast-food alley, whether at home or on the road, is all to the good, so I've included some of those businesses as well.

Cooking Schools and Cooking Classes

Sources of cooking instruction for home cooks, from beginners to knowledgeable enthusiasts and for incipient professional chefs, are detailed here. In addition to formal cooking schools and culinary career programs, I've included cooking classes given in retail stores, private homes, bed-and-breakfast inns, restaurants, or other locations.

Dining

Some people prefer to eat out and are always thrilled to discover a wonderful restaurant, either where they live or when they travel, whether it's a new place or a long-running culinary hit they just haven't tried before.

I have included information about a selection of restaurants culled from the many interesting and creative establishments throughout the state. I don't pretend that it is comprehensive, and I admit that it reflects my own culinary prejudices: the classic cuisines of France and Italy, as well as contemporary and fusion cuisine that blends in Japanese, Chinese, Thai, and other culinary strains. Innovative restaurants now also include modern Mediterranean, Southwestern adaptations of traditional Mexican dishes, and cuisine with strong Pacific Rim influences; you will find some of these restaurants listed as well. In larger cities and sophisticated resorts, I've chosen restaurants that are either cutting-edge or classic in terms of food, atmosphere, and service. In smaller communities, where the local tastes haven't yet matured to support many restaurants at those levels, I've tried to identify some of the best spots in town for a good meal, prepared and served with care.

Whether you are a restaurateur, a gourmand, a home cook, or a professional chef, please understand that any omissions are a matter of space and also my attempt to balance various resources available to the food-obsessed. This book should be viewed as a resource for learning about the ambience, the cuisine, and perhaps a bit of the history of some the state's most interesting places to dine—and the people who created them. For updates on the Colorado culinary scene, or to add your comments, please log onto www.culinary-colorado.com and share your thoughts and experiences with me.

In fact, I view this book as something of a mission. *Culinary Colorado* is an ode to the independents, the small entrepreneurs, the heart and soul of the food industry. Large national chains, in contrast, represent the anonymity and contrived concepts brought about by untrammeled growth along the Front Range and elsewhere in the state. My intent is to persuade readers to seek out distinctive places that prepare, serve, and sell authentic and honest food rather than factory-made, factory-portioned, and corporate-designed products. Even so, a few chains have managed to rise above the usual standard, and I have therefore included them in a section called "The Chain Gang" (see page 409).

I know that restaurants change hands, change chefs, or close altogether, but in order to keep this book lively and somewhat personal, I have taken the risk and talked about chefs who are on the job at this writing. Some of this information will be outdated by the time you read this, but that's the way it goes in the world of books. You won't find the days of the week and hours of the day that these restaurants are open, nor prices or price ranges or reservations policies. These things change too much. Each listing ends with the telephone number and, when available, website, so if a restaurant interests you, call or look it up.

Events

 Colorado is awash with food festivals and culinary events. I've personally attended virtually all of the big ones and many of the small ones. They are arranged in rough chronological order for each locale.

Retail

 Gourmet grocery stores, specialty butchers, and sources for cookware, tableware, and kitchen accessories also are identified. Because many food outlets carry some kitchen equipment, and cookware stores often carry gourmet foods, I consider these together within each chapter.

Wines

I have included a number of noteworthy retail wine stores, in particular specialty wine retailers throughout Colorado. (For information on the state's wineries, I suggest Alta and Brad Smith's *The Guide to Colorado Wineries*.) Many wine specialists regularly or periodically put on wine tastings and orchestrate increasingly popular in-home wine parties for customers, and arrange wine-pairing dinners in cooperation with local restaurants. While wineries and food-and-wine events may pour by the glass for wine tastings, present Colorado law prohibits liquor and wine merchants from opening bottles in their stores for customers to sample. In 2002, the state legislature voted to change to law, but the governor vetoed it, and at this writing, the prohibition against in-store tastings remains.

Other

If it doesn't fit in one of the preceding categories but might be of interest to epicureans, gourmets, and the rest of you reading this book, I've included it in a category titled "Other." You'll find information on miscellaneous topics such as mobile knife sharpening services, ethnic market tours, high-end wine storage, and more.

Recipes

Culinary Colorado is not a cookbook as such, but I couldn't resist the temptation to sprinkle a few recipes in it. Some are simple enough for any moderately experienced cook to follow, and others are complex and require a higher level of skill. But all are tasty and showcase the creativity of Colorado chefs.

What You Won't Find in This Book

Unless I drew the line somewhere, *Culinary Colorado* would have approached the size of an encyclopedia. Therefore, you will find food-service and retail businesses in this book but not ones that sell only wholesale or by mail order. I didn't ferret out the state's small ethnic restaurants or, for the most part, provide descriptions of ethnic grocers, for Susan Permut has done so in *Adventures in Eating* and *Denver's Ethnic Restaurants*. Both books were last published a few years ago, and I hope—in the interest of all food lovers—that updated versions will eventually appear.

Colorado's many fine caterers are not in this book either, but keep in mind that most gourmet grocers and some restaurants offer catering services. I haven't written about brew pubs, because it would seem odd to include brewmasters and microbrews while excluding wineries and wine makers in a culinary book. Nor have I included espresso cafés or bagel bakeries, though the best of them have fueled my culinary expeditions around this big, beautiful state.

The State of Colorado's Cuisine

Perhaps the single most important thing that I have learned in researching this book has been that the passion exists in Colorado for providing us all with the best possible food. I have traveled up and down the Front Range, to the mountains, and to Colorado's agricultural areas. I've attended cooking schools and visited bakeries, wine and cheese shops, farms and orchards. I've talked to chefs and others who are leading the charge for better, fresher, and, often, healthier food that still looks like art and tastes sublime.

During my travels, I have been awestruck by the amount of care, commitment, and plain hard work that goes into putting good, fresh food on our tables. Colorado is populated with organic farmers who hand-tend their fields and orchards, gourmet food stores that seek out truly special ingredients, cheese makers and cheese-sellers, butchers who hand-cut meat, bakers from whose ovens come masterful artisan breads and artful pastries, and chefs who really know food and care about every dish that emerges from their kitchens. Their passions enhance our quality of life beyond measure. We owe every one of them our thanks from the bottom of our hearts and from the top of our palates—and we should make it a point to patronize their businesses. Colorado Proud, a promotional program that encourages consumers— that's us—to purchase agricultural products that have been grown or processed in our state, reminds us to do just that.

Acknowledgments

I owe a debt to so many people for helping in the preparation of this book that it would take a chapter to list all the chefs, restaurateurs, bakers, wine makers and wine sellers, farmers, cheese makers, sommeliers, cooking instructors, store-owners, and others who have shared their knowledge and their passion. So thanks, gang. You know who you are. At Fulcrum Publishing, my deepest thanks go to editor-in-chief Marlene Blessing, managing editor Daniel Forrest-Bank, and copy editor Michelle Asakawa for their invaluable editorial guidance and expertise. And to my husband, Ral Sandberg, goes my gratitude for accompanying me on some of my culinary adventures.

The Front Range

Denver and the Metro Denver Area

Denver now has great eating. What was once a steakhouse type of town is a hotspot for fine food that is creatively prepared by talented chefs. Added to a core of long-standing restaurants that have withstood the test of time are new ones—many of them stylish in looks and cutting-edge in cuisine.

Denver also boasts four major cooking schools (two with highly regarded culinary career programs, one that offers both recreational and professional programs, and one geared for home cooks) and other cooking classes here and there. Artisan breads, exquisite pastries, fabulous cheeses, fresh and often exotic produce, gourmet products from around the world, first-rate meats, and fresh seafood are now readily available throughout the metro area. Cooking utensils from common to special-purpose are found both at retail stores and restaurant-supply houses that welcome home cooks. The best spots are concentrated in and around downtown Denver, Cherry Creek, and, increasingly, Highlands and Highlands North in the northwestern corner of the city. Suburban communities have their share of culinary resources as well.

Bakeries

Adagio Bakery

Adagio is the ultimate neighborhood bakery in one of Denver's most neighborly neighborhoods. Park Hillers stop at this friendly place for a sweet and an espresso, and neighborhood youngsters come in for ice cream—actually, sublime gelato from Gelato d'Italia.

Jerry and Mary Ellen Spinelli, owners of Spinelli's Market, a neighborhood grocery and fine-foods market (see page 76), established the bakery in late 2001 across the street from the market. They named it Adagio (Italian for "slow tempo") because they slowly grew their initial business and then carefully decided that Park Hill also needed a bakery. They enlisted Brenda Campbell, a professional baker who also brought with her some family recipes, including her grandmother's light and moist Orange Date Nut Cake.

Adagio uses only organic, nonbromated flours and other pure ingredients. Look for such excellent breads as baguette, kalamata olive baguette, Pugliese, focaccia;

healthy varieties like oatmeal, sunflower, whole wheat, and occasionally a distinctive English muffin bread, ideal for morning toast. Adagio's focaccia breadsticks are pulled with garlic, butter, and olive oil and rolled in Parmigiano-Reggiano—delicious!

Pies are another strong suit. Lemon meringue, Key lime, or a procession of fruit pies—apple, peach-raspberry, pumpkin, and others according to the season—are available at Adagio. As for cookies, Crybabies, subtly made with coconut and pecans, are house specialties. When almond biscotti are available, grab some. First-rate scones, Danish, brownies, fruit and cheese pastries, and occasionally hand-made croissants are also available.

Cakes are customarily made to order, though you might find something in the display case. Short-notice special orders for walk-in customers, in fact, are an Adagio feature. A customer might come in looking for, say, carrot cake, a fruit tart, or a particular pie. If Campbell has the makings or can run across the street to Spinelli's and get them, she will. "Come back in an hour-and-a-half," she'll say to the customer, "and I'll have it for you." That's a service you won't get in many places at any price.

Adagio Bakery, 4628 East 23rd Avenue, Denver; (303) 388-0904.

The Denver Bread Company

From a modest little bakery in northwest Denver come some of Colorado's most immodestly impressive breads. It is a bread bakery in the Old World sense. There are no tables inviting patrons to sit down, no espresso machines, no sandwich fillings, nothing encouraging customers to linger. Just about all it does is bake bread—and what breads they are!

The sturdy brick building was erected in 1906 to house Carson's Red and White Grocery Store. Later, when supermarkets put neighborhood grocery stores out of business, it became a studio of various types—dance, tae kwan do, and photography among them. Then, in 1994, Greg Bortz began baking bread there, and the combination of traditional artisan breads and the vintage building just feels right.

Flour fills the cracks in the old wood floor, flour sacks are stacked on pallets, worktables are centered in the large room, huge ovens line the walls, and tall baker's racks are for use, not for show. In fact, décor is little more than tomato-red paint on the lofty ceiling and a scattering of antique pieces—an old pie safe, an ancient glass display case originally to show off who-knows-what goods in an elegant retail store. In essence, the vintage brick building is a working bakery with a retail sales counter—and that's it, but who cares, because this bakery is about bread.

The signature bread is a three-pound *boule,* a dense and flavorful round loaf notable for its thick crust and irregular crumb structure. Other breads baked daily include whole wheat and white sourdoughs, white Italian and the rarer Italian *sfilantino,* as well as sensational scones, beautiful brioches, and tasty cinnamon twists. At his discretion, which normally includes just before weekends and holidays, Bortz might add olive bread, sun-dried tomato bread, raisin bread, Swedish peasant bread, rye bread, garlic twists, and focaccia, perhaps in various combinations.

In addition to such usual focaccia add-ins as sun-dried tomato and cheese, Bortz has fiddled—usually successfully—with such unusual combinations as pine nut–saffron,

Bluepoint Bakery

For a bakery that turns out boutique-style baked goods at commercial quantities for selected restaurant retail outlets, what gets Bluepoint Bakery the most media attention is their French Rustic Roll. CityGrille, self-described as one of Denver's power-lunch centers, serves its half-pound, hand-formed, chopped-sirloin on that unusual triangular bun, which is crusty, chewy, and altogether an appropriate foundation for so imposing a burger. Whenever CityGrille gets recognition, so does the Bluepoint Bakery. It is owned by the husband-and-wife chef team of Fred Bramhall and Mary Clark, who once cooked at such local restaurants as Tante Louise (see page 51), Chives, and Dudley's.

The couple started a retail bakery next to Oliver's Meat Market (see page 75) with a signature whole-grain Dakota bread, a dense loaf made with sesame, poppy, sunflower, and pumpkin seeds. Although there is no longer a Bluepoint Bakery retail store, Wild Oats (see page 426) carries Bluepoint's dense and delicious bread, and the bakery supplies such breakfast pastries as scones and breakfast bars to Peaberry's and independent espresso cafés all over town. You've probably eaten Bluepoint's baguettes, focaccia, and other specialty breads without even knowing it.

Bluepoint Bakery, 1721 East 58th Street, Denver; (303) 298-1100.

pear-walnut–Gorgonzola, blood orange–basil, and black diamond plum. He views such sweet, fruit-based versions as ideal holiday breads. In fact, the Denver Bread Company makes more of the holiday season than do most bread bakeries. For instance, Bortz has been known to infuse rosemary into the bread dough and twist it into wreathlike rings. In summer, when fresh fruit abounds, he also does dessert-like focaccia with blueberries or plums.

A native of Ithaca, New York, Bortz started working in restaurants as a teenager, learning on the job and eventually enrolling in the California Culinary Academy, where he was particularly drawn to pastry. He worked at the legendary Chez Panisse and started a wedding-cake business on the side. He moved to Italy for a year and then returned to Colorado, to bake at such restaurants as the Barolo Grill, Q's, Laudisio, and Mel's. While he was baking pastry, he was drawn toward bread, and when he started his own business, he decided on an artisan bread bakery. Still, you can never totally wean a pastry chef from sweets, and the Denver Bread Company does offer a few, such as cookies and biscotti. Bortz admits that he would love to add some pastry as well, but it is difficult to combine such delicate goods with the high heat at which the breads are baked.

If you are a breadaholic, you probably have inhaled the Denver Bread Company's breads in some two dozen of the city's better restaurants and perhaps bought a loaf or two in a gourmet food store or deli. But there's something about visiting the bakery, inhaling its wonderful aromas, and buying bread as newly baked as possible.

The Denver Bread Company, 3200 Irving Street, Denver; (303) 455-7194.

Devil's Food Bakery

Gerald Shorey has served as pastry chef at some of Denver's culinary temples—Mel's, Starfish, and Tante Louise among them. His pastries have also had featured roles in the Brown Palace Hotel's vaunted high tea service. Since 1999, he has operated Devil's Food Bakery on lively Old South Gaylord in Denver's vibrant Washington Park neighborhood. A steady stream of residents stop in for pastry and coffee to kick off the day. "Open bright and surly" is one of the bakery's whimsical slogans. The bright is right, but the surly is morning humor.

People from outside of the neighborhood who come to shop often make the bakery part of their Old South Gaylord pilgrimages. Business is brisk all day, as customers arrive for midmorning pick-me-ups, noontime breaks when the accent is on dessert, afternoon coffee, or something sweet to take home after dinner. Continental baked goods, especially filled pastries iced with a seamless crust of shiny chocolate, are the specialties, but everything is top quality and top taste.

The bright store is done up in Crayola primary colors, and if you hunker down at one of the handful of tables, you can watch a mixed procession of regulars who know exactly what they want and visitors who can't make up their minds approach the glass display cases filled with fine pastries. At Halloween, when Old South Gaylord is closed to traffic so that local youngsters can safely trick-or-treat at local stores, the budding epicures head straight for Gerald's place.

Devil's Food Bakery, 1024 South Gaylord Street, Denver; (303) 733-7448.

Gateaux

Brad High was a mortgage banker turned prep cook at the Brown Palace Hotel turned pastry chef. Kathleen Kenny was studying nursing at Metro State College. A fellow next to her was looking at a culinary book. She took one look—at the book, not the guy—dropped out of school and moved to Rhode Island to study pastry at Johnson & Wales University's culinary program. After a baking sabbatical in Vienna, she returned to Denver and eventually got a job at the Brown Palace, where she met Brad. In May 1999, they launched Gateaux on the fringes of the Golden Triangle. It quickly became known for totally gorgeous and outrageously delicious cakes.

People come for the wonderful pastries and sumptuous cakes, specialty tortes, tarts, pies, petit fours, pastries, cookies, and brownies—whether made and decorated to order or off the shelf—that are the stuff of instant legend.

Special-occasion cakes—wedding and otherwise—are Gateaux's forte. Just look at the ingredients: Cake flavors are almond, banana, carrot, chocolate, German chocolate, marble poppy, white, and yellow. Hold onto your hat for the filling selection, which is a choice of preserves, banana, Bavarian or chocolate Bavarian cream, buttercream or chocolate buttercream, cappuccino, coconut, cream cheese, fresh berries, ganache, hazelnut/praline, Grand Marnier, lemon curd, mint, tiramisu, and white or dark chocolate mousse. Icing choices are buttercream or chocolate buttercream, chocolate ganache, marzipan, rolled fondant, and whipping cream. It's hard to imagine anyone who can't find a combination to adore.

Besides the awesome choice of flavor combinations, Gateaux can produce whatever you might want rendered in butter—not just roses and garlands but a garden's assortment of flowers, ribbons, rolls, figures, just about anything—and in any color combo. Even their "standard" cakes are sublime. It would not be too far-fetched to call them edible works of art. The Tìramisu Cake, a symphony of chocolate candles, fins and flowers atop a divine cake, is celestial. If chocolate rings your chimes, try the Chocolate Praline Torte or the Chocolate Cookies and pastries in single-serving or petit-four size to tickle the eye as well as the palate.

There's a vaguely continental ambience to the store. Select a breakfast pastry or afternoon tea-type sweet and sit in the small shop to enjoy it, and you might feel as if you were somewhere wonderful in Europe. The peach walls, handful of tables and small, tastefully framed prints of continental scenes set the stage, but it's really the exquisite baked goods that will transport you to pastry heaven.

Gateaux, 1160 Speer Boulevard, Denver; (303) 376-0070 or www.gateauxpastries.com.

Le Délice

Le Délice is a fine little restaurant in Cherry Creek North, but what distinguishes it is that it doubles (or triples) as an authentic and excellent patisserie (pastry bakery) and boulangerie (bread bakery), directly connected with the restaurant. Long-time owners Maurice and Nicole Cochard set a very high standard for real French baked goods in Denver, and the present owner, Michel Coumes, has continued to fulfill that expectation since he took over in 2000. Coumes grew up in Provence (yes, Peter Mayle country), where he started helping in his grandfather's restaurant, a classic and nouvelle restaurant of considerable size. His culinary career took him to Paris for 12 years, but the climate and the pace of Provence remained in a corner of his heart. Colorado reminds him of that blessed region in the south of France—with hot sunny summer days and mountains nearby for summer hiking and winter skiing. In France, he might have become a chef-owner of a restaurant like his grandfather, or he might have opened a patisserie or boulangerie. Here, in the proverbial land of opportunity, he combines all three in one business.

When I first walked into the bakery through the restaurant, I was drawn to the pastry case like iron filings to a magnet. The gleaming glass case reminds me of a jewelry box, and inside, the colorful, artful and perfectly rendered pastries shine like edible jewels, made fresh every day. Napoleons, éclairs, tortes, cream puffs, rich chocolate creations of all shapes and sizes, and especially fruit tarts topped with a heap of fresh fruit and coated with a shimmering glaze.

Le Délice has a way with puff pastry. The croissants are flaky and perfect, wonderful butterfly-shaped cookies known as *palmiers* are baked to a perfect sugary crisp and shortbread-type cookies called *lunettes* are filled with raspberry. The bakery also produces excellent melt-in-the-mouth meringue confections, which manage, at the same time, to be light and airy, chewy and crisp. In all, the staff create more than two dozen pastries, all made from scratch—and one is better than the next. As a self-defined guardian of things French, Coumes has also set aside a corner of Le Délice to handle such charcuterie items as various pâtés, mousses, terrines, smoked fish, and specialty sausages. Among the sausage varieties Le Délice carries are *andouillette, boudin noir, boudin blanc,* garlic sausage, and a couple of unusual North African sausages. Most are sold frozen. Le Délice is a couple of doors down from the Continental Delicatessen (see page 66), and if you're a sausage lover, there probably isn't one you can think of that isn't available in one of these two places.

You can also go to Le Délice for a good sit-down meal (breakfast, lunch or dinner) in a pretty and pleasant restaurant. The menu changes seasonally, and daily specials take advantage of what's freshest and best that day. The food is very French, the presentation lovely and the experience relaxed and civilized. If you must eat at work, Le Délice will prepare a French-style lunch served on an attractive tray—brown-bagging with style. The restaurant also puts on monthly wine-tasting dinners that are a treat for the palate and informative as well.

Le Délice, 250 Steele Street, Denver; (303) 331-0972 or www.ledelice.com. A second Le Délice opened in 2002 on Boulder's Pearl Street Mall (see page 96).

Nonna's Bakery

This boutique-size neighborhood bakery is in good company: Sean Kelly's Clair de Lune restaurant is right next door; and Oliver's, a first-rate butcher shop, is across the street, as is Joy Wine & Spirits. Nonna's, Italian for "grandmother's," holds its own—even though there is really no *nonna* and it doesn't particularly specialize in Italian baked goods.

The bakery originally was established within Bella Ristorante in downtown Denver. It outgrew that modest start, but still presents itself as a small store with a tile floor, muraled wall and tasty wares displayed in vintage glass cases. The bread selection runs the gamut from hearth-baked breads with toothsome crusts to various flavored breads and even a shelf full of such healthy breads as banana walnut, cranberry walnut, and zucchini, offered by the slice or by the loaf.

Cookies, scones and bars, rich shortbread, appealing cakes, tempting tarts, and super pastries have won the hearts of virtually everyone in the neighborhood with a sweet tooth. But it's the chocolate desserts—sweet, rich, and utterly delicious—that are the most beguiling and bring neighbors back again and again.

Nonna's Bakery, 1306 East Sixth Avenue, Denver; (303) 839-1820.

Paris Bakery

For some of the best croissants this side of Paris, head for the Paris Bakery. Its unprepossessing setting in a strip shopping center between a vacuum-cleaner repair place and a mattress store does not begin to hint at the exceptional baked goods available there. Everything is done daily in-house.

The pastry counter practically fills the small store. It is loaded with croissants, plain or filled (chocolate is *magnifique*), plus a dazzling assortment of fruit-filled pastries, *palmiers,* meringues and such that look and taste as they would in a patisserie in France. The bakery also produces quality non-French items, including Danish pastries, pies, strudels, cinnamon buns, brownies, and coffee cakes.

As for breads, there are baguettes, of course, some topped with seeds, some plain, as well as *boule*, sourdough, seven-grain, and rye. The lace-curtained store is decorated with a simple mix of prints of Paris and certificates honoring baking excellence on the stucco walls. A couple of tables accommodate patrons, but essentially, this is a take-out bakery. Come early, for the bakery's most popular items go fast, especially on Saturdays.

Paris Bakery, 1268 South Sheridan, Denver; (303) 935-9353.

Pasquini's Baking

South Broadway's Antiques Row boasts a pair of eponymous storefront purveyors of fine baked goods and more—related in ownership by the Pasquini family but otherwise somewhat different businesses. Pasquini's Baking's scrumptious pastries and hearth-baked artisan breads made with organic flour are displayed in antique glass cases near the south end of Denver's best strip of antique shops. The walls of this stylish store are sponge-painted fuchsia, with an end wall done up in multicolored harlequin diamonds. Antique light fixtures cast a pleasant glow, while bunches of herbs and ropes of garlic are overhead reminders of the bakery's Italian roots.

The baking for all the Pasquini's establishments is done at this location. Breakfast pastries, desserts, and up to 20 different breads baked daily draw from many cultural influences: *ciabatta*, Pugliese and *pagnotta* from Italy, assorted sourdoughs and cinnamon raisin walnut from the United States, baguettes from France, and challah (Fridays only). The Italian influence that the bakery's name implies kicks in more strongly at lunch, when *panini* and grilled focaccia sandwiches are made with a variety of fillings.

Pasquini's Pizzeria, a few blocks to the north, offers appetizers, pizzas and pizzettas, pasta, calzones, subs, focaccia sandwiches, and pastries. When you eat inside with the pizza ovens in view, you'll feel as if you were in the heart of New York's Little Italy, Boston's North End, or one of the other centers of southern Italian lifestyle and cooking that are found in every Northeastern city but are rare in the center of the country. In summer, you can eat under a shaded awning with the Broadway bustle a few feet from your table.

Pizza comes with a thin crust (which Pasquini's calls Bianca Style), a thin crust pizza with a thick edge (New York Style), or thick crust (Sicilian Style) with a choice of toppings.

Pasquini's Baking, 1710 South Broadway, Denver; (303) 698-9393; Pasquini's Pizzeria, 1310 South Broadway, Denver; (303) 744-0917. Additional Pasquini's outposts in the greater metropolitan area are at 1336 East 17th Avenue, Denver; (303) 863-8252; and 816 Main Street, Louisville (old town); (303) 673-9400. The website for all is www.pasquinis.com.

Pretty Cakes

One of the simplest bakeries in town assembles what are some of Denver's most elaborate cakes for weddings and other special occasions. In 1991, Phyllis Cano, who once worked for Cakes by Karen in Boulder, opened her own modest business in a low-slung building in northwest Denver. There's nothing modest about her creations, however.

Cano produces the most complicated cakes—layers, pillars, towers, and fountains—and when you see the care she takes and the perfection of her work, the name she selected for her business becomes evident. As a baker, Cano isn't into exotic flavors (she does such basics as chocolate, yellow, white, and marble cakes with raspberry, chocolate, pineapple, and other standard fillings, plus icing of choice). It's the design and assembly that sets Pretty Cakes apart. Nothing is too ambitious or elaborate for her to tackle. She can assemble elaborate multitiered, multicolored cakes based on her design or your imagination.

Cano is the Pied Piper of fancy cakes in Denver. She teaches popular multiweek day and evening classes at the Emily Griffith Opportunity School (call 303-575-4801 to register and learn how to decorate a showy cake). Her cakes have been served to some of Denver's most illustrious locals and guests—including notable politicians and politicians-by-marriage. She baked for former First Lady Barbara Bush, and former President Bill Clinton, who invited her to a function in recognition of her status as a successful minority woman business owner. With his trencherman reputation, it's not inconceivable that he had extra helpings. Most of her customers don't have such name recognition, but they all know a pretty cake when they see one—and Pretty Cakes is where they go.

Pretty Cakes, 5211 Pecos Street, Denver; (303) 480-9622.

Rheinlander Bakery

You'll find one of Colorado's best German bakeries in charming Olde Town Arvada. Marco and Katharina Dimmer founded the Rheinlander Bakery in 1963, and their son, Ed, and daughter-in-law, Maro, still run it. "I started serving customers when I was nine," Ed recalls. "Some of my customers remember me being barely tall enough to see over the counter." He worked in the bakery all through childhood and even through college, and took over the business in 1986, the year he and Maro married.

The building dates back to the early 20th century and was "modernized" in the 1940s or 1950s—I'm not sure which former decade it reminds me of. Wooden floor-to-ceiling cabinets play off a large U-shaped glass counter displaying the wares, with a yellow awning suspended above. The store is luxuriously spacious by today's standards, with enough floor space for customers to wander from one display case to another without bumping into each other as they decide what to buy. When it comes to first impressions, however, the interior appearance—no matter how quaint—takes a backseat to the mouth-watering aroma of fresh baking.

The breads include two German ryes, multigrain bread, Kaiser rolls, Swedish *limpa*, Jewish challah, and other usual and unusual breads. During the holidays, the regular breads give way to such specialties from various countries as *stollen*, *babka*, and at Easter, challah made from colored dough so that the slices resemble rainbows.

The bakery is really a champion in the pastry and cake arena. Everything is made from scratch, using top-quality sweet butter, whole eggs, cream, quality nuts, and real fruit—and sometimes real rum, wine, and brandy. The Dimmers turn out rafts of authentic *Linzertorten* with sweet jam sandwiched between a shortbread crust; slices of *Bienenstich* topped with honey and almonds; *Nussecken,* classic cookies with almond-marizpan filling; those great almond drop cookies called *Florentiners; Schweineohren,* which translates to "pig's ears" but is in truth immensely appetizing; feather-light meringues; and more.

The Rheinlander Bakery also makes such popular American goods as cookies, cherry and apple turnovers, bearclaws, cinnamon rolls, coffee cakes, and other pastries, as well as biscotti that are as good as an Italian bakery would produce. I've spent a lifetime pleasurably trying to find *Apfelstrudel* that's as good as my Austrian grandmother made. Rheinlander Bakery comes close.

They also bake cakes, such as sinful Black Forest cherry, to-die-for Bavarian cream torte, rich chocolate mocha, and divine German seven-layer cakes with raspberry, lemon, or chocolate mousse. A few German boxed foods perch atop the cases, including Oetker baking products and tíramisu mix for those who like to make their own desserts too.

Rheinlander Bakery, 5721 Olde Wadsworth Boulevard, Arvada; (303) 467-1810 or www.rheinlanderbakery.com

Taste of Denmark

Danish pastry is not the only lure at this Lakewood bakery, but the excellent breads that emerge daily from the oven bring customers flocking in. Before Danish-born Ronnie Tronoe and his wife, Diana, launched this suburban bakery in a small neighborhood strip mall in 2000, Tronoe was the pastry chef for the Tivoli Deer Restaurant in exurban Kittredge. European-style display cases hold a dazzling array of pastries. There are authentic renditions of familiar fruit- and cheese-filled items. The Cinnamon Strip is the single best-selling sweet, and the Copenhagen Cookie resembles a small fruit tart, with apple-cinnamon the most popular flavor. Excellent cakes—some to order, some always or usually available—include a Danish cake made with vanilla custard and whipped cream that works spectacularly as a birthday cake and a chocolate ganache made with Belgian chocolate.

European-style multigrain bread, though not traditional, has gained favor in health-conscious Denmark recently. A Spanish-style fat-free, sugar-free bread that is nevertheless crusty and delicious is also popular. There are also classic French baguettes and a small Italian loaf called *la scarpa* after its shoe-like shape. Holiday specials from various cultures include hot-cross buns at Easter, traditional American pies and cheesecake at Thanksgiving, and Danish spice cookies at Christmas. The limited selection of lunch dishes includes scrumptious croissants with several kinds of fillings and, except in summer, individual pizzas.

The simple store is adorned with Danish travel posters on the walls and a handful of tables for customers who want to relax with pastry and coffee and breathe in the heavenly aromas that fill Taste of Denmark.

Taste of Denmark, 1070 South Union Boulevard, Lakewood; (303) 987-8283.

DENVER AND THE METRO DENVER AREA

Cooking Schools, Culinary Colleges, and Cooking Classes

Art Institute of Colorado Culinary Program

The Art Institute of Colorado is part of a chain of specialized, career-training schools in 30 cities, and Denver is one of fewer than 20 with a culinary program. The Institute was founded in 1951, and has been in Denver since 1994. Inside a commercial building off Broadway, the culinary school component, where you'll find hands-on learning and passionate and energetic students aiming for top-toque kitchen careers. The school grounds them in reality and gives them a firm foundation from which to launch into the profession of their dreams.

Three options are available—a one-year diploma program that involves just cooking and related skills, a two-year program that adds restaurant-management and business classes, bakeshop and nonculinary academic classes required for an Associate of Applied Science degree and a four-year Bachelor of Science in Culinary Management program. The school is accredited by the American Culinary Federation.

A few new students come straight from high school, but far more have had some restaurant or hotel experience, and roughly 40 percent are career-changers usually in their 20s or 30s. Some are well-educated home cooks, early retirees perhaps, who want to learn to cook like a pro. The Colorado Art Institute can accommodate them all. The school is set up with professional kitchens, more spacious than students will find in restaurants but equipped like the real thing.

No matter what length the program or the career goals, the schedule is pretty straightforward. Each class session lasts 11 weeks, with three sessions comprising the school year. Everyone starts with a basic skills class that serves as an introduction to food from the chef's perspective. Then the introduction to serious cooking begins, with a focus first on American regional cuisine utilizing classic French techniques applied to our own food traditions. Current Cuisine covers highlights of Asian, Mediterranean, and Eastern European cookery. Nutritional Cooking, of particular interest to aspiring personal chefs, teaches students to recognize basic nutritional needs, dietary restrictions, and recipe modification.

The school conducts three trips to Europe every year for firsthand—and first-palate—exposure to continental cuisine. The school also operates a full-on restaurant called Assignments (see page 31), where students cook, serve, and are fully immersed in the experience of running a fine eating establishment.

Art Institute of Colorado, 1200 Lincoln Street, Denver; (303) 837-0825 or www.aic.artinstitutes.edu.

Cake Crafts

To learn the fine art of cake decorating, check out the classes at this baking-supplies purveyor. Held in a dedicated classroom, the classes begin with four-session Cake Decorating I for beginners, followed by II for intermediates and III for advanced practitioners. They are held weeknights or Saturdays of consecutive weeks. Single-session classes cover such advanced skills as making gum-paste flowers and working with ChocoPan, a baking product that creates the appearance of fondant. Holiday classes on Christmas or Easter cookies, gingerbread houses, Halloween treats, and other topics are scheduled seasonally. There are also parent-child classes to help families share the joy of creativity in the kitchen. The teacher for most of the classes is octogenarian Helen Semba, an internationally recognized authority on cake decorating.

Cake Crafts, 401 South Broadway, Englewood; (303) 761-1522 or www.cakecrafts.net.

Cook Street School of Fine Cooking

If there were a beauty contest for cooking schools, this stylish LoDo school would walk away with top honors. This big, elegant space combines the warmth and charm of mahogany woodwork, bookshelves filled with cookbooks, hand-painted walls and the patina of natural brick, all within the soaring space of a fashionable urban loft. High stools are set at a butcher-block counter surrounding the spacious kitchen. Green-shaded glass lighting fixtures add a nice decorative touch while throwing light onto the counter.

The kitchen design reflects the pleasures of the table, and kitchens just don't get any better than Cook Street's. It boasts commercial-grade gas cooktops, a professional oven, and a granite demonstration island equipped with halogen lights. A separate baking and pastry kitchen features expansive work spaces in both marble and butcher block, plus what is referred to as "the jewel of the Cook Street kitchen": a custom-built wood-fired brick bread and pizza oven, the first oven of its kind built for a cooking school. The functional kitchen easily is transformed into an elegant dining space when instructors and students sit down to the meal they have prepared, eating off good china on tables set with white linens.

The setting is, at the same time, dramatic and congenial. Four levels of classes are offered: Classes for Home Cooks, Kids' Classes, Career Classes, and Semi-Professional Classes, the latter for serious home cooks who already have advanced skills. As such, it is Denver's most comprehensive cooking school.

Classes for Home Cooks

The most fundamental class is called How to Boil Water, a single hands-on session that covers the very foundation of classic cooking. Low-key and stress-free, it shows how fundamental skill levels are all that are needed to prepare a menu that makes for a reasonably impressive meal. Anyone who has been living on take-out prepared foods and microwavable foods but suddenly needs to awe a new love interest or out-of-town family members, or who is intrigued by good food and wants to start learning how to do it, can come away with enough skills to make Salade Citron, Coq au Vin, Roasted New Potatoes with Rosemary and Olive Oil, and Molten Chocolate Cake with Crème Chantilly. Not bad for a few hours of classes.

Classic Techniques I, which requires no previous class experience, is the prerequisite for II and III, which are based on the first series and utilize those skills, and focus on the regional cuisines of France and Italy respectively. Advanced Techniques is the capstone of this series. Beyond are the specialty classes.

The latest specialty series is the Sauce Series, taught by Executive Chef Michael Comstedt, who initiates students into the secrets of making authentic stock, which simmers at the heart and soul of French cuisine and is the essential foundation for that country's signature soups, sauces and other creations. From stocks come sauces, and the second of three sessions explore French sauce cookery, including the five Mother Sauces and their derivatives. Learn to control color, texture, flavor, and consistency through the use of classic sauce techniques, as well as the classic order of service and the art of food and sauce pairing. The final class in the series explores modern sauce constructions, using lighter ingredients and quicker methods to the sauces popularized in contemporary cuisine. This class explores cold sauces, pan sauces, vinaigrettes, marinades, and dessert sauces.

Pastry Techniques teaches the fundamentals of classic French pastry arts. Once you've actually worked with tart, puff pastry, and croissant doughs, made various sweet and savory fillings and assembled cakes, tarts, éclairs, Napoleons, and other dessert and breakfast pastries, these won't seem quite so miraculous anymore—but you will have a new appreciation for pastry chefs who make them perfectly, day after day. You yourself might not have the finesse of a trained pastry chef, but you'll know what goes into the creation of gorgeous French pastries. The Bread Series is similar in scope and scale. You'll work with yeast doughs and learn the basics of bread baking, including basic baguettes, *bâtardes*, sourdoughs and whole-grain loaves—all baked in that "jewel of Cook Street," the custom-built bread oven.

You can wrap Classic Techniques I, II, and III and Pastry Technique into one intensive program in the Semi-Professional Series, which essentially is a crash course leading to ready-for-prime-time culinary skills. If you are thinking seriously about a culinary career and want to enroll in the professional program, half of your already-paid Semi-Professional Series fees will be credited toward the Career Program. What a deal.

Professional Programs

The Career Program, whether in food or wine, consists of three months of classes in the school's 3,000-square-foot professional kitchen, followed by an optional three-month culinary study program in France and Italy. The menu-based curriculum revolves around carefully crafted daily menus that reflect the culinary traditions of particular regions of France or Italy. Students learn about each dish within its cultural and historical context during the lecture and demonstration portions of the class, and then break into teams to prepare the meal. With this approach, the school strives to push students beyond merely the mastery of recipes and techniques *sans* cultural context.

Graduates earn a diploma from the Cook Street School of Fine Cooking, which is a Colorado state-licensed trade school and is accredited by the American Culinary Federation (ACF), and also certificates from the International Wine Guild as a Chef of Wine Arts and Certified IWG Sommelier. All courses are also ACF-approved and count toward its certification of Professional Culinarian.

Social Programs

The school also offers social programs, including demonstration classes by visiting chefs. The Saturday Cooks class involves the commitment of a Saturday afternoon for cooking, followed by an excellent dinner for the cooks and even guests. Rush Hour Wines is a monthly wine-tasting with buffet sampling of matching foods prepared by the school's chefs and culinary students. It is social, it is educational, it is civilized—and it appears on many local foodies' list of favorite events. In the warm months, grilling classes take place on the patio, and the ambience is more cookout than culinary. The school runs a seminar room, rather grandly called the Wine Cellar, in a nearby building, in which International Wine Guild and other wine workshops and events are held that do not require kitchens. A shop in the entrance area carries some kitchen equipment and cookbooks.

Cook Street School of Fine Cooking, 1937 Market Street, Denver; (303) 308-9300 or www.cookstreet.com.

Cook's Fresh Market

This brilliant chef-owned gourmet food store (see page 67) offers cooking classes taught by professional chefs on the market's staff the second Sunday of each month, beginning at 12:30 P.M. The classes follow a particular theme—among them, French or Italian Classics, Barbecue Recipes and Techniques, Soups Galore, Wild Game Cookery, and Holiday Hors d'Oeuvres. The demonstration classes are currently held in the professional kitchen in the back of the store, but this will most likely change after a planned renovation of the store that will include a second kitchen custom-designed for cooking classes.

One of the market's greatest ideas for cooking enthusiasts who want to learn from a pro but cannot commit to a long series of classes is called Sous-Chef for a Day. This is a sensational opportunity to work side by side with the store's gifted professional bakers, butchers, pastry chefs, and real sous-chefs. Sous-Chef for a Day, which at this writing costs $185 per person, includes a monogrammed chef's coat (if you learn from the pros, you might as well look like a pro), an instant-read thermometer, a Forschner 10-inch professional chef's knife, a bottle each of extra-virgin olive oil and balsamic vinegar, and a $25 gift certificate to use in the store.

You can also book a cooking class in your home for yourself and up to seven of your family members or friends and learn to make a full meal consisting of an appetizer, a fish course, a game or poultry course, a meat course, and a dessert. Each participant receives a gift certificate as well.

Cook's Fresh Market, Belleview Promenade, 8000 East Belleview Avenue, Greenwood Village; (303) 743-4148 or www. cooksfreshmarket.com.

Johnson & Wales University

Step onto the handsome Johnson & Wales campus near the old Stapleton Airport; gaze at the lawn, the tall trees, and the mix of Gothic revival and modern buildings; and you'll think you're at an Ivy League College. In fact, it looks as if you might be in Rhode Island, where the school was founded in 1914 by the Misses Gertrude Johnson and Mary Wales as a business college to teach young ladies the new skill of typewriting.

Johnson & Wales has grown into five campuses in the United States (Providence, Rhode Island; Charleston, South Carolina; Norfolk, Virginia; North Miami, Florida; and, since 2000, Denver) plus one in Sweden, enrolling a total of 13,000 students. The JWU College of Culinary Arts is one of the nation's most highly regarded culinary schools. The Denver location looks so venerable because JWU inherited it. The leafy 30-acre campus dates back to the days when it was the Colorado Women's Academy, founded in 1890.

Within the walls of the beautiful old buildings and functional contemporary ones surrounding the central quadrangle are classrooms, dorms, and, most important for culinary students, first-rate professional kitchens. Five hundred students were enrolled in one- and two-year programs on the Denver campus during its fist couple of years of operation, with capacity doubling and four-year programs beginning in 2002–2003.

Four-year programs lead to degrees in Culinary Arts, Baking & Pastry Arts, and Culinary Nutrition, all of which include lab time (i.e., kitchens for cooking and baking classes), classroom time (academics), computer lab (self-explanatory), and externships (practical work in operating restaurants). The school is multiply accredited by the State of Colorado and professional culinary organizations.

JWU also offers a fast-track summer program for students who have had at least two years of restaurant experience and can pass a test demonstrating a core of knowledge and skills. Those who have passed can catch up on the first year's education in one pressure-cooker summer, gain advanced standing, and earn an associate of science degree in culinary arts in just one calendar year. On the other end of the educational spectrum is the Garnish Your Degree program for students who already have at least a bachelor's degree and want to switch to a culinary career. In one calendar year, they can add culinary skills on campus and through externships at local restaurants and also earn an associate of science degree in culinary arts. The 4-term curriculum on campus is followed by an 11-week internship at the Inverness Golf Club or The Broadmoor.

For aspiring chefs and bakers, JWU's kitchens—I mean labs, which *is* what the school calls them—are intentionally set up with different brands of ovens, broilers, burners, and even pots to give students hands-on experience with various kinds of hardware. A restaurant-style storeroom serves as a lab to teach purchasing and inventorying skills. The garde-manger lab is set up for butchering and meat-cutting, another lab accommodates the stocks-and-sauces kitchen, and others house the bakeshops. A 10-station bar teaches beverage-mixing and -service skills and serves as a venue for wine tasting (students under 21 aren't supposed to swallow; good luck!).

Expectations of students match those in the kitchens of fine restaurants. Everyone is required to arrive punctually and in a clean, ironed uniform. Cleaning up at the end of the class is part of the skill set too, as it is in culinary competitions and on the job. And graduates do get jobs—usually soon after graduation and in the restaurant or other establishment of their choice. Johnson & Wales alumni have racked up some impressive recent accomplishments, both in the restaurant business and in terms of culinary recognition. Providence grads Loren Falsone and Eric Moshier stayed in town and opened a restaurant called Empire. In 2000, *Food & Wine* magazine named them among the 10 best new chefs of the year. That same year, two J&W grads were on the team that earned four gold medals, one silver, and a grand champion award at the International Culinary Olympics in Erfurt, Germany.

The garde-manger lab is also the headquarters for the ice-carving club, which is called Chippers, one of several on-campus clubs in a school where there's no chess, cheerleading, debate, or other more traditional collegiate interests. Guest chefs frequent the campus, holding demonstration classes in the baronial splendor of Foote Hall, a treasured Gothic-style landmark. And in 2002, the prestigious Taste of the Nation moved to the campus (see page 58).

Johnson & Wales University, 7150 Montview Boulevard, Denver; (877) JWU-DENVER, (303) 256-9300 or www.jwu.edu.

Kathy Smith's Cooking School

These in-home classes—mostly demonstration, but some participation—for adults and children are offered on weeknight evenings between September and May. Taught by Kathy Smith herself or guest chefs, they cover such topics for the home cook as beginning cooking skills; baking and pastry; American regional cuisines; and French, Italian, Spanish, Mexican, and other ethnic cuisines. Smith also will teach private classes on request.

Smith's spacious kitchen accommodates up to 18 students. Other than baking and pastry, classes cover the preparation of a five- to six-course meal, which is happily consumed in her elegant dining room with suitable wines. In addition to those geared for the adult home cook, children's classes are also available. As many as 40 classes are offered each year. Most are single-session, but some, such as the introductory course for kitchen novices, are available as a three-class series.

Kathy Smith's Cooking School, 4280 East Plum Court, Greenwood Village; (303) 437-6882 or www.kathysmithcooks.com.

Panzano's Cooking with a Chef

Panzano (see page 46) executive chef Jennifer Jasinski shares her culinary knowledge and kitchen tips with kitchen novices to diehard foodies at monthly hands-on cooking classes, held at the restaurant on Saturdays from 10:00 A.M. to 1:00 P.M. Each Cooking with a Chef session covers a different topic, from winter soups to chocolate desserts, but all are designed to give students ideas, instruction, and, most importantly, insight into northern Italian cooking. These classes are followed by a light lunch, included in the price along with all that wisdom, practice, taxes, and gratuities.

Panzano, 909 17th Street, Denver; (303) 296-3525.

The Seasoned Chef Cooking School

The Seasoned Chef Cooking School, with classes directed at home cooks from the novice to the experienced enthusiast, is the embodiment of two women's dreams. Sarah Leffen, a passionate Denver foodie who was teaching cooking at Williams-Sonoma, fulfilled her dream in 1993 by opening her own cooking school. The school's symbol was a tall toque—and pretty soon eager home cooks were going to "the sign of the toque" for a few hours' immersion in the preparation of good food.

After five years, Leffen was ready to move on and planned to close the school. Then, in one of those serendipitous chains that change lives, the two partners who own the building where the school is located told their wives, who told their friend, Susan Stevens, a public-health specialist and cookbook author. Stevens bought and still runs the school, melding her love of good food, her desire to spread the gospel of food and cooking, and her background, which compels her to do good for people. Stevens' book, *Delitefully HealthMark . . . Cooking for the Health of It* might be on your shelf.

The Seasoned Chef's classes are taught by professional cooking teachers and also by some of the Denver area's most acclaimed chefs. Stevens remains on top of every aspect of the school's operation, including being a quiet, organized presence during class. Chefs who have taught there praise her orderliness and her adherence to the schedule, and students love the smooth way in which classes run. Whether demonstration or hands-on, classes run about two-and-a-half to three hours on weeknights and Saturdays. Hands-on classes are limited to 14, but for demonstration classes, expect that all six of the big round tables will be filled. Groups of friends who like to share an evening of food and companionship often sign up together. Many are repeat students, whom Stevens refers to as "my seasoned chefs." The bubbly and congenial ambience during such an evening reminds us all that good food is as much social as it is culinary.

Stevens also offers Cooking 101 "for the person who knows where the kitchen is but not how to use it." This course covers the basic skills that everyone must have. The first part of the two-session course is a demonstration class, followed by a hands-on class a few nights later. The Couples Cooking Workshop, a hands-on class offered once or twice in each of the school's four-month sessions, is the culinary version of the proverbial bicycle built for two. Four hands and two hearts can make one sensational meal, and this class not only teaches the basics but also cooperation and coordination in the kitchen. It is so popular that there's often a waiting list. There are also kids' cooking classes, knife-skills classes called Cutting Edge Workshops, baking and chocolate classes, low-fat cooking classes, cheese courses, ethnic and vegetarian classes, and classes focusing on specific upcoming holidays. Additionally, the Seasoned Chef organizes such off-campus programs as Saturday morning Asian Market Tour and Cooking Workshop and visits to the Cherry Creek Farmers' Market. Instructors and students make the rounds, buy the ingredients that interest them, and come back to the school to cook and eat it.

The clean and functional classroom, a large combined kitchen/dining area, is bright and cheery, with big windows and block prints on a food theme adorning the walls. Good acoustics help a lot when a chef is talking and cooking at the same time.

Stevens has assembled a cookbook called *The Best of the Seasoned Chef*, featuring 150 recipes created by the school's instructors and guest chefs (often with wine-pairing suggestions). "Chef Talk," a chapter of culinary pros' secrets, helps make cooking easier and more pleasurable, and a chapter called "Kitchen Savvy" demystifies food and recipe terminology. Even if you have never taken a class at the Seasoned Chef, this volume is a worthwhile addition to your cookbook collection. Seasoned Chef students receive coupons good for a 10 percent discount at Cooks Mart, Marczyk Fine Foods, Parisi's Deli, and Tony's Meats & Specialty Foods locations.

The Seasoned Chef Cooking School, 999 Jasmine Street, Suite 100, Denver; (303) 377-3222 or www.theseasonedchef.net.

Taste of Thailand Cooking Classes

Noy Farrell, owner of this well-regarded Thai restaurant, periodically offers cooking classes on the flavors and techniques of Thai cuisine. Each session of these participation classes, which are given on Mondays when the restaurant is closed, includes different specialties from the extensive Thai culinary repertoire.

Taste of Thailand, 502 East Hampden Avenue, Englewood; (303) 762-9112.

Warren Occupational Technical Center

This Jefferson County-run technical school includes a one-semester program leading to a certificate in restaurant arts, with optional second- and third-semester extensions for those seeking more extensive training. Externships in local restaurants are also part of the program. Classrooms, a huge kitchen accommodating up to 60 students, two dining rooms, and a restaurant provide the hands-on framework to train for a restaurant career.

Warren Occupational Technical Center, 13300 West Second Place, Lakewood; (303) 982-8600.

The Lakewood campus is also the site of the classwork for the American Culinary Federation's local chapter's three-year apprenticeship program, which leads to a degree from any of Colorado's 11 community colleges. Apprentices attend class on campus one evening per week on such topics as nutrition, sanitation, and restaurant management, and work in more than 30 restaurants, hotels, and caterers in the Denver metro area, which provide students with deep and broad hands-on experience.

ACF Culinarians of Colorado, 1937 Market Street, Denver; (303) 308-1611 or www.afchefs.org/chapter/co013.html.

Tony's Cooking School

Tony's Meats and Specialty Foods (see page 79) sells some of the best meat and seafood in town, has an awesome selection of gourmet ingredients, and carries a strong selection of fresh produce as well. When Tony's Bowles Village Market, the third location, was being designed, logic called for including a venue that might help customers learn what to do with it all. Therefore, the plan evolved to include a demonstration kitchen, located near the deli section.

Some markets offer cooking demonstrations during store hours, but Tony's Cooking School offers weekday evening demonstration classes taught after hours by in-house and visiting chefs. You can expect to find Mick Rosacci and Ben Davis on the roster at least every couple of weeks. Rosacci, one of Tony's sons who is also known as Channel 7's "weekend chef" and who writes food and wine columns for a number of local newspapers around Colorado, loves to get out of the office and lead students through recipes that take advantage of whatever is seasonal. Davis, a graduate of the California Culinary Academy, cooked in California and at several Michelin-starred restaurants in France, taught cooking in New Zealand as part of a culinary exchange program, and came to Denver to open Panzano. He is now executive chef for all three Tony's markets.

The store's set-up is conducive to demonstration classes because—with the addition of a high-capacity convection oven that Tony's bakers also use and instructors might—the kitchen is furnished much like a good home kitchen: four-burner range-top with built-in grill, normal-sized oven, double sink, and adequate but not overly generous counter space. Café tables for two or three are set right next to the counter, and bar-height tables with high stools are arranged behind them so that everyone can see. The instructor wears a microphone so that everyone can hear. With no one farther than one table from the action, questions are encouraged and interaction between instructor and students is easy.

Tony's Cooking School students tend to range from fairly new cooks to veterans with considerable experience in, and much enthusiasm for, the kitchen. Classes are scheduled from 7:15 to 9:30 P.M. Most are one session, though sometimes a multisession course is offered. Classes are built on an ethnic theme (Italian, Mexican, New Orleans/Cajun, etc.), an ingredient (chicken, salmon, herbs), or related techniques (Chef Davis's "Sauces Made Easy," for instance).Tasting classes are sometimes scheduled for cheese, olive oil, or another ingredient. Prices are reasonable, the food (in tasting portions, of course) is delicious, and participants receive a 10 percent discount on all cooking utensils, cutlery, cookbooks, and pantry items (canned or jarred food; the store is closed, so meats and such are unavailable).

Tony's Cooking School, 7421 West Bowles Avenue, Littleton; (720) 377-3680 (general store information). For cooking school information or registration, call (720) 377-3680. Class information is also available at www.tonysmarket.com.

Dining

Adega Restaurant and Wine Bar

Adega is Portuguese for a traditional aboveground wine "cellar." Adega in Denverese means a gorgeous LoDo restaurant built around a huge glass-enclosed wine room. Surrounding it is an elegant dining space, painted in a soothing palette of gray, cream, and black that creates a subdued décor and defers to the wine-room centerpiece. Dark-stained wood floors, an undulating white ceiling, subdued lighting and white napery and frill-free table settings add to the elegant look. Only the burnt-orange upholstery on the clean-line chairs infuses color into the monochromatic scheme. The transformation from Senorita's Cantina to Adega reportedly ran to more than $1 million—perfectly understandable for the culinary triumphs presented there.

Bryan Moscatello, the chef-partner, is a New Jersey native who was drawn to Aspen, where he worked first at the Ute City Banque and then under George Mahaffey at the Little Nell Restaurant. When Mahaffey left, Moscatello stepped in. He hung his toque in various other kitchens, including at the Chateaux at Silver Lake in Deer Valley, Utah, during which time he cooked at New York's James Beard House (see page 458). At the 2001 Food & Wine Classic at Aspen he met Kenneth Fredrickson, one of the world's few master sommeliers and a founding partner of Adega. Less than a year after Adega opened, Moscatello was named one of America's 10 best new chefs of 203 by *Food & Wine* magazine.

Fredrickson took a different route to LoDo. The Idaho native worked in the dining room and the kitchen at Charlie Trotter's in Chicago and Las Vegas and then joined Wolfgang Puck to create the wine and beverage programs for the Las Vegas versions of Spago and Chinois. In 1998, he went to Jackson, Wyoming, to open his own restaurant, Terroir, which quickly became the town's most creative and interesting restaurant, as well the Jackson Hole Wine Company and the Koshu Wine Bar.

In the process, he passed the Sterling Advanced Sommelier Course with the highest possible score and won an American Express Scholarship to the Court of Master Sommeliers' advanced course. In April 2000, he earned a diploma with the highest honors from that prestigious organization, becoming the 41st master sommelier in the United States and one of only 102 in the world.

Moscatello, Fredrickson, and a couple of partners who handle the crucial behind-the-scenes tasks teamed up to create Adega, which opened to great acclaim in 2002. The cuisine won kudos from Denver foodies for preparation and presentation, and the wines caused local oenophiles to swoon with joy. Even the style-mongers were thrilled at the beauty of the place.

For a close-up of the splendid cuisine Moscatello, sous-chef Russ Elliott, and their team contrive, gather a few friends and book the chef's table, set up in an alcove off the kitchen. Whether you dine in the kitchen or in the stylish restaurant, you will find the cuisine to be international in ingredients, contemporary in presentation, and classical in preparation. The menu is influenced by the seasons and therefore changes. Every item in every course is balanced in terms of color, texture, and form, and exquisitely and sparingly plated on pure-white china.

The wine bar menu includes Tastes, Meals, and Main Plate Selections. Tastes include such items as Prosciutto and Melon, Spoons of Truffle Potatoes and Scallops, and Crispy-Fried Mushrooms, and Brie with Tarragon Emulsion. Also noteworthy are the Charcuterie Platter with house-made terrines and sausages and the Artisan Cheese Plate. The Soup Sampler consists of three individual soups in cappuccino-size cups. The upscale Wine Bar Burger is topped with Fourme d'Ambert, a bleu cheese from France's Auvergne region, balsamic grilled onions, and bourbon barbecue sauce and served on a poppy seed bun.

Main Plate Selections is a mix-and-match idea whose time has come. You choose one item from each category: Protein (steak, chicken, salmon, pork, or duck), Starch (mac and cheese, potatoes, basmati rice, or beans), and Vegetable (corn, spinach, seasonal vegetables, sautéed mushrooms, and green beans).

The dinner menu does not overwhelm in size—a dozen or so dishes for each course are par—but it impresses in terms of variety, quality, and sheer creativity. Menu items change with the same dazzling frequency of a runway model—and they are just as dramatic and gorgeous. The menu is divided into Small Plates and Main Plates, all graced with whatever dishes that Chef Moscatello dreams up. In addition to perfect meats, fish, chicken, perhaps rabbit, a pasta or two, and a pasta-less vegetarian entrée grace the dinner menu. You can also order the Chef's Tasting Menu, six exquisite courses and, of course, wine to match.

Pastry chef Stephanie Cina—born and trained in Germany and engaged, among other places, as *démi-chef* patisserie at world-renowned Badrutt's Palace in St. Moritz, Switzerland—is as innovative and persnickety in the pastry realm as Chef Moscatello is in the main kitchen. She prepares eight to 10 desserts each day, roughly divided into fruit-and-cream desserts and chocolate creations. Chocolate is always a hit. White Chocolate Mille Feuille, Peanut Butter Parfait with a chocolate center, Warm Chocolate Gateau, and the gorgeous Chocolate Pyramid are as beautiful as sculptures and scrumptious as well. Her *panna cotta* and coconut crème brulée are grand renditions of these silky classics. She takes advantage of seasonal fruits, such as pears, peaches, and berries at their ripest, and also brings tropical fruits into play.

And then there are the wines. Soon after Adega was open and running, Fredrickson left the day-to-day (or should I say, evening-to-evening) operations to open a wine distribution business in Las Vegas. Sommelier Chris Farnum, who also partnered with Fredrickson in a wine shop called Reservelist (see page 84), now presides over the wine room, which has variously been reported to accommodate anywhere from 5,000 to 8,500 bottles—but who, besides the sommelier, is counting? With 800 wines, including 50 by the glass, it is fortunate that an expert is on hand to provide guidance and make suggestions, even though the wine list has pithy and helpful comments. Adega pours into wine glasses of eight or nine different shapes, so you'll be getting the perfect vessel for each wine you order.

Adega Restaurant and Wine Bar, 1700 Wynkoop Street, Denver; (303) 534-2222 or www.adegadenver.com.

Aix Restaurant

OK, let's get the pronunciation issue out of the way. Aix is pronounced "ex," as in Aix-en-Provence, a well-known town in France's sun-kissed land of olives, tomatoes, farm-raised pigs and chickens, and seafood from the Mediterranean.

Since July 2001, Aix has been Denver's own little corner of Provence. Two talented women chefs, Cyd Anderson and Rachel Woolcott, remade space once occupied by Sean Kelly's The Biscuit into a bright and stylish dining room. Mediterranean colors of lemon yellow and burnt orange were sponged onto the walls. Exposed steel beams, hardwood floors, a copper-topped bar, and hanging room dividers made of silky-feeling, crinkled wire mesh in metal frames add interest. Artist friends created such design as hand-blown glass lighting fixtures and paintings. On warm evenings the patio tables beside the wide sidewalk of the south side of Seventeenth Avenue are especially pleasant. Across the street are Marczyk's Fine Foods and the now-shuttered Cliff Young's, once Denver's most elite restaurant—and also one of the places where Anderson cooked.

Anderson and Woolcott describe their style as "American cuisine with French influences"—and a bit of an Italian accent too. The triad makes for happy juxtapositions of flavors, textures, and, colors. Aix isn't open for lunch and doesn't do daily specials. The owner-chefs prefer to focus on the best preparation and presentation of the items on the seasonally changing dinner menu with five to six appetizers, one or two soups, three salads, six to seven entrées, and about five desserts.

Anyone old enough to remember 1950s television will appreciate the play on words of the Hearts of Romaine Salad with Cyd's Caesar Dressing. Appetizers can be as light as the Aix Vegetable Terrine or as rich as Foie Gras au Torchon, accompanied by poached fruit and Sauterns *gelée*. The Grilled Filet Mignon, a staple on the menu since opening night, is served with braised baby bell peppers, golden raisin and hashed potato cake, and *poivre* compound butter. Expect also to find game, poultry, seafood, and a vegetarian entrée or two. Indulge in a raspberry-rosemary crème brulée with candied citrus zest offered in the spring, decadent Double Chocolate Torte accompanied by lavender *crème anglais,* or anything else that shows up on Aix's dessert menu. The Aix Cheese Platter, served with seasonal fruit, appears on both the appetizer and dessert lists.

Aix's wine list is strongest on California wines, followed by French vintages— more reds than whites, more whites than champagnes, more champagnes than dessert wines.

Aix, 719 East 17th Avenue, Denver; (303) 831-1296 or www.restaurantaix.com.

Assignments

This attractive restaurant isn't your average school chow hall. It is the living laboratory where students from the Art Institute of Colorado culinary programs (see page 20) hone their skills in the kitchen and in the dining room. One instructor runs the kitchen, and another oversees the dining room, but students do all the work as one of their 33-day terms. They spend half the time in the kitchen and half in the dining room, switching midway through. The idea is to teach not only culinary skills needed for the professional kitchen, but front-of-the-house hospitality skills as well. The restaurant also enables students to practice the teamwork necessary to put a meal out for customers, not under the bubble of a kitchen classroom.

Assignments is Denver's only culinary-school restaurant that is open to the public. It operates like a real restaurant, taking reservations and accepting credit cards. The menu changes every three weeks. As you eat, you can watch the student chefs through a large window that opens the kitchen to view, but unlike a restaurant open kitchen, you won't hear what's going on. Culinary students prepare and serve café-style lunches, fancy dinners, and a few multicourse formal feasts every year, when the full artillery of wine glasses, dishes, and flatware is rolled out and correct five-star service is mandated.

Dine at Assignments and you may be sampling the efforts of someone who will become a star chef someday. Think of it like buying a young artist's work—except you won't have to wait for the artwork to appreciate, for the payoff to the palate is immediate.

Assignments, 675 South Broadway, Denver; (303) 778-6625.

Barolo Grill

Barolo Grill, a Cherry Creek hotspot, has been attracting Denver's celebs and trendsetters since it opened in 1992. They come for the sparkling ambience, classy and brassy bar scene, very good Tuscan and Piemontese dishes, and one of the city's biggest wine lists. High prices have not made a dent in Barolo Grill's popularity. The dining room is achingly attractive, with soft colors, bright ceramics, big flower arrangements, and for-show bottles of wine to remind you about this restaurant's wine cellar, which boasts 700 vintages, largely from Italy.

Blair Taylor runs Barolo Grill with a deft hand, and Brian Laird became chef in late 2002. Menus change every couple of weeks, so this week's offerings might not be listed next week, next month, or during the same season next year. You can order à la carte or select the five-course Menu Piemontese with or without paired wines. It honors the splendid wine-gowing region of Piemonte, which displays a culinary kinship with nearby France.

The kitchen demonstrates a knack for taking tradition and tweaking it. Fried Minestrone, for instance, is a combination of the vegetables and beans of this most common of all Italian soups, which are mashed slightly, shaped into balls with polenta and fried. Porcini soufflé is a happy melding of the wild mushroom with the Italian name and cloud-light eggs whose provenance is French.

Barolo Grill has a special affinity for duck. Recent menus have contained the restaurant's signature, and very succulent, roast duckling made with Barolo wine, as well as creamy duck risotto, Pasticcio di Fegato d'Antara (duck-liver pâté encased in puff pastry), and various pasta offerings bathed in duck broth. Using virtually everything but the quack gives the Barolo Grill the imprimatur of European-style thrift and authenticity. So does the periodic appearance of sardines, rabbit, and organ meats on the menu.

Also punctuating this authenticity is Barolo Grill's practice of closing for two weeks for the staff's annual field trip to Italy. They meet chefs, talk shop, taste olives, sample olive oils and cheeses, and sip the local wines. They return, charged up and full of energy from their experience, which is then translated to thrill Denver diners.

Barolo Grill, 3030 East Sixth Avenue, Denver; (303) 393-1040

Beehive Restaurant

Behind a historic storefront just off Sixth Avenue lurks a delightful dinner-only restaurant, with exposed brick walls, flattering lighting, a small open kitchen, and a handful of immaculately prepared dishes. This intimate bistro offers elegant yet straightforward food prepared by San Francisco-trained Janice Henning, the owner/chef, coupled with a funky, mostly French wine selection orchestrated by her husband, Tim Elenteny, the wine expert. Henning takes good, organic food and turns it into simple but exquisite dishes that satisfy the eye and the palate. It's an understated neighborhood restaurant in feel but a precious dining experience in food.

Henning brings many influences to bear on her entrée list. She might offer her version of a popular Italo-American dish such as Sicilian Style Meatballs and Spaghetti. You know and I know that no one's Sicilian grandmother uses Coleman beef or adds pine nuts or currants to the sauce, but happily Henning does. She also offers flavorful and toothsome risotto; roast quail with a stuffing of cornbread, Swiss chard, and bacon; or a grilled rib eye steak served with gnocchi in a cheese sauce made with Bleu d'Auvergne and oven-roasted tomatoes. For each entrée, the menu suggests a suitable wine, available by the glass or bottle, selected, of course, by winemeister Tim Elenteny.

Beehive Restaurant, 609 Corona Street, Denver; (303) 832-5766 or www.beehivedenver.doc.

Buckhorn Exchange

A restaurant that has been around since 1893 must be doing something right. A restaurant that has survived and thrived in a area that was once in the hub of Denver's rail transportation system, stayed there while the neighborhood fallowed, and kept going until modern light rail practically began passing before the door must be doing something right.

What's right is the enduringly popular food—notably generous portions of dry-aged Colorado beef, plus such exotica and game as elk, pheasant, quail, alligator tail, and rattlesnake. Neither the meat-and-potatoes cooking style nor the décor, which is a combination of down-home and hunting lodge—complete with red-checked table-cloths, rare Native American artifacts, 120 antique firearms, and a lot of dead animals (including 500 trophy heads and stuffed birds!)—would normally put an eatery in the same culinary league as such places as Restaurant Kevin Taylor or Tante Louise, but its status as Denver's oldest restaurant elevates it to the top tier of Colorado eateries.

The Buckhorn Exchange, located in an 1888 building, boasts a hand-carved oak bar reportedly dating back to 1857—obviously a later import, because that was two years before the first settlers put down roots in what was to become Denver. The

Buckhorn Exchange holds Colorado state liquor license number one, which, in a sense, says it all.

For lunch, the selection runs to charbroiled beef, seafood and elk, burgers and sandwiches, and even salads and soups. Dinner, called "Supper" on the Buckhorn Exchange menu, is heavy on beef, buffalo, ribs, and game. You can order the Big Steak—big enough for a crowd. The biggest, enough to feed five, are three-and-a-half to four pounds. Combo plates feature such pairings as elk and pheasant, elk and two quail, and buffalo prime rib and pheasant. The "man-sized and man-style" entrées are not for the faint of heart or weak of stomach. They include Smoked Buffalo Sausage, Rocky Mountain Oysters, Sirloin Game Tips, Fried Alligator Tail, and Rattlesnake.

Buckhorn Exchange, 1000 Osage Street, Denver; (303) 534-9505 or www.buckhornexchange.com.

Campo de Fiori

Named after Rome's flower market and translating to "field of flowers," this Cherry Creek North restaurant is related to the Campo de Fiori restaurants previously established in Aspen and Vail. Elizabeth and Luigi Giordani own the three Campo in Denver, and in the mountains. The Cherry Creek location quickly created a buzz and with the see-and-be-seen crowd, who pour into the energetic space that glows with bright color and vibrant form. The walls are muraled, the floors hand-painted, the tables packed tightly, and the noise level matches the atmosphere.

Everything is beautifully presented and served with flair. The large menu lists dozens of dishes built on an Italian foundation and transitioning into the realm of contemporary cuisine—a little all-purpose Mediterranean, a little American. Steamed clams, for instance, could come from New England as easily as Italy. The restaurant offers a couple of simple, and simply delicious, grilled antipasto platters, one of grilled vegetables of the season, another of mussels, scallops, shrimp, and squid.

Campo de Fiori imports its dry pastas from Italy for some dishes and uses fresh pasta dough for others. Flat pastas. Round pastas. Shaped pastas. Plain pastas bathed in excellent sauces. Filled pastas. Gnocchi. Some served with meat, seafood, vegetables, or a combination. For *nuovo Italiano* cuisine and a sparkling atmosphere, you can't do much better than Campo de Fiori.

Campo de Fiori, 300 East First Avenue, Denver; (303) 377-7887.

Clair de Lune

During the six years that it was open, Aubergine was one of Denver's most acclaimed restaurants—and Sean Kelly was heralded as one of the city's top chefs. Exquisite Mediterranean regional cuisine, an obsession with fresh and usually organic ingredients, and impeccable service vaulted it to the top tier of local restaurants—and kept it there.

In February 2001, with young twins at home competing for his attention with the foodies who flocked to this high-profile restaurant and ready for a break from the long hours required of the owner-chef of a full-service establishment, Kelly pulled the plug on Aubergine. He took a sabbatical. He taught some cooking classes. He wrote a seasonal cooking column for *The Denver Post*. He caught up with himself and his family. In 2002, he came roaring back with Clair de Lune, a precious restaurant with just eight tables and a maximum capacity of 22 dinner guests. He downsized, but he didn't lose his culinary edge or his loyal following.

This jewel of a restaurant is as intimate and romantic as they come. Through Clair de Lune's large windows, you can watch the traffic of East Sixth Avenue whizzing by, but inside, all is ethereal. The textured walls of the small restaurant are painted as blue as the twilight sky. The table settings are simple yet elegant, and the two-stool bar indicates that this is a place to dine, not drink.

The kitchen is tiny and the menu is limited, but Kelly has not strayed from his insistence on the finest, freshest ingredients, nor has he lost his deft hand in turning them into exquisite dinners. He maintains a hands-on presence in the kitchen, the role that few chefs of his caliber chose to play. Kelly actually cooks, and his ever-changing menu is small enough for him to control without a large staff. He serves up a couple of appetizers, four or so entrées, and a like number of desserts.

During the spring–summer of 2002, a must-have-that starter was Antipasti Misti, a first-course feast of Spanish chorizo or salami, Roncal cheese, roasted peppers with cured olives and anchovies or sardines, and crispy-fried baby artichokes with basil aïoli, the latter one of the few Aubergine items that you can expect to find at Clair de Lune. Alternatively, it was Fruits de Mer—shrimp, Malpeque oysters, littleneck clams, and lobster in the shell, accompanied by exquisite sauces for dipping—available in three sizes, depending on the size and appetite of the party, and is one of the few constants on the Franco-Mediterranean menu.

The entrées change frequently—sometimes even daily. They include Sautéed Softshell Crabs, Pan-Roast Cumin-Rubbed Organic Chicken, Roast Colorado Rack of Lamb, Vegetable Tagine, Slow-Roasted Muscovy Duck, Pan-Roasted Tarragon-Sweetened Striped Bass, Lamb Rib Eye Provençal, Pomegranate Tart Chicken, and Oregon Porcini Mushroom and Spring Vegetable Fricasée. Something for those who prefer red meat, poultry, seafood, and vegetarian—and each one deliciously prepared, appropriately accompanied and presented with style and panache. Desserts are along the lines of a chocolaty Gâteaux Victoire, *panna cotta*, possibly the best strawberry shortcake you'll ever eat, and a Bay Leaf Pots de Crème, which nicks this classic French custard with a hint of an herb you'd normally find in stews.

Clair de Lune is as pricey as it is pretty, and the wines—mostly from California, with some from France and Washington State—are priced to match. They are selected by front-of-the-house manager/sommelier Kathy Hawkins, who previously did so at Micole, the restaurant that reigned briefly and beautifully in the former Aubergine space. The "Bubbles," as the wine list categories champagnes and sparkling wines, are mostly French. The restaurant is open for dinner only.

Reservations are recommended, and I'd add the adjective "strongly," for this is a small restaurant and happy guests do tend to linger. To keep things simple, the restaurant accepts only cash and checks. So when you dine at Clair de Lune, you *can* leave home without it and still get an extraordinary meal.

Clair de Lune, 1313 East Sixth Avenue, Denver; (303) 831-1992.

The Fort

Few restaurants so strongly reflect the passions and commitment of one person as does The Fort. The restaurant was the brainchild of Sam Arnold, former newspaper reporter, radio announcer, and advertising man by profession and historian by avocation. He is also a man with a vision—a vision stretching to Colorado's early days. In 1962, Arnold was browsing through old photographs at the Denver Public Library when a line drawing caught his eye. It depicted Bent's Fort, Colorado's first fur-trading post, built in the 1830s along the Santa Fe Trail. "I could live in a place like that," he remembers thinking.

Another thing that caught his eye was a seven-acre plot of land north of Morrison. Red rock formations and views of Denver captivated him. He bought the land and planned his house, an adobe recreation of the historic fort on the eastern Plains. He was refused a residential loan for such a structure, so Arnold decided to open a restaurant on the first floor, which would make him eligible for a Small Business Administration loan. While 22 construction workers from Taos, New Mexico, assembled 80,000 adobe bricks to build his dream house (and restaurant), Arnold immersed himself in the world of the original fort.

He researched books and diaries kept by trappers and traders, and learned that deer, elk, buffalo, and even cougar were eaten along the Santa Fe Trail in the 1830s and 1840s, and that duck, plover, teal, goose, turkey, and crane were the fowl of choice. When The Fort opened in 1963, buffalo steak was featured on the menu; now, 50,000 buffalo dinners are served there every year. Quail and guinea fowl remain on the menu as well.

Though long interested in food and food history, Arnold was not a trained chef, but early on, he decided he'd better learn. He studied with the legendary James Beard, enrolled in La Varenne Ecole de Cuisine, and took cooking classes in Asia as well. He also visited farms and ranches all over the Southwest to find ingredients that could be adapted for The Fort. In the process, he became one of the country's leading authorities on Southwestern foods. Dining at The Fort has been called "a living history culinary experience."

The Fort today is a large complex as busy as Bent's place on the trail—and as atmospheric a dining place as there is. A sign over the door welcomes guests in five languages. The courtyard features a fire pit and a teepee to acknowledge the original's role as a trading post with several Indian bands. Among the nine dining rooms is a garden patio overlooking Denver. Each one has a Southwestern-style beehive fireplace, and antiques, relics, and memorabilia adorn the walls. The menu features some classic dishes and some seasonal specials—including drinks straight from the history books. If you order a bottle of champagne, the cork will be popped with a tomahawk.

The Fort is a carnivore's paradise. An old cookbook in the Arnold family attic yielded a recipe for Beef Steak with Oysters, a signature dish of San Francisco's Palace Hotel and now a Fort specialty. The Fort serves more buffalo and elk than any other restaurant in the United States. Wild boar chop is sometimes served here, and you can also get buffalo steak or prime rib—or buffalo hump, sausage, barbecued ribs, center-cut shank prepared osso buco–style, or tongue, the latter a gourmet specialty in swank late 19th-century restaurants. The annual "awful offal" dinner features innards that people either love or loathe. Elk, Arctic musk ox, fallow deer, moose, mountain sheep, ostrich, and antelope appear on the regular menu or are served as specials.

Chilled rattlesnake cocktail is the restaurant's most popular appetizer, and Rocky Mountain oysters arguably the best known. These "oysters" have never seen the sea. They are the testicles of bison, calf, lamb, or even turkey, rolled in delicate Japanese bread crumbs called panko and deep-fried. The Fort's patrons certainly cannot be called gustatory wimps—nor can its cooks, who have to contend with such exotic ingredients.

Don't think of The Fort as a combination of theme park and culinary freak show. In fact, although the unusual offerings make good copy, the restaurant serves very good food based on more common ingredients, often with contemporary twists. Joining the restaurant as executive in mid-2002, The Fort's 40th-anniversary year, was David Woolley, who somewhat heroically tried to upgrade the culinary scene in the Arkansas River Valley with the short-lived Antero Restaurant outside of Salida. Woolley's cooking style has been called "modern American cowboy cuisine," and he brings that to The Fort.

Proving that our third president was way ahead of his time, The Fort's Thomas Jefferson's Tasty Roasted Guinea Hen, based on a Monticello recipe, is marinated in jalapeño and garlic and sprinkled with black sesame seed. And you can't get much trendier than Black Bean Warm Citrus Salad—or much more traditional, in an old New England way, than Colonial Lobster and Scallop Pie. Heirloom beans, crisp greens, four kinds of potatoes (including unusual tubers from an experimental farm in the San Luis Valley), and black quinoa (also from the San Luis Valley) are among the vegetables you'll find at the The Fort.

Don't miss dessert. Negrita, a mousse-like concoction, is a sublime chocolate dessert. Other specialties are Capirotada, a raisin-studded bread pudding, and Trapper's, a long-cooking cobbler featuring dried apples, applesauce, cider, brown sugar, raisins, and assorted seasonings, including copious quantities of dark rum. Vera Dahlquist, who came to work at The Fort when she was 80 years young, created the Caramel Canola Brownie. Holly's Adobe Rattlesnake Sundae was "developed" by Sam's daughter, Holly Arnold Kinney, when she was about 10 years old. She covered ice cream with the cinnamon-chocolate powder used for Mexican hot chocolate.

The Fort has made Sam Arnold, arguably, Colorado's best-known restaurateur. He has produced and hosted food shows on radio and television, written magazine articles, served as a spokesman on radio commercials, and authored such books as *Eating Up the Santa Fe Trail, Taste of the West, Frying Pans West,* and *The Fort Cookbook: New Foods of the Old West from the Famous Denver Restaurant.*

The Fort, 19192 Route 8, Morrison; (303) 697-4771 or www.thefort.com.

The Fourth Story

Just as every foodie loves the best efforts of talented, creative chefs and restaurateurs, every writer in the land loves independent bookstores run by passionate and knowledgeable people, and every serious reader in Colorado at one time or another visits the Tattered Cover in Cherry Creek. Browsing the bookstore's many titles— bestsellers, scholarly works, exotica, and Denver's best selection of magazines—is a wonderful way to wile away a few hours, and when hunger strikes, wandering upstairs to The Fourth Story for a good meal just caps off the day or evening.

The restaurant's library-like ambience suits the location. Bookshelves line some walls, large windows offer a penthouse-type view of surrounding rooftops, and art fills in the spaces. The solid wooden chairs would not be out of place in a library. In keeping with the bookstore environment, the menu categorizes the meal's courses as Chapter 1 for appetizers, Chapter 2 for soups and salads, Chapter 3 for entrées, and Chapter 4 for desserts. The restaurant had six chefs in seven years, the most recent being the talented Tyler Wiard, who previously cooked at Cliff Young's, Q's, Zenith American Grill, Napa Café, and Mel's Restaurant & Bar, during which tenure he was a guest chef at New York's James Beard House. He spent a year in California before returning to Denver and to The Fourth Story in 2002.

Wiard takes his inspiration for various cuisines and fuses them into his own version of contemporary American fare. Key ingredients include such currently popular items as foie gras, crabmeat, duck, mahi-mahi, ahi tuna, and various pasta shapes, grains, and seasonal greens. Wiard also offers swank and succulent versions of such eternally popular items as beef, pork chops, and trout. The menu changes frequently, and daily specials are offered as well.

Pastry Chef Syd Berkowitz offers just five crowd-pleasing desserts each day, such as flavored flan, tarts, and something chocolatey. The restaurant, which serves daily lunch and dinner, plus brunch, also hosts wine-maker dinners roughly twice a month.

The Fourth Story, Tattered Cover Bookstore, 2955 East First Avenue, Denver; (303) 322-1824 or www.fourthstory.com.

Hapa Sushi

The magic formula of good sushi, both traditional and inventive, and other Japanese and adapted dishes in a stylish setting has been imported from Boulder (see page 121) to Cherry Creek North. Wood floors and large windows set a sleek and attractive stage for Hapa's offerings, which closely resemble those served at the Boulder location.

Hapa Sushi, 2780 East Second Avenue, Denver; (303) 322-9554.

Japon

When he was a teenager growing up near Tokyo, Miki Hashimoto saw the movie *American Graffiti* and thought that it was just too cool. He dreamed of moving to America and owning a burger joint. Eleven years later, he was on his way to Los Angeles to work in a fashionable sushi restaurant and learn English. Hashimoto moved to Colorado in 1988, and seven years later, he opened Japon on Old South Gaylord near Washington Park.

Japon is as carefully arranged in terms of colors, shapes, and textures as an exquisite sushi tray. Blond wood, brushed stainless steel, and granite provide an attractive interplay to create a feeling that is at once soothing and energizing. Hashimoto adapted the Japon style when he later opened Japango in Boulder (see page 122).

Wonderful looks and wonderful flavors are Japon hallmarks. Both of Hashimoto's restaurants build their sushi creations—traditional sushi and sashimi, fusion sushi, and vegetarian sushi, the latter two made with Tamanishiki short-grain rice, which the owner-chef considers the world's best. His soy sauce is based on a recipe handed down through the very traditional Japanese family in which he was raised.

You'll find outstanding contemporary dishes at Japon. Magic Mushroom, a signature starter of avocado wrapped in halibut or salmon, is something the restaurant will only describe as "Miki's secret sauce." Spicy Calamari is sautéed in garlic butter and served with mushrooms. Salmon or Chicken Teriyaki and Mile High Tofu Spicy Miso Udon, thick noodles in a sea of miso soup, are among the popular main courses.

Japon isn't just a cutting-edge restaurant, but it has a cutting-edge website too. Log on, click on Fun Stuff and then on the Sushi Calorie Meter, and find out just what you'll be consuming if your order that opulent Sushi Boat. Click on Making Sushi at Home, and the site provides an on-line tutorial of sushi-making instructions. Hashimoto has fulfilled the first half of his teen dream, but being deflected from the second half (the burger joint) in favor of this fine restaurant and its Boulder offspring has been a dream come true for fans of Japanese and Oriental fusion cuisine.

Japon, 1028 South Gaylord Street, Denver; (303) 744-0330 or www.japonsushi.com.

Jax Fish House

Restaurateur David Query, whose eateries are known as lively places serving innovative combinations and excellent presentations, has brought one of his three successful Boulder restaurants (see page 114) to the site of Denver's former Terminal Bar & Café. Jax Fish House is now an established part of the LoDo dinner scene, though it is surprisingly considerably more subdued than the Boulder original. It presents the same (or almost the same) menu featuring fantastic offerings from the raw bar, great drinks, and even better seafood—bought fresh, cooked well, and presented with panache.

Jax Fish House, 1539 17th Street, Denver; (303) 292-5767 or www.jaxfishhousedenver.citysearch.com.

Jou Jou

Jou Jou, located in the Hotel Teatro, is the more formal Restaurant Kevin Taylor's playful cousin. Billed as an American bistro, it is moderately priced (OK, the high end of moderate) serving breakfast, lunch, and dinner. The high-ceilinged street-level restaurant offers stylish banquette seating and a good bar. One flight up is a cozy mezzanine with its own small bar. Granite tables, stylish tableware, and, most of all, the Kevin Taylor touch earns Jou Jou its place among Denver's top places to eat, and it

Kevin Taylor·

In 1987, a 25-year-old culinary prodigy named Kevin Taylor burst on the still-maturing Denver restaurant scene with Zenith American Grill. As one of the city's first restaurants to embrace "new American cuisine" with a special Colorado accent, it whetted the appetites of frustrated Denver foodies.

Taylor, a native son of Colorado, had been classically trained. He sensed food lovers' frustration and longing, and instinctively knew the time was right to update Denver dining. And Denver did devour virtually everything on Zenith's menu, but after 10 years, the lights went off at Zenith, and local foodies mourned. Meanwhile, Taylor opened Palette's at the Denver Art Museum in 1997 and both Bistro Jou Jou and Restaurant Kevin Taylor in the then-new Hotel Teatro in 1998. The following year, Zenith closed, briefly reinventing itself as Brasserie Z and then closing again for good. In 2001, things came full circle, when Taylor opened a Spanish restaurant called Nicois in the Zenith/Brasserie Z location. Then fate looped back on itself once more, when Nicois closed just after New Year 2003, only six weeks after Taylor's Dandelion in Boulder shut after seven years of serving some of that city's most precious food.

With the sour economy of the early years of the 21st century forcing such consolidation and regrouping, Taylor's fans concentrate eating at the three remaining restaurants that reflect his refined touch. They display variations on his signature culinary style, look different, and slot into different budgets, but they remain the vanguard of contemporary cuisine in Denver. In Taylor's interpretation, this means an artful combination of fresh ingredients in sometimes new and always interesting ways that are beautiful to behold and fantastic to eat. He contrives dishes that draw from various culinary roots to create his own style.

Yet within this harmony that flows across all three restaurants are nuances of ingredients and presentation. Furthermore, each establishment is designed with imagination and class, so that the entire dining experience is equally satisfying to the palate, eye, and spirit. If you like one restaurant, you'll most likely like the others, but never will you confuse them with one another.

shares Restaurant Kevin Taylor's well-stocked wine cellar. Located a short block from the Denver Center for the Performing Arts, it is my favorite pre-theater restaurant.

Among Jou Jou's top fusion creations are Steamed Mussels with Lemongrass, Chilies and Lime in Coriander Broth (Thai seasonings), Seafood Bouillabaisse with Yukon Potato and Saffron Aïoli Crostini (South of France, mostly), and Slow-Roasted Pork Loin with Cheddar Potatoes, Red Wine Cabbage, and Apple Butter (American-style comfort food). Jou Jou is also a place where a soup and salad can constitute a quick meal, you can order a satisfying burger and *frites,* and the desserts fly as high as the rest of the meal.

Jou Jou, Hotel Teatro, 1106 14th Street, Denver; (303) 228-0770.

Le Central

Located in a rambling building one block east of Broadway, Le Central feels like a corner of France. Owner Robert Tournier has created an unpretentious restaurant just south of downtown that serves such Gallic standards as French onion soup, pâté, escargots, bouillabaisse, mussels, coq au vin, and crème caramel in an intimate, non-stuffy atmosphere.

Executive chef Christophe Negrel, who worked in Provence including two years under the legendary Alain Ducasse, is a stickler for freshness and quality, bringing in seafood directly from Hawaii and Boston and selecting the best of everything from local purveyors. The mostly Provençal menu is tweaked daily to present diners with a wide variety of fresh, seasonal food.

Diners can always expect a selection of meat and poultry (chicken, pork, beef, lamb) and seafood (trout, snapper, bouillabaisse, paella, marlin), prepared in several ways (grilled, sautéed, roasted) and finished with traditional sauces, confits, *coulis*, and vinaigrettes. A vegetarian dish appears on every menu. If you want to know what Chef Negrel has planned for today, you can log onto the restaurant's website, where the menu *du jour* is posted.

Le Central has rightly made a name for itself with mollusks, known in French as *coquillages*. Perfectly cooked clams or mussels, prepared in various ways and served with all the French fries you can eat, are available at lunch and dinner. The Zagat Survey recently proclaimed that Le Central "puts muscle into mussels."

Executive pasty chef Jérome Dulas, a native of Bordeaux, says his ambition is to open a patisserie in Bayonne someday, and he doesn't mean New Jersey. Leave room for his *Gâteaux au Chocolat* (a divine soufflé-like chocolate cake), *Pain Perdu* (the Gallic version of bread pudding, here served with caramel sauce), *Mousse au Chocolat* (Dulas's silky version of this all-time favorite), *Clafoutis aux Framboises et Pommes* (shortbread-topped custard with raspberries and apples), Crème Brulée (made with crème fraîche), and *Tarte aux Poires* (pear tart with almond frangipane).

The wine list is extensive but not expensive. You'll find about 15 French and domestic reds and whites at $5 or under per glass and $14 to $24 per bottle at this writing, plus an additional 165 or so offered only by the bottle. The French wines are grouped by region and include all the majors. Featured wines are priced by the glass, by the bottle, or by the percentage of a bottle your party consumes. It's the only restaurant I can think of with such a customer-friendly policy.

Le Central is kid-friendly too—something you'll find all over Europe but less so in the United States, where parents often opt for corporate-owned "family restaurants." Keenly aware of young tastes, Le Central's children's menu offers *Poulet et Frites* (grilled chicken strips and French fries), *Pates aux Tomates* (pasta with tomato sauce), *Croque Monsieur* (grilled Swiss cheese and smoked turkey sandwich), and *Tartine* (grilled French bread topped with tomato sauce and cheese and served with a small green salad).

Le Central, 112 East Eighth Street, Denver; (303) 863-8094 or www.lecentral.com.

Le Délice

See description in "Bakeries" on page 15.

Mel's Restaurant and Bar

To anyone who associates the name Mel's and food with the diner of that old TV show, *Alice,* Mel's Restaurant & Bar will come as a delicious surprise. Pass under the festive awning, enter the restaurant, and steep yourself in the urbane atmosphere. The bar is a pleasant place for a before-dinner drink, but the tasteful dining room is the stage-setter for some of Denver's most dramatic food. Light walls, framed artwork, a light play created by various types of fixtures, rattan chairs, and clean, crisp table settings let the food take center stage.

There really is a Mel, namely Mel Master, who with his wife, Janie, left England for Provence in 1969. They founded Masterwines to sell little-known French wines, mostly from the Rhône Valley and Provence, in the United States, and Mel became a published expert on Côtes du Rhône wines.

The peripatetic couple eventually moved to California and then New York, where they teamed up with Chef Jonathan Waxman and opened Jams, an acronym for Jonathan and Melvyn's. It was one of New York's first California-style restaurants and became the *in place* in the 1980s.

In early 1995 Mel, Janie, and their son, Charles, opened Mel's Bar and Grill in Denver, and it became as hot in the Mile High City as Jams had been in New York a decade earlier. Charles now manages the restaurant, which remains one of Colorado's finest. Many of Denver's most talented chefs have at one time or another cooked there. The top toque at this writing is Jeff Saudo, who began his career in North Carolina and in 1999 moved to California to work under Thomas Keller at The French Laundry. After a year, he came to Denver as Sean Kelly's sous-chef at Aubergine. When Mizuna burst on the Denver dining scene under Mel's alumni, Frank Bonanno and Doug Fleischmann, Saudo became the chef de cuisine, and in June 2002 he moved on to Mel's as executive chef. His rise has been dramatic, and his creations are very, very good.

A number of Mel's sprightly, contemporary dishes appear both on the smaller lunch and more extensive dinner menus, presented by a fine waitstaff. Look for a Chef's Special Soup at each meal. Signature starters at both meals include Mussels "La Cagouille," inspired by La Cagouille in France, and Tomato, Mozarella, and Basil Napoleon, a combination of house-made mozzarella and ripe tomatoes that sings of summer bounty. Mixed Field Greens with balsamic vinaigrette and Grilled Salmon Nicoise, a composition of grilled salmon, haricots verts, potatoes, greens, and Niçoise dressing, are delicious.

Highlights of Mel's to-sigh-for dinners are outstanding fish dishes, which constitute about half of the entrée selections. Another house specialty is Duck "Two Ways"—crisp confit duck leg and maple smoked breast. You'll also find beef, pork, lamb, poultry, and vegetarian dishes—and perhaps two—on the evening menu.

Pastry chef Christopher Cubberly turns out about eight sublime desserts each day, and the dessert menu suggests sweet wines or suitable spirits for each. Lemon

Almond Genoise with warm berry compote, Classic Vanilla Crème Brulée, an Individual Key Lime Pie, and Banana Chocolate Chip Bread Pudding are wickedly good. The wine list is sorted by reds, whites, champagnes, and half-bottles, then sub-sorted by varietals or by country or region of origin. Alice, Vera, and Flo of *Mel's Diner* on the small screen never slung such hash.

Mel's Restaurant and Bar (founded as Mel's Bar and Grill), 235 Fillmore Street, Denver; (303) 333-3979 or www.melsbarandgrill.com.

Mizuna

This contemporary American-Mediterranean restaurant has ranked high practically since opening its doors in 2001. Named after a feathery salad green of Japanese origin, Mizuna was created by Frank Bonanno, the Culinary Institute of America graduate who presides over the kitchen, and Doug Fleischmann, who oversees the front of the house and is considered by many to be Denver's best maitre d'. Theirs is a fortuitous partnership, for the food is the peer of the service, and vice versa—and guests are the beneficiaries. Soft soothing colors set a discreet backdrop for the impressive food. The open kitchen invites you to watch the action, but in truth, once a plate is set before you, it's difficult to wrench your eyes away and see what's coming next.

Though Mizuna lays claim to a generally Franco-Italian Mediterranean style, its inspirations are far more wide-ranging. The signature appetizer is TK's Macaroni and Cheese, an all-American comfort food if ever there was one. Bonanno's adapted version, however, is a far cry from Kraft's boxed mac 'n cheese, but a velvety *beurre blanc* sauce of mascarpone and lobster instead of cheese. It was inspired by a dish created by Thomas Keller of the Napa Valley's legendary French Laundry—hence the initials TK. Excellent soups and fresh salads can also be preludes to selections from the small entrée list, which changes with the seasons, the market, method of preparation, accompaniments, whatever—but what they have in common is that they are always delicious and always beautiful.

Seared foie gras is a velvety dream. Mizuna's Caesar salad soars far higher than this reliable warhorse of the salad-course wars. Beef, pork chops, lamb, and perhaps rabbit please the carnivore. Bonanno doesn't shy away from putting organ meats on the menu either, so perfectly prepared that even people who would normally not risk ordering, say, sweetbreads are enraptured once they try. Seafood, poultry, and pasta round out the selections—and each creation is perfectly balanced.

The desserts are divine, not surprising because Bonanno was once a pastry chef. You'll find the likes of griddlecakes with house-made ice cream and Vermont maple syrup sauce, chocolate mousse, and crème brulée, perhaps flavored, to top off a very fine meal.

Mizuna, 225 East Seventh Avenue, Denver; (303) 832-4778.

The Palace Arms at the Brown Palace Hotel

Chances are that you've never been in the diplomatic reception room at the White House (at least I know I haven't), but if you're a fan of *The West Wing*, you might have noticed the wall-covering with what appear to be historic scenes in one of the reception rooms. The wallpaper, faithfully reproduced for the TV show, depicts an early interpretation of North American independence. Why do I mention this? Because the real rather than reproduced-for-television wallpaper hangs in only two places in North America: the White House and the Independence Room, a private dining room of The Palace Arms Restaurant in the Brown Palace Hotel.

Established in 1892 and a bona fide national landmark, the Brown Palace has hosted presidents and potentates, celebrities and citizens through much of Colorado's history. Its ultra-fine dining restaurant, The Palace Arms, is Denver's most sumptuous and traditional restaurant, but if no party is occupying the Independence Room, it's usually possible to pop in and take a look. The restaurant displays a timeless clubby elegance that you don't often find these days: manorial chairs upholstered in red leather, royal blue carpeting emblazoned with a *fleur de lis* design, perfect and precise table settings, and the attention and care lavished by a waitstaff captained by maitre d' Mehran Esmaili, one of the city's best.

Around the room hang 22 flags, replicas of Revolutionary battle flags and insignias from prominent explorations of the North American continent. The restaurant also displays priceless antiques, including a pair of dueling pistols that reportedly belonged to Napoleon and Josephine and an ornate 18th-century silver centerpiece commissioned by the British Royal Family. Not surprisingly, jackets are required and ties are encouraged for gentlemen at dinner, making this one of the few restaurants in casual Colorado that still bothers setting any such standards. With all that, the restaurant remains welcoming rather than stuffy, which is quite an accomplishment.

The glory of a Palace Arms meal matches the grandeur of the setting. The restaurant serves relatively light fare during lunch, but Chef Zach Bernheim pulls out all stops at dinner. The appetizers, soups, and salads are beyond wonderful, and yet the restaurant is, was, and probably always will be best known for its perfect renditions of hearty and gorgeously presented entrées. Beef Wellington with Prosciutto di Parma, Foie Gras, and Mushroom Duxelles Wrapped in Puff Pastry is made for two and carved at tableside—yet another Palace Arms nicety.

A platoon of eight pastry chefs under the command of executive pastry chef Sky Goble prepares all the baked goods and desserts served at the hotel. This job requires an overnight baker and an oven that never gets turned off. Divine desserts, toothsome breads, lavish tea pastries, gorgeous cakes for weddings and other occasions, and even Melba toast are made in-house. The Brown Palace's pastry chefs are among the best in the business, and their delectable desserts cap off a pricey Palace Arms feast that pleases picky palates.

The Palace Arms's wine list is legendary, with hundreds of reds, whites, and rosés, domestic and imported vintages, still and sparkling wines, moderately priced and over-the-top, costwise, to choose from. Nearly 50 wines are available by the half-bottle—a relatively huge choice for that size. The restaurant's knowledgeable sommelier will help narrow down the selection.

The Palace Arms occasionally organizes small wine-tasting dinners. An Evening with the Treasures of The Palace Arms at the Brown Palace Hotel is the elaborately named event that includes a rare tour of the restaurant's prized wine cellar,

---

Colorado Culinary History

A look through more than a century's worth of Brown Palace menus will tell you a lot about the state's changing—and not-so-changing—tastes in food. Meat in general and beef in particular has been popular since the hotel opened in 1892. The only time it was not available was on Tuesdays in 1917, when meat was reserved for servicemen. That year also marked a watershed of sorts in tastes for fowl and poultry. Before 1917, partridge, wild turkey, prairie chicken, Egyptian quail, and plover appeared on the menu, and duck was categorized by species: redhead, mallard, and wild. Pheasant and duck are still served, but they are farm-raised and generic.

Game was popular early on, declined, and now is on the upswing again. The Brown Palace now serves buffalo, elk, and rabbit. And of course, the hotel's restaurants still serve up that quality beef for which the Brown Palace has long been known.

---

champagne, a before-dinner wine tasting, and a feast as exquisite and elegant as this restaurant is capable of turning out.

Afternoon Tea at the Brown Palace has been a Denver tradition for more than a century. The basic version consists of a pot of properly brewed English tea and scones with Devonshire cream and strawberry preserves, savory tea sandwiches, and an array of classic tea pastries, served daily right outside The Palace Arms in the hotel's soaring atrium lobby, one of Colorado's most magnificent spaces.

The Palace Arms, The Brown Palace Hotel, 321 17th Street, Denver; (303) 297-3111 or www.brownpalace.com/dining/palacearms.html.

Palettes

This restaurant at the Denver Art Museum demonstrates eloquently how fine art and fine food go together. The atmosphere is avant-garde without being edgy, elegant without being stuffy. Light streams in through huge windows. The black ceiling grid recalls a Mondrian painting without the color. Room dividers resemble white stucco sculptures. Chairs are of a nouveau ladderback design, with light frames and black slats. The bar gleams like a polished stone sculpture. And diners get a view of a real sculpture on the plaza between the museum and the Denver Public Library.

The restaurant serves lunch and dinner whenever the museum is open. Kevin Taylor and Chef Michael Woods have cooperated on Palettes' menu, which is moderately priced and exhibiting the flair you'd expect. It is segmented into Small Plates (appetizers, soup, salad, and modest portions of pasta), Bigger Plates (substantial burgers and sandwiches, meat, and entrées), and Desserts. Signature dishes include Slow-Roasted Tomato Basil Soup with Sweet Fennel and Crème Fraîche; Rocket Salad with Goat Cheese, Dried Cherries, and Peppery Balsamic Syrup; Seared Tuna with Vegetable Stir Fry, Jasmine Rice, and Ginger Soy Broth; and Classic Crème Brulée with Butter Cookies and Berries. The wine list is exemplary, with special selections frequently added to coordinate with special exhibits at the art museum.

Palettes, Denver Art Museum, 100 West 14th Avenue Parkway, Denver; (303) 629-0889.

Panzano

When it premiered in 1998, the Hotel Monaco became Denver's first boutique hotel, opened by the Kimpton Hotel Group, a San Francisco–based company that was among the first to create wonderful new hotels within the shells of old buildings. Denver's stylish Monaco is located in the adjacent 1917 Railway Exchange Building and the 1937 Title Building. More to the point for a culinary book, another Kimpton policy is to run hotels, not restaurants. To that end, the company seeks talented restaurateurs and chefs to handle that end of the hospitality business.

Panzano, a casually elegant northern Italian eatery named after a place in the Chianti region, was installed in the new hotel, and in 2000, Jennifer Jasinski, a young culinary whiz of exceptional talent, became its executive chef. The native Californian started cooking as a youngster, enrolled in Santa Barbara City College's cooking program, and then attended the Culinary Institute of America.

Her pre-Panzano credentials include New York's Rainbow Room under Joe Baum and André Rene; the Hotel Bel-Air in Beverly Hills; Eureka in Los Angeles; and Spago, Wolfgang Puck's revolutionary restaurant in the City of Angels. Jasinski worked for Puck for a decade, including a sous-chef slot at Postrio in San Francisco, café chef at Spago in Las Vegas, executive sous-chef at Granita in Malibu, executive sous-chef at Spago in Chicago, and corporate chef at the Wolfgang Puck Food Company. She found time to do a stint at Ledoyan, a Michelin two-star restaurant in Paris. How lucky Denver is that she is cooking here!

Jasinski presides over a kitchen that, being in a hotel, must turn out breakfast, lunch, dinner, and weekend brunch every day of the year—and attend to the room services menu as well. She does so with aplomb, also managing to cook personally for chef's tables when booked in advance and teach a monthly cooking class as well (see page 25).

Panzano's large space is broken into three smaller sections. In front is the inviting bar area, the only one where smoking is permitted and guests can be seated without reservations. In the center is the bakery, with ovens and a marble counter on one side so that patrons may watch the action, and booths and tables on the other. Shelves laden with artfully arranged vases, pitchers, and ceramics hang in front of the plate-glass windows, providing a sense of separation from the street. Painted cherubs float merrily against a trompe l'oeil sky on the ceiling. The main dining area in the rear of the space features rich mahogany, deep and enfolding booths, tables, and another marble counter, this one right at the open kitchen where Chef Jasinski and her crew perform their magic.

Breakfast ranges from delicately continental, with house-made pastry, juice, or seasonal fruit and coffee, to gut-busting all-American meals. Quiche, eggs Benedict with prosciutto rather than Canadian bacon, filled ricotta pancakes, and house-made granola are among the specialties. Butcher paper covers the tablecloths during lunch service, when the European-style menu starts with antipasti, pizza, panini, soups, salads, and pasta before proceeding to the main course and dessert.

The dinner menu is an expansion and modification of the lunch offerings. Doughs for pizza and pastas are house-made. All produce is organic (anything with heirloom tomatoes is worth ordering); fresh mozzarella is first rate, and meats and seafood are prepared with the deftest touch. At lunch and dinner, a basket of focaccia and sun-dried tomato- and herb-infused olive oil for dipping appears on the table. Half-a-dozen antipasti, half-a-dozen pizzas, four or five house-made pasta dishes, six or so entrées (called, Italian-style, *secondi*) at lunch and a dozen in the evening, and four great desserts comprise the menu.

Specialties of the house? Salsiccia, a stand-out among Panzano's pizzas, combines spicy house-made sausage, caramelized fennel, goat cheese, and red pepper-infused oil. Zuppa di Mais (corn soup) is a silky and almost milky mélange of fresh corn, onion, garlic, and basil served with a slice of toasted *crostini* laid across the soup plate. Capellini al Pomodoro e Basilico is the Panzano version of "regular" red sauce Italian spaghetti. Angel-hair pasta with a flavorful tomato-basil-garlic sauce is available with or without shrimp. The Gnocchi con Cappa Sante combines house-made gnocchi, grilled sea scallops, Niçoise olives, oven-roasted tomatoes, and grilled zucchini bathed in lemon-oil broth. Ravioli ai Quattro Formaggi are plump pillows of house-made pasta filled with house-made ricotta, Parmigiano, fontina, and Gorgonzola and served with wild mushroom ragout.

Instead of conventional veal *osso bucco,* Panzano adapts it by using pan-grilled monkfish, wrapped in pancetta and presented with mascarpone polenta, roasted vegetables, and sherry-vinegar sauce. There are no substitutes for veal in Scallopine di Vitello, medallions of veal served with spinach, lemon, capers, and sun-dried tomatoes.

Additional à la carte side dishes (*contorni* on the menu) include oven-roasted seasonal vegetables, incredibly rich and creamy Polenta alla Mascarpone, Pare di Patate (mashed potatoes to you and me), and Spinaci Saltat con Pancetta (sautéed spinach with pancetta and roasted garlic cream that would put more stars in Popeye's eyes than Olive Oyl ever did). The house specialty dessert is tìramisu, over-the-top in richness, flavor, and beauty. Weekend brunch is an à la carte affair, combining breakfast and lunch favorites.

Line up a few foodie friends and book a chef's table at Panzano. Chef Jasinski will create a feast that is the equal of any in Colorado. Wine tastings can also be arranged, often in Panzano's charming wine cellar. And, of course, if you want to learn to cook Jasinski-style, her cooking classes are the place to get some tips and dine on the treats she prepares.

Panzano, 909 17th Street, Denver; (303) 296-3525.

Restaurant Kevin Taylor

Restaurant Kevin Taylor is located in the Hotel Teatro, a luxurious, theatrically themed hotel carved from a former office tower a block from the Denver Center for the Performing Arts. Regional American cooking with a contemporary interpretation and an unsurpassed flair are Chef Taylor's signature, and nowhere does he express himself more elegantly and eloquently than in his namesake restaurant.

This formal and elegant restaurant is a symphony of sage green and gold. It has soaring ceilings, beautiful artwork discreetly displayed on richly wood-paneled walls, custom alderwood armchairs upholstered in Scalamandré silk, and tables set with blindingly white and crisply starched linens, Bernardaud china, Christofle silver, and crystal stemware. It feels a little like an updated version of a fine *fin-de-siècle* restaurant in Paris, Vienna, or Madrid—the century being the end of the 19th, not the 20th. Serving dinners only, Restaurant Kevin Taylor is the special-occasion restaurant, the wooing-a-new-business-client, the cementing-an-important-business-deal restaurant, the I-want-to-make-this-meal-memorable–money-is-no-object restaurant.

Signature dishes include Pepper Seared Sashimi Grade Tuna with Jasmine Rice and Pot Stickers, Open Ravioli of Maine Lobster with Asparagus and Sweet Corn, and a two-lamb entrée—perhaps Roast Colorado Lamb Loin and Braised Lamb Shank with Niçoise Olive Sauce, or Rack of Colorado Lamb and Lamb Osso Bucco with Couscous, Medjool Dates, and Cardamom Jus. Four dishes, four influences: Oriental, Italian, Provençal, and North African.

The appetizers always include *foie gras* in a couple versions, diver scallops in some fashion, and caviar—beluga, golden ostera, and sevruga. To end the meal, pastry chef Jason LeBeau also performs such magic as Bittersweet Liquid Center Chocolate Cake, Fromage Blanc Cheesecake, and Individual Pear Tatin, most served with house-made ice cream or sorbet.

The service is as correct and professional as you'd expect in such a restaurant, and the wine list is simply one of Denver's best. Some 20 wines are available by the glass, and hundreds by the bottle. In fact, 5,000 bottles line the wine cellar, which also has tables accommodating a small group—a perfect setting for an intimate private party of people who love fine food and fine wines. Cynthia Meyers is the sommelier, while Imre Kraus, a second-level master sommelier, is general manager—and between them, there's a wealth of expertise to running the wine program as beautifully as the food service.

Restaurant Kevin Taylor, Hotel Teatro, 1100 14th Street, Denver; (303) 820-2600. The website for all the restaurants, www.kevintaylorrestaurantgroup.com, has links to pages for the individual establishments.

Strings

This uptown Denver landmark restaurant has long been serving great food in a great atmosphere. While other neighborhood culinary institutions have come and gone, Strings' heart beats on—and what a heart it is. Since 1993, this fine-dining restaurant has put on an annual Mother's Day feast called the "I Remember Mama" brunch for 150 women from Volunteers of America programs and from subsidized housing projects who have no local family. The event typically includes a fashion show or other entertainment, fresh flowers, Mother's Day cards, chocolates, and gifts from Neiman Marcus. There's even free transportation courtesy of Metro Taxi so the invitees have no reason not to get there.

The other 364½ days a year, this cheerful and stylish two-level restaurant hangs out its lunch, dinner, and brunch shingle for fashionable and fussy Denverites looking for a good meal, great service, and a fine atmosphere and are willing to splurge a little to get it. Fresh ingredients and flawless presentation come first at Strings. The kitchen embellishes on its well-regarded pasta and other Italian offerings by gleaning other influences from farther along the Mediterranean shore, as well as generous swaths cut by contemporary California cuisine.

The appetizer menu current at this writing featured Honey Smoked Tuna, Sesame Seared Scallops, well-garnished Carpaccio, and Roasted Portobello Mushroom. The latter two have been on the menu for some time. Soups come by the cup or the bowl, and salads from "Simple" to Caesar are other palate-teasers. Although the entrée list is wide-ranging, some people come to Strings just for the pasta—and many of these for the signature Penne Baguatta, toothsome tubes of pasta served with chicken, mushrooms, broccoli, and tomato cream sauce. The Laquered Duck Breast, inspired by the Chinese way with this flavorful fowl, is served with wild rice and a dried cranberry sauce—and it's also become a Strings signature. Pan-Roasted Calf's Liver augmented with applewood-smoked bacon is a treat. Well-loved desserts include silky crème brulée and ice creams and sorbets that come with fresh fruit and a cookie. Anything from the oven is awesome.

Noel Cunningham, Strings' salt-and-pepper-bearded owner, came into the restaurant business in an oddball way. He quit school early, self-educating himself by exploring everything from museum to mountains. When his father discovered that 14-year-old Noel was skipping school, he sent the young truant to work in an uncle's restaurant. He came into the culinary trade serendipitously and learned it well. For his up-by-the-bootstraps success in the restaurant business and his generosity to many local causes (Mother's Day and More, you might call it), Johnson & Wales University in 2002 awarded Cunningham an honorary doctorate.

Strings, 1700 Humboldt Street, Denver; (303) 831-7310 or www.stringsrestaurant.com.

Tamayo

Tamayo is a new Mexican restaurant, not a New Mexican restaurant. It is contemporary in décor, food preparation, food presentation, and service, a collateral relation to the many Tex-Mex restaurants in Colorado and the Southwest but bearing only the faintest family resemblance. The long, skinny restaurant with the huge south-facing windows and dynamite rooftop deck occupies a Larimer Square space long held by the Cadillac Grill. Just as Denver appeared to be tiring of automobile bumpers and horse saddles as design elements, along came Richard Sandoval, a native of Acapulco, son of a prominent restaurateur (his family owns Madeira's and Villa Fiore), and a graduate of the Culinary Institute of America. Sandoval won the 1992 National Toque D'Oro and was a member of the Mexican culinary team that traveled to Lyons, France, to compete in the Bocuse d'Or, a sort of culinary Olympics. He opened two French-accented restaurants called Savann in Manhattan and then a contemporary Mexican restaurant called Maya, again in New York. He called on his home region's culinary traditions, modernized it with a variety of ingredients and style of presentation—and a new restaurant form was born. A second Maya later opened in San Francisco.

Maya earned its reputation as much for its style as for its food. Not only did Maya's décor make a dramatic design statement, but Sandoval commissioned tableware for it, notably, distinctive three-legged bowls of black lava rock with silver inserts. Guacamole is served on the top tier, with chips on the bottom. With two Mayas going on the coasts, Sandoval looked to the middle of the country for a third. He chose Denver to launch Tamayo here and sold the two Savanns to concentrate on his culinary roots in the traditional cuisine of Mexico. He develops the recipes, but obviously, he cannot be everywhere at once, so he relies on chefs in each location to carry out his signature new Mexican style.

Denver's Tamayo is a long room bisected lengthwise by a custom wooden room divider. On the right is the dining room, with a view south toward Speer Boulevard and the Platte River Valley—or no view at all if the strong setting sun dictates lowered shades. On the left is the bar, dominated by a huge mosaic mural of famed 20th-century artist Rufino Tamayo, for whom the restaurant is named. He is known for mixing modern techniques with themes from Mexican folklore—much as Sandoval does with food at Tamayo the restaurant.

Don't even think about eating at Tamayo without ordering the guacamole. I imagine that Tamayo has one cook in the back who does nothing but peel, seed, and smoosh perfectly ripe avocados, mix them with just the right amount of subtle seasoning, and plunk a big dollop on the top dish of those distinctive serving pieces.

Other appetizer selections include Tamayo's updated Chile Relleno, filled with lightly sautéed seafood and Manchego cheese, and served in a black bean purée with *chile de arbol salsa, crema fresca,* and chive oil. The Quesadilla Surtidas is stuffed with Oaxacan cheese, *rajas* and zucchini blossoms, and topped with a homemade salsa. Dumplings stuffed with *huitlacoche,* a corn fungus that Sandoval and other Mexican connoisseurs call "the truffle of Mexico," swim in the ethereal Sopa de Elote, a creamy roasted-corn soup.

A standout among the entrées is Mole Poblano, grilled chicken breast with sautéed plantains that comes with a rich dark mole-poblano sauce. *Huachinango a la Talla,* marinated and pan-roasted red snapper, is served atop red cabbage and tomato. Separate bowls of rice and beans appear on the table too, so that you can select how much of these side dishes you have room for. And for gringos who think Mexican dining equals "combination plate," Tamayo's *Tampiqueña* consists of grilled, butterflied filet mignon with *rajas* potato gratin, a mole-cheese enchilada, guacamole, and cilantro oil.

The lunch menu offers appetizers, salads, open-face quesadilla sandwiches, and entrées, and you can assemble three items, starred on the menu, into a three-course lunch that will get you fed and out the door in an hour. The selection includes the wonderful *Tamal al Chipotle* (tamale), *Sopa de Tortilla* (tortilla soup), *Mole Poblano* (chicken mole), and *Champiñones Envueltos* (wild mushroom strudel).

There are, at this writing, a handful of Mayas and also a second Tamayo in Palm

Beach, Florida, but Tamayo was launched here, the vanguard of contemporary Mexican food in Denver.

Tamayo, 1400 Larimer Street, Denver; (720) 946-1433.

Tante Louise

This Denver classic has been serving outstanding French cuisine through Denver's notorious booms and busts since the early 1970s. And it has done so on East Colfax Avenue, an unlikely setting for a consistently high-caliber restaurant that resembles a French country inn.

The gracious home was built in 1917, but for more than half of its existence it has been a quiet, elegant, and romantic restaurant—a place that has aged as gracefully as fine wine or antique silver. More than half a century ago, it became a French restaurant called The Normandy. When it moved to larger space nearby in 1973, Corbine "Corky" Douglas III transformed it into Tante Louise and runs it to this day. Polished wood floors, diaphanous curtains, soft lighting, and crisp white napery all contribute to the romantic and elegant atmosphere that makes Tante Louise a special-occasion restaurant—or makes every dinner taken there a special occasion. In the summer, outdoor dining on a tree-shaded patio is an option.

Some of Colorado's best-known chefs have cooked at Tante Louise, including Jim Cohen, who went on to become executive chef at The Lodge at Vail and later at The Phoenician in Scottsdale; Mary Clark, who with Fred Bromhill now owns the Bluepoint Bakery (see page 13), and Duy Van Pham, who overlaid a subtle Southeast Asian influence on the French favorites. When he left midway through 2002 to launch Opal, Marlo Hix returned to preside over the kitchen where she had once been sous-chef. Hix, a Johnson & Wales graduate, took Tante Louise back to its roots just as the restaurant was celebrating its 30th anniversary. She backed off from her predecessor's Asian-influenced menu in favor of Continental classics and contemporary adaptations of French fare, some showcasing New World ingredients along with Old World techniques. Her half duck, redolent with cinnamon and orange and served with sweet potatoes, is an inspired cold-weather dish, as is a meaty loin of red deer served with gnocchi.

Sommelier Emma Healion presides over a cellar stocked with 600 domestic and imported wines. Not surprisingly, French vintages are emphasized. Tante Louise hosts periodic tasting dinners. Pastry chef Lisa Blette works magic with desserts, again including both classics and contemporary creations. Bread pudding has been a signature sweet since Tante Louise was a girl. To celebrate Tante Louise's 30th year, and to honor the fine chefs who have cooked there, the restaurant assembled a cookbook, available at the restaurant.

Tante Louise, 4900 East Colfax Avenue, Denver; (303) 355-4489 or www.tantelouise.com.

240 Union Restaurant

This beacon of fine cuisine shines amid the chains and hokey-themed restaurants in Lakewood's business-busy Simms–Union area. Established in 1989 by Strings owner Noel Cunningham in partnership with Michael Coughlin, who serves as the on-site general manager, 240 Union brought contemporary American cuisine to Denver's western suburbs and continues to transcend its surroundings in an uninspiring strip shopping center. Chef Matthew Franklin has been there since the beginning, and heads his crew in a 60-foot-long open kitchen, where they turn out vibrant and eye-appealing dishes at lunch and dinner.

The décor and cuisine are both contemporary American. Angular room dividers of polished wood bring the sprawling room down to size. The ceiling and some walls are white, other walls are bright red, and the painted surfaces that taper up to the big skylights are bright blue. The effect is chipper and upbeat, yet stylish. There is also a glass-enclosed "porch" overlooking the parking lot.

A wood-fired brick oven gives many of the dishes a particular flavor and sizzle. Not only the half-a-dozen or so daily pizzas, but roasted Prince Edward Island Mussels, whole fish, and some of the meats are roasted in it. Other meats are cooked on a mesquite grill. The menu changes with the seasons, and there are daily specials too.

Soups of the day, seafood *frito misto* with roasted garlic aïoli and grilled lemon, almond-crusted cakes, and buffalo carpaccio typify the starters, called Small Plates on the menu. The house salad is the whimsically named Leaves and Weeds, whose ingredients change with the season. You'll also find such excellent combinations as roasted pear with Bingham Hill blue cheese and pumpkin seeds, napped in pomegranate vinaigrette.

The brick-oven pizza shines, whether it's an artfully contrived California-style combo such as smoked salmon, avocado, tomato, red onion, capers, and sour cream; or fingerling potatoes, dried tomatoes, garlic confit, and goat cheese—or an almost-standard like Italian sausage, caramelized onions, and Gorgonzola. Pasta comes in similar renditions that are aggressively contemporary or near classics.

Some patrons come just for such hefty meats as a large pistachio-crusted pork chop, grilled New York steak, or braised lamb shank. Others are smitten with seafood entrées, including crusted grilled salmon, that brick-oven-roasted whole fish of the day, or 240 Cioppino, the restaurant's rendition of the classic San Francisco seafood stew. Poultry, including grilled duck, and a vegetarian dish or two round out the entrée selection. Everything is idyllically sauced and accompanied by interesting sides.

Pastry Chef Adon James similarly contrives totally whimsical desserts and adaptations of classics. The Vanilla Cream Crème Brulée with Season Berries and Mocha Panna Cotta are smooth and lovely. The Rustic Apple Tart is similar to apple pie but is made with a cornmeal-cheddar crust, while the Key Lime Pie is made with a macadamia nut crust and exquisitely plated with a frosted mint leaf, strawberries, and a froth of whipped cream. Pear Bread Pudding is rich with cashew caramel. And the Double Chocolate Mousse Tort is napped with raspberry sauce.

The California-heavy wine list leads off with "240 Union's First Wine Law." It is actually three laws in one: (1) I like it; (2) I don't like it; and (3) I'll only drink it if someone else pays for it. The restaurant offers a terrific wine list to choose from. More than 20 wines are available by the glass, and another eight or so are sold by the half bottle. The rest are categorized into Chardonnay, Simple Pleasures, and More

Than Just a Pretty Face (other whites and some rosés); and Comfort Zone Reds, Silver Linings, and No Wimpy Wines (reds of various sorts, from light and fruity to big, full-bodied selections).

With a combination of an attractive space, good food and drink, attentive service, and a light-hearted approach to seriously good food and wine, this restaurant works equally well for a civilized workday lunch or for a special dinner. And no part of town needs it more than Simms and Union.

240 Union Restaurant, 240 Union Boulevard, Lakewood; (303) 989-3562 or www.240union.com.

Vesta Dipping Grill

Vesta Dipping Grill is a soaring, many-columned space brought to a manageable, almost intimate scale with clever fabric drapings, booths that swirl like snail shells to encase groups of diners, and clever lighting. Serving dinner only, the restaurant presents a hip scene with terrific food—and a terrific scene with hip food. It's urban and urbane.

The mix-and-match concept is simple. Adapted Asian appetizers—such as Grilled Sesame Shrimp Satay, Ginger Crab Dumplings in wild mushroom-soy broth, and the Vesta Roll, a roll of rare tuna with wasabi cream sauce, cucumber, and pickled ginger salad—are followed by a choice of entrées. Chicken, tuna, salmon, pork, lamb, beef, and duck are seasoned, then grilled, pan-seared, or roasted. They are then skewered and brought to the table cooked. Diners select from more than 30 dipping sauces.

These sauces are adapted from Indian, Japanese, Mexican, Southwestern, and Spanish cuisines: abodo, black pepper aïoli, dried berry chutney, honey soy, mango-poblano salsa, miso, peanut sauce, pineapple ginger chutney, red pepper rouille, roasted corn, *salsa roja*, sweet chili ginger, three-citrus ponzu, wasabi cream, yellow chutney, and more. The menu suggests three sauces for each dish, but you can, of course, make your own combinations. After you've selected your meats and sauces, your next challenge is to narrow down the wines on the large list to the one or two that best match your dinner.

The skewering stops when dessert time comes, but many offerings do come with a unique Vesta twist. Traditional crème brulée, a great pie, and a house-specialty bread pudding are good renditions of fairly standard dishes. But Vesta's unusual ones include Dark Chocolate *Boca Negra* with White Chocolate Ganache and Matty's Daffy Apple, the restaurant's spin on the candied apple of the old-time country fair. Vesta's is a caramel-dipped apple rolled in sweet crunchy vanilla ice cream and chocolate syrup. Yum.

Vesta Dipping Grill, 1822 Blake Street, Denver; (303) 296-1970 or www.vestagrill.com.

Events

Captain Vino's Wine Tasting

Ongoing/Weekly—These informal, informational weekly wine tastings take place between 5:00 and 7:00 P.M. every Thursday evening near Parker, south of Denver. They are free and open to locals and visitors alike. Captain Vino's is informative and advocational, even for wine lovers who don't manage to attend a tasting.

    **Captain Vino, 10244 Progress Lane, Parker; (720) 851-6966
or www.captainvino.com.**

Great Chefs of the West

February—Roughly 1,000 supporters turn out for this annual fundraiser for the National Kidney Foundation of Colorado, Idaho, Montana, and Wyoming, which features tastings from two dozen or so leading local chefs, followed by a silent auction. In 2003, participating restaurants included 240 Union, California Café, Café Bistro, and Bruno's Italian Bistro. There is no wine tasting as such but a cash bar is set up. The venue is the Hyatt Regency Tech Center, done up stylishly enough to match the food.

    Details and tickets are available from the local office of the National Kidney Foundation, 3151 South Vaughn Way, Suite 505, Aurora; (720) 748-9991, (800) 263-4005, or www.kidneycimw.org.

Café Vineyard

April–May—Name notwithstanding, Café Vineyard is not a place but a one-evening wine-tasting benefit for the Arthritis Foundation in late April or early May at the Denver Marriott Tech Center. Launched in 1988, it attracts some 700 guests and is also one of the more reasonably priced such charity functions.

    More than 125 American and imported wines are poured in a two-and-a-half-hour period and food samples are served too. A silent auction is held with rare wines among the items up for bid.

    Purchase tickets at the door or in advance from the Arthritis Foundation, 2280 Albion Street, Denver, CO 80222-4906; (303) 756-8622, (800) 475-6447, or www.arthritis.org.

DAM Uncorked

April–May—This is a two-day wine event at the Denver Art Museum. Participants may register for one or both days. A Friday-night wine tasting is included with either, featuring wines from more than 30 notable wineries from all over the world, including vintages and reserves from Chateau Mouton Rothschild, Silver Oak Cellars, Clos du Val, Sterling Vineyards, Chalone Wine Estates, Broadbent Selections, and the Hess Collection. The second day of DAM Uncorked offers educational seminars led by locally and internationally recognized figures in the wine industry. The evening brings a live auction featuring rare and unusual wines from prominent local wine cellars and wine-related travel. Items appearing in previous auctions have included a bottle of 1929 Haut Brion and a three-day stay at a chateau in Beaune, France. A silent auction offers additional wine selections, travel packages, restaurant dining, and wine tasting packages.

Denver Art Museum, Civic Center Park, 13th and Acoma, Denver; (720) 913-0039 or www.denverartmuseum.org.

Asian Food Bazaar

May—The name "Asian Food Bazaar" is somewhat misleading, because the specialties prepared here are not pan-Asian but rather primarily Japanese, and it is not a bazaar in the usual sense of the word. There are no vendors selling their own individual wares or foodstuffs, but rather a festival of communal cooking from greater Denver's Japanese-American community. On the first Saturday in May, before sunrise, two dozen or more ladies begin cooking a handful of tried-and-true specialties for this food fest—just as they have every year since 1950. Sushi, beef teriyaki, and, in an ecumenical spirit, chow mein, are the main offerings. Fortune cookies and Japanese pastries round out the short list. A modest donation buys a heaping portion, available to eat in or take out. The Japanese-American Methodist church with the pagoda roof in which the Asian Food Bazaar is held also hosts other cultural events, including the Doll Festival the first weekend in April, which includes a traditional tea ceremony and flower arranging.

Simpson United Methodist Church, 6001 Wolff Street, Arvada; (303) 428-7963.

Taste of the Tech

May—Founded in 1892, the Denver Rescue Mission is one of the city's most venerable service organizations. Taste of the Tech, its annual fundraising food-sampling event held in late May, started in 1994. It currently takes place at the Sheraton Tech Center, a hotel in southern Denver's business development dedicated to technology. Some 20 local restaurants typically participate with tastings of their food specialties.

For information and tickets, contact the Denver Rescue Mission; (303) 297-1815.

Cherry Blossom Festival

June—To many, the words "cherry blossom festival" conjure images of the fragrant trees around the Tidal Basin in Washington, D.C. But Denver's Cherry Blossom Festival is more about culture, art, and food at Sakura Square on the northwestern edge of downtown. I'm not even sure that the area has any cherry trees, but they would be way beyond blooming when this engaging cultural festival takes place on a weekend in late June.

There, against the backdrop of the Tri-State/Denver Buddhist Temple, is the event that has taken place annually since 1972. The festival casts a spotlight on Japanese arts, crafts, martial arts, cultural presentations, artistic performances (especially dances and *taiko* drumming)—and of course, food. Volunteer cooks from the Japanese and greater Asian community prepare authentic dishes, some well known from restaurant menus and others new to non-Japanese diners. With such hefty inspiration of so many things Japanese, attendees often find it a bonus to stop at Pacific Mercantile, on the corner, for groceries and other food items—or at least for "Hawaiian shave ice," sold from a stand.

Cherry Blossom Festival, c/o Tri-State/Denver Buddhist Temple, 1947 Lawrence Street, Denver; (303) 295-1844.

The Greek Festival

June—Toward the end of June every year since 1965, the gold dome of the Assumption Greek Orthodox Cathedral on East Alameda has been a beacon for lovers of Mediterranean food in general and Greek food in particular. By the time the three-day event opens on Friday, the congregation's volunteers have been cooking up a storm for about six weeks. Denver's Greek Festival, reportedly one of the nation's largest honoring that ancient nation's traditions, is a really noncommercial event—without the intrusion of everything from Indian fry bread to bratwurst into what was originally a showcase for one particular and distinctive culture.

By contrast, the Greek Festival remains an authentic and sincere expression from that community. Volunteers make and roll acres of dough, mix gallons of entrée and dessert fillings, prepare oceans of syrup, and dole out mountains of chopped nuts. The cathedral's industrial kitchen is redolent with the enticing aromas of onion, garlic, mint, dill, basil, Greek oregano, and real sheep's milk feta cheese—and of course, meat being cooked or roasted and dough items being baked. In 2002, the *Rocky Mountain News* reported the oldest volunteer to be 93 and the youngest just four. Go to the festival and you'll find this labor of love expressed in such savories as *dolmedas*, *kalamaria*, gyros, *souvlakia*, *pastitsio*, and such sweets as baklava, *diples*, and *kourabiedes*. Festival admission is modest and includes an optional guided tour of the magnificent cathedral.

Assumption Greek Orthodox Cathedral, 4610 East Alameda Avenue, Denver; (303) 388-9314.

TableScapes

June—Think of a creative and well-set table as the stage on which the meal you've produced is performed. You may produce splendid meals—perfectly prepared and beautifully assembled—but when something falls short when it's time to eat, it might just be that stage. For inspiration, and to help a good cause, visit TableScapes, a three-day showing of 20 to 25 lovely settings to benefit the Assistance League of Denver.

The Compleat Gourmet, Tiffany's, Invitations Etc., and some of the city's leading home-furnishings and decorative-arts purveyors compete in the professional category, while 20 or more competitors set their stuff in the amateur category. Truth be told, some of these amateurs have had decorating training or experience and so set wonderful tables. Entrants select themes—such as a historic period, a holiday, or another culture—and select fabrics, dishes, glassware, flatware, centerpieces, and other decorative elements. During its first five years, TableScapes was held in early May. In 2002, it moved to the middle weekend in June, and there it might stay.

TableScapes, c/o Assistance League of Denver, 1400 Josephine Street, Denver; (303) 322-5205 or (303) 759-3137.

Cherry Creek Arts Festival

July—No one goes to the annual Cherry Creek Arts Festival just to eat. The state's largest juried art show is held over the Fourth of July weekend. Culinary Row, part of this huge three-day event held in Cherry Creek North, is set up on St. Paul Street and features food stands and a shady seating area. About a dozen restaurants and other food companies serve three or four items each. You certainly won't find them all to represent Denver's finest cuisine, or even necessarily its finest street food, but there's variety and cultural authenticity in that dozen.

Alphabetically they served up everything from a South American specialty called *alide gallina* from Chavin to the classic cold potato soup called vichyssoise from The Painted Bench. Culturally, the offerings traveled from Gourmet Cheese Steak (from Philadelphia Filly) and Breaded Chicken on a Stick (from Miller Concessions) to Exotic Fruit-Cheese Wonton (from Thai in Cherry Creek) and Valencia Paella (from Sevilla). The Culinary Row mix is about as wide-ranging and eclectic as the works by 2,100 visual artists from 49 states and five countries. Admission to the festival is free.

Cherry Creek Arts Festival, 2 Steele Street, Denver; (303) 355-2787 or www.cherryarts.org.

Dragon Boat Festival

August—Dragon boating is a 2,000-year-old tradition rooted in Imperial China that came to Sloan's Lake in August 2001 and quickly became a mega-hit on the Colorado cultural circuit. Within two years, 30,000 people were crowding around the lake to watch these elaborate rowed boats (calling them rowboats would hardly do them justice) compete. The colorful and exciting day-long event, in which oarsmen propel their craft across the water with graceful strokes and much teamwork, attracts many members from Denver's Asian communities—and anyone else who wants a quick journey to Asia without leaving town. The festival's busy Asian Marketplace features an entertainment stage for such performances as Chinese lion dancing and Japanese *taiko* drumming and, of course, food. Many of the Denver area's Asian restaurants, groceries, and civic and cultural organizations set up tasting booths.

The best source of information is the organizers' website at www.coloradodragonboat.org.

A House Toast

July–August—This wine-tasting event, held on a weeknight in late July or early August, benefits Habitat for Humanity of Metro Denver and features an assortment of quality, affordably priced wines from many of the wine-growing regions around the world. How appropriate for an organization dedicated to bringing quality, affordably priced housing to people around the world. The 2002 event was held at Dixon's Downtown Grill with wines selected by Corks Wine Store.

Habitat for Humanity of Metro Denver, 1500 West 12th Avenue, Denver; (303) 534-2929.

Taste of the Nation

July–August—Taste of the Nation, part of a country-wide fundraising effort that uses food festivals to combat hunger, is the city's biggest local event. Denver's is held annually between the end of July and mid-August, drawing thousands of participants and scores of restaurants and wineries. It is a testimonial to its high profile in food circles that many a festival now bears the name Taste of Someplace.

Denver, in fact, was the launching pad for the concept. In 1987, an executive with a nonprofit organization called Share Our Strength asked Pat "Gabby Gourmet" Miller and several chefs to help raise many for Meals on Wheels. Miller along with Noel Cunningham of Strings, and others developed the concept of using a series of culinary benefits to combat hunger and poverty. Taste of the Nation was launched that year and spread across the country. There are now more than 100 such culinary events in the United States and Canada, having become the continent's largest gourmet antihunger fundraising effort. In all, Taste of the Nation unites more than 6,000 chefs and restaurateurs in 70 cities and 65,000 guests to combat hunger while eating very well themselves. Denver's Share Our Strength initiatives have raised more than $2 million for local grassroots antipoverty, antihunger programs. Denver's event has moved around a bit since its inception, and in 2002, moved from Coors Field to the Johnson & Wales campus (see page 24).

For dedicated foodies, Taste of the Nation provides more than an opportunity to scarf up samples from dozens of restaurants. Taste a bit of this, a bit of that—lobster green chili, goose liver pâté, steamed crab legs, crab cakes, chicken curry, lamb riblet, hazelnut chocolate tart, coconut banana cream pie, and more—from many of Denver's top restaurants. Additionally, the event provides the opportunity to schmooze with the chefs (come at the beginning for the best interacting or stay until the end, when they—and you—might be tired but the crowd has thinned). You can also pick up menus and flyers for upcoming food-and-wine events to help plan your next eating adventures, and sometimes discount, two-fer, or free-item coupons to help subsidize them. The annual guide to participants and sponsors includes recipes, so you can try to replicate some of these delectables at home. At the silent auction, you can bid on food and wine items, art and memorabilia, dinners, and travel items.

The adult admission ticket ($50 in 2002) includes all-you-can-taste access to the food tasting and most wine-tasting stations. The VIP Ticket Package ($200 in 2002) turns an afternoon of "mere" fine food-tasting into an upscale experience. In 2002,

Who's Who at Taste of the Nation

Reading lists of restaurants can be as exciting as the phone book, but the lineup is so impressive and the contributions of restaurateurs, chefs, and wineries so generous that it is worth mentioning here. The chefs don't pull any punches when preparing sampling portions of their specialties. These were the 2002 participants, most of whom you can expect to see again:

Restaurants

240 Union
Appaloosa Grill
Avenue Grill
Bastien's Restaurant
BD's Mongolian Restaurant
Bravo Ristorante
Broker Restaurant
Brook's Steakhouse
The Brown Palace—Palace Arms
    Restaurant
Bruno's Italian Bistro
Buca Di Beppo
Croc's Mexican Grill
Del Frisco Double Eagle Steakhouse
Del Mar Crab House
Denver Chop House
Dixon's Downtown Grill
The Fourth Story Restaurant and
    Grill
Gallagher's
Great Northern Tavern and Brewery
Hilltop Cafe
Imperial Chinese Seafood
    Restaurant
Jax Fish House
Kendra's Kitchen
La Fondue
Lime
Luigi's Bent Noodle
Maggiano's Little Italy

Mattie's House of Mirrors
Mel's Restaurant and Bar
Morton's of Chicago
The Painted Bench
The Palm
Panzano
P. F. Chang's China Bistro
Ristorante Piatti
Roy's Cherry Creek
Strings
Sambuca Jazz Cafe
Seven 30 South
Sevilla Mediterranean
The Swan at the Inverness
    Hotel and Golf Club
Sahara Foodmart and Restaurant
Sullivan's Steakhouse
Sonoda's
Table Mountain Inn
Tamayo
Texas Land and Cattle Steak House
Tante Louise
Vasil's Euro Grille
Vesta Dipping Grill
Village Tavern
Wazee Supper Club
Westin Tabor Center
Wolfgang Puck Café
Wynkoop Brewing Company
Yia Yia's Eurocafe

VIP extras included courtesy valet parking at the campus (Quebec & 17th) and a VIP tent with preferred seating and table service with runners between the tent and the tasting stations. Events in the tent included cooking demonstrations by some of Denver's premier chefs and an exclusive wine tasting from Brown-Forman Wines USA.

Normally, tickets can be purchased in advance from a number of local restaurants and wine stores (a poster will alert you to their availability at a particular location) or at the door. The Johnson & Wales campus is at 7150 Montview Boulevard, which is actually on the corner of Quebec and 17th, southwest of the old Stapleton Airport. Parking is available at the old airport, with free shuttle service to the campus.

Taste of the Nation information is available from Volunteers of America, 2660 Larimer Street, Denver; (303) 297-0408 or www.voacolorado.org/taste.htm.

Big Bite: Take a Bite Out of Hunger

August—As something of an adjunct to Taste of the Nation (see page 58), Big Bite brings diners into restaurants rather than matching restaurants and diners in another location—all for the sake of hunger prevention.

Big Bite's magic number is 31. For 31 days in August, numerous metro Denver and Boulder restaurants participate by offering $31 *prix fixe* dinners in fine-dining restaurants and $31 dinners for two in more casual establishments. American Express donates two cents for every transaction paid for on the AmEx card, which might not be much per transaction but can add up.

Information and a list of participating restaurants is available on www.coloradorestaurant.com/bigbite.

Festival of Mountain and Plain . . . A Taste of Colorado

September—On Labor Day weekend, Civic Center Park is turned into a gigantic carnival, loosely wrapped around the theme of food. There's plenty to eat, including hot dogs, corn dogs, kettle corn, Asian and Mexican foods, ice cream, and, of course, beer, which some attendees consider a liquid food. Participants enjoy highly amplified entertainment on seven stages, carnival rides, a midway, 200 or more arts and crafts booths, the obligatory educational exhibits, and more. One section of the festival, set up in the Greek Theater, the classically inspired amphitheater on the park's south end, is devoted to more refined cuisine.

Out of the 30 to 40 participating restaurants, the best set up booths are in the designated Fine Dining Area and serve tasting portions of some of their specialties. Turn in some coupons for a ramekin of soup here, a small open-faced sandwich there, a spring roll elsewhere, grilled lamb nearby, and a fruit tart or piece of cake at other stands. Cooking demonstrations are held in a shaded, open-sided tent. Mostly, well-known local chefs prepare a dish or two, but occasionally a national star like Wolfgang Puck shows up as well. Actually, Puck's appearance is not too surprising since he has a restaurant at the nearby Denver Pavilions on the 16th Street Mall.

A new attraction in 2002 was "Ready, Set, Cook," a head-to-head culinary competition held Friday, Saturday, and Monday evenings. This inaugural event pitted top chefs against each other. Competitors included Mark Fisher, owner/chef of SIX89 in Carbondale, Richard Sandoval of Tamayo, and Sherry Yard, executive pastry chef of the Wolfgang Puck Dining Group.

The name Festival of Mountain and Plain . . . A Taste of Colorado is almost as big as the event itself, but people in general and those interested in food in particular tend to call it A Taste of Colorado. The festival packs 'em in—largely because there's something for almost everyone and because admission to this huge festival is free. Because the culinary aspect is so overwhelmed by all the other activities, A Taste of Colorado doesn't really compare to other serious food events in Denver or elsewhere in the state, nor does it pretend to do so. But it's an amusing diversion for residents and visitors during summer's final holiday weekend—and you *can* sample some good eats from good restaurants.

Festival of Mountain and Plain . . . A Taste of Colorado, Civic Center Park, Denver (mailing address: 511 16th Street, Suite 200, Denver, CO 80202); (303) 295-6330 or www.atasteofcolorado.com.

Oktoberfest

September—Denver's Oktoberfest takes place in early September, and though it comes before Munich's original, it is modeled after the most famous of all Bavarian festivals. The venue is Larimer Square, always a great place for a party but never more so during Oktoberfest, when German beer flows, German food is devoured, and German oompah music fills the air until midnight on Thursday, Friday, and Saturday nights and until 6:00 P.M. on Sunday, the festival's last day. Admission is free. Just pay for what you eat and drink.

Larimer Arts Association; (303) 685-8143 or www.larimerarts.com.

Red, White, and Brew

September—Despite the name that would imply beer as the beverage of choice, one of Denver's premier master wine-tasting and dinner charity events is Red, White, and Brew, established in 1994 to benefit the Mile High Chapter of the American Red Cross. The venue for this elegant six-course event generally held in mid-September is the Brown Palace Hotel, which certainly knows how to throw a party. Claude Robbins, a Master of Wine Arts, organizes the evening, which also includes a live auction. In 2002, one of the items was a basket of six top Bordeaux from France. The event attracts both aficionados of fine food and wine and Denver's charity-supporting social set, so it sells out fast.

For information or reservations, call the American Red Cross Mile High Chapter, 444 Sherman Street, Denver; (303) 722-7474 or www.denver-redcross.org.

March of Dimes Star Chefs

September–October—A major fundraising effort for the March of Dimes is the annual Star Chefs gala, a series of four sparkling culinary events held in four Colorado locations (Denver, Boulder, Colorado Springs, and Grand Junction) on four dates in the fall. Typically, each of the 15 to 20 participating chefs in each location prepares a single signature dish. Guests stroll around to sample what appeals to them while musicians play live music. The silent auction includes great dinners at restaurants where those star chefs cook, travel and lodging packages, signed sports memorabilia, and recreational opportunities from lift tickets to scuba lessons.

March of Dimes Chapter Headquarters and Denver Division,
1325 South Colorado Boulevard, Suite 508, Denver; (303) 692-0011;
www.marchofdimesco.org.

Great American Beer Festival

October—This is not a beer book, but I would be remiss if I did not at least mention the Great American Beer Festival. Founded modestly in 1982, it is now the nation's largest, with some 22,000 attendees sampling roughly 1,200 different beers, ales, porters, and stouts from 300 or so brewers and brewpubs. The event, which is held on two weekends in late September and early October, floods the Colorado Convention Center. In addition to general admission, an upgraded ticket includes the Connoisseur Session on one afternoon of the three-day event.

Information is available from the Association of Brewers, P.O. Box, 1679, Boulder,
CO 80306-1679; (888) 822-6273, (303) 447-0818, or www.beertown.org.

Wines for Life

October—Fine food, fine domestic and imported wines, and the best of beers are the draws for Wines for Life—established in 1982 to support cancer research. By the annual event's 20th anniversary, Wines for Life had raised more than $10 million, with the University of Colorado Cancer Center being the main beneficiary.

The afternoon event now takes place at the CityLights Pavilion on the grounds of the Pepsi Center. In addition to the wines available for tasting, dozens of bottles of rare, collectible, and just plain pricey wines are sold in a live auction. Even as the wines are poured, wine lovers come pouring in. In 2002, a reported 4,000 people were expected and 6,000 attended, making it—according to one report—the largest single-day wine event in the whole of the United States.

Advance tickets are sold in liquor and wine stores, mostly along the Front
Range but also in selected mountain towns. For information on Wines for Life,
call (303) 773-7581.

Nouveau en LoDo

November—One of the events at which Denver celebrates the annual release of France's Nouveau Beaujolais is a downtown wine gala to benefit the National Sports Center for the Disabled at Winter Park. With an *Iron Chef*-style head-to-head culinary competition, tastings of the year's freshest red wine as well as other vintages, music, and a silent auction, this is a fun and festive event, most recently held at Mattie's House of Mirrors.

For information, call (303) 777-6887.

Retail

AJ Restaurant Equipment & Supplies Company

You might not want to bother going to this flat-roofed, utilitarian building for any particular utensil or gadget, or to get in and out quickly. But definitely go if you are in the mood for serendipity. You might stumble upon something you've been looking for, new or used, at a very good price—or you might find something that you didn't know you wanted until you saw it. In that regard, AJ Restaurant Equipment is a little like a grab bag.

Located just west of Interstate 25 amid square and angled streets, this warehouse store is as tangled as the road map of its neighborhood. The aisles are tight, the shelves are crammed, and though there is order and organization, to the unschooled eye it might seem totally random. When I explored the place, a display at the end of one shelf was loaded with more sizes and shapes of ladles, scoops, and spoons than I could image in one small space. The steel shelves were loaded with baking tins, colanders, sauce pans, omelette pans, sauté pans, and more, both nonstick and regular. Mandolines, industrial-size pizza paddles, whisks, mashers, and sieves occupied other sections.

What else? Cast-iron fajita pans and wood trays to put under them. Authentic paella pans imported from Spain. Party trays. Lemon juicers. Chefs' aprons. Tongs. Stacks of cheap, utilitarian terrycloth towels that chefs use for everything from keeping their cutting boards clean and their knives wiped to protecting their hands from hot pot handles. Cake stands. Cake displays. Salsa bowls. Wine chillers. Soup tureens. The list goes on and on.

If you don't mind using some elbow grease, for some of the items are second-hand, you can find restaurant- or coffee shop–style dishes, sugar and grated-cheese shakers, squeeze bottles, and salt and pepper shakers. The back of the large store holds kitchen fixtures, from salamanders and deep fryers to stainless-steel pot sinks and refrigerators, some new but many used.

AJ Restaurant Equipment & Supplies Company, 3400 Mariposa Street, Denver; (303) 480-5000.

Asian and Middle Eastern Markets

The Silk Road, Spice Road, and Incense Road—those three legendary trade routes that stretched from the Middle East to the Orient—provided opportunities, honed over centuries, for the cross-fertilization of Mediterranean, Middle Eastern, Indian, and Asian cuisines. With the Denver area's Asian population soaring (at a rate of 67 percent growth between the 1990 and 2000 censuses), the Middle Eastern community growing as well, and many home cooks delving into Asian and Middle Eastern food, stores that sell once-exotic ingredients now abound.

They range from modest mom-and-pop stores to veritable supermarkets—the largest of them, in fact, located in stores that were once occupied by chain markets. Some are geared really to the needs of a particular ethnic community, with many food labels in languages other than English and few (or even no) English-speaking employees. Others have lots of English labels and English-speaking help and are happy to guide unknowledgeable customers through their complex cuisines and the ingredients for them. All of the bigger stores, such as the Pacific Mercantile, and some of the smaller ones, also sell cookware (including woks, steamers, rice cookers, and sukiyaki pans) as well as imported tableware, rice bowls, tea sets, and more.

An organized ethnic market tour, such as that offered through the Denver Free University is one way to get a fast introduction to this type of shopping. Some of these ethnic markets are closed or have limited hours in midweek, so call before you make a special trip to a specific one.

Here is a selection of some of the Denver area's most interesting sources for ingredients and sometimes prepared foods from the Middle East, the Indian subcontinent, Southeast Asia, China, Korea, Japan, and the Philippines across the sea:

Arash Groceries and Deli, 2159 South Parker Road, Denver; (303) 752-9272

Asian Market, 333 South Federal Boulevard, Denver; (303) 937-1431

Aurora Japanese and Oriental Super Market, 15401 East Mississippi Avenue, Aurora; (303) 750-5408

Bombay Bazaar, 3140 South Parker Road, Aurora; (303) 369-1010

D&C Manila Oriental Market, 564 South Chambers Road, Aurora;
   (303) 750-3970

Denver Shoji, 855 East 73th Avenue, Denver; (303) 289-1282

Indochina, 1045 South Federal Boulevard, Denver; (303) 935-0400

Indochina International, 1340 South Federal Boulevard, Denver;
   (303) 935-1600

Indus Imports, 3020 West Mississippi Avenue, Denver; (303) 742-4443

International Market, 2020 South Parker Road, Denver; (303) 695-1090

Krungthai Imports, 11700 Montview Boulevard, Denver; (303) 343-9450

Lao Market, 7302 Federal Boulevard, Westminster; (303) 428-3290

Laotian Oriental Food Store, 7141 Irving, Westminster; (303) 428-3694

Lek's Asian Market, 112 Del Mar Circle, Aurora; (303) 366-2429

Little Saigon Market, 375 South Federal Boulevard, Denver; (303) 937-8860

Lucky Oriental Market, 506 South Federal Boulevard, Denver; (303) 937-8105

Mekong Market, 1076 South Federal Boulevard, Denver; (303) 937-7271

Middle East Market, 2254 South Colorado Boulevard, Denver; (303) 756-4580

Ngoc Phu Asian Market, 3133 Peoria, Aurora; (303) 340-340-4186

Oriental Grocery Store, 7404 Irving, Westminster; (303) 430-4582

Oriental Market, 10260 East Colfax Avenue, Aurora; (303) 366-0454
Pacific Mercantile, 1925 Lawrence Street, Denver; (303) 295-0293
Pacific Ocean International Market, 2200 West Alameda Avenue, Denver;
    (303) 936-4845
Sabo Oriental Market, 1000 South Peoria, Aurora; (303) 363-1298
Seoul Oriental Market, 6150 North Federal Boulevard, Denver; (303) 650-0101
Tajmahal Imports, 3095-C South Peoria, Aurora; (303) 751-8571
Tejal International Foods, 10351 Grant Street, Thornton; (303) 450-4164

Cake Crafts

Cake Crafts offers the home baker the kinds of equipment and accessories that professional bakers and pastry chefs use for their finest creations. They carry lines like Wilton, Merckens, Bakery Crafts, Country Kitchen/Sweet Art, Lucks, Kopy Kake, Sweet Art Galleries, Chefmaster, and Life of the Party.

You'll find all manner of cake pans—round, square, oblong, hexagonal, flower-shaped, in the form of popular characters, and more in various sizes, as well as such supplies as molds, spatulas, pastry bags with various-size tips, brushes, and more. For wedding cakes and other elaborate special-occasion structures, you'll see such accoutrements as cake stands, tiers, fountains, stairs, bridges, figural toppers, and doilies. You can shortcut your decorating with pre-made icings and fillings in popular flavors, molded sugars, edible sprinkles of all sorts. Cake Crafts also offers cake-decorating classes (see page 87) and carries candy-making supplies.

Cake Crafts, 4015 South Broadway, Englewood; (303) 761-1522 or www.cakecrafts.net.

The Cheese Company

The Cheese Company, established in 1967, was Denver's first retail cheese specialist, carrying unusual cheeses when they were hard to find elsewhere in town. This bright and cheery store still is a beacon for food-lovers, especially those on the east side of the city.

It could really be called The Cheese, Sandwiches, Pickles, Crackers, and More Company, because it also sells all of the above. In addition to the standard deli and specialty sandwiches, you'll find freshly made entrées, salads, and dessert bars.

The shop sells such gourmet goods as Starr Ridge spreads from Phoenix, California Harvest Spreads from Santa Rosa, and Robert Rothschild Pretzel Dips from Urban, Ohio. Nostalgic New Englanders will appreciate the lineup from Stonewall Kitchen of Lake York, Maine, including scrumptious grill sauces, maple pumpkin butter, farmhouse pancake mix, and genuine maple syrup. From Goodwives of Lynn, Massachusetts, comes a line of frozen appetizers. Additionally, you'll find products from crackers to cookie dough, and if you're entertaining, there's a rack of paper party supplies too. And, oh yes, there's a nice little case of cheeses as well.

The Cheese Company, 5575 East Third Avenue, Denver; (303) 394-9911.

Compleat Gourmet & Gifts

Since 1984, this friendly store has been a magnet for south suburban cooking enthusiasts, people who entertain frequently, and those who just like to set a pretty table. Owners Barb Trexler and Joan Dennen stock it with mid-priced, well-designed, and well-made goods. The inventory runs to cookware, gadgets, table and kitchen linens, decorative items, tableware, flatware, and glassware.

For cooks, brands such as Chantal, Cuisinart, Cuisine Internationale, Good Grips, Küchenprofi from Germany, NorPro, Progressive, and Zyliss signal reliable quality. There are baking pans of various sizes, shapes, and materials, and gadgets galore. The Compleat Gourmet is the place for potato scrubbers, French bread pans, flexible spatulas, safety graters, locking tongs, whisks of all sizes and shapes, pastry and cake decorating supplies, and much more. Among the measuring devices is an endearing set of spoons for measuring "a smidgeon," "a pinch," and other cooks' favorites.

The store also carries beautiful handmade Colorado pottery, fine china and glassware, barbecue items, picnic and party goods, and home decorating items, including an extensive selection of themed holidays items for every event on the calendar.

Compleat Gourmet & Gifts, 7592 South University Boulevard, Centennial; (303) 290-6023.

Continental Delicatessen

Continental Delicatessen, established in 1969 by a Swiss-German family surnamed Gutknecht, produces authentic European specialty meat items for wholesale customers and for its own Cherry Creek North store, which offers many variations on the themes of Frankfurter, Wiener, and Bratwurst, as well as *Weisswurst, Bockwurst, Waadländer,* and other authentic sausages from various regions of Germany. Some more exotic varieties, such as numerous kinds of blood sausage, liver sausage, and other-organ-meat sausages, are sold frozen.

Freezers also harbor an ecumenical assortment of sausages from other lands, such as Hungarian and Italian sausages, Scottish bangers, chorizo, *kisk,* kielbasa, and *Saucisse aux Choux,* the latter from the Franco-German region of Alsace. Other frozen specialty foods include dumplings and pre-made *Rouladen,* thinly pounded meat rolled around a filling and ready for braising. The cheeses, which are primarily from Germany and Switzerland, include spreadable *Butterkäse* and *Bierkäse,* as well as Emmenthaler, Appenzeller, Swiss raclette cheese, cambozola (despite its Italian name, a German Brie-like cheese), Tête de Moine, and Gouda. Continental Delicatessen even carries *Quark,* a German favorite that resembles cottage cheese or ricotta, but with tang to ratchet it up flavorwise.

The small grocery selection focuses on foods from Germany or made in the German style. You'll find a range of seasonings, sauces, mixes, and dehydrated soups and broths from Knorr, Maggi, and Tello. Oetker baking products, various imported brands of cookies, chocolates, mustards, pickles, jellies, soups, and crackers—all staples among European food enthusiasts—fill the shelves. The delicatessen also carries good pumpernickel and rye breads, some from as close as Colorado Springs and some from as far as Milwaukee.

Continental Delicatessen, 250 Steele Street, Denver; (303) 388-3354 or www.continentalsausage.com.

Cookbook Café and Emporium

At the entrance to the Cook Street School of Fine Cookery is a relatively small retail shop and café that carries chef's knives and other professional-quality kitchen necessities, especially items required for or used in classes, as well as a good selection of cookbooks. It coordinates weekly knife-sharpening services with Rolling Stone (see page 23 for school location).

Cook's Fresh Market

This bright and lively store on the fringes of the Denver Tech Center is run by cooks for cooks and connoisseurs alike. Owners Ed and Kristi Janos, both Culinary Institute of America graduates, are gifted and experienced chefs—and Ed, in fact, is one of only 70 Certified Master Chefs in the United States. They operated restaurants in Michigan before moving to Colorado in the mid-1990s. Surveying the restaurant scene, they recall being "shocked by all the chains"—and so when they decided to open a fine food market, it was to counteract that pervasive situation, especially rampant in Denver's southern suburbs.

In May 2000 they opened Cook's Fresh Market, a store that fills several roles. It is a café where Tech Center workers go for breakfast or lunch, and a place that people stop on the way home to pick up something for dinner, either to prepare themselves or ready-to-heat. It is a specialty butcher, one of the few offering genuine prime meats, and it is a from-scratch bakery.

Fresh produce and herbs greet you as you walk in. Around the corner is a salad bar against the wall and a glass case with mouth-watering house-made prepared foods in the middle of the room. Round the corner past these prepared foods and another glass case gleams with fine cakes and pastries. Turn left again to the refrigerated case of rare imports and artisan cheeses that are the peer of any cheese specialty shop.

The meat, poultry, and seafood cases and the adjacent open kitchen occupy the entire back of the store, taking up much of its square footage, what with the butchering, baking, pastry decorating, and restaurant-style food preparation both for in-store sales and the thriving catering business. The kitchen remains the heart and soul of this multi-layered enterprise. In addition to positions at Cook's Fresh Market, Ed Janos and several other staffers teach at Johnson & Wales University's culinary program, as well as giving in-store cooking classes (see page 24).

Cook's Fresh Market's butchers have top-quality, all natural steaks and other beef cuts, pork, veal, poultry, and seafood available, but they also do the prep work for some of the most glamorous special-occasion or company dishes you can imagine. They will do a "TurDucken," a culinary *tour de force* consisting of a boneless turkey stuffed with a boneless duck stuffed with a chicken; an oven-ready beef Wellington with fresh foie gras, mushroom duxelles, and truffled Madeira sauce; and an assortment of specialty cuts of meat trimmed, stuffed, tied, and ready to roast. These are all dazzlers. The butchers will custom-cut meats any way you wish, and if you want specialty game, organ meats, or other exotica, they can order it for you. With the Janoses' restaurant contacts intact, they get their seafood directly from Boston, the South Atlantic region, and Pacific Coast purveyors.

Among its selection of artisan cheeses are some found in few other United States stores. Cook's also offers hard-to-find packaged, canned, and jarred imported and domestic foodstuffs. Tall stainless shelves are stacked high with an outstanding selection of gourmet and imported products, among them oils, vinegars, fine prepared dressings, basting sauces, specialty pasta and rice from around the world, Western and Asian spices and herbs, condiments of all sorts, and English candies and preserves, plus the Janoses' line of private-label sauces, salsas, and condiments. Freezer cases hold house-made frozen stock, and caviar, truffles in season, and other upper-end food products are carried here.

From the in-house bakery come breads made with King Arthur's unbleached and unbromated flour and the bakery's own yeast starter. The bread doughs are proofed for at least 16 hours, creating a somewhat sweet, toasty, and toothsome crust. The pastries and other sweets cover the range from chocolate chip cookies and brownies to pies and fruit tarts to beautifully decorated cakes and pastries. Seasonal specialties such as *stollen, panettone,* English plum pudding, and that gorgeous Yule log known in French, and at Cook's Fresh Market, as *bouche de Noël* are holiday items that grace many a Denver Christmas table.

Cook's Fresh Market, Bellevue Promenade, 8000 East Belleview Avenue, Greenwood Village; (303) 741-4148 or www.cooksfreshmarket.com.

Cook's Mart

Enthusiastic home chefs have been trekking to Cherry Creek North since 1980, when this terrific cookware store opened. Cook's Mart carries an impressive assortment of cookware from such makers as All-Clad, Calphalon, Chantal, Le Creuset, Cuisinart, Look, and Viking. Specialty cookware, often unbranded, ranges from Ableskiver pans to woks, and the gadget inventory ranges from apple corers to zesters.

The selection of bakeware and baking accessories is fabulous. Assorted pans, rings, shells, molds, sheets, boards, and ramekins form the core of the selection. Baguette pans, Bundt pans, cannoli forms, madeleine pans, *panettone* molds, popover pans, steamed-pudding molds, and tartlette tins are just a few of the specialty bakeware goods available. If those aren't exotic enough, where else can you find a special form for *Kranse,* a braided Easter bread from the German-Russian tradition; a special rolling pin for *lefse,* a Norwegian potato pancake that many consider the national dish; or a ribbed, Quonset hut–shaped form for an Austrian cake called *Rehrücken*— or, more to the point, where else can you get them all in one store?

Food preparation is made easier and more pleasurable with quality knives, and Cook's Mart carries the top-rated Henckels and Messermeister lines. Cook's Mart is also the place to go if you want, say, a baking blade or baking nails; a slicer for beans, butter, or mushrooms; a cherry stoner or a chocolate shaver; or any other unusual tool for the kitchen. If you are hunting for a super-specialty item, you'll find it here— and if you just go in to browse, you're likely to find a gizmo that you suddenly decide you need.

Cook's Mart offers mixers, food processors of various sizes, bread machines, coffee grinders, blenders, and electric cookers of all sorts from rice cookers to toaster ovens. There's also the requisite choice of electric and stovetop coffee makers and espresso makers, without which no kitchen seems to exist these days. If you want to know how to best use some of these products, whether you already own or are considering buying, check out the weekly in-store product demonstrations. Product lines include Bodum, Braun, Capresso, Cuisinart, Froth au Lait, Kitchen Aid, Krups, Maxim/Salton, Omega, Villaware, Waring, WestBend, and Zojirushi. The store also shows a full line of beautiful serving pieces.

On weekends, Cook's Mart offers samplings of foods from its gourmet food department stocks, which includes products from Bella Cucina, Cuisine Perel, El Paso Chile Company, Food & Wine, Prairie Thyme, Private Harvest, Republic of Tea, Robert Rothschild Farms, Stonewall Kitchen, Turtle Island, Wabash Valley Farms and Wind & Willow.

Cook's Mart gives a 10 percent discount to Seasoned Chef students and also offers services beyond the usual bridal registry. You can drop off your knives at the store for sharpening between Thursday and Saturday early each month, and they'll be ready for pick-up the following Tuesday.

Cook's Mart, 3000 East Third Avenue, Denver; (303) 388-5933 or www.cooksmart.com.

Denver Cutlery

This two-building complex just northwest of Denver is a mecca for restaurateurs looking for everything from a walk-in cooler and heavy-duty dishwasher line to a potato peeler—and it's a great place to stock up on no-nonsense items for the home kitchen at hard-to-beat prices.

Park behind the chainlink fence and the building to your left displays heavy-duty, commercial equipment—ranges so powerful that the building inspector in your town probably won't permit you to install one in your home, dishwashing lines, big grills, steam tables, and the like. The building to the right is where you can purchase utensils that will make you the best-equipped home cook on the block.

You'll find headhunter-sized stock pots (and ones more realistic for the home kitchen), bright copper bowls for whisking perfect egg whites, pizza pans and pizza paddles, restaurant-style plastic storage containers marked with measures so you'll know just how much flour or sugar you have left, ice cream tubs if you like to make your own, plus no-nonsense measuring cups, ladles, skimmers, whisks, and tongs of all sizes. In the trade, they call this "smallware" to distinguish it from the big equipment. Everything is displayed on steel shelving, so just grab what tempts you. Prices are the same for the home cook who comes in for a gadget or two as for the restaurateur buying in bulk.

Denver Cutlery's selection of knives includes such leading international brands as Dexter, Drescher, Forschner, and Henckels, as well as Den-Cut, the house brand distinctive for its primary-color plastic handles. Want a pouch-style scabbard to take your good knives to the weekend house or the vacation condo without damage? Denver Cutlery has them, as well as wood blocks for safe knife storage on your home kitchen counter. Have knives that need sharpening? Denver Cutlery will hone them while you wait.

Denver Cutlery is also the place to go if you want to decorate your family room or kitchen with a funky retro look; you can find diner-style booths, chairs, and barstools—all shiny chrome and vinyl. And to set such a table, you'll find restaurant-style salt and pepper shakers, a sugar shaker, and a covered glass container for drinking straws. If you entertain a lot and consider disposables a waste, Denver Cutlery sells restaurant-type dishes, glasses, and flatware. Buy them by the dozen for not much more than a couple of parties' worth of throwaway plastic.

Denver Cutlery, 1607 West 55th Avenue, Denver; (800) 705-2389 or (303) 433-6010.

Grassroots Market

Until recently, there was no need for a food store between Union Station and I-25, for most of the Platte River Valley was filled with railroad tracks. The railyards have shrunk, and in their place, a new urban neighborhood of apartment and loft towers has rapidly been built. The area is called Riverfront Park, and in 2002 downtown Denver's newest residential neighborhood got a new urban amenity: a good little grocery store. Located in a corner of the Promenade Loft Building, right near the Millennium Bridge that links Riverfront Park to LoDo and the rest of Denver, Grassroots Market draws its inspiration from stores in Italy and France, as well as urban markets in New York and San Francisco. With its shiny hardwood floor, gleaming stainless-steel shelves, butcher-block counters, and rows of track lighting below a ceiling of exposed ductwork, Grassroots Market certainly looks the part.

The store supplies residents with groceries to make something tasty for dinner that night, the downtown worker needing lunch (the market delivers to some downtown business areas), and visitors looking for picnic items to take to the nearby park.

Its gourmet delicatessen features artisanal cheeses, charcuterie meats, house-made soups, specialty sandwiches, and a selection of natural and organic grocery items. Breads include a choice of baguette, ciabatta, country loaf, croissant, focaccia, French rolls, Kaiser rolls, marble rye, pumpernickel, seven-grain, sourdough, and bagels. The deli offers a large selection of quality sliced cheeses and such fine meat brands as Niman Ranch beef, Black Forest, Honey Baked Ham, and Molinari salami.

Owner Tim Flowers' background is in fine resorts and restaurants, including Aspen's Hotel Jerome and the former Ritz-Carlton Aspen (now the St. Regis), Real Restaurants in San Francisco, and Rosewood in the British Virgin Islands, so he knows as much about five-star customer service as he does about good food.

**Grassroots Market, 2100 16th Street, Denver; (303) 433-6300 or
www.grassroots-market.com.**

Italian Delis and Markets

The Denver area boasts more Italian delis and markets than you might imagine. Among the items you'll find are excellent fresh Italian sausage, usually house-made and perhaps from long-held family recipes. Also showcased are such other *salumeria* standbys as imported ham, salami, capacola, sopresata, pancetta, and bologna that's light-years away from supermarket-style baloney. Some have fresh meat in a butcher counter and/or fresh produce as well. Many stock excellent dried pastas, as well as quality frozen filled pastas, such as ravioli, tortellini, manicotti, and stuffed shells, and layered dishes like lasagna. Shelves are laden with tomato products, excellent prepared sauces, olives, olive oils, aged vinegars, roasted peppers, pepperoncini, beans, tinned fish, and myriad other prepared foods for a classic Italian meal. And the cheeses you'll find: asiago, fontina, provolone, *locatelli,* Parmigiano-Reggiano, Grana Padano, Pecorino Toscano, Pecorino Romano, *scamorza,* and fresh mozzarella, occasionally house-made.

Most of Denver's Italian delis make sandwiches and/or have hot tables with house-made soups and prepared foods to take out. All sell bread from various purveyors (some better than others), and in addition to popular packaged Italian cookies such as biscotti, most also carry desserts (notably tíramisu and *panna cotta).*

Individual stores have additional specialties as well, items that people will cross town to buy: House-made pasta from Belefiore's. House-made mozzarella from Deli Italia. Pizza dough from Vinnola's. The metro area's Italian markets and delis are found predominantly in northwest Denver, where the city's Italian community was once concentrated, and in the western and northwestern suburbs. The small neighborhood stores, most of those listed here, are generally closed on Sundays.

Alberto's Italian Market, 6790 Sheridan Boulevard, Arvada; (303) 426-7300
Belefiore's Italian Sausage, 5820 West 38th Avenue, Denver; (303) 455-4653
Cansano Italian Market, 88 Lamar Street, Denver; (303) 466-3299
Carbone's Italian Sausage, 1221 West 38th Avenue, Denver; (303) 455-2893
Carmine Leonardo's Italian Sausage Meat and Deli, 7585 West Florida Avenue, Lakewood; (303) 985-3555, and 15380 East Smoky Hill Road, Aurora;
    (303) 238-7815
Deli Italia, 1990 Wadsworth Boulevard, Lakewood; (303) 238-7815
DeLorenzo's Delicacy Shop, 1801 Wynkoop Street, Denver; (303) 455-2893
Enrico's Italian Sausage, 8020 Chase Drive, Arvada; (303) 429-0750
Larusso's Italian Deli, 9134 West 88th Avenue, Arvada; (303) 940-9377
Old Fashioned Italian Deli, 395 West Littleton Boulevard, Littleton;
    (303) 794-1402
Parisi Italian Market, 4408 Lowell Boulevard, Denver; (303) 561-0234
Robert's Italian Deli, 6745 Ken Caryl Avenue, Littleton; (720) 981-7078
Salvaggio's Italian Deli, 2655 Pearl Street, Boulder; (303) 938-1981;
    1397 Pearl Street (take-out kiosk on the Pearl Street Mall), Boulder;
    (303) 545-6800, and 1107 13th Street, Boulder; (303) 448-1200
Spinelli's Market (see page 76)
Tony's Meat and Specialty Foods, three locations (see page 79)

Treppada's Gourmet Market and Café, 300 Second Street, Niwot; (303) 652-1606
Valente's Deli and Bakery, 7250 Meade Street, Westminster; (303) 429-0590
Vinnola's Italian Market, 7750 West 38th Avenue, Wheat Ridge; (303) 421-3955

La Groceria

Epicures in Aurora and Centennial don't need to go far for gourmet ingredients; fine meats and fresh seafood; a selection of cheeses, charcuterie, and baked goods; and especially abundant and well-prepared take-home items. They head for La Groceria, a food lover's jewel tucked into an unimposing strip shopping center.

Dee Pallasch, who established the store in October 2000, grew up in the retail food business in Cleveland, Ohio, where her family operated Baluh's Food Market. Her vision for La Groceria is to maintain the friendly sense of the corner grocery store of her childhood with modern convenience. La Groceria strives for the personal touch, while stocking and preparing foods that meet sophisticated tastes. Gourmet food products include seasonings, oils, vinegars, bread dippers, and lots of coffees and teas. Filling shelves, tables, and other display units are such lines as Busha Browne, Stonewall Kitchen, and Bookbinders'. Salad mixes, crab dip kits, and fondue fixings are shortcuts for the hurried cook.

Foods are prepared in the large kitchen that dominates the back of the store. La Groceria offers a weekly menu, including one daily soup and two daily hot entrées, usually with rice. These might include such sure-fire winners as Southwestern Chicken Stew, Chipotle Chicken, Orange Salmon, Cheese Ravioli, Game Hens Stuffed with Wild Rice and Apricots, Shrimp Scampi, Pot Roast, Baked Pork Chops with Caramelized Onion, or Ginger Beef. Additionally, La Groceria's popular rotisserie chicken has a different flavor each day, including basil, Tahitian, citrus-tarragon, oregano, and lemon-dill.

La Groceria's 16-inch pizzas, with house-made dough and a choice of quality toppings, are available ready to eat or to take home and bake. Also available are prepared appetizers, salads, and frozen soups. Fresh breads, lovely cakes, and pastries come from La Groceria's ovens, and Liks Homemade Ice Cream and imported and domestic specialty chocolates and candies satisfy the sweet tooth. La Groceria also makes commendable sandwiches and wraps, and a few high tables and stools at the front of the store accommodate those who wish to eat there.

La Groceria, Piney Creek Square, 15444 East Orchard Road, Centennial; (303) 766-5655 or www.lagroceria.net.

Latino Food Markets

Coloradans seem to take traditional Mexican, Tex-Mex, and border cuisine for granted. Excellent and often well-priced eating places that fall under the general "Mexican restaurant" category abound. Everyone has a favorite place or two and also a favorite dish or two, perhaps tacos on a hard or soft shell, enchiladas, burritos, fajitas, tamales, or the ubiquitous combination plate. Most of these restaurants serve such tasty and filling food that we tend not to bother making it at home.

However, adventurous home cooks are lately discovering the area's many Latino markets as sources of chilies, seasonings, fresh produce, and other essential ingredients of the cuisine. Small neighborhood stores abound, not just in Denver, but also elsewhere in the state—in fact, perhaps even more so in some parts—and supermarket-size stores specializing in Mexican products are scattered around the metro area too.

Wonderfully fresh peppers, tomatillos, avocados, mangos, and papayas can be found an aisle over from epazote, cilantro, Mexican oregano, *culantro, recao,* cumin, and other traditional seasonings. Many markets contain baking departments, or perhaps there is a *panaderia* right next door. Some stores also have meat or seafood departments, which sell authentic *chorizo* and more, and many offer house-made tamales and other specialties to take out or perhaps eat in at a handful of tables. Many are closed on Sunday. Here is a sampling of the Denver area's myriad Latino markets:

Avanza, 5801 West 44th Avenue, Denver; (303) 477-9967

El Azteca, 1065 Federal Boulevard, Denver; (303) 893-3642

La Casita, 4390 West 44th Avenue, Denver; (303) 455-2190

Chili Store & Kitchen, 4310-C Morrison Road, Denver; (303) 936-9309

Mercado Gigante, 3200 West Colfax Avenue, Denver; (720) 904-3830

El Mercadito, 3125 Federal Boulevard, Denver; (303) 561-0714

La Popular Mexican Food, 2033 Lawrence, Denver; (303) 296-1687

El Venado, 4120 Brighton Boulevard, Denver; (303) 298-8790

Marczyk Fine Foods

When this light and airy, 8,000-square-foot gourmet food market opened in Uptown Denver in April 2002, it truly was time for jubilation among local food aficionados. At its most basic, the store stocks foods for the home cook—both the long-time serious kitchen-jockey and the traveler who just returned from Europe and muses, "Why isn't the food here as good as the food there?"

Marczyk's specializes in the highest-quality ingredients, many of them imported, so that people can, indeed, prepare the highest-quality from-scratch meals at home. Neighborhood cooks quickly got into the habit of stopping after work for that evening's fixings, and as the word got out, cooking enthusiasts from all over metro Denver began making food-shopping pilgrimages.

Peter Marczyk, a Massachusetts-born stockbroker, was just such a passionate home cook, immensely caring about food, yet frustrated because he found no place in town where he could get quality meats and produce, a great loaf of bread, a rare imported ingredient for a particular dish, and even flowers for the table. Finally, the frustration got to him, and he and his wife, Barbara Macfarlane, a marketing and special events organizer, decided to fill that gap in the Denver food scene. They quit their jobs and spent three years figuring out what kind of fine-food store Denver would embrace. Their research included a coast-to-coast trip to look at upscale food markets. The result was Marczyk Fine Foods, literally a million-dollar baby, created in space that once housed a grim and dim nightclub—and not only the couple but also the entire neighborhood have rejoiced at the transformation.

The front of the store displays fresh produce colorfully piled in hefty birch bins. Macfarlane's brother, a master carpenter, made them, and she calls these wheeled bins "a simple, elegant background for elegant produce," including seasonal fruits and vegetables from local growers whenever possible. Under the theory that while customers have a love of cooking, they don't always have time, the produce department offers such things as trimmed green beans or washed organic spring greens in plastic zip bags—combining the straight-into-the-pot efficiency of frozen foods with the taste, texture, and eye-appeal of fresh. The store's ultimate conveniences are its Dinner at Home Kits, prepackaged ingredients for a home-cooked meal, ready to be picked up to save on shopping time.

The meat and seafood counters are exceptional by any measure. Marczyk's gets its meats, both fresh and charcuterie, from Niman Ranch, a highly regarded meat purveyor renowned in the food industry for producing premium meats from livestock raised humanely and naturally, with no hormones or antibiotics. It is well-marbled, dry-aged, and just about the best available. Butchers hand-cut sides of beef, pork, and lamb for the meat case or to order, grind the sirloin, assemble the kabobs, season Red Bird chicken, marinate fajita ingredients, and make fresh sausages. You can look through a large window to watch them at work in a cool room installed just for that purpose.

The seafood counter features an ice table on which fish and shellfish are displayed and lighted from below the ice bin to make the seafood even more enticing. The store tries to buy wild, not farm-raised, fish, and whole fish are cut to order. Seasonal selections include halibut and Copper River salmon from Alaska, black mussels from Prince Edward Island, scallops from the Gulf of Mexico, and Hudson River sturgeon.

The cheese section contains what is thought to be Colorado's only walk-in cheese cave, a pristine white-tiled room kept cool and humid. In the display case are artisanal cheeses from around the country alongside farmhouse cheeses from the British Isles, goat cheese from France, and other specialty cheese from many lands. Sometimes Marczyk's improves on the cheesemaker's original product. For instance, they make Camembert au Calvados, which involves boring small holes in Camembert wheels, dripping that classic apple brandy into it, and dusting it with excellent breadcrumbs. The subtle and delicious result is a tradition from Normandy, where both Camembert and Calvados originated.

Marczyk's buys from some of the Denver area's best bakeries. The breads come from Breadworks, Denver Daily Bread, Udi's, and TXO, a relatively new wholesale bakery that makes both traditional and unusual breads, including a fantastic baking-soda bread with a scone-like texture. Some are made up with charcuterie items, cheese, and vegetables into excellent sandwiches for lunch or a picnic in nearby City Park. Pastries, cakes, and cookies come from the Devil's Food Bakery, New World Baking, Nonna's, Trois Frères, and TXO.

The grocery section is chock-full of exotica: Custom-packaged dried fruits and nuts. Bubbie's pickles. New Skete Farms pancake mix. European and European-style butter. Sticky Fingers Bakery scone mixes. Packaged Piemontese crackers as big as cricket bats—well, not really, but they are free-hand baked and *very* large.

Scandinavian flat breads. Eduardo's pasta. Jars of Martin & Bassett herbs. Vail Mountain Coffee Roasters coffee. Peet's coffee. Scalfini pepperoncini and artichoke hearts. Divina roasted peppers. Mustards of various strengths, hues, and countries of origin. A couple of dozen olive oils. Argana oil, astonishingly orange in color and rich in taste—and hard to find. Countless vinegars. Hot sauces. Strianese canned tomato products. Imported tuna in cans and jars. Imported candies and chocolates. The list goes on and on and on. To help customers sort out the brands and flavors, Marczyk's hosts free tastings of oils, chocolates, chilis, hot sauces, and other gourmet goods—at least in summer, perhaps eventually at other times of year too.

Marczyk Fine Foods, 770 East 17th Avenue, Denver; (303) 894-9499 or www.marczyk.com.

Oliver's Meat Market

For more than 60 years, a rambling building just east of the intersection of Sixth and Marion has housed two businesses—a butcher shop and a grocery store—in one undivided space. The butcher shop is Oliver's Meat Market, founded in 1923 at Sixth and Pearl by the grandfather of Berry Oliver, the senior member of the current multi-generation owners. The dial of a treasured old wall telephone reads "Pearl 4629"—a number that countless Denver housewives called to order their meats in the old days.

Oliver's moved to the current site in 1939, sharing the generous space with Piggly-Wiggly, a well-known Southern supermarket chain with a few Denver stores. After the Piggly-Wiggly closed in 1952, a produce market called Greens and the Bluepoint Bakery took turns at the space. The Denver Deli is the latest roommate at this writing, but Oliver's draws most of the customers.

Oliver's business card has four names (Jim Oliver, Chris Oliver, Berry Oliver, and Rich Oliver), and a teenager representing the fifth generation in the family is already gaining experience in the business. The store looks the way you'd expect of a traditional, hands-on meat market: white walls, big old wooden meat lockers, meat hooks near the ceiling, butcher blocks that are really used rather than making a design statement, a 1937 cash register, black-and-white tile floor, and, most important, a friendly, knowledgeable butcher behind the counter—a guy who grew up in the business. This is the real thing—no shrink-wrapped meats languishing on Styrofoam trays in this fine place.

The glass case displays perfectly cut corn-fed beef, lamb, pork, veal, and chicken, which are custom-cut to order. The seafood section, though small by comparison, contains the freshest fish and shellfish—including excellent Atlantic varieties. A full-time sausage-maker makes an unbelievable 29 types, common and unusual, bulk and link, and raw, smoked, or cooked. This is the place to get the best bratwurst, andouille, boudin, chorizo, Swedish potato sausage, and others, in some cases made with traditional meats or optional buffalo, turkey, or chicken. Oliver's staff are particularly proud of their Linguisa sausage, a Portuguese specialty that is incredibly difficult to find in most of the United States. And well they should be proud. It took 15 years to get a good and authentic recipe—and now it's an Oliver's classic.

Oliver's Meat Market, 1312 East Sixth Avenue, Denver; (303) 733-4629.

The Restaurant Source

Supermarket-sized and recently renovated, this wholesale restaurant supply house is also open to the public. The inventory runs to about 8,000 food-service products, so there's very little in the way of food preparation equipment or restaurant-style tableware and barware that you can't get there—and at good prices to boot.

Like a supermarket, the showroom is divided into categories, including Chinese cooking implements, pastry-making equipment, chefs' equipment, and even pizza. In addition to the huge assortment of cooking and food-service items, you can find serving items such as big platters and chafing dishes, plus restaurant-size appliances and commercial furniture. The Restaurant Source is only open on weekdays.

The Restaurant Source, 5005 Washington Street, Denver; (800) 765-0274, (303) 296-1684, or www.restsource.com.

Spinelli's Market

When North Denver native Jerry Spinelli sold his bar and restaurant business in 1992, he and his wife, Mary Ellen (who grew up in Park Hill), cast about for something new to do. On a trip to New York, where Mary Ellen's brother lives, an idea was born. Her brother, a good cook, led them to his favorite greengrocer, his favorite fish store, his favorite butcher shop, his favorite bakery, and all the other little corner stores where he picked up ingredients to create his wonderful meals.

The Spinellis returned to Denver with the goal of opening a New York–style neighborhood market. They purchased dingy space in a Park Hill building that had been the first home of the Park Hill United Methodist Church (hence the castle-like crenellated roofline and bell tower), later a Piggly-Wiggly market, and finally a disreputable-looking cigarette and candy store. Everything improved when Spinelli's Market was born in 1994. "*Our* ambition was to create a neighborhood market," says Mary Ellen Spinelli. "*My* ambition was to create a memory for kids in the neighborhood."

They started modestly, with produce and a few other items, adding categories quickly. With the name Spinelli on the door (and Jerry's father being an immigrant from Calabria via Boston), the focus had to be Italian. Super-fresh produce and Belleverde pasta comprised much of the opening-day inventory, but that has changed, and now the market carries first-rate meats, seafood, cheeses, pastas, prepared foods, breads, cold cuts, packaged gourmet products, crackers, cookies, and candy. The fixtures remain simple and the staff remains friendly, but the shelves are now crowded with a dazzling array of sometimes-mundane but mostly upmarket goods, and Spinelli's reputation for quality has grown with it.

The market also has achieved Mary Ellen's goal and become a neighborhood landmark, much like the local stores of her childhood. When Spinelli's Market had been operating for about four years, the couple saw a party in preparation in the park kitty-corner from the store. They thought it was a block party to which, for some reason, they hadn't been invited. Then, a customer came in and urged them to come across the street. It turned out that 150 of their customers had organized a surprise party in the Spinellis' honor. The banner that the customers signed hangs prominently on a wall near the candy and ice cream in the front of the store.

The neighbors were honoring a wonderful neighborhood store, one that sells convenience items and, as Mary Ellen notes, "junk for the kids"—surely the memory-maker for the younger generation. For food enthusiasts, it's Spinelli's mix of house-made and commercial boutique brands that creates meals, which in turn create another kind of memory.

The list of brands in each category bespeaks quality and selectivity. Bread from Adagio, the Denver Bread Company, Bluepoint Bakery, and, on weekends, Breadworks. Vinnola's pizza dough. Bonne Maman and Hero preserves. Rocky Mountain Spice Company seasonings. Brianna dressings. Alessi breadsticks. Imported crackers and cookies from Broder, Delacre, Bahlsen, Jukes DeStropper, and Fekrum. Cold cuts from Buon Gusto, Malinari, Thurman's, and Maple-Glazed. Alessi risotto and *lentocchie*. Rice from Acquerello. Olive oils from Castelvetrano, Badalucco, Napoleon, Alessi, Carapelli, and Argumato, the last of which makes a sensational olive oil with tangerine. In addition to tried-and-true Belleverde, the pasta that launched a thousand Spinelli's products, there's pasta from Al Dente, DeVerde, and La Moliserva. The list goes on.

Spinelli's carries such excellent house-made products as pasta sauces, quiches, cold salads, and olives cured by Jerry Spinelli himself. Chef Chris Rogers, once executive chef at the now-shuttered Ice House, prepares some of Denver's best—and best-priced—to-go meals just for Spinelli's. Summer weeknight entrées often include Lime-Cilantro Tacos Pescado; Vegetarian Cheese Ravioli with Nut and Pepper Pesto, Broccoli Rapini, Wild Mushrooms, and Parmigano-Reggiano; and Chicken Breasts Stuffed with Crispy Pancetta, Goat Cheese, and Leeks over Garlic Mashed Potatoes. That's restaurant-quality fare at grocery prices. Sandwiches using premium ingredients are also available.

The deli counter, stretching across the back of the store, displays the aforementioned name-brand cold cuts, olives, salads, meat, and seafood. A good portion is devoted to one of Denver's best cheese selections, especially when it comes to Italian imports. That wonderful, grainy sheep's milk cheese called *pecorino*, mild and nutty *scamorza*, blue-veined Gorgonzola, flavorful *taleggio*, and the almost-sainted Parmigiano-Reggiano rank among the best. Additionally, Spinelli's carries Brillat-Savarin triple cream from France, goats' milk Gouda, dry Jack, Maytag blue, lemon-zest Stilton, an unusual Spanish blue called *cabrales* that is so intense and dusky that it looks like pâté, another intriguing Spanish cheese aged in wine and called Drunken Goat, and many, many more.

While Spinelli's was growing all these categories to the point where the once-sparse inventory filled the store, its staff had been baking in cramped space in the back. Recently, though, a new bakery was born when Spinelli's took over space across the street and launched Adagio (see page 11).

Spinelli's Market, 4621 East 23rd Avenue, Denver; (303) 329-8143.

St. Kilian's Cheese Shop

As the guiding spirit behind Hugh's American Bistro, Hugh O'Neill was one of Denver's superstar chefs. His restaurant won rave reviews and a loyal following, which turned into mourning when he decided to hang up his toque and seek more tranquil pastures. Since March 2001, Irish-born O'Neill and his Brazilian-born wife, Ionah deFreitas, have been running St. Kilian's Cheese Shop, close to home in Denver's vibrant North Highlands neighborhood. Denver may have lost the day-to-day efforts of a talented chef and restaurateur, but it has gained a splendid little neighborhood cheese shop. The awning over the front window reads, "Epicurean Essentials for Everyday Living." O'Neill and deFreitas provide such essentials as distinctive cheeses, olive oils, bread from the nearby Denver Bread Company, fine teas, and a small charcuterie selection.

The couple brings in as many raw-milk cheeses as possible, with a heavy emphasis on French and Spanish varieties in addition to made-in-America artisanal ones, lovingly displayed in a refrigerated glass case at the entrance to the small, narrow store. O'Neill unsurprisingly has something of a bias toward Irish farmhouse cheeses, which he offers when they are available—especially around St. Patrick's Day. In summer, St. Kilian's sells lots of goat cheese. Among those featured are gorgeous rounds with various toppings and edible organic flowers, from Harley Farms in Pescadero, California.

For O'Neill, "cheese is such a wonderfully simple food in its country of origin. There, it's usually peasant food," he says. "Here, it's become gourmet food. Customers come in, all nervous, and take a bottle of wine out of a bag, hold it up, and ask what to eat with it. I say, 'Just close your eyes and point.' Most of the time, it will be great, but if you don't like the combination, it's part of the discovery process. The only way to become an expert is to come with open curiosity, experiment, and decide what you like."

St. Kilian's Cheese Shop, 3211 Lowell Boulevard, Denver; (303) 477-0374.

The Truffle

Behind the welcoming yellow door is a yellow store called The Truffle. I walked in, took a few deep whiffs of the opulent aroma of blended cheeses that permeates this small specialty shop, and asked Kate Kaufman, who owns it with her husband, Dave, about the name. I wondered why they called it The Truffle instead of The Cheese, Curds and Whey, or Le Fromage. "We wanted to communicate the exotic, things that are hard to find and very special," she quickly replied.

The Truffle is really a cheese boutique, stocking an enormous assortment of first-rate, often hard-to-find hand-crafted cheeses—up to 85 varieties at any given time. Customers are invited to taste any of the cheeses, and The Truffle cuts to order any that you want to take home.

The couple are always looking for new specialty cheeses to add to the mix. During a road trip along the Pacific Coast and through the Southwest, they couldn't resist scouting for new cheese to carry even though they were on vacation. Upon their return, they secured a supply of *taleggio*-style cheese called Red Hawk and a blue cheese from Point Reyes Station, California. They also became the first shop outside of New England to carry cheese from Blythedale Farm in Corinth, Vermont. This 20-acre farm with just 20 cows is run by a husband-and-wife team, a partnership just like the Kaufmans'.

Cheese accompaniments available at The Truffle include caviar, olives, dried fruits, dry-cured meats, and a small assortment of French-style charcuterie. The shop also carries herbs and spices and unusual pastas such as chestnut tagliatelle and porcini or saffron fettucini by Rustichella d'Abruzzi. There are also sweets from The Chocolate Garden, pumpkin seed oil from the Austrian state of Styria, Carnaroli rice from Italy, and rare olive oils from California, Greece, Italy, and Provence. Not nearly from as distant a locale but very welcome are loaves from Boulder's Breadworks. And, of course, The Truffle does carry truffles in season plus truffle oil, truffle paste, and truffle flour year-round.

The Truffle puts on early-evening wine-and-cheese pairings and such other events as vinegar or olive tastings once or twice a month. When you visit, add your name to the mailing list for an informative, personal newsletter describing the couple's culinary adventures and their newest products.

The Truffle, 2906 East Sixth Avenue, Denver; (303) 322-7363.

Tony's Meats and Specialty Foods

There really is a Tony, and cooks in Denver's southern suburbs can thank him for creating one-stop shopping convenience for top-quality meats, super-fresh seafood, gourmet food items, baked goods, and truly terrific prepared foods. The Tony in question is Tony Rosacci, and the trio of excellent food stores that bear his name are way beyond the fulfillment of a dream he spun years ago. Rosacci, then a young supervisor for a Los Angeles supermarket chain, dreamed of starting a family-owned neighborhood meat market in a neighborhood that wasn't Los Angeles. The Rosaccis moved to Colorado in 1972, with Tony still harboring the dream.

En route to church one morning, seven-year-old Danny spotted a 7-Eleven that had just closed along Dry Creek Road and said, "Hey, Dad, that would make a good meat market!" Tony and his wife, Nancy, looked, saw the potential, and made an offer on the nondescript building. They solidified the purchase with a postdated check and approached the bank for a loan. The loan officer immediately turned the couple down. The next day, they put their house on the market to finance the dream.

The Rosaccis opened their old-fashioned butcher shop in 1978 with first-quality meats and a small selection of other items. Just as important, Tony's Meat Market offered first-rate service. One day a customer wanted a sandwich. Tony Rosacci sliced some ham and took a loaf of bread and some mustard from the shelf and put together a sandwich to order—the beginning of the store's deli. Later, Tony's introduced to Denver prepared foods for those who like to eat well but don't always have time to cook. Each of the three Tony's locations is now elaborately stocked beyond anyone's imagining a quarter of a century ago.

Tony's all-natural meats look immensely appetizing and have no added brines, chemicals, or mechanical tenderizing. Whether you select something from the meat case or request custom cuts, butchers hand-cut your selections—no prewrapped meats here. In addition to various cuts of beef, pork, veal, and chicken, you'll find smoked meats, kabobs, and homemade Italian sausages and bratwurst. Chicken breasts come preseasoned every which way.

The seafood counter displays an array of fresh fish and shellfish. In season, Tony's flies Copper River salmon in from Alaska daily. They'll cut whole fish to order and also sell what they call "Bundles," pre-selected assortments of seafood sold in quantity. If you can't find what you want fresh in the way of meats or seafood, you'll probably find it frozen. One freezer is devoted to cuts of elk, and another is stocked with mussels, Australian lobster tails, buffalo filet, goose, and more types of sausage.

The deli counter—a direct heir to that first ham sandwich—features Boar's Head, Buon Gusto, and Daniele cold cuts. And yes, they still carry great breads from Il Fornaio and Breadworks. Executive chef Ben Davis is in charge of the prepared foods—appetizers, entrées, party platters, and more—that are made fresh in a central kitchen and delivered daily to each location. The entrées, range from comfort foods like meatloaf and garlic mashed potatoes to more elaborate lemon-caper capellini and chicken saltimbocca. Pasta salads include such seasonal delights as Pasta alla Checcha with tomatoes, olive oil, and seasonings in summer and pasta salad with mushrooms and white truffle oil in winter.

Gorgeous cakes, pastries, and tarts emerge from the in-house bakeries. You'll find Napoleons and other classic pastries, bar cookies (lemon, white chocolate–raspberry, and others), cakes, scones, muffins, bagels, cookies, and neat little focaccia just right to accompany dinner for one or two people.

Other categories include a large variety of specialty and imported foods, fresh produce at supermarket prices, beautiful gift baskets, gourmet coffee, candy, giftware, wines, and the luscious output from an in-house bakery. You could fill your pantry with Tony's gourmet food items and never get tired of experimenting with the grand assortment of pastas, condiments, sauces, oils, vinegars, herbs, and spices. Most recently, Tony's added an olive-tasting bar in each of its stores—a special passion of Ben Davis.

With the opening of the Bowles Village store, Tony's launched a cooking school (see page 27) given in the demonstration kitchen as well as a small kitchenware department featuring Zyliss accessories, Trudeau nonstick utensils, and other common and uncommon brands. There are also some cookbooks and bright serving vessels for the output of your own kitchen or of Tony's.

The Rosacci family still runs Tony's: Tony himself still is the company's leader and standard-bearer. "Little Danny" Rosacci is the chief executive officer. Avie Rosacci Williams leads the sales team. Mick directs marketing and shares the family's passion for great foods in a weekly newspaper column that runs in a number of Denver newspapers. He also stars in live cooking segments on Channel 7 News on Saturday mornings. Both in print and on the air, Mick focuses on the preparation of currently fresh seasonal ingredients, using short, simple recipes but classic techniques.

Tony's grandkids—Anna, Nina, Lissa, Joey, Michael, Joshua, and Dominic—are now learning the business, just as their parents did before them. It looks as if there will be Rosaccis running Tony's markets for decades to come.

Tony's Original Market, 4991 East Dry Creek Road, Centennial; (303) 770-7024; Tony's Southbridge Market, 151 West Mineral Avenue, Littleton; (303) 795-7887; Tony's Bowles Village Market, 7421 West Bowles Avenue, Littleton; (720) 377-3680. The website for all is www.tonysmarket.com.

Wines

Corks

Smart and urbane Denverites looking for wines that are high in quality and moderate in price flock to Corks in the newly vibrant Platte River Valley. The vast majority of the bottles carried by this specialty store cost under $15, but all have been highly rated by wine critics or reviewed favorably in the wine press. "We don't just bring in stacks that some wine salesman is pushing," says Pam Glynn, who with partner Glenn Ehrlich opened the store in 2000.

The hip, modern store is done in light, bright colors. There's lots of glass and good light. Within this contemporary setting is marketplace merchandising. The store displays wines in open bins rather than on racks or wall shelves. Wines are grouped by style, not by country or varietal, so the reds are on one side of the room and the whites on the other. The wines are further apportioned into light-, medium-, and full-bodied subgroups. Each wine carries an informational label describing its origins, suggestions for food that goes with it, and the press it has received.

Glynn and Ehrlich have found that their customers enjoy poking around the bins, seeking out a wine that strikes them—and the marketplace ambience encourages that. Of course, there's advice and help available for anyone who wants it. For special occasions, Corks carries a limited amount of premium wine, which they call Dazzlers, as well as high-end champagnes and dessert wines. A small selection of spirits, wine glasses, accessories, openers, and other gadgets are offered too.

Corks' Wine of the Month Club allows customers the choice of redeeming certificates for wines one at a time or in multitudes. The store has held tastings at Dixon's, the Magnolia Hotel, and other venues.

Corks, 1620 Platte Street, Denver; (303) 477-5799.

Denver Wine Connection

Most wine connoisseurs find so little charm to warehouse-style big-box liquor stores, complete with glaring fluorescent lights, shopping carts, and supermarket-style checkout counters that they won't even enter. When it's a warehouse-type wine store, thrifty oenophiles tend to be a tad more tolerant.

The Denver Wine Connection was established in 2002 by Bob and Ingrid Grueter, who once owned Aspen Wine & Spirits, to provide a wide range of wines at attractive prices, albeit in a frill-free warehouse setting. The store's location along the Interstate 25 frontage road is not inspiring, but for some buyers, savings talk—as does the breadth of inventory.

Bottles are shelved by price, varietal, and region or country of origin. Imre Kraus, a second-level master sommelier, was on board during the Denver Wine Connection's launch period, which probably accounts for the rarer wines that are also available. He left to run Restaurant Kevin Taylor, but the legacy of a certified wine expert remains.

Denver Wine Connection, 1190 Yuma Street, Denver; (303) 825-8000.

Joy Wine & Spirits

This spacious purveyor of wines and spirits is the latest incarnation of a family business on site since 1963, when Tony Joy opened a pharmacy and liquor store at Sixth Avenue and Marion. Joy Pharmacy and Liquor filled customers' needs on several fronts, but eventually, the pharmacy was phased out and the store became a specialty wine and liquor store now run by Carolyn Joy. Her staff include an uncommon number of trained chefs, former winemakers, and brew masters—sometimes rolled into one knowledgeable person.

Joy's selects a wine of the month and puts out a very informative, opinionated flyer that gives a background on the region, a description of the winery and the wine, food-pairing information, and even cellaring potential for those who like to buy and store. It may also contain a suitable recipe that goes with the wine, thanks to the culinary talent on the Joy's staff. Unsurprisingly, where there is a wine of the month selection, there is also a Wine of the Month Club designed for gift giving.

The large selection of wines is organized by country, except for the back wall, which displays 100 wines for $10.99 or less. Additionally, Joy's offers 10 percent off non-sale wines every Wednesday, which is when value-minded regulars buy their week's wines. The store also does five tastings a year at nearby galleries or restaurants.

Joy Wine & Spirits, 1302 East Sixth Avenue, Denver; (303) 744-6219.

Marczyk's Fine Wines

When Marczyk's Fine Foods (see page 73) was being designed, provision was made for the eventual creation of Marczyk's Fine Wines in adjacent space. The 900-square-foot specialty wine room adjacent to the store's grocery section opened in early 2003. Labels include recognizable favorites as well as small farmhouse wines, though this small annex to the food store isn't aiming at the wine collector but rather at the food customer who is looking for what to drink right away. Wines are grouped by the food they pair with best—beef, poultry, lamb, seafood, dessert, and so on. In addition, the store sells good beer, fine cognacs, and apéritifs from around the world. If you're in a quandary over what to have for dinner, you can enjoy one-stop shopping both for gourmet food but wines to go with them—and wine-pairing advice is close at hand.

Marczyk Fine Wines, 770 East 17th Avenue, Denver; (303) 894-9499 or www.marczyk.com.

Mondo Vino

At the heart of North Highlands' small commercial area is a corner wine and

Wine Party Time
Grape Expectations

Bill Sauvigné is a gifted woodworker whose creations include clever wine racks and single-bottle holders. His creative spirit led him to encourage people's greater enjoyment and enhanced knowledge of wines—and perhaps, by extension, to need more wine racks. He has created a whimsical little kit that is essentially a wine party in a canvas tote bag. In the bag are instructions on throwing a wine-tasting party, a wine holder, scorecards, and ideas for tastings. It makes a neat gift for the nouveau oenophile in your life.

Grape Expectations, 236 West 13th Avenue, Loft 100, Denver, (720) 261-9745.

spirits store that has loomed large on Denver's wine scene since its 1999 opening. While other wine merchants cant heavily toward California and/or French and Italian wines, owner Duey Kratzer has stocked his bright and inviting store with great depth and breadth in other European wines, notably those underrated, relatively unknown wines from such places as Austria and the French part of the Rhône Valley.

He particularly favors the output from small wineries made from grapes grown by a single vineyard. Among the some 1,000 wines that he carries are those from Austrian regions with such tongue-twisting names as Burgenland, Gumpoldskirchen, Grinzing, Niederösterreich, Neusiedel, Nussdorf, Steiermark, and Wachau. Austria's white/red ratio is roughly 80 to 20, and of the whites Grüner Veltliner can be thought of as the most characteristic varietal. You can get a quick lesson in these wines or pick up some, which Kratzer feels provide more quality for less money than the better-known wines of nearby Germany. When he does the occasional wine tasting at such restaurants as the Highlands Gardens Café, you'll see what he means.

Mondo Vino occupies an attractive space, with high ceilings, exposed brick walls, a large mural of a vineyard and chateau, and beautiful wood shelves and racks on which you'll find both the unusual and unexpected. Regular and premium spirits and, of course, such fortified wines as ports and sherries are displayed as well. Along one wall is an enormous cooler for white and sparkling wines and for a significant selection of microbrews. A fine wine room in the back holds the rarest, costliest bottles favored by collectors and well-heeled connoisseurs. Wine racks, wine accessories, and wine books add to the mix.

Mondo Vino, 3601 West 32nd Avenue, Denver; (303) 458-3858 or www.mondo-vino.com.

Primo Vino

With its green walls, trellis-and-vine décor, and abundance of wine bottles, this boutique wine shop echoes the look of a vineyard or winery. Primo Vino is owned by Brad Vanderpool, who had previously worked with Blair Taylor both at Barolo

Grill and their wine business called Enotec Imports. He opened this attractive retail outlet in late 2002 to offer personalized service and cost-oriented pricing to what he perceived as an increasingly interested group of wine-lovers in Denver's northwestern suburbs.

Vanderpool's particular passion is in the wines of Italy, and specifically the wines of Tuscany, and he stocks these selections in breadth and depth. The store also carries fine wines from other European wine-growing regions, Australia, and California. You'll find the most precious bottles in an attractive bricked-in fine-wine room, but a massive walk-in cooler is the place to go for moderately priced whites, sparkling wines, and specialty beers and microbrews.

From the beginning, Vanderpool began maintaining a customer database, tracking their wine preferences. That way, when something appropriate for a particular customer comes in, he can alert him or her. Primo Vino also has established a wine of the month club, is planning an e-mail newsletter, and does winemaker dinners with DiCicco's Italian Restaurant just down the street.

Primo Vino, 5713 Olde Wadsworth Boulevard, Arvada; (303) 456-5347 or www.primovino.net.

Reservelist

When you read the word Reservelist, the free-association lobe of your mind probably will not instantly bring forth "wine store"—until you've seen the place. Once you've been there, the image of this hip wine boutique will be etched into your consciousness. That's just the way sommelier Chris Farnum, a partner in the store, wanted it. Soaring ceilings, thick pillars supporting decorative arches, circular fixtures of hanging lights, and wine-red walls make a spectacular backdrop for some 800 wines—and the store's temperature and humidity control system makes for the proper environment too.

Help is available from the knowledgeable staff, but you can also browse the store's wine and cookbook library or surf the Net if you want to do some of your own research. Wine bottles are racked, shelved, and slipped into pigeonholes, and their organization is orderly, like a good wine list. They are arranged by variety, region, intensity, and even in order of consumption, from apéritif to disgestif, but with countries, regions, and price ranges mixed in each attractive display area. Pretty neat.

Farnum's partner when the distinctive wine store opened in 2001 was master sommelier Ken Fredrickson, who a year later premiered the Adega Restaurant and Wine Bar (see page 29) with another team. Between them, Farnum and Fredrickson possessed the deep knowledge of wines to create an impressive inventory. Fredrickson has since moved out of state, but his sensibilities about wine are his legacy at Reservelist, where imported and domestic wines receive equal billing.

Reservelist procures small allocations of hard-to-find rare wines sought by well-heeled collectors, but most of the wines are affordable, and, being mindful of customers' budgets, the store's dynamic "20 for 20" program features 20 quality wines for under $20 each month. Beyond that, the wines are grouped by color and then by varietal. Reservelist is positively messianic about wine education—in the newsletter, on the website, and in person. Monthly tasting dinners were originally offered at Morton's of Chicago, but they are now—no surprise—offered at Adega.

Because Reservelist also encourages customers to hold wine tastings at home, the store will make up a tasting kit of three or four wines, paper bags for use in blind tastings, and tasting notes written by sommeliers. The wines in each kit represent varietals from different regions, for example, Sauvignon Blanc from New Zealand, the Napa Valley, Graves, and Sancerre. This allows the taster to compare wines of the same grape, but with vastly different flavor profiles.

The informative newsletter, "Reservelist Grapevine," makes holiday wine suggestions and also seasonal menu suggestions with recommendations for suitable wines. You might just run in to Reservelist for a bottle of wine, but don't be surprised if you stop to chat, leaf through a wine book, or just wander around in that inviting "wine-vironment."

Reservelist, Belleview Promenade, 8000 East Belleview Avenue, Greenwood Village; (303) 220-1945 or www.reservelist.com.

Tony's Wines

Of the three locations in this family-owned group of markets (see page 79), Tony's Original Market on Dry Creek Road also houses a small wine shop, which crams several hundred selected wines into just 670 square feet. Chef Andrews, a trained chef and the Rossacis' "wine guru," stocks what he considers excellent values. Even better is the $99 Special, a mixed case of selected wines.

Tony's Original Market, 4991 East Dry Creek Road, Centennial; (303) 770-7024 or www.tonysmarket.com.

The Wine Company

The Wine Company is a small, mid- to high-end retail store specializing in unique wines, beers, and spirits. The shelves all but overflow, opened and unopened cases are stacked wherever there is room, and track lights point to the wares with seemingly random direction. It comes across as an upbeat hodgepodge, not because of the sensory overload the store presents, but because of the knowledgeable and enthusiastic staff that knows its wines, offers value, and seeks to provide friendly, expert service. The inventory includes more than 1,000 wines, plus 250 microbrewed and imported beers. The resident oenophiles taste and evaluate something on the order of 249 wines each month. Little wonder that they are knowledgeable and enthusiastic.

The store's Wine of the Month Club comes in various permutations that allow members to explore the diverse world of wine. There are 13 sub-clubs within the main club to cater to special interests. Members receive a different wine each month along with a card describing the wine, including its history and origins, and giving some food-matching suggestions. They can come in to pick up their wine or have it delivered within the Denver metro area for a reasonable fee (currently $25 a year). Minimum membership is three months.

The Wine Company offers suggestions on wine and food matching, wine-cellar planning, and an e-mail newsletter. The store also puts on such specialty events as wine, beer, and spirit tastings, wine education classes, and winemaker dinners. Pretty heady stuff for so small a store.

The Wine Company, Cherry Hills Marketplace, 5910 South University Boulevard, Greenwood Village; (303) 795-1313, (877) WINECO6, or www.winecompany.com.

The Wine Seller

Lisa D'Alessio has spent a good portion of her life on the 600 block of East Sixth Street, where she runs the family wine and spirits business in a small, unpretentious corner store. In 1956, her parents started the dry cleaning business next door (they still own it), and in 1976, her dad, Herb, and her uncle, Joe, started J&H Liquors. With a demographic change in the neighborhood (Capitol Hill to the north, Country Club to the south) and the tilt of balance from hard liquor and beer to a commendable wine selection, it made sense to D'Alessio for the store's name to reflect its mix.

Small and unpretentious as it is, The Wine Seller has become known in the neighborhood for mid-range wines from France, Australia, and California. It also has been carrying Colorado wines nearly as long as they've been on the retail market. Most wines fall in the $10 to $13 range, but cheap jug wines aren't in the mix. Rather, D'Alessio prefers the products of small wineries that, she notes, get lost in bigger stores. Her store also sells a lot of high-end beer. D'Alessio holds almost-weekly wine tastings for her staff, and the store does periodic well-priced public tastings too.

The Wine Seller, 600 East Sixth Avenue, Denver; (303) 722-9459.

Wines Off Wynkoop

The address says 16th Street, but to find Wines Off Wynkoop, you have to wander down the alley behind The Tattered Cover. When Devany McNeill opened this three-level wine shop in 1997, success was not assured, but it naturally followed the trendy, artsy irreverent style established by LoDo pioneers. Prohibition-era posters hang on the exposed-brick walls, and wood floors carry out the patina of this historic district. As LoDo became Denver's hottest residential neighborhood, the neighborhood wine merchant gained a steadily growing following. Locals appreciate the friendly and helpful service and freely given advice—and especially the prices. More than 70 percent of the inventory is priced under $20.

In addition to California and the Pacific Northwest, imports from France, Italy, Chile, and Australia are well represented on Wines Off Wynkoop's shelves. Knowing what it's like to be a pioneer, the store is supportive of Colorado's nascent wine industry. It shows about 10 top Colorado labels, including Plum Creek, Canyon Wind, Cottonwood Cellars, and Grande River Vineyards.

Food-and-wine pairings are done with Dixon's and with The Fourth Story Restaurant at The Tattered Cover's Cherry Creek location. Case Logic is the clever name for the bimonthly buy-by-the-case deal, which carries a generous 20 percent discount on preselected bottles and seven cleverly named versions of the Wine of the Month Club.

Wines Off Wynkoop, 1610 16th Street, Denver; (303) 571-1012 or www.winesoffwynkoop.com.

Other

Accidental Chefs

Singles who (A) are interested in food, and (B) want to meet other singles who are interested in food participate in this informal cooking club, organized in 1999 by Diana Ohlsson, accountant by day, home cook by choice, and cooking instructor as her second vocation. She reasoned that participants can enjoy a great evening of socializing, and preparing and eating a meal—and who knows what romances will develop.

Monthly gatherings are held in the homes of volunteer members of Accidental Chefs, but hosting is not mandatory. Depending on the size of the kitchen, the group might range from eight to 14 singles—normally 50/50 men and women, generally in the "40-plus or -minus age range," Ohlsson reports. Some are regulars, taking part in most Accidental Chefs evenings, and new faces appear at almost every evening.

Participants send a check to the shopping crew to cover food costs and then show up, ready to prepare about 10 recipes that Ohlsson has assembled. Everyone cooks as part of a team and helps clean up. Individual levels of cooking experience vary, but the dynamics work best when the entire group's enthusiasm runs high both for cooking and for socializing. On any given month, there might be an ethnic dinner theme (Italian, German, Indian, Middle Eastern, French, Chinese, Vietnamese, Eastern European, Southwestern, Mexican, Cajun, or Caribbean) or another theme (recipes from the Chefs of San Francisco or Chefs of Hawaii, barbecuing and grilling, appetizers and hors d'oeuvres, spa cuisine, or vegetarian cooking). It's great fun—and tasty too.

Most of the participants have taken one of Ohlsson's classes at Denver's Colorado Free University, through which she has taught Cooking for Singles, the Gourmet Club, or the Art of Meeting Someone New and led Ethnic Market Tours. There's no guarantee that participants will hook up with someone special, but a good time and good food is a virtual certainty.

For more information, call Diana Ohlsson at (303) 987-1744.

Market Tours

The transition from buying everything at the nearest supermarket to seeking out specialty purveyors for particular types of exotic, ethnic food products and the freshest seasonal produce is a big one for home cooks. There are hurdles to shopping at ethnic grocery stores and even farmers' markets. Many of us who came of age in the environs of shrink-wrapped meats and poultry, produce shipped in from somewhere, and canned and packaged goods neatly categorized on shelves find it hard to change.

We might feel intimidated in a crowded ethnic market, where everything isn't labeled in English and we don't recognize many of the items or even know what to do with them. We may find it awkward to select what we want from piles of produce under the gaze of the farmer who grew it. Or we may simply be too time-pressed to explore on our own. Indeed, that habit of one-stop shopping is hard to break. Instead of a random foray to a farmers' market or exploration of ethnic grocery stores, sign up for a walk-through with a knowledgeable expert to quell the confusion.

Classes can be as short as three or four hours or take up an entire Saturday. Some instructors select just a handful of stops and walk the group through, which in mystifying ethnic grocery stores is particularly useful. Others cram as many stops as possible into the allotted time, giving the group an opportunity for a quick run-through and an orientation of where some of these stores are. There is not a "right" way and a "wrong" way to arrange such a class, rather a simple reflection of different styles. When you call for information or to register, inquire so you'll know what to expect. If you and some foodie friends like, you can inquire whether a school or individual instructor would organize a custom tour for your group.

Cooking instructors from such schools as the Seasoned Chef and the Cooking School of the Rockies (see pages 26 and 99) offer in-season farmers' markets tours. Normally, you'll tour the market, chat with growers, shop, bring your items back to the school, and then prepare and eat a meal. These schools also offer periodic ethnic market tours, as does Cooking from the Heart, which specializes in Chinese markets.

Denver's Colorado Free University of Denver (303-399-0093, 800-333-6218, or www.freeu.com) also offers an ethnic market tour.

Olde Town Winery

Christie and Don Angell had been producing homemade wine for some time when they purchased this five-year-old downtown Arvada winery in late 2002 and moved it to a new and more conspicuous location on Grandview Avenue, one of Olde Town Arvada's two main streets. The winery, complete with tasting room, is a true rarity in a metro Denver retail setting.

Christie, now the wine maker, offers tours of the small winery and explains the process of turning Colorado grapes into Colorado wines. Olde Town Winery makes Merlot, Chardonnay, Sauvignon Blanc, Cabernet Sauvignon, Zinfandel, and red and white table blends. Wines are available by the glass or by the bottle. The winery also sells wine accessories of all sorts. Hours are limited in the off-season, so call for opening times if that's when you plan to visit.

Olde Town Winery, 7505 Grandview Avenue, Arvada; (303) 901-2648.

Rocky Mountain Retinning

If the linings of your treasured copper pots are wearing thin, Rocky

Mountain Retinning will restore them for you. The process, known in the business as hand-wiping, assures a thick and even application of tin and gives it the patina that aficionados of that traditional cookware treasure. Rocky Mountain Retinning charges by inch, with measuring instructions available on its website. Its staff can also repair broken or damaged wire whips.

**Rocky Mountain Retinning Company, 3457 Brighton Boulevard, Denver;
(303) 295-0462 or www.rockymountainretinning.com.**

Rolling Stone

Darryl Hoffman started out as a grade-A, certified geek with a degree in information and computer science from the University of California at Irvine. He eventually segued into operations, sales, marketing, and contracts for a California high-tech company, but in 1995 he threw in the high-tech towel and started Rolling Stone, a circuit-riding business of sharpening knives for Colorado restaurants.

The one-and-a-half-ton Rolling Stone truck calls on customers anywhere from once a week to once a month to sharpen restaurants' knives—boning, utility, paring, carving, French, and cheese knives. Although chefs tend to be meticulous and compulsive about sharpening their knives as they go, these important tools of the trade all benefit from at least a professional pass on the fine-grit grinding wheel to smooth out bevels and still finer wheels to polish and buff the blades. Hoffman restores serrated knives too. The truck is also a smallwares outlet on wheels, with an assortment of knives, scissors, and gadgets for sale.

Rolling Stone has become something of a chain. In 1998, Jeff "Smitty" Smith, one of Hoffman's customers, persuaded him to buy a second truck. And a year after that, Hoffman added a third truck and hired Tom "Crash" Phillips to drive it. In 2000, Hoffman turned over a millennial leaf and spun off those two trucks to Smitty and Crash. After reading a *Denver Post* article on Rolling Stone, William Behrens contacted Hoffman about buying a franchise, and in 2001, Behrens, Mike Kosec, and Dan Bruntz all bought franchises. There are, at this writing, half-a-dozen rigs rolling and sharpening around Colorado.

**Regular stops include several cooking schools and cookware retailers.
Rolling Stone's address is 2815 West 144 Court, Broomfield, but that isn't
really important, because Rolling Stone is rarely there to grow moss.
For information on where and when to leave and pick up your knives,
call (303) 410-1722.**

Wine Storage of Denver and Winekeepers

"To buy good wine and not look after it properly is like not polishing your Rolls-Royce," says Hugh Johnson, coauthor of *The World Atlas of Wine* and other authoritative books. That quote from Johnson is the opening salvo on Wine Storage of Denver's website.

Wine Storage of Denver was designed as a service to restaurateurs who buy wines in quantity, private collectors, and people who order wines by the case or more and who may have no place to store it in the proper temperatures. This wine storage facility—calling it a warehouse seems too downscale—provides a secure facility and stable environment for fine wines.

External factors are controlled to minimize damage to expensive wines and to allow them to age properly. The facility keeps wine at what experts believe is a perfect 55 degrees. Humidity is 65 to 75 percent to prevent dried-out corks. Electricity is used sparingly to eliminate spoilage from light. And finally, WSD's concrete floors and brick walls are designed to minimize vibration. The minimum price ($12 a month at this writing) is based on storage of eight cases; the maximum is a private walk-in. Clients are assigned individual storage lockers that they secure with their own locks.

Reservelist, a high-tech, high-touch wine store in Greenwood Village (see page 84), now offers a similar service. It has established a facility called Winekeepers located near the new Mile High Stadium. Temperature- and humidity-controlled lockers are sized for one case or more, much more. The cost of such storage is determined by the number of cases.

Wine Storage of Denver, 202 South Kalamath Street, Denver; (303) 282-1655 or www.winestoragedenver.com. For information on Winekeepers or to arrange a tour, call (303) 477-0024.

Recipes

Hugh's New American Bistro may be gone from Old South Pearl (Hugh O'Neill is minding his St. Kilian's Cheese Shop in North Highlands now), but one of his divine soups lives on in this recipe.

Celery Root Soup

2 large celery roots, peeled and cut into ½-inch cubes
1 large yellow onion, peeled and finely diced
3 tablespoons olive oil or unsalted butter
2 quarts chicken or vegetable stock
1 bunch parsley, finely chopped
1 to 2 teaspoons kosher salt
freshly ground pepper to taste
8 tablespoons Spanish dry sherry
heavy cream and chopped parsley to garnish (optional)

In a large soup pot over low heat, slowly sweat celery root and onions in olive oil (or butter), stirring often, allowing the juices to come forth, about 20 to 30 minutes.

If mixture is dry and sticks to the bottom, add more oil or butter, or a splash of stock. Add remainder of stock. Simmer until thoroughly cooked, about 45 minutes. Remove from stove and purée in batches in a blender with most of parsley; season with salt and pepper to taste.

To serve, place a tablespoon of sherry in each bowl. Ladle soup into bowl and garnish with a swirl of cream, if desired, and a sprinkle of parsley. Serve immediately. Serves 8.

With to-die-for desserts, Panzano has solidified its position as one of Denver's most beguiling all-purpose restaurants. In addition to breakfast, lunch, dinner, brunch, or late-night bite, Chef Jennifer Jasinski knows her sweets. Here's one of her best. It's a complicated confection, but a worthy special-occasion effort.

Chocolate Velvet Crostada

Pâte Sucrée
3¼ cups pastry flour
½ cup granulated sugar
11 ounces (1⅓ stick) unsalted butter, chilled
2 egg yolks
3 tablespoons heavy cream

Combine flour and sugar in a mixer with a dough hook or in a food processor fitted with a steel blade, and mix until thoroughly combined. Cube butter and add to the flour mixture, mixing thoroughly until coarse and mealy (pea size). Combine egg yolks and cream, and add all at once to the flour mixture. Mix thoroughly until the dough forms a ball. Remove from bowl, cover with plastic wrap, and refrigerate for at least 2 hours. (You can make the Pâte Sucrée in advance and store in the refrigerator for two days or in freezer for up to one month, allowing it to defrost in the refrigerator.)

Preheat oven to 300 degrees and set out a 12-inch tart pan with a removable bottom. To make the pastry shell, remove dough from refrigerator and roll out to ¼-inch thickness, 1 inch larger than tart pan. Line the pan with the rolled-out dough. Cut a piece of parchment into a 12-inch circle, place on dough and add pie weights. Bake for 15 minutes, or until pastry is light golden brown. Remove from oven, remove pie weights and parchment, and cool.

Chocolate Pots de Crème Filling
4 cups heavy cream
1 cup milk
1 vanilla bean
1 cup sugar
11 egg yolks
9 ounces (9 squares) bittersweet chocolate, melted

Combine cream and milk in a 2-quart saucepan. With a sharp paring knife, cut vanilla bean in half lengthwise and scrape the inside of the bean into the cream and milk. Bring mixture just to a boil, remove from heat, and whisk in melted chocolate. Mix sugar and egg yolks in a large stainless-steel bowl, then slowly stir in the cream and milk mixture. (You can make the filling up to 2 to 4 days in advance.)

Banana Caramel Sauce
3 ripe bananas
2½ cups heavy cream
1 vanilla bean
3 cups sugar
1 cup water
¼ cup light corn syrup
4 ounces (1 stick) cold unsalted butter

Finely chop bananas with a knife. Combine chopped banana and cream in a saucepan. With a sharp paring knife, cut vanilla bean in half lengthwise; scrape the inside of the bean into the cream and banana mixture, and steep over low heat for 10 to 15 minutes. In a large saucepan (see note below), combine sugar, water, and corn syrup. Heat until mixture turns a rich brown color. Remove from heat; carefully stir in banana-cream mixture and butter. Strain mixture through a *chinois* or fine strainer.

Note: Be sure to use a large saucepan, because the caramel will foam up to three times its volume when you add the cream mixture.

Caramelized Banana
3 ripe bananas
granulated sugar

Peel bananas and slice into ¼-inch discs. Place slices in a heatproof vessel and sprinkle liberally with sugar. Place briefly under a preheated broiler or flame with a chef's blowtorch.

Assembly
½ cup creamy peanut butter
baked pastry, filling, sauce, and caramelized bananas, above
whipped cream (optional)
chilled dessert plates

Preheat oven to 275 degrees. Spread peanut butter all over the bottom of the prebaked tart shell. Pour in chocolate pots de crème filling until it comes to ½ inch of the top of the shell. Place on a baking sheet and bake for approximately 40 minutes, until the center is set. Cool in refrigerator for at least 1 hour. Carefully remove tart pan rim. Cut into 10 wedges.

Artfully decorate 10 chilled dessert plates with the prepared banana caramel sauce. Place one wedge atop the sauce, then lay 6 pieces of caramelized banana on each slice and garnish with whipped cream (optional). Serves 10.

Many of Tony's Meats and Specialty Foods' most successful recipes use the stores' fine meats, and many display their Italian roots as well. Executive Chef Ben Davis has braised a healthy chunk of meat using Mediterranean methodology in this recipe, which translates to Pork Cooked in Milk with Sage. In France, a similar recipe is known as *Porc à la Basquaise*.

Maiale al Latte

4- to 5-pound boneless loin of pork
kosher salt and freshly ground black pepper to taste
1½ quarts whole milk
2 tablespoons olive oil
4 tablespoons (½ stick) unsalted butter
5 cloves garlic, peeled and halved
1 small handful sage leaves
zest from 2 lemons (cut into strips with a vegetable peeler)

Cut most of the fat from the outside of the pork loin and discard. Generously season meat with salt and pepper. In a saucepan, heat milk over medium heat, watching carefully so that it does not boil. Set milk aside.

Heat a deep-sided, heavy-bottomed pan over high heat. Pour in olive oil. Add pork and sear on all sides until brown. Remove pork and pour off the fat. Reduce heat. Add the butter to pan. When butter is melted, stir in garlic and sage, and cook just until the garlic begins to color. Return pork to pan and add enough milk to come three-fourths up the side of the pork. Bring to a boil. Add lemon zest. Reduce the heat to medium-low. Cover pan with a lid, leaving it slightly askew. Simmer gently for about 1½ to 2 hours. The milk will have curdled during the cooking process, forming brown nuggets. Remove the meat, slice, and spoon the milk sauce over it. Serves 6.

Boulder and Boulder County

Oh, the Boulder one-liners. Fifty square miles surrounded by reality. The number of Boulderites it takes to change a lightbulb: 21—1 to change the bulb and 20 to relate to the experience. A college town where most students major in skiing and minor in partying. Colorado's tofu capital. America's most politically correct city.

There's a grain of truth—all right, a big kernel of truth—to all of them, but beyond the one-liners, clichés, and half-mocking, half-envious comments, Boulder is a beautiful, caring city where maintaining and enhancing the quality of life are high priorities for a good part of the citizenry. Eating well and staying healthy are two components to that vaunted quality of life. Boulder is graced with many restaurants that offer fine dining presented by immensely talented chefs, plus restaurants and foodstores that are dedicated both to healthful natural cuisine and eating well. Granola gourmet, you could call it.

The Pearl Street Mall, the city's main retail street, celebrated its 25th anniversary as a pedestrian zone in the summer of 2002, and in that quarter-century downtown Boulder developed into a regional dining and entertainment mecca. Boulder also boasts one of the best farmers' markets in the state, one of the best kitchenware stores in the country, the only wine retailer in North America owned by two master sommeliers, and one of the best cooking schools in the West.

Boulder's slow-growth, no-growth ethic, contrasted with Colorado's aggressive growth elsewhere, has resulted in an explosion of development in nearby communities, including other parts of Boulder County and adjacent Broomfield. What were, until recently, farming towns have been rapidly suburbanized, and some of the Boulder-style tastes and interests in good food have been spilling over to them as well, creating a mini-metro area around Boulder just a few miles northwest of the Denver metro area. The result is a Front Range that offers fabulous opportunities for foodies to dine, shop, and refine their own culinary skills.

Bakeries

Bavarian Bakery

The gingerbread-trimmed sign over this Longmont store says "Bavarian Bakery and Konditorei" (pastry bakery), and the sign to the right says "Restaurant." There's no more pastry, at least not at this writing, and the restaurant section is closed as well, but this longtime bakery is still turning out mountains of bread. Most is destined for wholesale accounts, but you can buy fresh bread on-site in 24- and 32-ounce loaves.

The selection consists of farmer's rye, German, farmer's dark rye, woodstove, sourdough, sunflower whole wheat, French white, multigrain, and cinnamon raisin. Six-packs of European dinner rolls are also available.

Bavarian Bakery, 613 Frontage Road, Longmont; (303) 676-1014.

Belgian Bakery

The Belgian Bakery offers authentic Old World breads, rolls, pastries, and cakes to eat in or take out. Napoleons, fruit tarts, éclairs, *palmiers,* the miserably misnamed but utterly delicious *miserable,* and other classic pastries can turn a proverbial cloudy day into a sunny one. Anyone whose treasured European memories include starting each morning with coffee and a Kaiser roll, with a brittle-crisp golden crust encasing a feather-soft interior, or a croissant that flakes with every delicious bite can replicate the experience at the Belgian Bakery.

Marleen Suy and Peter Blommaert immigrated to Boulder from Belgium in 1997. Her parents owned a bakery, he had worked in one, and the couple wanted their own. Blommaert remains the head baker. He and his small crew bake for both the original Boulder location and a newer store in Longmont, as well as for a handful of cafés and other commercial accounts.

The modest lunch menu offers three sizes and several flavors of quiche, a couple of salads, and a few sandwiches served on small baguettes. Even if you never set foot onto the Belgian Bakery's immaculate tile floor, you might have seen its vintage Citroën Deux Chevaux with plastic baguettes affixed to the roof parked out front or tooling around town.

Belgian Bakery, 3267 28th Street, (303) 449-7240; and 1127 Francis Street, Longmont, (720) 494-8660.

Breadworks

The funky Community Plaza shopping center holds one of the Front Range's most fabulous bread bakeries. When Larry and Kim Domnitz were starting Breadworks, they ordered a J. Llopis brick oven from Spain, importing the bricks and also a factory representative from Barcelona to assemble it. The 17-foot diameter oven, sizable enough to give the witch in *Hansel and Gretel* a major case of kiln envy, can bake up to 200 loaves at a time. Seven days a week, all-natural doughs go in and scrumptious, thick-crusted loaves emerge. Breadworks' recipes, quality ingredients, bakers' skills, and that unique oven combine into alchemy in the world of fine artisan breads.

Daily breads include such standbys as baguettes and *bâtards* in plain and seeded versions, *pain rustique,* a French sourdough called *pain au levain,* and Italiano. Some of these loaves are available in a couple of sizes. Breadworks is also Rollworks, baking rustic and focaccia rolls every day, the latter perfumed with roasted garlic and fresh rosemary.

The specialty breads are baked according to a schedule: Calamata olive-thyme on Monday, Wednesday, Friday, and Sunday; ciabatta on Monday through Thursday;

challah on Friday, before noon; fresh dill on Sunday; deli rye on Monday, Tuesday, and Friday; and so on through an awesome list that also includes *due formaggi,* green olive-sage, honey-whole wheat, Irish oatmeal, multigrain, fresh onion, *pain du campagne, panello de'Uva,* potato-chive, fresh rosemary, rye-raisin-walnut, semolina, and even fresh pretzels.

The bakery also turns out excellent scones, Danish pastries, croissants, muffins, Jewish apple cake, cornbread, tea cookies, popular American cookies such as chocolate chip and peanut butter, and brownies. Opening with just 2,300 square feet of space (modest considering the size of that oven), the bakery has since expanded to more than 6,000 square feet to accommodate both a bright and simple café and a pastry bakery with a more subtle oven than the Llopis behemoth. The pastry counter displays cheesecake, raspberry Linzer bars, Key lime tarts, and Key lime coconut bars. Breakfast pastries and coffee are, of course, popular, and the café is a good lunch spot as well, with sandwiches made with a choice of outstanding fresh breads, along with salads and soups.

Breadworks, 2644 Broadway, Boulder; (303) 444-5667.

Le Délice

In mid-2002, Le Délice, that Cherry Creek keeper of the Gallic flame (see page 15), opened a Boulder branch on the Pearl Street Mall. It is smaller than the Denver original, but the confections are just as good and just as gorgeous. This time, instead of having a French restaurant adjacent, Le Délice has partnered with a small Italian restaurant called Trattoria Girasole, which primarily serves foods of southern Italy, including soups, pizza, pasta, and sandwiches. The desserts, of course, speak across the doorway with a French accent. A sidewalk café stretches across both stores. Being north-facing, it offers relief as well as that good eating on a hot summer day.

Le Délice and Trattoria Girasole, 1430 Pearl Street, Boulder; (303) 544-0008.

Le Français

When Le Français debuted in 1982 as an authentic boulangerie, a cheer erupted from fans of true European breads, which were then seriously lacking on the Front Range. The bakery still cranks out splendid and totally authentic baguettes in a choice of white or wheat and various sizes, which are so fresh loaves emerge from the oven several times a day. Fans are still cheering.

In addition to being a bread bakery, Le Français produces masterfully rendered classic French pastries—fruit tarts, Napoleons, éclairs, *palmiers,* and other favorites. For a special occasion, it's hard to beat the cakes. They are so appealing that my husband and I were swayed to order a Mont Blanc as our wedding cake simply because the Frenchman who was baking at that time told us that he had made it for his own wedding. We figured if it was good enough for him and his bride, it was surely good enough for us. And it was.

Le Français, BaseMar Center, 570 Baseline Avenue, Boulder; (303) 499-7429.

The Lick Skillet Bakery

Once upon a time there were two restaurants in the funky mountain hamlet of Gold Hill, just west of Boulder: the Gold Hill Inn and the Lick Skillet Café. Both were institutions. The Gold Hill Inn is still in business, operating seasonally, but in the early 1990s, Lick Skillet closed its mountain location and reinvented itself as a bakery-café on Boulder's east side.

Improbably attached to a Total gas station, the bright little store has a few tables, a counter with a view of busy Arapahoe Road, and a big case filled with mouth-watering baked goods. Open from early morning to mid-afternoon, the bakery serves from-scratch breakfasts and light (and not-so-light) lunches. Lick Skillet's fresh-from-the-oven baked goods include generously sized muffins, scrumptious Danish pastries, cookies, cakes, and more that attract a mixed clientele of people commuting into or out of Boulder.

The Lick Skillet Bakery, 5340 Arapahoe Road, Boulder; (303) 449-7775 or www.lickskilletbakery.com.

Spruce Confections

Baking maestro David Cohen started out to be a musical maestro, at one point studying composition in Vienna. No one who lives in Austria can ignore the food, especially the pastries and cakes. Its capital city virtually institutionalized the art of baking *kuchen, torten, krapfen,* and other sublime sweets. Perhaps the unusual combination of all those inspiring Viennese pastries and Cohen's own creativity resulted in his notable baking skills.

Spruce Confections is located in a modest downtown store, but behind the plate glass, Cohen and his crew turn out a symphony of exquisite baked goods. The open kitchen—with its powerful mixers and high-capacity Blodgett baking ovens—is right behind the sales counter, so you can watch the bakers at work. Their breakfast pastries perk up many a Boulderite's morning, while cakes, tortes, cookies, pies, and patisseries brighten afternoons.

Muffins, scones, espresso–sour cream brownies, Mexican wedding cookies, coffee cakes, and fruit tarts beckon from the glass cases, but nothing sings out more seductively than the gorgeous layer cakes. If you need a special-occasion cake, Spruce Confections will make one to order that will be as scrumptious as it is beautiful—or, perhaps, as beautiful as it is scrumptious. For the health-obsessed or those with specific food allergies, breads like zucchini-pumpkin, vegan, and wheat-free oat-raisin cookies and vegan chocolate-chip cookies are like manna from heaven.

Spruce Confections also serves up nice light lunches such as focaccia with pizza-like toppings and tasty house-made soups. On balmy days, there's a real demand for the handful of sunny sidewalk tables in front of this fantastic bakeshop and the few more sheltered ones in a tiny courtyard next to the building.

Spruce Confections, 767 Pearl Street, Boulder; (303) 449-6773.

Cooking Schools and Cooking Classes

Cooking from the Heart

Mei Hamilton has been cooking since she was 12, preparing her mother's time-tested Taiwanese recipes for a family of eight. In 1979, she won second place in a regional cooking contest in Taiwan for a dish called Eight-Treasure Braised Duck. What validation of a young cook's skill! Nevertheless, she took a detour from the kitchen, earning three university degrees and landing in the high-tech world of computer programming before returning to the high-touch realm of cooking. She now shares the Chinese cuisine of her heritage, teaching at cooking schools and adult education programs in Longmont and Boulder—and also in her Longmont home, where she started Cooking from the Heart in 2001.

Hamilton's award-winning duck recipe of so long ago was complex in terms of ingredients and preparation. Her desire now is to develop recipes and teach people how to use Chinese methods and ingredients that are low in preparation time and high in flavor. We all know that traditional Chinese and other Asian cuisines are immensely healthy, so Cooking from the Heart could easily be called Cooking *for* the Heart. Hamilton is so determined that students will relax and enjoy their ventures into Chinese cuisine that she starts each class with relaxation exercises. That was a new one on me, but when you think about it, it makes sense to de-stress before concentrating on preparing the best food you can. The basic course serves as an introduction to Chinese cooking, while more advanced classes focus on authentic Chinese dishes that are often modified to American tastes and/or the skill level of her students in various classes. All classes include preparing four dishes in three hours.

Hamilton's logical, programmer-analyst thought processes come into play in her culinary syllabus. She starts with how to buy a wok, where to buy basic ingredients, and other important skills in preparing Chinese food efficiently. Hamilton asks her students to bring an apron, a favorite knife, and a cutting board—and they show up with curiosity and enthusiasm too.

She occasionally presents her Asian Market Tour and Dim Sum Treat in Denver. She needs at least eight people for the three- to three-and-a-half-hour program, shepherding her flock through the aisles of Asian markets, and introducing novices and experienced Chinese cooks alike to both ordinary and exotic ingredients. The group finishes by sharing a lunch of dim sum, delectable small dishes that you can think of as Chinese tapas.

Cooking from the Heart, 1238 Whitehall Drive, Longmont; (303) 678-9991.

Cooking School of the Rockies

Founded in 1991, this South Boulder cooking school is all things to all cooks: a few hours of culinary enlightenment to anyone with a passing interest in good food, week-long technique programs for serious home cooks, and professional cooking courses for those seeking culinary careers. The school is bisected into two kitchens— one with an island and overhead mirror that is designed for both small hands-on classes and larger demonstration classes for home cooks, and the other with serious restaurant equipment for the school's three professional programs and occasionally home-cook classes as well.

Many students exhibit the same passion for good food that caused Joan Brett, a lawyer, to start offering cooking classes in her home. Interest quickly outstripped that venue, so she established the school at the Table Mesa Shopping Center, where it now spreads across several storefronts. Brett's life since then has been more about tarts than torts, simmering than summaries, cookbooks than law books.

Classes for Home Cooks

The big main classroom, where most sessions for home cooks are held, is bright, functional, and frill-free with an enormous *batterie de cuisine* amply equipped for a whole class to be involved in preparation and cooking. When it's time to eat, tables are set with linen, restaurant china, stainless flatware, and real glasses. Nice. But fancy? Not really. What counts is a love for good food and an interest in learning to prepare it.

Some classes may be scheduled for a single evening or a full day on Saturday or Sunday—or a series. Single-session classes may be demonstration or hands-on, taught by regular instructors or guest chefs. They offer quick immersion into the food of a particular country or region, a particular ingredient, or a specific method of cooking. The schedule includes such broad and diverse subjects as Dim Sum Workshop, Stock Market (having nothing to do with Wall Street but making from-scratch stocks), Joy of Soy, French Bread, Savory Pastries, Hearty Vegetarian, Wilderness Gourmet, Cooking for the Week, Pasta Workshop, Regional Italian, Winning Salsa, Chocolate Extravaganza, Artichokes and Asparagus, Indian Cuisine Workshop, Thai Cuisine, Food in a Flash, and Sushi Madness. Additionally, the school hosts periodic evening wine-tasting and wine-pairing classes, as well as classes taught by noteworthy visiting chefs and cookbook authors from John Ash to Joanne Weir.

The school also offers specialty classes. If you take nothing else, ever, sign up for Knife Skills. Even long-time cooks are often awkward and inefficient when cutting, slicing, and dicing, to say nothing of mincing and julienning. If that describes you as it did me, this class will help. Take it, and then practice, practice, practice.

On selected Saturdays during harvest season, an instructor and students troop to the Boulder Farmers' Market, talk to growers, shop, and return to the school to prepare what they've bought. The school also has a table at the market, where you can pick up recipes, perhaps watch an instructor make a dish, or simply talk cooking. The Cooking School of the Rockies offers hands-on classes for children age 8 to 12 and teens age 13 to 16, as well as Corporate Kitchen team-building classes—no age restrictions there.

The cooking school's technique classes meet for five five-hour sessions either over five consecutive weeks or during one Monday through Friday period that lends itself to a cooking vacation. These classes—always small and always hands-on—are in-depth rather than quick immersion. They appeal to anyone with kitchen experience, whether follow-the-recipe-to-the-T types or confident cooks who adapt and perhaps create their own recipes but want to follow a thematic thread to learn right. The lineup includes Basic Technique (nicknamed Tech I at the school), Basic Technique II (naturally, Tech II), Country French, Mediterranean, Modern American, Italian, Asian, and Pastry.

The school's volunteer program is distinctive. Instructors of classes for home cooks—whether hands-on or demonstration—are backed by volunteer assistants. During the day, when tech classes predominate, one assistant sets up the room, assists the instructor with prep or any other tasks, clears away used utensils and dishes, and tidies the room after the class is done. A paid dishwasher handles the hard-core cleanup chores. Larger demo classes, generally given in the evening or on weekends, require several assistants to handle those tasks, plus serve the food and work as kitchen crew, washing dishes in the back. The pay-off is two-fold: the opportunity to learn while volunteering, and earning credits that may be applied to future classes. It's a great arrangement—and there's not another like it around.

Professional Programs

The Cooking School of the Rockies also has accredited professional programs for those seeking careers in the field. The classroom for aspiring chefs and bakers in all programs takes place in that fully equipped, state-of-the-art commercial kitchen, which was further upgraded in 2002.

The six-month Professional Culinary Arts Program, accredited by the Accrediting Council for Continuing Education and Training, emphasizes classical French technique. Each class session begins with a lecture, demonstration, and discussion about the day's menu. Then a maximum of 14 students work in teams to produce the planned meal, gaining extensive hands-on experience with preparation, cooking, and seasoning techniques. Afterward, the class savors and critiques the meal, followed by an additional lecture/tasting each day on a topic related to the curriculum.

To replicate on-the-job experience, positions such as student kitchen manager and team chefs rotate weekly. One of the real treats on the Cooking School of the Rockies' calendar is the semi-annual Culinary Gala, designed, prepared, and served by the current crop of graduates of the Professional Culinary Arts Program. It's always a sell-out.

Students can cap off their Boulder culinary education with a trip to France. The group visits Paris's fabled Rungis, said to be the world's largest wholesale food market, spends a week studying at the Université du Vin in the Rhône Valley, and travels to Avignon. There, students spend a week in a *stage*, an apprenticeship in the kitchen of a Provençal restaurant such as Oustau de Beaumanière, Le Bistrot d'Eygalière, and Restaurant Brunel. Visits to markets, wineries, bakeries, cheesemakers, and others, and additional experiences from seeing an olive-oil mill to participating in a truffle hunt can round out the trip.

The Pastry Arts Program is an intensive, hands-on 150-hour course spread over a one-month period and offered twice a year. It is so popular that the Cooking School's expansion in late 2002 was largely undertaken to enlarge the pastry section of the professional kitchen. Imagine learning, in just one month, how to make puff pastry, tarts, pies, yeasted sweet doughs, *pâte à chou,* pastry cream, lemon curd, ganache, cream fillings, buttercreams, layered cakes, meringues, *dacquoise,* brioche, *baba, savarin,* croissants, Danish pastries, biscuits, scones, muffins, chocolate candy, *confisserie, petits fours* and miniatures, mousses, custards, soufflés, fancy cookies, and even wedding cakes. This program can lead to a position as a pastry/dessert chef in a fine-dining restaurant, in a pastry and coffee shop, or as a baker in the fast-growing field of artisanal breads and fine pastries.

The Cooking School of the Rockies' most innovative professional program, called Chef Track, is a 24-week evening program designed for the career-changer. Students spend Sunday, Monday, and Tuesday evenings of the first 18 weeks training in the school's professional teaching kitchen, followed by a six-week paid, full-time externship in one of Colorado's top restaurants. The distinctive element of the program is the opportunity to work with a number of leading chefs who offer a restaurant position, mentoring, and, frankly, a foot in the door for graduation. If there is one common thread among the pros who back the Chef Track program, it's that "attitude is everything" in making it in the compelling, competitive world of the professional kitchen.

Cooking School of the Rockies, 637 South Broadway, Boulder; (303) 494-7988, (877) 249-0305, or www.cookingschoolrockies.com.

Expression Cooking Retreats

Deborah DeBord is a Ph.D. and cookbook author who organizes two-day, one-night cooking retreats in a charming cabin between Lyons and Estes Park. These cooking getaways are designed and priced for couples, and after the twosome has cooked, they can enjoy their efforts with wine and candlelight. DeBord herself, who does not call herself an instructor but rather a "guide," conducts them.

The next morning, DeBord suggests monthly themes for these retreats: Tapas y Vinos in January, Your Heart's Desire in February, Mardi Beads and Confetti in March, Cocina Oaxaca in April, the Comfort Kitchen in May, Pasta Pesto Presto in June, the All-American Grill in July, Partyhounds Celebrate in August, the Everyday Zen Practice of Kitchen in September, Abundant Autumnal Harvest in October, Wintry Soup Kettle and Rustic Loaves in November, and Festive Holiday Bakery and Non-Perishable Food Gifts in December. However, DeBord is flexible on this subject, and her clients tend to be so as well.

Expression—A Creative Retreat, 81 Cree Court, Lyons; (303) 823-0530 or www.expressionretreat.com.

School of Natural Cookery

A big part of the Boulder identity concerns holistic lifestyles, alternatives from everything for medicine to religion, and as an offshoot of that, a commitment to healthy eating, vegetarian food, and vegan options. Another big part of the Boulder identity involves quality of life—and that includes eating well, even if the diet is macrobiotic by philosophy and therefore Spartan by stereotype.

The Boulder School of Natural Cookery, established in 1983, helps students learn to cook without recipes and still prepare attractive, tasty meals within severe ingredient restrictions. Not surprisingly for this cutting-edge community, the SNC was one of the first in the nation to offer serious instruction for home cooks and aspiring professionals in this field.

Director Joanne Saltzman believes that cooking is an intuitive art, where the process of preparing food leads to individual understanding of our relationship with food. Further, she knows that a solid understanding of cooking theories and techniques creates a framework for culinary exploration where no recipes are followed, and all diets and cuisines can be accommodated—in fact, embraced. To this end, she has fine-tuned a curriculum that includes the art of preparing grains, beans, and vegetables.

The School of Natural Cookery's unique curriculum emphasizes vegetarian food preparation, with a goal of knowing how to prepare the ingredients you select and to do so intuitively, without recipes. Using the "language of chefs," an SNC concept, students can cook whatever is at hand and make it taste good.

Programs for Home Cooks

The Main Course, an eight-day program for home cooks offered several times a year, combines demonstration and hands-on classes. It can be taken as an intensive program, which includes communal boarding, or on a series of weekends. Among the skills taught and sensibilities raised are knife use, improvisation in the kitchen, and, of course, "the language of chefs." Most are totally vegan, using no animal or dairy products.

Students learn how to create grain, bean, and vegetable entrées; prepare soups and sauces; study tofu and tempeh; and make tempting desserts with whole sweeteners. The final session, in which the use of meat is an option, focuses on ethnic cooking. If your interests lie in the direction of sprouting, enzymatic food preparations, food dehydrating, how to improvise, and meal planning, the School of Natural Cookery occasionally offers classes on those subjects too.

Professional Programs

Aspiring professional cooks start with the Foundation Course, which includes the fundamentals of cooking: knife skills, kitchen safety, and the technique and theory of cooking. Food categories and preparations include tofu, tempeh, seitan, beans, vegetables, sea veggies, whole-dish grains, soups, sauces, meal composition, breads, cookies, pies, and cakes. In order to accommodate various dietary and philosophical needs, the program also offers alternatives to using wheat flour and dairy products, and baking with unrefined sweeteners. The repertoire covers seven different ethnic cuisines, party food forms, and how to build speed and coordination in the kitchen.

The SNC is one of the very few schools in the country to address the seemingly contradictory mandates of vegan eating and gastronomy in an advanced class taught by classically trained chefs. The "language of chefs" here becomes "the language of French cuisine," with an emphasis on artistry of presentation in the context of fine dining but without compromising idealism or dietary needs. With no fewer than four and no more than 15 students, classes are small and are in a five-cooking-station home kitchen in northeast Boulder. Classes also are offered in Albuquerque and Seattle.

School of Natural Cookery, P.O. Box 19466, Boulder, CO 80308-2466; (303) 444-806 or www.naturalcookery.com.

Sundays with Chef James Mazzio

James Mazzio has been offering cooking classes at ChefJam (see page 147), his catering business. This repeating series of four-week, hands-on cooking classes takes place on consecutive Sundays from 3:00 to 7:00 P.M. at this writing. In addition to an ability to pass along chefs' tips, tricks, secrets, and insights, Mazzio is an engaging extrovert with great stage presence, and visiting chefs also teach at ChefJam.

Participants cook a full meal during each class and then sit down to share it. The topics for each class jump around a bit so that a complete meal can be created. Each series starts with a fundamentals class focusing on such basics—new to some people, review for others—as knife skills, how to season and use spices, roasting, soufflés, and sauces. The second covers such varied topics as which cookbooks to read, how to time your meal, vinaigrettes, pasta, and ice cream. Topics for the third class are product awareness, which includes recognizing freshness and knowing how to buy seafoods and sorbets.

And the theme for the final class is something many home cooks agonize over: How to Create a Party, subtitled "Everything You Need to Know to Create an Amazing Cocktail Party." The ensuing "Tastes of the World" cocktail party is a global feast of tasty morsels from many traditions. Students are encouraged to invite family members or friends to join the cocktail party—sort of a graduation celebration for a crash culinary education.

ChefJam, 1200 Miramonte Street, Broomfield; (303) 404-2525 or www.chefjam.com.

What's Cooking

When What's Cooking (see page 140) moved into larger quarters in 2000, a new custom demonstration kitchen was constructed in a back corner of the store. Except for the fact that it is raised on a dais and has only two walls, it looks like a classy home kitchen with quality wood cabinets, granite countertops, double ovens, a large refrigerator, and a cooking island with a six-burner Viking rangetop and griddle.

Visiting chefs teach both hands-on and demonstration classes on Tuesday and Thursday evenings in the fall, winter, and spring. Some classes concentrate on one food category such as seafood, pasta, soups, appetizers, sauces, pizza, or sushi. Others focus on a particular ethnic cuisine, including Indian, Chinese, Mexican, and French. Pizza, sushi, and pasta classes just about have to be hands-on. Others might be hands-on or demo.

Cooking 101 covers fundamentals and is usually taught by Jon Inaba of the Cooking School of the Rockies. His 20-Minute Gourmet is geared for the time-pressed cook who nevertheless wants to do more in the kitchen than simply nuking something in the microwave. He demonstrates a medley of time-saving techniques that show you how to make real food from good ingredients in the same amount of time it would take to heat up an entrée prepared in a factory who knows how long ago and languishing ever since "in your grocer's freezer."

All classes run from 6:30 to 9:30 P.M. and are self-contained, with no serial classes in this program. Participants earn a 10 percent discount on any retail item purchased within two weeks of taking a class.

What's Cooking, 2770 Arapahoe Road, Lafayette; (303) 666-0300 or www.whatscookinginc.com.

Dining

Alice's Restaurant at Gold Lake Resort

In the early years of Colorado's mineral boom, the mountains above Boulder were filled with mining camps. One, Gold Lake, eventually became Gold Lake Ranch, a summer camp. Karel and Alice Starek bought the old camp in 1994 and transformed it into a spa resort, maintaining much of the original outward appearance while adding contemporary comforts.

A large log lodge, once the camp's dining hall, was totally refurbished to house Alice's Restaurant, a spacious, gracious, and refined place to dine. Resort guests take all their meals there, and day visitors are also welcome. Dinner and Sunday brunch are the most popular times for day-trippers.

Until late 2001, Eric Skokan presided over the kitchen, and Curtis Lincoln, the Culinary Institute of America graduate who followed as executive chef, carries on Skokan's Colorado contemporary style with his own overlay. The German-born chef has traveled extensively and honed his culinary skills in restaurants from Lake Tahoe to Nantucket.

With the increased emphasis on the spa component of the resort, which metamorphosed into Gold Lake Mountain Resort & Spa, the cooking style began to be described as "mountain spa cuisine." Whatever the name, the dishes that herald from Alice's kitchen under both chefs have invariably been tasty, gorgeous, and interestingly counterpointed, often with unexpected accompaniments.

The romantic restaurant boasts wood floors, low ceilings, and soft lights. One large table is surrounded by custom-made chairs with dramatic five-foot-high backs of polished pine that the big table feels like a room within a room. Twosomes and other small groups are seated at wooden tables, comfortably separated from each other but with conventionally sized chairs. Place settings feature heavy flatware, bulbous wine glasses, and interesting plates of various sizes and mugs made by two local potters.

Dinners at Alice's have been distinguished by lavish use of game, seafood, interesting grains, and, of course, fresh seasonal produce. Using natural and organic ingredients, Alice's kitchen even makes its own ice cream, cures its own olives, and mills its own flour for the breads, rolls, pastries, and cookies that are baked fresh every day.

The menu changes seasonally, but popular items over the years have included Farmer's Market Green Salad served with spicy grilled vegetables, toasted almonds, and a smooth red pepper crème; and a generous Grilled Elk Rib Chop served with sweet corn flan, black bean *relleno,* and cumin *jus*—an unexpected and subtle Spanish take on North American game. Alice's unusual persimmon cake is served with the contrasting flavors of black walnut ice cream and maple juice.

Chef Lincoln's Foie Gras with Black Pepper and Roasted Pineapple; Striped Bass with Corn Pudding, Citrus Sauce, and Wilted Spinach; and Chocolate Sponge Cake have won kudos too. In high season and on weekends year-round, there are always about nine appetizers, eight entrées, and six desserts to choose from. Peak-season and weekend dinners include the modest three-course "standard" *prix fixe* dinner or an optional seven-course tasting dinner, with or without paired wines. Midweek off-season offerings are more limited.

With a broad and deep wine list, Alice's has been arranging 50 to 60 multi-course tasting dinners a year, and under Skokan's tenure the resort also began offering cooking classes as part of its Culinary Escape packages. Gold Lake Resort and Spa and Alice's Restaurant are geographically close to Denver and other Front Range cities but light-years away in feeling, so it's a getaway that's not too far away and a culinary treat that's hard to beat.

Alice's Restaurant, Gold Lake Mountain Resort & Spa, 3371 Gold Lake Road (off Peak to Peak Highway), Ward; (800) 450-3544, (303) 459-3544, or www.goldlake.com.

Bácaro

Distantly named after Bacchus, the Greek god of wine, joviality, and, some would say, debauchery, Bácaro was inspired by the Italian portion of the Mediterranean. This stylish contemporary restaurant just west of Boulder's Pearl Street Mall features a congenial bar area and a tasteful yet sprightly dining space. Wines are a backdrop for the bar area, while a semi-open kitchen backs the dining section—obvious enough so that you know someone is cooking there, but not so obtrusive that the kitchen crew disturbs the diners. The dining patio boasts polished-granite tables for outdoor elegance and overhead heat lamps for chilly evenings.

Although Bácaro was launched as a northern Italian restaurant, it became somewhat more pan-Mediterranean, adding tapas and a subtle Spanish accent to some of its offerings. The tapas are especially affordable during happy hour (a generous three-and-a-half hours every evening). The dinner menu, extensive rather than overwhelming, is designed Italian-style, so that pasta properly appears ahead of the entrée course rather than as the main event—although Americans often start with a salad or soup, move on to pasta as the meal's centerpiece, and then order dessert.

For starters, Bácaro's Smoked Buffalo Carpaccio is hard to beat. Seafood, meats, and poultry form the backbone of the entrée list. You can even find saltimbocca, a Roman classic made with veal, prosciutto, and a healthy dose of sage. The classic Italian custard called *panna cotta* is flavored with orange and orange peel. The crème brulée, known in Italian as *crema al forno*, has a pistachio flavor. The sizable wine list tilts to domestic and Italian vintages.

Bácaro, 921 Pearl Street, Boulder; (303) 444-4888 or www.bacaro.com.

Carelli's

Based on the superficialities of location and outward appearance in a small strip mall just south of the University of Colorado's main campus, and perilously near a stack of towering dormitories, Carelli's doesn't make a powerful initial impression. Behind the bland façade, however, sits a good Italian restaurant that is as much all things to all customers—except a noisy college hangout—as any place in Boulder.

Businesspeople and "ladies who lunch" meet there in mid-day. Children are welcomed, so families abound in the early evening. Couples and groups of grown-ups show up later, some to enjoy a relaxed and romantic dinner by the fireside. It's understandable that Carelli's plays all these roles admirably, since the menu is large and varied, prices are reasonable, the waitstaff amiable, and the wine list and bar service are on a par with the food.

Greg Carelli launched the place in 1991 and remains a hands-on owner. The attractive and low-key restaurant has accents of brick, stone, tile, and a wall of triangular wooden racks stacked with wine bottles. The ceilings are high, the lighting is flattering (check out the string of aviation fixtures near the west end of the dining area), and the seating options are great. Tables and caned-back chairs provide most of the seating, but the best tables in the house are a quartet of high-backed curved booths on platforms. They provide a cocoon-like feeling and a view across the dining room. In winter, the tables near gas-log fireplaces are highly coveted, and a parking-lot patio is available for outdoor dining in summer.

Carelli's menu won't knock you out with punchy creativity, but it will satisfy you with ample portions and good renditions of traditional and adapted dishes, including daily specials. Lunches include enormous salads, satisfying pastas, sandwiches, pizza, calzone, and hot entrées. Dinner offerings are similar but tilt more toward the entrée camp. Fettuccini carbonara—pasta bathed in a blend of cream sauce, Parmesan cheese, Prosciutto, garlic, and mushrooms—is so rich that all but the heartiest eaters will surely take some home. With southern Italian roots, Carelli's makes a good marinara and uses it for eggplant Parmigiana and assorted pasta offerings. The wine list features mostly Italian and West Coast wines, many available by the glass.

The dessert tray displays cannoli, apple crostada, crème brulée, chocolate cake, carrot cupcake, chocolate mousse on a chocolate spongecake foundation, fruits in season, and Chocolate Lava Cake, a calorie bomb that may not be particularly Italian but is particularly delicious. Tiramisu, spumoni, and sorbet are also available, but they don't appear on the dessert tray.

Carelli's, 645 30th Street, Boulder; (303) 938-9300.

Chautauqua Dining Hall

Magnificently located at the base of the Flatirons, Boulder's Chautauqua Park claims a history that dates back to 1898, when it was established as a beat-the-heat retreat for Methodist teachers from Texas. It is the oldest continuously operating Chautauqua west of the Mississippi. The dining hall is one of the early buildings, but for years, little was done to improve it. The unheated restaurant, which operated seasonally, was popular for the setting and the views. The restrooms from that time are best forgotten.

For Chautauqua's centennial, partners Bradford Heap (of Full Moon Grill fame) and Richard Stein took over operations of the Dining Hall and treated the grand lady to a facelift, both in architectural and culinary terms. They brought the kitchen up to date, insulated and heated the building, upgraded the wiring and plumbing, cleaned and painted with respect to the building's historic appearance, and began serving breakfast, lunch, and dinner year-round—and yes, added new restrooms. The building has great bones, and the makeover was respectfully and simply done to enhance rather than disguise its appearance.

In contrast to the Full Moon Grill's northern Italian influences, Heap introduced young and vibrant Rocky Mountain cuisine to the dowager restaurant. Breakfast merges with lunch at the Chautauqua Dining Hall, combining into one long brunch— and there is also a traditional buffet brunch on weekends. Menu items represent the extremes of Boulder—nutritional rigor combined with let-it-all-hang-out comfort food. Breakfast-type entrées are therefore as varied as Trail Mix Pancakes and Vegetarian Tofu Scrambler in the healthy breakfast department and Angel's Huevos Rancheros and Flatiron Skillet, a belly-busting medley of eggs, bacon, onion, scallions, and cheddar cheese. Lunch-type choices range from a Roasted Vegetable Sandwich to the Classic Bacon Cheeseburger, naturally served with fries.

Regionalism creeps into the appetizer offering of Crispy Calamari and Rock Shrimp with an *ancho* dipping sauce, while the Crispy Trout Cakes intrinsically have more to do with the Rockies. Grilled Rib Eye Steak with Bleu Cheese Mashed Potatoes and Port Wine Sauce, Colorado lamb with seasonal accompaniments, and fried catfish with red beans and rice satisfy heartier appetites. The wine list segments selections by weight, color, and taste, but there are fewer high-end wines, more wines by the glass, and more microbrews.

The Chautauqua Dining Hall is at the peak of its popularity during the summer and is a favored pre-concert dinner choice for those attending a performance at the nearby auditorium, an equally venerable building. During the summer, a spot on the wrap-around porch is to be treasured. Winter is paticularly lovely when snow falls on the lawns, trees, and rooftops of Chautauqua and the hillsides to the west. With such unsurpassed ambience, good food, and a terrific wine and beer list, the Dining Hall today represents the best of classic Boulder interpreted in ways that those well-meaning teetotaling teachers could not have imagined a century ago.

Chautauqua Dining Hall, 900 Baseline Road, Boulder; (303) 440-3776 or www.chautauquadininghall.com.

China Gourmet and Spice China

An informal, family-run eatery tucked into a shopping center on North Broadway, China Gourmet seems at first glance not unlike scores of other Chinese restaurants in Colorado: simple décor, big take-out trade, and, for the eat-in crowd, the routine of ordering at the cashier's counter, setting your own table, and picking up your food at a window. The food is as good as any of the genre but rather standard too: such popular items as combination plates; egg drop and wonton soup; lo mein; sweet and sour and Kung-Pao everything; Szechuan and Hunan sauces on various meats, veggies and seafoods; and, because it's Boulder, a slew of vegetarian dishes, healthy steamed entrées, and a choice of white, brown, or fried rice.

The legendary blue menu is where China Gourmet earns its last name. For years it was printed only in Chinese, because the owners assumed that no one save Chinese customers would want the likes of Spicy Beef Tendon, Sautéed Tripe, or Pepper Squid. Chinese-fluent guests dug into platters of interesting-looking dishes that Westerners could just guess at.

Eventually, the secret leaked out as adventuresome Americans prevailed on Chinese friends to translate the blue menu and China Gourmet finally began printing an English version too. While some dishes indeed are unpalatable to most Westerners, many of China Gourmet's best ones are blue menu items that use familiar ingredients but in spectacular ways. Shredded Pork with Dry Bean Curd or Bean Curd Sheets, Crispy Chicken with Special Sauce, any of the Pan-Fried Noodle dishes, and especially the Vegetable and Tofu Hot Pot might just rank as the best Chinese dishes in the state.

The unprepossessing Boulder restaurant has spawned a descendant. David Fan, scion of the China Gourmet family, struck out on his own to open Spice China, a fancier and more expensive restaurant than his parents'. It is a welcome island of fine fare swimming in the sea of chain restaurants that engulf the Boulder Turnpike's Louisville-Superior exit in general and McCaslin Boulevard in particular.

The newer restaurant's extensive lunch and dinner menu serves some of China Gourmet's specialties, including the most popular and tastiest dishes on the blue menu. Also noteworthy is Spice China's devotion to Shanghai dishes, a welcome change from the usual Cantonese-Szechuan-Hunan offerings. In contrast to China Gourmet's simplicity, Spice China's soaring space is furnished with commodious tables, rounded booths, and custom Chinese artwork. There's a full bar, and a wait-staff to serve the meals.

China Gourmet, 3970 Broadway, Boulder; (303) 440-3500 and (303) 440-0999.

Spice China, 269 McCaslin Boulevard, Louisville; (303) 890-0999.

The Cork

Boulder is probably the only city of its size in the country that has more Indian,

Thai, and natural-foods restaurants than it does true steakhouses, but one of the latter has endured for decades. The Cork opened in 1969 as part of the Cork and Cleaver chain, which ultimately expanded to 70 restaurants. Alan Teran, then a new college graduate from Ohio who knew nothing about the restaurant business, was hired to open the Boulder location, Cork and Cleaver's sixth.

In 1975, the chain was sold and morphed into the Chart House, with Teran as divisional president until 1981, when he left the corporation and took over the restaurant, renaming it The Boulder Cork. As the 20th century drew to a close and tastes were shifting, the Cork broadened its menu and expanded its horizons to meet contemporary tastes, but hearty cuts of beef and classic American dishes remain at its core. Restaurant manager Donna Dooley has been on board since 1980 and Chef Jim Smailer since 1981. Both are now partners in the restaurant.

The Cork will eternally be known for its steaks, but this is not to say that it has been stuck in a culinary rut. Even though the menu once offered mostly steak, prime rib, and perhaps one fish or chicken dish, it is now overlaid with Southwestern, Italian, and Asian influences. Heck, there's even a veggie stir-fry. Fans of the restaurant's hearty pasta dishes are equally partial to the capellini with Roma tomatoes, fresh mozzarella, artichoke hearts, basil, and Parmesan. Grilled yellowfin tuna with shiitake mushrooms, pickled ginger, and wasabi mayo is a seafood standout. But many regulars go there just for the crab cakes.

The décor is a loose rendition of a Mediterranean villa, with stucco walls, tile floors, arches, and several dining areas that replicate the sense of being cozily indoors by the fire or outside on a shaded terrace. The wine list is strong on American vintages, and the desserts—particularly the cheesecakes and the signature mud pie—are Lucullan.

The Cork, 3295 30th Street, Boulder; (303) 443-9505.

European Café

In 1989, Chef Radek Cerney opened the European Café in a strip shopping mall, an unlikely setting for a refined restaurant serving exquisite Continental cuisine. For a time, he also operated a second European café in Denver, plus a couple other restaurants in the Mile High City, including highly regarded Papillon and Radex. Meanwhile, he handed the Boulder baton off to Executive Chef Lupe Gonzalez, who continues to run the European Café with the same care, attention, and creativity that were evident from the start.

Curtains across the lower half of the large front windows do a great deal to disguise the parking-lot view. Inside, shining glass tops over the tablecloths, subdued lighting, candlelight, paintings on the walls, and attentive service create a nurturing ambience. Snazzier restaurants, snootier restaurants, and costlier restaurants have come and gone, or come and stayed, in Boulder since the European Café opened, but few have been so good for so long.

Many of the dishes are European in derivation, among them Pâté of Duck Liver and Black Truffle, Baked Escargots, Sautéed Mushroom Salad, Pan-Seared Halibut Provençal, and many of the pastas. Other items have been inspired by flavors beyond

Europe, such as Spicy Thai Shrimp starter with coconut-yellow curry and sweet curry sauces, Cajun Grilled Ahi Tuna with citrus *beurre blanc,* and sweet soy and pickled ginger mashed potatoes. Gonzalez balances a modest handful of meat entrées, a couple more fish, perhaps a game item or mixed grill, and at least one vegetarian entrée. He favors jasmine rice and uses it often. Many dishes are available at lunch and dinner, others only in the evening.

You can't go wrong at dessert, whether you order cheesecake, crème brulée, or the signature Pompeii, a chocolate bag that holds an individual chocolate cake with a molten center and is served with *crème Anglais.*

The house prix fixe dinner, called Chef's Surprise, consists of a soup, a salad, an entrée, and a dessert of the chef's choosing. The server won't know what it is until he or she picks it up from the kitchen, and you won't know until it's set before you. To accompany the meal, select from the 130-bottle wine list. When I last looked, there was no such thing at the European Café as a surprise wine.

European Café, 2460 Arapahoe Avenue, Boulder; (303) 938-8250.

Flagstaff House

For more than three decades, the Flagstaff House has ranked as one of the top restaurants in the country, not just in Colorado. Located high on Flagstaff Mountain, some 600 feet above Boulder and surrounded by Boulder Mountain Park, it feels close to heaven. And because it occupies the site of a cabin built in 1929 and is therefore grandfathered into a place where no one will ever be permitted to build again, it will never have neighbors. Rusticity is history on this mountainside, for the Flagstaff House is an extraordinarily elegant restaurant with some of the most refined food around.

When the most special occasion is being planned—say a wedding rehearsal dinner or reception, a significant birthday or anniversary, or perhaps a retirement dinner—particular epicures think of the Flagstaff House. When organizations give awards to restaurants for food or wine or service, the judges think of the Flagstaff House. It has won many prestigious honors, including Colorado's only *Wine Spectator* Grand Award (since 1983), the Mobil Four Star Award, the Triple AAA Four Diamond Award, and the DiRoNA Award. When officials have needed a Colorado restaurant suitable for royalty, they too have thought of the Flagstaff House. During the visit of Emperor Akihito and Empress Michiko of Japan to the United States in 1994, the Flagstaff House was the only non-hotel restaurant on the royal couple's three-week itinerary.

The Flagstaff House is as expensive as all this implies, but it is also a prime example of the concept "you get what you pay for." What you get here is a wonderful space with a grandiose view, impeccable service, and some of the consistently finest food and best wines in Colorado, made that way by the Monettes, a family of gifted chefs and dedicated restaurateurs who have run the restaurant since 1971.

Don Monette has been the guiding spirit of everything that elevated the Flagstaff House to greatness. The views and ambience were always Boulder's best, but he elevated both the kitchen and the dining room to the pinnacle of Colorado dining. With exquisite cuisine, sensational service, unsurpassed atmosphere, and a world-class wine list, the Flagstaff House has never lost its edge. Don's sons, Mark and Scott, now divide responsibilities for the back and front of the house. After training in several Michelin Three Star restaurants in France and working at some well-known restaurants in New York City and Asia, Mark Monette came home to "the family farm" in 1985.

He brought back with him a style of cooking that combines classic French cuisine with Asian accents, one of Colorado's first chefs to make that culinary connection. He also was one of the first to change the menu daily to take advantage of the freshest seasonal ingredients. Early on, he had fresh fish flown in daily, ordered locally grown organic products where possible, and cultivated herbs in the restaurant's own organic garden.

Scott, who earned a degree in hotel and restaurant management and worked at fine-dining establishments in New York, Washington, and Virginia, is general manager, bringing a sharp eye for detail and the ability to make every guest feel special. His management and front-of-the-house skills complement his brother's skills in the kitchen. The menu changes with the seasons and always features ingredients that are exotic, pricey, and/or somewhat difficult to obtain in Colorado. The accompaniments are as sophisticated as the main ingredient—and it goes without saying that the presentation of each is elegant and creative.

First courses might include such delicacies as Pancetta Wrapped Quail with Maitake Mushrooms served with white truffle polenta and red wine sauce; Terrine of Foie Gras, Duck Liver Pâté, and Smoked Duck Breast with strawberry-black pepper marmalade and raisin-walnut toast; or Spicy Japanese-Style Venison Dumplings with onion confit and sweet pepper broth. And the first course that makes the Flagstaff House fit for an emperor? Beluga 000 Caviar, available with or without a half-bottle of Veuve Cliquot Gold Label Champagne.

Soups include Lobster Soup with shiitake mushrooms, sweet corn, and lobster chunks and Chilled Soup of Asparagus with lump crab and lobster. Salads are medleys of greens, other vegetables, and perhaps chopped nuts, shaved cheeses, a smidgen of smoked meat, or a touch of seafood.

Main courses can really be over the top. Mark Monette likes to accent many dishes with shellfish or other seafood, a wrap of pancetta to enhance and deepen the flavor of meat or poultry, interesting mushrooms, and foie gras wherever he can find a valid reason to use it. Consider a showstopper such as Copper River King Salmon and Foie Gras "Wellington," served with fresh tree oyster mushrooms, baby bok choy, parsnip purée, and Port wine sauce.

Even the "simple" steakhouse meats get the Flagstaff House treatment. Filet mignon is seared with three peppers and served with fresh trumpet royale mushrooms, gratin of Yukon Gold and sweet potato, and Pinot Noir sauce—with or without foie gras on the side. Dry-aged New York Angus strip steak comes with pancetta, Yukon Gold potato, Alba clamshell mushrooms, roasted garlic, caramelized pearl onions, and that Port wine sauce. For those who can't decide between meat or poultry, there's Rack of Colorado Lamb and Pancetta Wrapped Quail, accompanied by ratatouille vegetables, goat cheese, toasted pecans, and Italian white polenta.

The dessert menu is divided into two categories. One is the type of dessert you can decide on after you've polished off your entrée. This includes Hot Crisp Apple

Tart, Caramelized Pineapple Upside-Down Cake, and Hot Peach Baked in Brioche, each served with rich ice cream, flavor-matched to the main ingredient. If you like chocolate, don't miss the dessert listed as Our Infamous Chocolate Bag, which is indeed a bag-shaped container made of chocolate and filled with mousse of praline and toffee with warm bananas. Then there are the desserts that must be ordered in advance. It does, after all, take time to prepare a rum or Grand Marnier soufflé, a Hot Liquid Valrhona Chocolate Cake filled with liquid chocolate ganache, or a Hot Blueberry and Raspberry Gratin. A scoop of ice cream accompanies each.

When the Flagstaff House was renovated in 1998, the Monettes added a magnificent mahogany bar, which along with a cozy fireplace and rare crystal from around the world makes for a clubby space for a pre-dinner cocktail. The tiered restaurant seats 110 in the main dining room and 65 on the glass-enclosed terrace below. Diners gaze eastward through floor-to-ceiling windows at the procession of seasons or at the changing sky as evening becomes night. It is not uncommon to see deer browsing below in the twilight, before the city lights come on. The Vintner's Room, also added in 1998, is a private dining room for just 20 guests. One wall is stone, with a window opening to the restaurant's acclaimed 18,000-bottle wine cellar. The rest are glass, offering views of other parts of the sprawling restaurant and the rocky-topped summit of Mt. Sanitas.

That wine cellar and all it holds is another reason that gourmands hold the Flagstaff House in such esteem. The tome-sized wine list, 160 pages thick, includes boutique wines from the world over and features great depth in vintages from several California regions and from Bordeaux, Burgundy, and Champagne in France. The restaurant boasts a significant collection of Domaine Romanée-Conti Grand Cru Burgundies, more than 30 vintages of Dom Pérignon, one of the world's few complete Château Mouton Rothschild Collection artist paintings of labels (from 1945), more than 20 vintages of Australia's Penfolds Bin 95 Grange Hermitage, more than 15 vintages of Silver Oak Cabernet Sauvignon, and more than 20 labels of Williams-Selyem Pinot Noir.

Some of Boulder's most elegant events have taken place at the Flagstaff House, including fundraising events for important local charities. The annual Women, Food, and Wine Extravaganza has raised hundreds of thousands of dollars for women's fight against cancer, much of it coming from a gala dinner at the Flagstaff House. In 2001, before the Extravaganza's format changed, the highlight of the three-event fundraiser featured a five-course dinner prepared by some of the country's top women chefs and served with selections from women winemakers. It wasn't the first super-elegant event at the Flagstaff House, nor will it be the last, but it certainly will be missed.

Flagstaff House, 1138 Flagstaff Drive, Boulder; (303) 442-4640 or www.flagstaffhouse.com.

Full Moon Grill

Along with the nearby European Café and Zolo's and farther-afield Laudisio's, the Full Moon Grill offers the best dining in a shopping mall in Boulder. This small

---

A Heap of Good Eating

Bradford Heap is a local boy made good in the kitchen. Raised in Boulder, he worked at area restaurants throughout high school, caught a severe case of kitchen fever, and went on to study at the Culinary Institute of America, where he graduated with honors. He cooked at L'Orangerie in Los Angeles, La Folie in San Francisco, and Brava Terrace and Chateau Souverain, both in Napa Valley, as well as in France and Italy with such celebrated chefs as Alain Ducasse, Georges Blanc, and Carlo Cioni. In fact, Heap honors Chef Ducasse at the Full Moon Grill with the Risotto Nero Alain, a sublime symphony of slow-cooked rice, scallops, tomato confit, garlic, and champagne sauce.

He has been chef at the Full Moon Grill since 1994, and a year later he became a partner in that restaurant. In addition to cooking at the James Beard House in New York in 1996, he has been nominated for America's Best Chefs—Southwest Region by the James Beard Foundation. In 1997, he and partner Richard Stein took over the operation of the historic Chautauqua Dining Hall (see page 107), and turned it from a seasonal restaurant of great charm, historic significance, but sometimes rocky operations to one of Colorado's top dining destinations. With Bradford Heap responsible for two restaurants, he also relies on Chef de Cuisine Tim Bouse, a well-credentialed chef, to make both kitchens run smoothly.

---

restaurant occupies a modest, west-facing space in The Village, which locals think of as "McGuckin's shopping center" after the landmark hardware store. The setting sun blasts through the windows, so the blinds are usually drawn, which enhances the intimacy of the small space. This also blocks the view of the parking lot, not a bad visual byproduct since the dining area is a few steps down from auto-bumper level. The Full Moon Grill serves excellent contemporary northern Italian cuisine presented at lunch and dinner.

A tumbler of pencil-thin breadsticks awaits on the table to nibble on while you're deciding what to eat. A luncheon menu might display the perfect combination of Crispy Polenta and Grilled Pear served with Gorgonzola *dolce latte* sauce and toasted pine nuts, or a Braised Open Face Buffalo Sandwich with red wine sauce and soft polenta. If classic Italian is more to your liking, order Linguine Bolognese, but if you're in the mood for something from halfway around the world, there's Pan Seared Hawaiian Ahi Tuna with Beluga lentils, forest mushrooms, and roasted delicata squash in a red wine reduction.

With brilliant white tablecloths and simple but stylish tableware and glassware, the Full Moon Grill really shines at dinner, especially on a winter night when it is all candle-lit and romantic. Bresaola and Baby Arugula make a beautiful dried meat-salad greens pair. Tuscan Potato Gnocchi with duck livers, sage, shallots, and Parmigiano-Reggiano appears on the menu as an *antipasto,* but in my book, it falls in the more-potent-than-pasta category.

The kitchen has a way with mushrooms, making a porcini sauce for a vegetarian lasagna, a Forest Mushroom Risotto with free-range chicken and truffle butter, a Free-Range Chicken Filled with Wild Mushrooms that comes with soft polenta, Madeira, and white truffle emulsion, and a Roasted Quail Filled with Duck Breast and Forest Mushrooms, with sweet bread pancake and Port wine sauce. Among the entrées, the meats (braised Colorado lamb shank, grilled pork tenderloin, and grilled Angus steak), poultry (chicken and duck breast), and seafood (ahi, mahi mahi, and wall-eye—which together sound somewhat like a law firm) receive virtually equal billing.

Sorbets, gelato, tarts, *panna cotta,* and invariably delicious chocolate somethings are included on the dessert list. From course to course, dishes are seasonally appropriate and beautifully executed.

Wines from Argentina, California, and France as well as Italy are sorted on the wine list by taste, weight, and color. For that very special occasion, it includes estate-bottled and limited production champagnes.

Full Moon Grill, The Village Shopping Center, 2525 Arapahoe Avenue, Boulder; (303) 938-8800 or www.fullmoongrill.com.

Jax Fish House

Jax is a busy, noisy restaurant dishing up some of Colorado's best seafood. The bar—cojoined to serve as both the raw bar and booze bar—fills a large rectangle in the front part of the narrow restaurant. Bartenders mix killer martinis, pour sparkling and still wines, pull draught beer, and make a variety of drink specials. They also dispense several varieties of oysters, some of which are on early-evening special for much of the year.

In the immediately adjacent dining area, the jammed-close tables in back are covered with white butcher paper. Seafood art, fish and fishing geegaws, and even a stuffed alligator hang from the exposed-brick walls and high ceiling. The ambience at the dinner-only restaurant is boisterous and fun, much like an East Coast fish shack or oyster bar. David Query's touch is evident throughout the menu, which takes Atlantic, Pacific, and Gulf fish and shellfish and imbues with it suitable flavors and cooking methods from various parts of the world.

To whit, appetizers run from the expected Peel and Eat Shrimp to Pad Thai with Oolong Tea–Crusted Shrimp, and from Damn Good Crab Cakes, griddled and served with red pepper *Louie,* to Curried Shrimp Eggrolls with pineapple-jalapeño dipping sauce and a Killer Calamari with mango-chili *mojo.*

Entrées include Sesame Seed–Crusted Salmon with plum wine *beurre blanc,* hoisin barbecue sauce, calico rice, and snap pea and shiitake slaw; Alaskan halibut dusted with fennel pollen and honey powder and served with green gazpacho sauce, lemon-basil falafel, hummus, and sun-dried tomato-fig tapenade; Mississippi Skillet Catfish that is blackened or fried and served with skillet cornbread and white rice smothered with crawfish etouffée; and some of the best *cioppino* this side of San Francisco, made in a red wine and tomato basil-broth. I don't suppose that pigs fly, but—upon eating the Tuna "Filet Mignon"—I began to think that these fish say "moo"!

The Query Touch

After launching Q's Restaurant in the Hotel Boulderado (see page 119), chef David Query set out to establish his own Boulder-based restaurant group, and thus far has launched three very different, very popular, and very good restaurants in Boulder, but none of them bears his name: Jax Fish House, nearby Rhumba, and Zolo Grill—respectively specializing in seafood, Caribbean cuisine, and Southwestern specialties.

Query has made two forays into Denver; a second Jax in LoDo, and a new restaurant at the writing in the space previously occupied by Aubergine and Micole, called LoLa, serving *nuevo* Mexican/Southwestern cuisine. Except for such special occasions as wine-maker dinners at one of his restaurants, you won't find Chef Query in a kitchen night after night anymore, but his *corps de chefs* are very good about executing his ideas. In all of his restaurants, sprightly menus display a fine combination of melding and contrasting tastes and eye-catching presentations.

Just as steakhouses serve token fish entrées, Jax serves token beef—three dishes out of about 50 on the menu. One is a huge hamburger, and two are steaks. Like the seafood, it's the best, coming as it does from Niman Ranch, renowned for naturally raised animals. Desserts are simple. Wines tend to take a backseat to specialty drinks and microbrews at this fish house with attitude.

**Jax Fish House, 928 Pearl Street, Boulder; (303) 444-1811
or www.jaxfishhouseboulder.citysearch.com. There is a second
Jax Fish in downtown Denver (see page 39).**

John's Restaurant

When John and Nancy Bizzarro landed in Boulder in 1969, it was a small college town surrounded by farmlands. To John Bizzaro's eyes, this was reminiscent of Italy. Within five years, he was serving a multicourse, single-seating feast in an old house on West Pearl in a space he called Nancy's Restaurant. (That location later became Karen's, then the Café Louis, and is, at the writing, a new Indo-Nepalese restaurant called Sherpa, which shows what Himalayan people are reminded of by the Boulder area.)

Meanwhile, the Bizzaros turned another modest cottage, this time farther east on Pearl Street, into John's Restaurant, after all these years still one of Colorado's finest and most romantic places to dine. The Bizzaros have been running John's in that location since 1975. The ambience has remained modest and low-key. Dinner only is served in three small dining rooms with low ceilings, lace curtains, low lights, and an embracing atmosphere. Music plays in the background, unobtrusively yet nicely. John's is at once festive and familiar, a lovely combination.

Like so many early Colorado restaurateurs—and by "early" I mean the late 1940s through the early 1980s—Bizzarro tapped into a pent-up demand for what was considered exotic European food. Along with other ambitious and innovative proprietors, he catered to that demand and, in the process, elevated local restaurant meals from the meat-and-potatoes era into the age of fine dining. No one has done it better than John Bizzaro, who inherited his love of good from-scratch food from his Sicilian grandmother and has passed it on to his daughter, Stella, who is now the restaurant's pastry chef.

John's food has blossomed into a sophisticated blend, with French, Italian, Spanish, and subtle influences from other cultures, yet prepared on a firm foundation of classic cuisine. First-rate fresh ingredients are harmoniously matched for flavor, texture, and color, prepared with attention to detail, and meticulously and caringly served in that lovely, soothing place.

The menu, which changes according to the market and the chef's latest burst of creativity, won't overwhelm you in size (and neither will the wine list, for that matter). The dinner menu always includes two salads, a couple of soups, perhaps a mushroom dish or two (the exquisite King Oyster Mushrooms in *beurre noir* remains etched in my memory), and some of the best pasta dishes around. Tapping into his Italian roots, Bizzarro consistently includes outstanding ravioli; if the lobster-filled variety is on the menu, be sure to order it. Flat pasta, such as linguini or fettuccini, are made fresh on an antique, hand-cranked pasta machine and generally the basis for the restaurant's nightly vegetarian entrée. You may also find handmade gnocchi on the menu.

Entrées always include filet mignon, generally another beef dish, pork, lamb, poultry, and seafood. The sauces, seasonings, presentation, and side dishes change, but the basics remain. Atlantic Coast Bouillabaisse—a classic French seafood stew but with nontraditional touches (shrimp, scallops, salmon, blue mussels, and sea bass poached in tomato-leek-seafood stock with a hint of curry and a splash of cream)—reflects John's gentle eclecticism. The desserts exemplify the John's dining experience—elegant, simple, understated, and perfect. The choices tend to be on the order of a luminous crème brulée, a seasonally appropriate fruit tart, and some outrageously decadent chocolate creation.

John's Restaurant, 2328 Pearl Street, Boulder; (303) 444-5232 or www.johnsrestaurantboulder.com.

Mateo

Mateo takes its inspiration from Provence, the region of southern France kissed by Mediterranean breezes. The appearance of a corner of Provence on East Pearl in early 2002 was good news for Francophilic foodies, who have piled in for lunch and dinner since opening day. A lofty ceiling and exposed brick walls are remnants of Le Rocher, the previous occupant of the space, which was also French but fancier and pricier.

Just as in a bistro, you can stop into Mateo for a snack or a meal. The preparations are traditional country French, the welcome genuine, and the prices moderate. Owner Mateo Jansen's mostly French menu has some Italian touches and reflects good renditions of standbys rather than fancy flights of innovation. Go there for such dishes as Classic French Onion Soup Gratinée, Steamed Mussels Marinère, Classic

Croque Monsieur, Mateo Bouillabaisse served in an individual enameled pot, Steak Frites, Provençal Tomato and Onion Tart, and Wild King Salmon accompanied by the very Provençal Ratatouille, Pistou, and Pine Nuts. The *pommes frites* surpass American-styles fries by a country kilometer. Italian specialties include Penne Bolognese, Lobster Raviolo, and Porcini Mushroom Risotto.

Wine prices match food prices, which is to say that they are reasonable. As in France, where a very respectable and very affordable *vin ordinaire* is always available, Mateo offers carafes of red, rosé, and white, as well as wines by the bottle and the glass.

Desserts include a truly lemony lemon tart baked in a fine crust and topped with freshly whipped cream; Petit Pot au Chocolat, a sensuously dark and rich custard, served hot with an individual little pitcher of cream; and soothing sorbets to end the meal with the same simple style with which it began.

Mateo, 1837 Pearl Street, Boulder; (303) 443-7766.

The Mediterranean Restaurant

Back in the early 1990s, the Mediterranean Restaurant, which everyone calls "the Med," started the local trend toward foods and wines of this region. Located on the ground floor of an office building in space vacated by a Mexican chain restaurant, the Med features tile floors, stucco and tile walls, and beamed ceilings, along with accents of bright pottery, gleaming copperware, garlic and chili-pepper ristras, and green plants.

The lively bar area's high, zinc-topped tables can accommodate an overflow dinner crowd. Generously sized wooden tables and sturdy rattan chairs give patrons in the back dining rooms ample room to sit back and spread out—a good thing when the table is loaded with focaccia, a dipping dish for olive oil, and lots of little tapas plates, before the main course is brought out.

Chef Anthony Hessels has assembled an eclectic menu with palate-pleasers from Italy, Greece, France, Spain, and North Africa. Pizzas are made in an imported wood-burning oven, which produces crusts so delicious that the choice of toppings seems almost superfluous. Remember, I said "almost," because the toppings are varied and excellent as well. The Med does a fine job with seafood, particularly shellfish, and the pasta selections are also commendable. Spaghettini di Mare combines the two in a heaping bowl of pasta topped with mussels, shrimp, clams, and octopus bathed in an aromatic sauce.

Good mixed drinks and large selections of wine and beer are available. On warm days and evenings, the best bet is the large, landscaped patio—the closest approximation of a southern European courtyard in downtown Boulder.

The Mediterranean Restaurant, 1002 Walnut Street, Boulder; (303) 444-5335 or www.themedboulder.com.

PanAsia Fusion

PanAsia Fusion's menu is almost as big as the restaurant. The tiny, tasteful space was designed with Zen-like tranquility and is maintained in bandbox perfection.

Small tables, muted walls, subdued lighting, and minimalist décor create a setting that is, at once, energizing and relaxing. It's a little techie, but not too much so.

A trio of expatriates arrived in Boulder with a half-formed idea of opening a Bay Area–style noodle shop and Pan-Asia Noodle was born in 1997.

Initially, it served five types of noodles, including *udon* (thick Japanese eggless wheat noodles), *soba* (thin Japanese buckwheat and wheat noodles), *la mian* (a Mandarin special-occasion delicacy, hand-pulled from a five-pound ball of dough), *mian* (standard Chinese noodles), and rice noodles (eaten in China, Vietnam, and Thailand). Create-your-own rice bowls were on the menu too, plus occasional non-noodle specials that incorporated seafood and meat.

Now meat, seafood, and poultry join the noodle, rice, and vegetable-based dishes that have been featured since the beginning. The change was effected by Executive Chef Ian Nagelson, a Johnson & Wales University graduate who studied in France and cooked at a number of resort restaurants and at Brennan's in New Orleans, before lighting in Boulder. At PanAsia, he began blending dominant Pacific Rim flavors with European and American ingredients to create some of Colorado's most distinctive cuisine.

With Nagelson in the kitchen, PanAsia Fusion, as it was renamed, has blossomed into a better-rounded restaurant for a variety of tastes. For example, Chili-Encrusted Calamari with Beluga lentils and chili-cilantro aïoli share the appetizer billing with Cha Soba, green-tea noodles, a medley of Asian noodles and steamed vegetables served with dipping sauce, shredded daikon, wasabi, and scallion. Vegan Miso Soup, Sesame Asian Chicken Salad, Mango Seafood Salad, and Thai Grilled Beef and Arugula Salad satisfy various tastes and dietary restrictions.

The original noodle concept survives in such entrées as Seafood Noodle Soup, Beef Chow Fun, Szechuan Peppercorn Noodle Bowl and Pad Thai Bowl, a delicious rendition of the national dish of Thailand. Trout, beef tenderloin, baby-back ribs, rack of lamb, pork loin, and root vegetables are the main ingredients in the other entrées. Fusion recipes draw from the cuisines of France (*beurre blanc* with the trout, albeit flavored with wasabi and lime), Korea, India, Japan, the Philippines, the Middle East, and China's Szechuan province—often more than one in a single dish. There's even a hint of Mexico, with interesting salsa accompanying several of the dishes.

The kitchen's repertoire includes wok-searing, wok-frying, grilling, braising, and pan-frying. My favorite example of how PanAsia Fusion merits its last name? Yellow Fin Tuna and Lemongrass Risotto—grilled yellowfin tuna served over lemongrass risotto, with kaffir lime and coconut cream sauce, grilled tomato, basil oil, and steamed vegetables. A virtual United Nations in a single serving.

In addition to domestic and imported wines available by the glass and by the bottle, Asian and European beers, and an extensive selection of premium sakes and premium vodka, PanAsia offers myriad loose-leaf teas served in iron pots. In fact, the tea list is almost as long as the wine list.

The dessert list is small but as perfectly balanced as the restaurant's décor. Coconut Pots de Crème is a Burmese steamed coconut pudding, served with toasted coconut and fresh mango. Almost as exotic is the house-made Fresh Ginger Ice Cream, which also goes into the PanAsia Banana Split, along with coconut-encrusted fried bananas with green tea, red bean, and ginger ice cream and chocolate sauce. The Chocolate Gâteau is a moist flourless chocolate cake drizzled with raspberry coulis sauce.

Fresh flavors, lovely presentations, and moderate prices for interesting and healthy food make for a matchless combination. PanAsia Fusion is a beautiful place. It's a Boulder place. It's a place were aesthetic values flow seamlessly from surroundings to table and back.

PanAsia Fusion, 1175 Walnut Street Boulder; (303) 447-0101 or www.panasiafusion.com.

Q's Restaurant

David Query, who now operates Jax, Rhumba, and Zolo (see those entries), made the Hotel Boulderado into a culinary mecca when he opened Q's fine-dining restaurant on the hotel's mezzanine in 1990, quickly attracting Colorado gourmets and oenophiles who flocked there for excellent multi-course dinners in the light-and-lovely contemporary style. A year and a half later, Query left to start his own restaurants, and Culinary Institute of America grad John Platt bought Q's and stepped into the founder's shoes.

Q's moved downstairs in 1997 into larger and more visible space vacated by the rough-and-ready Teddy Roosevelt Grill as the hotel's breakfast, lunch, and dinner restaurant. The style is contemporary elegant—both in terms of décor and food, yet old-fashioned hexagonal tile floors, beefy columns, gorgeous leaded-glass fan-lights over the windows, and a high ceiling are reminders that the structure dates to 1909. Buff-colored walls, modern paintings, and subdued lighting bring an updated look to the dining room. Similarly, the cuisine is an artful melding of tradition and trendiness.

Platt and his kitchen crew carefully weave currently popular culinary threads into all Q's dishes. His inclination toward California cuisine was honed when he worked at the Ritz-Carlton Laguna Niguel, and he has refined it and added some other influences as well. Therefore, you'll find a touch of Asian, a *soupçon* of Provençal, a hint of North African, a bit of Southwestern, and a dollop of Italian in Q's dishes—fused in the most attractive, delicious, and agreeable ways.

The kitchen works with fresh, local, and, when possible, organic ingredients, and the menu changes seasonally. It includes the Organic Mixed Greens and Roast Rack of Colorado Lamb that most fine-dining restaurants in Colorado seem to feature, but it adds the Q's stamp of creativity as well. Examples? An appetizer of Grilled Quail and Prosciutto-Wrapped Melon with arugula or Hot Oil Ahi Sashimi dressed with sesame, lemon soy, and wasabi tobiko mixes East and West in just such a way.

The signature appetizer is Mano BBQ'd Shrimp Salad with lo mein, Napa slaw, and miso vinaigrette. More fusion, with roots in California cuisine. Salt Crust Lobster "Pot Pie," a seasonal starter, with *mirepoix,* white mushrooms, grainy mustard, and thyme, combines not-uncommon ingredients, flavorings, and preparations in a most uncommon way. The principle also runs through the entrée list, which might include Chick Pea Fritters and Couscous or a Strudel of Spinach, Mushroom, and Feta for

Boulder's large vegetarian population and Allspice-Cured Rotisseried Pork Loin, Soy BBQ Salmon Mignon, and Roast Grain-Fed Veal Shell Steak for those who love meats and seafood.

Q's presents the beguiling option of tasting menus—five courses at dinner and three courses at lunch. The dinner version includes two appetizer courses, a fish course, an entrée, and a dessert, with an optional expansion to include an *intermezzo* and a cheese course. Wines can be ordered by the glass or bottle—or paired with the tasting menu. The three-course lunch tasting menu includes a small appetizer, an entrée, and dessert, served with as much or as little speed as midday diners prefer. Q's manages to produce not only an exquisite tasting menu but at what is probably the least expensive of that caliber in Colorado—$50 at dinner and just $15 at lunch at this writing.

Pastry chef Mark Reese's excellent dessert menu includes distinctive twists on popular dishes. Perhaps you'll find Vanilla Bean and Honey Crème Brulée, Butterscotch Crème Brulée, or Bittersweet Chocolate Espresso Cheese Cake, a melding of tastes and textures to appeal both to cheesecake aficionados and chocoholics. There are always house-made ice creams and sorbets, seasonal tarts, and an Artisan Cheese Plate with fruit, spiced walnuts, and crackers.

Q's Restaurant, Hotel Boulderado, 2115 13th Street, Boulder; (303) 442-4880 or www.qsrestaurant.com.

Rhumba

Occupying space that once belonged to the sedate (and now long-defunct) Boulder Bagel Company is Rhumba, an island of Caribbean food and fun in the dry, mountainous "sea" of Colorado. David Query has partnered with Chef Joe Schneider in this popular restaurant. It's a scene—but a scene with terrific food in a unique nouveau-Caribbean style.

Almost-industrial design elements counterpoint with hanging plants and tropical accents and the bright tile mural by artist Cisco Manco combine to create an island-happy place. Its side patio is one of the best in town, and in warm months, overhead doors between the big bar and patio are raised to blend inside and outside seating in ways that you'd normally find only in the tropics.

Rhumba does one heck of a happy hour, with super drinks and great munchies. Chips and salsa at Rhumba means plantain chips and three salsas, one generally fruit-based. Other appetizers include *Rhum* Flamed Black Mussels with bananas and curry; conch fritters; Eddie's Black Bean Hummus, made of chickpea *roti*, toasted cumin *crema,* and grilled pineapple-mango *atjar;* and Sweet and Spicy Pork Dumplings with coconut basil dipping sauce. Like every other David Query restaurant, Rhumba's menu blurs cultural and regional lines when it turns out its innovative food.

You can get jerk chicken or mahi-mahi on a sandwich, but the entrées will really blow you away. It's hard to choose between such offerings as Leroy's Fried Catfish (a slab of blue corn–crusted fish served with coconut rice, black beans, mango slaw, and scotch bonnet tartar); Sesame Glazed Atlantic Salmon accompanied by warm spinach salad, spicy marinated tomatoes, shiitake mushrooms, roasted baby red potatoes, and mango-banana salsa; or Garam Masala–Crusted Halibut with yucca mashed potatoes, wilted spinach, candied ginger *beurre blanc,* and apricot *blatjang.* Other knockouts are the *Adobo*-Marinated Flank Steak with chipotle roasted potatoes, *chimichurri* asparagus, and charred tomato sauce; and Coriander Crêpes filled with roasted corn, shiitake mushroom, and poblano goat cheese, and served with griddled yam cakes, tamarind pineapple-jicama slaw, and charred tomato sauce. Desserts can be as sinful as the signature Chocolate Coconut Macadamia Nut Tart or as saintly as a fruit sorbet.

Rhumba, 950 Pearl Street, Boulder; (303) 442-7771 or www.rhumbarestaurant.com.

The Sushi Triangle

The popularity of Japanese cuisine and the profusion of Japanese restaurants have skyrocketed from exotic to mainstream, but Boulder has the greatest concentration in the tightest area. If you were to draw a line from Sushi Tora on 10th Street to Hapa Sushi and Japango across from each other on the Pearl Street Mall between 11th Street and Broadway and Sushi Zanmai a block north on Spruce Street, you'd have an oddly elongated triangle defining Boulder's three-and-a-half-block "sushi zone."

These four restaurants are different in looks and longevity but united in their outstanding selections of sushi and other Japanese specialties from miso soup to green tea ice cream—and the passion of their fans. All have sushi bars where you can watch the chefs prepare this traditional Japanese fare. Some Boulderites are loyal to one, while others go to whichever restaurant can seat them.

Hapa Sushi

Situated on the north side of the Pearl Street Mall, with a sunny sidewalk dining area fronting the narrow and deep restaurant, is Hapa. This hip and stylish recent addition to Boulder's Sushi Triangle is located in what can be considered sacred food ground, occupying the former New York Deli space. Whether or not pastrami and matzo ball soup hold any appeal, you will remember the storefront from *Mork and Mindy* if you're of a certain age or watch reruns of vintage TV shows.

The present restaurant doesn't purport to be pure Japanese but admits to inspiration from Hawaii. In fact, *hapa* is the island word for a melding of Hawaiian and American or something else. Hapa does a good job of combining a lot of Japanese with a little bit of this and that from elsewhere. The sushi menu is divided into "beginner," "intermediate," and "advanced" levels to sync with diners' level of adventurousness when it comes to spiciness, out-of-the-mainstream ingredients, or both.

Everyone has heard of the California roll, perhaps the first American-Japanese fusion sushi, but Hapa also offers a Philadelphia Roll, a Tootsie Roll, a Statue

Continued on page 122

of Liberty Roll—and more rakishly, a 69 Roll, a Foreplay Roll, and even an Orgasm Roll. Hapa still operates a small sushi and sake stand called Hapa on the Hill in the Fox Theater and a third location in Cherry Creek North in Denver (see page 38).

Hapa on Pearl, 1117 Pearl Street, Boulder; (303) 473-4730
Hapa on the Hill, 1135 13th Street, Boulder; (303) 447-9883.
The website for all is www.hapasushi.com.

Japango

Japango is niched into a historic building on the Pearl Street Mall, so the restaurant usually places a signboard announcing some of its 20 or so daily specials on the sidewalk out front. A deeply setback doorway and a long corridor lead straight to the sushi bar section of the spacious, stylish restaurant. A wooden awning is suspended over the elegant granite sushi bar. To the right of the oddly angled room are the tables, some on a platform, to give the semi-private sense of high-tech tatami rooms—with no sitting on the floor required. Soaring ceilings, light wood, richly colored walls, and enough brushed steel to qualify as a suitably trendy setting for trendy food result in a Feng Shui–compatible arrangement. In warm months, a south-facing deck in the back accommodates more diners.

Japango is owned by Miki Hashimoto, whose Japon (see page 38) is one of Denver's premier Japanese eateries. Both *sushiya* serve outstanding traditional and newer creations. This "nouvelle sushi" approach combines more ingredients in *nori* rolls or cones, plus dishes inspired by Japanese or other Asian culinary traditions. Among Japango's signature appetizers you'll find sautéed *hijiki*, a Japanese seaweed; *agedashi*, battered tofu in a wonderful tempura sauce; and grilled salmon *kasuzake*-style. You can order a combination of traditional sushi and sashimi or select the New Style Sashimi, drizzled with olive oil and soy syrup.

Entrées include beef filet (the nattily titled True Tender Filet), seasoned and served with rice and wok-tossed seasonal vegetables. The restaurant offers a galaxy of specials, from the traditional happy hour bargain sushi and drinks to an all-you-can-eat-except-sushi dinner for those with huge appetites. And at 9:00 P.M. on selected evenings, all guests are treated to complimentary sake.

Japango, 1136 Pearl Street, Boulder; (303) 449-0330 or
www.aaamenus.com/japangomenu.html (menu only; not restaurant website).

Sunflower

Many Colorado restaurants have evolved into using natural foods and organic ones wherever possible, but this bright restaurant east of the Pearl Street Mall was established on the principle of a first-rate dining experience using only such products. Vegetarians, vegans, and simply health-conscious and environmentally sensitive diners are presented with a choice of numerous gourmet dishes, not merely the token meatless offering that appears on virtually all restaurant menus today.

Sushi Tora

Set on a quiet side street a block and bit from the Pearl Street Mall, Sushi Tora has long attracted purists who want the finest, freshest sushi without frills. Duck under the curtain at the entrance and find yourself in Japan. A sushi chef utters a welcoming cry when you arrive. The space is intimate, décor is Zen-simplicity itself, and each portion of sushi is a work of art as well.

Sushi Tora has been slicing, dicing, packing, and rolling sushi since 1987, so it has its act together—and more. Magic Mushrooms enfolded in a salmon wrap and drizzled with a wonderful sauce is a signature appetizer. The super-fresh, immaculate sashimi continues to win raves. There's a daily chef's special (some regulars claim they've never seen the same special twice), but for the best sampling of Sushi Tora's top offerings, try a Bento Box, which includes several sushi favorites. The restaurant also serves a selection of cooked Japanese standards such as tempura and teriyaki in its small dining room.

Sushi Tora, 2014 10th Street, Boulder; (303) 444-2280.

Sushi Zanmai

Each customer who enters Sushi Zanmai, on Spruce Street "behind" the Hotel Boulderado, gets a raucous greeting and each one who leaves is sent off with an ebullient farewell. In between, there's the hustle and bustle of others being greeted or sent off, and karaoke on Saturday evenings as well. The most popular tables are in the front room, where the entrance, miniscule foyer, and sushi bar are located. The quieter back room, actually a side room, features a hibachi table for Benihana-style show-cooking. It is being redone at press time and could change.

Sushi Zanmai was one of the first to create fusion-style rolls, discovered by the college crowd and now popular with many sushi fans. So widespread are such creations as spider rolls and other relatively new offshoots of traditional sushi that many people don't even know that they were invented recently and not evolved over centuries. The restaurant is open for lunch and dinner, and especially in the evening, there's usually a line out the door.

**Sushi Zanmai, 1221 Spruce Street, Boulder; (303) 440-0733
or www.sushi-zanmai.com.**

To many people, "organic," "natural," and "healthy" are not necessary adjectives that can justly be used to modify "fine dining," but Sunflower pulls it off. John Pell established the restaurant in 1999 and called the restaurant's philosophy "natural fine dining." It was not his first venture into the genre. Pell opened the Five Seasons Restaurant in Boston in 1991 before moving to Colorado, where he, in turn, owned an organic orchard in Paonia, started Wildflower Catering in Basalt, opened a restaurant called Sunflower in Carbondale, and launched a natural-foods café in the Aspen Club.

When he relocated to Boulder, he took over the big corner space that had previously housed both Pasta Jay's and Rio Grande and turned it from party central into a bright, cheerful, and, yes, healthy-looking place. The name Sunflower, which suited it so well, was reborn.

The weekday all-you-can-eat lunch buffet features a changing selection of fresh organic greens and other produce, tasty house-made soups, and fine baked goods. It might just be the best salad bar in Boulder. Sunflower serves natural beef, buffalo, elk, seafood, and free-range poultry along with the grains, rice, pasta, vegetables, tofu, and tempeh that you would expect here.

Southeast Asia is Sunflower's strongest ethnic influence in its artfully plated, perfectly sauced dishes. Other knock-out flavors include a spicy tomato red, white, and roasted garlic sauce on the Calamari Romesco; steamed Manila clams in chili-ginger-coconut broth with fresh cilantro; sautéed Tempeh Scallopini with onions, mushrooms, garlic, white wine, lemon, and fresh herbs; and Grilled Duck Breast with mixed root vegetables.

Desserts include Triple Chocolate Mousse Cake, Fresh Fruit Crisp, Three Nut and Apple Tart, berry crisps, cheesecake, and fresh fruit sorbets in the flavor du jour. What other chefs might view as limitations, Pell sees as opportunity. Even the profiteroles come with butternut or soy ice cream, but the plate-licking-good chocolate sauce makes you forget that this isn't the full-on butterfat variety.

Sunflower serves lunch, dinner, and Sunday brunch. Coffees and teas are made with twice-filtered water, and even the wines come from organic vineyards. Critics and customers alike have described Sunflower as being an "only in Boulder" kind of place, and perhaps it is—but it is leading edge in many ways. It has given a name and pledged its whole-hearted commitment to "natural fine dining," which many chefs have now—to a degree—adopted.

Sunflower, 1701 Pearl Street, Boulder; (303) 440-0220.

Triana

Triana, just west of the Pearl Street Mall, was named after a fabled barrio in Seville where flamenco came to be. Bullfight posters adorn the walls, but everything else is modern. Set in soaring space once occupied by a used bookstore/art gallery, the restaurant manages to look intimate and spacious, contemporary and cozy, hip and elegant—all at the same time. High-backed semicircular booths line the room with tables in the center. One wall of rough-hewn stone projects a sense of antiquity, remarkable for a restaurant so young. In warm weather, the doors are thrown open to make the entire restaurant feel like a shaded sidewalk café. On winter nights, with candles flickering against the warm walls, there's no more romantic a place to dine.

The restaurant was launched by James Mazzio, named by *Food & Wine* magazine as one of the 1999 Top Ten Best New Chefs in America when he cooked at 15 Degrees, a downtown Boulder restaurant with a Roman candle–style life cycle. 15 Degrees opened, soared, and closed abruptly. The chef moved from one end of the

Pearl Street Mall to the other, bringing along all his creativity and classy cuisine, but with a Spanish accent. Mazzio put Triana on the map, and most recently Hosea Rosenberg, who had worked with Kevin Taylor, has kept it there.

Triana makes much of its tapas. Don't miss the cornucopia of sizzling shoestring potatoes, crisp-fried, sprinkled with salt and sugar, and heaped into a paper cone suspended from a wire frame. Alongside is a ramekin of romesco, a garlicky, roasted-peppery, almondy oily sauce from Catalonia. Ketchup with run-of-the-mill fries will never taste right again. Calamari, bacalao, and mussels appeal to seafood lovers, while many meat-eaters like Triana's pork kabobs. Salads feature organic greens, soups are outstanding (especially the gazpacho with shrimp and avocado), and entrées run the gamut from vegetarian to game, with a selection of meat, poultry, and seafood offerings comprising most of the menu.

Guests do not come to Triana for the food alone. Live entertainment—jazz, flamenco, fusion—is featured. The wine list is extensive and, of course, there's Port (provided by Spain's neighbor, Portugal). To my way of thinking, though, Spanish food yearns to be coupled with sangria. Triana's is a Zinfandel version augmented with Curaçao, apricot brandy, fruit juices, and fresh mint. Ole.

Triana, 1039 Pearl Street, Boulder; (303) 449-1022 or www.trianarestaurant.com.

Trios Grille, Wine Bar, & Home Gallerie

This exceptional restaurant has survived and thrived with obstacles overcome and perhaps a marketing consultant ignored. Trios is in downtown Boulder but not on the Pearl Street Mall. The undistinguished commercial building in which it is located presents no inviting storefront, meaning there is little spontaneous walk-in business. But Trios has triumphed. Pass through what resembles an office-building lobby and climb half a flight of stairs to a spacious bar/lounge, dimly and atmospherically lit to combine cocktail lounge class and wine-bar ambience. Trios boasts more than 300 wines served by the bottle and an impressive 50 by the glass. Live music—usually mellow jazz or rhythm-and-blues—is played every evening. A nightly happy hour and wine tastings periodically add to the Trios mix.

Beyond is an attractive dining room, whose subdued lighting, paintings on the walls, Flatirons views, hanging plants, and tables set with crisp white napery, candles, a fresh flower, and elegant stemware set a stylish tone. By day Trios feels like the kind of place local powerbrokers should be lunching, but at night, it has a special-occasion look—and a special-occasion wine list and food to match.

Trios' serves consistently good dishes drawn from a variety of cuisines, exquisitely presented and correctly served. You might find tamales from Latin America, pasta and pizza from Italy, and seafood prepared in the manner of one Asian country or another. Executive Chef John Trejo and his crew do it all with a seasonally-changing menu. The Home Gallerie is Trios's third component (restaurant, wine bar, and home-furnishings store—three, get it?), selling stylish furniture, home accessories, linens, glassware, pottery, and more to help make your home as good-looking as the restaurant.

Trios Grille, Wine Bar, & Home Gallerie, 1155 Canyon Boulevard, Boulder; (303) 442-8400 or www.triosgrille.com.

Zolo Grill

Zolo is hip and attractive, with exposed brick walls, gleaming wood floors, booths done up in diner vinyl, and free-standing tables with solid wood chairs. Artwork appropriate to the contemporary Southwestern food decorates the restaurant, including a large mural stretching across one wall. Although the large patio faces a parking lot and busy Arapahoe Avenue, it is partly screened by a brick wall and plants that make it attractive and pleasant despite a shopping-center location.

Margarita maniacs order the house Zolo-rita, a potent and flavorful version of this popular tequila drink, sensational with house-made tortilla chips, served with salsa or Zolo's dynamite guacamole. The appetizers, soups, entrées, and desserts shine at lunch, dinner, and Sunday brunch. Menu items that cannot be prepared in a vegetarian version are marked with a cactus symbol.

Zolo's dishes tend to be adaptations of Santa Fe versions of traditional Mexican and border food—except when they aren't. More than a few are prepared with decidedly Asian influences—with excellent results. For instance, the appetizer of steamed Prince Edward Island Mussels and Clams available with a choice of *tum yum* sauce of lemongrass, lime, and *galanga* root or saffron chili broth is about as fusion-y as a dish can get—then, too, there are the Blue Corn Dusted Turner Calamari, breaded and served with a garlic-lime *pequin* chili sauce, as well as the Maryland Crab and Shrimp Cakes with black beans, corn, creamy lime-cilantro vinaigrette, and chili aïoli.

More obviously Southwestern dishes come in decidedly contemporary versions and with the special David Query touch, interpreted and executed by Chef Rob Rosser. These include Lamb Picadillo Quesadilla with green apples, roasted Anaheim chilies, and jack cheese served with a tomatillo-lime and chipotle *crema;* tortilla soup with roasted peppers, jicama, radishes, tomatoes, and avocado in a smoked tomato broth with optional shrimp or chicken with *negro pasilla* chili-tequila BBQ sauce, corn tortillas, greens, rice, pinto beans, and choice of red or green chili; Pulled Pork Tamales filled with spicy braised pork and served with *salsa cruda,* rice, pinto beans, and choice of red or green chili; and the signature Barbecued Red Duck Chili Tacos. Zolo's Red Plate Specials are available at lunch Monday through Wednesday and at dinner Monday through Thursday. Getting through the filling drinks, appetizers, and entrées is daunting, but for those who have room for dessert, Zolo's banana cream pie is a winner.

Zolo Grill, The Village Shopping Center, 2525 Arapahoe Avenue, Boulder; (303) 449-0444 or www.zologrill.com.

Events

Oatmeal Festival

January—In 1997, merchants in Lafayette's Old Town were looking for a way to bring traffic back after a U.S. 287 bypass was completed. The resulting Oatmeal

Festival initially featured an oatmeal/oatmeal pancake breakfast, a parade, an eating competition, and a baking contest. Since then, oatmeal's health benefits have gained widespread attention, and the festival has become more health- and wellness-oriented.

It remains a day of small-town fun, but has attracted a big corporate sponsor, Quaker Oats. The company gave oatmeal-eating Lafayette residents their 15 minutes of fame in 1998, when 30 locals, who had taken the company's Smart Heart Challenge and eaten oatmeal at least once a day, appeared in a television commercial. The TV spot embedded the festival in the national consciousness.

The festival now attracts 3,000 or so people on a Saturday in late January. Events still include a breakfast, but the oatmeal bar now features some 150 toppings (said to be the world's largest toppings bar), including fresh and dried fruits, nuts, candies, sauces, and other grains. A 5K run/walk called the Quicker Quaker has replaced the parade. In 1998, the Oatmeal Festival gained a health fair component, with medical screenings and safety classes for children, plus other activities, oatmeal-related and not.

The Community Choice baking contest has been expanded to seven categories, and 78 contestants entered in 2002. The event isn't "culinary" in the conventional sense, but if you often indulge in the pâtés, opulent meats and shellfish, and luscious desserts prepared by chefs at food festivals and in restaurants in this book, you might want to add some oatmeal to you diet—if for no other reason than to counteract those indulgences. And if you're eating oatmeal anyway, why not celebrate it? The Lafayette Oatmeal Festival takes place in Old Town Lafayette, with the health fair and cooking competition at the Bob Burger Recreation Center.

Information is available at (303) 926-4352 or www.discoverlafayette.com.

Chocolate Lovers' Fling

February—Since 1981, the Chocolate Lovers' Fling, held early in February in the University of Colorado's Glenn Miller Ballroom, has provided funding for the Boulder County Safehouse and an opportunity for chocoholics to indulge in their favorite food. Until you've sniffed the chocolate-perfumed air, you cannot believe how good that ballroom smells at flingtime.

Up to 1,200 of the Boulder area's chocolate-obsessed attend the event, whose highlight is an all-you-can-eat chocolate foods tasting (and real chocolate lovers can eat a lot). Goodies are donated by local restaurateurs, caterers, chocolate shops, and markets. They have included truffles and bonbons, cookies and candy bars, chocolate-berry bread and chocolate mouse, tarts and cakes, brownies and clusters, fudge and ice cream, strawberries dipped in chocolate and molten chocolate poured over who-knows-what. It's not all confections, however. Sponsors donate beer, wine, milk, ale, ice cream, and such to sample along with the chocolates.

Other components in past years have included a chocolate dessert competition, one of the area's biggest silent auctions and a big-ticket-item live auction (an Audi A6 was auctioned off in 2002), and entertainment. The competition is appropriately called the Chocolate Challenge. Categories include professional chef and amateur chef, plus amateur and professional categories for sheer chocolate artistry, and people's choice. In 2003, the format changed to a sitdown dinner, which now means more variety to the edibles, less straight chocolate, and a higher ticket price.

Tickets are sold at several area businesses (expect to buy them at the Brewing Market in The Village, Ideal Market, Whole Foods, Rocky Mountain Chocolate Factory, all in Boulder, and Heritage Bank in Lafayette) and at the door. Information is available from (303) 449-8623 or www.ChocolateLoversFling.com. Do not call the Boulder County Safehouse hotline for Fling information.

Boulder Dandelion Festival

April—For a taste of old Boulder—"old" meaning idealistic, live-off-the-land hippie days—check out the annual Boulder Dandelion Festival. Women in granny dresses, men with ponytails, passionate herbalists, and first-wave New Agers earnestly promote the consumption of what many people consider to be a backyard nuisance. The festival is held on a Saturday in mid- to late April, before dandelion greens become bitter.

The festival began in 1998 in the backyard of organizer Dorje Root. Ten people showed up. Four years later the festival moved to Hedgerow Farm, an organic farm east of Boulder, which can accommodate a crowd, and more than 200 of Root's kindred souls appeared.

At this outdoor event, you can sample entries into the dandelion cook-off. Expect the likes of fritters made with dandelion flowers, sautéed dandelion greens, dandelion muffins, and dandelion pesto. You can also sample dandelion wine. In addition to the dandelion doings, you can attend lectures and workshops with herbalists and other speakers, buy handmade crafts, and send the children to have their faces painted.

Boulder Dandelion Festival, 2224 Nicholl Street West, Boulder; (303) 440-8164. Hedgerow Farm is at 8328 Valmont Road, east of Boulder. For cook-off entry information, call (303) 786-9755.

Taste of the Nation

April–May—Since 1989, Taste of the Nation has been one of Boulder's top food events. This annual showcase for the city's top chefs, coupled with wine and beer tasting, all for a good cause is part of the nationwide antihunger movement called Share Our Strength. The Boulder fundraiser benefits Community Food Share, the People's Clinic, and hunger-relief efforts in rural Colorado and even abroad.

In addition to the admission fee, 100 percent of which goes to the antihunger crusade, you can further express your generosity with a successful bid on an array of products and services in a silent auction—a fixture at charity fundraisers. Some are food-related; many are not.

The traditional timing for Taste of the Nation is early on a Sunday evening in late April or early May. The Glenn Miller Ballroom at the University in Colorado is set up with some 40 food-tasting stations, 20 wine stations, and 7 microbrew stations, many bedecked with elaborate floral arrangements and culinary decorations. The main attraction is the food, much of it prepared on the spot. Some restaurants and individual chefs have been participating since the beginning, while others are new. Establishments that wish to participate are wait-listed.

The three-hour event offers grazing on a grand scale. Dozens of chefs and their assistants offer such delicacies as tidbits of roasted quail, oysters on the half-shell, steak samplers, shrimp, samosas, crab cakes, sushi, seviche, pasta of various shapes and sauces, salads, cheese platters, artisan breads, and desserts, desserts, desserts. You can eat a little or a lot, and every time you turn around, someone is whisking away used plates and empty wine glasses. It may be stand-up eating, but because so many fine restaurants are involved, there's an overlay of service not found at many buffet-style events. Once the mad crush is over, chefs can be seen roaming around and sampling the offerings at one another's stations.

Tickets are usually available at Alfalfa's Market, Community Food Share, Cooking School of the Rockies, Liquor Mart, Whole Foods, and Wild Oats. For details, contact Community Food Share, 6363 Horizon Lane, Longmont; (303) 652-3663 or www.communityfoodshare.com.

Boulder Creek Festival

May—Memorial Day is *big* in Boulder, drawing tens of thousands of locals and out-of-towners to help kick off summer. This weekend-long celebration features everything from the classic 10K road race called the Bolder Boulder, which attracts upwards of 40,000 runners and walkers, to the Rubber Duckie Race, a community fundraiser down Boulder Creek. The Boulder Creek Festival is the umbrella under which many activities flourish.

Both sides of the creek between Ninth and 14th Streets are jam-packed with arts and crafts booths, dance and musical performances, informational booths for civic and non-for-profit organizations, rides, and, of course, food. No one pretends that this is a major culinary event, but you won't starve. The food ranges from mundane carnival eats to pretty darned good samples from local restaurants and bakeries. The outdoor food court, featuring a dazzling variety of traditional American and ethnic specialities, is usually set up near the library but is subject to change.

Boulder Creek Festival, 1002 Walnut Street, Boulder; (303) 449-3825.

95th Street Festival of Colorado Wine

June—Colorado wines, Colorado food, Colorado cooks, and several Lafayette, Colorado, restaurants are showcased in this late June festival, launched in 2002 at the Atlas Valley shopping center. The first one included children's activities, a 5K run around Waneka Lake, entertainment, and booths set up in the parking lot offering everything from spinal-alignment analysis to wine tastings. Other components are of interest to food and wine fans—and give the festival its focus.

The event does have the potential of becoming a major Front Range wine festival. Format and details could change as it gets refined, but in its first year, it kicked off with a Colorado winemakers' dinner at the Platinum Grill on Friday evening.

Saturday is the big wine day, with tasting tents set up in the parking lot.

Seventeen wineries participated in 2002. There is no charge just to wander around, but a modest admission charge covers a commemorative glass, tasting samples, and the opportunity to purchase those ever-improving Colorado wines by the bottle.

Meridian Wine & Spirits (see page 143), also at Atlas Valley, hosts a wine-tasting seminar, which included the principles of tasting for those who are just getting into wines. And throughout the afternoon, members of the Colorado Chefs Association give cooking demonstrations at What's Cooking (see page 140), another enterprise in the same shopping center. It is gratifying to see from the lines at the tasting booths that the notion of an East County wine event has merit. At the first event, far more people were queued up to taste and talk wine than to do or buy anything else.

What's Cooking also organizes a recipe contest for dishes that has to include a Colorado wine—and might do so again. Categories were appetizers, soup/salad, main entrée, and dessert. To enter, submit your recipe in advance (by mail to What's Cooking, 2770 Arapahoe Road #112, Lafayette, CO 80026; by fax (303) 666-6615 or by e-mail luhill@whatscooking.com). On contest day, you must bring the dish to feed six in "an attractive container," so leave the Tupperware at home. A panel of judges from the Colorado Chefs Association selects category winners on the basis of taste, appearance, and creativity, and there is also a Community Choice Award.

95th Street Festival of Colorado Wine, c/o Lafayette Community Events, 309 South Public Road, Lafayette, CO 80026; (303) 926-4352 or www.lafayettewinefestival.com. Wine-maker dinner reservations are taken directly by the restaurant.

A Moveable Feast

June–August—One of Boulder's most exclusive culinary events is the opportunity to dine splendidly in lovely private homes to benefit Blue Sky Bridge, a service organization that aids abused children and adults. A Moveable Feast started with two dates and now has expanded to three, with events once a month in June, July, and August. The maximum capacity for each evening is about 125 guests.

The food is lavish, the wines are excellent, and the ambience says "private dinner party" rather than "fundraising event." The entire group meets in one home for cocktails and appetizers, breaks up into more intimate groups of 10 to 30 for dinner in several other homes, and then meets again at still another home for dessert. The format and the menu change from year to year and from home to home. Some hosts are gourmet cooks who like to prepare the food themselves and are very good at it, while others serve courses prepared by a local caterer or top restaurant chef.

Information is available from Blue Sky Bridge, 2617 Iris Hollow Place, Boulder; (303) 444-1388.

Rocky Mountain Tea Festival

June–August—The Boulder Dushanbe Teahouse—a precious gift from Dushanbe, Boulder's sister city in Tajikistan—is one of the state's most gorgeous and exotic places to eat. This magnificent building of polychrome tile and carved wood is the site of the annual Rocky Mountain Tea Festival, held over a weekend in summer. Initially, the festival was held in early August, but by 2003 it moved to the last weekend in June—so check before you write it on your calendar.

You can admire displays of artistic, creative, historical, and whimsical teapots and related artworks, bring a child to the Mad Hatter Teddy Bear Tea Party, educate your palate at tastings, and enjoy a four-course dinner prepared by Chef Lenny Martinelli using tea as a cooking ingredient in all dishes. Topics for tea classes include cultural, spiritual, historical, occult (i.e., tea leaf reading), and gustatory aspects of tea. Playing on the exotic association with the Orient when tea appeared in the Western world, the sales area—where you can get books on tea, teapots, teas, and accessories—is called the Tea Bazaar and provides teas for tasting as well. A class in tea basics is offered for those uninitiated into the magic and mysteries of this universal beverage. While the Tea Bazaar and the teapot exhibit are free, there is a charge for other events.

If the festival doesn't fit into your schedule but tea classes interest you, ask Sara Martinelli, the restaurant's tea blender, what might be coming up. She sometimes organizes classes at the teahouse in conjunction with Naropa University. The class description for The Spirit of Tea, says that it "weaves together the contemplative and ceremonial aspects of tea drinking from around the world with the most up-to-date information on tea's health-giving and stress-reducing benefits." Pardon the pun, but if that's your cup of tea, contact the Naropa registration office, (303) 245-4800 or (800) 603-3117.

Rocky Mountain Tea Festival, Boulder-Dushanbe Teahouse, 1770 13th Street, Boulder; (303) 442-4993 or www.boulderteahouse.com.

Great Boulder Pie Festival Contest

August—When John Lehndorff was food editor of the Boulder *Daily Camera*, he instigated the addition of the Great Boulder Pie Festival Contest to the annual Victorian Fair held in August at the Boulder Historic Society's Harbeck House on University Hill. Lehndorff has moved on to become restaurant critic at the *Rocky Mountain News*, but the festival, which was established in 1995, endures as a fixture of Boulder's summer scene.

Entrants must register in advance for categories that include apple, fruit and berry, and nut and other, but cream, meringue, pumpkin, and custard pies are prohibited by health regulations. Professionals and amateurs may enter, and there are additional categories for children age 10 and under and for teens from 11 to 16 years. Each entrant bakes two identical pies, one for viewing and one for tasting. Prizes are the admiration of the community—and perhaps winners' names in the newspaper too.

Boulder Historical Society, 1206 Euclid Avenue, Boulder; (303) 449-3464.

Mall Wine Crawl

September—The Seed Wine Shop on the Pearl Street Mall organized the first Mall Wine Crawl in mid-September 2002. For more information, see page 143.

March of Dimes Star Chefs

September–October—A major fundraising effort for the March of Dimes is the annual Star Chefs gala, a series of four sparkling culinary events held in four Colorado locations (Boulder, Denver, Colorado Springs, and Grand Junction) on four dates in the fall. If you love good food, you might try to make it to all four—or at least a couple of them. Typically, each of the 15 to 20 participating chefs in each location prepares a single signature dish. Guests stroll around to sample what appeals to them while musicians play live music and bid on silent-auction items.

The Boulder event, which started in 1995, kicks off the series and takes place in September. It has most recently been held at the Omni Interlocken Hotel in Broomfield. Top local chefs who are stars on the Boulder culinary scene cook at Star Chefs events.

March of Dimes Chapter Headquarters and Denver Division, 1325 South Colorado Boulevard, Suite 508, Denver; (303) 692-0011 or www.marchofdimesco.org.

Harvest Fest

October—Community Food Share, the food bank serving greater Boulder and Broomfield, inaugurated its annual Harvest Fest fundraiser in October 2001. Held in a lavishly decorated section of FlatIrons Crossing, it included VIP shopping at Nordstrom's, a martini bar by Bloom's Restaurant, live entertainment, and both silent and live auctions. The main appeal for foodies is that top area restaurants prepare, present, and serve some of their specialties at an elegant sit-down dinner.

Community Food Share, 6363 Horizon Lane, Longmont; (303) 652-3663 or www.communityfoodshare.com.

Taste of Longmont

October—Since 1999, an evening in mid-October has been devoted to showcasing Longmont restaurants and microbrews at the Boulder Country Fairgrounds Exhibition Building. Approximately 1,700 people come to sample foods from the 20 to 24 local restaurants and caterers represented at the three-hour event.

In 2002, these included the Chef Extraordinaire BBQ Restaurant, the Meade Café, Colorado Rosecake Company, BK's Burrito Kitchens, Spelts Berry Natural Bakery and Restaurant, Whetstone Steakhouse, Bay Window Catering, Left Hand Tap House, Pumphouse Brewery, Johnny Carino's Country Italian Restaurant, Hunter's Restaurant & Pub, Chili's, Knot Hole Gifts 'n' Ice Cream, and Golden Corral. The mix of independent and chain restaurants drawing from various cultural influences and generally in the budget-to-moderate price range reflects Longmont's food scene. But because all participating restaurants must be Chamber of Commerce members, some of Longmont's better restaurants and food purveyors cannot participate.

With that caveat, tickets to this lively local event are sold in advance, with admission at the door a little more expensive. It includes all the food you'd care to sample, wine, local beer from the Left Hand and Tabernash brewing companies, and soft drinks. There's also live entertainment.

The Taste of Longmont is organized by the Longmont Chamber of Commerce, which also sells the tickets. The Chamber is at 528 Main Street, Longmont; (303) 776-5295.

Retail

Cen Tex Supply Company

This no-frills showroom is full of highly functional kitchen, serving, and table items designed for restaurants and caterers, yet it welcomes home cooks as well. Cen Tex sells utilitarian items at attractive prices, even if you are just buying a rolling pin or a rubber spatula.

Cutting tools are an important part of the *batterie de cuisine* whether the cuisine is a commercial or regular home kitchen. Cen Tex carries Forschner knives but also the less-known Dexter & Russell line of professional cutlery, dishwasher-safe and distinguished by textured and shaped polypropylene handles, and Serra Sharp by Mundial, which features a unique double-action edge that is scalloped on one side and microserrated on the other.

Cen Tex's professional versions of some common home-kitchen items include commercial bagel cutters, enormous potato mashers, and wire whisks fully two feet long that must be useful for the super-sized, industrial-strength stockpots, woks, and chef's pans from Wear-Ever and Pro-Advantage. These are great to own if you have the space to store them and often cook for a crowd. Need a lid for one of your own large pots or pans? Cen Tex offers them in various sizes. Pro-Advantage's skillets, saucepans, and omelette pans, with some models available in both nonstick and regular finishes, are more appropriately sized for most home kitchens. Stainless-steel mixing bowls and see-through plastic storage containers marked with measuring lines come in various sizes.

Cen Tex carries a terrific assortment of kitchen scales, pastry-making aids, and commercial-grade bakeware. Appliances range from huge commercial refrigerators and freezers to high-powered blenders and countertop convection ovens.

The showroom displays gadgets galore. One long slot wall is loaded with tongs, whisks, scoops, ladles, slotted and regular spoons, strainers, scrapers, meat mallets, and all manner of other tempting and useful kitchen items. One such is the Spoodle, a long-handled combination of flat-bottom scoop and measuring cup, both in slotted and solid versions. Dip into an ingredient container, and you immediately have the right quantity—provided, of course, that you remember your liquid ounce or milliliter conversions to tablespoons and cups.

For party service, you can buy chafing dishes, platters, and insulated coffee pots in a gleaming silver finish rather than coffee-shop brown and black plastic. If you do a lot of casual outdoor entertaining, prefer to use disposables, and can justify buying in quantity, explore Cen Tex's big selection of well-priced paper, plastic, and foam plates and cups.

Cen Tex Supply Company, 1750 55th Street, Boulder; (800) 660-4351,
(303) 442-8477, or www.centexsupply.com.

Cheese Importers Warehouse and La Fromagerie

Every day is Cheese Day in the 7,000-square-foot Cheese Importers Warehouse. Between 3:00 and 4:00 A.M., except on holidays, semis full of cheese begin rolling out to deliver to wholesale accounts within a 300-mile radius. Before long, deliveries of cheese from the cheesemaking corners of the globe begin coming in. Willow River Cheese Importers is the corporate name for this family-owned business, which was established in the mid-1970s.

The doors are thrown open to La Fromagerie, the warehouse's retail operation, at the more reasonable hour of 9:00 A.M. Bring a sweater or jacket, step into the cooler, and stroll "the street of cheese." You can find wheels of cheese, wedges of cheese, and containers of grated cheese. There are big cuts and little cuts, mild and sharp cheeses, aged and mellow varieties. There are 500 cheeses in all, from Wisconsin cheddar to the noble Parmigiano-Reggiano of Italy to some fairly exotic varieties.

Brie. Camembert. Chèvre. Triple crèmes. Gouda. Gruyère. They're all there—these wonderful cheeses from Italy, Switzerland, Austria, France, Spain, England, the United States, and Denmark. More than 40 domestic varieties of the Willow River Natural Cheeses, the house brand, including low sodium, reduced fat, raw milk, and rennetless.

La Fromagerie offers more than cheeses and cheese-related products. Since fine cheese and good bread go together like peanut butter and jelly, you'll want to check out the fresh baguettes and thick-crusted loaves of sourdough from the nearby Grizzly Creek Sourdough Bakery, which no longer sells directly retail. The deli makes hearty soups, focaccia sandwiches, and casseroles. Other temptations come from the espresso bar and olive bar and kitchenware section. French candies, Swiss chocolates, and fresh coffee round out the product mix.

Cheese Importers Warehouse and La Fromagerie, 33 South Pratt Parkway,
Longmont; (303) 443-4444, (303) 772-9599, or www.cheeseimporters.com.

Corner Gourmet

Boulder got its own little corner of gourmet-food heaven in late 2002, when the Corner Gourmet opened a couple of blocks east of the Pearl Street Mall in the space where Daily Bread started. That outstanding bakery was wrapped into Whole Foods Market (see page 424), but the legacy of fine food remains within those walls. The store is gorgeous, with rough-hewn stone columns, angled wood beams, Mediterranean-hued walls, discreet lighting, art-glass sconces, and artwork. If it weren't for the shelves and glass cases of food, you might think that you were in a gentrified European farmhouse instead of in a retail establishment.

Chef-prepared foods include veggie and Mexican lasagna, hand-rubbed and roasted beef tenderloin, flank steak with oyster sauce, Japanese cucumber salad, and all manner of other salads and soups—all take-home specialties of restaurant-quality.

Cheeses, which can be bought by the chunk, made up into sandwiches, or arranged on a cheese tray, come from top artisan cheese-makers from around the corner and around the world. The selection changes by availability, but you can expect to find cheeses made from cows' milk, sheeps' milk, and goats' milk, from mild to sharp, and from creamy and soft to hard and gratable.

Canned, packaged, and bottled products are high quality and highly unusual. They include such hard-to-find items as ultra-thin Moravian cookies, Rosebud preserves, Elizabethan Key lime curd, Misserie di Santeramo balsamic vinegar, Aunt Sue's salad dressings, Smith & Wollensky steak sauce, Religious Experience salsa, and Tartuf Langhe polenta and risotto. Dried pastas from Rustichella d'Abruzzi and Delverde come in various shapes and glorious colors. The Corner Gourmet carries Il Fornaio breads, Joseph Schmidt confections, and Bazzini nuts and dried fruits— straight from New York's Hunts Point Market, as the sign explains. But the Corner Gourmet is in Boulder, so it also sells Cliff and Luna energy bars.

You can perch on a designer stool at the counter on the Pearl Street side and watch the world go by, or on warm days take your meal or snack out to a small patio between the sidewalk and the parking lot. There, you'll have to be satisfied with regular plastic outdoor furniture.

Corner Gourmet, 1738 Pearl Street, Boulder; (303) 413-9000.

Ethnic Food Stores

Boulderites on the hunt for some exotic ingredient can, of course, drive to Denver to explore the myriad markets large and small, but they don't always need to. Several local grocers—a few of them concentrated in Tebo Plaza on 28th Street, just south of Valmont—offer Indian, Middle Eastern, Southeast Asian, and Far Eastern specialties. Here are some of the Boulder area's ethnic food stores:

Asian Deli & Seafood Market, 2899 28th Street, Boulder; (303) 449-7950
India's Grocery, 2877 28th Street, Boulder; (720) 565-0475, and
    780 West Baseline Road, Lafayette; (303) 666-9112
International Food Bazaar, 2855 28th Street, Boulder; (303) 415-1725
Mediterranean Universal Market, 2607 Pearl Street, Boulder; (303) 448-9552
Oriental Food Market, 1750 30th Street, Boulder; (303) 442-7830
Oriental Market, 12710 Lowell Boulevard, Broomfield; (303) 469-8038

Herb's Meats & Specialty Foods

In a city known for its vegetarians, vegans, and eco-idealists who eschew red meat for environmental or animal-rights reasons, an excellent meat market has been alive and thriving since 1976. Herb Dillard started the butcher store and sold it to Bob and Teresa Grass when he answered the siren call of retirement, but the look and the tradition of personal service of a classic neighborhood butcher shop remain.

The simple store is located in the BaseMar Shopping Center. Meats predominate in the white-enamel cases along two of the three interior walls and in the big freezer in the middle. Behind the cases, butchers hand-cut and hand-wrap beautiful fresh meats, which include all-natural beef, pork, lamb, and chicken. Herb's also makes up three kinds of freezer packs—Gourmet, Summer Grill, and Working Person's Pack.

Time-pressed cooks pick up tasty marinated meats and chicken. Appealing preparations include Teriyaki Pork Tenderloin, Teriyaki London Broil, Thai London Broil, Hot Cajun Pork Tenderloin, Island Pepper Tri-Tip, and Rosemary/Burgundy Lamb Round. In summer, the butchers skewer several flavors of pre-seasoned and marinated chicken and beef kabobs that need only grilling. Should you prefer to season your own, you can pick up marinades and dry flavorings by California Harvest, Gran Cucina, Lindeberg Snider, Lysanders, Stube, Take Me Home, and Herb's own house brand. An entire shelf is devoted to bottled barbecue sauces.

The store also carries many frozen items, but nothing that's supermarket-style, major-brand-name commercial. House-made stews, jambalaya, corn chowder, chicken Creole, pea soup, and more are frozen in rectangular packages, the better to stack into a modest freezer or even to pack into a cooler for a camping trip. A separate small freezer is dedicated to natural elk meat. You'll also find several varieties of Culinary Arts' *glace de viande,* high-quality frozen meat stock concentrates used by chefs to enhance the color and flavor of sauces, soups, and stews.

Italian-food lovers can find frozen meatballs, marinara and Alfredo sauces, and beautiful filled pastas, including stuffed shells, mushroom ravioli, cheese ravioli, and cheese tortellini. Herb's also carries excellent imported dry pasta. And for those in the mood for Mexican food, there are terrific frozen burritos, tamales, vegetarian green chili, chicken green chili, and just plain roasted and peeled green chilis. Chicken Cordon Bleu and Chicken Santa Fe are elegant little packets of cooked chicken breast with the appropriate sauces and seasons, and the frozen meatloaf mixture of seasoned beef or turkey addresses the occasional need for comfort food. In a way, though, just coming into Herb's Meats, with its nostalgic appearance, excellent service, and first-quality food is a comfort in itself.

Herb's Meats & Specialty Foods, 2530 Baseline Road, Boulder; (303) 499-8166.

In The Kitchen

Sandy Johnson, an enthusiastic and knowledgeable home cook, in August 2001 made her avocation into her business. After 16 years of toiling for the Colorado Department of Labor and Employment, she opened her dream kitchenware store in downtown Longmont. In less than two years, she moved into a brand new building.

The store stocks a number of top-name, high-quality brands of cookware, bake-ware, and accessories. Some are well known (such as Viking, Le Creuset, and Henkels), while others are exotic brands that display a favorable price-quality ratio, even without great name recognition. In the gadget and gizmo area, look for Cuisine International, GeoRena, GripEZ, Joyce Chen, NorPro, Progressive, SCI, Zyllis, and the tongue-twisting Spekspado Sevico. Two other less-known stand-out brands are Carlo Gianini, maker of elegant, all-stainless accessories, and LamsonSharp, which makes attractive wood-handled spatulas, tongs, and such. Both lines are decorative as well as practical.

In The Kitchen caters to the from-scratch cook with an inventory mix that includes a high proportion of specialized utensils and small appliances. Therefore, you'll find pizza sets, hand-cranked pasta machines, fish poachers, fondue sets, asparagus steamers, woks, avocado slicers, butter bells, apple wedgers, stacking multi-cookers that are conceptual heirs to Chinese bamboo steamers, tortilla makers, *ableskiver* pans from the Pennsylvania Dutch tradition, and canning supplies. Bakers like the choice of rolling pins and pans, plus pie-crust shields, pie weights, canapé cutters, cookie cutters, and other specialized accessories.

You'll also find *bouquet garni* bags for making your own herb mix, recipe cards (remember, before computers, when hand-written recipes were lovingly passed among friends and family?), garlic bakers, and mixing bowls of all sizes made of stoneware, stainless steel, and glass. Additionally, you'll find attractive wire mesh cabinet baskets, practical airtight stackable food storage containers by ClickClack, table and kitchen linens, woodenware of various kinds, copperware, and an entire shelf of vessels in which to make and serve coffee and tea.

Among gourmet food lines are Robert Rothschild Farms sauces and condiments, Peaberry coffee, Radiatori natural pasta imported from Italy, All Natural sauces to go on it, Pasta Planners meal-in-a-package kits, Sassafrass spreads, Plentiful Pantry soup mixes, Gigi Ann's assorted pickled garlics, Melina whole peppercorns, Quick Mixx crème brulée, pure vanilla extract from Madagascar, and Stonewall Kitchen's big line of mustards, dressings, and other condiments. Also on display are dispensers of several harmonious seasonings in one multipack from Dean Jacobs and Spice Library. Olive oils and vinegars from several makers are available too. And, oh yes, In The Kitchen carries Scharffen Berger chocolates, thought by many experts to be America's finest.

In The Kitchen, 1225 Ken Pratt Boulevard, Longmont; (720) 652-9386.

Peppercorn

Ever since I moved to Boulder and first wandered into this downtown store, I have wanted my life to be like Peppercorn—a life comfortably lived in a casually elegant, very stylish, and obviously creative environment that automatically carries the promise of good food, good wine, and great company. Walk in the door of this fabulous emporium and you might have the same aspiration. Come with enough cash, and Peppercorn can help you achieve it. Come on a more modest budget, and you can get the perfect treat for your own kitchen or table or as a gift.

Spread across a pair of adjacent storefronts on the Pearl Street Mall, Peppercorn is loaded to the rafters with an unsurpassed array of cookware, housewares, gadgets, kitchen appliances, cookbooks, gourmet foodstuffs, decorative accessories for the home, linens, glassware, fine china, cutlery, and flatware. Miraculously, the 12,000-square-foot store looks artfully designed and logically organized and not at all chaotic and cluttered. I'm not sure how the staff pulls this off, given the store's enormous inventory, but I'm glad they do.

Peppercorn opened in 1977, the year Pearl Street became a pedestrian mall, when foresightful future ex-hippies Doris Houghland and Rak Kraegel—only 27 years old at the time—started a modest cooking school and small gourmet kitchen store. The cooking school is no more, but the store has grown into one of the country's preeminent retailers of its type. This couple still runs the enticing store, which is now a treasured landmark on the mall, and any informal eyeball survey along the street reveals many shoppers toting Peppercorn's distinctive blue and white bags.

A trip to Peppercorn is a pure and simple pleasure for the food fanatic and cooking connoisseur. The eye-catching displays change frequently, but the organization of the merchandise is logical, so if you are going for, say, a mushroom brush, an extra disk for your Cuisinart food processor, or a rolling pin, and you've been in the store before, you'll know exactly where to go. I'm not claiming that you won't get distracted en route, but you won't be confused.

Peppercorn's great abundance of merchandise makes it difficult to get a descriptive handle on it. When I've written about other, more modest or more restrained cookware/houseware/tableware stores, I've often included a laundry list of lines they carry, to be useful to readers with a favorite brand of cookware, accessories, or food products. Peppercorn simply has so much that a list would take up an entire chapter. Someone (and I know not who) once called Peppercorn "the Smithsonian of cookstores." It's not far from the truth—except that, unlike at the museum, you can buy all the beautiful and interesting items on display on Pearl Street.

Walk into the original store, and on your right are the coffees and coffeemakers, straight ahead is a two-sided shelf of gourmet goodies, and on your left are brilliant displays of tableware, place settings, serving pieces, and/or decorative objects. Peppercorn is great at seasonal displays, so you'll find wonderful Christmas, Valentine's Day, Easter, and patriotic and other themes keyed to the calendar. I won't list all the brands Peppercorn carries, but I can't resist highlighting one that gives Peppercorn much of its signature style and verve. Your eyes will surely be drawn to the immensely stylish and colorful ceramics by Deruta of Italy's Raffaellesco. Vibrant majolica plates, bowls, cups, candlesticks, teapots, serving platters, and more have been handpainted in the tiny hilltop village of Deruta, above the Tiber in the province of Umbria, since 1358.

The back half of the store is the business end, with an eye-popping selection of cookware, bakeware, kitchen appliances, and gadgetry—some so exotic that it is designed to ease tasks that you might not even have thought of performing. Peppercorn has such turnover in Henckels knives (it carries both the four-star and the premium five-star groups) that this prestigious German line is always available at a discount. Ceiling-high bookshelves hold cookbooks devoted to a particular cuisine, ingredient, cooking technique, or geographic area.

Walk through the archway to the adjacent two-story section for fine china, crystal, silverware, linens for bed and bath, and fine lines of soaps and toiletries. Everywhere you look, you'll spot many items for the gracious home and for stylish entertaining. If you are getting married, you might want to register at Peppercorn and hope that your friends and family are very generous.

Even after all these years, Houghland keeps her finger in the Peppercorn's day-today buying and that seductive in-store merchandising. She is often called an "artist," but she dismisses her skill as merely good instinct. Whatever you call it, the bottom line is that Peppercorn reflects her style, her passion for both beauty and functionality, and her belief that coming into the store should be like coming into someone's home. No wonder I always feel like moving in.

Peppercorn participates in the Pearl Street Mall's sidewalk sales and offers great bargains. Even better deals are at the occasional warehouse sales. That's where I purchased my treasured and much-admired Portmeirion soup tureen. It's an extravagance that I never would have allowed myself at full price, but I bought well at the warehouse, and the Peppercorn people will be glad to know that I have given it a good home.

Peppercorn, 1235 Pearl Street, Boulder; (303) 449-5847, (800) 447-6905, or www.peppercorn.com.

Tundra Specialties

Tundra Specialties started out in 1991 supplying restaurants with plumbing equipment—pot fillers, pre-rinsers for dishes, floor drains, water filters, and other such unglamorous restaurant necessities. The company quickly expanded into the fun stuff—cookware, smallwares, serving pieces, and accessories, including many items suitable for the serious home cook. In 2001, it moved to the Gunbarrel area to a relatively large warehouse with a relatively modest showroom.

The showroom display changes every two weeks, so you might find just what you've been looking for, perhaps on clearance. But with 4,000 items in inventory, the chances are you'll have to ask for what you want. Someone on staff will either get it for you or accompany you into the warehouse. There, floor-to-very-high-ceiling shelves display virtually all restaurant needs and lots of home-cook wants, at attractive prices.

In addition to a deep overall inventory, Tundra Specialties takes advantage of manufacturers' specials and closeouts to offer across-the-board good values. Come in for, say, a sauté pan or saucepan of a specific size or a chef's knife of a certain length, and the warehouse is sure to have it—perhaps not in the brand you had in mind or even one that you've every heard of, but it will be there. Most home cooks do go there for heavy-duty cookware, bakeware, and smallwares (the restaurant trade term for what home cooks call gadgets and accessories). It's a whole tempting world of tongs, ladles, spoons, scrapers, salt and pepper shakers, and more.

Tundra Specialties puts out a catalog of restaurant-supply items—260 pages at last count—with unglamorous line drawings, specifications, and part numbers for everything from add-on griddle tops, aprons, and ashtrays to wire shelving, whisks, and youth chairs. The manufacturers whose products they carry range from Adcraft to Wyott. Tundra Specialties just as nice to a home cook who comes in for an ice cream scoop, a measuring cup, or a chinois strainer as for a restaurateur opening new business.

Tundra Specialties, 6390 Gunpark Drive, Unit A, Boulder; (303) 440-4142, (800) 447-4941, or www.tundraspecialties.com.

What's Cooking

In 1995, Luanne Hill opened a modest cookware store in Louisville. Local cooks flocked to What's Cooking for utensils, gadgets, gourmet foods, and, often, advice, and it wasn't long before the store outgrew its space. Just five years later, Hill and What's Cooking followed the big population migration that is turning East County from farmland to suburbia and moved to big bright space in a new shopping center in Lafayette.

Among the well-known brands of appliances, cookware, bakeware, and accessories are All-Clad, Cuisinart, Emerilware, GripEZ, Marcato, NorPro, Waring, and Zyliss. What's Cooking shows a lot of baking equipment and canning tools, perhaps as a last reminder of East County's fast-disappearing agricultural roots. Among the useful accessories are a pair of turkey lifters that make it easier to wrestle with that Thanksgiving bird, three-tier pie cooling racks, garlic bakers, butter warmers, French coffee presses, soufflé dishes in assorted sizes, and graters and peelers galore.

Copper, glass, wooden, and pewter pieces abound too—some to cook or serve in, some just for show. What's Cooking carries several less renowned but excellent makers. Revol is a line of attractive ovenproof serving dishes from France, while Danna Design comes from China but looks as if it could be Portuguese or Italian. Glassware, tableware, linens, and candles enable you to set a very pretty table. A back wall displays wine and cocktail glasses and bar accessories. In fact, you'll find all sorts of items for entertaining, from fondue pots to Willow Cheese Ball Mix, which comes in an assortment of flavors.

Gourmet food products come from some of the most interesting producers, including Karen's jams, pie fillings, and cookie mixes; Scandinavian Delights fruit preserves; Robert Rothschild Farms sauces; Stonewall Kitchen mustards; Santa Fe Seasonings jelly and honey products; and Pasta Partners handmade dried pasta in various shapes. Imported cookies, breadsticks, oils, and vinegars are obligatory these days, and What's Cooking carries them in abundance. Right under the olive oil shelves is an assortment of tiny dishes for dipping bread in this nectar of the olive tree.

Along with additional space to display her store's many wonderful wares, Hill designed the store with a full kitchen in the back of the retail sales floor. What's Cooking now provides food samples and has been able to offer classes in a far better environment than in the former space, where "makeshift" was the kindest description of the cooking facilities (see page 103).

What's Cooking, Atlas Valley Shopping Center, 2770 Arapahoe Road, Lafayette; (303) 666-0300 or www.whatscookinginc.com.

Your Butcher, Frank

Your Butcher, Frank is the classic small-town, full-service butcher shop. Behind the 30-foot meat counter, the butchers are traditionally attired with white shirts, ties, and aprons. They truly wait on their customers as in the old days. This Longmont meat market was established in 1980 by Frank Occhiutto, from whom the current owners, Lee Westcott and Ron Lamb (who began working at the market as youngsters in 1989) bought the business in 1998. They offer knowledgeable and excellent service, and sell hand-cut meats, with the beguiling just-off-Main-Street location a bonus.

All meats—beef, lamb, and pork—are USDA choice, hand-cut in the store, and then further custom-cut for individuals on request. The beef is aged at least two weeks. The lamb is local. The Farmland brand of pork comes mostly from Nebraska and the Dakotas, with some from Texas. The full deli features cold meats from Thurmann's, a top-line company.

Fresh sausages from their house recipes include breakfast sausage, sweet Italian, hot Italian, dynamite Italian (which is what they call their extra-hots), German and Polish bratwurst, and country-style sausages. Your Butcher, Frank has been Longmont's butcher for a long time, and if you start shopping there, it will most likely become yours too.

Your Butcher, Frank, 900 Coffman Street, Longmont; (303) 772-3281.

Wines

Boulder Wine Merchant

Under the gracefully curving retro roofline of the Community Plaza Shopping Center, an early Boulder strip mall restored to a trendiness, is one of the most complete wine shops for miles around. There is no artful lighting, no shelves custom-built of rare woods, in short no retail frills, but a wine inventory that is both broad and deep, and unsurpassed expertise within those simple walls. Two master sommeliers, Wayne Belding and Sally Mohr, display a passion and commitment not only to the wines themselves, but also to the selling of wines.

From the store's beginning in 1979, wine has been seen as an end unto itself, not as an afterthought to the beer-and-booze business. The concept of the knowledgeable wine professional is not unique today, but it was unusual when the store was established. Belding notes that in other countries, the wine trade is ranked as a profession, not unlike medicine or law—all of which require deep knowledge and on-going training to keep up in the field. Belding and Mohr philosophy is to "sell only good, carefully selected wines at fair prices, based on intensive and ongoing study."

The Boulder Wine Merchant stocks wines from the world over, organizing them geographically—South Africa, South of France, Italy, Spain/Portugal, and so on. Domestic wines are further subdivided into white, Cabernet, and Chardonnay, and there are also sections of the store devoted to Port/Sherry, dessert wines, and sparkling wines. Signs suspended from the ceiling identify each section.

I always peer into the intriguing glass case under the Old & Rare sign— intellectual curiosity, not any predisposition to buy a bottle with a three-figure price

Tale of Two Sommeliers

Wayne Belding, co-owner of the Boulder Wine Merchant, hails from New York's mid-Hudson Valley, which has since his youth become a serious Eastern wine-producing area. A lapsed geologist who found wine cellars more interesting than oil fields, he won the Denver Regional Competition and placed seventh in the finals in New York at the second Annual French Wine and Spirits Sommelier Competition in America.

Having made it through this grueling competition and, in fact, finding the examination experience stimulating, he began to pursue his master sommelier diploma when the Court of Master Sommeliers came to the United States in 1987. After passing the basic certificate course and advanced sommelier course, he became only the thirteenth American to earn the title Master Sommelier. He did so in Monterey, California, in 1990 and also earned the Krug Cup, bestowed on the person who passes all three parts of the master sommelier test at the same examination and attains the highest score of those tested.

As of this writing, only 51 Americans have passed the examination, and of those, only three others are based in Colorado—one being Belding's partner, Sally Mohr. Since 1996, Belding has been education chairman for the American Chapter of the Court of Master Sommeliers, and he has taught wine-service classes aimed at the hospitality industry and wine-appreciation classes for the wine-loving public since the mid-1980s, instructing well over 1,000 students in that time. He has also served as a judge at the National Restaurant Association Wine Classic in Chicago, the Colorado State Fair, and the California Wine Celebration in Denver, and been a featured speaker at the Epcot Food and Wine Festival, Telluride Wine Festival, the Taste of Vail, and the Rocky Mountain Wine and Food Festival. He is one of just five people on the permanent board of directors of the Court of Master Sommeliers and has been an owner of the Boulder Wine Merchant since 1985.

Sally Mohr began her wine career as a Boulder Wine Merchant employee in 1983 and became a co-owner in 1986. She earned her master sommelier diploma in 1995, just the second woman in the United States to achieve that distinction. She specializes in staff training and wine-list development for area restaurants. With her assistance, Restaurant Kevin Taylor received the *Wine Spectator* Best Award of Excellence in 1999. She has been involved in tastings, seminars, and wine festivals and has been a featured speaker at the Telluride Wine Festival, Epcot Food and Wine Festival, and Denver's Wines for Life. She has also judged in regional and international wine competitions.

To understand the high hurdles that must be conquered for master sommelier certification, contact the Court of Sommeliers, American Chapter, 1200 Jefferson Street, Napa, CA 94559; (707) 255-7667 or www.mastersommeliers.org.

WINES

tag. Last time, I saw a 1959 Pink Muscat from a winery identified as the Messandra Collection from the Crimean Republic. Most people, even most oenophiles, have no idea that Crimea ever made wines—especially in the height of the Communist regime in the Soviet Union. But such is the Boulder Wine Merchant's standing in the wine world that they have a bottle—until a collector purchases it.

On the other end of the spectrum are the wines displayed in the front of the store that were featured in that month's free newsletter. The monthly newsletter, also available on-line, is like taking a monthly wine class. The Monthly Wine Club is offered in eight options including the top-of-the-line Winelover's Preference and the Consummate Connoisseur's Collection. Members must pick up wines at the store, which provides a reason to go there at least once a month and see what's new or on special, or to pick up a bottle of something that Belding or Mohr just got in and would be perfect for that very evening's dinner.

Boulder Wine Merchant, 2690 Broadway, Boulder; (303) 443-6761 or www.boulderwine.com.

Meridian Wine & Spirits

The entire center of this spacious liquor store in booming Lafayette is taken up with black wire racks, with a wine bottle inserted into each pigeonhole. California wines are arranged by varietal, while wines from elsewhere are organized by state for domestic wines and by country for imports. A separate rack—no more elaborate or strategically placed than all the others—holds bottles categorized as "Selected Wines," which is the code phrase for "expensive."

Champagnes and other sparkling wines are shelved against a wall, near the glassware display from such makers as Vinca and Riedel. Along one wall is a long row of coolers displaying an abundance of chilled wine and champagne. Take one home and start celebrating. Jugs and boxes, while in inventory, are properly relegated to the back of the store, along with the pre-mixes and spirits.

Meridian was a sponsor of the first annual 95th Street Festival of Colorado Wine (in fact, the booths were set up in the parking lot right outside the door, see page 129). The store does occasional wine tastings at the Platinum Grill and sends out periodic e-mails to customers alerting them to in-store specials and events.

Meridian Wine & Spirits, 95th Street & Arapahoe Road, Lafayette; (303) 673-0220 or www.meridianwine.net.

Seed Wine Shop

As you stroll down Boulder's Pearl Street Mall, you might, at first glance, mistake the Seed Wine Shop for an art gallery. The hip, pared-down décor is the backdrop for positively artistic displays of bottles in back-lit elegance. Some are slipped into horizontal tubes, while others perch on shelves. Although the Seed projects an altogether high-end look, it prides itself on carrying quality wines for under $25 a bottle—many are far less. Wines are grouped according to type: light, medium, and full-bodied reds and whites, plus dessert wines and champagnes. One shelf is devoted to organics, and another rack displays premium wines.

Above each row of wine bottles is an information tag, not just to read and memorize but stacked on a peg so you can take one home with your bottle. Each tag provides the name of the wine, the country or region it is from, the name of the winery, the vintage, serving suggestions, and tasting notes. The Seed Wine Club offers three price levels and three options—all red, all white, or mixed.

The Seed Wine Shop sells an array of wine accessories. In addition to the usual glasses, racks, wine openers, and wine-glass charms, there are wine label removers and various versions of tasting note keepers. Seed specializes in setting up private tasting parties, so round up some fellow oenophiles and book a date.

In 2002, the shop organized the Mall Wine Crawl. Named after a now-defunct Halloween event, the Sunday afternoon roving wine tasting featured tasting portions of two appetizers and two entrées at four of the participating restaurants, with a food and wine presentation at each. Participants received a Seed Wine-tasting glass, tasting notes on the food and the wine, and a 15 percent discount on any wine orders placed that evening.

Seed Wine Shop, 1426 Pearl Street, Boulder; (303) 449 5900 or www.seedwineshop.com.

Smashing Grapes

You've got to love a wine retailer with such as whimsical name. Smashing Grapes has become a resource for East County wine lovers. Attractively decorated with buff-colored walls and light pine woodwork, it displays wine bottles clearly and respectfully. Domestic and imported wines are showcased, explained, and sold.

Smashing Grapes carries Riedel and other crystal wineglasses, other stemware, and decanters, wine racks, champagne buckets, and such small accessories as wine charms, corkscrews, and bottle stoppers. A wine-of-the-month club, classes, and wine-maker dinners, often at Proto's or Carelli's, help educate customers in the mystique and enjoyment of wines.

Smashing Grapes, 489 North Highway 287, Lafayette; (303) 604-2242 or www.smashinggrapes.net.

West End Wine Shop

Established in 1999 as the 8th Street Wine Library—a name that implied books about wine rather than wines themselves—this small shop still conveys the sense of cozy clubbiness implied by the original name. The rolling ladder that accesses the upper shelves is a remnant of that era, but when too many people wandered in looking for a book instead of a bottle, the store was renamed. It is stocked floor to ceiling with quality, mostly mid-priced wines from the world's major growing regions and a few of the lesser-known ones as well.

Established by David Cohen, the baker behind Spruce Confections next door (see page 97), and Joanne Keys, it is now owned by Keys and Manuel Sanchez. Keys has taken on behind-the-scenes tasks, so Sanchez is the one you'll most likely meet when you go in. Raised in Montreal by Spanish parents, he has a university degree in finance but was drawn into restaurants and wines.

Everyone who works at the shop has tasted all of the 350 wines in stock at any given time. Most bottles, primarily from small to mid-size wineries, are at drink-tonight prices, and you can always find monthly specials and case-end bottles on sale. The shop's Taster 6-Packs of half-a-dozen hand-picked wines at 15 percent off regular price make for a good way to sample wines that you might not otherwise try.

The West End Wine Shop frequently hosts wine tastings and wine-maker dinners at Bàcaro, Bloom, Dolan's, Mateo, Sunflower, Triana, Trios, or other fine Boulder area restaurants. The wines are selected on several themes. Some of the dinners are paired with wines from a specific country or wine region. Sometimes they are selected horizontally—say, a dinner paired with Cabernet Sauvignon, Chardonnay, or Pinot Noir/Zinfandel from various wineries or wine regions. Sometimes they are regional—say, wines of Tuscany or Piemonte, or they might feature a particular winery with food paired to match. Wine-maker dinners may even be selected on a particular theme—for example, American wines paired with traditional Thanksgiving dishes. One of the shop's specialties is customizing private wine-tasting events for home or business, so you can pick your own theme if you'd like.

West End Wine Shop, 777-C Pearl Street, Boulder; (303) 245-7077 or www.westendwineshop.com.

The Wine Experience

David and Tara Westfall, who both once worked for Soundtrack, became food and wine enthusiasts well before they got into the wine business. Their shared interest in cooking led to a parallel interest in wines and eventually decided to leap from electronics to wine selling. No pie-in-the-sky dreamers, these retail veterans thought hard about what kind of store they wanted. They agreed that it ought to be something "unique and different." Some focused thinking moved their dream from retail conceptualization to reality.

"What you find is a lot of warehouse stores and a lot of little places," David Westfall observes. "We didn't want to be a warehouse store, which has good values but little service. We didn't want to be a boutique, which has great service but not great prices or great selections. We wanted to give the customers everything: great prices, great service, great selection, and a great location."

And that's how The Wine Experience was born in 2001. This 10,000-square-foot store looks open and welcoming, with textured stucco walls painted in Tuscan orange. The floor is brick red. Though it is located in the burgeoning, built-yesterday FlatIron Marketplace, just off U.S. 36 between Denver and Boulder, it stands out as a shining example of an independent local retailer afloat in a sea of chain outlets.

The Westfalls met the challenge of organizing 2,600 wines by applying retail logic and describing them with clear and useful tags. California wines are arranged by grape—grouped according to such major varietals as Sauvignon Blanc, Chardonnay, and Pinot Grigio in the whites and Pinot Noir, Cabernet Sauvignon, and Zinfandel in the reds. Additional racks are labeled "other whites" and "other reds," for the likes of Syrah, Petite Syrah, and Shiraz-Cabernet in the reds and Riesling and Gewürztraminer in the whites. Washington, Oregon, and Colorado wines are arranged by state.

Imports from France and Italy are arranged by region: Bordeaux, Rhône, Burgundy, Loire, Piedmont, Tuscany, Veneto, and such. Imports from elsewhere are organized by country, with Argentina, Australia, Austria, Chile, and Germany well represented. Dessert wines, a fast-growing category, are grouped together and prominently displayed.

Most of the bottles are displayed on interesting and practical Australian pine racks—all comfortably below eye level. Three bottles of every available vintage are shown label up on the top shelf, with more slotted below, so customers don't have to stand on tiptoe or crawl on the floor to read the small print. (If you like the design and think the racks would go nicely in your wine cellar, you can buy one from The Wine Experience too.)

Champagnes and sparkling wines are displayed in an alcove, and next to it is a separate room harboring The Wine Experience's rare and collectible wines. If Colorado ever passes a law permitting retail merchants to hold on-site wine tastings, The Wine Experience is ready. Until that happens, its tasting bar is suitable for wine appreciation classes and vintner's seminars. Interestingly, the law already allows for sidewalk tastings of *Colorado* wines, and The Wine Experience periodically organizes them. The store also cooperates in winemaker dinners, with such area restaurants as Bloom, Il Fornaio, The Canyon Café, Q's, and the Boulder Chop House.

To enhance the wine experience, The Wine Experience carries just about every style and size of stemware that Riedel makes, plus wine racks, corkscrews, other openers, decanters, wine glass charms, martini shakers, bar sets, chillers, cocktail napkins, and more. There's also a good selection of books about wines. The Wine Experience also could be called The Beer Experience, with 300 beers—all bottled and chilled—in a huge cooler. Spirits are also available, largely as a convenience for customers who may come in for wine but want something else too.

The Wine Experience, 281 East Flatiron Circle, Broomfield; (303) 439-WINE or www.thewineexperience.net.

Other

Celestial Seasonings

The consumable, as opposed to consumer, product most associated with Boulder is Celestial Seasonings tea. In 1969, young Mo Siegel was gathering wild herbs in the mountains and brewing them into teas. Within a year, Siegel, his friend Wyck Hay, and their wives and friends were packaging a blend called MO 36 Herb Tea in hand-sewn muslin tea bags. The enterprise soon became a company called Celestial Seasonings, which grew into the best-known brand of herbal teas in the land.

OTHER

Some of the company's teas have become synonymous with the Colorado lifestyle: Red Zinger, Sleepytime, Wild Forest Blackberry. The hand-sewn mesh bags era is long gone, and teas are packed in a highly automated plant in Gunbarrel, Boulder's northeasternmost neighborhood. Long before the word "transparency" became a buzzword in government and corporate America, Celestial Seasonings lived it by offering free hourly plant tours so that people can see just what happens to their herbal teas before buying them. It is fascinating and informative.

Tours are offered daily except Sundays and holidays. Prepare to hang around before or after, especially in the warm months when the gardens are lovely. Celestial Seasonings retail shop sells teas and tea products, and a gallery displays original illustrations for the company's tea boxes. The cheery Celestial Café serves good breakfasts, freshly made and nutritious lunches, and light snacks that are perfect pre- or post-tour, plus 40 kinds of tea to sample.

Celestial Seasonings, 4000 Sleepytime Drive, Boulder; (303) 581-1202 or www.celestialseasonings.com.

ChefJam

OK. I know I promised that I wasn't writing about caterers, but ChefJam is the exception, included not because it is an excellent catering service but because of the man who established it and, more important, because it offers some unusual programs found nowhere else in the state. When James Mazzio, a peripatetic super-chef, established ChefJam in 2002, he trailed behind him one of Colorado's most impressive culinary resumés.

As a teenager, he worked at Main Line Seafood near Philadelphia, and then went to ski-bum in Aspen, where he incidentally moved up through the kitchens of Mezzaluna, the Silver City Grille, and Range and Rustique (formerly Renaissance, see page 319). Charles Dale, that rarified restaurant's owner-chef, mentored him, encouraged him, and helped him find work under such other well-known chefs as Daniel Boulud at Restaurant Daniel in New York and Thomas Keller at The French Laundry in the Napa Valley, California.

After six years, Mazzio became sous-chef at a short-lived Boulder restaurant called Diva. After it became 15 Degrees, Mazzio was elevated to the top-toque slot. During his tenure there, he was named one of *Food & Wine* magazine's best new chefs of 1999. Heady from that honor and with 15 Degrees slated to close because the building was to be demolished, he opened Triana (see page 124), a Spanish restaurant. After Triana, he founded ChefJam, which is what he is doing at this writing.

ChefJam programs include cooking classes (see page 103), Tuesday Tastings, and the Supper Club. Tastings are a series of free monthly samplings of ChefJam dishes served from 5:00 to 9:00 P.M. to potential customers and presumably anyone with a yen to try what Mazzio has most recently created. Pre-registration is required for these congenial events.

Supper Club requires no membership and charges no dues, except the modest cost ($50 at this writing) for a Mazzio-style three-course dinner, with a choice of appetizers, entrées, and desserts, and wine, beer, or soft drinks included. The menu changes weekly, and since this is not a restaurant as such, there isn't much point in detailing dishes here. Just know that fresh ingredients, local when possible, are assembled in the mostly French-Italian-Mediterranean mode that earned Mazzio so many honors.

ChefJam is located in a catering hall called the Miramonte Lodge. Rumors floating through the Denver culinary community at this writing indicate that Mazzio is looking to reestablish himself in the restaurant business, probably in Denver. Stay tuned, but meanwhile, give ChefJam's Tuesday Tastings or Supper Club a try.

ChefJam, Miramonte Lodge, 1200 Miramonte Street, Broomfield; (303) 404-2525 or www.chefjam.com.

Growing Gardens Cultiva Youth Project

Boulder's culinary conscience and good sense are exemplified in Growing Gardens' Cultiva Youth Project, a two-acre organic market garden operated by teenagers, some considered at risk, to introduce them to the concepts of growing, harvesting, and selling their product. The youngsters also tend a stand at the Saturday Boulder County Farmers' Market. Additionally, local chefs are committed to help these kids succeed and also support organic farming principles and practices. The Chautauqua Dining Hall (see page 107) has begun hosting an annual four-course fundraising dinner using Cultiva Youth Project's fresh produce. In September 2002, owner-chef Bradford Heap teamed with John Ash, Fetzer Vineyards' culinary director, to create the dinner.

For information on the Cultiva project or future dinners, contact Growing Gardens, 3198 North Broadway, Boulder; (303) 413-7248 or www.growinggardens.org.

Haystack Mountain Goat Dairy

Northeast of Boulder is Haystack Mountain, a grassy lump rising a few hundred feet above the plain. It might qualify as a mountain in North Dakota, but in Colorado, it's just a pimple on the landscape. Still, the nearby goat farm and dairy that adopted its name stands as tall as Longs Peak in the realm of goat cheese, not just locally but nationally. Haystack Mountain Goat Dairy produces farmstead cheeses— that is, cheeses made on the farm where the animals are located. Traditionally, this is considered the best possible scenario for producing outstanding cheeses.

The dairy's preservative-free cheeses are served at some of Colorado's best restaurants and sold at the Boulder County Farmers' Market (see page 464), in fine natural foods and gourmet stores, and at the dairy, which is open to visitors a few hours each week. The family-owned dairy handcrafts its simple, clean-flavored cheeses. The process goes like this: Acquire and care for a herd of goats. Milk the females twice a day. Heat the milk to pasteurize it. Cool it. Add a culture of vegetable rennet. Place in cloth cheese bags and suspend. When curds and whey separate and only curd remains in the bag, salt it and form it into chèvre. Package and refrigerate. Pass whey on to other farmers, who feed it to their livestock. This simple process that produces the perfect chèvre goes on every day in Haystack Mountain's whistle-clean cheese room, where workers in white rubber boots, long lab coats, and hair protectors perform this daily magic with goat's milk.

Under the Haystack Mountain label, you will find Boulder Chèvre, a delicate, semi-soft cheese akin to the classic Montrachet of France; Spreadable Chèvre, a soft cheese like French *chèvre fromage blanc,* made plain or flavored; Grateful Chèvre, a harder and more piquant variety suitable for salads, pastas, and hot vegetables; Boulder Chèvre en Marinade, cheese marinated in extra-virgin olive oil infused with garlic and Herbes de Provence; and feta, the traditional cheese of Greece, sold in brined whey and suitable for slicing or crumbling into salads or Mediterranean recipes.

Jim Schott, who had been a public school teacher and had held other educational positions, left the world of academe in 1989 for the world of livestock, early-morning milking, and cheese. He and his late wife, Arlene, purchased land north of Boulder, bought five goats, and learned the art of cheese-making. By 1994, the first full year of production, Haystack Mountain's goat cheeses won seven awards from the American Dairy Goat Product Association in Madison, Wisconsin, including a gold medal for *fromage blanc* and a silver medal for the signature Boulder Chèvre. Haystack Mountain also took one first place for its Boulder Chèvre with Rosemary and three second places (Chèvre Spread with Green Chili, Boulder Chèvre, and Chèvre in Marinade) at the 2001 American Cheese Society meeting in Sonoma County, California. Schott and his wife, Carol, operate the dairy, which has grown to 100 or so Nubian and Saanan goats and a staff of people as dedicated to goat-farming and cheese-making as is the family. "The flavor and craftsmanship of the farmstead goat cheeses made at Haystack Mountain Goat Dairy in Niwot are symbolic of owners Jim and Carol Schott's devotion to the land and to their animals," wrote *Profiles of America's Great Cheese Makers* author Linda Werlin, who certainly has seen her share of farms and cheese-making operations.

Kidding season, when the does bear their young, is from February through early July. You can visit the dairy, say hello to the goats, watch the cheese-making process, and learn about goat cheeses on Tuesdays or Saturdays between noon and 2:00 P.M.

Haystack Mountain Goat Dairy, 5239 Niwot Road, Niwot; (303) 581-9948 or www.haystackgoatcheese.com.

Pour

Boulder County's first California-style wine bar and tasting room was established in 2002 by Brandy Penrose, who had experienced and liked the concept in West Coast wine country. With no wine expertise other than as a consumer, she recruited Nathan Frye and Mat Meyer, members of the Society of Wine Educators, to staff the wine bar and run the weekly wine classes.

Pour resembles a tasting room at a winery, with artificial vines draped over the mirrors, a polished-stone wine bar, high tables for four, and regular-height tables for eight. Mellow jazz plays from the speakers, and wine art hangs on the walls. Open in the late afternoon and evening, Pour offers wine in a sociable and educational context.

Pour stocks 60 to 75 wines at a time, and 10 to 20 of them are changed out each month. Most customers order flights of wine, three or more 2-ounce glasses from a particular region or representing a particular varietal or blend. Frye or Meyer is on hand to guide patrons through the process of tasting, evaluating, and comparing. Pour also offers a selection of wine-friendly cold hors d'ouevres, to accompany wine tastings and as part of the cost of wine classes.

Pour is permitted to serve wine to be drunk on the premises by the flight, the glass, or the bottle—and it does. It may hold wine classes—and it does, every Wednesday evening. And it may sell wine accessories and books—and it does. What it is not permitted to do is to sell bottles of wine to be taken from the premises. So Pour has established a symbiotic relationship with Superior Liquor Market, right next door which may sell wines.

Pour, 1000 Superior Plaza Way, Superior; (303) 499-3335.

Tea Train

Tea Train began life as a business plan developed by Paul Cattin while he was in college. Since 2002, he has operated a long, narrow shop in a strip shopping mall on the outskirts of Longmont, that is a welcome oasis serving and selling fine teas from the world over. Pick a small table and have a scone and the tea of your choice—or sink into a sofa with a good book and tea. Soft music and a tranquil atmosphere will take you to a more relaxed place. Tea Train occasionally and irregularly puts on special events, including children's tea parties, tea talks, and tea tastings.

The store carries more than 100 teas, divided into geographical and varietal groups. There are black teas from India, China, Sri Lanka (formerly Ceylon), Africa, and Indonesia—plus flavored and blended black teas. There are green teas from China and Japan, as well as flavored and scented greens. Additionally, Tea Train stocks oolong, white teas, decaffeinated teas, both loose-leaf and instant, chai, various herbals (called tisanes in French), and fruit blends. It's also a place to get mate from South America, rooiboos from South Africa, or bobas from Korea, specialties you won't find in many other places. When it's hot out, you might want to try Teasings, tea-based smoothies with gingko, guarana, and ginseng, as good for you, herbally speaking, as they are tasty and refreshing.

Tea Train has an extensive mail order list, and Cattin is so eager to introduce customers to fine and often exotic teas that he offers a great incentives to try the store's merchandise. If you have any old tea around, bring it in and the Tea Train will trade it in, ounce for ounce, for one of its fine teas at a 25 percent discount.

Tea Train, 2201 Ken Pratt Boulevard, Longmont; (800) 655-1889,
(303) 651-1564, or www.teatrain.com.

Recipes

After years of blending tea, making tea, drinking tea, and promoting tea, it was only natural that a tea cookbook would emerge from the Celestial Seasonings braintrust. This chicken piccata recipe is from the *Cooking with Tea Cookbook* by Jennifer and Mo Siegel.

Lemon Zinger Chicken Piccata

3 cups water
4 Lemon Zinger tea bags
4 boneless skinless chicken breasts, pounded (about ?-inch thin)
1 clove garlic, minced
1 cup flour
salt and pepper to taste
2 tablespoons unsalted butter
4 lemon wedges

Bring the water to a boil the water and carefully pour into a large bowl. Add the tea bags and steep for 10 minutes, allowing the water to cool. Remove the tea bags, squeezing excess liquid into the bowl, and discard the bags. Add the chicken breasts and garlic to the liquid, and marinate for at least 20 minutes. Combine the flour and salt and pepper to taste in a large zipper-lock plastic bag. Add the chicken and shake the bag until the chicken is fully coated. Melt butter in a large frying pan over medium heat. Sauté the chicken on both sides until golden brown and cooked through. Serve garnished with lemon wedges. Serves 4.

High on the list of The Boulder Cork's signature dishes are tender, crisp-crusted crab cakes made from fresh, unpasteurized crabmeat. They strike the palate with the sweetness of the crabmeat and the brininess of the sea from which it comes. Chef Jim Smailer uses both fresh crabmeat and fresh bread crumbs, made by grinding quality French bread, to achieve the balance that makes this appetizer a perennial favorite.

Crab Cakes

6 tablespoons high-quality mayonnaise
1 teaspoon Dijon mustard
1 teaspoon Worcestershire sauce
½ teaspoon Tabasco sauce

¼ teaspoon white pepper
1 egg, lightly beaten
½ cup chopped fresh parsley
1 cup fresh bread crumbs, ground in the food processor
1 pound fresh, precooked lump crabmeat (Dungeness, blue, etc.,
    available at seafood counters), with any cartilage picked out
olive oil and/or butter, for sautéing

In a medium mixing bowl, whisk together mayonnaise, mustard, Worcestershire sauce, Tabasco, pepper, and egg. Stir in parsley and bread crumbs, then fold in crabmeat. Shape mixture into 12 balls, about 2 to 2½ inches in diameter. Flatten them slightly with your fingers. In a large nonstick sauté pan, heat a small amount of oil and/or butter (or Smailer's preferred 50/50 mixture), using just enough fat to keep the crab cakes from sticking to the pan. Sauté the cakes over medium heat, turning once, until browned on both sides and warmed through. (Since the crabmeat is pre-cooked, it only needs to be reheated.) Serves 6.

Sauce for Crab Cakes

The Cork serves its crab cakes with a tangy-sweet sauce made of mayonnaise, honey, Dijon, and a pinch of cayenne and dried dill weed.

The Cooking School of the Rockies has adapted this recipe for these popular and versatile mushrooms with flavored olive oil from *The Italian Country Table*. It is very quick and easy to make, and it works as an appetizer or as a portobello "steak" entrée.

Grilled Portobello Mushrooms with "Holy" Oil

2 large cloves garlic
½ teaspoon dried oregano
¼ teaspoon dried chilies or hot pepper flakes
½ cup olive oil
1 pound portobello mushrooms
salt and pepper to taste

In a blender, purée garlic, oregano, chili, and olive oil. If possible, let sit for an hour at room temperature to mellow the flavors. Remove the mushroom stems and save for another use. Clean the caps with a damp cloth or mushroom brush, and trim any bruised areas. Arrange the caps on a platter and season on both sides with the flavored oil. Marinate in oil mixture at room temperature for 15 minutes to about 2 hours. Heat grill, skillet, or sauté pan. Cook mushrooms, turning to brown on both sides. If sautéing, use medium-high heat until browned. When mushrooms are browned, move mushrooms away from the hottest coals on the grill or reduce heat to medium-low if sautéing. Cook 4 minutes longer or until tender to the touch when pressed. Serves 2 to 4.

To reach the old Lick Skillet Café, Boulderites and other Front Rangers would drive up Sunshine Canyon to Gold Hill. The no-longer-new Lick Skillet Bakery pays homage to the location of the original restaurant with its signature Sunshine Muffin. This all-natural nutrition bomb happens to be delicious too—good and good for you, just as Boulder likes its food. Robin Fine, a Lick Skillet baker, perfected this recipe, which uses a lot of bowls but makes one great batch of muffins.

Sunshine Muffins

1¼ cups cake flour
1½ cups whole-wheat flour
¾ tablespoon baking soda
¾ tablespoon cinnamon
¾ tablespoon salt
¾ cup raisins
1½ cup grated carrots
¾ cup almonds, crushed with a rolling pin
¾ cup shredded fresh coconut
1¼ cups peeled, cored, small- to medium-diced Granny Smith apples
4 eggs
5 ounces (scant ⅔ cup) real maple syrup
¾ cup canola oil
¾ tablespoon vanilla extract
¼ cup apple juice
nonstick spray
12 paper muffin or cupcake cups

Preheat oven to 325 to 350 degrees. Measure out the dry ingredients (the first five) into five separate bowls. Place the raisins, carrots, almonds, coconut, and apples into another medium-size bowl. Put the wet ingredients (eggs, maple syrup, and oil) into three separate bowls. Add a little of each of the first five ingredients to a large mixing bowl, and with the mixer running on medium speed, add a little of each of the three wet ingredients. Allow the mixer to stir until just combined, and scrape the bottom of the bowl if necessary, being careful not to overmix.

Repeat the process, adding a little more of the dry ingredients, then a little more of the wet ingredients, letting the mixer stir each time until just combined. Be sure to incorporate the ingredients at the bottom of the bowl. Add in the fruit-nut mixture last, stirring until just combined.

Coat a muffin pan with nonstick spray. Place paper muffin or cupcake cups into the pan, and thoroughly spray the insides of the cups and the top of the pan with nonstick spray again. Spoon the batter into the cups, filling them just to the top (not over). Bake for 15 to 20 minutes, checking them after 15 minutes. They are done when a toothpick inserted into the center of a muffin comes out clean, and when the tops of the muffins turn a dark orange color. Yields 12 muffins.

Colorado Springs and Pueblo

Although they are just 25 miles apart, Colorado Springs and Pueblo developed in polar-opposite ways. Colorado Springs and nearby Manitou Springs blossomed as getaways for well-heeled 19th-century industrialists, entrepreneurs, and their ladies, who were lured by the scenic beauty at the foot of Pikes Peak. The Colorado Springs gentry built elaborate mansions in that beautiful place and socialized largely with people like themselves. Nipping at their coattails in what is now called Old Colorado City was the city's more modest middle class, concentrated in a genteel aspiring neighborhood.

Pueblo started as a rough and tough trading post along the Arkansas River and began growing when the Denver & Rio Grande Railroad came through in 1872. Boom times came with the first Colorado Fuel & Iron Company blast furnace, and eventually enormous steel mills dotted the landscape. In contrast to the gentility and general WASPiness of Colorado Springs, Pueblo was a gritty industrial city largely populated by immigrant workers. They came from Mexico, Italy, Poland, Croatia, Serbia, Russia, and elsewhere, and lived in poverty, grime, and not always harmony while the bankers and industrial magnates elsewhere in town lived in considerable comfort.

Two world wars, a depression, and eventually technology changed the way people traveled. Even the rich no longer spent long summer weeks in elegant resorts or country homes, but began jetting for shorter periods to places around the world. The Colorado Springs/Manitou Springs resort era came to an end, replaced by touch-and-go tourism. Every family hit the road, and they came to Colorado Springs for a few days of exploring the city's abundant tourist attractions and activities. Even as the elegant lifestyle of the 19th century faded away, Colorado Springs developed into a major military outpost, housing active and retired personnel. Many had done tours abroad and developed a liking for foods from many lands. Meanwhile, Pueblo's steel industry withered away.

Colorado Springs and Manitou Springs always have had resort-related fine dining, while Pueblo has had its quirky ethnic eateries that have continued to serve the foods brought by the immigrant steelworkers so long ago. More recently, both cities have been maturing on the culinary scene. In most regards, Colorado Springs, the far larger and more prosperous of the two, is "ahead" of Pueblo when it comes to fine dining, but Pueblo is catching up. It boasts a resurgent historic district around its magnificent railroad depot and sell-out cooking classes at the local convention center. In Colorado Springs, restaurants and retail shops of interest to epicures are widely scattered around the sprawling city. The greater Pikes Peak region and its Pueblo extension offer an increasing number of such establishments, from the massive Broadmoor complex to small mom-and-pop food businesses.

Bakeries

La Baguette

Purists might sniff that La Baguette's loaves are not quite as crisp-crusted as they ought to be, but for legions of Colorado Springs residents who got their first taste of French- and Italian-style breads there, this bakery—now grown to four locations— has set the standard of what these baked goods should be like. Purists, step aside, for it's not a bad standard.

All the baking for all four stores, as well as for the restaurants and other commercial accounts that La Baguette serves, is done in the original Old Colorado City location. This large bakery-restaurant hums with activity at breakfast, lunch, coffee-break time, and early dinner.

The breads, available by the loaf or as the foundation of many sandwiches, include whole wheat, Parisienne, rosemary–red onion, olive, *ficelle,* rustique, raisin, pecan, Multi 6 Grain, walnut, and sandwich white. A number of these are also available as rolls. La Baguette's French Onion Soup is a Colorado Springs classic. From May 1 through mid-October, gazpacho is also on the menu, and regulars look forward to its appearance with the enthusiasm that bird-watchers reserve for the swallows' return to Capistrano. Breakfast pastries include huge croissants, filled and not. Later in the day you can order such lunch and early dinner entrées as escargots, various pastas and pasta salads, and individual thin-crust pizzas. The desserts include cream puffs, éclairs, crème caramel in a ramekin, truffles, and chocolate mousse.

La Baguette, 117 East Pikes Peak Avenue, Colorado Springs; (719) 636-5020;
2417 West Colorado Avenue, Old Colorado City, Colorado Springs;
(719) 577-4818; 4440 North Chestnut; (719) 599-0686; and
1420 Kelly Johnson Boulevard, Colorado Springs; (719) 598-5550.

Breadheads

Louis Borochaner, who previously baked at several top Arizona resorts and more recently at The Broadmoor, now performs his magic in his own artisan bakery and café in Manitou Springs. He's moved from preparing delicate pastries to baking the best hearty breads in the Pikes Peak region. Behind the warm and welcoming store-front, ceiling fans whirl over the soaring space, with gleaming hardwood floors, funky mix-and-match (or mix-and-mismatch) tables and chairs, prints on the wall, and food-and-kitchen antiques. Condiments are put out on an old Hoosier cabinet, but the rest of the antiques are there for show.

Borochaner bakes nine outstanding artisan breads: toothsome sourdough, walnut raisin, *ciabatta,* focaccia, *filcette,* Calamata olive, multigrain, caraway rye, and an outstanding French baguette, one of the most-often-baked artisan breads and one of the hardest to get right. On Fridays, he also does challah for the Jewish sabbath.

Those fine breads make excellent sandwiches. Oven-roasted turkey breast comes on multigrain. A special chicken salad enhanced with smokehouse almonds, apples, and fresh herbs comes on a buttery croissant. Veghead, a winning combination of roasted eggplant, zucchini, red pepper, and tomatoes with caramelized onions and crisp clover sprouts, is served with Middle Eastern hummus on Calamata olive bread. And the Muffaletta Focaccia Sandwich, offered in regular or belly-buster size, features hard salami, coppicola, pepperoni, provolone, and olive salad with Italian vinaigrette to help it all slide down. Breakfast items include wondrous Three-Grain Pancakes served with sweet butter and real Vermont maple syrup and Pain Perdue French Toast, made with true batter-dipped French bread and topped with pecans and cinnamon sugar. Children can discover the joy of genuine maple syrup too with the popular kids' breakfast of five silver-dollar pancakes. From-scratch breakfast pastries include Danishes, scones, muffins, bagels, croissants, and the Mountain Man Fat-Free Bran Muffin, a healthy power pastry that doesn't yield a bit on taste.

Among Breadheads' thin-crust individual pizzas, three-cheese, pepperoni, and chicken pesto are the simple ones. The two popular piled-up pizzas are Meathead (with five meats, cheese, and tomato sauce) and Veghead (the yin to Meathead's yang with roasted red onions, mushrooms, peppers, zucchini, garlic, Roma tomatoes, fresh basil, and mozzarella). There are super-fresh salads too.

Panzanotti is a hard-to-find traditional Italian bread salad stuffed into a fresh tomato, while the Fruithead Salad features seasonal fruits with an excellent honey-yogurt dressing and blueberry-sour cream muffin. Swiss Onion is Breadheads' signature soup, and there's also a soup of the day as well. Desserts—while in general not as elaborate as in Borochaner's Broadmoor days—include simple cookies, brownies, lemon bars, biscotti, or the more complex and beautiful fruit tarts, cakes, and pastry selections that vary according to the baker's whim and the fresh ingredients available. Breadheads also serves dinner (at this writing, it's open until 9:00 P.M. nightly except Monday and Tuesday). The menu changes weekly, and the dishes reflect the creativity, choices, and quality found earlier in the day.

Breadheads, 729 Manitou Avenue, Manitou Springs; (719) 685-2400.

Old Heidelberg Pastry Shop and Grindelwald Market

The corner of South Tejon and Las Vegas is *Das Deutsche Eck*—the German corner—of Colorado Springs. There you will find one of the city's best, and best-loved, bakeries and its most authentic German delicatessen (and do remember that "delicatessen" is a German word). Both businesses are owned by Germans—cousins, I believe—and are authentically middle European in style and substance.

Karl Schoenberger presides over the Old Heidelberg Pastry Shop located in a store that would be modest for a supermarket but appears gargantuan for a bakery. Everything is baked and decorated on-site—and what a sight it is. As soon as you walk in the front door, your eyes are drawn to two huge glass cases filled with an enormous array of cakes, pastries, coffee cakes, spongecakes, and cookies—all as delicious as they are appealing. You'll find such Continental favorites as Black Forest Cake, Sachertorte, and Rembrandt Cake, a sinful combination of white and chocolate cake filled with white and chocolate buttercream and frosted with chocolate and marzipan. In the European style, many of the confections are filled with or topped with fruits, nuts, or both. The bread rack is stocked with good versions of common breads and some unusual ones too, including an East-meets-West German Sourdough.

You can sit down on the café side of the store and indulge in sweet stuff. On the east wall is a large and fanciful mural of the Zugspitze, Germany's highest mountain, and through the plate-glass window on the west wall, you can gaze out at the Rockies.

Next door is the Grindelwald Market, a small grocery and deli in space that was once a taco stand. The rich, meaty dishes that are most favored in the traditional German and Austrian kitchen are not exactly in culinary favor these days, but this is the food I grew up on—and therefore I have a soft spot in my heart for it when it is done well. And Ingeborg Pauley is very good at homemade German and Austrian specialties like my *Grossmutti* used to make: *Leberknödelsuppe* (liver-dumpling soup), goulash and spätzle (respectively stew of Hungarian origin and fine-pressed dumplings that simply soak up the sauce), and other daily specials.

Grindelwald Market's deli section carries imported bratwurst, knockwurst, wienerwurst, and ham—and also cheeses from Bavaria, Holland, Denmark, and France. The grocery section is stocked with European packaged goods like Bahlsen cookies and biscuits and Oetker and Schawtau mixes, glazes, frostings, puddings, and other baking products). You'll also find good rolls, seeded and not. Pauley will build a great sandwich on one, or you can it take home to enjoy with sweet butter and jam. *Stollen* is available year-round, not just at Christmas, as is excellent marzipan.

Old Heidelberg Pastry Shop, 1109 South Tejon, Colorado Springs; (719) 634-1052; and 309-30 Austin Bluffs Parkway, Colorado Springs; (719) 536-0979.

Grindelwald Market, 1105 South Tejon, Colorado Springs; (719) 475-1414.

Pie-Eyed Pies

Pie-Eyed Pies was opened in mid-2002 by Debbie and Jim Conway and their neighbor Jackie Rickard. The Conways, who had sold Conway's Red Top Restaurants, a half-century-old local burger chain with four locations around the Springs, were looking for something a little different. Rickard and her late husband had once lived in Topeka and still raved about a small local pie shop there. The owner of that small Kansas business was willing to sell his recipes to the partners, and Pie-Eyed Pies was good to go.

They turn out fresh pies for takeout—fruit-filled, cream-filled, crumb-topped, meringue-topped, or some combination in flaky crusts. The popular fruit pies are made with fresh-frozen fruits, so most are available year-round. Other specialties include chocolate cream, French silk, Key lime, and lemon meringue, all available by the slice or as whole pies. There are even whole sugar-free pies for the diabetic (or perhaps dieting) pie fanatic. Pie-Eyed Pies also bakes quiches, chicken-pot pie, cheesecakes in several flavors, cookies, muffins, pecan rolls, and cinnamon rolls.

Pie-Eyed Pies, 2378 Academy Boulevard, Colorado Springs; (719) 622-1506.

Woodys Continental Pastries and Joanies Café

In 1987, James "Woody" Woodruff started working as a pan washer at Kohlhase's Bakery. He quit twice and was fired once, but he had learned on the job, in spite of the bumps in the baking road, and found that he was bitten by the Continental baking bug. In 1998, he bought the bakery and changed its name to his own, but it remains the old-fashioned, from-scratch bakery it was then. Woodys Continental Pastries still has a modestly sized and plainly appointed retail area—and a gigantic behind-the-scenes kitchen.

If it comes from the oven, Woodys does it. The bakery's repertoire runs to hundreds of items, as Woody describes it, "from donuts to wedding cakes." Pies, cakes and tortes, petits fours, cookies, Danish pastries, rolls, breads, muffins, quick breads, and other items are available in various flavors.

If the bakery has one signature item, it is coffee cake—but even that comes in 24 varieties. Among the savories are Woodys pretzels, house-baked and either plain or cheese-filled, the latter at first glance resembling a large baked potato oozing cheddar cheese. Enormous, softball-sized filled cream puffs are available with or without chocolate shavings. Cheesecakes come in New York–style (made with cream cheese) or German-style (made with *Schmierkäse,* a customer favorite from the Kohlhase era). Holiday items are predictably in high demand at Woodys.

In early 2003, Woodys expanded to the adjacent storefront and opened Joanies Café, offering breakfast and lunch. Joanies debuted with breakfast items, pizza, sandwiches, soups based on their own stocks, sandwiches on bread or bagels, deli fare, and a sprinkling of Southwestern dishes and also some more elegant, upscale baked goods than Woodys had previously offered.

Woodys Continental Pastries and Joanies Café, 2226 North Wahsatch Avenue, Colorado Springs; (719) 632-2592.

Cooking School and Cooking Classes

Chefs of the Front Range

Pueblo's downtown convention center is an attractive and well-appointed meeting facility. Put it, the excellent kitchen, and an accommodating staff into the hopper and then add the notion that interest in good food and wine is growing in Pueblo, and you have the ingredients for successful cooking classes.

Chefs of the Front Range is a series of demonstration classes offered in the convention center's commodious kitchen from 6:30 to 9:00 P.M. on four consecutive Tuesday evenings featuring chefs from Pueblo, Colorado Springs, and elsewhere. At this writing, classes were being offered in February/March, May, July, and November.

They have been sellouts from the beginning, and there is usually a waiting list. Just 25 people can be accommodated at each very moderately priced class, which includes a three- or four-course dinner, wine, and service by the convention center's congenial staff. Dishes are served as soon as they are finished, even as the chef goes on to the next. Among the culinary luminaries whom you might find at Chefs of the Front Range are Karen Briggs and Sally Greer, owner/chefs of Rio Bistro; Victor Matthews, owner/executive chef of the Black Bear Restaurant in Green Mountain Falls; Alys Romer, owner/chef of Alys' Fireside Café in Walsenburg; Calvin Silva, executive chef at the Pueblo Country Club; Dan Skay, a Culinary Institute of America graduate and executive chef at Pueblo's Parkview Medical Center (who probably doesn't often get to cook his award-winning cuisine during his day job); and Richard Warner and Mary Oreskovich, owner/chefs of the Steel City Diner. The Pueblo Convention Center's Executive Chef, Kit Recek, and Executive Sous-Chef, Ramon Gallegos, have taught classes and also facilitated guest chefs' use of their kitchen.

Thus far, wines from Cottonwood Cellars near Olathe have been paired with the chefs' foods, and convention center director Larry Ambrose, a dedicated food and wine enthusiast who might just have launched this series in order to feed his own interests, talks about wines and how they relate to food.

Even though seating is limited, anyone in Pueblo can tap into the Chefs of the Front Range's expertise. The Pueblo Community College's Center for New Media has been videotaping the classes for broadcast on the city's public-access television channels.

Pueblo Convention Center, 320 Central Main Street, Pueblo; (719) 542-1100 or www.puebloconventioncenter.com.

Pikes Peak Community College

Several culinary and baking tracks, leading to certificates or degrees and accredited by the American Culinary Federation, make up this local school's culinary arts curriculum. The culinary program is offered at the college's Centennial Campus, on the southern outskirts of Colorado Springs.

The programs combine academic basics and hands-on culinary experience—plus culinary academics for the degree program. Once a student has completed the culinary courses, he or she can apply for ACF certification by completing work requirements. The goal is for graduates to be prepared for positions such as secondary cook or station manager upon completion of the chosen course—and from there, advancement opportunities abound.

The Culinary Arts Degree program requires 68 credit hours of academic and culinary courses and results in an associate degree. The Culinary Arts Certificate program, designed for the student who is looking for a position as an entry-level cook, consists of 31 credit hours of cooking classes, plus completion or equivalency of four academic classes as well. The Baking Certificate program is similar, but with 28 credit hours in the pastry and dessert areas, plus equivalence of the same four academics.

Pikes Peak Community College, 5675 South Academy Boulevard, Colorado Springs, CO 80906; (800) 456-6847, (719) 540-7383, or www.ppcc.edu.

Restaurant Classes

Given the absence of the kinds of cooking schools that abound in Denver and Boulder, Colorado Springs area restaurants have been an invaluable resource for home cooks seeking to up their skills and food knowledge, but restaurants, chefs, and schedules come and go. During off-peak months (January through April), monthly cooking classes and wine seminars are given at The Cliff House. Executive Chef Deneb Williams instructs the weeknight evening, one-and-a-half-hour cooking classes. They include both demonstration and hands-on experiences and are held in the inn's boardroom. Afterwards students enjoy a gourmet dinner theme in the dining Room. Food and Beverage Director Julius Watson conducts the wine seminars. Classes are open to the public, with lodging packages also available.

The Broadmoor's cooking classes cover holiday theme and other topics. These moderately priced demonstration classes take place on selected Saturdays in November and December from 10:00 A.M. to noon in the hotel's West Ballroom. They are open to the public, but reservations are required. Call (719) 577-5733. In 2003, The Broadmoor inaugurated A Salute to Escoffier (see page 175), a food festival incorporating classes.

Colorado Springs area restaurants have also filled the city's cooking school gap by offering periodic on-site cooking classes. Initial plans for the Black Bear Restaurant's second site in Colorado Springs include incorporating a culinary school as well. Cooking classes were offered by two fine restaurants that sadly closed in 2002, Primitivo in downtown Colorado Springs and Old City in Old Colorado City. If their respective chefs, John Broening and Paul Jensen II, resurface, it is possible that they will again offer classes. For contact and reservations information on the restaurants that might be offering cooking classes, see the listings in the Dining section, below.

Dining

Black Bear Restaurant

The Black Bear Restaurant in Green Mountain Falls was once a rustic mountain restaurant with log-cabin construction that became a locals' hangout with cuisine that ran to burgers and other down-home food. Eventually renamed the Pikes Peak Pub and Grill (nicknamed the Pub and Grub by locals), its casual atmosphere remained.

When Victor Matthews Jr., a chef who had cooked and owned restaurants in New Orleans and Houston, decided in 1999 to trade the humid Gulf Coast climate for the cool precincts of the Rockies, he bought the Pikes Peak Pub. He reached back into its history and restored its original name but reached forward to introduce excellent contemporary cuisine served in a country setting. This was not a trivial undertaking. The old log building required a top-to-bottom makeover, starting with what can only be called deep cleaning and ending with new linens, tableware, glassware, and other fine-dining accoutrements. When the sign went up with the original name, the new version of the restaurant was in business.

The Black Bear is a unique melding of the old and the new. The front section of the building retains the casual pub feel while the back section has been turned into a fine-dining restaurant, necessitated by Matthews' slightly schizophrenic business plan. He knew that he wanted to wow Colorado Springs epicures and give them reason to drive up Ute Pass, but he wanted to keep loyal locals happy too. Especially in winter, the few hundred year-round residents in the hamlet of Green Mountain Falls were still counting on the Pub and Grub's burgers and chicken-fried steak. The Black Bear Restaurant feeds both types of clientele, with Matthews' burgers and such far better than anything from the old Pub and Grub days.

An assortment of gumbos, stews, and soups, plus Beer-Battered Fried Mushrooms and Hot Wings, are classic starters on the pub menu. Matthews fashions his "Almost-a-Pound Burgers" of beef-buffalo blend, and he makes his chicken-fried steak with Black Angus beef and loads it with house-made gravy, while the fresh-cut rib eye and filet mignon allow quality beef to shine on its own. Matthews continues the popular Thursday evening prime-rib special, with the musical accompaniment of jazz. Accompaniments on the plates are a choice of garlic mashed potatoes, home-style steak fries, Vidalia onion rings, or wild rice pilaf.

The true culinary interest comes when Matthews switches gears from his cook's cap to his chef's toque. His awesome menu changes constantly. Sublime offerings include such dishes as Imperial Lobster with Saffron Cream, lacquered duck, or something with precious truffles, which he brings in each fall. For the really adventurous eater, he occasionally offers an entrée that he calls Three Dragons. It may sound like something from a Chinese restaurant, but instead of egg roll, fried rice, and something stir-fried, his is a combination platter consisting of rattlesnake, snapping turtle, and alligator tail. The snake comes from Texas, the turtle from Louisiana, and the 'gator from Colorado's own San Luis Valley.

At the Black Bear Restaurant, the Black Angus is the cheap meat, for Chef Matthews also uses Kobe beef from Japan. These pampered *waygu* cattle are fed honey and beer and massaged with sake to produce the world's most marbled meat. It has traditionally been unavailable in America except on odd occasions and at $300 a pound, Matthews can't promise that it will always be on the menu, but it will be as long as long as he can procure it—he promises "at the best prices in the entire world."

The Matthews version of the traditional Chef's Table is unique. The chef sends out an *amuse-bouche* as a small diversion before he comes out and discusses the possibilities with you. He'll ask what you love to eat (and what you hate) and even what food allergies you might have, and return to the kitchen to customize a meal for you. There is no set number of courses, but the dishes always involve the freshest ingredients, prepared in the most innovative ways, to create a gastronomic *tour de force* evening after evening.

Special occasions call for special dinners, and the Black Bear Restaurant offers several each year. These include the annual Monet Dinner in mid-November. Matthews cooks from master Impressionist Monet's culinary journals. The chef actually travels to the famous painter's home in France prior to the dinner to bring back what he coyly describes as "all manner of surprises from Giverny itself." Mid-February brings the Valentine's Evening of Love, a feast featuring such seductive foods as champagne, caviar, oysters, truffles, chocolate, and more chocolate. Extravagant courses and *very* limited romantic seating.

The Italian Experience, scheduled for March, pays homage to Andrea Apuzzo, with whom Matthews trained. This great Italian master chef has never received the name recognition of some of his French counterparts, but foodies everywhere (as well as everyone who has ever seen *Sleepless in Seattle)* knows tiramisu, one of several now-standard dishes that he helped introduce in America.

You don't need a special theme dinner to indulge in the Black Bear Restaurant's excellent desserts. Some are exquisite executions of popular dishes, ranging from all-American pies made with fresh seasonal fruits or Italy's simple, and simply wonderful, *panna cotta,* while others are complex pastries appealing to the eye and palate.

When Matthews undertook the makeover, he stocked the wine cellar from scratch. "The restaurant had been open since 1959, and until I arrived here in March of 1999, they had never sold a single bottle of wine," he says. "I was lucky enough to discover a hidden underground room, actually an old bomb shelter, which I converted into the wine cellar." The Black Bear focuses primarily on less expensive California and Australian wines, but include some nice high-end selections, Colorado wines, and interesting finds. "Our wine list is not extensive, but we cover the bases very well."

Matthews and his Black Bear Restaurant have been winning accolades since he reopened the doors. The restaurant has received the highest ratings from food critics from all the Front Range media that have reviewed it, and Matthews won first place in the culinary competition at the Governor's Symposium for two consecutive years.

At this writing, Matthews is rumored to be setting his sights on a location for a second restaurant in Colorado Springs. In addition to being a top-ranked chef, he is a certified culinary educator (in fact, he staffs the kitchen at the Black Bear Restaurant with eager apprentices), and he hopes to open a culinary school. He has designed three professional curricula, of which what he calls the Institute of Fine Cuisine is the most advanced. His plan is to operate the school in a symbiotic relationship with the new restaurant. I can hardly wait—and neither can Colorado Springs foodies.

Black Bear Restaurant, 10375 Ute Pass Avenue, Green Mountain Falls; (719) 684-9648 or www.geocities.com/BlackBearRestaurant/.

Briarhurst Manor

In 1867, Dr. William Bell, a well-connected young Englishman, traveled to St. Louis to attend a series of medical lectures. When they were over, Dr. Bell—fired up with a sense of adventure in the chaotic "Gateway to the West"—decided to stay on in America for a while. He applied to be the expedition doctor with a railroad surveying party, but the position had been filled; however, a photographer was needed. Bell took a crash course in photography, purchased equipment, and was hired. Leading the survey was General William J. Palmer.

Their life-long friendship and successful business partnership was founded on a shared vision of building a corporate empire, which included founding the Denver & Rio Grand Railroad, and the towns of Colorado Springs and Manitou Springs. Bell returned to England in 1872 to marry Cara Scovell, and the newlyweds returned to Colorado to build a new home on the banks of Fountain Creek. They called it Briarhurst Manor. It soon became the social center of the community, hosting the internationally famous of the day. By 1876, when Colorado became a state, the demands of their 30 or so businesses were great on Bell and Palmer, but Briarhurst remained a refuge for Bell.

One winter night in 1886, while Dr. Bell was away on business, Cara awoke to a bedroom filled with smoke. The family escaped safely but lost almost all of their belongings. They "went home" to England but returned the following spring to rebuild. Their second, more elaborate home is now Briarhurst Manor. Their grandiose English manor house at the foot of the American Rockies is today one of Colorado's most elegant restaurants.

Drive through the archway leading to the grounds and the finely grained pink sandstone Tudor manor that recalls the architecture and landscaping of an English country house, complete with bubbling creek running through the property. You can tour the mansion before dinner, but the main event takes place in the elegant dining room. Flattering light, leaded-glass windows, and formal table settings reinforce the special-occasion experience.

The cuisine is a contemporary combination of modern American, French, and Italian dishes. Saged Deer Carpaccio with grilled Taos flatbread, sunchoke-olive aïoli, smoked corn salsa, and purple sage pesto melds the flavors of the Southwest and Italy. Bison and Shiitake Skewer is marinated and grilled with an apricot nectar and smoky Pikes Peak honey basting sauce and served with a cilantro-hazelnut reduction. Asiago croutons raft atop the Five Onion and Elk Consommé, gratinéed with Gruyère cheese. And those are just some of the starters.

Some entrées are made of commonly offered meats, game, and seafood, others of uncommon ones. Main courses include Braised Rabbit Dijonnaise, Pan-Seared Orange Duck Breast brushed with five-peppercorn sauce, Broiled Porterhouse of Veal, Blackberry Salmon, Roast Cornish Game Hen, Maroon Bells Trout, North Pork Elk Steak, Iron-Seared Scallops, and Plains Bison Top Sirloin. Two house specialties honor the original denizens of Briarhurst Manor: William's New York Strip and Cara's Steak Diane. The desserts—elegantly presented on a tray—are equally creative, complex, and divine, and a large and source-varied wine list complements the meal.

Briarhurst Manor, 404 Manitou Avenue, Manitou Springs; (719) 685-1864.

The Broadmoor

Few resorts in the nation have been as highly honored for lodging, amenities, and cuisine as The Broadmoor, a Colorado Springs landmark. The land at the base of Cheyenne Mountain that is now manicured golf courses and a sophisticated resort complex started as a dairy farm. In 1890, its owner, a Prussian aristocrat named Count James Pourtales, decided that building lots would be more profitable than dairy cows, and so he formed The Broadmoor Land and Investment Company. To

The Top Toque

Spencer Penrose was raised to appreciate fine cuisine. Like the rest of the men in his socially prominent family, he belonged to a gourmet cooking society in Philadelphia called the Rabbit Club. Penrose decided Colorado Springs needed a similar club and established one in 1911. Meetings were first held in private homes, with the hosts preparing the evening's feast. Later, Penrose built a clubhouse on Cheyenne Mountain with a Cooking Club kitchen. Then he turned his energies to creating The Broadmoor, but never lost his interest in food.

Astonishingly, The Broadmoor has had only four executive chefs since 1918. The first came on board a year before the hotel welcomed its first guest; Penrose hired 29-year-old Louis Stratta from Italy as chef, first to run a camp kitchen to feed construction crew and then for his true life's work, preparing opulent hotel meals once the doors opened.

On June 29, 1918, Stratta prepared an opening banquet of Velouté de Volaille Isoline with celery, ripe olives, and chives; Broadmoor Trout au Bleu with Sauce Exquisite; Braised Sweetbreads aux Perles du Périgord with Petits Pois Nouveau à la Français; Boneless Royal Squab, Potatoes Pasqualine, and Guava Jelly; Salade de Romaine et Cerises; Soufflé Glace Comtesse de Cornet; and Café Filtre. Most of us have to look into Escoffier to see what these fancy French classics might be, but Chef Stratta re-created it in its entirety for The Broadmoor's 50th anniversary in 1968.

Stratta ran his food fiefdom in an authoritarian, even autocratic, fashion, standing on a podium in the enormous kitchen and directing a cadre of sous-chefs, cooks, and helpers with a big chef's knife in his hand to emphasize his point. He inspected every plate before it left the kitchen. When he died in 1976 at the age of 89, after 59 years of service to The Broadmoor and its guests, three years of uncashed paychecks were found in his room at the hotel. He had a roof over his head at the best address in Colorado Springs, and the city's finest food under his control, so he probably figured he didn't need anything else. Stratta's Restaurant, in the spa/golf/tennis building, is named in his honor.

make the subdivision more attractive, he built The Broadmoor Casino and a small hotel. He operated a lot like developers of today's subdivisions, where cleverly furnished and nicely landscaped model homes and other amenities are designed to attract buyers.

The count's ruse didn't work. His project remained beset by financial problems, and the property eventually was converted into a boarding house and girls' day school. In 1916, an entrepreneur from Philadelphia named Spencer Penrose bought The Broadmoor Casino and Hotel and 440 acres of land at the foot of Pikes Peak. Riding the crest of the late-19th century penchant for grandiose plans and a brazen way of fulfilling them, Penrose commissioned a great hotel. Styled like an Italian Renaissance palazzo and massive in scale, Broadmoor Main was completed in a little

Stratta also left a tradition of mentoring. Longevity is not uncommon in The Broadmoor's kitchens, with many people working their way from basic entry-level jobs, often summer spots for students, to high positions in the resort's best kitchens. I think of The Broadmoor as something of a hothouse where Colorado Springs' culinary scene is nurtured. George Ferraro, who was born in Monte Carlo and worked at hotels in France and England before becoming executive chef of a hotel in Texas, visited The Broadmoor on a busman's holiday in 1962. Louis Stratta hired him, and when the legendary chef died, Ferraro took over as executive chef, serving until his retirement in 1981.

Henry "Hank" Trujillo started working at The Broadmoor at the age of 18. After a stint in the navy, where he went to cooking and baking school, he rejoined the resort, first as *saucier* and then as *garde-manger*, two early stepping-stones to higher ranks in the kitchen. Although he was an American of Native American and Hispanic descent, never apprenticed abroad, and never attended culinary school, he worked under European chefs and refined his culinary skills in The Broadmoor manner. By the time he retired as executive chef in 1992, he had been with The Broadmoor for 37 years.

Siegfried "Sigi" Eichenberger from Frohnleiten, Austria, began his culinary career as an apprentice at the Hotel Andreas Hofer in Tyrol before moving up through the ranks at various large hotels in Europe and the United States. Among other distinctions, he led the U.S. teams to numerous medals at the 1984 and 1988 Culinary Olympics. He was executive chef of the Opryland Hotel and owner/chef of Chef Sigi's Restaurant and the Wild Board Restaurant, all in Nashville, before moving on to The Broadmoor in 1992.

Young and full of talent, Chef Sigi, as he prefers to be called, has built on the classical foundations laid by his predecessors and updated them with more contemporary approaches to food and technique. He has introduced more American ingredients, lighter preparations, and more complex presentations on the plate. Yet, if called upon to do so in 2018, he will probably be able to re-create Chef Stratta's opening banquet for the hotel's centennial.

over a year by European craftsmen and artisans who worked around the clock. The turreted main hotel, four wings, and an 18-hole golf course opened on June 29, 1918.

The Broadmoor was more than showiness and grandeur. The well-traveled Penrose also insisted on a European-style level of service that was remarkable in America, especially so in a region that what was not really past its frontier days. By developing The Broadmoor, the Pikes Peak Highway, the Cheyenne Mountain Zoo, and other attractions and purchasing and promoting the Pikes Peak Cog Railway, it is fair to say that Spencer Penrose put Colorado Springs on the map.

Penrose appreciated fine food and fine wines and made sure that both were available to Broadmoor guests. He was, on the surface, an ardent opponent of Prohibition and took part in pro-repeal demonstrations—actions that displayed political correctness of the day. A wonderful 1933 photograph shows him in a two-wheeled cart pulled by a llama with an American flag in his hand and a sign behind him proclaiming, "Help Repeal the 18th Amendment." A millionaire rebel with a Main Line pedigree.

When it came to the fate of his own wines during Prohibition, Penrose was defensive as well as proactive. Thirty-eight cases of wines and spirits, that he had ordered secreted in tunnels that connected the original buildings, were not discovered until 1986. Today, Penrose's personal collection of international vintage wine bottles, some more than 200 years old, is displayed in Bottle Alley connecting Broadmoor Main's lobby with The Tavern. Some of the empties contain Penrose's handwritten notes indicating where the libation was purchased and consumed, and who was with him when he drank it.

Over the decades, The Broadmoor has often been expanded, remodeled, and repositioned—and of course, additional acreage was added. Broadmoor West, with more guest rooms and dining and meeting facilities; a second golf course; a beautiful spa; children's facilities; a dramatic swimming pool; and other enhancements have been built over the years. Most recently, in 2001–2002, the original hotel, Broadmoor Main, was completely renovated and restored. The project took longer than the initial construction, but it was done with such care and concern that time was not a factor. Neither was money. It cost $36 million. The result was all that mattered, and the result is that everything looks like a gleaming rendition of what Penrose's architects and craftsmen wanted, updated in scale and infrastructure but perfect in style and execution.

This is not a hotel book, but to write about The Broadmoor's position at the pinnacle of the Colorado culinary pantheon without putting it into context is to do a disservice to the resort and to the reader. The Broadmoor is a much-honored resort that truly deserves to be called world-class. Many claim it, but The Broadmoor is one of the few that lives up to the claim. It is the longest holder of the AAA Five Diamond and Mobil Five Star awards, the highest given by each organization. The Penrose Room and Charles Court, The Broadmoor's fine-dining restaurants, have each earned AAA Four Diamond and Mobil Four Star ratings and *Wine Spectator* and DiRoNA honors. I can't think of another place that has ranked so high so consistently, and for so long.

Quality reigns in every meal—every dish, in fact—whether in one of the grand restaurants, at the seasonal Pool Café, the casual Café Julie, or Espresso Broadmoor, delivered by room service, or at a banquet for hundreds. The many kitchens staffed by scores of chefs and cooks display a remarkable consistency in taking fine ingredients and preparing them with care, qualities that have been evident since day one. Virtually everything is made in-house, including all the baked goods, stocks, sauces, and pastries. Three restaurants do stand out, and if I were as effusive about them as I'd like to be, given their outstanding food and impeccable service, I'd be writing a whole book about Broadmoor cuisine.

Charles Court

Charles Court, a spacious restaurant in Broadmoor West, is known for its progressive American cuisine. Recently renovated, it offers splendid views of turreted

Broadmoor Main across Cheyenne Lake and twinkling reflections on the water surface. In warm weather, the shaded lakeside terrace is positively magical. In contrast to the opulent décor of the fine-dining restaurants across the way in Main, Charles Court is positively restrained. The restaurant foyer is a little on the glittery side, but once you pass this anteroom's curved partition, the restaurant presents itself as simple yet stylish. Custom-designed chairs upholstered in an understated floral print fabric, muted walls, generously sized tables set with white napery, and live green plants exude a sense of informal elegance.

The restaurant's American-oriented menu showcases The Broadmoor's commitment to American cuisine in general and Rocky Mountain fare in particular. Colorado Rack of Lamb, Charles Court Game Grill, and such innovative seafood dishes as Smoked Salmon–Grilled Ahi Tuna are totally contemporary. From breadbasket to after-dinner drinks, Charles Court serves dinner with unsurpassed style. It is, after all, one of the finest restaurants in one of the finest hotels on the planet.

Charles Court's wine list features more than 800 selections, with bottle prices at this writing ranging from $18 to $5,000. The cuisine is worthy of the high end, but no one will look askance if you order a modestly priced bottle. Winner of the *Wine Spectator*'s Best Award of Excellence and the Santé Award, Charles Court cellar stocks American, French, Italian, German, Australian, and New Zealand wines and vintage depth in Bordeaux, Burgundies, and California wines.

If dinner at Charles Court is great, experiencing the Chef's Table there is even better. When the restaurant and its kitchen were remodeled, special provision was made for a guest-friendly Chef's Table. Pass the glassed-in wine room to a tiled alcove just off the kitchen. The wedge-shaped table, tapering down to the end where the chef demonstrates and describes the evening's feast, can be set for as few as four epicures or as many as 12 or 14. Guests can choose their own menu or allow the chef to create a customized, multicourse meal.

The tapered table, a typically thoughtful Broadmoor detail, allows every guest a clear line of sight. The chefs presiding over the evening make a special point to appear frequently, explaining the dishes, sharing cooking tips, and doing as much tableside preparation as possible. The sommelier presents paired wines with equal care.

The Penrose Room

The Penrose Room is The Broadmoor's most formal and elegant dining room. Located atop Broadmoor South, which adjoins Broadmoor Main, its views toward Colorado Springs and Cheyenne Mountain are spectacular, but I find it hard to tear my eyes away from the gorgeous room and the artful dishes set before my dining companions and me. The thick floral carpeting, fruitwood chairs upholstered in striped fabric, classic tableware set upon cream-colored napery, and crystal chandeliers sparkling overhead combine to make for a romantic ambience. Live dinner music and nightly dancing recall a classier era than our own.

The cuisine is sophisticated, contemporary, and French with updated renditions of traditional gourmet fare and showy tableside preparation of many dishes. The appetizers include Escargots Sauté Bourguignonne and Caspian Sea Petrossian caviar, Maine Lobster, and Caesar salad. Chateaubriand of Beef, Filet of English Dover Sole, Grilled Colorado Rack and Loin of Lamb, and Breast of Muscovy Duck are featured entrées. The Penrose Room also has received numerous honors for cuisine and wine.

Lake Terrace

The Lake Terrace Dining Room on the mezzanine level of Broadmoor Main merits mention here because it is the hotel's original dining room and also because it is one of Colorado's classiest breakfast and brunch spots. Above a central fountain of Italian design is a coffered ceiling with a glass skylight. The room's classic proportions are reminiscent of mansions from the days of F. Scott Fitzgerald and *The Great Gatsby*—which, of course, was Spencer Penrose's era too. Grand windows frame picturesque views of Cheyenne Lake and the Colorado Rocky Mountains, and decorative garden chairs covered in flower-print fabrics surround the fountain.

Traditional breakfasts are served à la carte or buffet-style on Monday through Saturday, with a variety of egg dishes, pastries, pancakes, and continental offerings. The Lake Terrace Dining Room pulls out all the stops for weekend brunch, an extravagant buffet with more than 70 items. Ice sculptures, floral arrangements, and live classical piano music add to the classy scene. This brunch is not for small appetites. It includes prime rib, seafood, made-to-order omelettes, pâtés, Belgian waffles, blintzes, bagels, smoked fish, fresh fruit, and a wide-ranging dessert selection. Some people say that The Broadmoor's Bananas Foster are the best. I say that it's hard to find better food, better service, and a better atmosphere than at any of The Broadmoor's top restaurants.

The Broadmoor, One Lake Avenue, Colorado Springs; (719) 634-7711, (800) 634-7711, or www.broadmoor.com.

The Cliff House

In 1873, when The Inn was built along the stagecoach line between Colorado Springs and the rich mining center of Leadville, people were already coming to Manitou Springs for the town's healing waters. Three years later, Edward E. Nichols bought The Inn, changed its name to The Cliff House, and enlarged it to 200 rooms of remarkable luxury. The hotel boasted electricity, steam heat, a large dining room, elegant ballroom, library, sitting rooms, and even a bridal suite. Genteel guests sat on the shaded porch overlooking the town of Manitou Springs. Life was good.

Run by the Nichols family for seven decades, The Cliff House welcomed seemingly everyone who was anyone in the late 19th and early 20th centuries, particularly such entrepreneurs as P. T. Barnum, Thomas Edison, Harvey Firestone, Henry Ford, Zalmon Simmons, and F. W. Woolworth, as well as President Theodore Roosevelt, who was particularly enamored of Colorado and also felt comfortable in the same sorts of places that captains of industry did.

After the Nicholses sold the hotel in 1948, the grand building suffered a series of indignities. It became military housing, lost an entire wing to make room for a parking lot, became an apartment house of no distinction at all, and finally suffered a damaging fire in the early 1980s. The building was boarded up for 16 years, and the word "eyesore" does not even begin to describe how Manitou Springers felt about the place. But The Cliff House rose literally and figuratively from the ashes. It was renovated and restored to its past and present position of glory and glamour. From its reopening in 1997, fine cuisine has been as much a part of the renewed hotel as luxurious and romantic rooms and impeccable service. It's a real Cinderella story.

Everything about The Cliff House bespeaks a contemporary vision of Victorian grandeur, from the lovely porch, small lobby, and spacious adjacent music and sitting room to the immaculately furnished guest rooms, every one of which feels like a bridal suite. The original dining room is now the ballroom, where special group dinners are served. It is an interior room, but is at once elegant and intimate—and in contrast with many hotel ballrooms, does not feel at all institutional.

The atmospheric restaurant is simply furnished, with sparkling white tablecloths, napkins, and simple plates. By day, light filters in through the large, curtained windows, and in the evening, low lights and candles enhance the sweet, romantic ambience.

Craig Hartman, a nationally renowned chef, was the first to preside over the resurrected Cliff House's kitchen, earning it a quick reputation as a place for truly fine dining and a wine cellar to match. During his tenure there, Hartman represented Colorado at New York's James Beard House and also vaulted The Cliff House to Mobil Four Diamond status and also a *Wine Spectator* Award of Excellence. Hartman returned to the East, replaced in turn by the talented Jordan Wagman and, more recently, the equally talented Deneb Williams, who cut his culinary teeth in food-savvy Washington state. His parents named their baby Deneb after a star in the heavenly Summer Triangle—and he's a star for all seasons on the Colorado Springs culinary scene.

The Cliff House culinary style is "nouveau Continental," with liberal doses of Colorado favorites. The menu changes seasonally but always includes a small selection of appetizers, soups, and salads and eight to 10 entrées. Expect to find Colorado rack of lamb, Black Angus beef, duck, seafood (both fish and shellfish), pork, and poultry. Vegetarian dishes do not regularly appear on the menu, but the kitchen will prepare something on request.

Every dish is a symphony of colors, textures, and flavors. Williams, an enthusiast for seasonal ingredients whenever he can get them, prefers Copper River salmon, which has perhaps the shortest catch season on the planet. One of his inspired preparations calls for poaching the salmon in white peach court bouillon and presenting it on a bed of fiddlehead ferns (also seasonal), jicama, and julienned onion shoots, with a medley of champagne sabayon and Iranian Sevruga caviar with a deep-fried squash blossom perched against the fish.

Full dinners are along that order, but perhaps with dishes featuring heirloom tomatoes, blood orange sauce, free-range veal tenderloin, white anchovies, and other seasonal or specialty ingredients. And oh, did I mention that one of The Cliff House's cheeses might be Salers, a summer cheese from the Cantle Mountains made only between May and September? Seasonal once again.

The Cliff House has become one of Colorado's top places to stay and to dine—whether for a special occasion or simply because it's a place every aficionado of fine food, fine wines, fine service, and fine ambience should visit.

The Cliff House, 306 Cañon Avenue, Manitou Springs; (888) 212-7000, (719) 685-3000, (719) 785-2415, or www.thecliffhouse.com.

Craftwood Inn

Roland Brautwell built the Tudor-style mansion that is now the Craftwood Inn in 1912 as a coppersmith's shop. An Englishman, he was an architect, a builder, and a photographer in addition to being a metalworker. The fireplace hood and some of the lamps are examples of his work—which are reflective of the Arts and Crafts movement—and the stained-glass maidens from Italy and Japan that shine on the front column are souvenirs of his world travels. The former metal shop became one of Manitou Springs' most fashionable restaurants just before the United States entered World War II.

Fast-forward to 1988, when new owners Cris Pulos and Rob Stephens undertook major renovations to bring it up to date. They discovered a secret room in the attic containing artifacts from the past that revealed a rich cultural and artistic heritage of that Arts and Crafts period. The historic building sits on one-and-a-half beautifully landscaped acres, with a covered patio that is heaven on a warm evening. The romantic and elegant restaurant sets each table with fine linens, silver-plated flatware, lead crystal glassware, Royal Doulton English bone china, fresh flowers, and a candle.

Chef Jeff Knight, a master of new Colorado cuisine, performs magic with an unsurpassed selection of meat, seafood, poultry, game, and vegetarian items. Natural ingredients, local where possible, are hallmarks of this cooking philosophy. In addition to the usual beef-chicken-seafood-vegetarian dishes, he cooks such game as elk, venison, buffalo, caribou, wild boar, ostrich, pheasant, duck, and quail.

Want to try several? Order the Combination Appetizer, which consists of Pistachio Pesto Ravioli, Rouladen of Buffalo, Wild Game Quesadilla, and Sautéed Loin of Ostrich, or one of the mixed-game entrées. The Wild Grill combination features North American elk, seared loin of antelope, and braised venison sausage, while Game Birds is a mix of roast duckling, baked stuffed quail, and grilled pheasant sausage. Some of these are seasonal specials, but something comparable is offered at any time of year. Such exotica makes everything else on the menu seem prosaic, but it's not, for even the most ordinary ingredients, when selected for quality, combined creatively, and prepared with care, rise to sublime heights.

Speaking of sublime, there are the desserts. Chocolate Mint Pie, Apple Crunch Tart, Turtle Pie, Bittersweet Chocolate Paradise, Prickly Pear Sorbet, Craftwood Cheesecake, Jalapeño White Chocolate Mousse, and Hazelnut Crème Caramel are the stuff of dessert dreams. The wine list changes frequently but always includes a mix of quality domestic and imported wines, most available by the glass or the bottle.

Whether it's summer sit-under-the-patio awning time or winter, when fires are blazing in the two stone fireplaces and snow is swirling outside, the Craftwood Inn represents an uncommon, and uncommonly delicious, dining experience.

Craftwood Inn, 404 El Paso Boulevard, Manitou Springs; (719) 685-9000 or www.restauranteur.com/craftwood.

Gertrude's Restaurant

Gertrude's, self-described as offering "eclectic dining," is an Art Deco–inspired restaurant in Old Colorado City that serves up an alluring three-meals-a-day menu. Gleaming hardwood floors, plush banquettes, white tablecloths, and paintings by the talented Laura Reilly on the walls combine to make an attractive, sophisticated setting. On each table, you'll find a small lamp, a bottle of olive oil for bread-dipping, and an unopened bottle of wine. Hint. Hint.

There's no Gertrude in the kitchen. It's the province of owner/chef Robert Woolridge Jr., who presents fine vegetarian-friendly, but not vegetarian-exclusive, food. The breakfast and lunch offerings are tasty renditions of favorites. Added to that are such twists as Eggs Gertrude, a vegetarian version of eggs Benedict with avocado and grilled tomato in place of ham and an excellent lemon Hollandaise atop the poached eggs. Lunch features salads, pastas, and sandwiches that come with romaine lettuce, tomato, sprouts, mayonnaise, and Dijon mustard on a choice of spelt, sourdough rye, whole wheat, or baguette, accompanied by flavorful salsa and tortilla chips. Gertrude's serves a sit-down brunch on Saturdays and Sundays, a nice alternative to the ubiquitous buffet format.

Eclecticism kicks in at dinner, when the kitchen really shines. Just look at the first five items on the appetizer menu: wontons, shrimp wraps, Camembert with licorice Merlot, crab cakes, and bruschetta with hummus. Five appetizers, five influences. The house salad is dressed with an excellent balsamic vinaigrette that is also bottled for sale at the restaurant. Most of Gertrude's soups are vegetarian or vegan. Thai vegetable pasta and mushroom linguine, the two top pasta offerings, are in that mode too. Entrée choices are greatly international: Tex-Mex Enchiladas, Chicken and Sausage Choux with cream sauce and served over linguine, Tuscan Seafood Stew, Jamaican Jerk Pork Chops, and Chimi Churri, a filet mignon marinated, grilled, and served with a spicy Argentinean sauce and sautéed tomatillos—a top choice of non-vegetarian patrons. The menu suggests a wine for each entrée.

Gertrude's is essentially about fresh healthy food, which leaves room—or provides an excuse—for a sinful dessert, including its house-made ice cream. Among the baked goods, the house specialty is Chocolate Oblivion, a particularly outstanding version of this popular flourless cake.

Gertrude's Restaurant, 2625 West Colorado Avenue, Colorado Springs; (719) 471-0887 or www.gertrudesrestaurant.com.

La Petite Maison

This restaurant was established in 1975 in a vintage cottage in Old Colorado City. Inside the blue frame building, the décor is on the Mission end of the Victorian era, the ambience is country French, and the service is careful and caring. Pink walls flatter the complexion, white table linens flatter the food and allow it to be the star, and the pretty patio with white market umbrellas shading the tables is simply a feel-good place.

Chef Espiridion Moreno, who previously cooked at Chez Pierre, Primitivo, and the Blue Star, took over La Petite Maison's top-toque position in 2002, when the highly regarded Chris Adrian left to establish 32 Bleu, a club with fine-food overtones. Though La Petite Maison has had the image of being a French restaurant, Adrian let a lot of contemporary American influences into her menus. Moreno kept some of these touches but let the menu evolve into his own style, going more toward lighter, more Asian, more Southwestern preparations, especially at lunch. Other dishes remain in the contemporary Franco-American orbit.

Curried Shrimp Crêpes, served as a luncheon entrée with Snow Pea, Mango Salad, and Banana Chutney and as a dinner appetizer with just the chutney, remains a house specialty. A trio of green salads, each with something different—one with fresh mozzarella, peaches, and prosciutto; another with duck confit, dried fruit, walnuts, and blue cheese; and a third with pecan praline, Mandarin oranges, and feta—come with different versions of vinaigrette.

Shrimp cocktail with avocado relish, tuna in a broth infused with lemongrass, and a Southwestern-style crab cake are Moreno touches. Black Angus filet or another generous cut of beef, Colorado rack of lamb, free-range chicken breast, duck, a couple of fish, and a vegetarian pasta—each beautifully conceived and excellently sauced and accompanied with an appropriate starch and/or vegetable—grace the seasonally changing dinner menu. You might find a red wine reduction with this course, shallot *jus* with that, an heirloom tomato with another entrée.

Pastry Chef Summer Poulsen prepares lusty classics. Baklava, chocolate mousse cake, pecan pie, chilled lemon soufflé, or traditional French crème brulée and *pots de crème* lead the sweet parade. There's also a cheese option, perhaps a fine Camembert with grilled apple and lavender honey from Provence—that fruit touch so long a characteristic of La Petite Maison.

The wine list comes from a wide geographic range. Preliminarily divided into reds and whites, it is then subdivided into wines from California, France, Germany, Italy, Spain, and "the New Worlds" (Idaho, Oregon, and New Zealand). California and France are represented in the greatest depth.

La Petite Maison, 1015 West Colorado Avenue, Colorado Springs;
(719) 632-4887 or www.restauranteur.com/maison/index.htm.

Rio Bistro

Rio Bistro opened in Pueblo's vibrant, exciting, and innovative Historic Union District in 2002 with a stylish interior, a high ceiling, gleaming granite-topped bar, and tall-back chairs upholstered in mattress ticking that fits right in. This business operated with style, humor, and good food adds to the critical mass that hopefully will help all South Union enterprises succeed.

Rio Bistro is run by Karen Briggs and Sally Greer, sisters who epitomize long-term sibling cooperation. Back in 1978, they founded a wholesale food company in Denver. Tired of the rat race, they relocated to La Veta in 1994 to open a restaurant and cooking school. After another seven years, they were ready for some place bigger than La Veta yet smaller than Denver. They had been going to Pueblo to buy things they couldn't find in La Veta. Bingo!

They moved in Pueblo in 2001 and shared a position operating the Kid Rock Café at the Sangro de Cristo Arts and Conference Center. Their next enterprise was their own restaurant. Rio Bistro, with just 28 seats, is located in a space that locals still think of as a coffee shop called Perch's. The atmosphere is casual, the menu is of the chalkboard variety, the food is very good, and the prices are reasonable.

Preparation is done in a sprightly contemporary manner with equal attention given to eye appeal and taste. Among the starters, you'll often find steamed mussels, fresh shrimp cocktail, perhaps steamed artichoke, and a soup and salad. There is usually a choice of no more than about seven entrées—typically three meats or poultry, three seafoods, and a pasta or other vegetarian offering. All change frequently. One summer menu, for instance, included lovely broiled scallops with a hint of basil, extra-thick pork chops that had been marinated in beer, and orange roughy with a light crabmeat stuffing.

Rio Bistro's most distinctive dessert offerings are its signature Ice Cream Martinis, combinations of rich ice cream and a selection of liqueurs served in chilled metal martini glasses. Like the menu itself, the wine list is small—and like the food, the wines are selected for variety and are priced for affordability.

Rio Bistro, 126 South Union, Pueblo; (719) 253-0126.

Steel City Diner & Bakeshop

The Steel City Diner, directly across from Pueblo's handsomely restored railroad depot, is not a diner at all, but rather a small restaurant of charm and sophistication located in the Historic Union District, the most beguiling commercial area in this former steel town. By appearance, it is a pub, with gleaming dark wood paneling, black-and-white floor tiles, and mellow jazz on the sound system. By the palate, it is all about creative cuisine, prepared with passion and skill.

The restaurant is run by husband-and-wife team Richard Warner and Mary Oreskovich, both Culinary Institute of America graduates. He is originally from Chicago; she from Pueblo. He is the chef; she does the pastries. Both are remarkably good at what they do, and Pueblo—a city far more fine-food-deprived than Chicago—is fortunate to have them.

Ninety-five percent of the soups are vegetarian, and all are house-made. Warner uses Colorado products whenever possible. When he offers a meat dish, it is from grass-fed, hormone-free cattle and pork from the San Luis Valley or natural Colorado lamb. Starters (here, as in other trendy restaurants, called Small Plates) come from such different directions as the Asian-inspired Coconut-Encrusted Deep-Fried Prawns with Ginger-Plum Dipping Sauce, Crispy Southwestern Quesadillas, and Mixed Organic Field Greens with Maytag blue cheese, pomegranate vinaigrette, hazelnuts, and julienned vegetables.

Meat entrées like Colorado rack of lamb and cinnamon-cured, slow-roasted center-cut pork loin are each accompanied by a potato specialty. Chicken and fish suit lighter appetites, and meatless dishes include such standout pastas as the house-made Roasted Butternut Squash Ravioli with Marsala sauce, piñons, and lemon-rosemary aïoli.

Sublime seasonal fruit tarts, crème brulée, exceptional cakes, and other rich creations emerge from Oreskovich's oven. She makes her own ice cream using organic eggs and milk products. If you want an old-fashioned treat with a new twist, order her Steel City Diner Root Beer float, made with Thomas Kemper premium root beer and house-made vanilla ice cream, and if you just want a sweet nibble as you're strolling around the historic district, pop into the Steel City Diner and Bakeshop for a cookie or a brownie.

Steel City Diner and Bakeshop, 121 West B Street, Pueblo; (719) 295-1100.

Vita Bella Ristorante

Ballads recorded by Italian crooners wafting from sidewalk speakers might lure you into Vita Bella. Or, you might first stop and look through the large windows. There, in Pueblo's beguiling Historic Union District, is a stylish and spacious restaurant done in a monochromatic scheme of buff-colored tile floors and muted stucco walls. The back wall displays a mural of an Italian hill town, and if you continue to the way back, you'll see another mural—this one of one of the owner's grandfather's vineyards. Fresh flowers and a bottle of herbed olive oil grace every table.

Vita Bella's menu is more predictable than adventurous, but owners Lisa Trani and Marty DeJoy serve the kinds of Italian dishes Puebloans go for. The restaurant, which opened in March 2001, also has a children's menu, and with moderate prices, it is a good choice for a family that wants something better than Pueblo's ubiquitous chains.

You'll find good renditions of standard pasta shapes and sauces, plump layers of lasagna, enduringly popular eggplant Parmigiana, a nice selection of *panini* and pizza, and such well-loved desserts as spumoni and tìramisu. Vita Bella also does equally popular Italian dishes featuring seafood and chicken, and some items are more American than Italian, such as spinach and artichoke dip on the appetizer roster and fried shrimp. "Piccata" is a traditional method of preparing veal. Most American adaptations, for those who prefer not to eat veal, use white-meat chicken or perhaps turkey, but Vita Bella uses orange roughy filets.

You can enter Vita Bella from Victoria Street, where you've heard the Italian singers, or from the attractive courtyard in back. The latter, with its classical-shaped fountains, is quite the scene in summer. You can also enter the bar and the restaurant's smoking section from the courtyard. This has a nice side effect: if you prefer to avoid that scene altogether, simply come in the front door and stay in the restaurant section, with nary a whiff of cigarette smoke coming your way.

Vita Bella Ristorante, 310 South Victoria Street, Pueblo; (719) 543-2020.

Iron Chef Colorado Springs

The principle behind the TV cooking cult show *Iron Chef* has leapt from the Food Network to Colorado Springs. In March 2002, the Hospitality Expo at The Broadmoor hosted a competition called the Champion de Cuisine. Eight of the area's leading chefs faced off in an elimination tournament. The combatants—I mean, contestants—had one-and-a-half hours to create three or four original dishes using a secret ingredient that was unveiled in the last minute.

Chefs entering the starting gate were Chip Johnson of Briarhurst Manor, Brent Beavers of Sencha, John Broening of the now-shuttered Primitivo, Paul Jensen and Michael Kline of The Broadmoor, Christian Bowie of the Villa at Palmer Lake, James Africano of The Warehouse, and Christine Adrian then with La Petite Maison. Paul Jensen was the 2002 victor.

Tickets to watch the action were just $5. For information on or tickets to any future events, call (719) 633-3821 or (719) 785-8135.

Events

A Salute to Escoffier

January—The newest event on the Colorado culinary calendar is the first annual weekend-long Salute to Escoffier, orchestrated by the award-winning culinary team at The Broadmoor (see page 163). Launched in January 2003, the event honors Auguste Escoffier, the legendary French chef who worked with prominent hotelier César Ritz in the late 19th century and validated French cuisine with his groundbreaking book, *Le Guide Culinaire*. Escoffier, called the father of French cuisine, is also credited with bringing culinary arts to the professional level now enjoyed in restaurants today—and no one is better equipped to honor his contributions than the pros at The Broadmoor.

Plans are afoot to enhance future Salute to Escoffier programs to include a Friday-night wine tasting and additional classes, but during the first running, it started with relative modesty. It kicked off on a Saturday afternoon with A Taste of The Broadmoor, a splashy cooking demonstration showcasing traditional recipes from Broadmoor chefs.

The Saturday-evening highlight is the Escoffier Grand Buffet, a lavish and free-flowing dining extravaganza in the recently renovated Broadmoor Main building's Center Lounge, Pompeian Room, Lake Terrace Dining Room, Crystal Room, and Main Ballroom. In addition to fab food and wine, the event includes live entertainment and dancing. The Escoffier weekend winds down with a traditional Sunday brunch in the Lake Terrace Dining Room.

The basic Salute to Escoffier package includes all culinary events and feasts, as well as Saturday-night lodging. Friday and/or Sunday night can easily be added. When the Salute to Escoffier is expanded, the packages will be adjusted as well. The event benefits the Colorado Restaurant Association's education fund and The Broadmoor's Culinary Training Program and Scholarship Fund.

Reservations for and information about A Salute to Escoffier Weekend are available from The Broadmoor, (800) 634-7711, (719) 634-7711, or www.broadmoor.com.

Colorado Springs Wine Festival

March—This two-part festival benefiting the Colorado Springs Dance Theater is hands-down the most significant food and wine event in southern and south-central Colorado. This swanky annual event relocated in 2003 to The Broadmoor. It consists of a Friday night grand tasting with silent auction and a Saturday night dinner with live auction. Patrons can attend the event à la carte, going to the tasting, the dinner, or both, or go whole hog and make it into a full culinary escape that includes overnight accommodations at The Broadmoor.

As few as three and as many as six winemakers from one place, such as a California wine region or Oregon, pour at the grand tasting, and additionally 30 or so wine distributors are represented with their lines. About two dozen local restaurants set up tasting tables, providing samples of everything from hors d'oeuvres to desserts. In the past, these have included La Petite Maison, Primitivo, The Cliff House, Briarhurst Manor, and Blue Star, as well as Par Avion, a gourmet grocery store. The grand tasting makes for great grazing. Most guests are dressed in business attire or light dressy clothes for this stand-up, wander-around, and chow-down event.

Everyone pulls out all stops for the festive, black-tie-optional dinner the following night. The sumptuous five- to seven-course dinner is paired with participating winemakers' wines and many courses with specific varietals. The exquisite dinner is always prepared with care and served with panache.

The live auction has rare and collectible wines, dinners, and travel and lifestyle experiences up for bid, but it shines also because the auctioneers are sensational. The Colorado Springs Wine Festival brings in either David Reynolds or the incomparable Fritz Hatton, who also does the Napa Valley Wine Auction. Both men are from California and have reputations for being entertaining as well as knowledgeable, and listening to them is worth the price of admission, even if you don't bid on a thing.

Tickets are sold through the Colorado Springs Dance Theater, 7 East Bijou, Colorado Springs; (719) 630-7434.

Taste of the Nation

May—Colorado Springs is the local branch of the all-volunteer fundraising organization that supports hunger relief efforts as part of Share Our Strength, one of the nation's leading antihunger, antipoverty organizations. The local chapter hosts a food event that now draws 600 guests. For background on this worthy food festival, see page 58 in the Denver chapter. Locally in the Springs, it is held at the Sheraton Colorado Springs. As with all Taste of the Nation events, it is a wonderful opportunity to sample some of a community's most interesting foods, wines, and microbrews at a reasonable price—and for a most worthy cause.

For information on the date and location of future year's events, log onto www.tasteofthenation-coloradosprings.org.

Chile & Frijoles Festival

September—When people whom I talked to while writing this book asked me how I could cover so many facets of food and wine in just one year, I replied, a bit flippantly, that I didn't feel obligated to attend every chili cook-off in the state of Colorado. Still, Pueblo's annual Chile & Frijoles Festival—even if they insist on spelling it *chile* like the South American country—is remarkable for its size and its southern Colorado roots.

The festival was created in 1995 to celebrate the harvest of Pueblo-area chilies with authentic food, music, arts, crafts, and, of course, fresh and roasted chilies amid the atmosphere of an 1840s Spanish *mercado*. It usually takes place the third weekend of September on Historic Union Avenue. There, you can watch tortillas made in a traditional adobe oven and buy fresh-roasted chilies to take home.

Sports, art exhibits, and entertainment (including a jalapeño-eating contest) fill the schedule, but the heart of this free event remains the chili competition. Categories include red and green chili, *frijoles,* and salsa, entered in commercial/professional and nonprofessional/amateur divisions. You can submit your own best recipe or just come and enjoy the festival fun—as do more than 20,000 people every year.

Information is available from the Greater Pueblo Chamber of Commerce; (719) 542-1704 or www.pueblochamber.org/tourism/chile&frijoles.htm.

March of Dimes Star Chefs

October—The Star Chefs gala is a major fundraising effort for the March of Dimes (see the entries in the Denver and Boulder "Events" sections). The Colorado Springs event is usually held at The Broadmoor, with food by such local chefs as Aaron Bignell of Mona Lisa's, John Broening of the late Primitivo, and Lawrence Johnson of Briarhurst Manor.

March of Dimes Chapter Columbine Division, 421 South Tejon, Suite 236, Colorado Springs; (719) 473-9981 or www.marchofdimesco.org.

Retail

Cunningham's Market

This light, breezy downtown store is more than a mere deli. It is also a gourmet-foods shop, a restaurant, and a meat and seafood market that meets just about every basic food need with verve and style. Scott Cunningham, an émigré from the East Coast, decided to open a New Jersey–style deli in Colorado Springs. What he had in mind was a place that makes good Eastern pizza—thin crust, good sauce, choice of toppings—and a few other selected typical foods from Italian delis back there. What he ended up with was a specialty food store, a café, and ultimately a restaurant.

Floor-to-ceiling shelves stocked with gourmet foods, a handful of tables to accommodate the eat-in trade, and a pastry counter dominate the entrance to the store, the latter stocked with tempting pies, cakes, individual portions of tiramisu, tarts, and other sweets, and *ciabatta, rustica,* and baguettes, all made onsite. The deli counter makes to-order sandwiches, that Jersey-style pizza, salads, or more elaborate meals to eat in or take out—straight deli-format. Quality sliced meats and cheeses, breads, pâtés, olives, roasted peppers, and all manner of other palate-pleasing treats are attractively offered.

The entire back is devoted to foods that need to be refrigerated or frozen. Positively gorgeous individual portions of to-go foods, largely but not exclusively Italian, include beautiful double-meat lasagna, eggplant Parmesan, chicken Parmesan, barbecued ribs and chicken, and an array of salads. The baked dishes are so neatly sectioned into one-portion servings that the item you take home will be as eye-appealing as they are in the case. Beyond are super-fresh steaks, ground beef, pork, ribs, sausage, plain or seasoned chicken, skewers with various combinations of ingredients, and seafood. The large freezer holds both house-made creations and some from other quality purveyors, ready to take home and heat up. Cunningham's offers first-rate frozen appetizers, soups, sauces, and some sweets. On the gourmet-grocery shelves is a great assortment of American and imported goods, such as mustards, vinegars, oils, pasta, sauces, and condiments both from well-known and exotic brands.

In early 2002, Cunningham expanded into the adjacent store, blessedly replacing a Taco Bell. At lunch, the restaurant is more a gourmet café, with cooks stationed at two windows to create customized sandwiches, salads, and pasta combinations on the spot for lunchtime crowds. It's fast food efficiency with chef-made restaurant-quality taste. Dinner has been an on-and-off proposition, with concepts and chefs in flux since the store opened. Check its current situation if you're interested.

Cunningham's Market, 10 South Tejon Street, Colorado Springs; (719) 444-8686.

Ethnic Food Stores

Food stores from various ethnic traditions are scattered about the Colorado Springs area. These include Latino markets, Asian groceries, and specialty markets with imports from Europe. Some are only food stores, while others also offer prepared foods to take out, and perhaps to eat in a deli or restaurant set-up. Here are a few to explore:

Arirang Oriental Supermarket, 3830 East Pikes Peak Avenue, Colorado Springs; (719) 573-5743

Han Yang Oriental Supermarket, 3835 East Pikes Peak Avenue, Colorado Springs; (719) 570-1287

Hyundai Oriental Market, 217 North Academy Boulevard, Colorado Springs; (719) 597-0244

India Bazaar, 3659 Austin Bluffs Parkway, Colorado Springs; (719) 264-6995

Mollica's Italian Market & Deli, 985 West Garden of the Gods Road, Colorado Springs; (719) 598-1088 (see page 181)

Piemonte Italian Gourmet & Pasta Shop, 6530 South Academy Boulevard, Colorado Springs; (719) 540-2311

Saigon Oriental Market, 3744 Astrozon Boulevard, Colorado Springs; (719) 390-7454

Seoul Oriental Grocery Market, 2499 South Academy Boulevard, Colorado Springs; (719) 570-9999

Tamales El Carreton, 2031 East Bijou, Colorado Springs; (719) 632-9688

Taste of India, 4820 Flintridge Drive, Colorado Springs; (719) Colorado Springs; (719) 598-3428

Thai Orchid Market, 2487 South Academy Boulevard, Colorado Springs; (719) 550-9390

The French Store

When I was cruising along South Tejon for food finds, I saw a large sign over a storefront on a cross-street that proclaimed: The French Store. "Either it sells naughty lingerie or good French food," I thought and made a short investigative detour. To my joy, it was the latter. This no-frills shop stocks the fanciest French foods and fixings, either imported from France or totally French in style. Many of these products are available nowhere else in the Springs and in few other places in Colorado. The French Store, which opened on Valentine's Day 2000, is truly a gift of love to Francophiles and connoisseurs of French foods.

The shop sells classic specialties, ready-to-eat or as an ingredient, including impeccable *pâté de foie gras* and lesser pâtés, goose fat, goose *rillettes,* Provençal sausages, and imported cheeses. The imports aren't always from distant places. La Brea breads from California are ultra-artisan breads made French style, with fermented dough rather than yeast. It stocks an abundant selection of vinegars, which is good to know if you are particular about your salads. You'll also find olive oils, mustards, sauces, madeleines, chocolate truffles, and other sweet confections.

French cookbooks, breadbaskets, and all manner of tableware, linens, and serving pieces round out The French Store's inventory. But why is it all here? Co-owner Desirée Lewis, a Francophile who lived in California before returning to her native Colorado, explains, "I opened it because I couldn't find the things I liked. I got spoiled in California." Now she is spoiling Coloradans with French authenticity.

The French Store, 107 East Pikes Peak Avenue, Colorado Springs; (719) 473-2342.

Grindelwald Market

See Old Heidelberg Pastry Shop and Grindelwald Market on page 156.

Harvest Market

What was once known as Cunningham's Market West (see page 178) is now Harvest Market. The switch occurred in May 2001, when Derek Wall, a young California entrepreneur, decided that a gourmet food store in Colorado was to his liking and bought one of Scott Cunningham's two stores.

The gourmet deli underwent a change of ownership and name, but the philosophy remains similar. The store still carries fine imported cheeses, pasta, olives, gourmet condiments, natural meats, charcuterie, fresh seafood, and chef-made prepared and frozen foods, and this location remains convenient for residents of the northwest side of town, who stop by to dine in, take out, or buy ingredients to prepare at home.

Harvest Market, 4935 Centennial Boulevard, Colorado Springs; (719) 599-7747.

Michelle's Chocolatier and Ice Cream

John and Lois Michopoulos started making ice cream and fine confections in Colorado Springs in 1952, giving their business a Frenchification of their family name. In fact, there wasn't a Michelle, since the couple had four sons. Half a century later, the family still runs the business, which has now expanded to three locations. This is the place to go for locally made candies, which the family calls "kettle-fresh chocolates," for a special occasion—or just because they are so good.

Among the varieties, you'll find chocolate-covered creams, butter creams, caramels, nougats, crisps, butter almond toffee, Maraschino cherry cordials, honey almond nougats, English toffee, honeycomb and peanut butter crisps, and nuts (whole almonds, pecans, cashews, and Brazil nuts) dipped in milk and dark chocolate. Their signature candies include Gremlins, Imps, and Sprites (soft caramels topped, respectively, with pecan halves, salted Spanish peanuts, or roasted almonds dipped in milk chocolate). Their legendary chocolate-dipped truffles are offered in Amaretto, orange, rum, cappuccino, all milk, and hazelnut dipped in milk chocolate; Chambord, pistachio, mint, and chocolate mousse dipped in dark chocolate; and raspberry dipped in white chocolate. Michelle's also makes various wonderful fudges, brittles, and crisps—and their ribbon candies, made for Christmas, are a seasonal specialty.

Sandwiches, light meals, and fresh ice cream and special toppings, also available to take home, combine into great sundaes. On a warm day, find an outdoor table, watch the world go by, and enjoy.

Michelle's Chocolatier and Ice Cream, 122 North Tejon, Colorado Springs; (719) 633-5089; and 750 Citadel Drive East, Colorado Springs; (719) 597-9932. A metro Denver store is at Arapahoe Station, 6880 South Clinton Street, Greenwood Village; (720) 482-8390. The toll-free telephone order number is (888) 633-5089, and the website is www.michellecandies.com.

Mollica's Italian Market

This deli has been selling Italian food products and prepared foods since 1987, when it was established by Dom, Antoinette (Toni), and Jerry Mollica. This classic family enterprise is known for its Italian sausage, made from a recipe handed down by Toni's immigrant grandfather, Tony DeAngelis. Shelves and glass cases are stocked with house-made and prepared pastas and sauces, imported meats and cheeses, olives, pepperoncini, oils and vinegars, roasted peppers, spices, and many more old-country delicacies.

Tables in the middle of the deli are covered with red-and-white checked table-cloths for a satisfying sit-down meal. Italian and American sandwiches fill many a belly at lunch, but Mollica's dinner gives the place its rep as an authentic expression of Southern Italian culinary culture as practiced in the United States. On the simple menu are penne, a second pasta of the day, manicotti, lasagna, tortellini, and a choice of meat and meatless sauces, served with house-made soup or salad (order Mollica's own Italian dressing), and bread. Whole or half-portions are available, and if you order a half, you'll have room for the house-made cannoli or cheesecake. Wash it down with a glass of Chianti, top it off with an espresso, and you'll feel yourself transported in space and time to Italy—or at least, a Little Italy neighborhood in an East Coast city or perhaps Chicago.

Mollica's Italian Market and Deli, 985 West Garden of the Gods Road, Colorado Springs; (719) 598-1088 or www.restauranteur.com/mollicas.

Par Avion

Par Avion's bright red awning serves as a beacon for Colorado Springs foodies. This upscale specialty market with the aviation name (*par avion* is French for "by air" and is used to denote air mail) sells a matchless assortment of gourmet foods. Jim Sebastiani, one of just a handful of people in the United States (only five at the time of his induction, he reports) to attain the Guilde des Fromagers' cheese equivalent of serious sommelier status, and his son, Dart, established a specialty cheese store in 1996. They quickly added charcuterie and then began carrying other items on any gourmet cook's shopping list.

The modest 2,300-square-foot store—once a Circle K convenience store—is loaded with 300 cheeses, 40 to 50 varieties of fresh seafood on any given day, and an astonishing 3,000 gourmet packaged items, including close to 40 dried-pasta lines.

This makes it the Pikes Peak region's leading retail purveyor of outstanding and super-fresh meat, seafood, produce, and quality charcuterie, as well as packaged gourmet items literally by the thousands.

Along one side of the store is what the Sebastianis call the "wall of cheeses." Tall, glass-door refrigerated cases that once held Circle K's soft drinks now showcase Par Avion's array of cheeses, including all the quality favorites such as Brie, Camembert, Parmigiano-Reggiano, Gruyère, chèvre, Gouda, and so forth, from well-known and obscure domestic and foreign sources. Par Avion carries artisanal cheeses, some exotic imports from Europe rarely found anywhere west of the Hudson River.

Par Avion carries natural meats and poultry, including Golden Valley beef from Idaho, DuBreton pork from Canada, and all-natural chicken, but this is not nearly as unusual in the mountain West as the exceptional seafood. The store lives up to its name, directly air-freighting seafood fresh from the Atlantic, Pacific, and Gulf coasts and Hawaii. "Our fish was at auction yesterday and in our case today," says Dart Sebastiani.

This store also carries such seasonal seafood specialties as Copper River salmon from Alaska and pompano from Florida, and such exotica as Virginia black sea bass and Ipswich steamers. Par Avion flies in live Dungeness crabs and cooks them on site, rather than the usual precooked and packaged delivery. What is not feasible to carry fresh, Par Avion stocks in frozen form—including unusual sausages, super-size shrimp, *lutefisk* from Scandinavia, *haricots beurre* from France, beef and poultry stocks of various kinds, and even caviar.

The gourmet food products run the gamut from tinned fish to dessert items. In addition to the aforementioned pastas, Par Avion stocks a grand assortment of rice and risotto, olive and other oils, balsamic and other vinegars, tomato products, sauces, seasonings, condiments, and myriad other products. A small pastry counter displays lovely cakes and pastries. So extensive is their inventory, crammed into such modest square footage, that you truly have to see it to believe it.

Par Avion, 4510 Oro Blanco Drive, Colorado Springs; (719) 597-4545.

Pueblo Hotel Supply Company

This stucco-front restaurant and hotel supply house on the west side of downtown Pueblo sells functional kitchen utensils and tableware at hard-to-beat prices. You'll find an abundance of plates, platters, flatware, mugs, glassware, tongs, stockpots, oven grills, cutlery, pots, pans, casseroles, bakeware, and more. If you want to look cool in the kitchen, here's a place to get a chef's coat. The company likes to say that it sells "restaurant equipment and bar supplies from bottle openers to walk-in coolers; glassware to commercial stoves; salt shakers to popcorn poppers." And it does. At this writing, its inventory contains 10,372 line items from 237 manufactures and vendors. When you've cooked yourself into a stupor and your kitchen into a mess, this is even a place to find Diablo Carbon Kleen, a powerful agent that restaurants use to remove baked-on grease.

Pueblo Hotel Supply Company, 430 West Fourth Street, Pueblo; (719) 542-8857, (800) 566-7068, or www.restaurantsupplypueblo.com.

Seabel's Gourmet Shop

Locals go to this cute downtown Colorado Springs shop for gourmet products for themselves, or very likely, for someone else, since Seabel's is especially known for its wonderful gift baskets. You can select a themed basket for holidays or other occasions or buy gift-basket components à la carte, as it were, and have one customized. Seabel's stocks fine imported and domestic cookies and crackers, coffee, tea, pasta, scone mix, bread dippers, olives, syrups, preserves, spices, chips, and other snacks. The store also sells tableware, linens, and gift items.

Seabel's Gourmet Shop, 22 South Tejon, Colorado Springs; (719) 473-6709.

Also, Union Avenue Historic District, 105 West C Street, Pueblo; (719) 543-2400.

Seabel's lines are available at the Wooden Spoon, Pueblo Mall, 3541 Dillon Drive, Pueblo; (719) 542-2400.

Sparrow Hawk Ltd.

The whimsical caricature of a merry chef stands on the sidewalk during business hours to mark the entrance to Sparrow Hawk Ltd. It carries everything for the kitchen—in quantity and variety unsurpassed in Colorado Springs and unmatched in most kitchenware stores elsewhere in the state. Cookware and bakeware, kitchen appliances, and all manner of accessories fill the floor-to-ceiling shelves and hang from the walls and ceiling.

As I rambled through the narrow, maze-like aisles, I saw Forgiato utensils (spatulas, scoops, spoons) and other brands too, lots of teas and teapots, three shelves of peppermills, adorable egg whisks "sitting on" eggs, knives and peelers, serving stuff, wooden spoons, bowl scrapers, fondue pots, kitchen timers, and flatbread makers. There's glassware (lots of glasses, salad bowls, pitchers, plates), woodenware, mixing bowls, coffee makers, cookbooks, canisters, and baskets (for decoration and for bread), as well as many brands and types of pots and pans.

Appliances. Rolling pins. Boards of wood, marble, synthetics. Molds. Thermometers. Chinese steamers and woks. Lots of baking stuff, including three-tier cooling rack for pies. Forms in all shapes—used for everything (mousse, terrine, even Jell-O). Chantal bakeware. Grills and griddles. Whisks hanging from pot racks on the ceiling. Jillions of gadgets. Mixing spoons and bowls. And the list goes on. I can't imagine any home cook needing or wanting anything that doesn't appear somewhere in this wonderful filled-to-the-rafters kitchenware store.

Sparrow Hawk Ltd., 12 East Bijou, Colorado Springs; (719) 471-3235.

Spice of Life

Spice of Life is a cheerful place to go for a light breakfast or lunch, or for unusual coffees and teas, bulk spices, and hard-to-find gourmet food lines. It's both a deli/café and what owners Michael Conejo and Doug Lewis call "an ingredients emporium." Lunch always features a wonderful soup of the day, and its sandwiches, built with Woodys Continental Pastries' breads, and meats imported from Italy or by Saag's brand. Add the Spice of Life's from-scratch coleslaw, and you've got a terrific sandwich.

Floor-to-ceiling shelves are filled with quality coffees and teas, a whole wall of organic herbs and spices, exotic rices and beans, jams and preserves, cordials, and such interesting lines as Vineyard glazes, Brianna dressings, Torani syrups, and other gourmet brands. Most interesting are Conejo and Lewis's own specialties, such as a commendable replacement for Zaatar. This flower-based Israeli seasoning to their knowledge is not imported into the United States and is wonderful in Middle Eastern dishes. Locals come by just to stock up on the Cajun Spice Mix and Grandma Lela's Salsa, a perfectly balanced herb and spice mix that makes a first-rate seasoning for salsa, fajitas, *pico de gallo,* or even dip. Lela was Michael's mother's mother—and the recipe was hers. Doug developed a to-die-for chipotle mayonnaise, and Michael also does his own tamale sauce.

In addition to quality meats and cheeses, the refrigerated cases hold imported *tortas* from Italy (in flavors such as sun-dried tomato with or without pesto, sage, and Gorgonzola), imported olives (try the feta-stuffed green olives for a rare treat), and other unusual items. If you're heading up Pikes Peak on the Cog Railway or perhaps driving up and planning to picnic, Spice of Life customizes excellent box lunches; call by 10:00 A.M. and your selection will be ready when you swing by.

Spice of Life, 727 Manitou Avenue, Manitou Springs; (719) 685-5284.

Wines

Coaltrain Wine and Liquor

Back in 1981, Jim Little and Peggy McKinlay opened a little neighborhood liquor store north of downtown. Showing what was clearly impressive foresight, the couple determined that wines would become the drink of choice for many customers and began stocking high-end wines and liqueurs. Coaltrain Wine and Liquor was way ahead of the curve. Two expansions later, Coaltrain is still ahead of the curve—and Colorado Springs wine-lovers have responded. Wine sales now account of 70 percent of its business.

The store's location, in a hollow just off I-25, won't blow you away. Neither will the basic brick box that passes for architecture. But walk in the door, turn right, and prepare to be blown away by the huge assortment of wines—on shelves, on low displays, on high displays. Jim Little, who is football-player-size and not little at all, spent a decade as a restaurateur before opening Coaltrain. He is particularly interested in the relationship between the food his customers serve and the wines he sells. If you ask him which are his favorite wines, he'll probably say, "All of them."

Little and McKinlay have found people with similar passions about wine and wide-ranging knowledge about it for their sales staff. The most impressively credentialed member of their sales team at this writing is a graduate of the University

WINES

of Colorado at Colorado Springs and Peter Kump's New York Cooking School who worked at Sherry-Lehmann (New York's first prestige wine specialist and arguably still America's foremost wine/spirits retailer) *and* also was auction coordinator for Sherry-Lehmann and Sothebys fine-wine auctions.

Coaltrain's is known for the depth and breadth of California, Washington state, French, Italian, German, South American, South African, and Australian wines. There are Wines of the Month and extra values of the last bottles of wines. Sparkling wines—including rare champagnes—are also available, and the store was an early Front Range retailer of Colorado wines and remains a supporter of the state's growing wine industry.

Coaltrain sells various corkscrews, decanters, and nifty one-bottle wooden crates that serve as gift boxes, and organizes frequent winemaker dinners, often with The Cliff House in Manitou Springs (see page 168). The store also has done interesting special promotions, such as offering coupons good for a two-ounce sampling of a Wine of the Month paired with a complimentary appetizer at the Stagecoach Inn, also in Manitou Springs. Wines are good for the spirit—and also for the Colorado Springs Dance Theatre, and Coaltrain is a prime mover behind the annual Colorado Springs Wine Festival to support it (see page 176).

Coaltrain Wine and Liquor, 330 West Uintah, Colorado Springs; (719) 475-9700 or www.coaltrainwine.com.

Vintages Wine & Spirits

This lovely little specialty shop, located on the most vibrant and interesting block of South Tejon, has carpeting underfoot and walls lined with hardwood shelves on which an impressive array of wine bottles are displayed. In all, Vintages exudes the elegance of an upscale wine bar. It carries many familiar labels, wines from lesser-known wineries, and also some hard-to-get cult wines—a select group of high-quality, high-priced California wines, usually big reds, made in very small quantities by a handful of wineries. Cult or not, California wines are, predictably, important at Vintages, but the store also carries a commendable selection of French, Italian, and other imported wines.

Owners Eric and Michael Collins and their staff taste every wine they sell. The boutiquey shop's focus is on "hand-selling," to guide customers through the array vintages. Members of Vintages Wine Club get unusual and hard-to-find wines. There are three levels of wine-of-the-month membership, and the program can be customized with a choice of just one important wine—collectable or for a special occasion—or the maximum number of interesting wines suitable for everyday consumption.

Vintages selects a Wine of the Week and frequently hosts both tastings and wine classes, usually at Jack Quinn's restaurant just down the block. The wine classes, often led by Darby Gould of the University of Colorado at Colorado Springs and a noted local wine expert, focus on excellent values in moderately priced wines. The store also carries a limited assortment of spirits, including such rarities as absinthe and Williams with the pear in the bottle.

Vintages Wine & Spirits, 9 South Tejon Street, Colorado Springs; (719) 520-5733.

Recipes

Colorado Springs epicures miss Primitivo, which closed in August 2002. But it lives on in memories and through recipes. Executive chef John Broening used to offer this colorfully festive salad in summer, when Colorado corn is at its sweetest.

Corn and Beet Salad with Lime Vinaigrette

2 ears corn
1 medium red beet
1 tablespoon diced red onion
2 tablespoons chopped fresh cilantro leaves
3 tablespoons crumbled feta cheese
Lime Vinaigrette (below)
salt and freshly ground pepper, to taste
12 sprigs watercress

Shuck and boil corn. Carefully cut kernels from the cob and set aside. In a small saucepan, boil beet until tender. When cool enough to handle, peel, dice, and set aside.

Lime Vinaigrette
juice of 1 lime
pinch of sugar
salt and pepper, to taste
⅓ cup extra-virgin olive oil

Whisk together lime juice, sugar, salt and pepper. Slowly whisk in olive oil until emulsified.

To assemble, toss corn, beet, onion, cilantro, cheese, and Lime Vinaigrette together. Season with salt and pepper to taste and toss again. Arrange salad in a bowl and garnish with the watercress. Serves 6.

This seafood-and-pasta combination created by Briarhurst Manor executive chef Lawrence A. Johnson is a rich dish served in a rich atmosphere.

Sautéed Sea Scallops with Linguini
¾ to 1 pound fresh linguini
2½ pounds large sea scallops, sliced in half
¼ cup olive oil

1 tablespoons minced garlic
1 tablespoon minced shallot
1½ cups sliced shiitake mushrooms
1 cup diced red pepper, preferably Fresno
½ cup diced yellow bell pepper
1½ tablespoons flour
1½ cups heavy cream
¼ cup dry white wine
½ cup freshly grated Manchego cheese
lemon juice to taste
kosher salt
ground black pepper
minced chives for garnish
seasoned bread crumbs for garnish

Heat water for linguini. Assemble all ingredients for scallops and their sauce. Cook linguini according to package directions. While the pasta is cooking, prepare the scallops.

In a large sauté pan, heat olive oil over medium-high heat. Stir in garlic, shallot, and mushrooms, and cook for about one minute. Add scallops and peppers, and sauté until the scallops are starting to brown. Stir in flour; cook for about one minute. Add heavy cream, white wine, and Manchego cheese. Reduce heat and a cook on low heat for about one more minute. Stir in a few drops of lemon juice, and add salt and pepper to taste. Spoon the scallops and sauce onto cooked and drained linguini; sprinkle with minced chives and seasoned bread crumbs. Serve immediately. Serves 6.

Beautiful breakfasts are a hallmark of a stay at The Broadmoor. Whether you have breakfast in a dining room or patio overlooking the lake, or order from room service, you can order this healthy granola parfait to start your morning—or you can make it at home.

Sunrise Parfait
1 cup water
½ cup granulated sugar
¼ cup orange juice, fresh squeezed
12 fresh strawberries, sliced
1 large banana, sliced
2 cups vanilla yogurt
4 tablespoons granola
4 sprigs fresh mint for garnish

In a small saucepan over medium heat, cook water, sugar, and orange juice until mixture is reduced to a syrup consistency. Remove from heat and allow to cool. Pour over sliced strawberries. In 4 red wine or parfait glasses, evenly distribute strawberries and bananas. Place ½ cup yogurt in each glass and top with a tablespoon of granola. Garnish with mint and serve. Serves 4.

FORT COLLINS

Fort Collins

This northern Colorado city, set where the rolling plains start crumpling up against the mountains, would seem to be a good candidate for an abundance of interesting and innovative food. The thriving college town, home to Colorado State University, is growing fast, including an immigration of newcomers from far-flung corners of the country, a scenario that normally provides a ready clientele for quality restaurants. Its historic downtown is attractive and lively, boasting many locally owned businesses. Other than the fact that Loveland and Fort Collins will soon be cojoined by housing developments springing up between them and gobbling up farmland and grazing land, Fort Collins still lies in a largely agricultural area, providing doorstep availability of fresh products.

Yes, Fort Collins would seem to be a good candidate as a center of creativity and excellence in the food and wine areas. It is—and it isn't. It is because some truly interesting purveyors are located there. The city has several fine bakeries, fine two artisan cheese makers, a mushroom farm, a top cookware and kitchenware store, a fabulous wine bar, and even a place where you can bottle your own custom-made wine.

Yet for a city of its size—some 120,000 and growing—it has had problems supporting top-tier restaurants. There are many burger-and-beer pubs, pizzerias, Tex-Mex eateries, and Asian restaurants, many of which offer good, reliable food at moderate prices. Chain restaurants abound, but fine dining establishments have had a harder time making it. In what was heartbreaking for Fort Collins foodies, an ambitious French restaurant morphed into an all-purpose Italian eatery a few years ago and then faded away completely. A few shining eateries have hung on—and some have even thrived. If you like fine food and wines to match, patronize these establishments—or they'll never make it.

Bakeries

Babette's Feast

Babette's Feast was a French film whose best scenes centered on food, and it's also a French bakery and café in a shopping center on the east side of Fort Collins. Its owners adopted the name partly to honor the movie but mostly because baker Babette Wilson has the right moniker and skills to do the name justice. The kitchen of Babette Wilson's café turns out the foods she grew up with in a family of food lovers in Paris: baked breakfast goods, soups, quiches, salads, and especially pastries and other sweets. She learned to cook and bake from her mother and began a catering business in 1995. In December 2001, she opened this eastside bakery and café.

This sliver of a store between a Safeway and the local AAA office is small and precious. One of the reasons the café area is small is that the kitchen takes up a lot of space. The café walls are painted gold, with stencil work and judiciously placed mirrors as simple, elegant little decorative touches. Just six tables and a small counter accommodate customers for breakfast or lunch, with two more outside under the building's arcade. Along the right wall are the gleaming pastry cases.

Specialties include *tarte tatin, tarte bourdalouse, tarte bourdalouse chocolat,* chocolate *marquise* with or without berries, pear or apple in puff pastry, mixed fresh fruit tartlette, cheesecake, raspberry Napoleon, *pain au chocolat,* chocolate-dipped shortbread, coffee or chocolate éclair, coffee and chocolate *réligieuse.* Mousses—as common as chocolate or as unusual as passion fruit—have their adherents too.

Babette's meringues come plain or flavored and include chocolate meringues, raspberry meringues, and huge almond versions topped with slivered almonds. Where else in northern Colorado will you find perfect sugar-dusted *fraisiers* or *framboisiers?* And under a glass bell atop the pastry case are the madeleines, those biscuit-like cookies that are so perfectly French, baked plain or flavored with orange peel or orange and chocolate.

Babette's small bistro menu includes her lunchtime favorites. There are usually four soups: French onion, vegetable, cream of mushroom, and her rendition of *pistou,* a Provençal bean soup with pesto. Entrées are chicken Dijon with mustard sauce or Provençal with vegetables, beef *bourguignonne, coq au vin,* and an unusual French version of shepherd's pie. Salads are excellent, and sandwiches come on a baguette or other authentic French bread. Quiches include classic quiche Lorraine, tomato and basil, chicken with sweet peppers and mushrooms, Brie and mushrooms, smoked salmon, and the flavorful combination of blue cheese, bacon, and leek.

Babette's Feast, 1514 East Harmony Road, Suite B1, Fort Collins; (970) 223-0172 or www.babettesfeastcatering.com.

Maggie McCullough's Breadshop

This cheerful bakery and café across the parking lot from the mammoth Foothills Mall is friendly and inviting, with a black-and-white checkerboard floor, rose pink walls, bright oilcloth-topped tables, and miscellany of side chairs constitute the seating area for those who want to eat there. An assortment of hutches, armoires, and other antique pieces display gourmet food products and a good selection of cookbooks.

Many customers walk right by the seating area for the bakery counter to pick up loaves of delicious artisan breads of various types to take home. Yeast breads include French baguettes, *bémi*-cheese, French white, and farm bread, all baked every day. *Epi* resembles fused baguettes. *Padina* is made only on Monday and challah only on Thursday. Daily sourdoughs are country white, *levain,* rosemary, black olive, white wheat, multigrain, Jewish rye, and *levain* baguette, with or without seeds. Hefty two-pound loaves of two additional ryes, European and walnut, are baked on Friday, and pumpernickel comes out of the oven on Tuesday. Combination breads include ciabatta, rustic baguette, and cinnamon pecan baked daily, and *miche,* only on Thursday.

Everyday desserts include rich fruit bread pudding, beautiful fruit flans, and mini-tìramisus that are little towers of flavored mascarpone. Also emerging from the ovens are marbled chocolate meringues, raspberry coconut bars, rocky road brownies, walnut brownies, fruit pies, filled croissants, muffins, and coffee cakes. For special occasions, Maggie's artistic and memorable cakes are the peer of the finest specialty pastry shop. Several are visual standouts. The romantic Princess Cake features white *génoise* with raspberry filling, whipped cream, and marzipan topped by a rose. Jean's Package looks like a stack of gift-wrapped boxes tied with edible ribbons. The Porcelain Poppyseed Lemon Cake is dome-shaped, rather like a rimless Derby hat, topped with fondant. There is also a small cheese case, stocked with petite Basque, Gruyère, montchevré goat cheese, vintage Irish cheddar, Stilton, *cambozola*, and FolEpi baby Swiss. Great Midwest jalapeño morel and leek jack suit those who want flavored cheeses. Cheeses from award-winning Bingham Hill and MouCo are popular with customers who make a point of supporting local cheeseries.

Maggie McCullough also offers Continental Sausage's brats and wieners, plus More Than Gourmet tubs of *démi-glace* and other sauce bases. Shelved gourmet goods include Bella Cucina pestos in cute squat jars and sweet toppings, Farmhouse and L'Oublio olives, Davina roasted peppers, Stonewall Kitchen chutneys and sauces, and a baker's rack filled with various oils, dressings, and mustards. For great baked goods, a satisfying breakfast or lunch stop, or a commendable assortment of gourmet food products, Maggie's is a good choice.

Maggie McCullough's Breadshop, 116 East Foothills Parkway, Fort Collins; (970) 282-8460.

Olive Street Bakery

This no-frills bakery and café just off College Avenue sports simple peach-colored walls, fluorescent lighting, a linoleum floor, and a handful of tables that remained from the many years that it was a Fort Collins classic called the Old Town Pastry Shop. When Lut and Olivier Campé purchased the bakery from Patrick and Winona Tillard in late 2002, they weren't eager to redecorate immediately but chose to get down to the business of baking and let their delicious output speak for itself—just as their predecessors had. The Belgian-born Campés kept the most popular items from the Tillard era and added some specialties of their own. They renamed the business both to reflect its location and also as a play on Olivier Campé's first name.

The freshly baked breads and elegant pastries shine like jewels from the plain cases and simple shelves. Olivier graduated from culinary school in Belgium where he baked before becoming pasty chef at Mirabelle in Beaver Creek (see page 273). There's not a sweet tooth that can't be seduced by his sensuous cream puffs; chocolate or vanilla éclairs; fruit or vanilla Napoleons; lemon or fresh seasonal fruit tarts; cakes; mocha, chocolate, or fruit mousse; *fraisiers;* cheesecakes, or *croix de Savoie,* a custard-filled puff pastry dusted with powder sugar. For a smaller nibble, buy cookies individually or by the dozen. Chocolate macaroon, cinnamon crispy, large or mini *palmiers*, butter cookies, and plain or chocolate meringue cookies are just the ticket.

Breads from the Old Town era include baguettes, Parisian and *Epi* loaves, white loaves, wheat with or without walnuts, sourdough plain, with walnuts or with walnuts and olives, sun-dried tomato, seven-grain, pumpernickel, pesto, farmers, onion, herb, and mozzarella-cheddar.

Olive Street Bakery has fine plain and filled croissants and other outstanding baked goods for breakfast. Lunch-time offerings include filled croissants, *croque monsieur* sandwiches, quiches, individual pizzas, and a soup du jour served with a freshly baked roll. If you're having a party, you can order savory or sweet bite-size pastries to glaze the festivities with a sophisticated French touch.

Olive Street Bakery, 120 West Olive Street, Fort Collins; (970) 482-9875.

Cooking Classes

The Cupboard

Northern Colorado's best and most complete cookware store also leads the way in cooking instruction with two-and-a-half-hour weeknight classes, held in the store's demonstration kitchen. They focus heavily on the cuisines of other nations and are often taught by natives of those countries and sometimes by local or visiting chefs. Classic Indian Cuisine; Italian Seafood Appetizers; Fish I, II and III; Turkish Cooking; Sushi; American Regional Fusion; and Tamales were on recent schedules,

Classes on a particular technique, such as Sauces and Sautéing, or a particular approach to food and cooking, such as One-Course Meals, are also offered. The classes—hands-on, demonstration, or a combination—are limited to 14 participants. Additional participation classes directed at the "junior chef" aged 11 and older introduce kids to the mysteries of the kitchen. Wine pairings and wine tastings are limited to 20 students and last three hours. Each student leaves class with a collection of recipes and a coupon for 10 percent off nonelectric, nonsale purchases within two weeks.

The Cupboard, 152 South College Avenue, Fort Collins; (970) 493-8585 or www.thecupboard.com.

Dining

Braddy's Downtown Restaurant

In this stylish downtown restaurant, which opened in late 2001, some of Fort Collins' most interesting meals are served. Abstract paintings are sparingly and perfectly placed on pastel walls. The lighting is soft. The table settings are as white and clean as a new canvas, waiting for strokes of the artist's brush to bring them to life. The woodwork is blond. A large stone fireplace and aspen trees "planted" in a room divider serve as decorative accents to remind diners that Braddy's is, indeed, a Colorado restaurant. The total effect is one of a light, airy, and inviting place to dine.

Co-owner and chef Don Braddy moved to Fort Collins in 1968 when he was seven years old. He attended graduate school at Colorado State University, studying creative writing and cooking on the side. The restaurant business eventually beckoned more powerfully than ultimately finding his words on the printed page. Cooking at various Fort Collins restaurants, he often mused, "If I had my place, I'd do it this way. . . . "

Braddy's vision—a mix of his own poetic, artistic, and creative calling and an answer to what was long a real need in the local restaurant scene for fine dining—has resulted in what is usually referred to as "the best restaurant in town." It offers the combination of carefully prepared food made from fresh ingredients, caring service, and an inviting atmosphere. The menu changes seasonally. It does not overwhelm in size or complexity, but it is carefully balanced, using fresh ingredients, local whenever possible, to create a distinctive style. For want of a better phrase, Braddy characterizes it as Modern Western American. That means more than Bingham Hill and MouCo cheeses and Hazel Dell mushrooms. It means Colorado trout, lamb, and poultry, American in foundation with clean and simple preparation and excellent flavors and presentation.

A recent fall menu, for example, included Trout Fritters, Shrimp Relleno, and Avocado Shrimp Roll. The section featuring lamb, beef, and tuna carpaccio; beef, tuna, or salmon tartare; oysters on the half shell, and seviche is called Raw Stuff. The fact that it is on the menu at all demonstrates how far Fort Collins palates have come, while the warning, "High risk! Intense flavor! Big fun!" shows that all patrons are not ready for such prime-time dishes.

Entrées are all beautifully presented and well-sauced. Examples of standbys with Chef Braddy's delicious twists are Bacon-Wrapped Filet Mignon with Cabernet Sauvignon Jus; Pork Tenderloin with Roasted Corn, Green Chiles, and Tomatillos; elk medallions, marinated in Jack Daniels and served with a mushroom garlic sauce, and Beef Tournados, the restaurant's signature entrée, are sublime. You'll also find seafood, poultry, other game, and a vegetarian selection or two.

The desserts are simple, and all (except a plate of imported cookies) are house-made. Chocolate mousse, New York–style cheesecake, crème brulée, or fresh fruit with cream are predictable—and predictably good. Chocolate and lemon soufflés can be preordered for Monday through Thursday evening dinners—and I applaud any kitchen that will take the time to whip up this ethereal creation. The offering of Mixed Nuts, Chocolate, and Moldy Cheese is another example of how Braddy's puts itself out for the how-far-diners-have-come segment of the clientele.

The wines come from Australia, California, Chile, Colorado, France, and Germany. Braddy's offers the option of wine pairings with all courses and schedules periodic wine-maker dinners. Frankly, restaurants of this caliber are not uncommon elsewhere in Colorado, but Braddy's has broken a culinary barrier in Fort Collins, and local epicures are fortunate for the addition.

Braddy's Downtown Restaurant, 160 West Oak Street, Fort Collins; (970) 498-0873 or www.braddys.com.

Fish

Fish serves, well, fish. There are finny fish, shellfish, sashimi-style, and fish soups and chowders. You can select raw fish from the small retail market and have it cooked to order (grilled plain or with a suite of Southwestern accompaniments, blackened, poached with sauce, Parmesan-breaded and baked, or cornmeal-crusted and pan-fried) or take it home to cook yourself. Brown paper covers the tabletops, and a small stash of crayons is available in case you are so inspired by the fish theme that you want to draw your own instead of filling yourself up with the flavorful bread that comes to the table by the half-loaf.

The starters include soups that change daily but might include Fisherman's Stew and New England Clam Chowder, each hearty enough for a meal (especially when you use bread to mop out your bowl). The menu is fairly small, but there's a catch of the day that expands it from what appears on the printed page. Seafood comes in predictable dishes (shrimp scampi, fish and chips, sesame-seared ahi tuna, and the like) and in unexpected ones (Parmesan trout, curry stir-fry, and blackened steelhead sandwich, as some examples). The fact that there is now a restaurant serving fresh seafood in this part of the state borders on the thrilling.

Fish serves four specials at lunch, six on weeknight evenings, and up to eight or nine for dinner on weekends. An informal atmosphere (remember the brown paper); a small and modestly priced wine, beer, and beverage list; and breads and desserts from Maggie McCullough's round out this place for, well, fish

Fish, 150 West Oak Street, Fort Collins; (970) 224-1188.

Jay's Bistro

This sleek and spare space, furnished with stylish wooden chairs, a wall of wines, a double-sided fireplace, and a swirly wrought-iron room divider, is the most recent incarnation of the twice-relocated Jay's Bistro. It is a congenial place for good food, good drinks, wine, and live jazz. The wine list covers the gamut, from workmanlike selections from the big California wineries to expensive imported champagnes with price tags well into three figures. Wine flights of three two-ounce tastings are poured for those who like to compare and contrast. Some customers come in just for some of the best martinis in town.

If you had to tag the food with one culinary word, it would have to be American—but one word won't do, for it is American with a contemporary fusion twist. Seafood is showcased with Jay's hot and cold oyster bar. There's a nod in the general direction of Spain with a tapas selection. The restaurant also serves cooked-to-order "pan-roasted" soups, a unique and innovative concept. The lunch options of fine sandwiches and salads indicates Jay's aim to please all palates. Also pleasing are the moderate prices at lunch, dinner, and Sunday brunch, making it a well-priced, locally owned Fort Collins favorite. In fact, it has been voted in the Taste of Fort collins as the best for gourmet food as well as the best special-occasion restaurant.

Jay's Bistro, 135 West Oak Street, Fort Collins; (970) 482-1876.

Nokhu on Canyon

Named after the Nokhu Crags, a distinctive rock formation near Cameron Pass west of Fort Collins, this downtown restaurant contrasts a soft atmospheric dining space with the stainless-steel and brightly illuminated edginess of an open kitchen. The comfortable lounge and bar area and a private dining room in a former bank vault provide more contrast within Nokhu's walls.

Theo Ott, the chef and a co-owner, inserts influences from distant lands into his cuisine. Among the first-course offerings, for example, fresh oysters are served with a lemongrass-garlic-ginger sauce. Citrus-Cured Salmon Nori Rolls come with a thick soy sauce and a shallot-wasabi dipping sauce. Local mushrooms from Hazel Dell form the basis for Shiitake Mushroom Egg Rolls, served with lemongrass and soy sauces.

Entrées cover the seafood/meat/poultry/vegetarian spectrum. On a recent menu, Maine scallops were dusted with *ancho* powder, seared, and served with black-rice pancakes, lemongrass, and saffron *crème fraîche,* combining an American mollusk with the flavors of the Southeast and Asia. Duck was smoked, flavored with *poblano* pepper and jasmine spiced tea, and served with Brie and sherry-orange vinaigrette. A hefty flank steak of buffalo came with peanut *mole* and roasted garlic mashed pota-toes. Colorado rack of lamb was crusted with cilantro, garlic, and brandy and served with five-spice butter sauce and forbidden rice, both derived from the Chinese kitchen. Ott likes to add flavors of the southwest, Asia, and other traditions to main-stream ingredients.

Desserts are also creative adaptations on old and new themes. Nokhu's S'mores are a sweet, moist spin on the old campfire favorite, and Flourless Chocolate Cake is a rich, elegant version of a currently popular dessert. The wines include domestic and imported vintages. Aware of the challenges that have beset ambitious Fort Collins restaurants, Ott provides additional incentives to dine there, especially early during midweek. At this writing, Monday features a very reasonable *prix fixe* dinner that includes two glasses of wine, and on Tuesdays, bottles of wine are half-price.

Nokhu on Canyon, 211 West Canyon Avenue, Fort Collins; (970) 493-5777.

Pulcinella Ristorante

When I was growing up in Connecticut, a sophisticated treat was to go to Little Italy in New York, where waiters were wannabe (or former) opera singers who serenaded as they served. This Fort Collins restaurant, which dishes up some of the city's best Italian fare, replicates that experience with live opera every second Tuesday evening between September and May. It's a particular cultural kick to couple cuisine and a favorite art form in the country of the cuisine's origin.

Pulcinella is also a trip across a cultural gap from the mountains and plains of Colorado to the coast of southern Italy. With white walls, tables simply set with white napery, and an imported fountain for ambience, it "feels" Italian. Antonio Race and his wife, Mary, opened Pulcinella in 1991. Race (pronounced rah-chay) hails from the small town of Miliscola north of Naples. His father was a lifelong fisherman and farmer and his mother a traditional Italian housewife, meaning that he brought home fresh ingredients that he caught or harvested and that she was a fabulous cook. She practiced her art on her family, feeding five on the bounties of the sea, as well as with local produce, meats, cheeses, bread, fresh pasta, and, of course, wine. Her meals were made with love and eaten in conviviality. Young Antonio learned about the joys of culinary expression from his mother. What is now cutting-edge is in his bones and in his blood—and the high prices, for Fort Collins, derive from some entrepreneurial strain in his gene pool.

Pulcinella's primarily Neapolitan menu changes seasonally. The items aren't particularly unusual—Caesar salad, seafood antipasto, prosciutto and melon, gnocchi, lasagna, pastas of various shapes and bathed in various traditional sauces, veal, rack of lamb—but the execution is excellent. Pulcinella's tasting menu, called Veritá Artistica Culinaria, translates roughly to "the true art of cuisine" and features tastings of four main courses and dessert, with or without paired wines.

The wine list, which runs to 45 pages and some 800 wines, starts with a quick course on how to decode Italian wine labels. You'll need it—as well as the guidance of your server. Another way to familiarize yourself with the wines of Italy is by attending some of the very moderately priced wine education evenings, with appetizers, every Friday, currently at 5:00 P.M., or the wine-pairing dinners on the last Sunday of the month between September and May.

That epic wine list details fine wines from Abruzzo, Basilicata, Campania, Emilia Romana, Friuli Venezia Guilia, Lazio, Liguria, Lombardia (Lombardy), Marche, Molise, Piemonte, Puglia, Sardegna (Sardinia), Sicilia (Sicily), Toscana (Tuscany), Trentino Alto Adige, Umbria, and Veneto—all organized by region. Some are represented in great depth, other more exotic regions with just a wine or two. You'd be hard pressed to find a larger selection of Barberas, Barbera blends, and Chianti Classicos anywhere. Chef Race has put his imprimatur on some of his favorites. Pulcinella also offers a good selection of California wines, but I say order Italian, for "when in Rome. . . . " Or perhaps, as aficionados of excellent Italian food and wine might say, when at Pulcinella's. . . .

Pulcinella Ristorante, 2100 West Drake Road, Fort Collins; (970) 221-1444 or www.pulcinellaristorante.com.

Events

Wine Fest

May–June—Wine Fest, an annual event raises money for Disabled Resource Services. Like the Super Bowl, each Wine Fest is identified by Roman numerals. Wine Fest XIX, which took place in 2002, for the first time had a wine-maker dinner appended to it. Traditionally, 300 to 400 wines from are poured, including such Colorado wineries as Augustina's Winery, Bookcliff Vineyards, Canyon Wind, Carlson Vineyards, Colorado Cellars, J. A. Balistreri Vineyards, Stoney Mesa Winery, Trail Ridge Winery, and Two Rivers Winery. The event also features a silent auction and a raffle.

The University Park Holiday Inn hosted the fest's first wine-maker dinner, which featured selections from the Robert Mondavi Winery paired with food provided by Wild Oats Market and local purveyors such as Canino's Italian Restaurant, Maggie McCullough's Breadshop, and Nico's Catacombs. Given that it was the first dinner held in tandem with the Wine Fest, its format could change in future years.

For tickets or information, contact the Disabled Resource Services; (970) 482-2700 or www.fortnet.org/winefest.

A Taste of Fort Collins

June—This annual event, established in 1997 to benefit Special Olympics, is held at the Colorado State University Oval. It is part food fest and part family festival—a little like Denver's Festival of Mountain and Plains...A Taste of Colorado (see page 60), but on a far smaller scale, drawing 20,000 people on a single day.

Twenty-five local restaurants form a food court that gives the festival its theme, as well as an eaters' selection of favorite eateries. In addition to the modest admission fee, restaurants offer sample portions for a reasonable price (just $3 per item in 2002) and encourage festival goers to cast their votes based on a substantial sampling. Attendees who vote are eligible for prizes, and the winning restaurants earn a "Chef's Cap" roving trophy and a year's worth of bragging rights. The 2002 popular-vote winners from the food court were Panino's, Best Overall; Fish, Best Local; Star of India, Best International; Woody's Wood Fired Pizza, Best Hand Held Fare; Most Creative, Island Grill; Most Friendly, Taj Mahal; Carraba's, Tastiest; and Ben & Jerry's, Just Desserts. The Coors Beer Garden and the Ciao Vino Wine Pavilion provided food to go with the drink.

A fun feature added in 2002—and of considerably more interest to food televiewers—was the Taste of Fort Collins inaugural "Steel Chef" competition. Local chefs competed before a taste panel and the public for the title of top northern Colorado chef. During three rounds, they created several main courses from mystery ingredients presented minutes prior to each round. Fort Collins' version of *Iron Chef,* the popular cult program on the Food Network, debuted with Don Braddy of Braddy's Downtown; Hiroshi "Nimo" Nimota of Nimo's Sushi Bar & Japanese Restaurant; Brad Rossini of Pulcinella Ristorante; and Rick DeHearder and Mike Seaman, the team from Jay's Bistro; and others. Rossini was named the 2002 Steel Chef Champion. Other Taste of Fort Collins attractions include a children's fun zone, a juried art show, and live entertainment.

A Taste of Fort Collins; information from (877) FC-TASTE (328-2783) or www.atasteoffortcollins.com.

Retail

City Drug

This downtown pharmacy features, among other nondrug and nonhealth items, a couple of shelves crammed with well-priced gourmet foodstuffs, many imported. Chocolates come from Valar, Lindt, Stonewerck, and Yves Fleurs. Gourmet flavored vinegars include Hengsterberg and Cuisine Perel, which makes wonderful Late Harvest Riesling and Blood Orange vinegars. I also spotted Krüegermann pickles, mustards from several makers, and Oetker baking products, but I have a sense— not confirmed by the cashier, who didn't seem to know much about these food products—that the store carries some items regularly and others when they are available. If you find such imported condiments and sweets irresistible, stop by while downtown and see what's displayed. The good shelves are right near the front door.

City Drug, 101 South College Avenue, Fort Collins; (970) 482-1234.

Colorado Cherry Company

For locally made jellies, jams, marmalades, and similar categories of preserves and flavored ciders, stop at this unusually specialized store outside of Loveland, south of Fort Collins. Cherry flavors, alone or in combination with other fruits, predominate, but you can also get both commonplace and exotic fruit preserves. What can be more common than peach, strawberry, or blueberry—and what can be more unusual than dandelion, pomegranate, or prickly-pear cactus? Wild chokecherry, neither the most commonplace nor the most unusual flavor as well as indigenous to this region, is considered the house specialty.

Other condiment categories carried by the Colorado Cherry Company include chutneys, honeys, mustards, olives, pickles, relishes, and assorted syrups. The store also sells wonderful house-made ciders by the glass or the jug and freshly baked pies, whole or by the slice. Take the lot home, or find a riverside table for a sweet little picnic on the spot. The Colorado Cherry Company is open daily during the summer tourist months and weekends from Labor Day through Christmas.

Colorado Cherry Company, 1024 Big Thompson Canyon Road, Loveland; (888) 526-6535 or (970) 667-4141.

The Cupboard

When The Cupboard opened in Fort Collins' Northern Hotel building in 1972, it was little bigger than a cupboard. The 750-square-foot space displayed some pottery, some baskets, and some kitchen gadgets. Over three decades, owner Carey Hewitt, who bought out his original partner in 1979, relocated the store to its current site on South College and expanded and remodeled it several times.

The Cupboard now carries one of Colorado's best selections of cookware, kitchen appliances, gourmet foods, table linens, and cookbooks—and yes, there's still plenty of space for decorative items like pottery and baskets, and kitchen gadgets are perennially big sellers. Near the front of the store the most tempting items are displayed—those shiny pots and pans, the gadgets hanging on a wall, the gleaming case filled with gourmet chocolates, and some of the colorful pottery and tableware that so many customers fall in love with at first glance. There's a magnetic pull to the place, as you are drawn through the labyrinthine aisles to find the store's other treasures. More cookware. Shelves of coffeepots, espresso makers, coffee grinders, tea kettles, and teapots—and a whole wall of teas to go with them.

Roam around some more, and you'll find a huge display of Henckels knives. A section filled with such name brands of cookware as Calphalon, Chantal, Cuisinart, Multiclad, CopperTri-Ply, Joyce Chen, and Lodge Cast Iron. Colorful and artistic pottery from eastern Europe. Glassware. Pewter. Woodware. Tabletop items. Bar accessories. The treasures unfold shelf by shelf. Some decorator accessories, all on the unusual side. Seasonal specials at holiday time.

Gourmet foods take up a whole, significant—and rather magnificent—section near the middle of the store. A substantial made-in-Colorado subsection showcases food products from all over the state, including Aspen Leaf Gourmet sauces and marinades, Bear Meadow products, and many other made-in-Colorado lines. The Cupboard also carries honey from Jerry Dittrich (whom locals know as "the bee guy") and toffee from Vern's Toffee House (which locals consider simply the best rendition of this confection around).

The demonstration kitchen in the rear of the main floor was added in 1994 for cooking classes (see page 191). Upstairs, in the so-called "loft" area—the mezzanine, really—are baskets, linens, and a fabulous selection of cookbooks. Two thousand or so titles comprise a veritable cornucopia for people who devour cookbooks for recipes or for the sheer pleasure of it.

More than inventory, however, The Cupboard is about service. Most of the staff have been working for Hewitt for at least five years, and loyal customers view them as a resource for food, cooking, and serving advice. One long-time manager said of her boss, "Carey started out modestly. He learned retail on the job himself, and now new hires learn from him. His role is now a conductor, not of a junior high band but of a full orchestra." When it comes to food- and cooking-related products or subjects, The Cupboard is Fort Collins' concert hall.

The Cupboard, 152 South College Avenue, Fort Collins; (970) 493-8585 or www.thecupboard.com.

The Tea Table and Miss Attie's Tea Room

The Fort Collins areas boasts two tea rooms—one strictly retail and the other serving afternoon high tea and light meals. Since it opened in late 2001, The Tea Table, a small shop on a side street just off College Avenue, has brought out all the tea lovers in Fort Collins—in fact, in a good swath of the northern Front Range. Laurie Bricker, a nutritionist by training who is herself hooked on teas, established the store to supply what she herself had found difficult to obtain locally.

The small quaint shop is filled with teas, traditional and electric teapots, tea cozies, tea cups, tea infusers, tea measures, antique tea spoons, linens, and all the other accoutrements of formal tea service, including such English delectables as jams, jellies, butters, preserves, both orange and lemon curd, and clotted cream cookies. Whip up some cucumber sandwiches, add scones, and other baked goods from one of the fine local bakeries—and you can virtually replicate the flavors and rituals of an English tea.

One wall is devoted to about 100 teas: black teas, green teas, and herbal teas. Most are available as loose teas, the way connoisseurs prefer them, and some are in tea bags, which purists think of as "starter teas." New and featured teas are written on a board. The Tea Table's Tea of the Month Club is a must for teaholics. Sign up and you'll receive three ounces of a different tea on the first week of every month of the year. You can select from the black, green, or herbal tea plan; the Adventure Plan with a preselected rotation of different teas, or the Surprise Me Plan, which also is a rotation of different types of tea, but you won't know in advance what you'll be receiving. I've never thought of tea drinking as an adventure type of activity, but the Tea Table's Adventure and Surprise Me Plans almost have me convinced that it can be.

Miss Attie's Tea Room is located in a spacious, antique-filled 1910 four-square in Loveland that serves as the perfect backdrop for traditional afternoon tea. The owners, Linda and Jim Otterman, have the tea ritual down cold. Tea is steeped and poured at tableside into lovely porcelain cups on Wednesday through Saturday afternoons, accompanied by a beguiling afternoon menu that includes a selection of loose teas, delicate sandwiches, beautiful scones and jam, and pastries.

Miss Attie's also serves lunch, early dinner, and Sunday brunch. The menu is small but varied with a soup of the day, a couple of salads, several sandwiches, and moderately priced hot entrées offered at lunch; entrée salads, meat or seafood selections, and pasta dishes are available at dinner. Many customers eat there just for the changing but luscious cakes and pastries. Miss Attie's also sells tea sets, new and antique cups and saucers, a great selection of fine teas, books on tea, pretty stationary and gift cards, and tea bric-a-brac of all sorts.

The Tea Table, 105 West Mountain Avenue, Fort Collins; (970) 221-5520 or www.theteatable.com. Miss Attie's Team Room, 1140 North Lincoln Avenue, Loveland; (970) 278-9757 or www.missatties.com.

Wines

Wilbur's Wine and Spirits

This busy purveyor of wine, beer, and harder stuff has the most fun of all with its commendable selection wines—and also plays on wine words, calling itself Wilbur the Wine Wizard and Wilbur Wine Nation. Much of the store's impressive stock of wines is displayed on attractive shadow-box shelves.

There are wines from all over the vinicultural world. Go into the store, or even visit the website, and you'll be peppered with information—practical and trivial alike—on regions, varietals, and even specific growers. Wilbur the Wine Wizard does impress with a range of knowledge on such matters.

In addition to carrying the usual array of domestic and imported selections in moderate price ranges, Wilbur's stocks a limited inventory of rare wines and also carries organics. There's a Wine of the Month Club, as well as a featured Wine of the Month and Wine of the Week to snare the interest of wine lovers—whether or not they are club members. The store is also a good source for all manner of wineglasses and other glassware, barware, wine accessories, books on wine, journals for wine-tasting notes, and wine racks.

Wilbur's Wine and Spirits, 200 West Foothills Parkway, Fort Collins; (800) 988-WINE (988-0463), (970) 226-8662, or www.beveragenation.com.

Other

Bingham Hill Cheese Company

Tom and Kristi Johnson—he a watershed scientist and she first a biologist and then a patent attorney—plunged into cheesemaking in late 1999. They did it not from a platform of long-standing interest in fine food in general or cheese in particular, but out of general dismay at the homogenization of the United States. Distressed by the tidal wave of chain restaurants, big box stores, and factory-made, overprocessed, and overpackaged foods, they were at the same time casting about for a lifestyle change.

As part of their transition, Kristi had started a Slow Food chapter (see appendix, page 450) in Fort Collins. A chance channel flip to a Martha Stewart television segment in which she extolled the glories of what Kristi remembers as "funky cheeses" sparked their interest in American cheesemaking. The couple discovered the growing interest in handcrafted specialty cheeses, and a new business was born. Bingham Hill, named after the place where the first settlers of what is now Fort Collins lighted, burst onto the Colorado food scene and beyond.

"We both have science backgrounds," she notes. "We knew microbiology and scientific technique, but we didn't know about pumps and electricity and refrigeration and mechanical stuff." They learned the mechanics, even as they developed cheeses from whole, raw nonhomogenized, organic cow's milk. To say that they are quick studies is putting it mildly.

Their first success was Rustic Blue, a blue-veined cheese with a cheddar-like texture. In 2000, before Bingham Hill was a year old, they entered it in a major American Cheese Society competition, where it was judged as the Best Blue. It won a bronze medal at the U.S. Cheese Championship the following year, quite a validation for the new microcheesery. It remains the signature cheese.

Bingham Hill has added more beautifully formulated and whimsically named cheeses. Ghost Town developed serendipitously. One day, Tom forgot to punch holes in some Rustic Blue, so that the blue veins never developed. The Johnsons sampled the cheese and found it to be Colorado's version of Parmesan. It grates and melts beautifully, and placed high in the 2001 U.S. Cheese Championship before it even had a marketing name.

Harvest Moon, an innovative raw cow's milk cheese, is one of several washed-rind cheeses in Bingham Hill's repertoire. Washed-rind cheeses are dipped into a liquid during the aging process to promote the growth of exterior mold that enhances the cheese's flavor. A wheel of Harvest Moon's finishes with an orange-colored rind that resembles a mid-autumn full moon rising over the plains. Angel Feat, another washed-rind cheese, is rubbed with a starter culture so that it ripens from the outside, a rare feat in the art of cheesemaking.

Poudre Puffs are named after the Cache le Poudre River, which flows through Fort Collins. In Bingham Hill's inimitable product description, Poudre Puffs resemble "a Camembert doing a Dolly Parton impression—rounded fuzzy white mounds which taste like truffles and sweet cream." With an herb coating, juniper berries, and crushed peppers, Poudre Puffs become Tumbleweed, because that's sort of what they look like.

Fresh & Simple is a group of spreadable cheeses made of simple cow's milk and cream cheese combined in enticing ways: Garlic, Parsley, and Chive; Tuscan Herb (rosemary, garlic, sage, and oregano); Roasted Green Chili; Dill; Basil and Garlic; and Plain, which showcases the pure cheese flavor.

Also in 2001, the Johnsons were approached by a sheepherder from the San Luis Valley who wanted to know if they might be interested in buying his milk. They agreed and started making first a fresh cheese and then Sheepish Blue. These were the first, and might still be the only, sheep's milk cheeses made in Colorado. This seasonal washed-rind blue cheese, now a mixed-milk version, is wrapped in grape leaves and ages for five months.

The year 2002 was another big one for the Johnsons. First, their Rustic Blue won a silver medal at the biennial World Cheese Championship against 49 blue, or bleu, cheeses from 10 countries. Then their cheeses won six awards at the annual American Cheese Society competition out of 473 cheeses entered by nearby 200 U.S. and Canadian cheese companies. Angel Feat and Fresh & Simple won gold medals, while Poudre Puff, Tumbleweed, Sheep's Milk Fresh Cheese, and Fresh & Simple Garlic, Parsley, & Chive all took silvers. Pretty impressive for a cheesery not yet three years old.

You can visit the Bingham Hill Cheese Company and sample cheeses in their small retail outlet. Look through the window and you might see something going on, like milk being poured into vats or curds being scooped out. The cheeses are also available in selected cheese shops, restaurants, and farmers' markets.

Bingham Hill Cheese Company, 1716 Heath Parkway, Fort Collins; (970) 472-0702 or www.binghamhill.com.

Ciao Vino

Antonio Race's Pulcinella Ristorante (see page 195) is well known for its outstanding wine list. He became messianic about educating his customers about wines, hosting frequent wine tastings and wine-pairing dinners. In December 2000, he took his cause one step farther and partnered with Patrick Laquens to open Ciao Vino, a downtown wine bar where you can hang out, sip wine, listen to music, nibble, and socialize. Race later pulled out of Ciao Vino to concentrate again on his restaurant, and Laquens now runs the show.

Laquens grew up in New Orleans, apprenticed as a chef there, and then ran a kitchen for Antonio Race. Laquens also operated a private chef service, created more than 30 six-course dinners with paired wines, worked in the Sonoma County vineyards at harvest time, and along the way got a master's degree in philosophy. Now he is Ciao Vino's general manager and wine buyer, and he helps customers delve into the subtleties of wines.

Ciao Vino's cellar includes 300 selections, with more than 47 available by the glass, poured through a state-of-the-art wine preservation system to ensure the highest level of quality from the first glass to the last. While Pulcinella is heavy on Italian wines, Ciao Vino also pours wines from the United States, France, Germany, Spain, Australia, New Zealand, South Africa, Argentina, and Chile. For those who prefer other spirits, there are also premium liquors and both domestic and imported microbrews.

Man and woman do not live by wine alone, so Ciao Vino offers a limited menu of imported cheeses, smoked meats, smoked and marinated fish, caviars, pâtés, foie gras, marinated vegetables, olives, olive oils, sandwiches, salads, breads, and desserts. Call it gourmet bar food.

Both wine and food selections are offered in monthly "flights" in order to maximize the wine/food education. For example, a three-glass comparison of Chardonnays from France, Australia, and California might be paired with a selection of salmon from Maine, Norway, and Scotland. Four wine flights are constructed every week, and the wines by the glass are continually rotated to maximize a diversified experience. In addition, the schedule calls for a weekly public wine tasting, broadcast live over the Internet, where the Ciao Vino experts are joined by wine makers from around the world who educate attendees about the viticulture processes and about specific wines.

For customers, learning about wine is optional—though it's hard to avoid at Ciao Vino. For employees, it's mandatory. Education is the hallmark of the establishment's philosophy. Every employee is required to write a three- to five-page paper on a prescribed wine topic every two weeks.

Committed as Ciao Vino remains to wine education, it is no plain classroom but rather a gorgeous and dramatic example of Italian decorative flair. Nine thick columns with ornate capitals support arches that vault to over 13.5 feet. The walls and floors have the appearance of old wine cellar stone, accented with an elegant mahogany bar with cherry panels. A grand piano looks gorgeous and makes beautiful music. The north wall features an iron-encased, walk-in wine-storage room with the best table in the house. As no original Michelangelos were available, four 6-by-4-foot reproductions hang on the west wall. In addition to fine wines and great food, there's live jazz nightly and an informal festive ambience.

Ciao Vino, 126 West Mountain, Fort Collins; (970) 484-8466 or www.ciaovino.com.

Hazel Dell Mushrooms

Hazel Dell owner and grower Jim Hammond cultivates fresh organically grown mushrooms on hardwood sawdust and wheat bran mixed with water and steam-sterilized in a special plastic bag that has been "inoculated" with the desired fungus. The mushrooms are incubated at 75 degrees for 3 to 13 weeks, depending on the species, and then moved to the temperature-controlled and humidified harvest room into which fresh air flows, an environment designed to simulate the conditions of a tree fall in a forest. You can visit the farm on weekdays to see the process and buy mushrooms on the spot.

Hazel Dell sells both uncommonly fresh versions of common mushrooms and some more unusual varieties at the farm, at selected farmers' markets, and especially to high-end restaurants whose chefs insist on fresh and local. The varieties you're likely to find are oyster, king oysters, shiitake, lion's mane (a.k.a. bearshead or monkeyhead), portobello/crimini (which is the same species at different times in the growing cycle), and *maitake* (a.k.a. hen of the woods).

Hazel Dell Mushrooms, 3925 County Road 32, Fort Collins; (970) 226-0978.

MouCo Cheese Company

In mid-2001, Birgit S. Halbreiter, whose parents are master cheese makers in Germany, and her husband, Robert R. Poland, began hand-producing small batches of outstanding Camembert-style cheese—a variety that originated in Normandy in the 18th century. The cheeses quickly gained a following among chefs and cheese lovers alike. This soft, creamy cheese with a distinctive nutty bouquet is made in a pristine cheesery, monitored by Halbreiter, trained as a dairy laboratory specialist. You can buy cheeses from a small retail outlet on-site and also tour the cheesery by advance reservation (they let no one but the cheese makers in during certain steps of the process).

MouCo Cheese Company, 1401 Duff Drive, Fort Collins; (970) 498-0107 or www.mouco.com.

Vintages

Walk into Vintages, and you'll be hit with the heady, grapey bouquet of aging wine that you inhale in wine cellars around the world. Even though you are at street level, Vintages' look and feel are winery/wine cellar as well, with stenciled stucco walls, arched doorways, cool tile floors, and wine-making paraphernalia scattered about.

At this wine-making and bottling shop, you can ferment and bottle your own private label wines. You need only to have the patience for a six- to eight-week process from selection to completion. You start by choosing the varietal or blend that you want to have. Seventeen types of wine grapes and wine-grape juices, seven from Italy, two each from Chile and France, and one from Australia are available, as are the makings for fruit wines.

Then, you consult with wine maker Lino Di Felice, who has been handcrafting wines since 1983 and founded Vintages in 1999. He'll work with you to fine-tune your selection to your taste. Want a wine that is "softer," "rounder," more or less "oaky," "fruitier," "drier" or not, and the other permutations that a particular grape can undergo on its way to being wine? Di Felice takes it from there, until it's ready for bottling. Meanwhile, you can design your own label—and Di Felice says that he has seen as much creativity in the graphics area as with customized wines. Some customers make the same wines again and again, while others experiment.

You then come in and bottle your own wine, with Di Felice on hand to walk you through the process. The filling and corking apparatus is semi-automated, so you don't have to be a mechanical genius to do it—just mind the instructions. You'll walk out with a batch of 26 bottles of wine made just for you—at a fraction of the store-bought price. Most people come in for wines that are ready to drink at bottling and reaching full maturity in one-and-a-half to two years for those who like to put wine aside. At this writing, De Felice was quoting the price for these of $4.80 to $5.75 per bottle, which he believes is comparable to $15 to $20 bottles at retail. Of course, if you buy retail, you can get a discount on mixed cases and aren't committed to a relationship with 26 bottles of the same wine. Vintages' late-maturing wines reach full maturity in three to four years, currently at $6.55 per bottle, and according to Di Felice, comparable to $25 to $30 at retail.

These days, the height of wine fashion is the limited output of small, little-known wineries. I submit that there's not much smaller than your own private-label wine, in quantities as modest as 26 bottles.

Vintages, 120 West Olive Street, Fort Collins; (970) 484-9813 or www.vintageswine.com.

Recipes

When Martine Deboodt, an accomplished and enthusiastic cook, moved to Fort Collins from Belgium, she set about searching for foods she liked. Ecstatic when the Bingham Cheese Company was established, she began adapting some of her favorite recipes to include those artisanal cheeses. She has now written a book called *Belgian Gourmet Cooks Colorado Cheeses,* from which this appetizer cheesecake recipe that uses three Bingham Hill cheeses is taken.

Original Blue Cheesecake

4 cups Bingham Hill Fresh & Simple cheese (plain)
6 ounces Bingham Hill Rustic Blue
pepper to taste
6 egg whites
¼ cup Bingham Hill Ghost Town, grated
sliced radishes and chopped parsley for garnish
crackers

Preheat oven to 325 degrees. In a food processor fitted with a steel blade, combine the Fresh & Simple cheese, Rustic Blue cheese, and pepper (or combine in a medium mixing bowl with an electric mixer). In a bowl, beat egg whites into a froth and fold into cheese mixture. Lightly coat a 9-inch springform pan with oil or non-stick spray. Spread mixture evenly in the bottom of pan. Sprinkle top with grated Ghost Town cheese. Bake 35 to 40 minutes or until center of cheesecake is firm. Remove from oven and let cool. Refrigerate for at least 2 hours or as long as 24 hours. Remove cheesecake from pan by inverting onto a serving plate. Garnish with radish slices and chopped parsley. Serve with crackers. Serves 16 to 18.

Note: This recipe can alternatively be served as an appetizer with a salad and also makes a fine filling for quiche.

The Northern Mountains

Steamboat Springs

Steamboat Springs is trying to balance its long-time traditions as a ranching community and the latter-day lifestyle brought about by its status as a major ski resort. Locals keep the Winter Carnival alive, support Howelsen Hill—Colorado's best local winter and summer recreation venue—and fight to preserve the surrounding landscape from excess development.

Still, becoming a vacation destination has brought resources to Steamboat Springs that ranchers could not have envisioned half-a-century ago—which has benefited locals and visitors alike. Tourists' needs, wants, and wallets have added a veneer of fine interior design, original art, and culinary resources to the town scene. This, in turn, has made Steamboat Springs attractive to lone eagles, telecommuters, active retirees, and well-heeled newcomers who want certain amenities to go with the wide-open northern Colorado scenery.

Just three miles south of Steamboat Springs' downtown, at the base of the eponymous ski mountain and its attendant resort development, are hotels and condos for thousands of guests plus commercial space with restaurants, nightspots, and retail shops. Private homes—many quite opulent—flank the resort and its ski runs. The directional signs now call the resort center "Mountain Village," but to avoid confusion with several "Mountain Villages" in Colorado and elsewhere in the Rockies, I've identified businesses located there as being at the Steamboat Resort as opposed to the original town of Steamboat Springs.

The downtown scene remains lively and fun. Along a five-block stretch of Lincoln Avenue, the main street holds most of the dining, partying, and shopping. The core of the sprawling Steamboat Resort development is built on several levels. Gondola Square is directly at the base of the gondola and ski lifts and is the center of sports activities. Nearby Ski Time Square is actually more of a roadway than a square, while Torian Plaza feels like a series of interconnected plazas and squares. Among them, these little commercial pods at Steamboat Resort and the straightforward main street/grid layout downtown assure that no epicure or oenophile living in or visiting greater Steamboat Springs will go hungry or thirsty.

steam boat Artist Gallery
southside of St. west end of town.
f.m. Light. sons western wear.

207

Bakeries

Albrecht's European Bakery

The core of this simple and spacious bakery is the business end—scales, big mixers, pastry boards, refrigerator, cooler, and ovens. The cases filled with sweet temptations are in the front of the store, with a line of tables stretching along a side wall. A nice patio in back is like an oasis on a summer day.

The formidable bread selection includes French baguette, country French, sourdough, pesto, five seed and grain, rosemary-olive, pumpernickel, Russian black bread, six-grain, Bavarian rye, and New York rye baked daily. Sandwiches made with those wonderful breads are available too. Baker Pamella Albrecht-Wedel does it all, from cookies and strudels based on family recipes to the judicious application of tips, tricks, and recipes from culinary school for the most elaborate specialty cakes and delicate pastries.

As a girl, Pam Albrecht baked with her grandmother, turning out wonderful desserts, cookies, and other homemade sweets that often display Eastern European roots. She built on this time-honored way to get a feel for dough with formal training in a Florida culinary school. Eventually she moved to Steamboat Springs, where she met her husband, Scott Wedel. He is in the computer field, but when they decided to open a Continental-style bakery, he became a credible bread baker. Still, Pam remains the *pâtissière extraordinaire.*

She offers such great-tasting scratch-baked goods from fresh and natural ingredients as exemplary strudels (apple, cherry, and Hungarian stretched dough), continental pastries and cakes (hazelnut, marzipan, chocolate, chocolate mousse, Dobos, Black Forest, mocha, chestnut, and more), coffee cakes (French, marzipan, blueberry, custard pecan, Swedish, and something intriguingly called Swedish flop, which I didn't try because there was none left when I visited), and puff pastries (cherry, blueberry, and apple). Muffins, scones, cookies, and rugallah also come in a choice of flavors. Try the donuts—small, beautifully textured, nongreasy circles available in glazed, sugared, or plain versions—and you'll never want to go "Dunkin'" again.

Albrecht's European Bakery, Sundance Plaza, 1250 South Lincoln Avenue, Steamboat Springs; (970) 871-7999.

Blue Sage Bakery

Blue Sage is primarily a wholesale bakery, supplying its first-rate breads to restaurants and retail shops all over the Steamboat Springs area. It does sell at retail in a limited way through the former Wally's Pizza that it bought and now also operates.

Pizzas come in deep-dish, double-dough, or thin varieties, by the pie or by the slice—if you're in the mood.

Blue Sage Pizza and Bakery, Central Park Plaza, 1809 Central Park Drive, Steamboat Springs; (970) 870-8600.

Winona's

This engaging downtown bakery and café turns out fresh breakfasts and lunches, but most of all, scrumptious baked goods made in-house daily. Kristy and Scott Fox own Winona's, a pleasing and inviting spot with red tile floors and pine paneling hung with hand-painted tiles made by a local artist. Eat-in customers slide into solid wooden booths near the front windows or tables. The glass case displaying those tempting baked goods is in the back.

Some locals come in just for their daily fix of Winona's cinnamon rolls. Not fancy enough to qualify as pastries in the formal French sense, Winona's other baked goods are rich and delicious. It's difficult to decide when the choices include lemon squares, chocolate raspberry cake, the locally legendary Chocolate Sin Brownie and the house special, a rich chocolate chip cookie layered with cream cheese and topped with ganache. It is called the Fox Square, in honor of the café's owners.

You can select an ardently healthy breakfast from the fruit and grain food groups or something soul-satisfying from the Egg-Stravaganza list. Other choices include various types of fluffy pancakes with house-made honey butter and great scones. Lunch presents a large choice of house-made soups and salads, hot and cold sandwiches and hoagies, and the whimsically named Wicked Wraps and Qiller Quesadillas. Prices are reasonable and portions are ample.

Winona's, 617 Lincoln Avenue, Steamboat Springs; (970) 879-2483.

Cooking School and Cooking Classes

Colorado Mountain College

The Steamboat Springs campus of Colorado Mountain College, a string of schools across the state, offers an array of single-session, noncredit, low-cost cooking, and food courses for home cooks taught by some of the area's best chefs.

Some courses go beyond traditional kitchen skills. Take, for instance, Wild Game from the Field to the Table, with Erik Skinner, an appropriate name for an instructor who promises to "take wild game from the field to butchering to marinade" and also teach students how to sauté, grill, and jerk meats and fowl that they have hunted.

Colorado Mountain College, Alpine Campus, 1330 Bob Adams Drive, Steamboat Springs; (970) 870-4444 or www.coloradomtn.edu/ campus_alp/home.html.

The Home Ranch

The Home Ranch is Colorado's only guest ranch meeting the high standards of a Relais & Chateaux member in terms of accommodations and gastronomy. Of 469 members in 51 countries on the current roster, 45 are in the United States (just six are in the Rocky Mountains and only two are in Colorado). In order to enjoy Chef Clyde Nelson's refined food, you have to be a guest (one-week summer minimum stay but only two nights in winter).

During selected weeks during the slower season, Nelson puts on hands-on cooking classes. The typical program includes a wine and hors d'oeuvres reception before dinner, followed by three days with a hands-on class either in the morning or afternoon and an optional demo class the other half of the day. Hands-on classes total five hours, and the spirit is light-hearted and fun, yet the learning is real—not surprising for such an award-winning establishment as The Home Ranch.

Nelson imparts such basic kitchen techniques as the roasting, grilling, and sautéing of meats, fish, and vegetables and the preparation of sauces, stocks, salsas, soups, and appetizers. Baking classes include dinner rolls, sandwich bread, pizza and focaccia, tortillas, various types of pastry dough, and complete desserts. Because the setting is, after all, a ranch, campfire cooking and barbecue are also on the program.

The Home Ranch, 54880 Routt County Road 129, Clark (mailing address: P.O. Box 822, Clark, CO 80428); (970) 879-1780 or www.homeranch.com.

Vista Verde Ranch

Chef Jonathon Gillespie, a graduate of the Culinary Institute of America, often welcomes guests to his kitchen, hosts daily wine tastings, and also offers weekly cooking classes, just for Vista Verde Ranch guests. These hands-on classes last about two hours and include such specialties as Rosemary Flat Bread, Salmon Roulade, Gooey Chocolate Cake, and Chocolate Truffles. In summer, his class on cooking with wild edibles is a seasonal delight—and he is the culinary spirit behind the Wild Edible Feast, an annual fundraiser held at the ranch to benefit a local environment organization (see page 219). For more details on the ranch and its cuisine, see the Steamboat Springs Dining section.

Vista Verde Ranch, Seedhouse Road, 31100 Routt County Road 64, Clark (mailing address: P.O. Box 770465, Steamboat Springs, CO 80477); (800) 526-7433, (970) 879-3858, or www.vistaverde.com.

Dining

Antares Restaurant

Antares is one of the brightest stars in the heavens, and its namesake restaurant is one of the brightest stars of Colorado cuisine. Antares, one of Steamboat Springs' bastions of New American cuisine, adds a strong overlay of Asian flavors—a sub-theme of Southwest—and dishes graced with wine-based sauces.

Situated in the historic Brandywine Building half a block off Lincoln Avenue, the restaurant contrasts traditional décor and contemporary food. Wood and flagstone floors, sturdy oak tables, and a warm fireplace seem to say, "Be comfortable and eat well." The ambience conveys solidity and endurance, while the food is innovative and creative—just the way owner Paul "Rocky" LeBrun wants it.

Start with a salad of ripe mango and avocado over field greens served with a plum-ginger dressing. Or try the Potato Asparagus and Chipotle Soup or Asian Pear Salad, made with those wonderful firm pears that are shaped like apples that are ever more readily available in Colorado. Accompanied by gorgonzola and walnuts and dressed in a champagne vinaigrette, it is a combination to jumpstart the palate.

The restaurant divides main courses into two categories. "Suppers" are moderately priced and include pastas, salads, chicken, and perhaps another dish or two. "Entrées" are heftier and pricier. The kitchen uses a lot of *tournedos,* a French cut of lean beef tenderloin. You can order surf and turf in, oh, a jillion restaurants, but Antares vaults its version above the bar by combining a Maine lobster tail with a *tournedo* and an unusual port-horseradish sauce. Called *Tournedos Le Brun,* this house specialty is served with a Port-shallot sauce, accompanied by angel hair pasta. That preparation also appears as the centerpiece of the mixed grill, a platter featuring three meats or game. On a recent menu the trio consisted of *tournedo* with a wild mushroom-Pinot Noir sauce set into gustatory flight with quail and duck napped in ginger-plum-serrano sauce.

Veal and lamb have their place on the menu, as does Elk Crosby, which features three sautéed elk medallions finished with a Merlot glaze and—what else—dried Bing cherries. You might find a special seafood combo of swordfish and halibut or some other pairing. Ruby Trout Mexicali is given a light coating of crushed cashews, sautéed, and finished with chipotle cream sauce and fresh pineapple *pico de gallo.*

The small dessert list offers a relatively simple ending for such complex earlier courses. The trio of house sorbets refreshes, the Grand Marnier Crème Brulée soothes, but if you want just one more hit of flavor contrasts, try the house-made vanilla ice cream topped with blueberries sautéed in Frangelico. Steamboat Springs' fussy food and wine fans delight in the atmosphere, the food, and an award-winning wine list.

Antares Restaurant, 57 1/2 Eighth Street, Steamboat Springs; (970) 879-9939.

The Cabin

The Cabin is the Steamboat Grand Hotel and Conference Center's fine-dining restaurant. In fact, the only modest thing about The Cabin is its name. The word *cabin* implies some sort of homey rusticity, but this cabin is big in every respect: a sizable hotel restaurant in the largest lodging property at one of Colorado's largest ski resorts, serving large portions of hearty food.

The Cabin is a study in masculine-style rusticity: solid hand-crafted tables inlaid with wrought-iron designs, deep booths, commodious armchairs upholstered in leather, hefty tableware, and Western-style art on the ruggedly finished walls. The room is cleverly subdivided by "groves" of bark-on aspen trunks. The food also happens to be very good, which prevents it all from being overkill. The culinary style is steakhouse fare thickly veneered with Contemporary Colorado cuisine.

Applewood house-smoked salmon with chive corncakes, asparagus, and *crème fraîche*, and Baked Cambozola Cheese with roasted garlic, sweet tomato jam, and flat-bread crisp are among the interesting, contemporary starters to whet hip appetites. A vegetarian specialty such as flaky-crusted strudel filled with forest mushrooms, roasted peppers, eggplant, and spinach is decidedly 21st century. The house specialties are beautifully cut, amply portioned, and perfectly cooked USDA prime beef, native fish, natural poultry, and game. Seven cuts and sizes of beef appear on the regular dinner menu, ranging from modest eight-ounce filet mignon and small prime rib to hefty 16-ounce portions of T-bone and prime rib.

Elk, pheasant, thick-cut pork chops, buffalo rib eye, rack of lamb, and rainbow trout all evoke culinary images of Colorado. Salmon, on the other hand, swims nowhere near the Centennial State. Pan Roasted King Salmon Osso Bucco, is onion-crusted fish served with creamy herbed polenta and *beurre blanc*, is a specialty. Executive Chef Patrick Lowe, who among other assignments was host-chef at the *Food & Wine* Magazine Classic at Aspen (see page 326) for eight years, has taken the meaty menu and tarted it up with beautiful renditions of that contemporary Colorado cuisine that he favors, and if that means naming a fish dish for a meat dish, so be it.

The Cabin sub-specializes in fondue. The cheese fondue, recommended for two or more, is listed under the appetizer menu, but I'm happy to order one of the lighter appetizers or a salad plus this rich fondue to share and call it dinner. At the back end of the menu is The Cabin's Toblerone Chocolate Fondue, warmed at the table and served with pound cake and fresh fruit.

The ample wine list, which is heavy on California vintages, was assembled to harmonize with Lowe's menus. The menu divides the wines by color and type, referred to as "Shades of White" and "Shades of Red." Therefore, you'll find Light to Sweet Whites, Chardonnay, Adventurous Whites, Bubbly Whites, and Crystal Whites, Light Reds, Merlot, Cabernet, Adventurous Reds, and Crystal Reds. Most of the wines in the "Crystal" categories are priced in the midrange and are also available by the glass.

The Cabin, Steamboat Grand Hotel and Conference Center, 2300 Mt. Werner Circle, Steamboat Resort; (970) 871-5700 or www.steamboatgrand.com.

Café Diva

This sensational restaurant was not part of any grand plan, but rather grew rather serendipitously. Planning isn't everything, for the Café Diva now rests firmly on Steamboat's top tier of wining and dining spots. And rightly so. Seth Cheiken had restaurant jobs starting in his teens, mostly cooking at fast-paced, family-owned Italian places in Connecticut. After earning a degree from Union College, he moved to Steamboat and started working in restaurants. What else does a graduate in psychology do in a ski town?

Meanwhile, with years of restaurant and hospitality industry experience, Paul Underwood had decided that Steamboat needed a wine bar. By the time he and Cheiken met up, he had already signed a lease for a small space in Torian Plaza. They decided to team up, with Cheiken whipping up hors d'oeuvres to accompany the fine wines Underwood would be pouring.

The Café Diva opened in December 1998 with 12 seats and a kitchen outfitted with two Coleman camping stoves. Just a few weeks later, a purveyor accidentally delivered three whole salmon rather than the three pounds of smoked salmon Cheiken had ordered for one of the hors d'oeuvres. With his chef's adrenaline pumping, he assembled what he had on hand—a bag of rice that he had planned to cook for a quick staff dinner, some pistachios, some mangos, and other odds and ends—to make a hastily conceived dinner.

They equally hastily bought a chalkboard to announce that night's special: pistachio-crusted salmon with mango rice. The special sold out—and word spread quickly that the new Café Diva served great food. Cheiken quickly developed a weekly rotation of three appetizers and three entrées that he could prepare in his limited kitchen. Evening by evening, the Café Diva morphed from wine bar to restaurant.

Cheiken is not a classically schooled chef, but his aptitude and enthusiasm came to the fore while the wine bar was transitioning. Learning on the job as a youngster gave him flexibility in the kitchen, and immersing himself in the culinary philosophies of Escoffier, Child, Hazan, and Trotter raised his skill level and his commitment to excellence.

After another shot of serendipity, Cheiken, the extroverted perfectionist, moved away from the stove and out to the front of the house, where his interaction with customers is as caring and enthusiastic as are his skills in the kitchen. Arriving in Steamboat Springs was a superbly talented young chef named Kate van Rennselaer. She had graduated from New York's prestigious French Culinary Institute and following an externship there was hired and ultimately became a sous-chef under the great Jean-Georges Vongerichten at Manhattan's ultra-trendy Jean-Georges Restaurant.

At a previous restaurant called Vong, Vongerichten had pioneered the fusion of the cuisine of his native France and that of Asia. At Jean-Georges, he brought it to new heights, developing his signature minimalist perfection—and van Rennselaer proved to be a quick study, but with family in Steamboat she answered Colorado's siren call. Meanwhile, Café Diva had grown to 65 seats with a real kitchen that boasts a 10-burner stove. Van Rennselaer now adds her light and Vongerichten–inspired touches to Cheiken's foundation of slow-cooked stocks and sauces.

The combination is inspired and continually evolving. The small and exquisite menu changes seasonally. You can expect unexpected dishes, always prepared with care, served with enthusiasm, beautifully plated, and tasting divine. One season, the prime filet mignon is pepper-crusted and perches atop wilted spinach greens and a potato-leek pancake, accompanied by horseradish sauce and dried-cherry chutney. Another season it is wrapped in pancetta and served with forest mushroom ragout and roasted-garlic mashed new potatoes.

If Café Diva has any signature dishes, these are Crab and Tomato Bisque, a Vegetarian Spring Roll appetizer with carrot-ginger and soy-mignonette dipping sauces, and Caesar salad that appears as a half-wedge of romaine lettuce with made-to-order dressing and Pecorino-Romano cheese.

What of the wines in what had begun as a wine bar? There are about 350 selections from all the major wine-producing regions. Many are available by the glass or in two-ounce tasting portions, so you can build your own flights. The menu arranges them by country and the wine-growing area or varietal. Therefore, the "White Wines—United States" list includes Sauvignon Blanc–Fumé Blanc, Chardonnay, and Other Varietals. The "White Wines—France" section is divided into the wines of Alsace, Burgundy, and Other Regions. You'll also find whites from Australia, Germany, Italy, New Zealand, and Spain. "Red Wines—United States" includes Pinot Noir, Red Zinfandel, Merlot, Cabernet Sauvignon, Meritage Blends, and Other Red Wines. French reds are sorted into Bordeaux, Burgundy and Rhône Valley-Languedoc, while Italian reds are divided into wines from Tuscany, Piemonte, and Other Regions. Reds from Spain, Chile, and Australia, dessert wines, and champagnes complete the roster.

The Café Diva's main characteristic, however, transcends culinary talent, up-to-the-minute cuisine, the pleasantly low-key décor, delightful patio for summer evenings, and stocked wine cellar: It is the passion and commitment of the people who run it. These traits come through with every perfect plate.

Café Diva, Torian Plum Plaza, 1875 Ski Time Square Drive, Steamboat Resort; (970) 871-0508 or www.cafediva.com.

Cottonwood Grill

Just before the Christmas–New Year rush in 2000, the doors to the new Cottonwood Grill were thrown open. This beautiful restaurant, specializing in Pacific Rim cuisine, was an instant hit. How could it be otherwise? The décor bespeaks Zen-like tranquility with curved, peach-colored walls hung with selected pieces of interesting Asian art. During the warm months, the restaurant opens its large patio overlooking the Yampa River and, even better, provides a handful of tables on the grass right at riverside.

The restaurant was started by Peter Lautner and Michael Fragola, a pair of owner-chefs who came to the Cottonwood Grill concept via different culinary roots but now cook in perfect harmony. Fragola, a veteran in Steamboat kitchens, was the executive chef at La Montaña, a long-running, ever-popular Mexican–Southwestern restaurant, has the instinct and experience to know what kind of food will fly in Steamboat Springs. Lautner, a Culinary Institute of America graduate, was executive chef at New York's Club 101 and later at Reebok's headquarters in Boston, who brought into the mix cutting-edge culinary trends.

Start with Shrimp and Thai Basil Sticks (Gulf shrimp with Thai basil and ginger in crispy spring roll wrapper, served with Asian vegetable slaw and sweet and spicy chili sauce); Yampa Valley Lamb Potstickers with ginger, garlic, and chilies in a steamed dumpling with *mirisol* chili and *ponzu* sauces; or pan-seared crab and shrimp cakes served with sweet red pepper, garlic, water chestnuts, and a wasabi aïoli atop field greens.

Entrées include crisp free-range chicken breast seasoned with lemongrass, garlic, kaffir lime, and chilies; duck spiced with sun-dried cherries and Sichuan peppercorns, served with cracked-coriander bok choy and curry-fried noodles and finished with a cherry-Merlot sauce; orange-marinated, grilled Gulf shrimp, served with a light coconut red curry sauce, sesame sugar snap peas, and lemon cilantro rice; or perhaps Thai pork, marinated with Chinese-sounding hoisin and ginger—*and very, very good.*

Among Pastry Chef Jennifer Holbrook's sublime desserts is Cottonwood Torta, a dark chocolate cake filled with chocolate mousse, topped with Callebaut chocolate ganache and served with house-made caramel sauce. Her subtle Ginger Crème Brulée with a chocolate shortbread cookie is creamy and dreamy. She usually makes a tart of some kind too, perhaps Apple Tatin, caramelized Granny Smith apples on a flaky pastry tart with a gorgeous vanilla ice cream tower and fresh seasonal berries, or a fresh fruit tart in season. She's great at cheesecakes, and her fruit sorbets are best in summer, when produce is perfect.

The wine list features many mid-range wines by the bottle or the glass and some exceptional, hard-to-find expensive vintages as well. Mirroring its wine selections, the Cottonwood Grill is both a relaxed place for a night on the town (or near the river, to be precise) and a special-occasion restaurant calling for the finest wine or champagne.

Cottonwood Grill, 701 Yampa Avenue, Steamboat Springs; (970) 879-2229 or www.cottonwoodgrill.com.

Hazie's and Ragnar's

The Steamboat ski area was one of the first in Colorado to feature good food on the mountain. In addition to the usual self-service eating facilities, Steamboat has long boasted two real restaurants, Hazie's and Ragnar's, that meet the standards of people who are as fussy about the meals set before them as they are about the quality of the snow. In addition to serving civilized, European-style lunches—with a nice bottle of wine if you like—both of these seasonal restaurants also offer fine dinners some nights of the week.

The massive, multi-level Thunderhead day lodge perches on a plateau at the top of the eight-passenger gondola, and Hazie's Restaurant spreads along the top floor with great views across the Yampa River Valley. It also provides a gracious alternative of a sit-down lunch at an attractively set table to the usual ski-area self-service cafeteria ambience. Because it is in the building where the gondola unloads, nonskiers can enjoy the Hazie's experience without slip-sliding across the snow.

Named after the late Hazie Werner, member of an early Steamboat Springs family and mother of three renowned Olympians, Hazie's serves daily lunch and nightly dinner through most of the ski season and an excellent Sunday brunch during the summer. As you are escorted upstairs to your table, your glance will probably light upon the dessert tray displayed on an antique sideboard. If you're like me, you'll remind yourself to save some room.

The food inspirations are taken from many sources, with a little of this and a little of that. Three of the signature dishes served at both lunch and dinner are conch chowder, Caesar salad tossed with aged asiago cheese (and anchovies included on request), and Oysters Selana, a spinach-artichoke casserole topped with bacon-wrapped oysters and Jarlsberg cheese. Otherwise, the menus for the two meals deviate from each other. Lunch features more salads, a modest selection of entrées, and a great choice of generously portioned sandwiches.

Dinner—for which reservations are required—is from a smaller but more refined à la carte menu, with interesting ingredients prepared with a classic flair. Locally smoked trout, Prince Edward Island mussels in Thai coconut curry sauce, petite lobster tail and scallops over angel hair pasta, half a Muscovy duck barbecued with an Asian-style ginger-honey-soy glaze, grilled rack of lamb, and a vegetarian Cornucopia Acorn Squash stuffed with orange quinoa and a garden of vegetables are among the options. The wine list is dominated by California vintages and well-balanced between reds and whites. Those desserts are too good to be mere tray-toppers. Try the Sinful Chocolate Decadence Cake or the warm apple crisp with vanilla bean ice cream.

On the lower level of a smaller day lodge at Rendezvous Saddle, partway down one of the most popular ski runs, is Ragnar's. Norwegian in looks and culinary tradition, it has an attractive and homey, Scandi-country look—most inviting on a snowy day, when people tend to linger over lunch.

Velkommen tel Bords—Welcome to the Table—is Ragnar's message. Ragnar's Fiskesuppe, a creamy fish chowder in the Norwegian style, is a souper-warmer-upper on a cold day. I love salmon in countless ways, but Ragnar's thinly sliced gravlax—raw cured salmon—with dill-mustard sauce is my favorite. Swedish meatballs made of beef and pork are served over pasta with a rich sour cream–dill sauce. It's listed as an appetizer, but it's rich enough to be an entrée.

Scandinavian Chili is made with sautéed venison, onions, garlic, chili spices, and three-bean chili red wine sauce. Wienerschnitzel in the classic Viennese mode, Seafood and Wild Mushroom Pot Pie, and a daily pasta special are also offered. *Smørrebrød* is Norwegian for sandwich, and Ragnar's selections include a Croissant Club and a Yampa Valley Beef Burger, a cheeseburger made of local beef and a choice of cheeses. Among the desserts are excellent pastries, mousse, and fresh berries, a real touch-of-summer treat on a winter day.

On Thursday, Friday, and Saturday nights and more frequently during holiday periods, Ragnar's also serves dinner to the mellow accompaniment of live acoustic guitar. Access is via gondola and snowcat-drawn sleigh. Dinner includes a plate of cold appetizers, a choice of *Fiskesuppe* or French onion soup, a choice of eight entrées, and a dessert selection. The entrées run the gamut from the Vintner's Filet, a mesquite-grilled filet of beef tenderloin, or Herb Grilled Venison for carnivo-rous diners to a gorgeous Wild Mushroom Potato Stack, with sautéed mushrooms layered between potato pancakes, for vegetarians. Ragnar's is open from early December through early April. Reservations are recommended for lunch and required for dinner.

Hazie's, on the mountain at Thunderhead Lodge; Ragnar's, on the mountain at Rendezvous Saddle; information and reservation number for both, (970) 871-5150. The website for the Steamboat ski resort is www.steamboat-ski.com.

The Home Ranch

Dude and guest ranches have a reputation for casual Western ambience and copious quantities of traditional American fare—meat and potatoes, pies and cobblers, anything that might be dished out from the back of a chuck wagon. Rustic cabin lodging, a good horse program, and a passel of family-friendly activities are standard. But times have changed, and a number of ranches have ratcheted up their culinary goals and standards of hospitality. None has flown higher than The Home Ranch along the Elk River Valley northwest of Steamboat Springs. It is Colorado's only guest ranch selected as a Relais & Chateaux member. Consider this: Relais & Chateaux, an international association of noteworthy privately owned hotels and inns and gourmet restaurants, is renowned for its high standards, both in terms of accommodations and gastronomy. Of 469 members in 51 countries on the current roster, 45 are in the United States (just six are in the Rocky Mountains and only two are in Colorado).

The Home Ranch attained this level by creating elegant and luxurious cabins, advancing the traditional dude-ranch horse program to the level of a world-class equestrian center, and hiring a chef who knows fine food. Chef Clyde Nelson strikes a balance between sophisticated cuisine and what is expected in a place whose last name is Ranch. The dining room displays elegant Western style, with a soaring beamed ceiling, massive river-rock fireplace, country-style lighting, and generously sized tables. During summer high season, when ranch guests only are permitted, the meal plan includes breakfast and lunch served buffet-style, with family-style meal service at dinner.

Winter is The Home Ranch's quieter and more accessible season. Not only is the high-season minimum one-week stay reduced, but outside guests are welcome for lunch or dinner. Dinner is a five-course feast—one of the best in the Steamboat Springs area. No matter what the season, the full-time pastry chef produces fresh breakfast pastries, breads, rolls, and desserts. Winter is also the season when Nelson offers cooking classes during selected weeks (see page 210).

The Home Ranch, 54880 Routt County Road 129, Clark (mailing address: P.O. Box 822, Clark, CO 80428); (970) 879-1780 or www.homeranch.com.

The Swiss Haven

Erik and Laura Binggeli run an authentically Swiss restaurant in the heart of downtown. From house-made soups to specialty desserts, you'll feel as if you have indeed migrated to the Swiss Alps. The pretty dining room is set up with white table-cloths over cloths of red and small shaded oil lamps on each table. A pianist sometimes plays.

The Swiss Haven serves house-made soups, Bündnerfleisch (air-dried beef), Bauernteller (a platter featuring Bündnerfleisch and other specialty meats, cheeses, and cornichons), or a variety of fondues, either as appetizers or for the main course. In addition to classic cheese fondues available with various kinds of cheeses, The Swiss Haven offers *Fondue Chinoise,* where the meat is cooked in broth rather than oil, and Exotic Fondue, with beef and shrimp marinated in an Asian-style soy-ginger sauce before you dip it.

The restaurant also serves raclette, a memorable Swiss classic in which a particularly meltable cheese is heated under a special hot iron, scraped off and served portion by portion with cornichons, small pickled onions, and boiled potatoes. The Swiss Haven literally beefs up this traditional presentation by adding *chippolata* sausage, New York strip, chicken breast, or shrimp to the classic mix.

Entrées are named after Swiss places. The Eiger is a marinated portobello mushroom served with Béarnaise sauce, the Gotthard is grilled chicken breast served with curry sauce, and Zuriberg is thinly sliced free-range veal in a mushroom-cream sauce. It is the local special of Zurich. These are all served with *rösti*, coarsely grated potatoes, sautéed to doneness, or cheese *spätzli*, free-form dumplings bathed in a cheese sauce.

Sometimes The Swiss Haven goes international—sort of. During Bavarian night, as is done every Friday during the summer, the featured attraction is a sausage sampler platter, house-made potato-onion tart, pretzels, a choice of several kinds of hearty meat, and dessert, all to the sounds of live piano music.

Desserts include chocolate fondue, apple strudel, and a Swiss chocolate vermicelli, which in Switzerland (and at The Swiss Haven) is not a pasta dish but a sweet chestnut puree that, when pressed out, resembles that extruded pasta specialty. There's a full bar (and a bar menu too) and a good selection of imported and domestic wines, including several Swiss wines that are not often imported into this country.

The Swiss Haven, 709 Lincoln Avenue, Steamboat Springs; (970) 871-1761.

There is also a Swiss Haven at 325 South Main Street, Breckenridge; (970) 453-6969, under different ownership (see page 253).

Vista Verde Ranch

This guest ranch in the broad valley of the South Fork of the Elk River has become almost as well known for its fine food as for its classic dude-ranch activities. It has earned the Mobil Four Star rating for its cuisine as well as its other guest services. The ranch's day-to-day dinners soar, and its special dinners approach those in fine hotel and independent restaurants.

For guests gathered in the warm and cozy confines of the ranch dining room, Chef Jonathon Gillespie prepares ambitious and exquisite seven-course winemaker feasts. One memorable menu started with a Salmon Tartare "Ice Cream Cone" à la Thomas Keller (he of the famous French Laundry in Yountville, California); climaxed with Roast Loin of Cervena Venison on Dried Fruit Compote with Maytag Blue Cheese Whipped Potatoes, Slow Roasted Golden Beets, and a Port Wine Dèmi-Glace; and finished with Red Wine and Cassis Poached Pears with Homemade Cinnamon Ice Cream and a Hazelnut Tuile Cookie, all accompanied by a procession of matched wines. This noteworthy dinner was paired with Estancia, Franciscan, and Simi wines. Another Vista Verde innovation is the "progressive" winter winemaker dinner, with courses served at different places on the ranch that are accessible by skis, snowshoes, or horse-drawn sleigh.

Even without the special occasion of a winemaker dinner, fine dining and the enjoyment of wine wines are a major part of the Vista Verde experience—so much so that the ranch puts on special dinner-and-entertainment programs for young children to enable parents to enjoy an adult dinner and adult conversation. Gillespie also offers some cooking programs (see page 210).

Vista Verde Ranch, Seedhouse Road, 31100 Routt County Road 64, Clark (mailing address: P.O. Box 770465, Steamboat Springs, CO 80477); (800) 526-7433, (970) 879-3858, or www.vistaverde.com.

Events

Wild Edible Feast

May—Yampatika, Steamboat Springs' nature association, has been holding an annual fundraiser at Vista Verde Ranch since 1998. The day before the banquet, local naturalist Karen Vail leads a volunteer group that goes gleaning in the woods and meadows for edible plants. Typically, these include such native species as cattails, wild onion, fiddlehead ferns, nettles, mint, piñon pine nuts, sweet cicely root, dandelion, edible violets, and, of course, Yampa root, which is related to the carrot.

Jonathon Gillespie, Vista Verde's chef, creates a feast from those ingredients, supplemented by purchased foods. He generally tries to include trout, elk, or other ingredients that are also found in the wild in the area. One year, he also fixed crawfish cultivated from Steamboat Lake. The five-course gourmet feast generally includes hors d'oeuvres, soup, salad, entrée, and dessert, accompanied by wine. There is also a silent auction to benefit not-for-profit Yampatika and its conservation efforts.

For information, call Yampatika, 57 10th Street, Steamboat Springs; (970) 871-9151 or www.yampatika.org.

Steamboat Mountain Brewfest

September—This one-day festival, held in conjunction with the annual Fall Foliage Festival, is a family-oriented arts and crafts event with a beer chaser. Rocky Mountain breweries offer beer tastings, food vendors tickle the palate, and live entertainment adds a musical component.

For information, contact the Steamboat Springs Chamber Resort Association, 1255 South Lincoln Avenue, Steamboat Springs; (970) 879-0880 or www.steamboatchamber.com.

Retail

The Homesteader

If the word *homesteader* calls up the image of pioneers living in sod huts on the prairie, think again. Steamboat Springs' Homesteader sells fine cookware, bakeware, kitchen accessories, tableware, table linens, and gourmet food products—all a far cry from the cast-iron pot in which those original homesteaders cooked virtually everything. Steve and Daniela Kennedy own the store. She is from Switzerland, so the couple seeks out unusual European brands when they are making their several-times-a-year family visits.

The Homesteader's customers can select from Calphalon, Le Creuset, Chantal, and All-Clad cookware and sturdy ceiling pot racks to hang them from at home. The store also carries Kuhn Rikon pressure cookers from Switzerland. Shelves hold seductive specialty appliances—blenders, food processors, blenders, juicers, waffle makers, and more—from such quality makers as Cuisinart, Waring, and Kitchen Aid, plus a terrific Solitaire double-beater mixer.

Customers can stop at the small coffee and tea bar to fuel up or calm down or buy their favorite beverages coffees and teas, and utensils and appliances in which to prepare them. An array of coffee beans, ground or whole, and teas, bagged or loose, dominates the front corner of the store, alongside tea pots, coffee pots, and a good selection of conventional coffee makers and espresso makers, including machines from Capresso and Nespresso.

The gadget wall is loaded with lines like OXO Good Grips in regular and mini-size—the latter mounted on magnets—Factotum by Gianinni, Movli, NorPro, Trudeau Ergonomic, Westmark, and Zyliss. Some brands are familiar to kitchen gear-heads, but the Kennedys keep discovering others in Europe. For outdoor or stylish tabletop cooking, dining, and entertaining, there's an array of grilling accessories, fondue pots, pepper grinders, and specialty service pieces.

Generous front-of-the-store space is devoted to gourmet foods, including one shelf with just Colorado products such as Bear Creek Bread and Gigi Ann's bread mixes; Colorado Mud brownie mix; and Kim's Gourmet Sauces, Mountain Sunrise, Prairie Thyme, Rachel's Smokin' Sauces, Sunshine, and Westwood jams, jellies, preserves, and conserves. Cotswold Cottage scone mixes boast of producing scones "in the British tradition," but it could be called Colorado Cottage too, because the recipe is formulated for higher elevations.

From out of state, and out of the country, come excellent oils and vinegars in various flavors and from various makers. Pastas are from Benedetto Cavalieri, Pasta Partners, and Saperi di Casa, with David Gourmet pasta sauces and Bella Cucina pestos to put on them if you don't make your own. Other lines include Miss Scarlet's olives, Rice River Farms gourmet rices, King's Cupboard dessert sauces, Stonewall Kitchen preserves and condiments, and Melino's preserves from Germany. Salsas and hot sauces come from Desert Pepper, Jump Up & Kiss Me, Dave's, and other makers. British biscuits, Scottish shortbread, Aunt Lola's cookie mixes, and bread mixes from Great Bakes and Highland Sugarworks are the specialty baked goods at The Homesteader.

The Homesteader, 821 Lincoln Avenue, Steamboat Springs; (970) 879-8689, (907) 879-5880, or (800) 321-4702.

Market on the Mountain

To find this small on-mountain convenience and liquor store, look at the store below Montaña's. The signs over the storefront don't say "The Market," or anything like it. They read "Beer Wine & Spirits" and "Grocery & Deli," but it is the Market on the Mountain that sells all the conventional stock-a-condo stuff, from corn flakes to crackers to Campbell's soups, but it also has above-average breads, prepared foods, and gourmet products.

The breads come from Blue Sage, a fine local wholesale bakery, and La Brea from California. The fresh salads include Greek Pasta, Artichoke Pasta, Red Pepper Pasta, Fresh Fruit, and Old-Fashioned Potato. Cascade Farms organic jams, Inglehofer mustards, Stonewall jams and vinegars, Redmond RealSalt sea salt, MacDougall's organic wild rice, A's Do Mar imported tinned tuna, Dal Raccolta vinegar, Peloponnese roasted peppers, Padua Coltibuono olive oil, and even such exotica as Crosse & Blackwell condiments can elevate meals fixed in the basic condo kitchen above the norm.

The Market's wine room carries numerous well-known, mid-priced reds and whites, grouped by varietal on steel shelves, and premium wines—$100 and up—are on a shelf near the cashier. The Market on the Mountain won't satisfy all your culinary needs or wine wants, but for one-stop shopping practically at slopeside, it's hard to beat.

Market on the Mountain, Village Drive at Apres Ski Way, Steamboat Resort; (970) 879-2965.

True Value Hardware

This all-purpose hardware store on the western outskirts of Steamboat Springs carries everything from paint to wingnuts, but it also has a commendable kitchen tools department with an above-average selection of housewares and small appliances. Pots and pans come from Chantal, Mirro, NorPro, WearEver (including Meyer Analon Cookware by WearEver), plus cast-iron and Hi-Side skillets by SilverStone.

Gadgets by NorPro (including an elegant all-stainless hollow-handle group), OXO Good Grips, GripEZ, Chef'n, GoodCook and wooden implements from Gourmande represent the kinds of brands that you might expect to find in specialty stores. This True Value also carries Chicago Cutlery and Krona by NorPro kitchen knives, as well as knife holders to store them in and boards to cut on. There's particular depth in pressure cookers, canning equipment, and bakeware. Check out WearEver and Air Bake, which makes slotted cookie sheets and other items for use in convection ovens. Mixers, blenders, toasters, coffee pots, espresso makers, crockpots, and rice cookers include Avanté heavy-duty toasters, Black & Decker, Hamilton Beach, Lectrix, and Osterizer—and, oh yes, George Foreman grillers.

Steamboat True Value Hardware, 2989 Riverside Plaza, 29595 West U.S. Highway 40, Steamboat Springs; (970) 879-8014.

Wines

Bottleneck

This downtown liquor store keeps going more heavily into wines, with about 300 wines occupying most of the modest space. The front of the store has the magnum sizes, jugs, and smaller bottles from the same wineries. In the middle are specials, while the good stuff is in back. An antique grape press is in the center of this section of this store, where better wines—mostly from U.S. wineries—are sectioned by varietal. One shelf is devoted to Australian and Chilean wines. A small glass-topped case displays a selection of high-end and older wines. Bottleneck organizes fundraising wine tastings for such local cultural organizations as the Steamboat Springs.

Bottleneck, 734 Lincoln Avenue, Steamboat Springs; (970) 879-1255.

Vino

Steamboat Springs has several places where you can buy wines, but there is just one dedicated wine specialist—and that's Vino. This small wine store is simple yet attractive, with a spatter-painted concrete floor, warm yellow walls, and sturdy oak wine racks. But looks don't make the store. Commitment and expertise do, and with an abundance of both, Vino draws wine-lovers not only from Steamboat Springs but all over northwestern Colorado.

Vino's slogan is "Life's too short to drink bad wine," and owners Lisa Leyshen and Michael Kirlan devote themselves to making sure that no one does. Leyshen is a former assistant beverage director at Snowbird, Utah, and Kirlan was a sales representative for a bicycle company. But wine has long been the couple's passion. Before they got into the business, they loved wines and made great efforts to learn as much about them as possible, but they realize that not everyone shares their penchant for self-education. When they opened Vino in early 2001, their mission was to help people understand wines.

The store specializes in small-production wines from mostly family-run artisan wineries. You'll find labels from France, Spain, New Zealand, Australia, Washington, Oregon, and Colorado—with five or six Colorado wineries represented. Vino's particular depth is in small wineries from Spain and the less-heralded regions of southern France, but also from New Zealand, Australia, and Oregon. "You won't find Kendall-Jackson or Mondavi in the store," Kirlan says, then after skipping a dramatic beat, adding, "except for Private Reserve."

Leyshen and Kirlan taste every wine they carry, and they are beyond happy to talk to you about wines in general or any particular varietal or region. Vino hand sells virtually all of its wine, puts out an informative newsletter, and organizes special wine events. The couple has done tastings at True Value Hardware and winemaker dinners at Café Diva. Leyshen and Kirlan assemble a monthly mixed case of six reds and six whites at a 25 percent discount, while customers who prefer to mix-and-match bottles for their own case from any 12 reds or whites in the newsletter reap 15 percent savings. The store also stocks a limited but intense group of specialty beers, both microbrews from this country and exotic imports, and also invites customers to create their own six-packs. There is also a shelf of glasses and wine accessories.

Vino, 435 Lincoln Avenue, Steamboat Springs; (970) 875-1183.

Wine Rack

Visitors staying in condos at the base of the Steamboat ski area often pop over to the Wine Rack for a bottle to drink with the dinner that's just about to go on the stove or under the broiler. This small store carries mostly domestic wines, and mostly from the better-known wineries in California, Oregon, and Washington. The selection is sorted by varietal, with a greater proportion of reds than whites.

The Wine Rack stocks Steamboat Springs Cellars wines, made by the town's only winery from Palisade grapes—certainly not the finest wine in the barrel, but a nice souvenir. Whether domestic or imports from France, Italy, Spain, and a few from Germany, most of the Wine Rack's wines fall into the "reasonable" price category. Still, the store does carry late-harvest Rieslings, dessert wines, and some other premium bottles, as well as liqueurs and spirits.

Wine Rack, 1850 Ski Time Square Drive, Steamboat Resort; (970) 879-0485.

Other

Guided Gourmet Hikes

Hardcore backcountry explorers would hardly consider the Steamboat ski area's self-described "exhilarating 1½-mile trek" to be much of a workout, but for those who spend more time in the kitchen or at the table than on the trail, it qualifies. This summer program, inaugurated in 2001, consists of a ride up the Silver Bullet

Gondola, a hike with a guide who will share his or her knowledge about mountain flora and fauna as well as the area's history and geography, and a picnic at the Four Points Hut. The uphill route involves a 640-foot elevation gain. Most groups walk in fairly leisurely fashion, taking 1¼ to 1¾ hours.

The "picnic" is actually a buffet-style lunch put on the resort's executive chef, Liz Wahl. Enjoy the hike and then dig into the international cheeses, croissants, baguettes, fresh Italian pasta, seafood salads, assorted fruits, peppered and sliced round of beef, smoked turkey, country ham, salmon filet poached in wine and herbs, fresh chocolate-dipped strawberries, éclairs, summer cobblers with mountain berries, and wine, of course.

Good as the food is, it tastes even better in the clear mountain air and sunshine. At this writing, the hikes are offered on Tuesdays and Thursdays, beginning in midmorning and timed so that hikers arrive at Four Points right around lunchtime, where Chef Wahl's feast awaits.

Steamboat Ski Area, 2305 Mt. Werner Circle, Steamboat Springs;
(800) 922-2722, (970) 871-5191, or www.steamboat.com.

Off the Beaten Path

Steamboat Springs' congenial bookstore–café is a popular spot for breakfast, lunch, morning coffee, afternoon tea, or early-evening light dining—along with outstanding book-browsing. Located on a side street just half a block from Lincoln Avenue, the store is a favorite of locals and a must for visitors. The café portion of the business occupies a big sunny room that feels like an enclosed porch, with some spillover tables in the main room. Breakfast pastries, good soups and sandwiches, toothsome sweets, and beverages comprise most of the chalkboard menu. Many of the dishes are house-made, and others come from good mostly local suppliers. There's variety, freshness, and quality, which, along with the feed-the-mind ambience of the bookstore, holds considerable appeal.

Off the Beaten Path Bookstore, Coffeehouse, & Bakery Café, 56 Seventh Street,
Steamboat Springs; (970) 879-6830.

Spasso

If you're seeking a cute place for an on-mountain bite—whether a snack or a light meal—look no farther than Spasso. With its Mediterranean décor and pleasant patio, the little shop starts serving specialty coffee drinks in the morning and pours wine well into the evening. Accompaniments include pastries, tarts, muffins, scones, croissants, and breads in the morning, and a variety of sandwiches on baguettes, ciabatta, and focaccia for lunch or a light dinner. Soup, salad, antipasti, bruschetta, or a cheese plate are other nice options. Some people come just for the gelato, excellent Italian ice cream house-made from a base to which fruit purees, cocoa, vanilla, mocha, and other flavors are added.

Spasso, Torian Plum Plaza, Steamboat Resort; (970) 871-1488.

Recipes

Café Diva Chef Kate Van Renselaer assembles beef Wellington-inspired steaks. The recipe is a little on the involved side, but certainly doable for an experienced home cook—and sauce and mushroom ragout, if made in quantity, can be frozen and defrosted for the next time.

KVR Beef Wellington

4 center-cut beef tenderloin steaks
kosher salt and fresh cracked pepper to taste
about 3 tablespoons olive oil, divided
1 clove garlic, peeled and minced
1 shallot, peeled and minced
½ pound baby spinach, washed
4 puff pastry rounds cut the same size as the steaks, brushed with butter and
    baked until golden (use frozen puff pastry and bake according to package
    directions)
1 cup Sauce Périgourdine (recipe below)
½ cup Mushroom Ragout (recipe below)
4 tablespoons Gorgonzola butter (2 tablespoons unsalted butter and
    2 tablespoons imported Gorgonzola, mashed together)

Preheat oven to 425 degrees. Season steaks on both sides with salt and pepper. In a large skillet over high heat, heat olive oil and sear steaks on both sides for about 1 minute per side, until medium browned. Transfer steaks to an oven-proof pan and bake in preheated oven for about 5 minutes for medium rare. Let steaks rest at room temperature for an additional 3 minutes. While steaks are in the oven, add a little more olive oil to skillet, and add garlic and shallots and sauté briefly, being careful not to burn the garlic and shallots. After just a few seconds, add all the spinach, season with salt and pepper, and cook, tossing rapidly in pan with tongs.

On the center of each of four plates, place a puff pastry round, top with a few spoonfuls of mushroom ragout, then lay the steaks on top the mushrooms, and top each with a tablespoon of gorgonzola butter. Ladle the Sauce Périgourdine around the Wellington, and serve. Serves 4.

Sauce Périgourdine
3 tablespoons olive oil
1½ cups portobello mushrooms, finely diced

¼ cup shallots, peeled and minced
2 teaspoons minced garlic
1 carrot, peeled and minced
2 stalks celery, minced
2 teaspoons chopped fresh thyme
1 bay leaf
2 teaspoons brown sugar
1 cup Madeira
¼ cup sherry
¼ cup cognac
2 ounces veal glace (*glace de veau*, available in gourmet food stores)
2 ounces chicken glace (*glace de poulet*, available in gourmet food stores)
¾ cup dry white wine
2 teaspoons black truffle peelings
2 teaspoons unsalted butter
kosher salt and fresh cracked pepper, to taste

In a sauté pan over medium-high heat, heat olive oil. Add mushrooms, shallots, garlic, carrot, and celery, and sauté until soft. Add thyme, bay leaf, and brown sugar, and sauté until sugar dissolves. Deglaze pan with Madeira, stirring up bits that cling to the bottom of the pan. Then add cognac, sherry, veal and chicken *glaces*, and white wine, and reduce to sauce consistency. Add truffle peelings, swirl in butter, and season to taste with kosher salt and fresh cracked pepper.

Mushroom Ragout
2 tablespoons olive oil
¾ cup red onion, peeled and finely diced
2 tablespoons brown sugar
2 tablespoons unsalted butter
kosher salt and fresh ground pepper
1½ cups mixed wild mushrooms, diced
1 tablespoon mixed fresh herbs (thyme, rosemary, oregano)
2 tablespoons sherry
2 teaspoons veal *glace*

In a sturdy saucepan over medium-high heat, heat olive oil. Add red onion, brown sugar, butter, and salt and pepper, and cook, stirring occasionally, until onions are caramelized. Add mushrooms and herbs (and another teaspoon or two of butter if needed, as the mushrooms will absorb the moisture). Cook, stirring, until mushrooms are golden brown. Deglaze pan with sherry. Stir in veal *glace*. Reduce heat to low and cook until ragout is thickened. Adjust seasoning by adding more salt and pepper, if needed.

No matter now sophisticated they may be, guest ranches cultivate a down-home persona, and what can be more down-home—other than, perhaps, canning your own peaches—than homemade ice cream? Vista Verde has perfected this banana ice cream.

Roasted Banana Ice Cream

4 very ripe bananas, peeled
2 cups heavy cream
2 cups half and half
1 cup sugar
1 vanilla bean, split and seeded
2 eggs
8 egg yolks

Preheat oven to 350 degrees. In a lightly oiled pan, roast peeled bananas for 5 to 10 minutes until very soft. Meanwhile, in a medium saucepan, combine cream, half and half, half the sugar, and vanilla bean over medium high heat. Bring to a simmer, then whisk in the eggs, egg yolks, and remainder of the sugar. As soon as cream mixture comes to a boil, slowly pour in the eggs and whisk to combine. (It is important to do this step slowly, or you will end up with scrambled eggs.) Return the mixture to the saucepan and over medium-heat, stir the mixture constantly with a wooden spoon until it is *nappe* (coats the back of the spoon). Purée the bananas and stir them into the thickened mixture. Strain into a container set in an ice bath. Cool completely. Freeze in an ice-cream machine. Makes 1 quart.

Ragnar's was one of the first on-mountain, table-service restaurants at a Colorado ski resort, and it has served one of the most interesting menus, winter after winter. This rich Norwegian chowder, a longtime Steamboat classic, has been fine-tuned by various chefs over the years. This is the version refined by the resort's executive chef, Liz Wahl.

Ragnar's Fiskesuppe

1 pound sweet butter, divided
1½ cups flour, divided
½ pound carrots, peeled and diced
½ pound celery, diced
½ pound yellow onions, peeled and diced
1½ tablespoons clam base (available in gourmet food stores)
1 bay leaf
1½ teaspoons ground fennel
¼ teaspoon cayenne pepper

1 teaspoon thyme
1½ teaspoons dried tarragon
1 pint (2 cups) water
1 pint (2 cups) clam juice
½ cup dry white wine
¼ cup milk
¼ cup heavy cream
4 tablespoons (¼ cup) brandy
1 8-ounce can of chopped clams
½ pound shrimp, peeled and deveined, or other seafood of choice

To make roux, melt ½ pound (2 sticks) butter in a medium saucepan over low heat. Whisk in 1 cup of flour and continue cooking and stirring until flour begins to turn a light beige. Set aside.

In a large saucepan, melt remaining ½ pound (2 sticks) of butter over medium-high heat. Add carrots, celery, and onions, cover, and allow to sweat for 5 minutes. Stir in remaining ½ cup flour, mixing well. Add clam base and seasonings and stir. Add liquids and cook covered over medium heat for 30 minutes (or longer). Stir in reserved roux until completely blended and soup begins to thicken. Add reserved clams and shrimp or other seafood. Bring to a boil and cook for 2 to 3 minutes. Serve immediately. Serves 8 to 10.

Winter Park, Fraser, and Granby

Southern Grand County is an immense valley of beautiful mountain-ringed ranchland, anchored by the Winter Park resort. The ski area and the namesake town of Winter Park are just west of Berthoud Pass, beguilingly close to Denver, and also accessible by the Ski Train, which runs on weekends during winter and once a week during the summer. The ski area has been around since 1939, welcoming skiers and more recently snowboarders—and also summer hikers, mountain bikers, and folks who simply like to kick back and admire the spectacular mountain scenery.

U.S. 40 snakes over Berthoud Pass and is the main route through downtown Winter Park and other Grand County communities. Winter Park and Fraser between them have some 30 places to eat, most falling into the casual category. Lots of Italian, lots of burgers, lots of Tex-Mex, and a smattering of fine-dining establishments. Fraser is the closest to the ski town, tiny Tabernash is beyond that, and Granby is just a few miles up the road. Grand Lake Village, a classic summer resort town enviably situated between the west side of Rocky Mountain National Park and eponymous Grand Lake, is at the eastern end of the county. They are not known for an abundance of culinary features. Some of the area's most interesting food is served at guest and dude ranches, but most of these serve only to overnight guests. This is beginning to change. Winter Park is in the early phases of the kind of concentrated base-village development that Keystone, Copper Mountain, Steamboat, Breckenridge, Beaver Creek, and other ski resorts have—and with that will come more restaurants of greater variety and more sophistication. They always do.

Meanwhile, just outside of Granby, SolVista Golf & Ski Ranch has launched its own master-planned enlargement, and nearby ranchland and open areas are being converted into golf courses and pricey golf-oriented communities, which could bode well for Grand County food-lovers, a group that has been in enforced culinary hibernation for decades. A few good restaurants, bakeries, cafés, and food festivals have kept them going. Stay tuned to see what happens as construction picks up steam.

Bakeries

Base Camp Bakery & Café

From early morning, this cheery bakery puts out from-scratch bagels, muffins, scones, croissants—and full breakfasts too. Midday baked goods include cinnamon rolls, cookies, brownies, and fruit bars. Lunch options include wraps and sandwiches on a choice of freshly baked breads. House-made soups, daily specials, salads, and a full espresso bar make this a good choice for a quick meal. If you want a tasty box lunch to take on a picnic, call ahead and they'll make one up for you.

Base Camp Bakery & Café, Park Place Shopping Center, 78437 U.S. Highway 40, Winter Park; (970) 726-5530.

Carver's Bakery Café

Carver's has been around for years, producing fresh baked goods and from-scratch breakfast and lunch offerings long before they were commonplace. There always seems to be a line at this quaint and cozy cabin tucked in behind the Cooper Creek Square shopping center.

Hand-rolled bagels, excellent pastries, and some of the best breakfasts in ski country roll out of Carver's kitchen. The lunch offerings include the usual repertoire of soups, salads (in a bread bowl if you like), and sandwiches that range from healthy grilled veggie sandwiches to traditional American clubs and BLTs that are as good as they get. Dinners are heartier, with everything from soup to pastries made on site. Carver's remains one of Grand County's grand places for breakfast and lunch—and I salute its longevity and consistency.

Carver's Bakery Café, Cooper Creek Square, 93 County Road 7, Winter Park; (970) 726-8202.

Ian's Mountain Bakery

There is an Ian behind Ian's Mountain Bakery. Ian Daugherty operates a place that is a highlight for locals and visitors to Granby—people whose day begins, and sometimes ends, with great baked products. Scones and breakfast pastries start the day. Soups and sandwiches made on those excellent breads keep it going. And desserts to take home are the sweet capstone.

Daugherty is the only baker in this part of Colorado with French ambition and the skill to pull it off. Among his artisan breads, baguettes are standouts. Just to prove that Ian's is no one-note bakery, the jalapeño cornbread is the best around. The pastries, including a divine *pain au chocolat*, are topnotch, and the cheesecakes are so good that locals have taken to ordering them made into wedding and other special-occasion cakes. Daugherty has developed cheesecake recipes with more than 30 flavors in the fruit-coffee-toffee-swirl realm and another 10 that are liqueur-based. Every one of them is as gorgeous as it is tasty, so it's no wonder that they have become legendary.

Ian's Mountain Bakery, 358 East Agate Avenue, Granby; (970) 887-1176 or www.rkymtnhi.com/businesses/ians/.

Dining

Caroline's Cuisine

The pleasing restaurant at the Soda Springs Ranch, a resort located half-way between Granby and Grand Lake, is known Grand County–wide as the place to get French and Italian specialties that are a little fancy, a little bistro-style, and always excellent. Caroline's also offers well-made American pub-type dishes to suit the unadventurous diner. The setting is casual and charming, with glass tops over flower-print tablecloths, Valentine-red napkins, and country-type decorative touches.

The regular menu, though rather small, touches a number of culinary bases, but if there were a market for an all-French restaurant in this corner of Grand County, Jean-Claude Cavalera could comply with style and authenticity. Being realistic, however, he cooks for the clientele—and for the popular adjacent bar, where pub food is de rigeur. Caroline's menu balances between such (relative) exotica as escargots and mushrooms sautéed in garlic butter, frogs' legs, and carpaccio with such dishes from the standard U.S. repertoire as half-pound burgers, chicken breast and steak sandwiches, and Caesar salad topped with blackened chicken breast.

House specialties include blackened, grilled jumbo tiger shrimp served with rice and red-pepper *pico de gallo* and Antipasto Fettuccini Alfredo, a rich pasta dish made with marinated artichokes, mushrooms, roasted bell peppers, sun-dried tomatoes, and herbs served with a Parmesan cream sauce. Additionally, Cavalera makes seasonal menu changes and uses market-fresh ingredients for nightly specials. You might find corn chowder, fresh mussels, pork with apples in a Norman style, or duck, the latter roasted with rum or folded into an enchilada or given another possible permutation.

The rich desserts include profiteroles, almond butter cake with strawberries, meringue-topped spumoni tower, Sour Cream Apple Tart, and Chocolate Cake Sundae, which consists of an individual cake and all the makings of a chocolate sundae.

In addition to wines from a well-balanced wine list, Caroline's is known for its specialty drinks and coffees. Order an anise-flavored *pastis,* and you'll feel as if you are in the South of France, even if the guy at the next table door is wolfing down tortilla soup, his wife is nibbling on the house salad, and the kids are digging into chicken fingers with barbecue sauce and fries.

Caroline's Cuisine, Soda Springs Ranch, 9921 U.S. Highway 34, Granby; (970) 627-8125, (970) 627-9404, or www.sodaspringsranch.com/cc.htm.

Deno's Mountain Bistro

Not much to look at from the outside, simple on the inside, and offering a menu that isn't at all unusual, this Winter Park restaurant nevertheless has snared both a

Wine Spectator Award of Excellence and a DiRoNA Award (see page 452) as a noteworthy restaurant. These honors are all the more remarkable—shocking, even—because Deno's is a casual and extremely reasonably priced ski-town restaurant and sports bar where promptly producing large portions is the most valued attribute that a kitchen can display.

Deno's Onion Soup Gratin is a perennial favorite, and the Soup of Yesterday, a whimsical twist on the perennial soup of the day offered almost every place else. The salads are fresh, the steaks are aged, and the seafood, poultry, hand-tossed pizzas, pastas, and vegetarian dishes are popular too.

Most locals who are only into the food scene are bewildered that this restaurant ever copped those awards, but the excellent and extensive wine program is the reason. The roughly 70 selections on the "short" wine list represent some of the more moderately priced wines, and bottles of currently popular wines are displayed in a case near the dining room. The "long" list has about 250 wines, including the more expensive vintages, and those bottles are locked in a climate-controlled wine room. Deno's carries wines from California, Oregon, Spain, Australia, France, and Italy, with about 10 available by the glass, including a nightly featured wine.

The pub menu and lunch menu are both lighter and more casual than the evening offerings, although Angel Hair Pomodoro and Chicken Linguini Alfredo, two favorites from the dinner menu, are also available in midday. Fine dining at Deno's? Not really. But respectable and hearty food at very reasonable prices? Yes, indeed. And then, there are those awards. . . .

Deno's Mountain Bistro, 78911 U.S. Highway 40 (downtown, next to Cooper Creek Square), Winter Park; (970) 726-5332 or www.denosmountainbistro.com.

Fontenot's Cajun Café

The heat and spirit of The Big Easy are transported to the Rockies in this lively New Orleans-style bistro. Opened in 1986 and owned since 1990 by Chris and Linda Moore, Fontenot's serves moderately priced, flavorful (sometimes downright spicy, in fact) fare at lunch and dinner. Gumbo, red beans and rice, jambalaya, and po' boys with fillings as varied as *andouille* sausage to Philly cheese steak are midday specialties. Light dinners are available, but most folks come in to be stuffed from starters to desserts. Entrée specialties include Cajun-style peel-and-eat shrimp, Bourbon Street Catfish, crawfish ettouffée, and a seafood sampler called the Rajun Cajun Combo. Asian flavors appear with Teriyaki Mahi burgers and Sesame Seared Salmon on the menu, as do Italian influences in the form of fresh linguini with a choice of house-made sauces. The sizable wine line features California and some Australian selections.

Fontenot's Cajun Café, Park Plaza, 78711 U.S. Highway 40, Winter Park; (970) 726-4021.

Gasthaus Eichler

When this charming inn was established in 1988, it provided Winter Park with some needed culinary variety. Family-run by Hans and Hanne Eichler, it retains the spirit of an authentic *gasthaus* (guesthouse) transplanted to Colorado's high country. Upstairs in this Bavarian chalet-style building are 15 spotless guest rooms. Downstairs is a large restaurant known for well-executed German classics, as well as many lighter and more contemporary offerings, all served amid charming European-style décor.

Despite the Gasthaus Eichler's strong German accent, some of the dishes are from elsewhere, including such starters as Italian-inspired venison carpaccio and French-influenced mussels *marnière*. More typically Germanic or Alpine appetizers include wild mushroom strudel and the hearty potato pancakes. The cuisine of central Europe again shines in the main course, where you have a choice of several schnitzel preparations, bratwurst, *Rindsrolladen* (braised beef rolls), or *Kasslerippchen* (smoked and grilled pork chops served with sauerkraut). The chef's specialties are a little more cosmopolitan and varied. Salmon en Croûte, Crispy Cedar Plank Duck Breast, Grilled Vegetable Napoleon, and Red Deer Medallion demonstrate the range of the kitchen's repertoire. Everything is appropriately accompanied by suitable side dishes—and everything is very good.

Among the desserts, apple strudel and Linzer Torte maintain the Germanic tradition. Other popular sweets include New York Cheesecake and Kahlua Toffee Chocolate Mousse Torte. The wine list is modest enough in size that it is simply divided into "house," "red," "white," and "champagne," but it offers sufficient variety to match the cuisine. Earlybird specials, rare in ski country, make the Gasthaus Eichler all the more attractive.

Gasthaus Eichler, 78786 U.S. Highway 40, Winter Park; (970) 726-5133, (303) 717-3537, or www.gasthauseichler.com.

Lodge at Sunspot

The lovely Lodge at Sunspot, near the unloading area of Winter Park's Zephyr Express high-speed chairlift, is a fine mountaintop restaurant. With big beams, a soaring ceiling, huge windows, and fieldstone floors, it is architecturally commanding. The food is darned good too, which is remarkable, because it operates seasonally, meaning that longevity among the cooks and servers is never assured.

Enter into the lodge's massive foyer and the self-service restaurant is on the left and the lovely sit-down restaurant on the right. Winter dinner is served on Thursday, Friday, and Saturday nights. There are two options: a buffet and a sit-down feast. For either, you reach the Lodge at Sunspot via a magical ride in an enclosed gondola car that is hooked onto the chairlift cable. You can also take a mountaintop ride in a snowcat-pulled sleigh before you dine. For vacationers, an evening is generally a culinary and experiential highpoint of a ski trip to Winter Park.

Skiers can avoid the cafeteria crowds with a relaxed sit-down lunch when the restaurant serves ample portions of well-prepared soups, salads, hot entrées, and desserts. Start dinner with a tasty soup (especially the cream of mushroom), the perfect start to a meal whose "appetizer" was a ride in the cold night air. Among the entrées, The Lodge at Sunspot is known for its preparation of elk medallions, rack of lamb, and seafood dishes. Leave room for dessert. Tíramisu fans are in heaven, and the fresh strawberries, raspberries, and blueberries, served with either ice cream or thick cream, are a real treat in midwinter two miles above sea level.

The Lodge at Sunspot, Winter Park Resort, Winter Park; (970) 726-1446 for dinner reservations or www.skiwinterpark.com for general resort information.

Marvin's Hideaway Park Restaurant

Front Rangers with fond memories of Marvin's Garden Restaurant in Denver, diners who experienced the culinary renaissance of the Ranch House Restaurant at Devil's Thumb Ranch, or guests who dined at the now-defunct Restaurant On The Ridge can now find Marvin Bronstein, the creative chef who wowed patrons at those establishments, ensconced in his own place at the north end of downtown Winter Park. Marvin's Hideaway Park Restaurant serves what Bronstein refers to as his "passionately prepared upscale, modern mountain cuisine."

Best of all, he delivers—perhaps it is his nature to be giving and caring. For 15 years, he worked as a nurse-practitioner in the pediatrics department at the University of Utah. While on a trip to New Orleans for a medical conference, he had what he calls an epiphany. "I was sitting in a restaurant there, and suddenly I realized, all this incredible food is out there, and I could be making it," he recalls. End of medical career. Start of culinary career.

After working his way through kitchens in Park City and Salt Lake City, Utah, and then in Los Angeles, he opened the State Beach Café in Santa Monica. After an earthquake in 1994 destroyed the building, Bronstein left quake country for Denver, where he established Marvin's Garden and then went on to several other Front Range restaurants. After two years as executive chef at Devil's Thumb Ranch, he and his sister, Donna Truitt, created the Restaurant On The Ridge at Meadow Ridge. The food won raves. The wines won raves. Bronstein and the restaurant were cited by *Gourmet* magazine in the 2001 best-restaurant issue.

Marvin's Hideaway Park Restaurant has adopted many of the quality features of Restaurant On The Ridge. The menu changes seasonally, with local products used when possible. This mix-and-match chef likes to surprise with combinations of his own imagination. Appetizers (called Openers) include Chicken Fajita Eggrolls (wonton wrappers stuffed with Southwestern chicken, bell peppers, and jalapeño Jack cheese, served with lime-cilantro dipping sauce and a dollop of crème fraîche), Goat Cheese Gnocchi bathed in a pesto cream sauce, and Venison White Bean Nachos (tricolored tortilla chips, white bean-venison chili, Mexican cheese, fresh cilantro, and sour cream).

Entrées (called Main Events) include Game Cassoulet (slow-simmered game sausage, forest mushrooms, lemon, and herbs in a Romano-herb *boule)*, and Rocky Mountain Trout (whole boneless trout stuffed with crayfish tail meat, scallops, and shrimp wrapped in bacon, roasted, and served with rice or quinoa).

There are weekly special entrées as well. One ski-season roster included Roast Atlantic Salmon napped in browned butter–parsley sauce, Charbroiled Flatiron Steak with Devil's Tongue Steak Sauce, and Seared Elk Medallions napped with black truffle–caper *démi-glace*. Bronstein has always displayed a fondness for game (that, in fact, is what impressed *Gourmet*) and also for trout. Dessert specialties include Maple Pecan Crème Brulée, tìramisu, and house-made ice cream.

The wine list tends to affordably priced selections from various wine-growing areas, all available by the glass. Chef's Cellar Selections is a program of small-batch, usually handcrafted selections from lesser-known wineries and often not available in Colorado, plus a sampling of hard-to-get selections from name wineries. These wines are poured into elegant Riedel stemware, a Restaurant On The Ridge consideration transplanted to Marvin's Hideaway. Wine flights are an option, with Pinot Noirs always available and other varietals changing. You can even order a flight of bourbon if the spirit moves you.

Marvin's Hideaway Restaurant serves lunch, dinner, and weekend brunch. Downstairs from the restaurant is Get to The Point, a relaxed spot offering family favorites, lighter and more casual fare, and tapas, as well as light jazz, often live.

Marvin's Hideaway Park Restaurant, 78259 U.S. Highway 40, Winter Park; (970) 726-7660 or www.marvins.biz.

Ranch House Restaurant & Saloon

Devil's Thumb Ranch is a grandiose spread that fills different roles. It provides charming hideaway lodging for a romantic getaway or quiet family retreat. It offers horse-drawn sleigh rides in winter, fly-fishing in summer, and horseback rides both in summer and during midday even in winter. It is one of Colorado's best, and best-known, cross-country skiing and snowshoeing centers. And its restaurant, located in the original Yaeger family homestead, built in 1937, is one of the finest places to dine in the area. You can mix and match by staying there, playing there, dining there, or any combination of those pleasures.

The lounge area, which is the "saloon" part of the restaurant's name, is as warm and cozy as a bar can be. On weekends, there's live acoustic music. If you are dining, you will be led into either the main dining room or the outer dining room, which resembles an enclosed wrap-around veranda. Knotty-pine walls, white tablecloths, and a sprinkling of artwork and Western memorabilia create a pleasingly rustic, yet romantic, ambience. Windows in the main dining room overlook the outer dining room, whose big windows in turn overlook the Devil's Thumb spread. There's no better setting for lunch with a view of the Continental Divide. Good as the food is in the bright light of day, this restaurant really shines at dinner.

The New American cuisine menu changes seasonally. Starters include crisp salads, plated appetizers, and fine soups. Winners include hearty Sea Bass and Corn Chowder, a creamy cross-pollination of seafood and corn chowders; and Grilled Spicy Thai Shrimp Skewer in red curry and lemon basil curry served over cucumber slaw and immaculately seasoned, and crisp-fried Blue Crab and Lobster Cake with a sweet-sour pink grapefruit rémoulade.

Among the entrées, you'll always find beef and game items, such as impeccable Black Angus beef tenderloin, New York strip, Black Buck antelope medallions, pan-roasted pork tenderloin, New Zealand lamb chops, and buffalo meatloaf, all served with the perfect sauces, side dishes, and condiments.

Bob Fanch, who with his wife Suzanne owns Devil's Thumb Ranch, has a buddy who is a commercial fisherman on Cape Cod. Ranch House Restaurant diners receive the beneficiaries of their partnership in the form of seafood delivered weekly fresh from the boat. Depending on the season, New England cod, striped bass, bluefin and yellowfin tuna, scallops, and lobster appear on the menu. Clearly, all don't come from the *Sea Fever II*, but all the seafood is as fresh as can be.

There's always cheese tortellini prepared either with seafood or vegetarian-style, but the signature vegetarian offering is a terrific strudel bursting with sautéed vegetables and served with vodka cream sauce and pistachio rice. Top your dinner off with a selection from the wine list that keeps getting better and with a sublime dessert.

Ranch House Restaurant & Saloon, 5350 County Road 83, Tabernash; (970) 726-5633, (970) 726-5632 for general information, or www.devilsthumbranch.com.

Wildcreek Restaurant

Winter Park dining options took a giant leap forward in 2001, when Ron Custer, former manager of the ski area's Club Car Restaurant at Mary Jane, took the old Rome on the Range and remade it into the Wildcreek Restaurant. The 30-foot vaulted ceiling held up by lodgepole beams, large windows, and subtle Western motif provide a suitable setting for what quickly became known as serving some of the best and most creative food in the valley.

Everything at lunch and dinner is house-made from scratch, mostly by classically trained cooks. Midday options include appetizers of shrimp satay or brick-oven flatbread served with marina sauce and mozzarella. The latter is also a bar-menu favorite. Featured lunch attractions also include a grilled tuna steak with perky wasabi mayo, a comforting meatloaf sandwich with marinara and smoked mozzarella on a baguette, or a substantial sirloin burger topped with portobello mushrooms, pancetta, and cheddar cheese that puts your basic bacon cheeseburger to shame.

Dinner offerings cover an ever-wider swath of world cuisine, creatively conceived and well executed. Nagamiki roll, loosely adapted from the sushi counter, features thinly sliced New York strip steak rolled with portobello mushrooms and scallions, then grilled and served with a teriyaki glaze. Poached Asian pear served with baby bib lettuce, toasted walnuts, and creamy raspberry dressing makes for a refreshing salad. Entrées satisfy meat lovers, including elk medallions *au poivre*, fillet of beef wrapped in smoked bacon, and grilled, roasted pork loin with a wonderful Rainier cherry stuffing.

Linguini Montelcino, something of a house specialty, is served with sautéed sausage, prosciutto, fresh tomatoes, spinach, red chilies, garlic, and olive oil. The Purse is a gorgeous vegetarian specialty, composed of grilled vegetables encased in puff pastry and sauced with fresh herb and mushroom velouté.

Mostly domestic and some imported wines are categorized on the well-balanced wine list by varietal, with just a handful of the less expensive wines also offered by the glass. The desserts are as varied in provenance as the entrées. Chocolate Mousse Cake, tiramisu, bread pudding, ice cream, and Apple Pecan Upside Down Cake. Dessert wine pairings are suggested for each.

After 10:00 P.M., as the last crumb of dessert and last drop of wine are being consumed, Wildcreek shows its wilder side. Especially in winter, the crowd gathers upstairs around the four billiards tables, at the bar, and in the lounge area, for live music on Friday and Saturday nights and a party atmosphere all the time. In summer, Wildcreek's outdoor dining is just the best.

Wildcreek Restaurant, 78491 U.S. Highway 40 (downtown), Winter Park; (970) 726-1111 or www.wildcreekrestaurant.com.

Events

Chef's Cup Race and Benefit Dinner Dance

January—Speed in the kitchen and speed on the slopes. Skills with a skillet and skills on snow. Agility running gates in a race course and agility running plates through a dining room. Such are the talents required to triumph at this annual two-pronged event. The Chef's Cup Race and Benefit Dinner Dance takes place on a Thursday and Friday in mid-January for the benefit of the Winter Park Competition Center—and anyone who loves to eat.

On Thursday, four-person teams of chefs, servers, dishwashers, and bussers compete to see who is the fleetest team on the hill. It's an out-of-the-restaurant event where everyone in the kitchen is created equal—with the best of equals being the one who is the best ski racer. On Friday, the chefs reign again. They prepare a gala feast for the evening dinner-dance at West Portal Station, the day lodge that is fancied up for the occasion. Winter Park and Fraser Valley restaurants try to outdo each other in the culinary arena for an evening meal that lights up a January night. In 2003, Marvin Bronstein, owner-chef of Marvin's Hideaway Restaurant, (see page 234) cooked his way to first place in the culinary competition, and attendees feasted on his and other chefs' creations. Beer and wine are complimentary, and the attendant silent auction includes gift certificates to a number of the participating restaurants. You can count on fab food, music for dancing, and a great midwinter time.

For ticket information, call the competition center, (970) 726-1590.

Rocky Mountain Wine, Beer, & Food Festival

August—For one Saturday each August, West Portal Station morphs from a sporty day lodge into a showcase for great food, wine, and microbrews. This festival was established in 1985 as a fundraiser for Winter Park's renowned National Sports Center for the Disabled (NSCD). You'll see folks wheeling around in their chairs, balancing food, wine, or navigating the crowded aisles on crutches. The NSCD has helped them fulfill their sports dreams, and they support the NCSD in return—and sample great eats and great drinks.

The three-hour extravaganza includes food from more than a dozen Grand County restaurants, something like 200 wines, and about 100 domestic, imported, and microbrewery beers. Restaurants offering tasting portions at this event have included the Gasthaus Eichler, Grand Lake Lodge, the Lodge at Sunspot, and the Restaurant On The Ridge. The wines are from all over, but most of the microbrews are from Colorado. The usual format is for some of the participating restaurants to offer wine-pairing or beer-pairing dinners a night or two before the festival.

Before the doors of West Portal Station are unlocked for the afternoon tasting, one-hour wine and beer seminars take place. Scheduled for late in the morning of the main event, the seminars provide a good prelude to the tasting. A silent auction with many sports, travel, and lifestyle items is also part of the festival. The admission ticket is good for all you can eat or drink during the three-hour main event, but tickets for the wine and beer seminars are available only that day. Seating is limited, so come early.

For tickets, call the National Sports Center for the Disabled, (303) 316-1545, (800) 420-8087, or www.nscd.org.

Flamethrowers High-Altitude Chili Cook-off

September—Every Labor Day weekend since 1978, chili lovers and, more importantly, official judges sanctioned by the International Chili Society have singed their tonsils at the Flamethrowers High Altitude Chili Cook-off at Winter Park.

Two competitive events are rolled into this two-day chili extravaganza. Saturday is the official Colorado State Chili Cook-off, a qualifier for the Rocky Mountain Regional Chili Cook-off, held the very next day and at the very same location. The regional contest in turn is a qualifier for the World Chili Cook-off, in Reno, Nevada, and definitely the big time in the realm of chili cooking.

Lest you think this is a frivolous event, know that—as in all serious cooking competitions—there are rules, a schedule, and real rivalries going on. Categories are red chili, green chili, salsa, and an open category for the most creative chef (which may have as much to do with his or her outfit as for the recipe). Entrants must bring their own cook stoves, ingredients, and utensils. With the exception of canned or bottled tomatoes or tomato sauces, no precooked ingredients are allowed in ICS Traditional Red or Chili Verde entries. No beans or fillers are allowed either, although portions dished out later to the public must have beans.

Another sign that this is not a trivial event? It's the sheer quantity of chili that gets prepared and gets eaten. Cooks are required to prepare a minimum of one gallon of chili for the judges and an additional two to three gallons of "sampling" chili (that's the stuff with the beans) for the public. Salsa and open division cooks may bring prepared or "doctored up" chilies or salsas to be submitted to the judging panel. After the judges have completed their tasting, the public is invited to sample recipes from subtle to searing. Cook-off admission is free, but the tickets required to sample the entries benefit the National Sports Center for the Disabled.

In addition to the hot stuff (and not-so-hot stuff), the cook-off includes entertainment (not surprisingly, salsa music), a Shoot 'n' Shout Contest (contestants toss back a shot of tequila and produce the loudest holler they can), and the jalapeño eating contest. Not haute cuisine, to be sure, but a whole lot of fun—and for a very good cause.

Winter Park Resort, Winter Park; (970) 726-5514 or www.skiwinterpark.com. The website for the International Chili Society cook-offs is www.chilicookoff.com.

Arts, Aspens, & Eats

September—A whimsical, wonderful, and unusual Grand County annual event is this tour of some of the area's most charming bed-and-breakfast inns, complete with the opportunity to taste food prepared from B&B cookbook recipes. Half of the participating B&Bs are open on each of the days of the two-day tour, which takes place over a weekend in mid-September (often when the aspens are displaying their golden autumn splendor) and supports Grand County Habitat for Humanity. The admission fee is modest, but the chance to visit the area's quaint inns is priceless.

Tickets are available in advance at most of Grand Country's visitors' centers and chambers of commerce, as well as at several local businesses. For information and ticket sales locations, call (970) 725-3640 or (970) 726-5346, or log onto www.colorado-inns.com/tour.htm.

Wines

Bottle Pass Liquors

Though small in square footage, Bottle Pass Liquors looms big among food- and wine-lovers. Grand County's most complete and most knowledgeable wine specialist is packed with wines in a wide range of styles and prices from one wall of large bottles to a section of high-end cabernets.

Largely because customers come in and request specific vintages that they've had before, California wines predominate, but the Australian wine selection has increased threefold since Bottle Pass staffers and customers have become aware of the favorable price-quality ratio from Down Under.

The store also carries a lot of French wines, but currently fewer from Italy, Spain, and other European nations. From the Southern Hemisphere come interesting wines from Argentina and South Africa, plus value wines from Chile. Canyon Wind, Grand River, and Plum Creek are the Colorado wineries represented on Bottle Pass Liquors' shelves.

Bottle Pass Liquors, Fraser Valley Shopping Center, Fraser; (970) 726-9476.

Other

Dashing Through the Snow

Sleighride dinners are not uncommon in the resorts of Colorado's high country, but this long-time sleighride operator offers six-course dinners on three different themes on different nights of the week—and that alone puts it a cut above most operations and their one-size-fits-all dinners. The horse-drawn sleigh ride to a dinner cabin far back on a 3,000-acre ranch sets the tone for the pleasurable evening to follow.

After a ride through the snowy countryside, guests are welcomed into light and warmth with hot chocolate or steaming cider and live entertainment by local artists. Each dinner starts with an appetizer, salad, and soup. The entrée choice is large rib eye, chicken, salmon, or a vegetarian offering, most often a squash casserole or similar. Dessert closes the meal.

The country dinner is hardly a gourmet event, what with chicken-fried steak, meatloaf, and such, but the wild game dinner, at this writing offered one night a week, is a feast for connoisseurs of elk, venison, and other game meats. Like all such operations, which have horses as well as people to feed, the dinners are pricey, but Dashing Through the Snow's bring-your-own policy saves on the cost of wine.

Dashing Through the Snow, 1400 County Road 5, Fraser; (970) 726-5376.

Recipes

Depending on the season and his inclination, Marvin Bronstein of Marvin's Hideaway Restaurant serves these tasty pillows of goat cheese with a simple fresh basil tomato sauce, a light pesto cream sauce, and an Alfredo sauce, all with great results. Bronstein considers six gnocchi to be an appetizer portion.

Goat Cheese Gnocchi

1 pound goat cheese
2 egg yolks
2 whole eggs
1 cup all-purpose flour

Combine all ingredients in the bowl of a standing mixer. Using the paddle attachment, beat on medium speed for about 2 minutes until well combined. Cover bowl with plastic wrap and chill well for about 2 hours or longer. Bring a large pot of salted water to a boil and then reduce to simmer. Drop the dough by the teaspoonful into the simmering salted water. When the gnocchi rise to the surface and float on the simmering water, cook for about another minute. Remove gnocchi with a slotted spoon and place on a heated plated on a pool of the sauce of your choice. Serves 6.

Delicious deep-sea fish at over 10,000 feet above sea level is something of a modern-day miracle. The Lodge at Sunspot serves this entrée with roasted tricolored potatoes and sautéed baby vegetables.

Pecan-Encrusted Deep Sea Grouper with Brandied Apricot Cream Sauce

10 grouper fillets
salt and ground white pepper to taste
2 cups all-purpose flour
2 cups egg wash (eggs diluted with small amount of water)
2 cups pecans, toasted and finely chopped
clarified butter, as needed
Brandied Apricot Cream Sauce (recipe follows)

Preheat standard oven to 375 degrees or convection oven to 350 degrees. Season fillets with salt and pepper to taste. Dredge in flour, patting off excess. Dip into egg wash and coat with chopped pecans.

In sauté pan at medium temperature, melt clarified butter. Sauté fillets until one side is lightly browned. Turn fillets onto an ovenproof pan and finish in the oven, about 7 to 10 minutes. To serve, ladle 3 tablespoons of sauce over each fillet. Serves 10.

Brandied Apricot Cream Sauce

½ teaspoon ground allspice
2½ cups (1 pound) dried apricots, cut into small dice
2 cups apricot brandy
¼ cup shallots, peeled, finely diced, and slowly cooked in unsalted butter until soft
2 cups heavy cream, heated to reduce
4 tablespoons (½ stick) unsalted better, softened
salt and ground white pepper to taste

In a dry saucepan, heat allspice for 30 seconds. Add apricots, brandy, and shallots. Simmer until liquid is reduced to ¼ cup. Add cream and reduce until sauce coats the back of a spoon. Stir in butter. Season to taste with salt and pepper. Keep warm until ready to use; do not let sauce boil.

The Central Mountains and Wine Country

(I-70 Corridor)

Breckenridge and Keystone

Given its prominence in skiing circles (led by three ski resorts that each tally a million or more skier/snowboarder visits every winter), its waves of summer tourists, and, most of all, its increasing census of new full-time residents who migrated from the Front Range and elsewhere, you'd think that Summit County would boast an abundance of really outstanding restaurants and a vibrant, consistent culinary scene. While the former isn't exactly true, a calendar peppered with special food events does help to fill the void.

Breckenridge is, at the core, a Colorado old mining town that has blossomed into a mega-resort with lodging development on the ski area's flanks and increasingly elsewhere around town. Copper Mountain and Keystone were both designed and built as ski resorts, complete with lodging and visitor services. These resorts and the nearby towns of Dillon, Silverthorne, and Frisco have many restaurants, especially in the Tex-Mex, steak, pizza, and informal Italian ilk, but surprisingly few have great culinary ambitions. Those that do tend to be found in Keystone, among the Rockies' first to claim a place on the Colorado culinary map with restaurants that catered to sophisticated palates. For a time, Keystone also promoted cooking classes designed for people who enjoy fine dining and wanted to recreate Keystone's style of gourmet dining at home. These classes are no more, but the resort does have a model professional cooking program in conjunction with Colorado Mountain College.

When he was with Keystone, Chef Bob Burden's monthly cooking classes drew a combination of loyal local fans and vacationers. Breckenridge too needed a culinary shot in the arm, and Burden, who moved there, now provides it. Still, Breck's cookware store closed, and some of the town's restaurant sites have recently shifted downmarket. For instance, the Adams Street Grill, a Breckenridge bastion of hip American fare, closed and was replaced by a branch of the Bubba Gump Shrimp Company chain. Sad.

I hold great hope for Copper Mountain. It is in the throes of a major redevelopment, with an attractive base village rapidly taking shape. I along with other Colorado foodies anticipate that some day, really good restaurants should occupy some of the new commercial space. Keystone can be expected to stay on top of Summit County's culinary heap—and, with luck, the nearby nonresort communities, where so much of the retail and service sector and good selection of mid-range restaurants are located, will also boast some fine dining and perhaps a cooking school and a cookware store.

Bakeries

The Blue Moon Baking Company, Butterhorn Bakery Café, and Clint's Bakery-Café

You have to search a bit to get a really great dinner in Summit County, but finding outstanding baked goods takes nothing more than a slight detour off the interstate. Pulling off at a Silverthorne or Frisco exit for a hit of coffee and a freshly baked scone, muffin, Danish, bagel, or other breakfast treat has become almost instinctive for me on a morning drive to the High Country. Clint's, in downtown Breckenridge, is a bit farther afield, but in philosophy, menu, and quality, it is not unlike the B-team.

Blue Moon and Butterhorn are always packed with locals, lining up for excellent breakfasts—whether continental-style light or full-on American fill-'er-up type—and satisfying reasonably priced lunches. The two bakeries are similar in style, ambience, and offerings. In both, the staples are soups, salads, and sandwiches, all house-made and fresh. Between meals, folks stop in for fresh bread or rolls and something for dessert, notably excellent cakes, pastries, and cookies. Both bakeries are in the casual, order-at-the-counter mode, though Butterhorn also offers the option of table service.

Clint's offers filled breakfast croissants, breakfast and lunch wraps, and enormous freshly baked bagels, plain or as the basis for hearty breakfast or lunch sandwiches. A daily quiche, house-made granola, and from-scratch soups are popular as well. Clint's slow-roasts coffee on-site in small batches every day, and the coffee bar always offers five fresh-brewed types.

The Blue Moon Baking Company, 253 Summit Place, Silverthorne; (970) 513-0513.
Butterhorn Bakery Café, 408 West Main Street, Frisco; (970) 668-3997.
Clint's Bakery-Café, 131 South Main Street, Breckenridge; (970) 453-2990.

Cooking Schools and Cooking Classes

Beaver Run Cooking Classes

Bob Burden is something of a Pied Piper when it comes to Summit County classes for the home cook. He used to hold culinary programs at Keystone, and when he moved to Breckenridge as Beaver Run's executive chef, in charge of the totally remodeled Spencer's Restaurant, he took his enthusiasm for and interest in teaching cooking with him. Both locals and vacationers have responded.

Because there are so many regulars, the menu and the theme are always different. Held monthly (usually the evening of the second Thursday of the month at this writing), these classes give a maximum of 16 home cooks the rare opportunity to use a real commercial kitchen—and a recently refurbished one at that. Wearing chef's aprons and tall white toques, they get to feel like the real thing too.

Classes start with champagne and introductions—and then the cooking starts. "I won't let you touch my knives or hot oil, but you can do anything else," Burden tells his attentive audience of food enthusiasts. Participants can do "anything else," but in reality, they often don't. The format is a combination of hands-on, demonstration, and inclusion of dishes or components of dishes prepared in advance by Burden and his team of chefs.

Burden, a sous-chef, or the pastry chef offer detailed explanations of each dish that has been fully or partially prepared, as well as those that the class makes. Unusual though it is in the all-or-nothing realm of cooking classes, this system works. Students get oodles of information on ingredients, technique, and presentation, and they do just enough stirring, mixing, sautéing, cake decorating, or whatever to feel that they are cooking and not just watching. Besides, preparing and dining on a six-course feast in a semblance of leisure in just three hours would be a daunting challenge, so a little shortcutting is practical.

After the cooking part, students doff their toques (which they may take home) and aprons (which must be left) and move to a lovely private dining room at Spencer's for the meal they have had a hand in preparing. Each course is paired with a suitable wine, with the sommelier's explanation of why the pairing works. Beaver Run Cooking Classes are perfectly balanced between education and information in the culinary realm and a really nice multicourse wine dinner in a lovely setting—all at a very reasonable price.

Beaver Run Resort, 620 Village Road, Breckenridge; (970) 453-8755 (direct line to Spencer's, which handles cooking class reservations) or www.beaverrun.com.

Colorado Mountain College

Colorado Mountain College's Culinary Arts program is designed to fast-track students into the kitchen. Classroom studies include the theory, science, and classical foundations of modern cuisine, plus business courses designed to prepare students for today's food service industry. These subjects require only one day of classes. The other five days are devoted to the apprenticeship program, which by graduation time means a student will have racked up at least 6,000 hours of real-life work experience.

The community college applies American Culinary Federation (ACF) Apprenticeship Program guidelines to its affiliation with Keystone, a partnership that has helped set the standard for culinary apprenticeship in the United States. The program's goal is to teach classical skills in a hands-on environment. It's the ultimate work-study deal, with students classified as full-time employees and paid a competitive wage and benefits package.

Every six months during their apprenticeships, students rotate through various properties to provide a broad range of experience in real-life kitchens. This means different workstations, different menus, and work under different chefs. Graduates receive an Associate in Applied Science Degree in Culinary Arts from Colorado Mountain College, and Certified Cook credentials from the American Culinary Federation.

Colorado Mountain College, Breckenridge Center, 103 South Harris Street, Breckenridge (mailing address: P.O. Box 2208, Breckenridge, CO 80424); (970) 453-6757; and Dillon Center, 333 Fiedler Avenue, Dillon (mailing address: P.O. Box 1414, Dillon, CO 80435); (970) 468-5989. The website for all CMC campuses, centers, and programs is www.coloradomtn.edu.

Dining

Alpenglow Stube, Keystone Ranch, and Ski Tip Lodge

Keystone Resort restaurants were offering fine dining when many of its competitors couldn't do much better than steak and baked potatoes. Of Keystone's 30-odd food-service outlets, three restaurants stand out. While they are of various styles and vintages, this trio allows the resort to maintain its edge as a resort where one can dine well. Most are at peak activity during the ski season, with summer being the second season.

Although Keystone, and therefore Vail Resorts Inc., its parent company, runs all the food service, each restaurant maintains a distinctive culinary style, and with individual chefs given considerable leeway to exercise their creativity. Keystone restaurants have been lauded with AAA Four Diamond, *Wine Spectator,* and DiRoNA honors.

Ski Tip Lodge is the most venerable. Built in the late 19th century as a stagecoach stop on the west side of Loveland Pass, it looks and feels much like an old New England Inn. In the 1940s, it became a private residence for Max and Edna Dercum, who also operated the rambling structure as a guest lodge to house skiers from the Arapahoe Basin ski area high on the pass. Max Dercum later established Keystone, which opened for the winter of 1969–1970. It was one of Colorado's first planned lift-and-lodging resorts, but Ski Tip has never become obsolete.

The fledgling resort soon opened the lakeside Keystone Lodge and built scores of condominiums tucked into the trees. Nevertheless, Ski Tip long remained a haven, off by itself up Montezuma Road. It still rents out a few quaint rooms on a B&B basis for people who love that homey touch, but most people know it for its outstanding restaurant. Since the entrepreneurial Dercum era, Keystone has been corporate-owned and increasingly development-oriented.

Relatively new homes and condominium complexes press in so closely to Ski Tip that the inn's long-standing sense of isolation and tranquility has been diluted—until you walk in the door, and then you're back in a quieter, more congenial era.

With low-beamed ceilings and charm to beat the band, the dining room still exudes a mellow, nurturing ambience. Dinners are four-course affairs with choice of menu for each. The cuisine is described as "sophisticated American," and it is indeed. There are generally five entrées—meat, game, poultry, seafood, and a vegetarian offering, each with the accent on sophistication. Foie gras (in an appetizer or as part of the stuffing for roast turkey), unique sauces and chutneys, divinely and unusually flavored whipped potatoes, and other palate-pleasing bursts explode from the menu.

In style and scale, **Keystone Ranch** is the yang to Ski Tip's yin. Located in the golf course clubhouse, this grandiose log lodge is an expansion of an old homestead from the days when the Ranch was still a ranch. Its six-course gourmet dinners are also American feasts, but with a distinct Colorado and Southwestern (and occasionally Asian) slant.

Start with a choice of appetizers and a soup. The signature Ranch Kettle Soup is described as "reminiscent of mountain flavors," a way of saying a lot of ingredients are combined into a hearty brew. Appetizers on a recent menu included Grilled Margret Duck Breast, Sesame Seared Ahi Tuna, Lobster and Dungeness Crab Ceviche, and Venison Lunettes. Each one is as carefully presented, with choice accompaniments, as if it were an entrée.

A crisp salad and an intermezzo of granita, fruit ice, or sorbet are preludes to the entrée course. Main-course choices on that recent menu read like a culinary symphony—and the presentations of each combination are works of art: Roast Rack of Colorado Lamb with maple whipped sweet potatoes, shallot-Dijon sauce, and a mélange of grilled celery root and carrots; Range Fed Veal Loin with mustard seed-speckled Israeli couscous and white wine veal sauce with wild mushrooms; Grilled Filet of Aged Beef with scallion-herb *rösti* potatoes, horseradish corn relish, and Zinfandel *jus lie*; Applewood Roast Plains Pheasant with wild cherry risotto, natural sauce, baby squash, and pearl onions; or Grilled Pork Tenderloin with Chimayo polenta, baked chayote squash, and "Colorado sauce." The vegetarian option called Alpine Garden is perhaps the prettiest of all, consisting of a potato basket filled with curry-braised spinach, grilled palm hearts, and roast pepper sauce.

An enticing possibility for the adventurous diner is Ranch House Chef's Table, a nightly creation of fresh seafood and game. Keystone chefs do play a game of musical kitchens, so this was the brainchild of David Welch, who had been chef at Ski Tip before becoming top toque at the Keystone Ranch. As at Ski Tip, the server will tell you about the glorious desserts of the evening after the entrée has been cleared.

Ski Tip and Keystone Ranch offer fine dining at resort elevation, but the third top-of-the-line restaurant is also at the top of one of the mountains. The Outpost is a dramatic log day lodge perched at 11,444 feet atop North Peak. It consists of two parts, a self-service cafeteria by day that turns into the good family dining spot called Der Fondue Chessel, and the Alpenglow Stube, which serves outstanding skier's lunches and fine dinners.

The Outpost is ski-in, ski-out, so the Alpenglow Stube provides guests with fur-lined slippers to keep their tootsies toasty while they dine. And dine they will—whether it's a leisurely lunch or a sensational dinner. The setting resembles a European mountain hunting lodge—or at least a European mountain lodging of my fantasies, but without the trophy heads that make me uncomfortable when their relatives are on the menu.

In any event, the chefs put on truly fine meals two gondola rides from the base area. There's a show kitchen, so you can watch them at work if that is your wont. Moreover, the kitchen crew does this twice a day, serving one of the most elegant and sybaritic skier's lunches in all of Colorado and then ratcheting up their efforts even more for dinner.

The dinner menu displays a mixture of outstanding Alpine-Bavarian dishes and Colorado contemporary cuisine. Pine Cone Pâté, a house specialty almost since opening day, contains goose and duck foie gras. It is named for another of its ingredients, *pignoli* (pine nuts), which come from pine cones—as well as for the pine cone that garnishes each plate. It is served with house-made lingonberry preserves and pumpernickel bread soaked in *Kirschwasser*, a potent European brandy made of cherries.

The Wild Game Grill, another signature dish at this two-mile-high restaurant, is a platter laden with rib eye of musk ox, loin of wild boar, and caribou chop, each marinated and served with its own unique sauce. For more conventional connoisseurs, the Alpenglow Stube presents beautiful slow-roasted duck breast, Colorado rack of lamb, pan-seared tuna, and beef tenderloin. There's always a vegetarian delicacy too.

Particularly interesting for a group is the *dégustation* menu, which means "chef's choice." Each member of the party receives a customized dinner of the chef's choosing, a perfect arrangement for a group that wants to trade bites. Top any meal off with the crème brulée, a house specialty made with sweet cheese, fresh berries, and toasted almonds. Other desserts include flourless chocolate torte, poached pear filled with white chocolate-mascarpone mousse, and a wonderful Baked Fromage, cheese wrapped in a delicate pastry package, baked, and served with a fruit compote, often figs and apples. All three of these Keystone restaurants have excellent wine lists geared toward their cuisine.

Keystone Resort, Keystone; the activities (and dining reservation) numbers for the entire resort are (970) 496-4386 and (800) 354-4386. Direct line to Ski Tip Lodge, (970) 496-4202. The resort's website is www.keystoneresort.com.

Blue River Bistro

This acclaimed restaurant, established in 1991, and winner of numerous awards when the Taste of Breckenridge was a noteworthy annual gastronomic event, serves some of downtown Breckenridge's best lunches, a selection of 75 martinis, a commendable wine list, tasty dinners, and late-night appetizers and desserts for those with the off-hour munchies. It is not an Italian restaurant as such, but Italian influences predominate.

Have Yourself a Chocolate Little Christmas

Chocolateville U.S.A. has been a holiday tradition since 1998, when Keystone Pastry Chef Ned Archibald first created this sweet scene. He typically spends five months and something on the order of 750 hours planning, molding, and carving 850 pounds of semisweet, milk, and white chocolates from Switzerland and France to create his annual masterpiece, a real display of a *chocolatier's* highest art and craft.

Archibald's 280-pound semisweet chocolate mountain is covered in powdery snow. At the bottom, he creates Chocolateville, an entire alpine village, a running "chocolate" waterfall, a working train, trees, and two Nutcrackers weighing 120 pounds each. Chocolateville U.S.A. is on display at the Keystone Lodge from mid-December through the end of the holidays.

Fried calamari, fresh mozzarella served with Roma tomatoes and basil oil, a significant list of pastas, and a popular chicken picatta entrée certainly are Italian. But who, in the Old Country, would relate to Toasted Jalapeño and Cheese Ravioli served with fresh tomato salsa, sour cream, and avocado mousse? Few, I'd wager, but it's a very good appetizer.

Pastas, which comprise the major part of the menu, similarly come in classic, adapted, and far-out versions. There's fettuccine with a choice of Alfredo, marinara, red-roasted pepper, or Bolognese sauce, or basil or sun-dried tomato pesto. Eggplant Parmesan, meat and vegetarian lasagna, and angel-hair pasta with fresh tomatoes, basil, and garlic in a light wine sauce. Fairly Italian, right? But add the optional marinated tofu, and you're off in another culinary hemisphere. Additionally, the Blue River Bistro serves hand-cut steaks, poultry entrées, and seafood dishes.

The majority of the wines are domestic, with the list divided into "Light and Lively Whites," "Rich and Round Whites," "Bright and Flavorful Reds," "Champagnes and Sparkling Wines," and "Ports."

Blue River Bistro, 305 North Main Street, Breckenridge; (970) 453-6974 or www.blueriverbistro.com.

Briar Rose Restaurant

The Briar Rose, located just off Breckenridge's Main Street, was named after the Briar Rose Mine, located high on Peak 10—not after Rosemary Schardt, who with her husband, Bill, has owned this popular spot since 1984. The building was once a boarding house, and it is entirely possible that miners who toiled in the original Briar Rose fueled up in the historic building that is today the Briar Rose Restaurant. Victorian décor ties in these two eras in Breckenridge's history. The vintage bar boasts an antique diamond-dust mirror, so stop for a cocktail or a glass of wine and admire yourself.

The restaurant offers moderate prices, a friendly and welcoming atmosphere, and a combination of food that pleases meat-and-potatoes types and more adventurous diners. You can launch into your meal with Crab Stuffed Mushrooms, baked escargots, or Beer-Battered Coconut Shrimp. You won't have to decide whether you ought to begin with a salad, because you *will* begin with a salad—the house version (or the optional Caesar) that comes with every entrée.

The restaurant's reputation rests on consistently fine steaks and succulent slow-roasted prime rib in 12-, 16-, or gut-busting 24-ounce portions. The Briar Rose, one of the first in town to specialize in game, puts tenderloin of elk, caribou, and ostrich on the menu, each accompanied by a suitable sauce. There's always seafood and poultry as well. Rocky Mountain Ruby Trout is served either with Grand Marnier sauce or with toasted almonds. Salmon Papillote is baked with wine, lemon, and herb butter. Gulf shrimp are stuffed with crab and served on Newburg sauce, a rich sauce of butter, egg yolks, cream, and sherry. This once-popular sauce is infrequently offered nowadays, but still is rich and flavorful. Pasta primavera and another vegetarian dish are available nightly.

As a passionate advocate of introducing children to real restaurants, I applaud the Briar Rose's children's menu. To be sure, offerings such as chicken fingers, prime rib, fried shrimp, and spaghetti and meatballs are targeted toward the small fry whose early eating-out experiences center on small fries (and the burgers that accompany them at fast-food outlets), but nevertheless the Briar Rose is genuine, the service is not "self," and restaurant manners are encouraged. Briar Cheesecake, the restaurant's special chocolate bread pudding, ice cream (plain or assembled into a sundae), or a dessert of the evening cap off the meal. The children will probably opt for the ice cream.

Briar Rose Restaurant, 109 East Lincoln Avenue, Breckenridge; (970) 453-9948.

Café Alpine

This restaurant, located in a charming house off Breckenridge's Main Street, doesn't serve food of the Alpine region. Rather, the name reflects Breckenridge's Alpine setting, for the food is international and much more southerly and easterly in provenance, which Chef Keith Maloney prefers to the Irish food of his ancestry.

Tapas from Spain dominate the appetizer menu (there's a tapas wine bar too, if you want a light bite). Additional starters include Caponata Bruschetta with Asiago from Italy, Chicken Satay with Thai Banana Peanut Sauce, Baked Peppercorn Brie with French Bread and Fresh Fruit, and Blackened Tuna Sashimi with Wasabi, Pickled Ginger, and Shoyu Sauce. Soups and salads display a similar crosscultural bent.

While beef and lamb dishes are offered, Café Alpine entrées are heavy on interesting treatments of seafood and poultry—a welcome contrast to many of Breckenridge's meat-oriented restaurants. Grilled Sea Scallops with Lemon Pepper Pasta, Smoked Mozzarella, and Tomato Cream Sauce is adapted Italian. Southwestern Ruby Red Trout with Warm Rattlesnake Bean Salad and Avocado Crema indeed reflects contemporary Southwestern cuisine. Chili-Rubbed Rocky Mountain Chicken with Pico de Gallo Ravioli in Ancho Posole Broth is an amalgam of both of those influences.

San Francisco Seafood Cioppino from the West Coast and Medallions of Beef with Creole Grillade Sauce from the Gulf Coast bring two American culinary traditions to the Colorado mountains. The Braised Lamb Shank goes Indian—not Native American, but from Asia—by its immersion in a red curry-coconut broth accompanied by "Bombay condiments." The Vegetarian Viet-Thai Peanut Stir Fry comes with Black Bean Sweet Chili Sauce and Jasmine Rice.

Elaborate desserts include Lemon Napoleon served over Berry Compote and Chocolate Mouse Tower with Raspberry Sauce and Chocolate Ganache. In winter, the cozy fireplace beckons. In summer, when lunch is also served, the outside dining area is pleasant. The wine list runs to a hundred or so selections, of which some 40 are available by the glass.

Café Alpine, 106 East Adams Avenue, Breckenridge; (970) 453-8218.

The Hearthstone

The building housing The Hearthstone dates back to the early 1880s, when Christ Kaiser, a German immigrant butcher, built himself a home. It survived a fire in the 1940s and was later renovated for restaurant use. Dick Carleton and Jane Storm purchased the building in 1989 and renovated it once more into a warm and comfortable restaurant with a Victorian-style exterior and a very contemporary kitchen that turns out old standbys as well as genuinely interesting culinary creations.

Even if you don't dine at The Hearthstone, you might stop by during happy hour, when appetizers are priced two-for-one. Jalapeño-Stuffed Shrimp is a house specialty, and other apps include Venison Carpaccio with Sun-Dried Tomatoes and Onion Compote; Baked Brie with Fresh Fruit, Berry *Coulis,* and Pepper-Infused Pastry; and Smoked Trout Platter with Herbed Chèvre, Red Onion, Capers, and Lemon. Some dinner guests don't bother with the à la carte appetizers, because all entrées come with a choice of New England clam chowder, Three Onion Soup, or a house salad.

The Hearthstone specializes in such rich meat entrées as Colorado Lamb Chops, Filet au Poivre, Filet Mignon, and Pueblo Grilled Pork, but it also offers more contemporary fare like Tilapia Pepita, a filet of farm-raised fish encrusted in pumpkin seeds and finished with sun-dried tomato *beurre blanc;* Granola-Crusted Elk Chop, made with a garlic granola and served with blackberry démi-glace; and Tuna with Asian Horseradish *Beurre Blanc,* fresh-cut, spice-rubbed ahi tuna medallion served with a sweet soy reduction and a rice-noodle cake. Other seafood, poultry, and vegetarian options are also available.

Featured desserts include the signature White Chocolate–Raspberry Bread Pudding served with rum-infused caramel sauce; Chocolate Marquis, a divine Frangelico-infused chocolate and hazelnut mélange served with fresh fruit and berry compote; and house-made sorbet—or ice cream *du jour* in a house-made cone.

The wine list offers close to 200 selections, including two dozen available by the glass. Domestic wines from California and Oregon predominate, but there are also imports from Europe, Australia, South Africa, and Chile. The list sorts American wines by varietal, and imports are categorized as "More Great Reds" and "More Great Whites."

The Hearthstone, 130 South Ridge Street, Breckenridge; (970) 453-1148 or www.stormrestaurants.com.

Pierre's Riverwalk Café

Main Street, Breckenridge, has a corner of France in the form of Pierre's Riverwalk Café. Established by Pierre and Catherine Luc, he a French-trained chef who first stepped into a kitchen at the age of 14, the attractive restaurant is a sophisticated addition to the Summit County dining scene.

The seasonally changing menu offers French classics, contemporary French dishes, and modern American fare with international influences, conceived and assembled by classically trained Chef Pierre. The combinations are so well and proudly thought-out and so beautifully presented that the chef asks guests not to request substitutions. That's confidence in the kitchen—even more so when you consider that it's an open kitchen so guests can watch the action.

Among the French classics are onion soup, escargots, and lobster crêpes. From there on, the dishes fan out to include ingredients and cooking methods from other countries too. For instance, for crab ravioli folded into a dill-flavored shrimp mousse, the chef begins with a rather French mixture, encases it in Italian pasta dough, and serves it with a smooth saffron sauce. The Caesar salad is topped with traditional Parmesan and also goat cheese. Colorado rack of lamb is crusted with a mixture of Dijon mustard, herbs, and bread crumbs, then served with its natural juice perked up with fresh rosemary and roasted garlic, and garlic mashed potatoes. Natural juices flavored with fresh tarragon enhance the pan-roasted half-chicken, served with fresh asparagus and those wonderful garlic mashed potatoes.

Ris de Veau Vol au Vent, is a classic French favorite, of veal sweetbreads sautéed with a sauce of tomatoes and black olives. Asian flavors subtly appear on the menu too. Consider the filet of beef steeped in a Thai marinade and served with a sweet potato *gallette,* black rice, and shiitake mushrooms. Desserts are freshly baked in-house, and the wine list features 100 selections, primarily from France and the United States.

Pierre's Riverwalk Café, 137 South Main Street, Breckenridge; (970) 453-0989.

Spencer's Steaks & Spirits

Spencer's, a long-running Breckenridge restaurant, has a bright and stylish new look, thanks to a makeover in 2002. Bob Burden came from nearby Keystone to serve as executive chef for the restaurant and all other food service at Beaver Run Resort.

Located slopeside near the bottom of Peak 9 and operating as the only full-service restaurant in one of the resort's largest lodging properties, Spencer's sets up buffet-style breakfast and lunch. Dinner starts off with selections from an extensive 30-item soup and salad bar. Additional appetizers include Coconut Shrimp with Ginger-Spiced Orange Marmalade, Seared Ahi Tuna with Wasabi Cream Sauce and Gari Shanga (pickled gingerroot), Lime-Seared Scallops with braised spinach and crisp bacon lardoons, and escargots with mushrooms, Parmesan, and garlic butter — and French bread for sopping it up.

Burden and his kitchen crew know how to make up a good sauce to fancy up such solid American favorites as herb-roasted prime rib, grilled rib eye, filet mignon, and New York strip, all perfectly cooked. Pork chops, medallions of lamb, center-cut pork chops, and tender Colorado farm-raised venison steak are additional specialties. Seafood selections include pesto-crusted salmon, rainbow trout with *beurre meunière*, and shrimp scampi broiled with garlic, white wine, and lemon and served with a rich fettuccine Alfredo.

Among Spencer's very good desserts are Baked Alaska, mousse (chocolate, hazelnut, and/or mocha), crème brulée, a towering brownie sundae, and the signature Chocolate Pyramid. The showpiece features a hard-chocolate shell filled with chocolate mousse.

Spencer's Steaks & Spirits, Beaver Run Resort, 620 Village Road, Breckenridge; (970) 453-8755.

The Swiss Haven

Breckenridge is one of two Colorado ski towns with a Swiss Haven restaurant. For the fondue and raclette offerings, owner Matt Garrett uses the same ingredients and basically the same techniques. For a description of the food see the Steamboat Springs chapter (page 217), but he has added more salads, and his dessert list is different. Breckenridge's Swiss Haven does a signature White Chocolate Cheese Cake, a Three-Layer Chocolate Terrine (white, milk, and dark chocolates), and a different apple strudel.

The Swiss Haven, 325 South Main Street, Breckenridge; (970) 453-6969.

Events

Applause!

Various months—Fundraisers for the Breckenridge Music Institute and National Repertory Orchestra, which go under the umbrella name of Applause!, have included musicales, hiking, biking, and food and wine events. Specifics change from year to year, season to season, but they have included culinary opportunities from picnics to black-tie galas, including one ushering in the Millennium. Many of the events take place in patrons' private homes.

A Seafarin' Soirée on a party boat on Lake Dillon started with a bon voyage champagne toast before the boat set sail for a gourmet luncheon on a "secret island". A couple of years later, it was organized as a two-boat flotilla. Such a midday soirée is certainly a novelty at the Summit County's 9,000-plus-foot elevation.

An Immovable Feast included cocktails, dinner by Hearthstone Catering (yes, the same enterprise as the restaurant), a mini-concert, dancing, and both silent and live auctions. A Colorado Collaboration of Wine, Music, and Food included jazz, a Colorado wine tasting with Steve Smith and Naomi Shepherd of the Grande River Vineyard, and a sampling of fine food. The French Connection was a grand evening of cocktails, brass band music, and an elegant country French buffet.

Bach, Beethoven, and Brunch is a perennial favorite to kick off the holiday season, and Here We Come A-Caroling, topped off by killer eggnog and a holiday feast, has continued it. A 16th-Century Olde English Yuletide Madrigal Dinner has pulled out all stops, with such more or less Elizabethan features as madrigal singers, merrie men, and even the boar's head procession.

Dinner on the Titanic replicated the last supper on the superliner's infamous final voyage. A Cooking School—A La Chinois was a hands-on cooking class and dinner with Bobbie Moran, who studied at La Varenne in France, taught international cuisine at the University of Wisconsin, and later owned her own cooking school.

A couple who had lived in Spain hosted Olé Olé—A Tapas Buffet. First tapas and then Spanish *postres* (desserts) brought the tastes of Andalusia to the heart of the Rockies. Mediterranean Mystique was a cornucopia of Spanish tapas, Italian antipasti, and dishes from Greece and Turkey. A Symphonic Soirée and Elegant Buffet, this one in the evening, included chamber music followed by a buffet dinner with fine wines. A Colorful Collection of Classic Colorado Culture and Cuisine, another culture/cuisine combination, provided an opportunity to see works from an art historian's private collection and enjoy a Colorado menu of trout, lamb, beef, and house specialties from a fine hotel.

Billed as a "global gourmet feast," Bon Appétit! Buon Apetito! Bueno Apetito! was a multinational, multicourse buffet feast. A Cuisine Collectable promised "exotic flavors, designs, and entertainment" and "an evening of many surprises"—and delivered. Carnevale a Venezia brings the seductive tastes, music, and costumed pre-Lenten revelry to Summit County, while a Taste of Thai echoes the exotic flavors, fragrances, and textures of this memorable Asian cuisine. But lest you think Applause! is all about fine cuisine, one of the enduring popular events is the annual Pig Roast and Barbeque, featuring both roast pork and lamb with all the trimmings.

Big Reds by the River was a wine tasting of red wines and an international menu of red foods, including Big Red Bean Torte with Red Salsa, Crimson Gazpacho, Salmon on a Bed of Red Lentils, Mixed Garden Greens (and Reds), Roasted Red Pepper Hummus, Summer Pasta with Fresh Tomato and Sweet Basil Sauce, homebaked "B-reds," and Zebra Brownies in Red Raspberry Purée. You just never know what creative direction those clever Applause! organizers will take next.

Applause!, c/o Breckenridge Music Institute, P.O. Box 7068, Breckenridge, CO 80424-7968; (970) 453-9142. Send for a seasonal brochure, or call Sherrie Calderini at (970) 453-8556 or Bobbie Moran at (970) 262-0688 to see what's on tap.

Wine, Jazz, and Art Festival

August—Keystone's annual Wine, Jazz, and Art Festival kicks off with a Friday night concert and continues with a weekend of juried art and tastings of some 300 wines. If they wanted to make the name any longer, organizers could call it the Wine, Food, Jazz, and Art Festival, because there are culinary components too.

Admission to the festival, which takes place at River Run Plaza from 1:00 to 5:00 P.M., and to the wine and culinary seminars is free, but food sampling is priced à la carte and you must buy a souvenir wine glass needed for the wine tasting. The festival, which also includes several jazz combos and a juried art show, benefits the Summit County Arts Council and the Summit County Middle School French Club. Bon appétit.

Keystone Resort, Keystone; (800) 354-4FUN or www.keystoneresort.com.

Colorado Barbecue Challenge

August—Okay. Barbecue isn't haute cuisine, but it's an American tradition that does merit mentioning, especially when a cook-off attracts something on the order of 80 of the nation's top barbecuers. Especially when, at 9,100 feet, it is the nation's and purportedly the world's highest-elevation barbecue contest. Especially since it is Colorado's official barbecue competition. Especially since it has been going on since 1992, with 5,000 or so people now showing up over a Friday and Saturday in mid-August. The event even has a title sponsor, so it's officially the Coors Barbecue Challenge, which is a good fit because nothing goes with barbecue like beer.

The competitors, who refer to themselves as cookers, vie for prize money (a total of $8,000 in 2002) and take their craft very seriously. They set up their equipment, which ranges from relatively simple grills and kettles to elaborate custom-made rolling kitchens. Secret sauces, time-honored smoking techniques, slow braising, and other tricks of the trade abound within the barbecuing fraternity.

Categories are Ribs, Beef Brisket, Pork (shoulder, Boston butt, picnic cut), Chicken, and Miscellaneous. Under the latter, contestants have entered lamb, rattlesnake, and even ostrich meat, as well as the occasional vegetarian dish. Additional categories are barbecue sauce/salsa, side dishes, and desserts, plus a Kids' Kook-Off. Awards are given for entrants evaluated by an official judges' panel, and there also are People's Choice honors.

Admission to the event is free. You can buy tasting tickets and sample to your heart's (and stomach's) content. Contestants are not required to sell their food to the public, but most do—and the local Rotary Club benefits. The cook-off also features lots of entertainment, mostly in the country-and-western, old-time rock and roll, and bluegrass genres, as well as a concurrent crafts show in Historic Park.

Information (and entry forms if you are so inclined) are available from Town of Frisco, P.O. Box 4100, Frisco, CO 80443; (800) 424-1554, (970) 668-5276, or www.townoffrisco.com.

Taste of Keystone

August–September—If you've always wanted to eat at the sky-high Alpenglow Stube, the historic Ski Tip Lodge, the elegant Keystone Ranch restaurant, or any of the other Keystone eateries where the resort's top chefs preside, you can sample some of their creations at the annual Taste of Keystone. For me, the opportunity to compare dishes from those three restaurants without moving more than a few steps is reason enough to attend, but for the record, the other participants with particularly interesting food include the Keystone Lodge's Bighorn Steakhouse and the Garden Room, and Der Fondue Chessel located atop North Peak.

Under normal circumstances, there's more casual dining at the Edgewater Café, Gassy Thompson's, Great Northern Tavern, Ida Belle's Bar and Grille, Kickapoo Tavern, Out of Bounds, and RazzBerrys, and for the Taste of Keystone, they put out their best creations too. For a facility geared to large group meals, the conference center's big catering kitchen offers surprisingly refined dishes as well, and you can sample it too. Handmade chocolates, yummy cookies, and ice cream from Calories satisfy your sweet tooth.

Held for four delicious hours at Keystone Village, this event is free. You just pay for what you eat. From its inception at least through 2002, food tickets were just $1 each—and each taste required between one and three tickets. Live music and children's activities round out the festivities, which benefit Summit County's Mountain Mentors program.

Keystone Resort, Keystone; (800) 354-4FUN or www.keystoneresort.com.

Toast of Breckenridge

September—On Labor Day weekend of 2002, Breckenridge launched an ambitious new culinary event, which organizers hope will become an annual food and wine celebration. The organizers might decide to continue but change the fine points, so don't take year one as a forever-after format.

In 2002, the three-day Toast of Breckenridge kicked off on Friday evening with a Grand Food and Wine Tasting at Main Street Station. A hundred wines were poured, the products of five area microbrews were tapped, and local restaurants whose chefs showed off their culinary prowess included Blue River Bistro, Café Alpine, The Hearthstone, Maori's, Quandary Grill, Southridge Seafood Grill, and the St. Bernard.

Saturday was devoted to two very different spotlighted activities. The Wine and Nine Golf party at the Breckenridge Golf Club was the kind of cross-fertilized event that inspired golfers to drive harder and aim better (at least the intent was there) and made oenophilic nongolfers rethink their lack of participation in the sport. Wine and spirit tastings and prizes on each of nine holes made this the golf party of the season.

Saturday also featured a Celebrity Chef cooking demonstration and picnic with Anita Lo of Annisa in New York City, one of *Food and Wine* magazine's best new chefs of 2001. Lo's demonstration was on weaving influences from the Middle East, Asia, and North Africa into a coherent sensibility and breathtaking culinary creations. Maori's supplied the picnic lunch that accompanied this wonderful event.

Late in the afternoon, the Sub-Dudes, something of a Colorado cult favorite, played their New Orleans–spiced music from the Maggie Pond stage. The mix of R&B, roots rock, and gospel country sounds paired well with the tastes of participating wines, spirits, and local microbrews. For anyone still able to sip another sip or eat another bite, local restaurants put on wine-pairing dinners. The first annual Toast of Breckenridge wrapped up with a Sunday champagne brunch prepared by Quandary Grill, with bubbly from Southern Wines and Spirits.

Workshops, seminars, and an on-going wine auction were sprinkled throughout the weekend. The wine curriculum ranged from Wine Tasting 101, highlighting the fundamentals of how wines are made and the basics of tasting, through an advanced workshop called Tasting the Masters' Way. Sommelier Jay Fletcher guided participants through the tasting techniques taught at the Court of Master Sommeliers. Those new skills could be put to good use at the Sherry, Port, and Champagne seminar, hosted by Christopher Rowe who explained how "the royal trinity of processed wines" are made, from the Solera system of Sherry to the riddling racks of Champagne. It was a sensory and educational journey through the countries that produce these wines. Rowe also conducted a workshop on New World dessert wines from the United States and Australia.

Anyone who harbors a dream of operating a vineyard got some enlightenment from Barry Collier, a city boy who traded his Mercedes in for a tractor and a pickup truck and developed 26 acres in Sonoma County into Hillside Vineyards, where he grows ultra-premium wine grapes. He has become known for running the finest Zinfandel and Cabernet vineyards in California. Other seminars and tastings focused on the wines of the Rhône Valley and Tuscany, as well as one just on Pinot Noir wines.

The first annual Toast of Breckenridge benefited the Summit Foundation and the Breckenridge Outdoor Education Center. Ticket options included a weekend pass, with or without the golf event, or admission to individual events. Packages including lodging were also offered.

General information on Toast of Breckenridge is available from (720) 359-1065 or www.toastofbreckenridge.com. For festival ticket information, call (800) 455-7334, and for packages including overnight accommodations, call (800) 465-2168.

Oktoberfest

September—Breckenridge jumped on the Oktoberfest bandwagon when it launched its late-September version in 1995. Main Street between Lincoln Avenue and Adams Street is closed for three days of food, fun, and—of course—beer. Local restaurants and bakeries dispense German specialties from bratwurst to strudel, and American and other foods are available too, all at street-fair prices.

The Friday evening of the weekend event features a brew master dinner, which is similar to a winemaker dinner but with German beers paired to each course. The 2002 dinner was held at Poirrier's at the Wellington, but that restaurant has since closed, so the dinner's future is uncertain at this writing.

Information on Oktoberfest is available from the Breckenridge Resort Chamber, 137 South Main Street, Brechenridge; (970) 453-5579, (970) 453-5260, or www.gobreck.com.

Wines

Ridge Street Wine

Anne Dowling, one of the country's top freestyle skiers, prepared herself for life after competition by immersing herself in the wine business. She was a sales representative for a small wine company, but recalls, "I got sick of being in my car." She decided to combine her skiing with her growing interest in wine and went to France for an extreme competition and also to travel and learn the language. As she traveled around France, she saw unpretentious little wine shops all over the country, which planted a seed in her mind. After injuring her knee and having "plenty of time to work on a business plan," she opened Summit County's first—and, at this writing, still only—specialty wine shop.

Ridge Street Wine opened on Ridge Street in the fall of 2000, and a year later moved to a distinctive yellow cottage on Main Street in Breckenridge. Friendly and knowledgeable service and a commitment to wines distinguish this enterprise. Ridge Street Wine carries about 60 percent domestic wines, with the remaining 40 percent from all over the wine world. The rack of under-$10 bottles is popular with budget-watching customers.

The shop organized a wine club that at this writing has 160 local members, which is impressive considering that Breckenridge is still a small town. The club meets in members' homes to taste, discuss, and delve into wines. Members enjoy a 10 percent discount at the store. Ridge Street Wines also carries stemware, openers, wine charms, coasters, and other wine accessories, as well as books on wines.

Ridge Street Wine, 301 North Main Street, Breckenridge; (970) 453-7212.

Other

Gourmet Cabby

Not everything that this food-delivery service will bring to your Breckenridge door qualifies as *haute cuisine*, but some of it certainly does. Perfect for the don't-want-to-cook tonight, don't-feel-like-going-out resident or visitor, Gourmet Cabby delivers food from casual pizza places to some of Breck's better dining spots, including the Blue River Bistro, The Hearthstone, and the St. Bernard. The service operates from 11:00 A.M. until 11:00 P.M., takes your order for more than two dozen restaurants (plus wine, beer, spirits, soft drinks, pet food, and more), and speeds it to you for a 15 percent service charge. If you like to cook but hate to shop, Gourmet Cabby will deliver groceries for you, even stocking your rental condo before you arrive. Scott and Vivien Teetsel established the service for the 2000–2001 ski season under the name Mountain Express Cuisine and have been rushing meals around Breckenridge ever since.

To order a meal (or a menu if you don't have access to one), contact Gourmet Cabby at (970) 453-7788 or www.gourmetcabby.com.

Recipes

Keystone chef David Welch offered this favorite condiment at Ski Tip Lodge, where he served it warm with fish or chicken. He also likes it with chips or tortillas and recommends making it in quantity, putting some up in jars, and storing it in the refrigerator for future use. Make it during Colorado's peak sweet-corn season.

Corn Chutney

2 tablespoons sweet butter
½ cup brown sugar
1 pound fresh corn kernels
10 fresh tomatillos, peeled and finely chopped
1 bunch scallions or green onions, root end removed and
    green and white parts finely chopped
2 cloves garlic, peeled and finely chopped
1 red bell pepper, stemmed, seeded, and finely diced
1 medium onion, peeled and finely diced
1 Poblano chili, stemmed, seeded, and finely diced
1 tablespoon chili powder (Red Molido preferred)
1 teaspoon salt
1 teaspoon freshly ground black pepper
1 teaspoon dried leaf oregano
½ cup balsamic vinegar

In a saucepan over medium heat, melt butter and brown sugar, stirring to mix. Stir in all of the vegetables and all of the seasonings except for the balsamic vinegar. Adjust heat so that mixture maintains a lively simmer. Cook, continuing to stir, until the vegetables are cooked. Add the vinegar and continue cooking. Remove from heat until ready to serve. Allow to cool before putting in jars.

Bob Burden oversees the busy kitchen at Beaver Run Resort and Conference Center, and he also teaches popular classes to home-cooking enthusiasts at Spencer's, the resort's recently revamped restaurant. You'll find that this rich and aromatic soup is quick to cook and serve.

Chicken Coconut Soup

1 stalk lemongrass
1 teaspoon whole black peppercorns
3 kaffir lime leaves
1 teaspoon dried galangal (also known as Thai ginger, Siamese ginger, or Laos ginger and available in Asian markets)
1 teaspoon olive oil
3 cloves garlic, peeled and crushed
3 tablespoons chopped green onions
½ teaspoon red curry paste (available in Asian markets)
2 green chilies, roasted, peeled, seeded, and diced
3 cups rich chicken broth
1 pound skinned and boned chicken breast, trimmed of fat and finely sliced
1½ cups coconut milk
2 cups cooked straw mushrooms (or canned, drained and rinsed)
1 tablespoon fish sauce (available in Asian markets)
1 tablespoon fresh lime juice
1 tablespoon cornstarch, soften in ¼ cup cold water
1 teaspoon fresh ginger, peeled and chopped
3 tablespoons fresh chopped cilantro

Tie lemongrass, peppercorns, lime leaves, and *galangal* in cheesecloth or in a sachet bag (available at kitchenware stores). In a medium saucepan over medium heat, heat olive oil. Add garlic, green onion, curry paste, and green chilies and cook, stirring frequently, for about two minutes. Add chicken stock and cheesecloth or sachet bag. Bring to boil, turn down heat and simmer for 20 minutes. Add chicken breast, coconut milk, mushrooms, lime juice, and ginger, and bring to a rapid boil. Stir in water/cornstarch mixture. Thicken until the soup coats the back of a wooden spoon. Removed seasonings bag. Garnish with fresh cilantro and serve. Serves 4 to 6.

The Vail Valley

In 1962, three ski lifts were constructed and a small village center was established on a former sheep meadow along Gore Creek and U.S. 6, a two-lane roadway winding across the Colorado Rockies. On December 15 of that year the lifts began operating, and Vail instantly became America's most talked-about ski area. In less than four decades, Vail Mountain grew into the largest, grandest ski mountain in the land, and the small village mushroomed into a sophisticated and glamorous resort, spawning a long strip town. Vail today is bisected by Interstate 70, which itself was built to supplement parts and supplant other sections of U.S. 6.

Vail Village has expanded eastward to East Vail, abutting the lower flanks of Vail Pass and the U.S. Forest Service land. To the west lie Lionshead, Cascade Village, and Eagle-Vail. Two valleys over the Vail ski area owner plotted and built Beaver Creek, a super-luxury, controlled-access mountain. In the valley below, Avon exploded from a sleepy crossroads, and a ski and golf resort called Arrowhead created west of Avon, was sucked into the Beaver Creek megalith. Then, still another development sprang up between them in Bachelor Gulch. Even farther west, rural little Edwards also saw explosive growth. If the Eagle-Vail airport is considered the western terminus of what is today promotionally called the Vail Valley, it now sprawls some 30 miles, all the way from Vail Pass.

Growth was fueled by new ski lifts, golf courses, and thousands of condominiums and homes. Vail, Beaver Creek, Arrowhead, Cordillera, and Singletree sport multi-million-dollar homes and condominiums. Even the timeshares are pricey. Hotels and inns have been built or rebuilt to accommodate tens of thousands of overnight guests. Those people all have to eat—and they like to eat well.

To foodies, Vail has become a feast of orgiastic plentitude. The Vail Valley boasts dozens of first-rate restaurants of all styles, mostly in the mid-high to way-upper price ranges. A comprehensive roundup could fill a book. The gastronomes of *Zagat Guides* love Vail. So do the star- and diamond-dispensers from AAA and Mobil. DiRoNA and *Wine Spectator* regularly honor Vail Valley restaurants for cuisine, ambience, wines, and service. It's big-city quality in the Colorado Rockies. Vail is hard to beat when it comes to fine dining.

There's no shortage of special food-and-wine events in the Vail Valley and no shortage of charities eager to benefit from the generosity of those who like to eat and drink well. The Taste of Vail is one of Colorado's most prestigious food-and-wine events. Beaver Creek has three major events on its annual calendar.

Excellent specialty wine merchants, from-scratch bakeries, and a couple of attractive retail stores carrying top-quality utensils and accessories for the passionate home cook make the Vail Valley into a complete culinary center. About the only thing still missing is a good cooking school, but that too may someday come to the Vail Valley.

Bakeries

Alpenrose

The Alpenrose is a commendable Continental restaurant overseen by owner/chef Peter Haller who has for more than 25 years offered fine lunches and gorgeous dinners in four small, intimate dining rooms and one beguiling south-facing patio. But I include Alpenrose in the bakery section purely because of what awaits just inside the door. Vail has a plentitude of fine-dining restaurants, but few bakeries of this caliber, consistency, and longevity.

The long pastry counter near the entrance is filled with authentic European breads, pastries, and cakes, including various sorts of strudels, fruit tarts, chocolate pastries, cream-filled treats, and cookies. As a restaurant Alpenrose is very fine but not totally unique in the Vail context, but as an authentic Middle European patisserie and *confiserie,* it has few peers and no betters, not only in Vail but anywhere in Colorado.

Alpenrose, 100 East Meadow Drive, Vail; (970) 476-3194.

Avon Bakery & Deli

Walk into the Avon Bakery & Deli, and you'll understand why "bakery" comes before "deli" in the establishment's name. On the right, behind a wire rack stocked with the day's fresh loaves, is a mammoth Italian bread oven. A canvas conveyor inserts 120 proofed lumps of dough into the oven's maw at a time. Since the dough is wet when it comes out of the proofer, the baker can't handle it too much. He neither weighs nor measures, but quickly eye-cuts each loaf, resulting in extraordinary rustic breads, each free-form loaf shaped slightly differently from the next. Inside the baking behemoth are the stone decks necessary to create the hard-crust breads that are an Avon Bakery hallmark.

Dan Trush and Mark Strickland, who had worked together on Zino's opening crew, established the bakery in 2000. Trush had previously baked bread at the Grouse Mountain Grill and Ham's Bistro in Boston. Strickland's Vail Valley pedigree includes Sweet Basil, where he worked with Jonathan Sharon, who in turn came aboard to cook at the "deli" part of Avon Bakery & Deli. In fact, even the lower-level members of the cooking line were at fine Vail Valley restaurants before joining the upstart bakery. The appeal, rare in a ski town, is a five-day workweek with two consecutive days off.

Trush says that Strickland "has always been the bread guy," and it was he who came up with most of the new bakery's recipes and methodology, but the sourdough came from Trush's Boston years. Regardless of their provenance, all the breads are made from organic flours and other top-quality ingredients.

In addition to killer ciabatta and the Boston-based sourdough, made in full loaves and bread-bowl sizes for soup, they bake baguettes, focaccia, scones, cookies, and more.

The sign over the door may say "deli," but the food is way better than usual deli fare. Jonathan Sharon builds genuinely gourmet sandwiches, with quality meats, cheeses, salads, and accompaniments, and makes his own stock for at least two soups and two entrées every day. At this writing, the place is open for breakfast, lunch, and the earliest of dinners, but this could change in the future.

"We were all tired of fussy fine dining," says Trush. "We wanted to do something fun with good food in a casual atmosphere. We're all hands-on." Check 'em out. When you're leaving Beaver Creek, turn right when you see the Starbucks. The bakery is a few storefronts to the right of the coffee chain—and its baked goods are a whole lot better.

Avon Bakery & Deli, 0025 Hurd Lane, Avon; (970) 949-DELI or (970) 949-4907.

Bonjour Bakery

Until recently, Edwards offered little more in the way of baked goods than cellophane-wrapped, preservative-laden sweets sold at convenience stores. Michel Battaglin changed with Bonjour Bakery, located in the heart of Riverwalk, booming Edwards' new main street. Behind this bright storefront are tables covered with checked cloths, cases and racks stacked with freshly baked French pastries and breads, and a counter where sandwiches, soups, coffee, ice cream, and other desserts can be ordered to eat in or take out. The artisan breads include sourdough, sun-dried tomato, and baguettes leading the popularity parade.

Bonjour Bakery, 1st and Main, Edwards; (970) 926-5539.

Columbine Bakery & Café

The Columbine Bakery, around a few corners from Exit 167 off Interstate 70, is an excellent Continental-style bakery in a small strip mall with a Domino's Pizza at one end and a Mexican grocery store at the other. If you could see over the sloping parking lot, which forms something of a visual berm, the view would be of a City Market and Wal-Mart. In the bakery business, location isn't necessarily everything.

Columbine Bakery was one of the earliest enterprises in the western end of the valley to display a commitment for the art and craft of preparing fine fresh food and first-rate baked goods. The immaculate shop features a long pastry display case, a wall of breads and rolls, and some tables and chairs. From the ovens in the back comes a profusion of excellent European-style baked goods. From the kitchen comes light, casual, and utterly delicious food, including soups, sandwiches, salads, and quiches. Owners Daniel and Ronda Niederhauser fill the shelves with a daily effusion of buttery pastries, flaky croissants, toothsome cookies, and great artisan breads and rolls. Whether you take out or eat in, be sure to leave room for dessert, many along the lines of fruit-filled somethings or cheese-filled something elses. Daniel Niederhauser grew up in a restaurant family in Switzerland and began training at a small-town bakery that was essentially what he and Ronda run today. He attended trade school for pastry chefs, but when he moved to Captiva Island, Florida, in 1984 it was to cook in a restaurant with the odd name of Mucky Duck. While his purpose was to learn American food preparation and restaurant operations, he kept honing his baking skills by creating custom cakes.

Florida didn't do much for the native of a country with lofty mountains, cool summers, and snowy winters. He moved to Vail in 1987 to become pastry chef at the Westin Hotel (now the Vail Cascade Resort and Spa) and became pastry chef at Beano's Cabin (see page 265). Niederhauser saw a niche for fine European breads and pastries, as well as affordable meals in a casual atmosphere. The bakery named for the Colorado state flower provides just that.

Columbine Bakery & Cafe, 51 Beaver Creek Place, Avon; (970) 949-1400 or www.co-biz.com/columbinebakery.

The Market at the Larkspur Restaurant

The Larkspur Restaurant, a fine-dining establishment in the Golden Peak Lodge (see page 271), has within it a bakery and café called The Market, where, slope-bound skiers and riders stop in the morning for a coffee and pastries and at midday for a quick soup-and-sandwich type of lunch. Because of its location in a ski-area day lodge, Larkspur must produce quantity as well as quality. The restaurant bakes 400 pounds of artisan bread in over 20 varieties every day for sandwiches and for breadbaskets on the table at sit-down skiers' lunches and at dinner too.

The Market at Larkspur Restaurant, 458 Vail Valley Drive, Vail; (970) 479-8050 or www.larkspur-vail.com.

Cooking Classes

Grilling Classes

Summer means grilling or, as many people refer to it, barbecuing. Anyone can toss a burger or a steak on the grill, but tips and secrets of great grilling are harder to come by. The spacious slopeside terrace of the Park Hyatt Beaver Creek is the venue for free summer grilling classes given by Executive Chef Pascal Coudouy. Nonguests as well as hotel guests are invited to attend. At this writing, the classes were scheduled on the third Saturday of June, July, and August from 5:30 to 6:30 P.M.

If the format remains, one class will continue to cover red and white meat, another fish, and the third smoking meats and fish. Through 2002, Coudouy also offered a prix fixe meal featuring the dishes he had demonstrated that evening, along with other courses and suitable accompaniments. In fall 2002, the fine-dining Patina

Restaurant closed and was replaced by an upscale family-style restaurant called Bivans. It is possible that the special after-class dinners will be offered there.

Park Hyatt Beaver Creek, Beaver Creek; (970) 949-1234 or www.beavercreek.hyatt.com.

Dining

Allie's Cabin

Located on a bench at the top of Beaver Creek's Haymeadow beginner area in a grove of aspen, this large log lodge offers views of the village but is surprisingly unobtrusive from below. Only open for dinner during the winter, it is reached by snowcat-towed sleigh or snowshoes—the latter for diners who want to work up an appetite. Since it is a romantic and subdued restaurant, relatively few people actually take the snowshoe option.

Gleaming wood floors, a soaring stone fireplace, massive wrought-iron chandeliers, and impeccable table settings provide an elegant backdrop for this upscale steakhouse. The kitchen always sends out a small *amuse-bouche*, a teaser to "amuse" the palate while guests decide what to order. A strudel filled with rare mushrooms and goat cheese served as such an overture during the winter of 2002.

Ambitious appetizers include Sweetbread Vol au Vent, Pan Seared Foie Gras, Grand Marnier of Duck Napoleon, and Colorado Crab Cakes. While crab is as native to Colorado as the mythical jackalope, the Colorado-created dish of bluepoint crab and *panko* (Japanese cracker crumbs) is a winner. Entrées include Colorado rack of lamb, beef tenderloin or porterhouse, pheasant breast, veal rib chop, and baked salmon, each with a distinctive and well-matched sauce and the right side dishes. And, unlike the upscale steakhouse chains, you won't have to pay extra for the accompaniments.

For reservations (required), call (970) 949-9090.

Beano's Cabin

As with Allie's Cabin, Beano's Cabin isn't a cabin but a huge log lodge, with high ceilings, large windows, and an open kitchen. The restaurant is located amid aspen trees near the bottom of Larkspur Bowl. Access from the ski area base is via snowcat-pulled sleigh in winter, and horses, horse-drawn wagon, or vehicle in summer.

The five-course prix fixe dinner features outstanding creative American cuisine. Guests may choose their preferences for three of the five courses. From the appetizer menu, selections include Pan-Seared Buffalo Carpaccio, Scallops Poached in Butter, Warm Goat Cheese Tart, or Beluga Caviar Gâteau. Main courses offer such excellently

Exclusive On-Mountain Restaurants

When English aristocrats of the sort presented in *Gosford Park* began skiing in the Alps, they had little interest in mixing socially with the below-stairs types represented by the local farmers and tradesmen who inhabited the villages that became ski resorts—or with even skiers of lesser pedigrees. The solution was the establishment of private clubs high on the mountains of St. Moritz and other exclusive resorts where lunch could be taken in leisure and in the company of the right sort of people.

Beaver Creek was the first resort in Colorado to import the concept, though in our mountains, a titled lineage traceable back to William the Conquerer, or at least Henry VIII, isn't nearly as important as the ability and willingness to pay a hefty initiation fee and commensurate dues. It's all rather like a golfing club, but without the fairways and greens, or like a London gentleman's club, but without the leather chairs and impeccable butlers. Beano's, set in a secluded clearing high on Beaver Creek, Allie's Cabin lower down on the mountain, and the Game Creek Club (see page 270) on the fringes of Vail's Game Creek Bowl are private on-mountain luncheon clubs during the ski season. If that were all, they would not appear in these pages. In contrast to the old English clubs, the Vail Valley's counterparts do throw their doors open to anyone for dinner. I have no idea whether this egalitarianism is a result of U.S. Forest Service policy requiring that the public have access to facilities built on public land, whether Vail Resorts found another opportunity to derive revenue from these luxurious mountain restaurants, or a combination of these. Whatever the reason, people who love to dine well and stylishly are in luck. For visitors, all three rank as memorable "mountain experiences" and not merely resort dinners.

conceived and prepared dishes as Honey-Rubbed Rotisserie Duckling, Rocky Mountain Rainbow Trout, Wood-Grilled Venison, and Colorado Rack of Lamb, all appropriately accompanied. Desserts selections might include Cappuccino Crème Brulée, Hot Spice Apple Crumb Pie, and Bourbon Pecan Torte.

For reservations (required), call (970) 949-9090.

La Bottega

In the heart of Vail is La Bottega, a congenial Italian restaurant run by Stephen and Elisabetta Virion. The adjacent wine bar, called La Bottega del Vino, pours excellent wines—in both variety and depth—while the restaurant's menu features specialties of northern Italy and Tuscany. La Bottega started small, more a deli than anything else, in space formerly occupied by a bagel shop and expanded to two adjacent storefronts.

The daytime menu displays stone-oven pizza, bruschetta, and American-style sandwiches and salads. Vail insiders stop in for the Tuscan-style oven-roasted chicken, available for take-out only. In the evening, the restaurant serves pasta in all shapes along with beef, veal, lamb, seafood, and rabbit. The menu changes daily, so that you will find different but well-executed dishes in all of these categories. The space is dim and atmospheric, and the prices—for Vail—remain moderate.

La Bottega, 100 East Meadow Drive, Vail; (970) 476-0280 or www.labottega.com.

Campo de Fiore

For information on the genesis and cuisine of Campo de Fiore, see the Aspen chapter (page 305).

Campo de Fiore, 100 East Meadow Drive, Vail; (970) 476-8994 or www.campodefiore.net.

Chap's Grill & Chophouse

The Vail Cascade Resort & Spa anchors the western end of Vail's sprawling ski terrain. With a chairlift right outside the door, it is a desirable ski-in, lift-ride-out resort hotel. The recently redone Aria spa and fitness center rank among Colorado's finest, and its restaurant, also recently renovated, quickly became the place to go in the Vail Valley for hearty meals in a generously sized space. Formerly a mostly Continental restaurant called Alfredo's, the hotel dining room has reemerged as Chap's Grill & Chophouse.

It has been reenergized as well, offering three meals a day and quickly garnering a reputation for its exceptional prime meats and other hearty fare, skillfully prepared and beautifully served in an upscale Western setting. In the evening, which comes early in winter peak season to this resort tucked up against a steep, north-facing slope, the large dining room—with its high-backed booths, banquettes, and free-standing tables ringed by large, sturdy chairs—manages to feel both grandiose and cozy. At breakfast and lunchtime, it is suffused with light. In summer, the patio is an extension to the dining room, with quaking aspens, deep-green conifers, and swift-flowing Gore Creek just beyond the railing.

Chap's quickly earned its stripes for hefty cuts of prime beef, veal, pork, lamb, buffalo, and game specialties. Less heralded are fine seafood entrées, pasta selections, and vegetarian options. Because it is the only dining room in an award-winning hotel, Chap's is also one of the rare really good restaurants to welcome families with 10 kid-pleasing entrées, and the waitstaff is as attentive to juniors' needs as to adults'.

The signature appetizer is generously cut Portobello Fries, served with house-made steak sauce. Other knockouts include citrus-marinated Maine Lobster Cocktail with avocado, Baked Maine Mussels in an aromatic garlic-Chardonnay broth, corn-meal-battered Firecracker Oysters with chili-garlic, and Santa Barbara Prawns with a house-made cocktail sauce. And if you can't decide, try the Seafood Sampler, an inviting mélange of fish and shellfish.

Chap's meals never leave much room for dessert, but diners somehow manage to squeeze sweet stuff somewhere. How could they not, with such house temptations as Chocolate Lava Cake, Ginger Crème Brulée, Mission Fig Tart (or other seasonal fruit tart), Mocha Java Bomb, or Banana Bread Pudding. Sure, there are house-made sorbets, but few diners have the willpower to go light when rich remains an option from the first course to the last. If you're dining at Chap's, plan on a before-dinner cocktail or a glass of wine (and hors d'oeuvres if you just can't wait) or an after-dinner something in the Lobby Lounge, one of Vail's best piano bars.

Chap's Grill & Chophouse, Vail Cascade Resort & Spa, 1500 Westhaven Drive, Vail; (970) 479-7014, (800) 420-2424, (970) 476-7111 (resort number), or www.vailcascade.com.

Cucina Rustica

See "The Wildflower and Cucina Rustica" entry in this chapter.

Game Creek Club

Vail's equivalent of the two Beaver Creek "cabins" (see page 266) is the Game Creek Club, a mountain manor that more accurately styles itself as "a European-style chalet." The kitchen matches the grandeur of the space. Heavy table settings featuring heavy pewter place plates, hefty flatware, and impressive stemware hold their own in the baronial space.

The prix fixe dinner presents itself with weighty choices for each of four courses. Soup du jour, house-cured gravlax, bluepoint crab cake, Beluga caviar, carpaccio of venison, duck confit, and seared foie gras are prepared differently at different times. The Game Creek Club is probably the only place at 10,000 feet above sea level that has ever offered Diver Sea Scallops with Crispy Sea Urchin.

Fresh salads are followed by a choice of entrées. The kitchen does different preparations of striped bass, yellowfin tuna, lamb shank, venison, elk, grouper, halibut, veal, breast of chicken or capon, caribou, and a vegan entrée. Desserts include seasonally appropriate tarts, pastries, and other baked, frozen, and refrigerated items. Access for winter and summer dinners and summer Sunday brunch is via the Eagle Bahn gondola from Lionshead, followed by snowcat or van shuttle.

For reservations (required), call (970) 479-4275.

Grouse Mountain Grill

One of my favorite kitchen magnets reads, "Don't trust skinny cooks." If you buy into that logic, Grouse Mountain Grill Executive Chef Rick Kangas ranks as the Vail Valley's most trustworthy chef. "The dining room is big, the chairs are big, the food is big, and the chef is big," he affirms.

Kangas, indeed a big man, grew up in Montana, where his grandmother owned two restaurants and his mother worked in food service. As the oldest of five children, Rick often cooked family meals, with his working mother available for telephone instructions or consultations. He cooked his way through college, including at Many

VAIL'S EURO-CLASSICS

Alpenrose, Pepi's Restaurant, Swiss Chalet, The Tyrolean, and Swiss Stübli

Vail Village is often described as "a Bavarian village in the Colorado Rockies." To my eyes, its core isn't as much Bavarian as it is pan-Alpine, with chalet-style structures that are a little Bavarian, a little Tyrolean, a little Swiss, and a little American.

When Vail was founded, the skiing life and the traditions and styles of the Alps were intertwined. The town still has several restaurants that serve the rich food of that region. Don't be surprised by such trappings as a waitstaff clad in dirndls, loden, or lederhosen, along with rustic tablecloths in a folk pattern, knotty-pine walls, and beer steins. On the menus, you'll likely find schnitzels, sausages, sauerbraten, and strudels, as well as classic meat and cheese fondue, pork, and veal. Desserts are classically European too—and so are the wines. Some have updated their menus with lighter dishes, more salads, seafood, steaks, lamb, and game, but at their heart, their roots tap deep into the soil of the Alps.

Pepi's Restaurant, established in 1964 in the Gasthof Gramshammer, is the oldest. Its Antlers Room specializes in gourmet game dishes and tableside preparation, once the ultimate in fine dining and still a kick when done well. The **Swiss Chalet,** one of several restaurants (and the most European) in the sprawling Sonnenalp Resort, is the newest. **The Alpenrose** is as much a pastry shop as a restaurant (see the Bakery section in this chapter), while **The Tyrolean** opened in 1972 and was serving game from the beginning. All four are family-owned and -operated, just as they would be in the Alps. In fact, the Langeggers, who have run The Tyrolean since the beginning, also own a ranch near Silt, where they raise game.

Over in Beaver Creek, the **Swiss Stübli** fills the same role, offering Swiss and other Continental classics derived from the traditions of neighboring Italy and, occasionally, France. In addition to *Bündnerfleisch,* fondue, and raclette, you'll find a salad of fresh buffalo mozzarella and Roma tomatoes, various pastas, and a wonderfully summery *vitello tonnato,* veal saltimbocca, and other dishes from Italy, alongside chilled vichyssoise from France.

Alpenrose, 100 East Meadow Drive, Vail; (970) 476-3194. Pepi's Restaurant, Gasthof Gramshammer, 231 East Gore Creek Drive, Vail; (970) 476-4671; Swiss Chalet, Sonnenalp Resort, 20 Vail Road, Vail; (970) 479-5429 or (970) 476-5656. The Tyrolean, 400 East Meadow Drive, Vail; (970) 476-2204. Swiss Stübli, Poste Montane Lodge, 76 Avondale Lane, Beaver Creek; (970) 748-8618.

Glacier Hotel in Glacier National Park, where the head chef mentored his early moves toward a culinary career.

Rather than inaugural years in trendy California wine country restaurants or *stages* with Michelin-starred restaurants, he perfected his skills at places like the Rocky Mountain Pasta Company in Bozeman, the Stock Exchange and Broadway Bistro in Billings, and eventually back to Glacier as *sous-chef* at the Lake McDonald Lodge. He always took time to travel and broaden his knowledge, hitting San Francisco, New Zealand, Australia, and—extensively—Europe, where he ate, learned, and absorbed.

Kangas landed in Vail in 1989, initially as chef at Blu's Restaurant. His arrival coincided with Colorado's culinary awakening, so his growing sensibilities and the town's growing sophistication and interest in food were in synch. He continued to expand his culinary perspective and also learned more about pairing wines with foods, a skill that was not in great demand in Montana when he was growing up. In 1993, Kangas, along with David Dowell, formerly of Cyrano's in Vail, and restaurant manager Tony McNally, opened Grouse Mountain Grill in Beaver Creek's Pines Lodge—and there he remains.

The restaurant is known for huge portions and often unexpected combinations. The jumbo pork chops, practically the size of the dinner plate, are perennial favorites, sometimes served with orange-mustard sauce, red cabbage, and apple compote, and other times coated with pretzel crumbs and paired with mustard sauce. That's not the only snack food Kangas uses as an ingredient. He also devised a Ritz Cracker–Crusted Walleye on sweet lemon lettuce with dill tartare sauce. Incredibly, these dishes, which sound as if they come from a 1950s' women's magazine, taste more sophisticated than the descriptions would indicate—and they demonstrate out-of-the-box thinking and gutsy experimentation. More conventional dishes include such he-man entrées as grilled 10-ounce tenderloin of Limousin beef with herbed mushrooms; dry-aged prime New York steak with Maytag blue cheese, roasted onion, and port reduction; and elk rib chop with parsnip-potato *rösti* and huckleberry brown butter. Another Kangas hallmark is potato bread. Each evening, he creates a different potato flatbread, flavored with something unusual. Scallops, onion, cheese, and an assortment of herbs are offered one time, and curry tomato relish and duck sausage on another. He also is one of the few American chefs with the nerve to attempt a house-cured prosciutto.

Many Colorado restaurants boast about using fresh local ingredients. The Grouse Mountain Grill does them one better, with its own produce gardens downvalley in Edwards, where six kinds of heirloom tomatoes, salad greens, herbs, and root vegetables are grown, supplemented by fresh produce from other growers. Still, it is a sign of Kangas' commitment to freshness and quality to grow what he can. Salads aside, even seasonal specialties have heft and presence on the plate. A recent summer menu featured roasted rack of Colorado lamb with goat cheese and potato tower, a modest 7-ounce cut of grilled Limousin beef tenderloin steak with potatoes and tomatoes, and Cranberry-Braised Colorado Buffalo Short Ribs with a truffle dumpling, which started as a seasonal entrée but might make it to perennial status.

It's a challenge to eat light at the Grouse Mountain Grill—ironically, until you get to dessert. Fresh Seasonal Berries, Mountain Huckleberry Shortcake, and Sorbet of the Day with Fresh Berries aren't too, too rich. Then again, that same dessert list also suggested Apple Bread Pudding, Cinnamon Ice Cream & Bourbon Caramel Sauce, Classic Crème Brulée with Shortbread Cookie, and the endearing Chocolate Cake and a Cold Glass of Milk.

Zagat ranks the Grouse Mountain Grill as the top Regional American Restaurant in Colorado. It has also earned the AAA Four Diamond Award and the *Wine Spectator* Award of Excellence for its extensive, mostly American wine list. In addition to cooking at the James Beard House in New York, Kangas was invited to Epcot's International Food and Wine Festival in 2000, and he also returns to Montana for occasional food events there. You might even catch him cooking for the cameras on the Public Broadcasting System, Food TV Network, and on the box of gourmet cookware that he endorses. He's a big guy and hard to miss.

Grouse Mountain Grill, The Pines Lodge, 141 Scott Hill Road, Beaver Creek; (970) 949-0600 or http://beavercreek.snow.com/menu.grouse.asp.

Larkspur Restaurant

Larkspur serves informal lunches, gourmet dinners, afternoon drinks, and morning coffee and pastries, which makes it a little like a hotel restaurant, except that it isn't in a hotel. It is located in Golden Peak Lodge, the snazziest, ritziest base lodge in all the Colorado Rockies. There's a ticket window, a ski rental operation, restrooms, and all those usual day-lodge services—plus one of the finest restaurants in Vail. In fact, this finest of all base-lodge restaurants in ski country, is open full-bore during the winter season, on a reduced schedule in summer, and closed in spring and fall.

Walls of cream, beige, or lemon join pale wood and stone floors to create a simultaneously upbeat, substantial, and sophisticated look. Room dividers, harmonious changes in wall treatment, and clever lighting make the big space more intimate.

Local star chef Thomas Salamunovich owns and operates Larkspur with his wife, Nancy Sweeney. Salamunovich worked as a line cook during his first ski-bum experience in Vail and graduated from the California Culinary Academy in 1984, when California cuisine was in its infancy. He honed his skills in France at Michelin three-star restaurants under Paul Bocuse and Lucas Carton, and at Élysée Gaston Lenotre, a Michelin two-star restaurant. He also worked in Poilane Boulangerie, arguably France's best-known bakery, and for a small family-owned bistro in the French countryside.

Eventually he returned to San Francisco's leading-edge restaurant scene, including cooking with Jeremiah Tower at Stars and at Wolfgang Puck's Postrio. He came to Colorado with a resume that landed him the top spot at Sweet Basil, where he cooked for seven years, before opening Zino Ristorante (see page 283). Then came Larkspur in late 1999, where Salamunovich has created dishes that are French at the core, using fresh ingredients and impeccable culinary technique to turn out food that is sometimes deceptively simple and yet always elegant. Dramatic and imaginative renditions abound on the menu that changes seasonally and includes many specials.

Among the dishes on recent menus was a complex Roasted Five Onion Soup. Vine-Ripened Tomato and Mozzarella Tower with Basil and Parmesan Crostini is a Caprese salad turned into an artful sculpture. Glazed Sonoma Duck and Petaluma Free-Range Chicken use poultry from California's wine country. Black Truffle and Potato Gnocchi mates a hearty ingredient and a delicate one, a daring act of culinary tightrope walking. Petite Doughnuts with Godiva mocha sabayon is a hauntingly satisfying dessert. Raspberry-Studded White Chocolate Cream with Kir Royale, berries, and bittersweet chocolate sauce takes dessert and complements it with a classic apéritif to bring a dinner full circle.

The coveted Chef's Table, right by the kitchen, features smaller portions of a multicourse feast that enable Salamunovich to let his creative juices really flow. He says, "We allow ourselves to think more architecturally and artistically to keep the customer amused and excited throughout the meal." The customized menu accommodates guests' dining preferences and dietary restrictions, but imagination knows no bounds when it comes to preparation or presentation. Each course is served on a different piece of china—and sometimes no china at all. A Salamunovich signature is food served unconventionally—on skewers, in glassware, even on cleaver blades.

Wine Spectator lauded Larkspur with an Award of Excellence beginning in its inaugural year. The spectacular wine list is divided by region and by varietal, with depth in Californian, French, Italian, and Spanish vintages and especially in champagnes and sparkling wines. Two dozen or so are available by the glass.

From the outset, Larkspur set and has maintained its high standards, despite the challenge of that high-traffic, base-lodge location that, on the surface, would seem to defy the possibility of fine dining.

Larkspur, 458 Vail Valley Drive, Vail; (970) 479-8050 or www.larkspur-vail.com.

The Left Bank Restaurant

Vail turned 40 in 2002, and for more than three-quarters of its existence, The Left Bank Restaurant has drawn lovers of French cuisine. From 1959-1961, young Luc Meyer embarked on a culinary education in the classic European tradition with an apprenticeship at the legendary Restaurant de la Pyramide in Vienne, not far from Lyon, then at L'Oustau de Baumanière at Les Baux de Provence.

He worked in Switzerland and Canada, before landing in the Bahamas, where he met his wife, Liz. The couple lived in St. Croix in the U.S. Virgin Islands until the allure of palm trees paled, and they settled in Vail, opening The Left Bank Restaurant on Thanksgiving Day 1970. The Left Bank, located in the venerable Sitzmark Lodge, is still considered a Vail bastion of traditional fine dining. Meyer's kitchen turns out French *classiques*, with a decided tilt to the Mediterranean part of the country, derived from his days in Vienne. Liz Meyer handles the dining room, which a charming example of country French grace and is even furnished with family antiques.

Among the stellar starters are escargots, authentic French onion soup, and house-made pâté de foie gras. La Soupe de Tomate en Surprise is an aromatic tomato soup topped with a pastry crust. The surprise is that the dough is puffed up by hot soup and browns beautifully, making the presentation look more like a soufflé than a soup. Le Steak au Poivre Blanc, a distinctive pepper steak finished with a sauce of cream, brown stock, and Cognac, has been on the menu since day one. Other long-time house specialties are bouillabaisse and Le Carré d'Agneau Rôti à Ma Façon, which in plain English means rack of lamb. Meyer's version features Colorado lamb brushed with Dijon mustard, rolled in Provençal bread crumbs, roasted to perfection, and portioned for two to share.

The Left Bank was one of the first Western Slope restaurants to bring in super-fresh seafood. The breads are baked in-house, and the dessert cart rolls along with beautiful baked goods, crème brulée, tìramisu, and floating island. The Left Bank's gorgeous chocolate soufflé takes time, as does the signature fruit tart (peach tart in summer, pear tart in winter), served with house-made sorbet, so it's advisable to order it well in advance.

Most of the 400 wines are from France, with a smattering of American selections. The menu suggests some wine pairings. Some 20 wines are available by the glass–seven or eight each of red and white wines, a fine champagne, and four late-harvest dessert wines, including the coveted nectar released by Chateau d'Yquem.

In contrast to other Vail restaurants that promote and advertise heavily, the Meyers are low-key, turning their attention toward exquisite cuisine and impeccable service. While The Left Bank is a white tablecloth kind of restaurant, children are welcome, just as they are in France. Also as in France, off-season at the resort is off-season for the owners. The restaurant closes between mid-April and mid-June and between early October and mid-November. You should know that reservations are virtually mandatory and The Left Bank does not take credit cards, so bring cash—lots of it. Perfection does, after all, carry a price.

The Left Bank, 183 Gore Creek Drive, Vail; (970) 476-3696.

Mirabelle at Beaver Creek

In contrast both to the gray concrete that characterizes most buildings in Avon and to the monumental edifices of Beaver Creek just up the hill sits an inviting farm-house, more than a century old. Located near Beaver Creek's security gate, the simple frame house could have fallen prey to development ambitions. It is something of a miracle that it was never demolished to make way for something grander, and for foodies, it is a culinary landmark as well as a historic one.

The old homestead houses Mirabelle at Beaver Creek. It is also home to owner-chef Daniel Joly and his wife, Nathalie, who have quarters upstairs. The nearby barn, built in the 1860s, is one of Eagle County's oldest buildings. The farmhouse was built in 1898 and expanded in 1902. This is a long time ago by Colorado building standards, but in Belgium, where Joly was raised, it is only yesterday.

At the age of 14, Daniel informed his father, an architect, that he intended to become a chef. His father found a kitchen job for him but predicted that this was a passing fancy. His father was wrong. At 18, Joly enrolled in a Belgian culinary school and just two years later was named the country's best young chef. In 1988 he fast-tracked to the United States, becoming executive sous-chef at Restaurant Million in Charleston, South Carolina, before moving to Colorado and filling the same billet first at the Restaurant Picasso (see page 274) and then at Camberley's. Meanwhile, Luc Meyer, owner of The Left Bank in Vail (see previous entry), had established Mirabelle. In 1992, he hired Joly to become executive chef, with Nathalie overseeing the dining room. Seven years later, the Jolys bought the restaurant.

Many honors have been heaped upon both chef and restaurant. Mirabelle has steadily received four stars from Mobil, DiRoNA honors, and the *Wine Spectator*

Award of Excellence, and Joly has cooked at the James Beard House in New York. He is the rare expatriate member of *Les Maîtres-Cuisiniers de Belgique,* a highly selective society of Belgian master chefs. Most of the 80 members are owner-chefs (*chef eigenaar* in Flemish, in case you're interested) of restaurants in Belgium. Joly is the only member in the United States. While Daniel is fanatical about being a hands-on chef in his own kitchen, Nathalie takes on front-of-the-house chores with panache. For diners who think of Belgian food as *waterzooi* and other heavy stews, the food is a revelation. A little of Belgium, a little more of France, and a lot of contemporary threads are woven into the Mirabelle tapestry.

Named after a yellow Alsatian plum, Mirabelle spreads warmth as surely as that first sip of mirabelle plum brandy. The old farmhouse is painted in historically appropriate creamy white with brown trim. In summer, lavish baskets overflowing with bright flowers hang above the front porch railings. The dining area reflects the original farmhouse floor plan, with some walls opened up to link rooms that are graced by and polished hardwood floors, green carpet, green and white walls, and harmonizing wallpaper. The tables are elegantly set with designer china, sparkling crystal, and golden flatware on pure-white linen tablecloths.

Chef Joly, an unremitting foie gras fan, offers as the specialty-of-the-house appetizer Hot Foie Gras with Mirabelle Plum Coulis and Caramelized Golden Apples. Grilled Colorado Lamb Chops, crusted with the traditional seasonings of garlic, parsley, and rosemary, appear on the menu with the description "in my granddaddy's style." This signature dish remains a constant on the menu that changes about every six weeks. Other dishes showcase Joly's departure from classic cuisine into the realm of contemporary Continental and beyond. I'm going to bet that his Belgian progenitor never made Lightly Spiced Crab Egg Rolls with red ginger, rice vinegar, and a salad of baby greens or Lobster and Calamari Casserole with artichoke, Roma tomatoes, and basil broth and an adornment of vegetable crisps.

The nightly four-course chef's menu can be seamlessly paired with wines from a cellar that stocks more than 200 imported and domestic selections. Desserts are based on the classic pâtisserie repertoire, but a little different, and at least a little better, than you're likely to find in most other restaurants. And if you want a *digestif* to cap the feast, order a shot of potent plum brandy—made, of course, with mirabelle plums.

Mirabelle at Beaver Creek, 55 Village Road, Avon; (970) 949-7728.

Restaurant Picasso

Restaurant Picasso debuted in 1989 as the elegant dining room of a grandly proportioned 28-room lodge in the middle of a vast and ambitious planned second-home development called Cordillera. The lodge was set high on a mesa overlooking the Eagle River Valley, and all around were "Lot for Sale" signs. The tract, now so heavily built up, was then still quite bucolic. The Lodge at Cordillera doubled its size to 56 rooms, and surrounding it, on those once-vacant lots, are multi–million-dollar mountain mansions. The gated community positions itself as a golf resort, with fairways and greens etched onto historic ranchland that has been wrapped into the 6,800-acre development.

Restaurant Picasso has been a constant in this period of intense growth. Its subtle, subdued colors suggest an Old World atmosphere. A fireplace here, a Picasso there, an eye-catching view elsewhere create a warm and worldly ambience. The Wine Cellar, private dining space for groups of up to 16, was added in 1997.

Early on, chefs came and went, but Fabrice Beaudoin has had staying power, developing a style of light interpretations of classic European fare that has maintained its reputation for excellence. Often cited for honors from *Wine Spectator* and DiRoNA, this gourmet restaurant is appreciated equally for the Picassos on the walls and culinary artistry evident on each plate that emerges from the kitchen. Divided into several small spaces, the restaurant displays a triumph of elegant intimacy.

The menu changes seasonally and features the iconic ingredients of contemporary American cuisine—frisée lettuce, arugula, field greens, duck breast, carpaccio, risotto, house-made pasta, seared tuna, diver scallops, Colorado lamb, crème brulée, seasonal fruit tarts, and a host of other wonderfully fresh ingredients prepared carefully and served with panache in a lovely setting.

Chef Beaudoin a pioneer Vail area with wine-pairing dinners, drawing from a 3,700-bottle cellar and matching selections, two per course, to the evidence of his prowess and creativity in the kitchen. The extensive wine list with a focus on French and Californian labels (with some Spanish and other selections thrown in) still combines well with Beaudoin's innovative menu.

Restaurant Picasso was once Cordillera's only place to eat, but with all those golf courses, the resort now also offers opportunities elsewhere on the huge spread. The Timber Hearth Grille serves New American cuisine with a southwestern flair, Chapparal is a steakhouse, and Grouse on the Green is a pub. Still, Restaurant Picasso remains at the pinnacle in terms of fine wining and dining.

Restaurant Picasso, The Lodge at Cordillera, 2205 Cordillera Way, Edwards; (800) 877-3529, (970) 926-2200, or www.cordillera-vail.com.

SaddleRidge

SaddleRidge, a complex of luxurious condominiums, was built slopeside at Beaver Creek as a private corporate conference center. An indoor pool that resembles a boathouse, a library boasting such Western artifacts as General Custer's parade hat and Buffalo Bill's desk, and a soaring restaurant with a ceiling reminiscent of the hull of a wooden ship were among the amenities designed to be enjoyed by the privileged elite. One circumstance led to another, and SaddleRidge is now operated by Vail Resorts.

The restaurant is open to the public, so we can all be part of the elite now. Chef Geordy Ogden's specialties are wild game and seafood, often with Southwestern or Asian flavors. Start with Quesadilla de Canarditas, blue-corn tortillas filled with duck confit and *queso fresco* and garnished with cilantro *crema* and *salsa cruda,* or with Modern Tuna Sashimi, sliced ahi tuna drizzled with hot sesame chive oil and served with *wakame* salad. Prefer Mediterranean fare? Try the Greek-Style Octopus, with grilled vegetable salad dressed with ouzo saffron dressing.

Mixed Game Burgundy Style consists of braised buffalo and elk with potatoes, carrots, onions, and mushrooms in red wine sauce. Carnivorous traditionalists prefer the likes of Grilled New York Strip with garlic mashed potatoes, sautéed vegetables, blue cheese, and red wine *glace*. Those whose tastes run to Thai, healthy, or meatless are indulged with dishes like Glass Noodle Bowl, with stir-fried vegetables, fried tempeh, and coconut curry broth. Top desserts include Warm Chocolate Cake with espresso cream and shaved chocolate, classic crème brulée, and a mini–banana split with caramelized bananas.

Some people show up just for classy appetizers and a game of eight-ball on SaddleRidge's antique billiards table. Desserts and fine port are often served in front of a roaring fire. Indulge in them, and you might just return for a full meal.

SaddleRidge, 44 Meadow Lane, Beaver Creek; (970) 845-5450, (866) 395-3185, (970) 845-5456 (resort number), or www.beavercreek.snow.com/menu.saddleridge.asp.

Sonnenalp Resort Restaurants

There is no more authentically European resort hotel in the United States than the Sonnenalp Resort in the heart of Vail Village. Colorado's luxurious Sonnenalp is a sister property to the original Sonnenalp, founded in 1919 by Adolf and Eleanor Fässler in the Bavarian Alps. Today, the original Sonnenalp still thrives, as does the New World version run by the Fässlers' grandson Johannes and his wife, Rosanna. Three Vail Village properties are now under Sonnenalp management, each with an on-site restaurant: The Sonnenalp Resort of Vail is an elegant 90-room suite-hotel, the Austria Haus has been turned into a high-end timeshare, and the Swiss Hotel and Spa, and the Singletree Golf Club down the road in Edwards, all come under the Sonnenalp umbrella.

Despite the German name, **Ludwig's,** in the Sonnenalp of Vail, serves contemporary American cuisine at dinner in an elegant and stylish setting. It also puts on in-season wine maker dinners and such occasional food-oriented activities as preholiday cookie decorating workshops conducted by a chef. **The Swiss Chalet** (see page 269) in the Swiss Hotel building specializes in cheese and meat fondues and authentic raclette with two nightly seatings. **The Bully Ranch,** along with Ludwig's located in the main building, is the Sonnenalp's casual lunch and dinner restaurant, specializing in Southwestern fare, burgers, and other beef dishes amid the kind of casual Western atmosphere that European guests expect in the American West. **The King's Club** does traditional afternoon tea and evening cocktails or cordials. **Balata** at nearby Singletree serves contemporary, upscale Colorado cuisine at lunch and dinner.

Sonnenalp Resort of Vail, 20 Vail Road, Vail; (800) 654-8312, (970) 476-1639, or www.sonnenalp.com.

Splendido at The Chateau

No restaurant more fits the Beaver Creek image of grandeur, understated elegance, and majesty in the mountains than the immodestly named Splendido at The Chateau. It is not, however, false immodesty. Splendido is every bit as lavishly appointed as its name would suggest. Located in the grandiose resort property called The Chateau, it is a dining room of proportions that indeed are reminiscent of a French chateau.

Under high ceilings and huge chandeliers, swag draperies frame massive windows and formal armchairs surround generously proportioned tables that are elegantly set with imported linens and tableware. The picture is one of sophisticated elegance and (dare I say it?) splendor. Only the open kitchen along one wall brings a note of American informality to this faux-Euro-aristocratic setting. British-born and Colorado-raised Chef David Walford ski-bummed at Vail restaurants in the 1970s before deciding that he wanted to be a chef. He trained with Masa Kobayashi at Auberge du Soleil in Napa Valley and with Udo Neschutneys at Miramonte in St. Helena, California. He put in an obligatory and enlightening year in France, working *stages* for Roland Mazère at Le Centenaire in Les Eyzies and Bernard Loiseau at La Côte d'Or in Saulieu. The prodigy next worked in San Francisco's Masa and then returned to Vail as executive chef at Sweet Basil in Vail, a position he held for nine years.

Meanwhile, the Vail Valley had changed greatly. The space that is now Splendido opened in 1994 as Chadwick's with Chad Scothorn, who now captains Cosmopolitan in Telluride (see page 378), as the first chef. When Scothorn left, Trey Holt revamped Chadwick's and reopened it as Splendido, named after Splendido in Portofino, Italy—which indicates that sign on the door isn't as boastful as it might seem. When Holt moved on to open Toscanini (see page 279), Walford moved down the valley and up the hill as Splendido's executive chef.

On the seasonally changing international menu, Provençal, Italian, and contemporary American flavors predominate. Walford's background is reflected in the European-based dishes, while the American aspect comes in with steady and creative use of the kitchen's wood-fired oven, with mesquite to feed the flames, as well as with East Coast seafood in many dishes. If there is one house specialty, however, it is close-to-home Colorado rack of lamb. Always wood-oven-roasted, it might be napped with rosemary-olive *jus* and a silky sheep's milk cheese soufflé in the cooler months or perhaps lightened with chickpea and olive fries and grilled cherry tomatoes in summer.

Walford often has ravioli on the appetizer menu, sometimes lobster ravioli with lemon, tomatoes, leeks, corn, and basil, and others duck ravioli with squash, white beans, and browned butter. He also likes beet salads. He might offer a Roast Beet and Blood Orange Salad with pistachio vinaigrette and a blue cheese crisp, or a Beet and Endive Salad with walnuts, pear, and Gorgonzola *cromesqui*. Alaskan halibut might be paired with king crab and Italian parsley sauce or with Jerusalem artichokes, buttersoft Savoy cabbage, and grilled endive.

Into Splendido's wood oven go Atlantic salmon, young chicken, elk loin, Maine sea scallops, and any number of other ingredients, and out come perfectly roasted bases around which to build beautifully artistic creations. Walford has a field day with fresh wild mushrooms, delivered by a local gleaner whose forays to the best spots in the nearby mountains yield wild puffballs, chanterelles, cèpes, and whatever else comes along to grace seasonal menus in appetizers, salads, and entrées. The small and tight dessert menu lists half-a-dozen offerings, many of which incorporate seasonal fruits, plus crème brulée, sweet soufflés, mousse, and house-made *sorbets*. California wines dominate the 300-item list. Along with The Wildflower and Mirabelle, it is a Vail Valley holder of four stars from Mobil. The restaurant and Walford have garnered numerous other culinary honors as well as the loyalty of well-heeled locals, second-home owners, and vacationers who love the splendid ambience, the quality, and the service.

Splendido at The Chateau, 17 Chateau Lane (also known as Scott Hill Road), Beaver Creek; (970) 845-8808 or www.splendidobeavercreek.com.

Sweet Basil

Cognoscenti have been trooping to Sweet Basil since it opened in the heart of Vail Village in 1977. Then a small restaurant in a far smaller resort, it was the first place in with contemporary cuisine combining American food and classical French technique in exciting new ways. The concept is old toque now, but a quarter of a century ago it was cutting-edge.

Sweet Basil was established by Kevin Clair, who had intended to go to medical school but was sidetracked by a restaurant job. After graduating from the University of Denver's School of Hotel & Restaurant Management, he did *stages* at two Michelin three-star restaurants, Rousseau de Beaumanière in Provence and Maxim's in Paris. He arrived in Vail in 1975 and two years later opened his own precious restaurant, which has since been expanded twice and remodeled at least that often.

Clair stills owns Sweet Basil and oversees the big picture, but he leaves the day-to-day kitchen activities to others. Some of Colorado's top culinary talents have cooked there. Bruce Yim has been Sweet Basil's executive chef since 1999, following Robert Salamunovich, who left to establish Zino, then Larkspur. Before that, Yim attended San Jose State University and intended to go to the Culinary Institute of America, but he was derailed by top kitchens on both coasts. He cooked his way up the culinary ladder starting at Le Pavillon and Le Fleur in Washington, D.C., followed by Café Royale in Philadelphia, the Polo Lounge and 21 Club in New York, Harry's Bar and Harry's Dolce in Venice, and finally Postrio, Bix, and Ristorante Ecco, all in San Francisco.

The executive chefs who followed Clair have earned many honors for the restaurant. There have been DiRoNA awards and *Wine Spectator* Awards of Excellence since 1994, and Yim became the latest Sweet Basil chef to cook at the James Beard House in New York. Between a three-and-a-half year stint at Postrio and his first executive chef position at Bix, Yim worked for a time as photographic food stylist for Williams-Sonoma cookbooks. His years at so many leading restaurants, his food-styling stint, and his instincts for food combinations keep him on the culinary forefront of fusion cuisine, that open-minded and creative combination of French, Mediterranean, Asian, and other influences.

Sweet Basil is a sizable and unpretentious restaurant that conveys a bit of the bistro style. Lunch on the terrace on a summer day is a delight, but dinner within Sweet Basil's hallowed walls is what gourmets think of as heaven. Those walls are simple and barely adorned, the lighting is subdued, the napery is white, and the table settings are pared-down—all to let the food speak for itself. While much of the menu changes seasonally, evolving to evermore refined combinations of flavors and presentation, some dishes have been favorites since Kevin Clair was in the kitchen.

Ingredients can assume different identities in different seasons. A recent summer menu featured seared foie gras with Colorado peaches and *vin cotto*. In winter, the foie gras was integral to a Napoleon with black pepper genoise and blood orange–ginger marmalade. The Napoleon concept was executed in a wild mushroom Napoleon with cippolini and truffle vinaigrette. The summer version of the baby field green salad comes with house-made mozzarella, the winter version with potato fritter and creamy blue cheese–apple vinaigrette or with mango salsa, macadamia nuts, and Point Reyes blue cheese. In summer the grilled double-cut pork chop comes with a sticky rice spring roll and black bean vinaigrette, and in winter it sports a cauliflower gratin and apricot-sun-dried tomato sauce.

Pastry Chef Charles Broschinsky executes great renditions of such classics as crème brulée, warm apple tart, and house-made ice cream, but his creative juices flow with such unusual offerings as the signature Hot Sticky Toffee Pudding Cake with Dark Rum Sauce and Vanilla Whipped Cream or the intensely seasonal Peaches and Cream made of ripe Palisade peaches, French cream, and vanilla and raspberry sauces. The Chocolate Tasting—a milk chocolate terrine, warm dark chocolate pudding cake, and house-made chocolate *sorbet*—is a chocolate lover's fling on a single plate. Hard to decide? Order the dessert sampler for everyone at the table to share.

Sweet Basil's Chef's Tasting Menus change several times a year. The five-course feast, with or without paired wines, is available for full tables only. The *amuse-bouche* is normally a seafood, followed by soup, an appetizer, a meat dish, and a dessert. Among the more than 300 selections gracing Sweet Basil's wine list are imports and domestic wines, heavy on French and Californian vintages. Selections from elsewhere are called "Alternative Whites" and "Alternative Reds." Sweet Basil also offers excellent champagnes, half-bottles, "Large Bottles," and by-the-glass selections.

Sweet Basil, 193 East Gore Creek Drive, Vail; (970) 476-0125 or www.sweetbasil-vail.com.

Toscanini

This rink-side restaurant in the heart of Beaver Creek Village is an Italian restaurant writ large. Though the stylish space is grand, clever furniture placement and glass room dividers bring it down to a surprisingly intimate scale. Lacquered bentwood chairs, simple table settings, and lights low enough for atmosphere but bright enough to read the menu add to the hip elegance of the place.

You know you're at a serious Italian restaurant when you notice that on your table are three olive oils and a balsamic vinegar, but no salt and pepper (of course, you can request these seasonings if you wish). Read Toscanini's slogan—*La Fame é la miglio salsa,* or "hunger is the best sauce"—and you know that there's both attention to the food itself and a light-hearted approach to it.

Chef Chris Dressick grew up in Connecticut, where he worked in Italian restaurants. This hands-on training that what he calls "a culinary education in the school of hard knocks" was the foundation for the way he cooks today. His food emphasizes the beauty in the simplicity of fresh ingredients, prepared from scratch and with authenticity and honesty. Produce and legumes come from western Colorado whenever seasonally possible, but his prosciutto must be Italian. He prefers grass-fed lamb from New Zealand and Australia and Argentinian beef. Dressick and his crew work in an open kitchen, preparing individual pizzas, fresh pasta, and rotisserie-roasted meats. Antipasti Castelvetro, a selection of Italian cured meats, house-made mozzarella stuffed with basil, and prosciutto, is an eminently sharable appetizer. So is Aglio Arrosta, a garlic bulb with extra-virgin olive oil and herbs, roasted soft to spreadability and served with Parmesan.

The pizzas sizzle, the pastas sing, and the meats are first-rate. Orecchiette e Tartufo, cute cup-like pasta that translates to "little ears," is tossed with black truffle oil, garlic, anchovies, and Parmigiano-Reggiano. Pizza Anatra is a fusion pie made with duck confit, caramelized onions, grilled *traviso,* and Gorgonzola *dolce.* Never would such a pizza even be recognized in those Connecticut red-sauce Italian restaurants, but is it ever wonderful. *Cacciagione* is an Italian name, but the red-deer chops come from New Zealand, and the accompaniments of sweet-potato custard, spinach, candied garlic, rosemary, and Marsala come from Chris Dressick's fertile imagination.

Sinful specialty desserts include a luscious semi-frozen chocolate hazelnut mousse called *semi fredo.* The *zabaglioni* is kissed with fennel, spiked with Galliano, and baked on fresh berries served with house-made gelato, which in my mind is like three desserts in one. Torta Cioccolata, Toscanini's tìramisu, layers hazelnut ladyfingers with chocolate mascarpone. Strucolo Fritti is a fabulous mélange of crisp Italian strudel dumplings with cinnamon gelato and bourbon caramel. Contrary to the prevailing sense that small children have no place in big, fancy restaurants, Toscanini takes its cue from eateries in Italy, or perhaps from those Connecticut spots, and makes a children's menu available until 6:30 P.M.

The huge wine list is practically all Italy, with whites occupying one category and reds are subdivided by region, with depth in all. Dessert wines and sparkling wines, both Italy's *spumante* selections and token grand French champagnes, are also available. You can dine grandly at Toscanini, and your wine selection will equal the cuisine.

Toscanini, Market Square, Beaver Creek Village Plaza, Beaver Creek; (970) 845-5590.

Vista

Since the development of Beaver Creek, Avon has borne the image as the exclusive resort's gateway—a development at the doorstep right off I-70 that one passes through on the way to ski or to dine. Vista was the first to fill what had been a gastronomic gap between Vail to the east and Beaver Creek above. Locals know that its quality and sophistication approach the Vail Valley's top-tier resorts but at more moderate prices.

Located in Benchmark Plaza, a distinctive building whose streetside façade resembles a ship's prow, Vista is simple, with artworks on friendly yellow walls and clean, crisp table settings. The food, not the décor, is clearly the focus.

Owner-chef Michael Glennon started his career at Chillingsworth, a noteworthy bed-and-breakfast inn on Cape Cod, where he met his wife, Janine. A friend suggested that Sweet Basil in Vail needed line cooks, so off they went. In classic ski-town fashion, he cooked and she waited tables. The next stop was the Montauk Seafood

Grill, where Michael became sous-chef and then chef. That restaurant's owners had enough faith in the Glennons' vision to invest in Vista, but the couple runs the show.

Vista is a toned-down version of culinary Vail that brings interesting American/Thai/Italian cuisine, artful presentation, and caring preparation and service to Avon. While Glennon goes for fresh ingredients, he doesn't seek out, or pay for, the costliest or more exotic. Vista is therefore not a place where you will find diver-plucked sea scallops, quail, foie gras, or anything with truffles. Meat, poultry, seafood, and vegetarian dishes are always on the menu, but none of it is too precious, too exotic, or too expensive.

Glennon steams Prince Edward Island mussels in Thai red curry and coconut milk broth, braises veal shortribs and serves them with garlic mashed potatoes and suitable vegetables, and makes a traditional Bolognese sauce, but with untraditional elk, and serves it atop fresh pasta. He even suspends chicken chunks and seasonal vegetables in a fine matrix, tops the mixture with a house-made crust, and bakes it into the kind of chicken pot pie that you wish your grandmother had made. A Seared Cumin-Crusted Yellowfin Tuna served on *wasabi* mashed potatoes and sautéed baby bok choy with a soy-ginger sauce is another signature.

The wine list is segmented by location (California, Australia, France, and the Pacific Northwest) and light-hearted in terms of categories. It groups wines into red and white "Food-Loving Companions," "Sparklers," "Light and Refreshing," "Big and Bold Brunettes," "Sassy Redheads," "Luscious Blondes," "Fruitful Wines," and "Soft, Sassy and Smooth." What constitutes a "brunette" wine? The big reds—Cabernet Sauvignon, Merlot, Petite Sirah, and Zinfandel. When you think about it, that's right on. So is Vista—right on in terms of food, ambience, style, and price.

Vista, 48 East Beaver Creek Boulevard, Avon; (970) 949-3366 or www.vistarestaurant.com.

Vue

The luxurious Park Hyatt Beaver Creek Resort and Spa's new ultra-fine-dining restaurant reflects the hotel's stature, service, and award-winning reputation. Vue, an intimate 36-seat dining room, opened in late 2002. Normally, I wouldn't even mention something so new, but since hotels like the Hyatt don't change their restaurants frivolously, it will probably be around for a while. The design is plush-plus, with an opulent and elegant interior and a view of Beaver Creek Village and its skating rink. Hence the name Vue, which is French for view.

Perhaps more to the point, the hotel's executive chef, Pascal Coudouy, has the credentials to pull it off. A native of a ski village in the French Pyrenees, he cooked at Chez Pierre in Paris and La Belle Époque in Nice, before coming to New York's United Nations Plaza Hotel in 1987, then Gascogne Restaurant and Le Périgord, also in Manhattan. The lure of the mountains was strong, and Vue provides him the opportunity to extend his culinary reach. Predictions in the ephemeral realm of gourmet restaurants are risky, but I'll stick my neck out and recommend this one for anyone with refined tastes and a generous dining budget.

Vue, Park Hyatt Beaver Creek, Beaver Creek; (970) 949-1234
or www.beavercreek.hyatt.com.

The Wildflower and Cucina Rustica

The Lodge at Vail, an enduring resort hotel just steps from the VistaBahn chairlift in the heart of Vail Village, has one exceptional restaurant, The Wildflower, and one very good one, Cucina Rustica. The former is classically European with contemporary internationalism, and the latter is firmly Italian. Between them, they serve breakfast, lunch (indoors and al fresco in summer), and dinner.

Except for the floral motif, there is nothing wild about The Wildflower. Understated, elegant, impeccable, and finely tuned to diners' desires, this refined and civilized restaurant carries on the noble tradition of European ambience and service in the heart of America's number-one ski town. The restaurant has been steadily honored as a Mobil Four Star restaurant—astonishingly, the only one in Vail until this writing and one of only 13 in Colorado. The Wildflower has won numerous DiRoNA Awards and *Wine Spectator* Best Award of Excellence honors and keeps ranking as number one in Vail in the annual *Zagat Guide.*

The décor displays understated opulence, with gold walls stenciled with white garlands and massive arrangements of real flowers. One of The Wildflower's secrets is that every table feels like the best in the house, either near a large window, in a quiet corner, next to a magnificent floral arrangement, or in some other way special.

The Wildflower assembles an exemplary mélange of culinary tracks that comprise the best in modern American food. The menu changes often in order to take advantage of the finest, freshest ingredients at the market that week or that day and also to reflect seasonality. Fusion influences reign. Entrée selections feature contrasting flavors, colors, and origins—and sometimes on the same gorgeously presented plate: Napoleon of Maine Lobster and Cajun Fried Green Tomatoes embellished with Buttermilk-Whipped Purple Potatoes, Chanterelle-Corn Sauce, and Lobster Oil. Five-Spice Marinated Muscovy Duck Breast, seasoned in such a classic Chinese way, with very French duck confit, Italian-inspired risotto, and a divine tomato-leek fondue. Chili-Rubbed Game Hen with Poblano-Polenta Cakes. Marinated Nebraska Ostrich with Yukon Smashed Potatoes and Colorado Cherry Compote.

The *dégustation* tasting menu comes paired with wines for each course. From the ever-changing soups and starters to the equally ever-changing desserts, The Wildflower turns out first-rate dinners. The constants are a broad and deep wine list and, most of all, that gracious, attentive and correct service.

Cucina Rustica is no more rustic than The Wildflower is wild—unless you interpret "rustic" to mean some country-ish decorative elements, a big stone fireplace, and gleaming bare-wood tables rather than double tablecloths. The breakfast buffet is lavish, the winter skier's buffet is one of Vail's best sit-down lunches, and dinner is well-conceived, -executed, and -served. It is also less pricey than The Wildflower. Salads and appetizers are mostly steeped in Italian tradition. Think of Gorgonzola and Roast Fennel Salad, Tenderloin of Beef Carpaccio, Prosciutto-Wrapped Cantaloupe, and Roasted Fennel and Chestnut Soup, and you get the idea of the Cucina's orientation.

The mozzarella is hand-pulled, the gnocchi house-made, and house-made pastas, whether flat and sauced or filled, are pure Italian or slightly adapted. Smoked Chicken Ravioli, Roasted Eggplant Ravioli, Fettuccini Bolognese, and Butternut Squash Gnocchi give you an idea of the pasta range. Veal, chicken, and seafood entrées share equal billing. Veal Osso Bucco, served with polenta, candied squash, and *gremolata* (the classic garnish of finely minced parsley, lemon peel, and garlic) is as good as it gets. Spit-Roasted Apple Cider–Brined Pork Loin with Fennel Mashed Potatoes, Roasted Red Onions, and Apple *Démi-glace* meld Italian and America flavors, perfectly appropriate for its location.

The Wildflower and Cucina Rustica, The Lodge at Vail, 174 East Gore Creek Drive, Vail; (970) 476-5011 or www.lodgeatvail.com.

Zino Ristorante

This vibrant, two-story Italian restaurant drew nascent downtown Edwards into the net of places where good, freshly made food can be had. Its appeal is it's a festive buzzin' casual, high-spirited restaurant that won't, by Vail Valley standards, break the bank. The restaurant is located on the two lower floors of the Inn at Riverwalk, the north anchor of Edwards' booming retail scene, but it doesn't feel or look like a hotel restaurant.

The high-ceilinged room is split horizontally. The main entrance is located on the mezzanine level, where you can stop at the Z-Bar, have a drink, and look down on the dining action below. The open balcony is rimmed by a custom wrought-iron railing, and the zinc-topped mahogany bar in European bistro style. On the level below, the hip restaurant has been packing 'em in since it was launched in spring 1999 by Sweet Basil owners Kevin and Sally Clair and a crew that cut its teeth in that esteemed Vail establishment. Zino's patio, overlooking the Eagle River, is one of Colorado's best, and two riverside bocce courts always are a draw for a rousing game or two before or after dinner.

The signature appetizer, Zino's Iron Skillet Roasted Mussels, comes to the table in the hefty pan in which they were cooked. The skillet is placed on a wrought-iron stand, and everyone digs in and also dips fresh house-made bread into the aromatic broth. Other long-running starters are the Crispy Calamari with Lemon Chili Aïoli and the Antipasti Platter, laden with prosciutto, tomato bruschetta, artichoke hearts, house-made mozzarella, roasted eggplant, and mixed olives.

Pizza from the wood-fired oven is offered with such trendy combinations as wild mushroom, mozzarella, and truffle oil; caramelized balsamic onion, Gorgonzola, and rosemary; and pepperoni, sausage, and pancetta. The classic tomato, mozzarella, and basil combo satisfies purists for whom pizza dough must be topped with red, white, and green.

House-made pasta specialties include Capellini with Shrimp, Scallops, Calamari, and Puttanesca and Rotolo Filled with Spinach, Eggplant, Portobello Mushrooms, and Gorgonzola Sauce. Signature entrées are Wood-Oven Roasted King Salmon with Wild Mushrooms, Saffron Orzo, Arugula, Peas, and Walnut Gremolata, and Free-Range Chicken with Parmesan Mashed Potatoes. Desserts include the restaurant's interpretations of Italian classics as *panna cotta,* pressed chocolate cake, lemon tart, gelato, and Zino-Misu, an inspired version of tìramisu.

Gather a small group and book the Chef's Table, usually set up at a commodious booth ringside to the open kitchen, where six to ten diners have a front-row seat for the culinary action at two nightly seatings. Larger groups are accommodated at a long table under the spiral stairway, a much better setting than it sounds. The chef asks whether anyone has food preferences or dietary restrictions, and then the five-course feast begins. It can be paired with wines from Zino's mostly Italian and American wine list, and it ends with a sweet and coffee.

Zino Ristorante, 23 Main Street, Edwards; (970) 926-0444 or www.zinoristorante.com.

Events

Beaver Creek Culinary Classic & Celebrity Chef Ski Race

February—There's nothing like the heat of the kitchen to counteract a cold, snowy February weekend, and there's nothing like a ski race of any sort to remind you why cold, snowy Februarys are so divine. Put them together into a weekend of food, pastry, and wine pairings; let the chefs loose on the mountain for a fun-filled celebrity-chef ski race; and you have all the makings for a mix-and-match event that belongs in the mountains on, yes, a few days in February.

The Beaver Creek Culinary Classic, established in 1999, has a serious culinary side and an exuberant outdoor sporty side. It brings leading chefs together to cook and mingle with each other and with attendees on terra firma and on the snowy slopes. The most recent format includes a welcome reception and a five-course dinner at Splendido on Thursday night, followed by the ski race on Friday. Saturday night features concurrent events, five-course dinners both at Toscanini and Mirabelle, plus the Culinary Classic, a walk-around wine and food tasting at the Park Hyatt Beaver Creek Resort and Spa. A champagne brunch at the Grouse Mountain Grill served as the classic's finale. Big-name visiting and home-town chefs prepare these feasts.

Admission to the food events can be purchased individually or as a full package, with or without skiing and with or without lodging. The schedule has been tweaked since the event was created and can continue to change from year to year.

Information on the Beaver Creek Culinary Classic & Celebrity Chef Ski Race is available at (800) 404-3535 or www.beavercreek.com. To purchase tickets to any of scheduled festival events, call (888) 920-2787.

Taste of Vail

March–April—One of Colorado's most anticipated, and most acclaimed, yearly food and wine events is the Taste of Vail. The highlight is a dynamite mountaintop picnic, signaling the time when Colorado and visiting foodies are ready for the impending spate of culinary events coming in spring and summer to Front Range cities and mountain town alike.

It begins with Wednesday-evening registration—and the sublime and special Founder's Dinner, a reunion dinner of the restaurateurs and chefs who conceived of the festival, and wraps up with a dressy Grand Tasting on Saturday night. In between are all sorts of enlightening events in the refined world of food and wine. Admission tickets to the Taste of Vail can be ordered as a full feast or à la carte, with individual tickets to specific events. Various Vail Valley charities have been beneficiaries since the inaugural in 1990, and about 3,000 people now attend.

Serious connoisseurs sharpen their palates at as many excellent and impeccably organized wine-tasting, food, and related seminars as can be squeezed into three days. Unlike other major festivals that schedule simultaneous sessions, the Taste of Vail offers just one at a time. If it isn't of interest, there's time to slip to the slopes for a few runs. The Vail Cascade Resort is the main venue, and there's a chairlift right outside the door. Sessions range from the fundamentals of taste and tasting to highly sophisticated discussions of food and wine subtleties. Guest chefs and lecturers change from year to year, but variety of topics is a constant. Additionally, most of the 35 participating Vail Valley restaurants from Allie's Cabin to Zino Ristorante schedule prix fixe wine-maker dinners on free evenings.

In 2002, these seminars and tastings included Wine 101 and *Umami*. Wine 101 introduced understanding and judging the balance of wine components and developing a "palate memory." The *umami* seminar introduced the concept of the "fifth taste," understood in Asian cultures to be an elusive satisfaction-inducing taste that cannot be defined by the sweet, sour, salty, or bitter tastes defined in Western concepts.

The Taste of Vail manages to convey almost scholarly information, but it also maintains some sense of fun that goes so well in a resort venue. Specialized wine seminars in 2002 also included topics like "Life Beyond Chardonnay and Cabernet," an enlightening (in every way but calorie-wise) dessert seminar, and "Blind Man's Bluff: A Double-Blind Tasting Seminar" in which participants couldn't even see whether they were tasting a red or white wine and had to shift the senses of taste and smell to a higher plane. "The Grape Debate: Nature versus Nurture" explored the issue of whether great wines are made on the vine, in a well-developed vineyard and under ideal conditions, or in the winery, by an experienced and knowledgeable wine maker.

The seminars are typically presented by exceptionally knowledgeable food and wine experts, but not necessarily of the TV celeb stripe. Presenters in 2002 included Jerry Comfort, culinary director of Beringer Blass Wine Estates in St. Helena, California; sommeliers Chris Farnumand Ken Fredrickson, whose partnerships have included Reservelist (see page 84) and Adega (see page 29), both in Denver; and guest chef Don Yamauchi, the award-winning chef-partner of Le Francais in Wheeling, Illinois. Yamauchi prepared the keynote Wine & Food Pairing Luncheon, and Comfort introduced and explained the wines paired with each course.

The mountaintop picnic is accessible to nonskiers by Eagle Bahn gondola to a plateau made festive with tasting tables set up by top local restaurants and a tent where wines are poured and poured and poured. Sometimes Vail snares a late-season storm that day and you get snowflakes in your wineglass; sometimes it's hot and your sorbet melts before you can eat it. Organizers prepare for either by setting up some picnic tables in the open air and others under canvas to accommodate weather that might be snowy, sunny, or a bit of each during the afternoon bacchanalia.

On Saturday evening, everyone gets dressed to the nines (which for chefs means sparkling whites) for the Grand Tasting. In 2002, it featured 35 top local restaurants, 60 leading wineries from the world over, and 1,300 attendees. The Taste of Vail is a great way to wind down the ski season, rev up the summer food season, or both.

For Taste of Vail information and tickets, call (888) 311-5665 or (970) 926-5665, log onto www.tasteofvail.com, or e-mail info@tasteofvail.com.

Beaver Creek National Pastry Competition & Culinary Festival

June—The requirements for winning, say, the Pillsbury Bake-Off are bush-league compared to what should be required just to breathe the same air as the contestants at the annual Beaver Creek National Pastry Competition. This first-class annual event takes usually occurs the weekend following the *Food & Wine* Magazine Classic at Aspen (see page 326).

The Beaver Creek festival, sponsored by *Bon Appétit* magazine and Beaver Creek Resort, turns the practice of the most refined pastry and confectionary skills into a spectator sport. From its inception in 1999 through 2001, it was a two-day international team competition with a dozen three-person teams vying to make the most elaborate possible chocolate showpiece and sugar showpiece, plus trays of bonbons, *petits fours*, frozen desserts, plated desserts, and three identical cakes judged for taste and perfect, uniform appearance. The proceedings resembled high-level figure skating competitions. Watching eight judges from seven countries measure entries with rulers and calipers and get down at eye level with cake tops, I was reminded of skating judges when the compulsory school figures were still part of competition.

In 2002, this big international team event moved to Las Vegas, and the format at Beaver Creek was scaled down. Now, five solo pastry chefs each create one piece that incorporates both pastry and confectionary art. The rules are still exacting, but with a far small contestant field and fewer hours of competition, everything is simpler. The 2002 showpiece, for instance, had to be half cake with no more than four ingredients, including a preordained percentage of chocolate.

Whether in team or solo competition, the showpieces reflect a theme. In 2001, the last year of the team competition, the theme was "Hollywood," and in 2002, when the solo format kicked in, the theme "magic" had to be incorporated into a half-chocolate and half-sugar figural showpiece, at least 24 inches high. One chef spun a unicorn of sugar, and another sculpted a chocolate rabbit and magician's top hat.

Observing these pastry artists compete is sheer fascination for anyone who has so much as frosted a cupcake. Admission is free to view the six-hour pastry-a-thon in Beaver Creek's Village Hall and Park Hyatt Hotel. This competition is such a spectacular show the creative process is done in the eye of the public and the eye of the camera. Some people wander in and out of Village Hall to glance at the proceedings, while others stay for hours, transfixed by the chefs' practice of their art and craft. Identical kitchens are set up side by side, but chefs are shielded from each others' view. The competition is intense—and the scene is tense as competitors race the clock even as they bake, frost, melt and temper chocolate, color, spray, marbleize, melt, pull or cast sugar, sculpt, and perform any number of other culinary tricks, trying to be creative and precise, mindful of the unrelenting time clock.

The 2002 contestants were Andrew Shotts of New York's Chocolate Loft Pastry School; Patrice Caillot of the St. Regis Hotel, also in New York; Richard Carpenter of the Registry, Naples, Florida; Anil Rohira of Albert Uster Imports, a Maryland-based purveyor of Swiss culinary products; and Chris Hammer of the International School of Confectionary Arts in Gaithersburg, Maryland. The chefs do it for the glory and also compete for a $10,000 cash purse. Therefore, everyone is a winner. First prize is $4,000, second is $2,500, third is $1,500, and fourth and fifth are $1,000. Not too shabby for an afternoon's work, you might think, but on second consideration, it's a small monetary reward for a lifetime of refining skills to such a level. Experience pays off, because the 2002 winner, Chef Caillot, and runner up, Chef Rohira, were contestants in the previous year's team event.

Concurrent with the enrapturing Beaver Creek National Pastry Competition is the resort's Culinary Festival. Local chefs give cooking demonstrations, and Beaver Creek and Avon restaurants and bakeries set up tasting booths. Wine-tasting, children's activities, and live entertainment round out the event, which takes place in the center of Beaver Creek Village. Admission is free, but you must pay for food and beverage tastings. Some people make a culinary weekend of it, taking advantage of specially priced multinight lodging packages.

Information on the Beaver Creek National Pastry Competition & Culinary Festival is available from (888) 323-7612 or www.pastrychampionship.com. General information on Beaver Creek is available from (970) 845-9090 or www.beavercreek.com. Lodging may be booked through (800) 404-3535.

Pro-Am Duck Confit Cook-Off

August—In the land of chili cook-offs and barbecue competitions, the annual Pro-Am Duck Confit Cook-Off stands out as a carefree gastronome's dream—and a cholesterol-obsessed health fiend's nightmare. Confit, now viewed as a delicacy, is an old French way of preserving duck meat, which is salted and cooked slowly in its own fat. The cooked meat is placed into a crock and covered with the rendered fat, which seals and preserves it.

Craig Bale, a wine rep and confit aficionado, conceived of the late-summer cook-off and persuaded Dan Sidner, the similarly impassioned managing partner of Zino Ristorante (see page 283), to host the event. Sidner, in fact, had put on a foie gras cook-off in 1998 but was so taken with the confit concept that he switched. Duck '99, Double O't Duck, 2001: A Duck Odyssey, and Duck Version 2.002 are history as of this writing, and who knows what future cook-offs will be called?

Sixteen local chefs and a handful of amateurs vie for prizes, and the 150 or so attendees get to sample the rich creations. In 2002, first place went to Chris Dressick from Toscanini for duck confit over bread pudding and boysenberries, which seems like a hearty appetizer and a dessert in one dish. Runner-up was Geordy Ogden of

SaddleRidge for a duck confit taco topped with guacamole, black beans, and salsa. Franco-Mexican—a new trend, perhaps?

For information on the Pro-Am Duck Confit Cook-Off, call Zino Ristorante at (970) 926-0444.

Vail Valley Wine Auction

August—Auctions are anticipated annual extravaganzas in wine-growing regions from France to California, where vintners and buyers meet to trade—both wine and wine lore. Fine food goes with fine wine, and the convivial and civilized aspects of the wine business are nurtured along the way. Vail's wine auction is a charity event open to the public. It is also an opportunity to examine and buy serious wines, as well as to sample the cuisine presented by four leading local chefs.

The auction, usually held at the Vail Marriott Mountain Resort, begins with a Friday-evening blind tasting, hors d'oeuvres, and the first of two auction previews. For oenophiles, the tasting is the prelude for the main event, Saturday's thrilling live auction of rare wines from wineries, wine professionals, and private collectors. On a typical schedule, the doors open in mid-afternoon for the second preview, followed by an elegant four-course wine-maker dinner and finally the live auction. Each participating chef prepares one course for the dinner. In 2002, attendees enjoyed an appetizer of Peachwood Smoked Atlantic Salmon with Cucumber Fennel Rémoulade and Alpenrose Rye by Luc Meyer of The Left Bank; Fantasy of Potato Crusted Shrimp, Seared Scallop, and Avocado Salad by Daniel Joly of Mirabelle Restaurant; an entrée of Pistachio- and Herb-Crusted Colorado Lamb T-Bone with Butternut Squash Rösti and Minted Plum Wine Sauce by Dean Waziry of Marriott Mountain Resort; and Napa Valley Harvest Strudel with Elderberry Sauce and Crème Anglaise by Daniel Niederhauser of the Columbine Bakery.

For information or tickets, contact the Vail Valley Wine Auction, (970) 926-1494, (800) 341-1494, www.vailwineuaction.com, or e-mail epsm@colorado.net.

Vail Festival Italiano

September—Vail certainly doesn't have a Little Italy, or a Little Anyplace Else, but it has a nucleus of Italian-American–owned business that can pull off an approximation of the hometown festivals that their proprietors grew up with. Rick Scalpello, a local event organizer who hails from Pittsburgh, filled a perceived void and put on the first Vail Festival Italiano in September 2002, with Italian and other food stands, Italian wine tasting, music, crafts, Vespa scooter rides, and kids' activities—and even a kids' food and gelato booth.

Bagali's, La Bottega, Campo de Fiori, Pazzo, Valbruna, and Grappa Wines & Spirits, with obvious ties to the old country, participated, with the Alpenrose, Blu's, and Joe's Deli in on the act as well. Chicago-born Paul Ferzacca, owner/chef of La Tour, took temporary leave from the kitchen of his fine-dining landmark to introduce a deep-dish pizza that he calls Zacca-Za at the first Vail Festival Italiano. There may be a Zacca-Za pizzeria in Vail in the future, but festival '02 goers had the first taste. The Vail Farmers' Market coincided with the Sunday of the two-day festival, held at the

Crossroads parking lot and along Meadow Drive.

For information on Vail Festival Italiano and its future, contact (970) 328-1182.

Oktoberfest

September—Colorado is ahead of the calendar curve when celebrating Oktoberfest, Bavaria's famed fall event. This is understandable, because it could be snowing when October rolls around. Vail, built from the ground up in an Austro-Bavarian-Alpine style, is such a natural setting for Oktoberfest that it stretches its version over two post–Labor Day weekends in September.

Vail's Oktoberfest is a beer and music festival, rather than a culinary event, a number of fine restaurants that serve quality Austrian, German, and Swiss food are represented. The venues could change in the future, but currently the first weekend takes place at Lionshead and the second in Vail Village.

Details are available from the Vail Valley Chamber & Tourism Bureau, (970) 477-4007 or www.visitvailvalley.com.

Wine Harvest Party

September—Hundreds of locals mark the third Saturday in September or thereabouts on their calendars, descending on the Eagle-Vail Pavilion for the area's best, and only truly affordable, one-evening food and wine event. This fundraiser for the Eagle Valley Humane Society is known for its modest entry fee to support a popular local cause for paws. Started in 2000, it is a sell-out for the sips, the nibbles, and the exuberant fun. David Courtney, co-owner of Beaver Liquors, decided to bring to the Vail Valley non-black tie kind of wine event for locals on a budget that benefited a charity they liked to support.

In 2002, wines from Churchill Cellars in nearby Wolcott were poured, a blind-tasting table was set up to provide a wine-education component, and such restaurants as Ti Amo, The French Press, Vista, Bartelli's Deli, and the Gourmet Cowboy set up tasting stations, as did Mountain Flour, known valley-wide for its excellent desserts. Courtney has joked that this event is becoming "a mini Taste of Vail." Well, not quite. It's still informal and unserious. Courtney orders wine grapes from California and invites attendees to stomp away, just like the madcap Lucy and Ethel did in a classic episode of the legendary television comedy *I Love Lucy*. Grape-stompers crush enough grapes to make 25 cases of wine, which are uncorked at subsequent Wine Harvest Parties.

For Wine Harvest Party tickets and information, contact Beaver Liquors at (970) 949-5040.

Mountain Microbrew Festival

November—Vail's Mountain Microbrew Festival, inaugurated in November 2002 to benefit the Vail Breast Cancer Awareness Group, drew microbreweries from as far away as Colorado's northeast (Smiling Moose Brewery from Greeley and C. B.

Potts/Big Horn Brewery and Cooper Smith's Pub & Brewery from Fort Collins) and southwest (Carver Brewing Company from Durango and Smugglers Brewpub & Grille from Telluride).

Additionally, the festival featured tasting stations with the hearty specialties, mostly German, that go so well with beer: roasted *Weisswurst* with sauerkraut, fried chicken sandwiches, pretzels with spicy mustard, and apricot-filled donuts. (I'm not sure the latter go all that well with beer, but they sure were tasty.) Aria Spa offered mini spa treatments, and Helmut Fricker oompahed his way around the room. As the saying goes, a good time was had by all, so you can expect there will be future Mountain Microbrew Festivals too.

Vail Cascade Resort & Spa, 1300 Westhaven Drive, Vail; (800) 420-2424, (970) 676-7111, or www.vailcascade.com.

Wine Symposium

November—The annual two-day Wine Symposium and Wine Makers Dinner at the Park Hyatt Beaver Creek was launched in 1999 and focuses on California wines with a graceful acknowledgment of the European antecedents to American viticulture and winemaking.

The 2002 program included seminars and panels conducted by such wine authorities as Richard Anders, formerly a Boulder wine-seller and currently the manager of Peak Wines International; Jay Fletcher, master sommelier and fine-wine specialist for Southern Wine & Spirits; Fred Halloway, wine maker at Santa Barbara's Cambria Winery; and Christopher Rowe, Southern Wine & Spirits' director of education. Two sessions are held concurrently, with the most popular sessions offered twice over the two days, so you'll have a good chance of getting in.

The Saturday-evening Wine Makers Dinner is a six-course bacchanalian feast orchestrated by the hotel's Chef de Cuisine, Pascal Coudouy. The 2002 dinner started with the Chef's Selection of Specialty Canapés and Cheese Fondue, paired with Artesa Carneros Chardonnay (Napa Valley, 2001). The appetizer featured Asian Mixed Greens with Leeks, Smoked Duck, Tomato Confit, Parmesan Shavings, and Truffle Vinaigrette, accompanied by Cambria Julia's Vineyard Pinot Noir (Santa Maria Valley, 1999).

The entrée was Roasted Lamb Saddle with Truffle and Bacon Potato Gratin, White Asparagus, Red Cabbage, and Thyme *Jus,* with Geyser Peak Block Collection, Vallerga Cabernet Sauvignon (Napa Valley, 1998). As a postlude, the chef prepared Seared Foie Gras with Fresh Figs, Toasted Brioche, and Goat Cheese *Quenelle,* paired with Napa Valley Dolce. Finally, the dessert course rolled in, featuring a Decadent Chocolate Dessert Selection and Port Tasting. For those willing and able, luxury bourbons and scotches were also available.

Added in 2002 was the Masquerade Ball on Friday evening, where guests were invited to come in costume or at least with a mask—or to dress casually. Organizers promised that "the wines will be in disguise. Each winery will be pouring its 'signature' vintage as well as a 'masquerade wine.' Guests bobbed for clues to unlock the mystery and unmask these blind wines." If it's deemed a success, the masquerade will most likely continue. The wine event is promoted as a package including two nights of lodging at the luxurious spa hotel in the heart of Beaver Creek Village.

Park Hyatt Beaver Creek Resort & Spa, Beaver Creek; (970) 949-1234 or www.beavercreek.hyatt.com.

Retail

Foods of Vail

Some of the Vail Valley's fanciest gourmet fare comes from a remarkably simple storefront in an out-of-the-way strip mall in Avon: Foods of Vail, a gourmet food store and deli that started out as a caterer and branched out with a retail store offering quality take-out. Customers can dip into the tureen for the soup of the day, pick a salad, order a good sandwich, on home-baked bread, and for dessert, find an assortment of fresh cookies, bars, and other baked goods.

Selections also include an assortment of prepared and frozen appetizers, soups, filled and unfilled pastas, sauces, and entrées. The store's slogan is "Making Your Home the Best Place to Eat," and owner Tracey Van Curan and her crew make it happen. The regular appetizer and entrée selection, called "Dinner in a Dash," includes good versions of such popular offerings as Thai Spring Rolls, Miniature Quiches, Oriental Dumplings, Chicken and Wild Rice Casserole, Thai Chicken Curry, and Beef Bourguignonne. Daily specials might include Rosemary Seared Rack of Lamb, Citrus Dill Salmon, or Garlic-Rubbed Prime Rib, and the catering menu features more—and more exotic—selections. For home cooking, Foods of Vail sells such fine ingredients as dried forest-mix mushrooms, Stonewall Kitchen chutneys and relishes, Jim Town Fig and Olive Spread, Fontera Mexican ingredients, and Dahlia's Exotic Flavor Pastes blended with the spices of Cuba, China, Thailand, and India.

The store also carries American artisan cheeses, interesting imported cheeses, sumptuous pâtés, cured meats, sausages, smoked fish, gourmet crackers, at least a dozen olive oils, aged balsamic vinegars, grilling sauces and marinades, salsas, mustards, and an assortment of excellent breads, breadsticks, and cheese sticks. Many of the store's baked goods, ice creams, and sorbets come from Mountain Flour, a local company run by Shawn Smith, former head pastry chef at The Lodge at Vail, which now supplies some of the finest restaurants and hotels in the Vail Valley.

Foods of Vail, 150 East Beaver Creek Boulevard, Avon; (970) 949-0282.

Kitchen Collage & Linens

Kathy Rohlwing, who once worked at Boulder's Peppercorn, owns a store in Edwards' Riverwalk Center that is the Vail Valley's largest seller of things for kitchen and table. Attractive displays will entice you to buy something—a cooking utensil, a piece of specialty bakeware for the dessert you're planning, or something you want, like a set of dishes or a gadget that you've never seen before but suddenly lust after. The gadget wall is laden with the most imaginative cooking accessories, and Rohlwing says she sells more of these items than anything else.

Cookware includes Emerilware, the trademark line of one of TV's hottest chefs, plus such classic and reliable brands as All-Clad, Calphalon, Cuisinart, and Henckels. Bakeware comes in various materials—including Pyrex—shapes, and sizes. Rolling pins, pastry boards, baking sheets, and cookie cutters are also stocked.

Kitchen Collage's tableware can be loosely described as country-style, but from several countries: brilliantly hued Amalfi from Italy, Portmeirion from Wales, and slipware from Portugal, as well as delightfully painted glassware—plates, bowls, butter dishes, and glasses. Serving pieces are of various kinds and shapes, and the selection of tea sets, from dollhouse-size to regular-size, is substantial. To finish off the table decoration, select some candlesticks and candles.

But what to cook? There's a small selection of cookbooks and a larger one of gourmet foods. Kitchen Collage sells various packaged breakfast fixings, several brands of prepared sauces and condiments, excellent pasta, and specialty teas—the better to enjoy that new tea set. Pie in the Sky Double Fudge Brownie Mix, made in Colorado for our elevations, just about flies off the shelf. A large linen department sells kitchen, table, bedroom, and bath linens. There are also bath oils, soaps, and other toiletries—after all, you can't spend all your time in the kitchen.

Kitchen Collage & Linens, Crystal Building at Riverwalk, 34323 U.S. Highway 6, Edwards; (970) 926-0400, (888) 239-4743, or www.kitchencollage.com.

To Catch a Cook

Behind a modest storefront tucked amid the rabbit warren of Vail's Village Inn Plaza pedestrian lanes nestles To Catch A Cook. This elegant store extends far back into the building, creating a deep and dramatic retail space that displays tableware and decorative ware as if they were art objects and yet offers a fine assortment of practical items for the cooking enthusiast. Tile floors, attractive lighting, and mellow music set the suitably classy tone for this classy store.

To Catch A Cook is geared to the Vail lifestyle and is organized to anticipate that some customers might be more interested in entertaining than in cooking. At the front of the store are the gorgeous serving pieces, linens, tableware, and purely decorative objects for the stylish home. Customers can assemble sets, buy pieces, or pick up entire place settings from such makers as Simon Pearce from Ireland; Vieri, which looks Italian or Portuguese but is actually from North Carolina; and Le Comptoir de Famille, a line of solid French everyday or bistro tableware that is positively retro, and therefore trendy. The shop also sells table linens, glassware, and candlesticks.

Farther back are the practical kitchen items. One cabinet displays fine chef's knives. Shelves hold pots, pans, and such kitchen appliances as blenders, food processors, and espresso makers. The gadget wall displays a tempting selection of items that make cooking and baking easier. The store carries unusual bar accessories, most convenient given the presence of a liquor store right around the corner. Upscale gourmet food lines occupy a large section, and there's even a selection of appealing paper napkins, plates, and such for a casual night at home.

To Catch A Cook, 4 Village Inn Plaza, Vail; (970) 476-6883.

Wines

Beaver Creek Fine Wines

If you're holed up in Beaver Creek and are in a hurry for a nice bottle of wine, zip over to this small store tucked into an arcade on the Plaza Level of St. James Place—or call for a delivery. The small jewel of a shop resembles a wine library, with bottles lining the Euro-rustic pine shelves and cozy armchairs where you can contemplate your selection. Carefully culled wines from the world's wine-growing regions join some specialty beers and spirits.

For Jack Vesey, manager of Beaver Creek Fine Wines, the business and personal passion are one and the same. He is an expert and collector of Burgundy wines and visits vineyards in France and Spain whenever he can to expand his wine knowledge. Driven to seek perfection, he has admitted that it sometimes takes up to a decade to collect just the right wines to offer a complete survey of wines for a particular tasting theme for a tasting or dinner. He has moderated the Burgundy Seminar for the Taste of Vail (see page 284).

Beaver Creek Fine Wines, St. James Place Arcade, 210 Offerson Road, Beaver Creek; (970) 748-9055.

Beaver Liquors

Located on the bottom level on the backside of an undistinguished building in Avon, Beaver Liquor's hard-to-find entrance looks much like an underground garage made over into a retail store. Once inside, you won't be too impressed either by the standard booze-and-beer selection crammed into the brightly lit room. But things start looking up (or down) when you spot the sign over the stairs directing you to the wine cellar, displaying all the looks and ambience lacking upstairs. The cellar is actually elegant, with subdued colors, piped-in classical music, and bubbling fountains and wine barrels as decorative accents for the stunning assortment of wines.

The wine cellar, located 14 feet underground, stays at a constant 53 to 57 degrees year-round. Its huge inventory is subdivided into several specialty rooms. Wines from California and France are carried in enough depth to merit their own rooms. Italy, Australia, Argentina, Germany, other U.S. wine-producing areas, and other countries have to share one large room. Rare wines and champagnes are displayed in another room. And still another room is a walk-in humidor called the Cigar Room.

While Beaver Liquors' customer base is broad, the store's irreverent logo, a somewhat salacious lip-licking tongue appearing on T-shirts and other promotional paraphernalia, has something of a cult following among young customers. Locals of drinking age are attracted by the good prices (especially the end-of-season, stock-up-now sales). Beer drinkers like the enormous selection of microbrews and big-brewery beers, as well as the Beer of the Month Club. Those who prefer spirits have a vast choice as well and may never make it downstairs to the wine cellar.

Some serious wine connoisseurs don't even know what the store looks like. Second-home owners and vacationers often pre-order their beer, wine, soda, and spirits before they arrive. Beaver Liquors also organizes numerous wine tastings, often at restaurants like Splendido up the hill in Beaver Creek or at Vista, right around the corner. They also specialize in tastings in private homes. Those homes, of course, are mostly up the hill.

Beaver Liquors, 110 East Beaver Creek Boulevard, Avon; (970) 949-5040 or www.beaverliquors.com.

Grappa Fine Wines and Spirits

The only unusual thing about this liquor store on the backside of the Vail Village Inn is that fine wines with high price tags are located on shelves within view of the cashier. Walk down a flight of stairs and you'll find yourself in Vail Village's only wine cellar.

Green bins along the walls, and shelves and crates set on the tile floor are loaded with moderately priced wines, arranged by country. France and California are the major "countries," but you'll also find Australian, German, Italian, South African, and Spanish wines. Many are from small vineyards. Grappa, established in 1988, promotes an in-store wine-of-the-month special, often introducing wine-lovers to these less-known vintages. Grappa is also carrying more Colorado wines.

Grappa Fine Wines and Spirits, 32 Village Inn Plaza, 100 East Meadow Drive, Vail; (970) 479-WINE (479-9463).

Peregrine Wines & Spirits

Peregrine was established in 1968 and relocated to a modest location in the Crossroads Mall in 1970. This small shop displays wines on the stocked-full shelves, but owner Dick Neal prides himself on ferreting out vintages, even exotic ones, that customers request. "Tell me what you want, and I'll make it happen," is his oft-used line. When someone comes in, raving about a wine he or she had somewhere, Neal will try to track it down—and he often succeeds. Dick Neal is the Dick Tracy of wines in the Vail Valley.

The store's strength and his expertise lie in wines from California, France, and Italy. Reds and whites are grouped by color and varietal, with countries and regions mixed. The décor is all about wines—bottles on open shelves, rare wines behind locked glass, a wine map of France on the wall, and wine-case ends fronting the cashier counter. Peregrine does wine specials and extends case discounts to any mix a customer wants—and that includes microbrews.

Peregrine Wines & Spirits, Crossroads Mall, 141 East Meadow Drive, Vail; (970) 476-5441.

Riverwalk Wine & Spirits

Almost half of this corner store on the south side of Edwards' booming Riverwalk business district is devoted to wines—everything from Gallo jugs to Grands-Echezeux. About half of the wines are domestic, mostly from California, Oregon, and Washington wineries, but some hail from Colorado. The imports come from all over the wine-growing world.

Riverwalk Wine & Spirits, Riverwalk Center, 34295 U.S. Highway 6, Edwards; (970) 926-8111.

Other

À La Car

Snuggled up in that exquisite, luxurious, and costly condo, are you? Have a hunger for fine food but don't want to mess up that stylish kitchen? Call À La Car to deliver food from Vail Valley restaurants as casual as Pazzo's Pizzeria and as elegant as La Tour or Mirabelle—normally within an hour of ordering. Some restaurants prepare a special menu for À La Car delivery, while others offer their full selections. House and delivery prices may be different, and there is, of course, a delivery charge. Gratuities are also expected. But when you're both hungry and happy at home, À La Car's service is hard to beat.

À La Car; (970) 476-3663 or e-mail alacar@vail.net.

Gourmet Snowshoe Tours

Snowshoeing and eating well aren't automatically related, but posh Beaver Creek puts on guided snowshoe tours that include a gourmet lunch. You don't need to join this pricey tour to snowshoe along more than 20 miles of snowshoe and cross-country trails maintained by Beaver Creek's mountaintop trails. Simply buy a ticket and board the Strawberry Park Express lift, which you can ride up and down with snowshoes. However, to get the expertise of a naturalist-guide, to find the trails suitable for your energy and ability and offering the most panoramic views, and to dig into a hearty and well-made lunch, you do need to book a tour through the Beaver Creek Cross-Country and Snowshoe Center.

Lunch is delivered up the mountain via snowmobile, so hot stuff like soup remains hot, cold stuff like salad is cold, and everything is fresh when you eat it.

Frankly, the lunches have not always merited the adjective "gourmet," but since Avon Bakery & Deli (see page 262) has been catering them, they have been first-rate. A guided tour isn't a wilderness experience but rather a civilized way to get some fresh air and exercise—and a good lunch too. Depending on the weather, you'll eat at an outdoor picnic table or indoors in a heated trailside yurt.

Beaver Creek Cross-Country and Snowshoe Center, Beaver Creek; (970) 845-5313 or www.beavercreek.com.

Recipes

Portobello mushrooms often are described as the meatiest fungi, both in terms of taste and texture. Sliced and deep-fried, they are a Chap's house specialty appetizer, served with the restaurant's house-made steak sauce.

Chap's Portobello Mushroom Fries

6 large portobello mushrooms
2 egg whites
1 cup all-purpose flour
2 tablespoons cornstarch
1 cup cold water
salt and cayenne pepper to taste
oil for frying
freshly grated Parmesan cheese and white truffle oil
    (available in specialty food stores) to taste
Steak Sauce (recipe below)

Clean the mushroom caps and scrape the black gills off the underside with a spoon. Cut into ½-inch strips. Whisk egg whites to a creamy consistency. Combine ½ cup flour, cornstarch, ½ cup cold water, and salt and cayenne pepper, and fold into the egg whites. Dredge the mushroom strips in the remaining ½ cup flour and then dip into the seasoned batter. Heat oil in a heavy skillet until hot but not smoking and fry mushroom strips until golden and crisp. Serve in a bowl, sprinkled with Parmesan cheese and white truffle oil, and steak-sauce on the side.

Steak Sauce
1 white onion, peeled and chopped
2 garlic cloves, peeled and chopped

2 slices bacon, chopped
½ cup red wine
½ cup balsamic vinegar
2 tablespoons bottled teriyaki sauce (or soy sauce)
4 tablespoons mango chutney
1 teaspoon chipotles in adobo sauce (available in small cans)
½ cup ketchup
salt and black pepper, to taste

In a saucepan over medium heat, sauté onion, garlic, and bacon, stirring frequently to avoid burning, until onion and garlic are soft and light brown. Deglaze pan with red wine, balsamic vinegar, and teriyaki sauce. Turn down heat to low and simmer for 5 minutes. Add remaining ingredients and simmer 10 minutes. Blend in a food processor until smooth. Cool and serve with Portobello Fries (or steak). Serves 4 to 6.

This pasta recipe is a perennial Sweet Basil favorite, on the menu since the late 1980s. Its origins predate Chef Bruce Yim, but it has remained on his menu as one of the restaurant's signature dishes. Chef Yim made a subtle change in this Sweet Basil classic by adding the jalapeños and saffron.

Saffron Linguini with Lobster, Bay Scallops, Shrimp, and Crème

1 quart heavy cream
¼ cup dry white wine
⅓ cup shellfish poaching liquid (fish stock or canned clam juice
   can be used as a substitute)
3 shallots, peeled and chopped
salt and white pepper to taste
juice of one lemon
1 tablespoon canola/olive oil blend (Sweet Basil uses an 80/20 blend)
12 tiger shrimp, shelled and deveined
½ pound bay scallops
½ pound cooked lobster meat (if you use a whole lobster,
   poach a 1 to 1½-pound lobster and reserve liquid for the sauce)
1 pound saffron linguini*
3 tomatoes, peeled, seeded, and chopped
½ bunch scallions, green part sliced thinly
2 jalapeño peppers, seeded and sliced
pinch of saffron

*Sweet Basil makes its own fresh saffron linguini, and if you make your
own pasta, you can prepare saffron linguini too. Otherwise, fresh or dried
unflavored linguini is acceptable.

Make sauce first (as early as the day before): In a saucepan over medium-high heat, reduce cream by about one-fourth. In another saucepan over medium-high heat, combine wine, poaching liquid or stock and shallots and reduce to almost a syrup. Add this thick liquid to cream, stirring until well blended and of desired consistency. Season with salt, pepper, and lemon juice. Strain and set aside, covered.

Cook linguini in a large pot of boiling salted water until al dente. Meanwhile, in a large chef's pan over medium-high heat, sauté shrimp in oil until pink and tender. Add scallops and lobster meat. When ready to serve, warm the sauce and finish with chopped tomato, scallions, jalapeño, and saffron. Adjust seasoning to taste. Pour seafood and sauce over drained linguini, and toss. Serves 4 to 6.

The following recipe, a versatile standby at The Wildflower, originated as a warm vinaigrette used as a sauce for a squab appetizer. It was adapted as a cold marinade for quail on a summer menu and can be used as a marinade for poultry or other proteins without any changes. Chef Thomas Newsted suggests it as a dressing for a cold salad. He recommends top-quality ahi tuna, seared rare, sliced, and combined with olives, vine-ripened tomatoes, arugula, *haricots verts*, yellow beans, and basil. This cold dish could be accompanied by endive and such greens as frisée, watercress, mâche, red oak, arugula, and/or field greens.

Tangerine Vinaigrette

    1 teaspoon chopped, blanched orange zest (method follows)
    1 tablespoon minced shallots
    2 teaspoons minced garlic
    2 teaspoons chopped fresh tarragon
    2 teaspoons chopped fresh cilantro
    2 tablespoons white wine vinegar
    1 tablespoon fresh orange juice
    ½ cup corn oil
    3 tablespoons tangerine oil (available in specialty food stores)
    salt and freshly ground black pepper to taste

To prepare orange zest, using a vegetable peeler, cut strips from the outermost (orange) layer of a fresh orange. Heat a small amount of water in a small saucepan to boiling and blanch orange zest three times, shocking it in an ice bath after each immersion in boiling water. Remove from water, drain, and chop finely.

Combine chopped zest, shallots, garlic, tarragon, cilantro, vinegar, and orange juice in a medium bowl. Mix the corn oil and tangerine oil together, then slowly whisk them into seasoned vinegar–orange juice mixture until emulsified. Season to taste. Makes 1 cup.

Aspen and the Roaring Fork Valley

No town shines more brightly on the Colorado culinary firmament than Aspen. The story of this former mining town has been told over and over. Its growth from virtual destitution into a glittering summer and winter destination is the stuff of history, myth, legend, and reality. It is now a playground and getaway for the rich and famous, the rich and infamous, and the not-rich-at-all who are bewitched by the magnificent scenery, the incredible outdoor sports opportunities, the beauty of the buildings and the people, and the cachet.

Fleets of Lear jets pack the local airport during high season. The top international retailers have set up branches in the historic downtown. Aspen is the place to shop for such items as jewelry, furs, designer clothing, expensive active sportswear, and top-line sporting goods from fly rods to snowboards. Prada, Fendi, Dior, and Baccarat all have established retail beachheads in Aspen. Think of it as Rodeo Drive in the Rockies.

Consumption tends to be conspicuous, but the scenic beauty is priceless. Set along the Roaring Fork River and in the midst of four mountainous wilderness areas, Aspen is a glittering fairyland both for outdoor recreationists and those in search of the pampered good life.

And food standards are as lofty as everything else. Aspen's only important annual food and wine event is arguably *the* most important food and wine event in the nation, attracting visiting chefs, restaurateurs, and wine experts. Aspen's chefs are among the nation's most talented, and its best restaurants are among the most fashionable and desirable in the land. The historic downtown core is the center of the culinary action. The most stylish, most talked-about, and most expensive of them are located within a few square blocks, but fine dining is also found elsewhere in the Roaring Fork Valley. In fact, the Aspen lifestyle has crept down valley to Basalt, El Jebel, and Carbondale—and even as far as Glenwood Springs.

Some people in Aspen do love to cook (or purport to) and they pack into Cooking School of Aspen classes and shop at several excellent kitchenware stores in the area. But the main gustatory experiences in and around town involve being cooked for—hence the unsurpassed concentration of great dining opportunities and the land-office business for caterers and private chefs in town.

Even though "rich" is the dominant gene on the Aspen firmament, the town has a genuine conscience. The arts are generously funded, and townspeople enthusiastically support preservation of open space and wilderness surrounding Aspen—at least once they have *their* mountain mansion where they want it and as big as they want it. There's even a culinary conscience. When word came out that the slow-growing Chilean sea bass was being overfished to the point of endangerment, Aspen restaurateurs rallied to banish it from their menus. "Fresh," "organic," and "local" are naturally watch words by which Aspen chefs live and cook.

Aspen's first boom was launched by the successful quest for precious metals. Its second came from the discovery of outstanding skiing on its snow-covered slopes. Its third, and current, boom has been fueled by high-figure real estate transactions— and perhaps by exquisite food and expensive wines served in gorgeously designed restaurants. Bon appétit, Aspen.

Bakeries

Grana Bread Company

Some of the best and most unusual breads in the Roaring Fork Valley are baked in a light-industry complex between Basalt and El Jebel. Area restaurants and retail outlets boast of carrying its artisan breads. Though a few tables in front invite customers to sit down with freshly baked pastry, a designer sandwich, and an espresso or cold drink, the Grana Bread Company is mainly a wholesaler.

Grana's logo shows a woman removing steaming loves from the oven on a bread paddle with mountains in the background—a romantic image for some very down-to-earth breads. Crusty loaves, baked fresh daily from organic ingredients, include *pagnotta*; white and wheat ciabatta; an unusual wheat bread called *casareccio*, made with dough rolled in sesame seeds; hearty, seeded Dakota bread; honey multigrain; sourdough; Roaring Fork rye; self-leavening *levain*; and *pain de campagne*, Grana's signature French country bread. The bakery makes at least one additional special bread each day: Tuscan harvest, holiday bread, Italian fig, cinnamon raisin, black olive, or challah. When Colorado growers are harvesting produce, everything from rhubarb to roasted chilies might be incorporated into a seasonal bread.

There might be others that have escaped my notice, but Grana Bread is the only Colorado bakery I've found to offer *Bire Wecke*, a Swiss bread made with dried fruits, and *bara brith*, an aromatic Welsh bread made with cinnamon, cloves, nuts, and fruit. When you're standing there breathing in the aromas of fresh breads wafting from the big bakery area, you want to buy at least one of each.

Grana Bread Company, 0050 Sunset Drive, #5, Basalt; (970) 927-1060.

Main Street Bakery & Café

From a modest one-story building of vintage brick come tray after tray, rack after rack of first-rate, freshly baked scones, muffins, Danish pastries, and croissants in an assortment of flavors to start the day. And don't forget the breads and rolls, which emerge hot and aromatic too.

The ambience is a quaint throwback in a town where power breakfasts now rule, even among visitors who might think that they left their power positions at home. On any winter's morning, you'll find breakfasting locals and visitors, browsing through the morning newspaper, sipping a hot beverage, and either nibbling on one of these great baked goods or forking into substantial pancakes, egg dishes, and more. Steamed-up windows enhance the café's sense of being a warm refuge from the chill of daybreak. In summer, breakfast is also served on the patio, and some customers take their to-go goodies to Paepcke Park, just across the street.

The baking doesn't end when breakfast is over. The bakery's old-fashioned pies, brownies, cookies, and cakes are addictive. Thrifty locals know that the morning's pastries sell at two-for-one prices from mid-afternoon to closing, which also means that the next day's crop will again be freshly baked. Ditto for the breads, baked daily and available to buy by the loaf, for the best toast in town, or to clamp around sandwich fillings later in the day.

Reasonably priced, quality lunches include hearty soups, stews, and chowders; pot pies; stir-fries; a variety of sandwiches on that house-baked bread; and excellent salads. Just remember to leave room for dessert.

Main Street Bakery & Café, 201 East Main Street, Aspen; (970) 925-6446.

Cooking School

Cooking School of Aspen

Aspen boasts a phenomenally high proportion of top chefs in relation to its modest year-round population. Some work for cutting-edge restaurants, others cater *Town & Country*–caliber parties, and some preside over private kitchens in upgraded West End Victorians or mountain mansions high above town. The Cooking School of Aspen taps into these local tremendous talents and also books big-name visiting chefs

Rob Seideman was a writer, a writing instructor at Colorado Mountain College, and founder of the Aspen Studies School of Writing, which brought visiting writers from all over the country to hold seminars in Aspen. He also had a love affair with food. At one point, Seideman's wife, Kelly Hall, observed, "You love to cook as much as you love to write, and you're a great teacher. Why don't you do some cooking seminars? You don't even need to fly chefs in [to teach]. The best in the world are here." Soon Seideman was organizing classes in Aspenites' home kitchens. For the host or hostess, the class was free. Everyone else paid. It was informal, informative, and fun.

He launched the Cooking School of Aspen in January 1998 in a tight alley off East Hyman Street. In the small but elegant and intimate classroom the school holds demonstration classes (called "At the Chef's Table: Dinner and Demonstration") and full participation classes (called "In the Kitchen: Hands-On Classes"). It also offers really cool kids' cooking classes. These junior chefs grow up to be comfortable and happy in the kitchen, the type that pack the school's adult classes. Ethnic and advanced technique classes, all including wines paired to dishes of the day, are geared to dedicated home cooks. For novices, the personable Seideman himself teaches "Clueless in the Kitchen: A Two-Day Workshop for the Beginner Home Chef."

Local chefs who regularly teach at the Cooking School of Aspen are a virtual Who's Who of Aspen area culinary talent. The roster of visiting instructors is a jaw-dropper for dedicated foodies. Recent demonstration classes have been taught by such luminaries as the legendary Jacques Pepin; Tony Mantuano, of Chicago's Spiaggia Restaurant; James Boyce, of Mary Elaine's at The Phoenician in Scottsdale; and Coleman Andrews, editor-in-chief of *Sauveur* magazine.

Wine makers and winery chefs hold wine workshops, and authorities in related food fields have presented at the Cooking School of Aspen. For instance, cheese meister Steve Jenkins, a passionate and outspoken cheese buyer from New York's heralded Fairway Market and author of the award-winning *Cheese Primer,* has presided over a wine-paired tasting of sensational, virtually unknown cheeses from the French and Italian countryside. What an eye-opener and palate-stretcher to learn about such handmade artisan cheese, and to understand bite by bite what is lacking in the factory-produced cheeses that prevail in this country.

The Cooking School of Aspen also organizes field trips—and what field trips they are. Some are strictly local. Such offerings as the "High-Altitude Gardening, Wild Foraging, Preservation, and Cooking" workshop help participants understand and maximize their use of Colorado's bounty of the land. "The Two-Wheel Gourmet: A Food and Wine Mountain Bike Hut-to-Hut Tour," is a local program geared (pardon the pun) to the food-loving off-road cyclist and the hard-pedaling food-lover. A different chef cooks in each stop along the 10th Mountain Hut System Route. Only in Colorado!

Culinary Adventures are overseas vacations that don't require lungs and legs of steel but rather dual passions for food and travel. These trips feature cooking classes, visits to food artisans, dinners at top restaurants, and cultural and scenic experiences. Recent adventures have included "On Safari: South Africa" and "A Food & Wine-Walking Tour of Emilia Romagna and Liguria."

Sommeliers preside over the wine room and tasting bar and what has to be the most congenial weekday après-ski, après-hike, or après-whatever happy hour in town. Sommelier Frank Todaro is in charge of this cozy corner in the back of the Cooking School of Aspen, pouring wine by the taste, by the glass, or by the flight—and being as informative or unobtrusive as you might want.

Walk down a few steps to the school, and before you get to the kitchen-classroom or the wine bar—or even if you never go there—check out Epicurean Alley. This compact retail area sells exotic salts from around the world that can really make a difference in the way each salt-bearing dish turns out, plus estate-bottled olive oils, Scharffen Berger chocolates, Wüsthof Trident kitchen knives, a great assortment of cookbooks, and more. It's not a full-fledged kitchen store by any stretch, but the unusual range of merchandise fills some empty niches in kitchen or pantry. For other needs, Les Chefs d'Aspen (see page 331) extends a 10 percent discount to Cooking School of Aspen students.

Cooking School of Aspen, 414 Hyman Avenue Mall, Aspen; (800) 603-6004, (970) 920-1879, or www.cookingschoolofaspen.com.

Dining

Ajax Tavern

Shlomo's and its big south-facing deck were, for years, Aspen's most casual ski-and-be-seen spot right after the lifts closed. Located at the bottom of the Little Nell slope at the base of Aspen Mountain, the Nell Bar was an institution. It was also the antithesis of chic—except for the pedigrees (social and celebrity) of the clientele. The scene changed when the base area was redeveloped. First came the luxurious Little Nell Hotel, and in 1994, the Shlomo's site became the trendy Ajax Tavern.

The culinary brain trust responsible for Tra Vigne, an acclaimed eatery in California's Napa Valley wine country, built this stylish restaurant and brought in Nick Morforgen to head the kitchen. The beautiful people who had formerly been content with casual Shlomo's now set their culinary sights much higher. Even though the big deck rocks at the end of the ski day as it did in the era of Shlomo's and the original Nell Bar, the Ajax Tavern is a year-round mecca for foodies.

Morforgen's cooking won all sorts of awards, but he eventually left the Roaring Fork Valley. His replacement, Greg Topper, later moved across town to open his own namesake café (see page 324), and in 2000, Dena Marino, who had cooked under Topper, was tapped to run the Ajax Tavern's kitchen. At 26, she seemed improbably youthful to wear so high a toque, but she quickly proved to be up to the challenge. Cooking since she was a child in northern New Jersey, Marino's family goes back to Calabria, so when she helped in the kitchen at home, it was at such tasks as making from-scratch pasta and the toothsome sauces that go with them. After graduating from the Culinary Institute of America, she moved to California and ultimately rose to sous-chef at Tra Vigne and then at the Ajax Tavern.

Marino builds on her family's recipes, her CIA training, and three years at Tra Vigne. Her cooking style has moved up the boot from Calabria to Italy's Alpine region, encompassing many regional Italian influences along the way, but all with a modern CIA overlay. The simple, sleek, sophisticated dining room glows with the warmth of Italy when the waitstaff brings out plate after plate of her hearty yet sophisticated soups, pasta, seafood, and meat entrées—and oh yes, truffle fries when available.

Rarely does anyone miss dessert at the Ajax Tavern, particularly a sublime blood-orange cheesecake with a blood-orange sauce and a touch of chocolate. The wine list, heavy on California and Italian vintages, continues to be one of the best in Colorado—and for the retro-trendy, Ajax Tavern offers cleverly named martinis in many flavors and a humidor filled with expensive cigars.

Ajax Tavern, 685 East Durant Avenue, Aspen; (970) 920-9333 or www.ajaxtavern.com.

Cache Cache

This stylish restaurant, decorated in flattering tones of ochre, cream, and table-linen white, and bathed in equally flattering light, has been serving Provençal cuisine since 1987. That was before Peter Mayle burst on the American literary consciousness with tales of his love affair with Provence, before the Mediterranean region was viewed as a hotbed of fine cooking, before "country French" was as linked a phrase as "luxury condominium," before Aspen had a myriad of truly fine-dining choices.

Cache Cache's pedigree is pure. French-born Philippe Mollicchi and Marie Casanova opened it as a tiny 14-seat bistro, which became such a hit they soon needed more space and more staff. Maitre d' Jodi Larner joined Cache Cache in 1990 and became general manager in 1991 and partner in 1992. Rick Hession, a Canadian-born entrepreneur, bought out Mollicchi and Casanova and joined Larner, his long-time friend, as partner in 1996. They still oversee the front of the house with élan and panache, no small task in a restaurant grown to seat 108 inside and an additional 55 outdoors in balmy weather.

Georgia-born Chef Christopher Lanter is an avid Francophile, having spent some of his early years in Paris and apprenticed in France, where he developed a particular affinity for the foods and cooking style of Provence. When he returned to the United States, he cooked at Jean Georges and Le Barnardin, both in New York, before heading west to Aspen's Caribou Club to be sous-chef.

The Cache Cache menu changes with the seasons, but you can expect to find such dishes as Black Mussels with Pernod, Tomatoes, Garlic, and Onions in Lobster Broth and the signature Potato-Zucchini Cake with Herb Cheese and Baby Salad on the appetizer list any time. Expect also to find seared Hudson Valley foie gras, though it might come with a Corn Pancake and Onion Compote, with Honey-Roasted White Figs, or with another accompaniment. Cache Cache is known for its terrines: foie gras, pork, duck liver pâté, or a country terrine of rabbit is often on the menu.

Among the beautifully balanced seafood, meat, and poultry entrées are such house favorites as Osso Bucco in Marsala Sauce, Grilled Tenderloin of Pork, Colorado Rack of Lamb, and such vegetarian entrées as Couscous with Harissa Sauce. The bouillabaisse, which the menu calls Marseille Seafood Stew with Croutons and Aïoli, is as good as this Mediterranean specialty ever gets.

Lanter doesn't shy away from organ meats either. His menu includes calf liver, with or without onions; veal kidneys with sautéed spinach and bacon-shallot sauce; and an appetizer of Veal Sweetbreads with Chive Gnocchi and Mâche Salad. Lanter likes to slow-roast chicken and duck on a nonpiercing rotisserie, allowing the juices to stay in and his seasonings to enhance each bird's intrinsic flavor.

Everything is served with grace and style in the aesthetically simple setting of an upmarket bistro. The wine list boasts 500 selections and 4,500 bottles from very moderately priced to astronomical. Among the French wine regions, Burgundy, Bordeaux, and Rhône are most deeply represented, with Italian and domestic wines also available.

Cache Cache is known by locals and visitors as a lively and fun gathering spot (for many, inspiration comes from the house specialty drink, nicknamed The Bomb) and by romantic couples as an atmospheric place to dine and make eyes at each other over a bottle of fine wine and fine food.

Cache Cache, 205 South Mill Street, Aspen; (970) 925-3835
or www.cachecache.com.

Campo de Fiore

Elizabeth and Luigi Giordani met in 1986, when she was attending Michigan State University and he was on what he thought would be a "short vacation" in the United States. They eventually landed in Aspen, got jobs waiting tables (what a surprise in a ski town), and only two years later opened Campo de Fiore. They, their relatives, and their friends built and decorated the small restaurant, and Luigi, who had attended culinary school in Rome, became the chef, and Elizabeth started hostessing.

Campo de Fiore quickly earned a local reputation as a place for very good and very authentic food served in a lively and friendly atmosphere by a knowledgeable staff. Two expansions later, the Giordanis catapulted their concept over the mountains and have since opened restaurants in Vail and in Denver, bringing in on-site partners to keep the culinary lines clean. To date, these partners have all been either Italian-trained or Italian-Americans steeped in the culinary traditions of the Old Country.

Aspen remains the mother ship of the Campo de Fiore fleet. This first location offers outdoor courtyard dining in summer and a warm and inviting dining room done in traditional Italian colors and textures set the stage for a procession of courses, from a sizable antipasto selection to rich desserts. The simple menu offers an excellent selection of artfully rendered Italian regional classics from various parts of Italy, some updated to mesh with contemporary, Colorado, or local tastes. The ingredients are first-rate, the pastas are house-made and fresh, and the portions are ample. Campo de Fiore boasts a large—and largely Italian—wine list.

Campo de Fiore, 205 South Mill Street, Aspen; (970) 925-8222, (970) 920-7717, or www.campodefiori.net.

The Century Room

When the Hotel Jerome was built in 1889, it was said to rival The Ritz in Paris in terms of luxury and appointments. Built by Jerome K. Wheeler, former president of Macy's in New York, it was state of the art, boasting hot and cold running water in 15 indoor bathrooms for 90 rooms, steam heat, electrification, and one of the West's first elevators. In keeping up with the Ritzes, the hotel also installed a real French chef in the main kitchen and a German horticulturist in the hotel hothouses to grow fresh vegetables through brisk Colorado winters.

As long as the mineral boom lasted, the hotel was one of the swankiest in the country. With Aspen's decline, the hotel suffered too, and Wheeler himself was forced into bankruptcy. A Syrian-born frequent Jerome guest named Mansor Elisha first leased and then, in 1911, bought the hotel for back taxes. Long-term boarders then paid $10 a month to live at the Jerome, joined by traveling salesmen and other short-term guests who came through town.

Between the world wars, Aspen's population swung between 300 and 800 souls—down-and-out-miners, merchants, ranchers, and people who in some way were keeping Pitkin County afloat. During the Depression, Elisha's son Lawrence ran the hotel, which remained the center of Aspen's diminished social life. The culinary highlight was Sunday-evening chicken dinner—for 50 cents—including musical entertainment. The simply furnished dining room had bare-wood floors, single-bulb hanging light fixtures, and spare bentwood chairs, but with white cloths draped over the tables, it was still the best place in town to eat.

During World War II, soldiers from nearby Camp Hale put their new skiing skills to use on Aspen Mountain, and Aspen's postwar renaissance began when Chicago industrialist Walter Paepcke arrived with highfalutin' notions of establishing Aspen as an intellectual and cultural center. Using the hotel as a base, he founded the Aspen Institute, and ultimately the Aspen Music Festival and School, the International Design conference, and the Aspen Skiing Company were established within the Jerome's brick walls.

The hotel's own renaissance included the addition of more bathrooms, the installation of furniture bought at auction from Chicago's famous Palmer House, and the addition of an outdoor swimming pool in a garden adjacent to the hotel. In the mid-1980s, a couple of owners later, the Jerome was massively rebuilt, its skeleton reinforced with steel trusses, rewired, replumbed, its façade restored, and its interior restored to the Eastlake décor fashionable a century before. Original light fixtures, door hardware, tiles, and vintage furniture—some found in hidden corners of the old hotel—were restored or reproduced, supplemented by period interior architectural features such as fireplaces, windows transoms, cherrywood doors, and some furniture from a St. Louis mansion. When the Jerome celebrated its centennial in 1989, it was again one of the grandest hotels in the West. A new wing, carefully furnished to match the old, added 66 luxurious rooms to the 27 in the original building.

Close the history book and direct your attention to The Century Room, the Jerome's landmark fine-dining restaurant. This opulent space is furnished with historic accuracy. You can dine in an atmosphere of yesteryear, complete with gleaming mirrors, crystal chandeliers, period wall coverings, plush tufted banquets, manorial chairs, and perfect table settings. Todd Slossberg, a talented executive chef, has had to carry the dual burden of high expectations and history in creating and executing dishes to match the room.

Slossberg discovered the joys of the table as a teenager on a family trip to Europe, where he was awed by the pleasure people took in eating a meal and also by how well regarded chefs were there. "I realized that chefs were more than mere cooks, but shapers and creators of experience. I am still intrigued by food's power over the senses," he recalls. A Culinary Institute of America honor student, he was recruited to be sous-chef at the Hotel Jerome and in 1995 was elevated to executive chef. He now enjoys the respect and regard he noted as a teenager in Europe. Indeed, he was twice nominated as the James Beard Foundation's Best Chef in the Southwest.

Slossberg's ambitious dinners suit the opulent setting and at the same time meet contemporary expectations and tastes. His menu changes seasonally, always reflecting regional influences within the general category of contemporary American cuisine.

Occasionally, the region is as narrow as the Roaring Fork Valley. One of his signature entrées, for instance, is called Buffalo Prime Rib with Crispy Gold Potatoes and Red Onion Démi-Glace. It might be that Slossberg simply likes the sweetness and color of red onion, but I prefer to think that it's also a nod to the Red Onion, an enduringly popular watering hole a few blocks over on East Copper Avenue.

Another subtle tribute to Aspen traditions is Elk Tenderloin with Roasted Vegetable Hash and Cranberry Bourbon Reduction. Elk, native to the Rockies, have long been hunted. Hash goes back to mining days. And bourbon? Jerome guests have enjoyed their whiskey at Jerome Bar throughout the hotel's history, except during Prohibition, when it was turned into a soda fountain. Slossberg's Colorado rack of lamb is reputedly the best in town. In one presentation, it is plated with Sharp Cheddar Potato Purée and Thyme Lab *Jus*. Caribou, trout, salmon, and beef are among the other Western specialties prepared with the refined Slossberg touch.

The Century Room's excellent wine list and careful service keep up with Slossberg's cuisine. The restaurant is a perpetual DiRoNA award winner and holder of a *Wine Spectator* Award of Excellence. The hotel has been honored with numerous awards in the hospitality industry, and is a member of The Leading Hotels of the World and Historic Hotels of America.

The Century Room, Hotel Jerome, 3300 East Main Street, Aspen; (970) 920-1000, (800) 331-7213, or www.hoteljerome.com.

Conundrum

Conundrum's entrance—a gleaming expanse of glass and steel with a revolving door at the front—looks like a fancy boutique. If you like, you can think of the restaurant as an exclusive dining boutique, where the most artfully presented culinary creations await the discerning patron. The décor is elegant, with deep banquettes lining the walls hung with landscape paintings, stylish wood chairs, and simple yet classy table settings.

The restaurant was founded in 1999 by George Mahaffey, who as chef at The Restaurant at The Little Nell was nominated three times for the James Beard Foundation Best Chef in the Southwest and won in 1997. In fact, while at the Nell, Mahaffey collected culinary honors as if they were poker chips. He gambled them on his own place, and he seems to have hit the jackpot.

Actually, he gambled mostly with his own reputation, not with cold cash—and his reputation for quality and creativity made Conundrum a winner. When Mahaffey left the Nell, Aspen epicures missed his fine food. He had connected with the Signature Restaurant Group, which tried to lure him to Chicago. Mahaffey, who preferred Aspen, struck a complicated deal to take over Signature's disappointing Asian fusion restaurant and turn it into Conundrum. It was win-win. Mahaffey created his dream restaurant, Signature turned a miss into a hit, and his fans followed him to Conundrum.

Jim Cohen, formerly with Tante Louise and The Phoenician, signed on as Conundrum's executive chef—a double-whammy in the kitchen. Mahaffey sets high standards, and Cohen maintains them, adding his own creative input. Mahaffey

Mountain Cuisine

Most major ski companies in the United States operate the restaurants at the bottom of the lifts and on the hill. The gourmets in the human resources department hire the chefs, the epicurean corporate bean counters set profit goals, and hired designers research, create, and execute a theme for each eating place. The results are predictably mixed—and almost always impersonal.

The Aspen Skiing Company (and Aspen Highlands when it was under separate ownership) developed in a more European mode, leasing on-mountain restaurants to independent operators. Even though the company has now taken many of them into the corporate fold, the legacy of the individual and individualistic creators remains. Aspen skiers do not take easily to change, and the ski company has taken pains to retain the differences among the on-mountain eateries in terms of style, décor, and cuisine.

To get a spot, either eat before noon or after 1:30 in even the most casual self-service spot, or make a reservation if you opt for a sit-down table-service lunch. Here's where skiers and snowboarders eat on high at Aspen and Snowmass:

Aspen Mountain

The Sundeck

Aspen's first mountaintop lodge designed by legendary local architect Fritz Benedict was totally rebuilt in 1999 to reflect modern tastes, times, and needs. The original dated back to the days when it was necessary to ride a daisy chain of double chairlifts from the base area to the summit. Now it's a fast 12-minute ride on the Silver Queen gondola. The new Sundeck summit lodge still has a huge fireplace, but a scramble-system cafeteria, a double wok station for instant stir-fries, and a gourmet salad bar have replaced the snaking cafeteria line. Hot food no longer gets cold while waiting to pay. And if you don't feel like skiing, you can always hang out at the bar (ride the gondola down, please) or veg in a lounge chair on the Sundeck's sundeck.

About once a month, on full-moon winter nights, the Sundeck opens in the evening for limited food service (pizza, full salad station, noodle bowls, kids' menu, and a full selection from the grill), hot beverages, and a cash bar. Live entertainment and moonlight snowshoe tours are offered too. Tickets are sold at the Gondola Ticket Office, and further details are available by calling (970) 429-6971.

Also at the Sundeck, but essentially off-limits, is the Aspen Mountain Club, an exclusive members-only luncheon club with stunning design details and a fine menu of hearty mountain-style fare. You can't get in on a whim, but I mention it in case you have enough disposable income to join or get invited and want to know where you're going—or simply are curious about what's behind that door.

The general phone number for both the Sundeck and the Aspen Mountain Club is (970) 925-1220.

Bonnie's

Aspen Mountain regulars meet to eat at Bonnie's at the bottom of Tourtelotte Park. Bonnie's still serves memorable food, and the people-watching can't be beat—especially from the deck on a sunny day. Born as Gretl's and a great part of the Aspen story, Bonnie's specializes in house-made soups, designer pizzas, and excellent sandwiches. Still independently run, Bonnie's is also the repository of divine hot apple strudel.

When you fork into a scrumptious slice, raise a fork to Gretl Uhl, the woman who brought this Austro-Bavarian specialty to Aspen. Gretl grew up in Garmisch-Partenkirchen, Germany's preeminent ski resort, where she learned to ski and to bake. She started ski racing in 1941 and was a German National Ski Team member until 1951, by which time she had married fellow ski racer Sepp Uhl.

In 1953, the young couple moved to Aspen to teach skiing at the nascent resort. Gretl supplemented their modest instructors' income by baking European desserts for the few local restaurants that then existed. More than a decade later, the Aspen Skiing Corporation decided to build an on-mountain restaurant. Gretl, who grew up where such dining facilities were the norm, persuaded the company to let her run it—and so she did, until 1980.

In an age when burgers, hot dogs, and canned soups were common ski-area fare, she served the food she grew up with: homemade soups, stuffed cabbage and stuffed peppers, beef roulades, and other then-exotic German dishes. Her flaky and flavorful apple strudel became the stuff of legend. Gretl's Restaurant was *the* lunch spot on the mountain. It would not be a stretch to credit her for pioneering the concept of on-mountain dining, rather than merely refueling, as part of the American way of skiing. After the lease ran out for her namesake restaurant, she moved her strudel to the Merry-Go-Round Restaurant at Aspen Highlands, then an independent ski area.

Things have changed—but they haven't. The Aspen Skiing Company (as the corporation was later renamed) bought Aspen Highlands. Gretl's on Aspen Mountain became Bonnie's, and there, Gretl's famous strudel remains on the menu, a culinary tribute to Gretl, who passed away in the winter of 2002.

Microbrewed beers, good wines, and the regular array of less interesting mountain beverages are also available at Bonnie's. **(970) 925-4218.**

Gwyn's

Gwyn's also typifies the musical restaurants game played on Aspen's mountains. Gwyn's, located at the bottom of Ruthie's Run, used to be called Ruthie's Restaurant. Gwyn Knowlton, who established Gwyn's High Alpine over at Snowmass, relocated her eatery to Aspen Mountain, and then she herself moved on to the Aspen Club and Spa, but her name is still on the door of the slopeside restaurant. Gwyn's sit-down lunches feature such contemporary specials as elk tenderloin, tempura scallop salad, and ahi salad. The building also houses the more casual

Continued on page 310

Alpine Café, an above-average cafeteria for breakfast items, soups, pasta, salads, and bar food. **(970) 920-6308.**

Aspen Highlands

Cloud Nine Café

This old warming hut is now Aspen's most authentically Alpine mountain restaurant. Aspen Meadows chef Andreas Fischbacher took the half of the building at the top of the Cloud Nine Chairlift that the ski patrol wasn't using and upgraded it into the kind of genuine mountain bistro that he knew so well from his native Austria. Two sublime and genuine daily specials—one hearty and meaty, one veggie and lighter—highlight a menu that also includes soups and salads, house-made crêpes, sinfully rich desserts, and a small wine list. The Soup Bowl section is for lighter food and faster getting back to the slopes. The café's interior is charming and cozy, and the views from the deck toward the Maroon Bells are picture-perfect. **(970) 544-3063.**

Merry-Go-Round

Ever wonder why this mid-mountain eatery looks familiar—in a can't-put-my-finger-on-it sort of way? This sprawling restaurant, far wider than it is deep and with huge windows facing uphill, was once a Safeway supermarket in Grand Junction. In the days when Aspen Highlands was a frugally operated independent mountain, the store was dismantled, trucked to Aspen, and hauled up the hill to the base of Scarlett's Slope. Despite the efforts to disguise its provenance with the long-ago addition of one of the best decks in Colorado, the Merry-Go-Round retains its funky ambience, resisting any subtle efforts to be upgraded or upscaled. Its most popular dishes are down-home too, including burgers, brats, sandwiches, Mexican dishes, and sweet stuff for afterwards. It is rumored that the offerings will be upscaled for 2003–04. Prices are still reasonable, down to the wines. **(970) 925-8685.**

Buttermilk

Bump's

Although Bump's isn't on the mountain but rather at the bottom, I mention it because it is operated by the owners of Ajax Tavern (see page 303) and Tra Vigne, so it's worth sacrificing panoramic views for that level of base-lodge food. Excellent breakfast items, freshly smoked salmon, Caesar salad, oven-baked focaccia pizzas, chili, prepared-to-order pasta specialties, house-made desserts, and après-ski snacks vie with each other for the best-of-Bump's honors. **(970) 925-4027.**

Cafe West

This small restaurant at the bottom of West Buttermilk, and therefore not totally on the mountain either but usually reached on skis or snowboard, is perennially one of Aspen's best-kept lunch secrets. Still, those in the know go there for house-made soups, authentic crêpes, filling and well-filled sandwiches, salads, and delicious desserts. The outdoor deck catches the sun during a good part of the day. **(970) 920-0960.**

The Cliffhouse

Lunch is secondary to the scenery that The Cliffhouse atop Buttermilk offers from a fantastic deck. But then again, the mountaintop restaurant serves up pretty good grub. The regular cafeteria offers regular cafeteria fare, but the Mongolian barbecue makes The Cliffhouse unique in all of skidom. Select from a choice of meats, fish, tofu, vegetables, oils, sauces, and spices, and the cooks grill it all up for you in a flash. **(970) 920-0933.**

Snowmass

Cafe Suzanne

This is Snowmass' answer to Buttermilk's Café West, a place to get French country fare on a Colorado mountain. House-made soups, the French grilled-cheese sandwich known as *croque monsieur*, various crêpes, good desserts, and daily entrée specials—and wines to go with them—make this an appealing ski stop. When the weather permits, the Café Suzanne fires up the outdoor grill. **(970) 923-3103.**

Gordon's and High Alpine Restaurant

When Gwyn Knowlton pulled up stakes from Snowmass and moved to Aspen Mountain, Gwyn's High Alpine became Gordon's, and High Alpine took on a separate identity. The restaurants share a building at the top of the Alpine Springs chairlift. Gwyn's looks kind of Bavarian and is known for such brunch-style dishes as eggs Benedict, as well as for desserts. **(970) 923-5188.** The High Alpine Restaurant can launch the day with breakfast pastries and keep it going with soups, pasta dishes, sandwiches, salads, and, in clement weather, outdoor grilled fare. **(970) 923-3311.**

Sam's Knob

Sam's Knob is a prominent mountain feature—and it features a prominent mountain restaurant of the same name. Located at the top of Lifts 3 and 5, this extremely busy lunch spot offers the best views across to Mt. Daly and Garret Peak, up toward the Big Burn slope, and down toward the valley. It offers a full menu of light or hearty lunch dishes, available both as self-service and for table service. **(970) 923-6220.**

Continued on page 312

Ullrhof

Ullr is the Norse god of snow, and Ullrhof at the base of the Big Burn is Snowmass' snow central after a storm. It dishes up fiery chili, rich stews, salads, and fresh baked goods. The large deck offers grill selections and a bar—when it isn't snowing. **(970) 923-5143.**

Up 4 Pizza

Ullrhof is at the bottom of the Big Burn Superchair, and Up 4 Pizza is at the top. This glorified warming hut serves pizza by the slice with either traditional or gourmet toppings. For non–pizza-lovers, if there is such a thing, Up 4 Pizza could also be called Up 4 Soup, Up 4 Chili, or Up 4 Sandwiches. Everyone, it seems, dials into Up 4 Dessert. Lounge chairs on the snow provide relaxing and people-watching opportunities on sunny days. **(970) 923-0464.**

claims that his motto is "More class, less sass," but in truth, his restaurant is both classy and sassy.

The restaurant is named after 14,022-foot Conundrum Peak, Conundrum Creek that flows from its flanks, and perhaps even the Conundrum Mine. Taking elements from all of those Conundrums, it is decorated in subtle variations on the greens and golds of mountain summers and aspen trees in autumn. Ascending the grand staircase just might feel like climbing a mountain after you've put away an entire Conundrum feast. Robust and often earthy flavors, deep as a mineshaft, resonate from each exquisitely arranged plate. The only Conundrum not evident at the stylish restaurant is Conundrum Hot Springs, a legendary clothing-optional spring deep in the backcountry. At Conundrum, the only clothing option seems to be expensive, more expensive, and most expensive garments.

Well-dressed diners start with such signature dishes as Lobster Soup with a Sauté of Lobster, Wild Mushrooms, and Chervil; Trio of George's Smoked Salmon Firecracker Prawn and Crabcake with Spicy *Tobiko* Sauce and Opal Basil Salad; or Seared Hudson Valley Foie Gras with Caramelized Pineapple and Cippoline Onions with "100-Year-Old Balsamico." Entrées include Grilled Elk Loin with Caramelized Apples, Sweet Onions, and Sugar Peas with a Sun-Dried Cherry Sauce; Almond Dusted Filet of Turbot with Sautéed Baby Bok Choy, Fresh Water Chestnuts, and Shiitake Mushrooms, and Lemon-Ginger Sauce with Vanilla Bean; and Grilled Beef Filet Mignon with Green Chile Mashed Potatoes, Tortilla Salad and Jalapeño Hollandaise. The vegetarian Cauliflower Agnolotti is composed of house-made pasta stuffed with cauliflower mousse. Flavors mingle in innovative ways. Presentations delight.

Like many of the appetizers, soups, and entrées, desserts shift with the seasons. Look for a bittersweet chocolate cake that truly is more chocolaty than sugary, Banana Milk Chocolate Napoleon, or the whimsically named "Remembrance of Things Past," combining house-made *madeleines* with a distinctive Earl Grey ice cream. The wine list is long and strong, with 500 selections, most from Italy, France, or California but also wines from Spain, Austria, and Portugal.

Restaurant Conundrum, 325 East Main Street, Aspen; (970) 925-9969 or www.decarorestaurantgroup.com/index_conundrum.html.

DINING

Krabloonik Restaurant and Kennel

In 1974, Stuart Mace (see page 317) gave 55 sled dogs to his protégé Don MacEachen, who had worked with him at Toklat for four-and-a-half years. Entrusting MacEachen with his huskies was an act of faith and affection. While Mace already believed that his health and age would not permit him to continue the strenuous routine of operating his Toklat kennels, he lived more than 15 years longer—enough to confirm that his trust was not misplaced.

MacEachen established a kennel at Snowmass and named it Krabloonik, after the first lead dog that that he had raised for Mace. These broad-chested, wide-shouldered–hybrids of the three original sled-dog types, malamute, Eskimo, and Siberian—with long legs and wide paws ideal for Colorado's mountains and powder snow are canine powerhouses—who pull the sleds for rides all winter long. In a rambling log structure plastered onto the side of a hill, overlooking high mountains, a deep valley, and the kennels housing more than 200 dogs is a restaurant. Fine dining in so beautiful a setting and dogsled rides make for a unique combination. In winter, you can do one, the other, or both. In summer, you can only come to eat and look at the dogs. Only dinner is served during the summer, while both lunch and dinner are offered in winter. The restaurant is basically rustic and homespun, but new Western stylishness has crept in. Through the large picture windows are daytime or moonlight views of Mt. Daly and Capitol Peak, though in the evening, the sunken fire pit vies with the windows for guests' attention.

Krabloonik is known for its Wild Mushroom Soup, freshly baked breads, home-made preserves, smoked meats from its own smokehouse, and game. Other starters include Krabloonik Smoked Trout with Creamy Horseradish, Wild Game Tartare, Baked Brie with Pears and Lingonberries, Southwestern Gravadlox Napoleon with Toasted Tortillas and *Salsa Fresca*, Lollipop Boar Chop with Aged Balsamic Glaze over Onion and Fennel Confit, and Scottish Pheasant *Galantine*. Entrées continue in the same mode. Rack of lamb, trout, and salmon are found on menus all over the state, but Krabloonik's Culinary Institute of America–trained chef Matt Maier spin results in Rocky Mountain Trout Sautéed with Rock Shrimp, Tomatoes, and Marjoram; Grilled Atlantic Salmon with Blood Orange Glaze and Roasted Yellow Pepper Puree; and Roasted Rack of Colorado Lamb with Rosemary and Grain Mustard Glaze and Mint Julep *Au Jus* are the restaurant's renditions of these favorites.

Game specialties include Boneless Breast of Quail over Roasted Cranberry-Apple Polenta with Balsamic Maple Glaze; *Escallope* of Wild Boar with Sauce Normandy; Grilled Noisettes of Caribou with Truffle Spice *Démi-Glace*; Roasted Loin of Elk with Pecan Herb Crust and Morel Mushroom Cream; Medallions of Fallow Deer with Olive Oil, Garlic, and Soy Grilled and Topped with a Ginger Teriyaki. Among Krabloonik's most popular, and priciest, entrées are two combination game platters, one of caribou, wild boar, and quail and the other of caribou, elk, and fallow deer. The three-course prix fixe winter lunch includes a starter, an entrée, and a dessert.

The large wine list features domestic wines as well as selections from Australia, Chile, France, Italy, Spain, and South America. The list is divided by color, region, and varietal, with a decent assortment in several price categories offered by the glass. Because the Wild Mushroom Soup and homemade preserves are so popular, Krabloonik now makes them available for retail purchase to take along or have shipped—but not by dogsled.

Krabloonik Restaurant and Kennel, 4250 Divide Road, Snowmass Village; (970) 923-3953 or www.krabloonik.com.

Montagna

From the day in 1989 that The Little Nell Hotel opened at the base of Aspen Mountain, it joined the pantheon of the town's most acclaimed properties. Ninety-two luxurious rooms, elegant public spaces, matchless convenience to the Silver Queen gondola, and the precious Restaurant at the Little Nell were all part of the picture. Chef George Mahaffey put the elegant, three-meals-a-day Restaurant at the Little Nell at the culinary pinnacle, matching the hotel's high level of hospitality.

Chef Mahaffey is now running Conundrum (see page 307), and after a few changes of guard in the kitchen under the old concept, the restaurant was remade into Montagna. It is less formal but just as stylish and, most important, just as good. Beyond Montagna's Bar, adjacent but distinct dining rooms flow easily from one to the other. Off the expansive main dining room are a private dining room (important in celeb-heavy Aspen) and an exquisite Wine Room (very important for a restaurant with an extensive wine cellar).

Executive Chef Paul Wade, who previously cooked at The Tides in Miami Beach, the Peaks Resort and Golden Door Spa in Telluride, The Cotton House on Mustique in the West Indies, and Five Palms Beach Grill in Kihei, Hawaii, has been on duty since Montagna's opening just before Christmas 2000. He has traded his tropical culinary persona for mountain cuisine—clean, tight, and identifiable, but international in its derivations. House favorites are seafood pot-au-feu, wood-roasted wild salmon, elk with roasted potatoes, and house-smoked tenderloin of beef.

Montagna features a monthly prix fixe menu focusing on a different mountain region around the world. Wade researched and concocted accurate dishes that encapsulate the tastes of the Andes of Chile, the Drakensburg Mountains of South Africa, the Alps of both New Zealand and of Europe, the Himalayas of Nepal, the Atlas Mountains of Morocco, and the Blue Mountains of Australia. Wade thinks globally, but he acts locally as a strong supporter of the green market. He prefers to buy from local and domestic growers to ensure that ingredients are as natural and wholesome as possible, including local potatoes, onions, corn, tomatoes, apples, peaches, and grapes.

Wine director Richard Betts maintains a refrigerated wine cellar of more than 11,000 bottles of the finest wines from throughout the world's wine regions and heads a team of three sommeliers. Monthly tasting menus and occasional wine-maker dinners are scheduled throughout the year.

Montagna, The Little Nell Hotel, 675 East Durant Avenue, Aspen; (888) 843-6355, (970) 920-4600, or www.thelittlenell.com.

DINING

Olives Aspen

I was vaguely tempted to put Olives in "The Chain Gang" chapter, because when it opened at the St. Regis Aspen in 1999, it became the tenth restaurant by that name. Todd English, one of America's star chefs, opened the first Olives a decade earlier in Boston, bringing Mediterranean-inspired cuisine to Beantown, and he has sprinkled Olives elsewhere on the American fine-dining landscape. But having promised subjectivity, I decided to keep Olives here, for local recipes join English's creations on the menu.

Olives Aspen is distinctive, engaging, and casual—in a classy St. Regis sort of way—with buffed pine floors, coffered ceilings, ochre walls hung with artworks, rich earthtone fabrics, antique accents, classy table settings (are those tablecloths by Frette?), wrought-iron chandeliers and wall sconces, baronial chairs, and an exhibition kitchen faced in imported marble and hand-painted tiles.

English established some of the dishes that are considered signatures at Olives, but he is smart enough to give his talented chefs latitude in adding their own creations to the menu. At a culinary festival in Hawaii, English met Jason Rogers, formerly *chef de cuisine* at the Vail Cascade Club and sous-chef at The Whitehall in Chicago. Impressed by Rogers' work, English offered him a job at Olives Aspen. Rogers has been there from opening day, and two years later, when he was just 27 years old, he was elevated to executive chef.

Todd English and, by extension, Olives restaurants have made their reputation on complex dishes served in large portions. Generously cut rack of lamb, pork rib eye and shortribs, thick-cut tuna and halibut, rich house-made duck sausage, mountains of mashed potatoes flavored with this or that, creamy risotto, and Paella Olivacious, a toothsome arborio rice with lobster, clams, mussels, shrimp, roasted chicken, *and* chorizo. Even the tapanade is complicated. I've heard that it is composed of 15 varieties of olives.

Such abundance is par for the Olives Aspen course. Interestingly, however, a more modestly sized dish is a signature. Shaped like miniature hats, Olives' tortelli are filled with puréed butternut squash whipped into mousse-like airiness, bathed in a brown butter, and served with sage and Parmigiano-Reggiano.

No dessert is more sinful than the silky Very Vanilla Soufflé and the Fallen Chocolate Cake, dark and rich and seductive to a fare-thee-well. For nostalgia and fun, order S'Mores and you'll get house-made marshmallows, graham cracker shortbread, a thick chocolate-hazelnut paste, and a tabletop hibachi-type "campfire" to cook them on.

The wine list is 500 or so selections strong, much imported from the Mediterranean region that inspired the menu. The wine service parallels the food service in terms of graciousness, attentiveness, and knowledge. Rogers assembles "spontaneous tasting menus" with paired wines on Thursday, Friday, and Saturday nights.

The Legacy of Stuart Mace

To understand the magic of the Pine Creek Cookhouse, you have to know a little about Ashcroft and Stuart Mace. Ashcroft, a mere dozen miles from Aspen, was platted in 1880. Within three years, the booming silver camp mushroomed to 2,000 inhabitants, but the silver bubble quickly burst, and by 1885 the population fell to just 100. In the 1930s, the abandoned mining town was going to be the site of a future ski area, but World War II intervened. After the war, Stuart Mace, a former commander of the 10th Mountain Division's canine corps, moved his family and his sled dogs to Ashcroft. Mace family members remain there to this day. *Sergeant Preston of the Yukon,* a television series of the late 1950s, was filmed there, with Ashcroft standing in for Alaska and the heroic TV mountie driving Stuart's huskies.

The remains of the town, mostly original structures and a few built for television, comprise a National Register Historic Site. Stuart Mace and his wife, Isabel, became the de facto guardians of the achingly beautiful 9,500-foot-high valley. Their daughter, Lynne, operates Toklat, a gallery showing fine works by Native American and Western artists in a rambling, rustic building that was once a lodge and restaurant. Toklat's long-term future is uncertain, but it will remain in the family's hands as long as Isabel, who is well into her eighties at this writing, lives. Despite the development pressure radiating out from Aspen to every corner that is not under federal or other protection, this deep pocket of the Castle Creek Valley remains much as it did when Stuart and Isabel were young. Many people hope that it continues that way.

The Pine Creek Cookhouse, an atmospheric restaurant at the edge of the wilderness, is also part of the Mace legacy. Stuart and Isabel's son Greg and his wife, Christina, opened this remote restaurant in 1971. Their building, originally constructed in the 1930s as a skeet-shooting lodge near Basalt, was later moved to its present location where it served as a hunting lodge and a scout camp. John Wilcox bought the cookhouse from the Maces in 1984.

It is possible that the existing restaurant building will eventually be replaced by a larger facility with a better kitchen and more behind-the-scenes storage. But I, along with other admirers of the family who saved the valley, hope that, if ever and whenever a new Pine Creek Cookhouse is built, the spirit of Stuart Mace will be honored in the design and the execution. I am confident that the food will be good and hope the magical setting will remain pristine and priceless.

Dinner (and to an extent lunch or brunch) is a production, and an expensive one at that. But you can enjoy the ambience at the bar, where a more modest menu is available. Even so, Olives Aspen isn't really about modesty. It's about grand food in a grand setting.

Olives Aspen, St. Regis Aspen, 315 East Dean Street, Aspen; (970) 920-7356, (970) 920-3300 (hotel number), or www.stregisaspen.com.

Pine Creek Cookhouse

Deep in the Castle Creek Valley, just one-and-a-half miles south of Ashcroft, Toklat, and the winter road closure is the Pine Creek Cookhouse. In summer, you can drive to the door. In winter, Castle Creek Road is plowed only as far as Ashcroft, so you reach the restaurant on skis or snowshoes or in a horse-drawn sleigh. (Cross-country skis and snowshoes are available for rent at Ashcroft Ski-Touring, right at the winter road closure.)

Under a roof supported by huge whole-log timbers and beams, the Pine Creek Cookhouse serves generous buffet lunches (soups, salads, pasta, entrées, and dessert) to cross-country skiers and hikers. In the evening, it puts on pull-out-all-stops romantic dinners for couples and congenial dinners for families or groups of friends.

The sophisticated menu changes twice a year. The dinner menu starts with the chef's appetizer selection, followed by a choice of the soup of the day or a salad, a choice of entrées, and dessert. Dinner entrées include such winter specialties as Grilled Colorado Lamb Chops with Sun-Dried Apricot Chutney, Quinoa Tabbouleh, and Infused Mint Oil; Rocky Mountain Rainbow Trout with Walnut-Basil-Encrusted Shrimp Scampi and Warm Southern Sweet Potato Salad; Pine Creek Hot Smoked Salmon on Warm German Potato Salad with Horseradish Cream and Basil Purée; Pistachio-Crusted Caribou with Maple Mashed Yams, Gorgonzola Fondue, and Huckleberry *Jus;* and Herb-Roasted Free-Range *Poussin* Stuffed with Wild Mushroom Risotto and Natural Pan Juices. Summer specialties using seasonal ingredients include Rabbit Confit with Arugula Salad, Confit of Shallots, Honey, and Ginger; Diver Scallops with Yukon Potatoes, Braised Leeks, and Beluga Caviar Finished with Lobster Champagne *Beurre Blanc;* Jack Daniels-Marinated Elk Tenderloin over Sweet *Pommes* Anna and Sautéed Dandelion Greens; and Wild Mushroom Risotto made of Black Truffles, Seasonal Wild Mushrooms, and Mushroom *Jus* with Fresh Herbs.

Also available are such complex vegetarian dishes as Grilled Vegetable Pie of Eggplant, Asparagus, and Shiitake Mushrooms with Oven-Roasted Grits, Tomato Fondue, and Goat Cheese. The kitchen produces daily special desserts featuring fruits and the ever-popular chocolate. The Pine Creek Cookhouse serves wine, beer, and spirits, but mainly, it serves scenery and the setting. As delicious as lunch or dinner may be, even fine food plays second fiddle to the drop-dead views of Star Peak and the surrounding Elk Mountains.

Pine Creek Cookhouse, Castle Creek Road, Aspen; (970) 925-1044 or www.pinecreekcookhouse.com.

AUTHOR NOTE: *Just as this book was going to press, the Pine Creek Cookhouse burned to the ground. With no winter road maintenance closer than a mile from the restaurant, firefighters could not reach the site to save even a timber. Owner John Wilcox promises to rebuild, but it is difficult to determine how soon that could be accomplished.*

Piñons

Piñons, occupying the second floor of an unremarkable building, doesn't advertise a lot, but it doesn't have to, for its loyal following and stellar reputation keep the reservations book filled.

ASPEN AND THE ROARING FORK VALLEY

Aspen's Franco-American Star Chef

Charles Dale is a soft-spoken, impeccably mannered restaurateur, but he doesn't captain the front of the house. Rather, he is a Colorado power chef, a major culinary talent with a reputation honed by meticulous renderings of French cuisine. Updated classics are Dale's hallmarks—at Renaissance, the first of his two establishments, at earthier bistro-style Rustique, and now at Range.

Raised abroad amid titled and privileged Europeans, Dale's culinary career path into the heat of the kitchen might seem at odds with the cushy life he could well have led. His father was a U.S. vice-consul and later private adviser to Prince Rainier of Monaco. Charles spent his early years with Crown Prince Albert and Princess Caroline in the palace, where refinement in food and service was practiced. The family returned to the United States when he was 11, and he was enrolled in Manhattan's Lycée Français.

Dale earned a degree in romance languages and art history from Princeton University but went to New York to break into the music business. His father's successful bid on a cooking class at a silent auction charity fundraiser turned Dale's attention to cooking rather than rock and roll as an outlet for his creativity. He studied at Peter Kump's New York Restaurant School and apprenticed with Alain Sailhac, then chef at New York's famed Le Cirque. For several years, he bounced back and forth between some of the best restaurants in New York and France, including cooking under Daniel Boulud at the Plaza Athénée Hotel New York, then back to France to the kitchens of Jean-Paul Lacombe in Lyon, and eventually returning to Le Cirque as chef *saucier* when Boulud took over the kitchen there.

Perfection reigns at Piñons—in the kitchen, in the dining room, in the décor, among the waitstaff. The restaurant is a study in elegant Ralph Lauren-type rusticity with high ceilings, richly painted walls, hanging lights with pierced shades, polished wood, and even leather-bound menus branded with the restaurant's logo.

Piñons was created in 1988 by chef Rob Mobalian and maître d' Frank Chock. Their lofty standards of cuisine and service have been maintained over the years. Mobalian moved Piñons firmly into the camp of Colorado cuisine, which is American with a decided cant to southwestern regional ingredients. It remains known for Chef de Cuisine Dave Merlina's beautifully presented roasted lamb chops, sautéed pheasant, and various cuts of such big game as elk and venison.

Start with Tuna Tartare, Seared Diver Scallops, Lobster Strudel, Caviar, or something modest like the Freddy Salad, a house specialty of romaine lettuce, bacon, tomatoes, and a creamy herb dressing. (Someday, I'll find out why Freddy merits having a salad named after him.) In addition to Piñons' storied lamb and game dishes, entrées include equally sublime fresh seafoods, such as Piñons Pan-Seared Number-One Ahi with Baby Beets and Wasabi Potato Cake and a rich port reduction; Grilled Wild King Salmon with Miso-Glazed Stir-Fry Vegetables, Buckwheat Noodles,

Three years later, Dale joined Aspen's Hotel Jerome, and in June 1990, only 31 years old but with a wealth of experience, he went out on his own. He opened Renaissance in space formerly occupied by a fish market, on what was then considered a fringe block of downtown Aspen. How quickly things change. There are no fringe blocks these days, and Renaissance was a player in the turn-around.

Renaissance was a beauty from the get-go, but it was the refined cuisine, which Dale characterizes as "the alchemy of fine dining," that catapulted it into the top tier of restaurants in the West. Along with the later addition of the R Bar, a casual lounge sharing the Renaissance kitchen, the restaurant remains a warm, welcoming, and surprisingly cozy place. In 2003, he remade Renaissance into Range.

In 1995, Charles Dale was the first Coloradan to be named by *Food & Wine* magazine as one of the Best New Chefs in America, and he was twice nominated by the James Beard Foundation as Best American Chef in the Southwest. He often teaches at the Cooking School of Aspen, is a regularly featured guest chef on Crystal Cruises and at the Santa Barbara Wine Auction, and has cooked sellout dinners at the James Beard House in New York City, most recently in 2003 to debut Range's menu and concept.

Not content simply to run two of Aspen's best restaurants, Dale has released his own line of made-in-France food products under the St. Dalfour label and with his wife, Aimée, co-authored and published *The Chefs' Guide to America's Best Restaurants.* Next? A cookbook entitled *Haute Rustic Cuisine.* If I had written the former, Renaissance would be included, and if I wrote the latter, I'd be proud to feature rustic recipes of Rustique's caliber. And next, perhaps, is an ode to Range's Western cuisine.

and Mustard Sauce; and Grilled Ruby-Red Trout with Vegetable *Riso,* Mexican Shrimp, Kalamata Olive-Tomato Ragout.

A vegetarian entrée is always available too, and in deference to well-heeled clients' waistlines or arterial condition, the menu also reminds patrons that all entrées can be grilled, served plain, and accompanied only by steamed vegetables. After that, dare I mention dessert? Sommelier Jeff Walker is primed to suggest the right wine selection for your taste and for your meal.

Piñons, 105 South Mill Street, Aspen; (970) 920-2021.

Range (formerly Renaissance) and Rustique

The opening of Renaissance quite simply changed the way Aspen thought about food and the venue in which it is served. On all levels, it set the highest aesthetic standard, with a softly lit dining room done in soothing rose, earth tones, and natural wood; paintings on the walls, and subdued lighting. With impeccable service, exquisite cuisine built on the foundation of French culinary classicism, and stratospheric prices, Renaissance flourished for more than a dozen years. Renaissance's dishes were

ASPEN AND THE ROARING FORK VALLEY

unusual, exquisite, and expensive—and constantly changing, with a menu somewhat altered every night to reflect the season's and the day's best and freshest ingredients. Honor upon honor were heaped upon Renaissance itself and upon owner/chef Charles Dale.

But times change. As the 21st century cranked along, such indulgences as Beluga Caviar Bites on a Savory Lemon Tart with Chive Crème Fraîche; Wild Rice Bisque with Roasted Pheasant Galantine and Black Trumpet Mushrooms, and Mountain Bouillabaisse of Lobster, Nantucket Bay Scallops, Clams, and Veal Cheeks with Saffron and Cayenne Pepper Froth seemed like over-the-top excess.

Renaissance's sublime five-course Chef's Tasting Menu, and for Herculean eaters, a nine-course feast with mostly imported wines from the 550-selection cellar, had run their culinary course. With a growing family and Dale's own roots had tapping deeper into Western soil, he longed for simplicity—and so did his customers.

In April 2003, just as *Culinary Colorado* was going on press, Dale lowered the curtain on Renaissance, and in June, the space reemerged as Range, a restaurant featuring what Dale calls "Foods of the New West." He has tapped into the bounty of the Gold Rush states—the land between the Rockies and the Pacific Coast—and created a wave of innovative but simple dishes that shine with all the finesse that the kitchen at Third and Hopkins is famous for producing, no matter what the name of the establishment or the provenance of the cuisine.

Just like the chefs of France, who depend on nearby farmers and fishermen for the freshest local products, Range utilizes what is local—though the "locality" reaches all the way to the Pacific and even Alaska. Range's Foods of the New West are based on the best fruits, vegetables, and herbs from the Western Slope in season, and from the West Coast year-round, plus naturally raised and hormone-free meats, river fish and Pacific species. Dale set a high bar for himself, previewing Range's dishes for fussy foodies at the James Beard House in New York before the remodeled space in Aspen welcomed its first guests.

Range, which will be solidly open by the time this book comes out, will present a more casual face than elegant Renaissance. Range is modern, warm, and inviting, with a hardwood trellis affixed to the curved back wall, and grid lights suspended over the booths and tables. Significantly, in a time of economic stress, prices are about half of its predecessor, and the wine list—like the food—is from the American West. "Now people are coming to eat well rather than to have a transcendental experience," Dale notes. Renaissance provided transcendental experiences for 13 years, and Range will extend the opportunity to eat well—very well, in fact—to a wider clientele.

Range is not Dale's first venture into more casual dining. He opened Rustique in 2000 as a perfect counterweight to Renaissance-first-rate food, but with less formality and lower prices. Dale describes it as a bistro, and so it is-down to the beamed ceilings, hanging dried herbs, and paper cones in which the *pommes frites* are served.

Range, 304 East Hopkins Avenue, Aspen; (888) 311-CHEF (2433),
(970) 925-2402; check the previous website, www.renaissancerestaurant.com,
which might still be valid with a link to Range, or a Range site might be up.
Rustique Bistro, 216 South Monarch, Aspen; (970) 920-2555 or
www.rustiquebistro.com.

Sage

The Snowmass Club, the Aspen area's first and still leading golf resort, has been massively renovated in the past several years including numerous new private homes and villas, a redo of the lodge, and a Sage Restaurant makeover in a high-country bistro style. This restaurant amid the golf fairways and greens serves three meals a day.

Chef Mitch Levy studied at Oregon's Western Culinary School. An externship at The Little Nell brought him to Aspen, and after cooking at other local restaurants, he took over Sage's kitchen. He uses Colorado products when possible and is fanatical about house-made everything, including breads, stocks, and smoked meats and fish. The menu changes four times a year, with innovative dishes—some homey, some cutting edge—flowing from the kitchen. A recent fall menu featured entrées that ranged from the succulent and meaty Grilled Pork T-Bone with Caramelized Onion and Roasted Garlic Marmalade, Swiss Chard, Butternut Squash, and Gorgonzola Orzo to vegetarian Crispy Grilled Eggplant with Roasted Tomato Fennel Sauce, Provolone, Swiss Chard, and Goat Cheese. The adjacent Sage Bar & Living Room presents a smaller, more casual menu.

Sage offers splendid mountain and golf course views from its dining room and patio, the latter excellent for Sunset Suppers, earlybird specials between 6:00 and 7:00 P.M. Four-course wine dinners every Wednesday often sell out, so if you are visiting the Aspen area, make reservations.

Sage, Snowmass Club, 0239 Snowmass Circle Drive, Snowmass Village; (970) 923-0923 or www.snowmassclub.com.

SIX89 Restaurant & Winebar

One of Aspen's best restaurants is actually 30 miles downvalley in Carbondale. SIX89 Restaurant & Winebar is located in a rambling red brick Victorian house in the heart of downtown, occupying the kind of generous space that would cost a fortune in Aspen and purveying Aspen-quality cuisine at lower-than-Aspen prices.

A series of intimate dining rooms beautified with gleaming mahogany woodwork, fresh flowers, and crisp white napery are backdrops for the ever-changing dishes, and contemporary art on the walls. In summer, the pleasant, secluded patio is the primo spot, and herbs thrive in a garden behind the restaurant.

Owner/chef Mark Fischer, a biologist by training, gravitated toward the professional kitchen. He graduated as valedictorian from the Pennsylvania Culinary Institute and cooked at Aspen's high-toned Caribou Club, San Francisco's Fog City Diner, Le Cirque and Mesa in New York, and Table 29 in Napa before launching SIX89. In his own restaurant, he prepares what he calls "world cuisine," claiming no allegiance to any one culinary strain but drawing from many. Actually, his allegiances are evidenced in his unstinting support of local growers and wine makers.

The menu changes with the seasons, the week, and even the day. In summer, it might feature such items as local heirloom tomato salad, Westphalian ham with fresh figs, lamb brochettes with mint and cracked-pepper vinaigrette, grilled rack of lamb with spring onion and mint gravy, or pork T-bone. There's always some sort of

Japanese Influences in Aspen

Takah Sushi, Kenichi, and Matsuhisa

If it hasn't hit Aspen, it's not a food trend. All-purpose, formal French, bistro French, northern Italian, and Colorado contemporary have all established their places in the Aspen culinary pantheon. And so did **Takah Sushi,** becoming Aspen's first Japanese restaurant and its most enduring. Chefs in this intimate restaurant have been shaping rice, slicing fish, rolling nori, and showcasing all the other sushi-making skills for more than 20 years.

Paper umbrellas, kimonos displayed as artwork, and cozy booths characterize the décor, but diners at the sushi bar take notice of little other than watching the chefs at work and eating some of the best sushi around. Takah Sushi is still proud of a *New York Times* article that once described it as offering "the best sushi between Manhattan and Malibu." Since the early days, the restaurant has branched out with a somewhat more Pan-Asian menu, providing an intriguing journey through the rich flavors of Pacific Rim cuisines without leaving the Roaring Fork Valley.

Kenichi opened in 1991 by sushi master Kenichi Kanada and partner Bill Rieger, who took Japanese food in the direction of healthy Asian cuisine. Kenichi prepares both notable classic and contemporary sushi creations and other dishes across the spectrum of ingredients and influences. Of the various talented sushi chefs in Aspen, Kenichi's Kyomi Sano puts on an exacting culinary show while preparing some of the best sushi around. Tatsumaki Crab Cake, fresh Dungess crab encased in a wonton shell and served with sambal-pickled ginger sauce, is a noteworthy appetizer specialty. Others include Hot Spring Rolls, Blackened Tuna, and

carpaccio, ahi tuna carpaccio with wasabi aïoli being one of the favorites. Vegetarian offerings include such items as local organic vegetables with cornbread shortcakes and smoked tomato vinaigrette and vegetable *mu shu* crêpes with a crispy soba noodle cake. The more robust winter menu features the likes of lamb with tomato-apricot chutney, red-curry mussel stew, braised veal cheeks, duck rellenos, and venison with apple-smoked bacon. At any given time, the desserts might include pumpkin cheesecake, macadamia nut tart, maple crème brulée, seasonal fruit tarts, and homemade ice cream.

Fischer divides his offerings into small plates (appetizers), bowls (soups, stews, and other liquid creations), greens (salads, of course), large plates (conventional entrées), and sugars (desserts, natch). SIX89 is also known valley-wide for its moderately priced bar menu consisting of a small plate, a large plate, and a sugar, served at the bar or at one of the zinc-topped tables, and for its excellent wine-maker dinners. Fischer also offers what he calls his Random Acts of Cooking, where he creates meals especially to a table's particular tastes and culinary preferences and serves a customized feast family-style on hand-painted platters.

Nega Maki, rolls of grilled filet mignon, asparagus, roasted red peppers, and spicy black beans.

These days another Kenichi chef, Bodhi Durant, fuses Japanese, Indian, Thai, Chinese, and other traditions into such originals as Oriental Roast Duck, Macadamia Nut-Crusted Colorado Lamb Chop, and Buddha's Angel Hair, wok-seared angel-hair pasta with seafood and Asian vegetables. Such combinations demonstrate Kenichi's successful melding of Oriental and Occidental cuisines. Diners have a choice of sushi bar or tatami room, and there is a take-out counter as well.

Matsuhisa, which opened for the 1997–1998 winter season, rounds out the local eateries with sushi bars and Japanese traditions. As the Aspen outpost of an international group of Japanese gourmet seafood and sushi restaurants, it could also find a place in "The Chain Gang" chapter. Not many owners of restaurant chains win high culinary honors, but Nobuyuki "Nobu" Matsuhisa was named one of America's 10 Best New Chefs of 1989 by *Food & Wine* and was a nominee for the James Beard Foundation's 2001 Outstanding Chef Award. This talented chef's mix of Japanese and world cuisines has spread also to Las Vegas, Los Angeles, London, Malibu, Miami's South Beach, Milan, New York, Paris, and even Tokyo, with restaurants operating under the name Nobu, Ubon, or, as in Aspen, Matsuhisa.

At Matsuhisa, wasabi-pepper sauce, spicy or light garlic sauce, or black bean sauce are the condiments of choice for ultra-fresh house-specialty seafoods. Matsuhisa also prepares filet mignon, lamb, and chicken with a choice of sauces.

Takah Sushi, 420 East Hyman Avenue, Aspen; 970-925-8588. Kenichi, 533 East Hopkins Avenue, Aspen; (970) 920-2212 or www.kenichiaspen.com. Matsuhisa, 303 East Main Street, Aspen; (970) 544-6628.

The wine "cellar" is a glass-front, climate-controlled wine wall in the dining room with a commodious 2,400-bottle capacity. Just as Fischer roams the world for culinary inspiration, the wine wall displays global bounty, with selections from California, Argentina, Australia, France, Italy, Oregon, and Colorado wineries down the road in Hotchkiss or elsewhere on the Western Slope.

SIX89, 689 Main Street, Carbondale; (970) 963-6890 or www.SIX89.com.

Syzygy

The mostly-end-of-the-alphabet name of this sizzling Aspen restaurant (pronounced si-zeh-jee) comes from the Greek, alluding to an alignment between heavenly bodies—or, in this restaurant's case, between imaginative cuisine and hot jazz. Chef Martin Oswald takes ingredients that are currently as trendy as Syzygy itself and combines them in a thoroughly modern menu. In course after course, you'll find tiger shrimp, tuna tartare, Maine lobster, Hudson Valley foie gras, Colorado rack of lamb, elk, beef tenderloin, Black Mission figs, pancetta, and other popular ingredients.

Signature dishes, seasonal dishes, and special dishes all emerge from Oswald's kitchen, immaculately prepared and carefully presented. He adores such perky and distinctive flavors as lemongrass, Kaffir lime leaves, and curries. A judicious and imaginative use of produce characterizes many of his creations—julienned apples in the cucumber stuffing for the cured salmon, grilled pineapple to offset tempura lobster, and the like. Desserts include Syzygy versions of such classics as crème brulée and sorbets in various flavors.

Oswald hails from Styria, Austria, still a mostly rural province. His mother grew her own vegetables, herbs, and fruits. Neighbors supplied meats, dairy products, and honey. Mushrooms came from the woods, and wild berries from mountain meadows. Home-cooked family meals were the rule. He maintained that connection to fresh local ingredients and careful, caring preparation as he moved into professional chefhood. In the European style, young Martin began an apprenticeship in a nearby restaurant when he was 15, and by 20, he had his first chef position. He moved on to the kitchens of a prestigious group of spa-hotels, where he learned about such healthy foods as grains, beans, and vegetables. When he came to the United States in 1989, Austrian compatriot Wolfgang Puck hired him to work at Postrio in San Francisco, where he learned about the magic of Asian flavors. The mountains called, and Oswald moved to Sweet Basil in Vail, a launching pad for many Colorado culinary careers.

As executive chef at Syzygy, he melds those diverse experiences into what are basically European and Asian dishes with an American twist—or perhaps American dishes with a European or Asian twist. The wine list boasts 600 selections from all over the wine world, including, yes, Austria.

Syzygy, 520 East Hyman Avenue, Aspen; (970) 925-3700.

Topper's

Chefs at name restaurants usually set their sights on opening their own glamor restaurants or working for an establishment with a higher level of cuisine, style, and price than their previous kitchen. Greg Topper, formerly with the oh-so-toney Ajax Tavern (see page 303), did the opposite. He left that chic restaurant to open his own place that is, by objective standards, downmarket. His modest café next to Clark's Market offers quality and value along with the level of food Ajax diners grew to expect when he cooked there.

Topper's is a small, informal café serving pizza (here called flatbreads), pasta, popular Aspen Bowls (toothsome combinations of vegetables with or without meat, plus a choice of polenta, potatoes, rice, or beans), sandwiches, and desserts to eat on the spot or take out—all at prices that are bargains by Aspen standards. A modest selection of dinner entrées is also served. Recipes are prepared from scratch from fresh natural ingredients—and the results are surprisingly epicurean for so modest a place.

Where else, at this level of informality, can you get pizza with truffle oil? Or venison chili with spicy crème fraîche and a buttermilk biscuit? House-made sausages? Grilled New York strip steak with Maytag blue cheese, baked potato, and veal *démi-glace*? This is not surprising, really, when you remember that it is the brainchild of the guy with Ajax Tavern on his resume.

Topper's, North Mill Station, 300 Puppy Smith Street, Aspen; (970) 920-0069.

Willow Creek Bistro

Aspen Highlands was long a renegade ski mountain, with creaky old lifts and a funky base area, part A-frame day lodge and part rambling office building that resembled a rickety old motel. That changed when the Aspen Skiing Company bought Highlands, replacing the lifts, opening more ski terrain, and partnering with a developer to create a "village" at the base, created in the modern Colorado mountain mode with huge buildings of stone, big timber, and stucco. The complex contains retail space, eating space, condominiums, large homes, and an upscale fractional ownership property called the Ritz-Carlton Club.

Willow Creek Bistro, located in the Ritz-Carlton Club, is a culinary bright light. Chef Matthew Zubrod, late of the Vail Cascade Club and Spa (now the Vail Cascade Resort and Spa), is the chef. As a hotel restaurant, it serves three meals a day, but Zubrod's culinary inclinations show at dinner, when he offers an intriguing menu of flavorful foods inspired by many regional cuisines. He uses seasonal ingredients, sometimes in several variations on a single menu.

Typical starters include Maine Mussels in Chardonnay Broth, Pan-Seared Hudson Valley Foie Gras with Peach Jam, Colorado Cheese Plate, and Firecracker Oysters with Chili Garlic Sauce and Corn Relish. The showstopper is a Seafood Trilogy of Santa Barbara Prawns, Oyster Shooter, and Maine Lobster Cake. A recent summer menu featured Heirloom Tomato Gazpacho with Maine Lobster and Basil, and Sweet Olathe Corn and Jalapeño Soup. One soup showcased a favorite ingredient from the East Coast, the other a major crop from just over the mountains in western Colorado.

Entrées are divided into three categories: "From the Sea," "From the Land," and "Vegetarian and Pasta." Super-trendy dishes include such complex productions as Day Boat Halibut with Roasted Tomato Broth and Olive Oil–Poached Purple Potatoes; and Prime Filet with Potato Cake, Portobello Mushroom, Caramelized Shallot, and Cabernet Reduction. Others are rooted in American comfort foods, but with a little trendy flip. These would be such dishes as Braised Lamb Shanks with Goat Grits, and Dry-Aged Shell Steak with Macaroni and Cheese au Gratin. The new village at the Highlands base is still working at becoming a real place, but Zubrod is a real chef turning out really good food.

Willow Creek Bistro, Ritz-Carlton Club Aspen Highlands, 0075 Prospector Road, Aspen; (970) 429-2327.

Events

Food & Wine Magazine Classic at Aspen

June—For three glorious, glamorous gustatory days in the middle of June, Food & Wine Fever grips Aspen. The town hosts one of Colorado's most important annual culinary events. Correction, make that one of *the nation's* most important culinary events. The *Food & Wine* Magazine Classic at Aspen, which everyone in the know calls "Food & Wine," draws star chefs, vintners from leading domestic and international wineries, important hoteliers and restaurateurs, and thousands of dedicated or wannabe foodies. If there's a hot new trend, an emergent regional cuisine, a creative method of presentation or plating, or a new wine-growing area, it'll show up first and big at Food & Wine.

Aspen magazine quoted Jimmy Nadell, once chef at Aspen's exclusive Caribou Club and later at the short-lived Bistecca Toscana in Carbondale, as recalling, "One of my favorite memories is from '89, when Jean-Georges Vongerichten came to the festival and did a demo of his famous molten chocolate cake, the individual cake with the warm, runny center. Pretty soon, chefs from all around town, and the country, were imitating that cake." Such is Food & Wine's influence in the small, tight culinary world.

The event itself started small. In 1983, in an effort to spur summer business in the Aspen area, Gary Plumley, owner of the Aspen wine store called Of Grape and Grain (see page 332), and Bob and Ruth Kevan, who operated Snowmass Village's Chez Grand-mère restaurant (see page 393), launched a modest event with an ambitious name: Aspen/Snowmass International Wine Classic. Some 350 people—largely locals—attended. Within three years, *Food & Wine* magazine became the Classic's title sponsor. The publication's clout meant that the aristocracy of American cooking made appearances. The headliner, of course, was Julia Child, who is credited with awakening the country's palate and introducing French cookery.

The divine Julia and other great chefs presided over cooking classes, signed books, and rubbed elbows with adoring fans—and the nation's top culinary stars still do. The introduction of the talented 10 who were anointed by the magazine as America's Best New Chefs of the year was added as a feature in 1986, and a decade later, more than 50 previous recipients came to Aspen for their 10-year reunion. By that time, the event was attracting 5,000 people, which is the limit even this large festival can accommodate.

Today, a group of white-capped tents that resemble the Denver International Airport terminal transplanted to Wagner Park serve as the temporary landmark where Food & Wine is held. The St. Regis Aspen, the Wheeler Opera House, and other nearby buildings now also house many key events, including a full schedule of cooking demonstrations, wine tastings, and product samplings. Elsewhere, coveted by-invitation-only parties take place in Aspen's best restaurants or catered in private homes.

Seminars geared for food and wine professionals are now open to anyone who wants some behind-the-scenes insights in how top restaurants operate. These trade seminars deal with back-of-the-house issues, but recently, the trade program has been expanded into something akin to an outreach effort enabling customers to get the most out of their dining experience. The seminar called "How to Restaurant— Getting the Most from Your Dining Experience" has become a staple on the Food & Wine menu. Conceived of by Danny Meyer of New York's Union Café and other top eateries, it guides attendees through the fine points of fine dining, from making reservations to resolving discrepancies on the bill. Some people who have attended this session claim that the festival's high price of admission is a worthwhile invest-ment in getting the most for later dining experiences.

Nowhere else is the line between the glamorous show-biz aspect of the current culinary scene and sheer creativity and boldness in the kitchen so blurred as at Food & Wine. Both culinary professionals and fussy connoisseurs rush to buy their tickets. They don't come cheap. In 2003, Food & Wine's earlybird three-day admission was $825—with reserve wine tastings from top wineries up to $250 extra each. This does not deter dedicated epicureans or oenophiles. Passes typically sell out in February. (It must be all those bargain-hunters who book quickly, because any remaining tickets cost $925 after March 15.) Aspenites—both socialites and the local hoi polloi—vie to volunteer, donning aprons and helping at the event. There's even a waitlist for 900 volunteer slots.

Cooking demonstrations under canvas and in hotel meeting rooms alternate with morning and afternoon sessions when the big tents are open for the twice-daily Grand Tasting, and happy hordes descend on scores of long tables where wine makers from the world over pour their wines. You can sample wines that you've never even heard of before. Some attendees work the aisles, happily sipping 'til they're tipsy, while others soberly and seriously do the taste-and-spit routine, meticulously taking notes. Purveyors of gourmet foodstuffs from almonds to caviar offer samples, and a handful of makers and distributors of cookware, fine kitchen gadgetry, and appliances display their lines as well—sometimes employing star chefs who prepare small tasting portions of their own specialties.

When the big tents are closed, people who haven't stood in a food line since their boarding school cafeterias happily do so for a hard folding seat in a tent or cavernous hotel ballroom, where temporary kitchens are set up for top chefs' scheduled cooking demonstrations. The organization is slick, and the chefs come on like clockwork. Each demonstration kitchen features overhead mirrors above the prep and cooking area and television cameras wired to closed-circuit, big-screen monitors to bring every chop, whisk, mince, stir, and sizzle into sharp focus for all.

Until it became unwise for her to be at Aspen's elevation, the legendary Julia Child used to pack 'em in like no one else, and in recent years, Food & Wine has attracted such contemporary celebrity chefs as Mario Batali, Rick Bayless, Daniel

Boulud, Bobby Flay, Emeril Lagasse, Jacques and Claudine Pépin, Wolfgang Puck, Steve Raichlin, Charlie Trotter, Jean-Georges Vongerichten, and Patricia Wells. For many Food & Wine-goers, it's all about watching real pros strut their culinary stuff. People queue up for cooking demonstrations by name chefs. Most have cooked for an audience before and are not shy about public appearances. They are engaging speakers, and many encourage questions even as they cook. The showstopper is a head-to-head *Iron Chef*–style cook-off, held in parallel kitchens set up in a cavernous St. Regis function room. The event pits big-name chefs against each other in a timed competition, with the audience as judging panel.

Wine authorities include such luminaries as Andrea Immer, Jancis Robinson, and Joshua Wesson, and leading wine makers from around the world also are there in force. Groups of vintners from a specific wine-growing country or region, or even a single vineyard, orchestrate tastings for anyone wishing to build his or her wine knowledge. At coveted and costly reserve tastings, offered for additional fees, leading vintners pour their rarest vintages for a limited number of participants. Hosts include some of the nation's leading wine experts. In an evening that resembles nothing so much as a coming-out party, the nation's 10 anointed Best New Chefs make their debuts at the Classic. They don't curtsy, but they sure do cook. Though they already preside over restaurants with stellar local and regional reputations, this is a national showcase, where each prepares one dish for an opulent buffet dinner at the Hotel Jerome. For the 800 guests who cram into the Jerome's historic rooms, it's a 10-course tasting menu.

So many events, so many people, so much food, and so much wine is crammed into three days that Food & Wine takes on a life of its own feeling like a community— a temporary community, largely under canvas—devoted to the dual cults of fine foods and fine wines, the cornerstones of the epicurean lifestyle.

Food & Wine Magazine Classic at Aspen, 1120 Avenue of the Americas, New York, NY 10036; (212) 382-5600 or www.foodandwine.com/ext/classic/index.html.

Rocky Mountain Brewers Festival, Snowmass Village Chili Shoot-Out, and Taste of Fall Wine Festival

August and September—Two events, while not strictly "culinary," draw the chili and beer crowd to Snowmass Village. The annual Rocky Mountain Brewers Fest in recent years has attracted 40 microbreweries to compete for annual People's Choice awards for the beer of the year, based on aroma, appearance, flavor, body, drinkability, and that elusive but important criterion of overall impression. People 21 and older may taste these beers, and a bluegrass band or other group provides entertainment to sip by.

The annual Snowmass Village Chili Shoot-Out takes place on a Saturday afternoon toward the end of August. The Snowmass Village Mall is turned into an arena where amateur chefs and restaurants duke it out to see who makes the meanest, spiciest, baddest chili in the whole Roaring Fork Valley—and at this event, the fork— or more accurately, the spoon—does roar. Categories include flavor, texture, blend of spices, and overall appeal and presentation. People's Choice and Excellence in Chili honors are also awarded. The entry deemed to be the very best chili in the valley wins the coveted Water Buffalo Horn Trophy. (For the record, the crew that operates the D&E Snowboard Shop and also Ink! Coffee, a popular café and hangout, keeps winning—but with a different recipe each year.) If hot stuff suits your palate and you want to sample all the chilies, just buy a ticket. Live entertainment, including blue-grass music, and ice-cold beer on tap help the chili go down.

Summer's wrap-up at the Snowmass Village Mall, often coinciding with the turning of the leaves, is the Taste of Fall Wine Festival. There are food and wine tastings, plus such harvest-time traditions as apple bobbing and pumpkin painting. It's also the time that Snowmass Village retailers clear out their summer merchandise with sidewalk sales.

Details on all three are available from the Snowmass Resort Association at (970) 923-2000 or www.snowmassvillage.com.

Retail

The Butcher's Block

In the world beyond Aspen and before the 21st century, the local butcher shop was a fixture of many a downtown. How gratifying that the nation's most exclusive and most expensive ski town still has such a store. The Butcher's Block anchors Aspen to the reality of buying ingredients and assembling a meal. It has been on South Spring Street "forever," according to my Aspen-dwelling friends. "Forever" is actually since 1973, when Jack Frey, who learned meat-cutting in the army, opened his butcher shop.

When you walk in, the low ceiling, functional fluorescent lighting, and white-enamel refrigerated cases remind you that you are in a true meat market, not in a food boutique. A big case front and center displays top-quality hand-cut beef, lamb, veal, and pork. "We don't sell a lot of hamburger," acknowledges manager Jim Strickbine, but says that big, beefy steaks such as rib eye, sirloin, and tenderloin are in great demand. Aspen cooks also go there for poultry, specialty meats, game (buffalo, elk, venison, and rabbit), and sausages. Sausages range from Louisiana-style andouille to German- and Austrian-style wieners—not exactly sausages from A to Z but nearly so. The butchers make their own Italian sausage, and the store gets other styles of sausage from first-rate purveyors.

The Butcher Block also has super-fresh seafood. In addition to ever-popular salmon (whole, steaks, fillets, or smoked), trout (fresh or smoked), and shrimp (raw in-shell, raw peeled, and cooked), also carries sushi-grade seafood, abalone, calamari, all sorts of crab in-shell and crabmeat, eel, frog legs, shad roe, scallops in-shell, smelt, and stone-crab claws. Also in stock are many other makings of a fine meal, including Grana bread from Basalt (see page 300) and *panko* crumbs from Japan, excellent olive oils, several balsamic vinegars, hand-raked French salt, Rice River rices and grains, dressings and marinades, dried fruits and mushrooms, and fine preserves. Keep looking and you'll find several kinds of tempting pâtés from Les Petits Cochons, truffle butter, caviar, Echiré butter churned in France, and other refrigerated delicacies. The cheese case holds several English Stiltons, including layered Stilchester, lemon Stilton, and cranberry Stilton; Explorateur, a criminally rich triple cream from France; fontina, Parmigiano-Reggiano; various blue cheeses, and many others.

Behind the glass doors of freezer case is frozen beef, veal, and chicken *glace de viande,* an excellent base for fancy saucery. *Haricots verts,* the incomparable green beans from France, and lobster tails share space in the case with quality frozen appetizers. The store also carries a limited assortment of produce, including organic greens and fresh morels in season. What a treat.

The Butcher's Block's deli lunches include roasted chicken or baby back pork ribs, made-to-order sandwiches, storied meatloaf, cheese, and several good salads on good bread and with the toppings of choice. There are also three or four house-made soups every day, to combine into one of the best—and best-priced—soup-and-salad lunches in Aspen.

The store also maintains its tie to the local community is with its annual block party—The Butcher's Block block party, get it? Many autumns ago, Frey had lots of ground meat left over after the leaf-peepers had left and the skiers were still weeks away. He began grilling burgers and giving them away, free, to locals. Annual rumors float through town that "this year's" party will be the last. Some year, it might be, but as of this writing, it was still a tradition that connects Aspenites with the best-quality meat and one of the town's most enduring food businesses.

The Butcher's Block, 415 South Spring Street, Aspen; (970) 925-7554.

Epicurious

Epicurious, the Roaring Fork Valley's newest gourmet food store, was opened in late 2002 by Chris Norvell. With 20 years of Aspen restaurant experience under his belt—most of it working the front of the house—he developed a sense for local tastes and food needs. The store's pared-down and clean décor features a black-and-white checked floor, white walls, chrome refrigerated cases, and chrome shelves. "All the color is on the shelves," says Norvell—and it is, in bright packages of gourmet packaged goods from the world over.

Epicurious also sells custom-cut meats, produce, and super-fresh seafood, the latter from five different sources, including one from whom Norvell only buys tuna. Cheeses are international, with selections from England, Holland, France, and artisanal cheeses from domestic makers. Tasting samples are often set out. Among common prepared foods are steamed shrimp, meatloaf, crab cakes, and other favorites. Epicurious also sells pastries and other desserts from local bakeries and Grana bread.

Epicurious, Orchard Plaza, 400 East Valley Road, El Jebel; (970) 963-8353 or www.myepicurious.com.

The Kitchen Cupboard

You might expect Culinary Institute of America graduate Amy Hausman to be cooking, say, at the Snowmass Club, where she was sous-chef, or any of the another fine Aspen area restaurants. But Hausman became interested in making it possible for others to cook well for themselves and in 1992 she opened a tiny store called The Kitchen Cupboard in Basalt. With her culinary background, she does what few other cookware retailers are able—or willing—to do: give accurate and appropriate baking and cooking advice to her customers. Not only do they pick her brain when they are in the store, but they often phone, in mid-kitchen crisis, for an emergency consultation.

The store has expanded since it opened in space not much larger than a cupboard, but it still is, let's say, cozy—and it still is full of goods, gadgets, and gifts for the home cook. If some desired item is not in stock, The Kitchen Cupboard will order it. "We like to think of ourselves as a Williams-Sonoma, but in a smaller space," Hausman deadpans.

The inventory includes everything from pricey, heavy-duty Kitchen-Aid mixers to little hand gadgets that cost just a few dollars. Top-of-the-line All-Clad, Calphalon, Chantal, and other quality cookware adorn the shelves. Walls are hung thick as ivy on an English cottage with all manner of accessories, gadgets, and gizmos— both common and hard-to-find items. There's also a good selection of gourmet condiments and seasonings, and an extensive cookbook assortment.

The Kitchen Cupboard supports of Colorado artisans, both makers of gourmet food products and those who work in pottery, glass, or fabric arts. A top seller is Betsy Bingham Johns'elk-, moose-, flower-, and fish-themed pottery dinnerware that suits the mountain lifestyle and its currently popular décor. In addition to special orders and cooking advice, The Kitchen Cupboard has a wedding registry, makes gift baskets, produces an annual catalog that comes out each fall, and puts on three sales a year, the big one between Christmas and New Year's and smaller ones in spring and fall.

The Kitchen Cupboard, 207 Basalt Center Circle, Basalt; (970) 927-3634.

The Kitchen Loft

If you need a package of nails, some putty, a bag of potting soil, a gallon of paint, a saw, and a wire whisk, you can enjoy one-stop shopping in the Miner's Building. The main level and basement sell hardware supplies, and the mezzanine contains The Kitchen Loft, which offers such practical things as small appliances, Pyrex storage containers, kitchen clocks, flatware sets, and a small battery of cooking utensils and accessories. It also carries pewter, glassware, table linens, area rugs, Italian pottery, a riot of brightly colored Fiestaware, and a sweet line of Polish pottery. And, if you need a little help from above for your next dinner party, there's a Bible corner on the same floor.

The Kitchen Loft, 319 East Main Street, Aspen; (970) 925-5550.

Les Chefs d'Aspen

A corner store in the historic heart of downtown Aspen is filled with both practical and fun items for cooking and serving. In this most elegant and aggressively decorated town, the top kitchen shop shows its considerable inventory in what looks like randomness. It isn't random, of course, just full of great stuff stacked on tables, on glass shelves, on wire shelves, hanging on the wall or from the ceiling, or suspended from any other available space. Rambling through a series of small rooms, this family-owned retail shop sells all manner of quality cooking utensils and kitchen gadgetry. Leading brands prevail. Considering the space limitations, the store manages to show profusions of just about every category.

In addition to the pots and pans, accessories, and appliances for the kitchen, the store carries a large line of elegant Christofle flatware. Keep looking and you'll find a wall of candles, shelves of party goods, a bright display of Majolica, barware, gourmet grocery items and seasonings (a number of them local), coffee blends, stoneware, and more. Upstairs is the baking room crammed with tins, baking and roasting pans, molds, cookie sheets, pastry tubes, racks, measuring cups of all sorts, kids' cupcake-making kits, and turkey platters, even when it's not Thanksgiving. Another upstairs room is full of table linens, tableware, and year-round holiday items. Christmas stuff is major.

When *Travel/Holiday* magazine's super shopper Suzy Gershman profiled Aspen shopping opportunities, she cited the store for "a huge array of all things Calphalon or Cuisinart, as well as inventive, international touches, such as vintage silver-plate French flatware, pieces of Italian Vietri pottery, and hand-painted platters from Zimbabwe." That, in a proverbial nutshell, summarizes the store's variety—and of course, it carries nutcrackers too. Les Chefs d'Aspen maintains strong ties with the most kitchen-savvy and cooking-crazy Aspenites, whether resident or visiting, by offering a 10 percent discount to Cooking School of Aspen students.

Les Chefs d'Aspen, 405 South Hunter Street, Aspen; (970) 925-6217 or (800) 769-6226.

Wines

Aspen Wine & Spirit Company

This all-purpose store carries spirits, beer, and lots of wine—domestic and imported wines, by the jug, by the bottle, by the case, or presumably by the carload. There's everything from basic and budget to high-end and exclusive. Located next to Clark's Market, it offers convenience as well as selection and variety.

Aspen Wine & Spirit Company, 300 Puppy Smith Street, Aspen; (970) 925-6600 or www.aspen.com/wineandspirit.

Of Grape and Grain

This tiny shop is big time in the wine world. It has racked up more than 80 percent of its sales in wines since its opening in 1975—quite remarkable for those early days.

Founder and owner Gary Plumley, who laughs that "it's a long time to have the same job," is important in the world also as the instigator of Aspen/Snowmass International Wine Classic, which became the *Food & Wine* Magazine Classic at Aspen (see page 326).

Plumley watched the festival grow, but he has kept his business modest. Now in its second (and presumably permanent) location, its modest 1,200 square feet are stocked with spirits, beer, and (overwhelmingly) wine. The small store's wooden shelves are loaded with about half domestic and half imported wines. Domestic wines are shelved by varietal, and imports by region. Those coveted sale bottles are grouped in the middle of the store. Wines from pricey collectible selections to sale bottles priced at less than $10 fill the store. It is also chock full of knowledge. Plumley and the people who work for him fan out on annual trips to wine country, where they visit wineries, talk to wine makers, sample wines, and come back full of impressions and knowledge, especially about what Plumley calls "less than mainstream wines." From the north of Italy to the south of France to the Pacific Northwest of the United States, Of Grape and Grain has been there.

One practice that regular patrons truly treasure, as they have for over a quarter of a century, is that Of Grape and Grain marks prices on the bottles with wax china markers than come off easily, rather than those sticky labels that always leave a gummy residue. It's a small nicety, when you bring wine as a host or hostess gift, or put it on your own table, to have a clean bottle. Of Grape and Grain does occasional wine-tasting dinners, usually at Willow Creek Bistro (see page 325).

Of Grape and Grain, 319 East Hopkins Avenue, Aspen; (970) 925-8600.

Recipes

Charles Dale, the award-winning chef who established Renaissance Restaurant, then Rustique Bistro, and later Range, has this favorite on the menu at Rustique, where it is listed as "Risotto from My Childhood." Considering that a good part of his early childhood was spent in the Royal Palace in Monaco, you can figure that this recipe is meant for royalty. Rustique Bistro offers daily variations on the risotto theme. Here is the popular mushroom version.

Risotto from My Childhood

2 tablespoons sweet butter, divided
1 white onion, peeled and finely diced
½ pound arborio rice (an Italian short-grain rice)
½ cup dry white wine, plus a dash extra

4 cups chicken stock (reserve ¼ cup)
1 teaspoon salt (or to taste)
2 tablespoons olive oil
2 pounds assorted mushrooms (shiitake, chanterelle, portobello, etc.), sliced
2 shallots, peel and minced
1 garlic clove, peeled and minced
1 tablespoon fresh rosemary and thyme, chopped
salt and pepper to taste
2 tablespoons heavy cream
¼ cup grated Parmigiano-Reggiano cheese

In a stainless steel coated, 4-quart saucepot, melt 1 tablespoon butter. Add onion and sweat over medium heat. Add rice and stir to toast lightly, but not color deeply. When the rice feels dry and is just about to stick, add ½ cup white wine and stir until absorbed, about one minute. From the 4 cups of chicken stock, immediately add enough to barely cover the rice, stirring constantly. When stock is absorbed, add more stock, again enough to cover rice, and also add the salt, stirring. Repeat until all the liquid is absorbed, and the rice is *al dente*. Set aside briefly.

In another saucepan, heat olive oil over high heat. Sauté mushrooms until they soften and give up their liquid, stirring frequently. Stir in shallots, garlic, and herbs; stir briefly. Add remaining splash of wine, and stir until absorbed into mushroom mixture. Add a small amount of stock to moisten, and salt and pepper to taste. Keep warm.

Return the saucepot of risotto to the heat. Stir in the reserved ¼ cup of chicken stock. Add reserved 1 tablespoon of butter along with cream and cheese. Correct seasoning with salt and pepper, and serve in a bowl, topped with sautéed mushrooms. Serve optional additional freshly grated Parmesan cheese. Serves 8.

Rob Seideman, founder of the Cooking School of Aspen, has a quiver of treasured recipes that he cooks himself and uses in his classes. Here is a quick but colorful, and even luxurious, recipe for shrimp on greens that he says is a favorite among favorites.

Pan-Seared Shrimp over Greens with Sambuca Dressing

1 bag assorted prewashed salad greens (available in supermarkets)
1 pint fresh whole strawberries (preferably with stems on),
    rinsed and sliced into fans
1 pound medium or large shrimp, peeled and deveined
1 cup Sambuca

Dressing:
½ cup grapeseed oil
juice of 1 lemon

½ tablespoon mustard
1 shallot, peeled and small-diced
¼ cup rice vinegar
salt and freshly ground black pepper to taste

Place greens in four plates, and garnish the perimeters with sliced strawberries. In a fry pan, heat just enough grapeseed oil to coat the bottom of the pan. Over medium-high heat, fry shrimp on one side until golden brown. (Take care not to stir-fry. Just let shrimp cook undisturbed.) With tongs, turn shrimp, and fry on other side until golden brown. (Take care not to overcook.)

On four plates, place shrimp equally over greens. Without returning pan to burner, add Sambuca to deglaze, then set over reduced heat. Meanwhile, whisk together dressing ingredients.

When Sambuca is reduced to almost a glaze, add dressing to pan. Continue reducing until desired consistency (about half the initial amount). Pour dressing generously over salads, including a drizzle over the strawberries. Serves 4.

Grand Junction and the Grand Valley

Grand Junction is western Colorado's de facto capital—the largest city, shopping mecca, transportation hub, and college town. Its charming and historic downtown boasts delightful retail stores, numerous government offices, several good places to eat (alas, often only open for breakfast and lunch), and an invitingly landscaped main street. While it is lively during the day, downtown quiets down early on most evenings, but the framework is there for a happening place, both for great food and great entertainment.

The city also is the gateway to Colorado's highest profile and most significant agricultural area—agribusinesses and grains on the eastern plains notwithstanding. Just east of Grand Junction is Palisade, the epicenter of Colorado's fabulous stone-fruit orchards, most of them family-owned. Apricots, cherries, nectarines, plums, and, above all, peaches thrive in the hot summers, mild winters, and irrigated fields of the Grand Valley.

In addition to orchards and the occasional truck farm growing vegetables and herbs (many organic), the Grand Valley boasts numerous vineyards and on-site wineries. South of Grand Junction, the Delta-Olathe area is known primarily for fabulous sweet corn, and northeast of those towns (and still close to Grand Junction) is the Paonia-Cedaredge-Eckert area with, yes, more orchards, more farms, and more vineyards. The three top culinary events in the immediate Grand Junction area respectively celebrate local peaches and regional wines. The Palisade area has been called the Rocky Mountains' Garden of Eden, and that's not really too far off the mark.

With bountiful fresh produce that both home cooks and professional chefs swoon over, you might think that Grand Junction also abounds in good restaurants. Alas, it is not yet Colorado's answer to California's Napa or Sonoma Valleys. This growing city of roughly 100,000 people still lags in terms of fine dining and chefs able and willing to put out innovative, contemporary cuisine. At this writing, much the town's best food is found in a few ethnic eateries and several bakery-café combos.

Still, there is hope. One first-rate restaurant, Chefs' New World Cuisine, has won awards excellent, offers sophisticated fare, and has developed a loyal following. If local foodies are fortunate, more will follow. Perhaps graduates of Mesa State College's culinary program are or soon will be ready to raise the bar in local dining options. An excellent cookware store and classes for home cooks also help increase culinary awareness. Many of the Grand Junction area's newcomers show up with palates intact and presumably seeking more great places to eat. Let's hope they are soon able to find them.

Bakeries

The Cake Cottage

The Cake Cottage specializes in elegant wedding cakes, customized birthday cakes on any theme, or even great off-the-shelf (or, rather, from-the-case) cookies and pastries. The store is simple, but the cakes are complex. They include 3-D cakes in the shapes of teapots, dolls, ships, cars and many other subjects. All are made to order, with free-hand design of considerable imagination and artistry. Cake flavors include Carrot Walnut, Italian Coconut Cream, Chocolate Fudge, White Almond, Hazelnut Torte, White Chocolate Pound Cake, and Chocolate Mousse Cake. Each one is augmented by the ideal filling, topped with fine icing, and perhaps sprinkled with chopped nuts or shaved chocolate. The execution is positively artistic.

The Cake Cottage also offers beautiful muffins (and who would have thought that a muffin could be a thing of beauty?), several types of classic French pastries, some Italian pastries, or cookies. The Italian fruit tarts, made with a cookie crust, pastry cream, and apricot glaze, are noteworthy. For something simpler, The Cake Cottage also does Florentines, lemon bars, and other fairly plain cookies. There are a few tables and carry-out service.

The Cake Cottage, Village North Plaza, 2889 North Avenue, Grand Junction; (970) 244-8672.

The Crystal Café and Bake Shop

Caryl Rudofsky, a self-confessed "lapsed nurse," started baking since she was a child in a Minnesota Scandinavian family. While she was still in nursing, her husband, Harley, managed a Denver jazz club. When he decided to open for brunch, she started cooking. Eventually they moved to Lake City, where they operated the Crystal Lodge for 16 years and in 1994, they migrated to Grand Junction, where they opened a bakery and café named after their previous business.

The Rudofskys like to travel, often to Italy, where Caryl always tries to take a cooking class. She slowly began infusing the Crystal Café's menu with Mediterranean touches. "I like the clean flavors of the Mediterranean," she says. "They use wonderful fresh things, especially the best from their summer gardens." And so does she. The first-rate baked goods put the Crystal Café on the map, but the medley of made-from-scratch breakfast and lunch dishes—some with clear Mediterranean roots and others with the spirit of freshness and simplicity—have kept it there.

Locals and visitors alike start the day with sumptuous glazed muffins, huge cinnamon rolls or pecan rolls, handmade bagels, sensational scones, and more. (Save the brownies, available in several flavors, and the cakes, tarts, cookies and other baked treats for later in the day.) There's usually a line for the bakery section of the long, deep space, so if you have time, sit down at a butcher-block–top table, enjoy the same setting, and sample some of the foods, straight from the kitchen.

Breakfast entrées include pancakes, French toast, omelettes, and other egg specialties, a veggie scramble, and a house-made granola. If you order toast or a roll or a scone, know that the peach, apricot, strawberry, or sour cherry jam that comes with it is also house-made—and of organic fruits. Even the Western Slope's occasional gray day is brightened with a cup of coffee and pastry in front of you and diffused light coming from the domed skylight overhead.

Lunch includes hot and cold sandwiches, from-scratch soups, salads, quiches, and those tempting desserts. If there's something you have your heart set on, come early. Caryl, her thrifty Scandinavian roots rising to the surface, prepares no more than she thinks will sell because, "I'd run rather out than waste." The Crystal Café also offers a few varieties of wine by the glass or bottle, a small selection of microbrews, and a handful of unusual bottled waters, fresh squeezed lemonade, natural soft drinks, and cider—fine accompaniments to the sprightly menu choices.

The Crystal Café and Bake Shop, 314 Main Street, Grand Junction; (970) 242-8843.

Main Street Bagels

In addition to 15 varieties of bagels that give the business its name, this big, lively bakery and café in the heart of downtown Grand Junction makes such artisan breads as baguette, country sourdough, walnut raisin, olive, Asiago cheese, ciabatta, classic French, country rye, rosemary, multigrain, challah, and assorted specials. They are available by the loaf, and they make fine sandwiches as well, as do the bagels.

The breads are made fresh daily, and the bagels are baked hourly, which is pretty much a hectic New York pace rather than one typical of laid-back western Colorado. The deli and bakery occupy one half of this double storefront, and the restaurant takes up the other. A full juice and smoothie bar and a selection of gourmet coffee drinks round out the picture. A second store is off Main Street.

Main Street Bagels, 559 Main Street, Grand Junction; (970) 241-2740, and 2486 Patterson Road, Grand Junction; (970) 241-9553.

Slice O' Life

After her marriage and a move to Colorado, North Dakota native Mary Lincoln started baking out of her home. "All of a sudden, the curtains parted, and I said, 'I could have a bakery.' I saw what was in front of my face," she recalls. She opened Slice O' Life in 1980, baking her from-scratch doughs and batters with natural products, long before this was a trend. Many of her recipes were handed down by her mother, grandmother, and family friends in North Dakota, as well as Grand Valley friends. The rest are derived from her own dreams, tinkered with, adjusted, and perfected.

Slice O' Life offers 11 different breads each week, including the signature, All-Grain. While not an artisan variety, this soft, multigrain sandwich bread serves as a foundation for a sandwich made on the spot to eat in or take out. Other breads include banana-nut, pumpkin, and vegetable, a vitamin- and mineral-rich loaf made with carrots, red onion, green pepper, and assorted grains, seeds, herbs, and honey.

The bakery uses every local fruit in pies, and turns out toothsome cookies, mouth-watering breakfast pastries, and delicious bar cookies. Salted Peanut Chews, Hello Dollies, Berry Cups, North Dakota–style rhubarb bars, individual bread puddings, Australian cream buns, and more emerge from Spice O' Life's ovens. The house specialty is Mary's Cheesecake, made with semi-sweet chocolate chips on top. Harvest time is also fresh fruit pie time, and Mary also freezes local fruit in season to use later, but that's as far as she will go in straying from her all-fresh ways.

Her children grew up in the bakery. Daughter Anna worked there until she got a full-time government job. Son Curt started making ice cream sandwiches when he was 11, using Slice O' Life's butter wafers filled with his own ice cream. When Mary's husband, Tim, turned a growing fruitcake operation over to Curt, he passed the ice-cream sandwiches down to younger brother Matt.

The sandwiches remain a popular hometown treat, and the fruitcakes have taken on a life of their own as successful mail-order gift products. The recipe—a blend of local peaches, pears, plums, apples, and cherries soaked in a blend of fresh apple juice and rum—is fine enough to redeem the reputation of the holiday fruitcake. To showcase Palisade peaches, Slice O' Life's fabulous Peachcake is an amalgam of sweet peaches steeped in rum and orange juice and baked into a rich almond-butter batter. The mail order operation sells these and also handles other local gourmet food products. But there's nothing like stopping in this informal bakery, filled with great scents, ordering a pastry or a sandwich, and sitting at one of the simple tables in the front of the store while all of Palisade stops in for something fresh from the oven that probably harkens back to Mary Lincoln's North Dakota past.

Slice O' Life, 105 West Third Street, Palisade; (970) 464-0577, (866) 4646-0577, or www.sliceolifebakery.com.

Cooking School and Cooking Classes

Carol's Food & Gifts

Carol Leinberger started teaching Asian cooking back in 1976, and while she now runs the most important Asian grocery store in western Colorado (see page 346), she still conducts evening classes about every three weeks in the winter. Call it building a new customer base, if you like, or realize that she loves to teach and is good at it.

The participation classes take place in the big professional kitchen in the back of the store. In a basic class, she introduces an Asian salad, rice, and two or three entrées to cover the most fundamental and simplest techniques. Typically, these are dishes familiar to Westerners, such as kung pao chicken and "something fried," perhaps a sweet-and-sour dish or other popular standby.

She customizes classes, either to a particular regional cuisine or to a level of complexity beyond basic. She promotes what she calls party classes, typically five couples who view cooking and eating as both entertainment and as a chance to get together and socialize with friends. And isn't that what good cooking is all about?

Carol's Food & Gifts, 2814 North Avenue, Grand Junction; (970) 245-3286.

The Country Cook

Tom Favor, Grand Junction's Country Cook, zealously spreads the word about classic cuisine, especially French country, Italian country, and Cajun, the latter a specialty and a particular passion. He's been on local television. He teaches well-attended adult-education classes organized through Parks & Recreation. And he holds custom classes in his own kitchen. To take the academic formality out of the situation, he calls them "visits" to his home. Most are demonstration classes, with students seated around a huge kitchen table and Favor presiding over the workstation on a higher countertop, which he jokingly refers to as "the pulpit."

While he uses such light verbal touches that made him a successful salesman, he now preaches the gospel of great, simple foods prepared with the underpinnings of classic technique. "We have an amazing breadth of food resources in the valley," he says, noting that since moving to Grand Junction in 1998, he is astonished at how few locals are cognizant of the abundance or really take advantage of it in their own cooking.

Favor grew up in Wheat Ridge, attended Mesa State University, worked around the world, and became interested in food. While living in Arizona, he realized that he really wanted a career as a chef. "I was 38 when I entered a professional kitchen for the first time," he says of his epiphany. He left the corporate world to shuck oysters at a Cajun restaurant for $4 an hour and moved from restaurant to restaurant to learn from one chef after another. He gravitated toward French kitchens and French chefs, which provided everything that he was looking for. This exposure to this cuisine inspired a number of trips to the French countryside to experience firsthand the national dishes and the personalities of the people who prepared them.

After he and his wife, Nancy, returned to Colorado and settled in Grand Junction, Favor began musing, "I wonder if anyone else wants to learn what I've learned." It turns out that they do. He has developed about 50 Country Cook programs, which appeal primarily to competent home cooks who want to extend their culinary and creative range. Among his popular programs are holiday menus beyond the stuffed turkey with traditional fixin's; "Carnivores' Carnival," focusing on meat recipes; and "Mexican Fiesta," which introduces more refined classics than Tex-Mex favorites. Each of his classes—I mean, visits—includes an appetizer, an entrée with suitable accompaniments, and a dessert.

The Country Cook; for information, call (970) 858-8845
or e-mail thecountrycook@onlinecol.com.

Mesa State College

This Grand Junction college offers the region's only professional culinary training program. Called the Colorado Culinary Academy, it meets American Culinary Federation requirements and includes National Restaurant Association Professional Management Development courses. Graduates earn the associate of applied science degree and also a Certificate of Occupational Proficiency. The culinary program is offered at the Tilman Bishop Unified Technical Education Campus, so if you hear locals talking about the UTEC culinary school, it is the same thing.

Technical cooking and baking classes are held in a state-of-the-art kitchen and bakery. Other courses include dining room management, menu planning, food service supervision, cost controls, purchasing, marketing, and computer applications for food service. Students put this combination of kitchen and classroom skills into play at Chez Lena, a full-service public breakfast and lunch restaurant.

Mesa State College, UTEC, 2508 Blichmann Avenue, Grand Junction; (970) 255-2600, (888) 455-2617, or www.mesastate.edu

Dining

Il Bistro Italiano

Brunella Gualerzi comes from the Italian village of Bibbiano, located where the Pianura Padana meets the Apennine Mountains—rather like the greater Grand Junction area where the agricultural land of the Grand Valley butts up against the Grand Mesa. It is the land of Parmesan, prosciutto, and porcini—respectively among the planet's best cheese, ham, and mushrooms. She and her husband, Ron Hall, bring these traditions to Grand Junction to Il Bistro Italiano, and indeed, it is *the* Italian bistro in Grand Junction, serving contemporary and traditional Italian food. The décor is mostly modern, with marbleized walls, updated Mission-style chairs, a wavy ceiling, and suspended halogen lighting. The straw-wrapped Chianti bottles on the tables come across as retro chic, not a cliché.

Lunch features a small selection of starters, a bigger choice of salads, a large offering of *panini* on fresh-baked focaccia, an even greater choice of fresh pasta, and enough desserts to last through the afternoon. The dinner menu loses the *panini* but adds more appetizers (including a very good cheese platter with roasted peppers and balsamic-cured onions) and a couple of excellent soups (artichoke-Parmesan is a house specialty). Pastas include various shapes, sauces, and all sorts of combinations, from a trendy mélange of prosciutto, shrimp, avocado, and cream sauce flavored with white wine and thyme over pasta to such classics as Bolognese lasagna.

On the small entrée list, veal is the meat of choice, chicken prepared various ways is the poultry, and there is usually one fish. Interesting house-made pizzas are served with salad. Desserts include profiteroles, tiramisu, bread pudding, chocolate cake,

---

Ristorante Numero Uno

Pantuso's Ristorante, established in 1962, claims to be the oldest Italian restaurant between Denver and Las Vegas. It is located on Crossroads Boulevard, behind the Grand Vista Hotel in Grand Junction.

---

parfaits, and *panna cotta* bring satisfaction to the sweet tooth. The wines are mostly from Tuscany and other regions of Italy, and Caffe LaVazza is freshly brewed. The final Italian touch? The check comes with Pantini, small, chewy, and deeply flavored candies.

Don't leave Il Bistro Italiano without Gualerzi's fresh-baked bread and house-made pasta (tomato, spinach, chestnut, tomato-basil, and buckwheat), available at a retail sales counter at the front of the restaurant.

Il Bistro Italiano, 400 Main Street, Grand Junction; (970) 243-8622.

Chefs' New World Cuisine

A low and undistinguished building along a major arterial houses Grand Junction's first culinary oasis. Chefs' New World Cuisine serves arguably the best food in town. The name recognizes United States' assimilation of many different cultures, and Chefs' combines many flavors, ingredients, and cooking styles in often nontraditional ways. The restaurant, in short, does fusion cuisine without exactly calling it that.

Lyndal Hunt and Dave Dame met at Arizona's Scottsdale Culinary Institute, and graced Grand Junction with cuisine of the quality and complexity that previously had been lacking. With artwork on the walls and soft jazz in the background, the soothing décor provides a subdued background for the food. The walls are peach, the linens and tableware are simple and stylish, and the service is so prompt and still unhurried that relaxation rules. No matter how hectic the day or searing the summer heat, the atmosphere at Chefs' is calming and (in summer) cooling.

Chef Lyndal Hunt sends out a small *amuse-bouche,* a tiny taster from the kitchen, And Sommelier Dave Dame, who runs the front of the house with graciousness and aplomb, presents the wine list. Will it be a California wine, the region that dominates the list, or a selection from France, New Zealand, Austria, or Colorado?

The dinner menu, which changes every six to eight weeks, is modest in size but major in quality. It includes about four appetizers, half-a-dozen items on the soup and salad list, eight or 10 entrées, and a handful of desserts, with seasonal products used when possible.

To start, should it be New Zealand green-lip mussels in Thai coconut curry? Cucumber and beet salad with yogurt-mint dressing? Or perhaps Caesar salad with Chefs' dressing? There are almost as many preparation methods and presentations as there are entrées. On a recent menu, beef tenderloin filet, swordfish, and chicken breast were grilled, while the salmon was crusted with sesame seeds and served over salad, the halibut was steamed in vegetable juices and lemon *en papillote*, and the veal was simmered in a ratatouille and served over pasta. The dessert menu features similarly varied offerings. At the end of the hot day when I visited, I could think of nothing better than house-made ice cream and sorbet with fresh fruit.

Chefs' New World Cuisine, 936 North Avenue, Grand Junction; (970) 243-9673 or www.gjchefs.com.

The Winery

When The Winery opened in 1973, its name was prescient. The wine industry was not even a spot on the western Colorado horizon—and The Winery's quality beef and spuds, served on substantial wood-topped tables in a comfortable, clubby restaurant, were considered the epitome of a good meal. In the intervening decades, wines and wineries have flowered, and Colorado culinary sensibilities have skyrocketed, but quality beef and spuds are still, well, the meat and potatoes of business at The Winery.

The dinner-only restaurant is tucked into an alley just off Main Street. Beyond the heavy, carved-oak door is a foyer paneled with wine-case ends. Dark barnwood covers the bar and dining room walls, with light filtered through a collection of gorgeous stained-glass windows providing much of the illumination. Wine barrels and a few hanging plants bring the high-ceilinged dining room down to scale.

The focused dinner menu features a few appetizers, several cuts and sizes of premium-quality aged beef, a little pork and lamb, a couple of seafood entrées, and a small selection of popular desserts. Order an appetizer or stroll over to the salad bar and bring your heaped plate back to your table. Notice that you're eating off lovely, mostly-blue pottery dinnerware, with "The Winery" discreetly etched into a corner of each plate. There may be two alike, but it doesn't seem that way. Local potter Jeff Pike custom-makes this dinnerware.

Strangely, close inspection of The Winery's 150-item wine list reveals that it is very light on Colorado vintages—at least at this writing; California selections predominate, with France, Australia, and Washington also represented. Additionally, The Winery pours Ports from Portugal and Sauternes from France with or instead of dessert.

The Winery, 642 Main Street (Seventh and Main), Grand Junction; (970) 242-1000.

Events

Grand Valley Spring Barrel Tasting

May—In 2003, eight leading wineries from the designated Grand Valley American Viticultural Area participated in the first annual barrel tasting, a preview event of young wines from each to enables you to better understand the winemaking process. Participants purchasing a two-day Tasting Passport ($50 the first year) were entitled to on-site tastings at and tours of all the wineries, food pairings, and a monogrammed souvenir wine glass, plus a 20 percent discount on wines and gift items purchased during the event. Those visiting all eight wineries additionally were entered in a contest for eight wine-oriented grand prizes. Lodging specials in the Grand Junction/Palisade area are offered for Barrel Tasting guests.

Details are available from the Grand Valley Winery Association, P.O. Box 99, Palisade, CO 81526-0099; (970) 464-5867, (303) 399-7586, or www.winebarreltasting.com.

Viva El Vino

May—Viva El Vino, which benefits the Junior Service League of Grand Junction, an appropriately name for a lively event that ushers out spring and welcomes summer nearby Colorado wine country. Launched in 1990, when Colorado's wine industry was in its infancy, the festival also gives wineries an opportunity to showcase the year's new releases.

Viva El Vino's schedule promises "wine, food, and music." Roughly 900 people attend the event that typically takes place on a Saturday evening at the Adam's Mark Hotel. It spreads from hotel function rooms to the patio and to tents set up on the lawn. Food and wine tasting stations intermingle, making it easier to mix the hotel's hors d'ouvres and suitable wines. In addition to Viva El Vino, the league also produces a well-regarded cookbook as a fundraiser.

To purchase tickets, check at Fisher's Liquor Barn, 2438 F. Road; Gift Baskets Galore, 2454 Highways 6 and 50; Unique Expressions, 336 Main Street; and Coronado Liquors, 569 32 Road; or contact the Junior Service League; (970) 243-7790 or www.westoftherockies.org.

Peach Fest

August—The Grand Valley grows some of the best peaches in America, and Palisade is unquestionably the state's peach capital. Not long after John and Jean Harlow planted Palisade's first peach trees in 1882, early valley families to start partying around the peach. Nobody knows precisely when celebrations started, but town records indicate that Peach Days were popular as long ago as the 1880s, and the modern festival started in 1968.

This usually sleepy rural town roars into sweet life at the annual three-day Peach Fest. Today it's more than just peaches. Community organizations and food purveyors, including a number of Grand Junction's best, set up booths and provide lots of live entertainment. The event generally kicks off with free peach ice cream and a street dance on Thursday evening. Merriment continues on Friday evening with a barbecue dinner buffet and band concert.

Saturday is the big day, beginning with the Lion's Club Breakfast and ending with an evening benefit concert. Between are a downtown parade, the much-anticipated

Big Beauty Peach Contest, and the even more anticipated announcement of the winner of Town Grouch "honors."

The food lovers' highlight is the annual Palisade Peach Fest Recipe Contest. Traditional categories are Pies, Cakes, & Tortes; Miscellaneous Desserts; and Non-Dessert Miscellaneous, which could include peach soups, salsas, sauces, chutneys, and such. The three top places in each category earn cash prizes, and a professional category was most recently added. The contest entry form is available on the festival's website—as are winning recipes from past contests.

Palisade Peach Fest, c/o Palisade Chamber of Commerce, 319 Main Street, P.O. Box 729, Palisade, CO 81526; (970) 464-7458 or www.palisadepeachfest.com.

Colorado Mountain Winefest

September—With the explosive growth of the Colorado wine industry, the Colorado Mountain Winefest, held annually on the third weekend of September, has grown right along with it. It is now one of the premier wine events in Colorado and is gaining in importance in all the West. Since it began in 2001with just a handful of wineries it , now includes some two dozen wineries and 5,000 guests.

Friday evening wine-maker dinners take place in several area restaurants, giving chefs and restaurateurs the opportunity to show off their finest creations and presentation to match the best Colorado wines that accompany these feasts. Collectively called the Grand Harvest Celebration, these dinners always sell out, so book early if you're interested. Local establishments hosting these dinner in 2002 were the Adam's Mark Hotel, Il Bistro Italian, Chateau at Two Rivers, Chefs' New World Cuisine, Chez Lena at the Colorado Culinary Academy, and La Dolce Vita.

Saturday festivities begin at 8:00 A.M. with something typically Colorado, even in the context of wine and food: a bike ride. The annual Bike Tour of the Vineyards attracts 1,000 cyclists who pedal through Colorado's wine country on a 25-mile ride past the area's wineries, fruit orchards, and vineyards.

The Festival in the Park (Palisade Park, that is) begins around 11:00 A.M., about the time the cyclists come rolling in. Winery representatives present their wines, chefs demonstrate their specialties, and there are an ice carving demonstration, wine competitions, and even a grape stomping contest, all to the accompaniment of live jazz or other music. Professional and amateur wine makers compete for medals and bragging rights in the realm of Colorado wines. Commercial wineries compete in Best of the BEST, Fruit Wine, Red Wine, White Wine, and Rosé Wine categories. Amateurs compete in all but the Rosé Wine category. A panel of judges awards gold, silver, and bronze medals.

Culinary demonstrations were introduced to the Colorado Mountain Winefest in 2000. Guest chefs at these Saturday afternoon demonstrations included Mike Pizzuto, consultant to the School of Culinary Arts, the Cook Street School of Fine Cooking, and the American Culinary Federation; Robert Emiltzer, executive chef at The Palace Arms in The Brown Palace Hotel; Chris Rybak, food and beverage director at Keystone and president of the ACF Culinarians of Colorado; Darran Herbst, executive chef at Denver's Metropolitan Club; and Greg Seever, executive chef at the

Front Street Café in Fairplay. The festival concludes with the Winefest Heart Gala, a jovial and stylish Saturday-night dinner that proves that heart-healthy food can be very tasty. This semiformal, multicourse dinner held at the Bookcliff Country Club includes Colorado wines, live entertainment, and an auction.

Colorado Mountain Winefest coincides with harvest time on the Western Slope, so area wineries, which always welcome visitors, add other incentives to stop by. Tasting rooms are open. The art of winemaking is explained, and some of the wineries provide entertainment and appetizers too. And if you buy a few bottles or cases of wine, you'll make them really happy. Sunday has its serious side too, with a seminar on grape growing in Colorado or some other meaty (or should I say, fruity?) topic.

The Colorado Mountain Winefest is an à la carte event, with separate tickets for all components. Reservations for the wine-makers' dinners must be made with the individual restaurants, so check the website or call (800) 704-3667 for the current year's participants. For details on registering for the Tour of the Vineyards, contact Event Marketing Group, (303) 635-2815 or www.emgcolorado.com. Advance tickets for the Festival in the Park are available at numerous Western Slope wineries and selected Front Range wine specialty retailers and liquor stores, or can be ordered by phone or on-line from the Colorado Mountain Winefest (below).

Colorado Mountain Winefest, 2180 Meadow Court, Grand Junction, CO 81503; (800) 704-3667 or www.coloradowinefest.com. Reservations for the Winefest Heart Gala can be made at (970) 241-4577.

Apple Jubilee!

October—The Museum of Western Colorado operates Cross Orchards Historic Farm, a living history museum that honors and documents early–20th-century life in orchard country. You can explore the original bunkhouse, barn, and apple orchards. Fresh apple cider and traditional apple dishes are featured at the annual Apple Jubilee!, established in 1979. It now includes hay-wagon rides, a pumpkin patch, and, in the spirit of living history, demonstrations of ice-cream making, butter churning, and cooking on a wood stove. There is a modest admission charge .

Cross Orchards Historic Farm, 3073 F Road, Grand Junction; (970) 434-9814, (970) 242-0972, (888) 488-3466, or www.wcmuseum.org.

March of Dimes Star Chefs

November—The Grand Junction portion of the March of Dimes annual Star Chefs gala (as described in detail in the Denver Events section) finishes up the four-night, four-location series in Grand Junction in November. Participating local chefs in 2002 were Lyndal Hunt of Chefs' New World Cuisine, Massimo Perucchini of La Dolce Vita, Deborah Perrone of The Cake Cottage, Dina Tarasciwicz and Holly Garcia of DMT Culinary Adventures Catering, Wayne Smith of the Colorado Culinary Academy at Mesa State College, Case Bricker of Adam's Mark Hotel, Brett and Christie Antczak of NorthStar Catering and Distinctive Design, Kimberly Scott of

Odie's Fine Chocolates, Sterling Bock of Java Junction, and Mike Henderson of Marco's Pasta and Pizza.

March of Dimes Western Slope Division, 518 28 Road, Suite A103, Grand Junction; (970) 243-0894, or www.marchofdimesco.org.

Retail

Carol's Food & Gifts

In Denver and even in smaller Front Range cities, there are Japanese grocers and Chinese grocers and Indian grocers and Thai grocers and so on. In Grand Junction, perhaps in all of western Colorado, there is Carol's. This large, immaculate store caters to Japanese, Chinese, Filipino, Hawaiian, and other Asian customers—and to non-Asians who have learned there is more to Asian ingredients than Kikkoman and La Choy. Carol's Food isn't a butcher shop or a greengrocer, but it is a commendably comprehensive source for other Asian staples of all sorts.

Carol Leinberger, whose own heritage is Japanese, requires that with very few exceptions, the products she carries all are labeled in English in addition to the countries of origin. Sacks of all kinds of rice, a staple in so many cuisines, get deserved attention and space. The shelves are laden with a mind-boggling array of soy sauces, because the Japanese, Chinese, and Hawaiian styles are so very different. The same goes for fish sauces, spices, teas, and other seasonings, nuts and seeds, packaged or in bulk. Cans of seafood products, preserved products, special produce, and more invite serious study, but the store also stocks what she calls "general" Asian ingredients for Americans who aren't quite ready to plunge into totally unfamiliar food territory. Refrigerated and frozen specialty foods are also available.

The store carries an assortment of steamers, woks, specialty utensils, and especially rice cookers, and also a good selection of cookbooks with recipes of foods from various nations. Carol herself has been teaching Asian cooking since 1976 and has long operated this store to supply ingredients to her students. She still conducts classes (see page 339), but the retail store has become the focus of her efforts.

Carol's Food & Gifts, 2814 North Avenue, Grand Junction; (970) 245-3286.

Culinary Corner

Culinary Corner, established in 1981, occupies one of the Mesa Mall's major crossways and is chock-full of first-rate cookware, bakeware, knives, and kitchen gadgets. Regulars stop there just to see what's new (and something always is), and even casual browsers are lured in by the aroma of fresh espresso from the coffee bar at the front of the store. Partners Jackie Laumann and Beth Zasinski, hands-on owners who know their clientele well, fill their store with top brands of major items but also boast one of the best gadget inventories of any similar establishment in the state. Culinary Corner prides itself on being among the first stores to stock innovative accessories as soon as they come on the market.

What variety will you find there? Slant-bottom measuring cups so that the gauge is readable from above. Big-grip gadgets that are easy on anyone's hands and indispensable for a cook or baker with arthritis or other hand problems. Kake-Kut and Pie-Kut for even slices. Micro Egg Cups for cooking eggs to soft or hard "boiled" doneness in the microwave. Kebab skewers shaped like circles to fit on the grill better than the conventional straight ones—and kebab racks to elevate those standard straight skewers from the grill surface. An ingenious wok is designed to fit onto an outdoor grill. Pizza shears. Tablecloth weights for outdoor dining. Silicon whisks for nonstick pans. Microplanes in various sizes, including superzesters for soft cheeses. Retro-style, manual citrus juicers. Bud's Rollers, a line of handmade wooden rolling pins, including a tortilla roller made just for the store. Adjustable measuring spoons. Select-A-Spice. Individual springform pans, as well as the more common small tart pans. Whipped-cream dispensers. I could go on and on, because Culinary Corner's selections go on and on.

Of course, there is also mainstream kitchenware on Culinary Corner's stainless-steel shelves, including conventional and nonstick lines from such important makers as Calphalon and Scantel. Dough Makers' pebble-surface bakeware and soft silicon bakeware are recent concepts in fabrication that home bakers report on favorably, while waffles, sandwiches, and *pizzelle* cook outrageously well on InterBake by Villa Ware. Culinary Corner also stocks a large selection of Henckels knives and other necessities for any home cook, plus a way-above-average choice of canning supplies, a necessity for locals who take advantage of the Grand Valley's seasonal bounty.

While kitchen implements are the store's major focus, fine gourmet food products from local, domestic, and imported lines include flavored and plain olive oils, coffee from four suppliers including one from nearby Palisade, Torani syrups, designer teas, sauces, salsa, syrups, mixes, and much, much more from fine makers. Table and kitchen linens, locally made canister sets, and a snazzy line of acrylic trays, plates, and glasses add indoor and outdoor good looks to the Culinary Corner–stocked home.

You can tell that customers love to cook when you gaze at the cookbook shelves that are well-stocked and ever-changing, and note that the selection of recipe boxes, recipe cards, and other recipe organizers is enormous—signs that customers read recipes, prepare them, and share them, and another way that Laumann and Zasinki show how firmly they have their fingers on the pulse of Western Slope cooks.

Culinary Corner, Mesa Mall, 2424 U.S. Highways 50 and 6, Grand Junction; (970) 245-9892 or (800) 748-2841.

Enstrom Candies

You can buy Enstrom's renowned toffee by mail, phone, or the Internet (tens of thousands of customers do). You can find it at two Enstrom's retail stores in the Denver area. However, nothing beats a visit to Enstrom's immaculate Grand Junction plant, open weekdays from 7:30 to 3:30. Walk through the candy store and press your nose to the plate-glass window to watch Enstrom's toffee-meisters at work in the candy kitchen.

Mountains of butter by one-pound blocks, chocolate by the 10-pound mega-bar, cream by the barrel, sugar by the 100-pound sack, and almonds by the super-carton are turned into some of the best almond toffee on the planet before your eyes— 52 70-pound batches a day. The toffee is cooled, hand-cut, and hand-packed. No less an authority than the legendary Florence Fabricant raved in *The New York Times* that "the gold standard has to be Enstrom's Almond Toffee."

That has been true for decades. Chester K. "Chet" Enstrom started working at Bathel's Confectionary, an early Colorado Springs ice cream and candy maker. He had been hired for the ice cream operation, but candy was his interest, so he learned candy-making after his regular work hours at half-pay—"because," his boss said, "you're tired." In 1929 Enstrom and his bride, Vernie, loaded up their Model T and made their way to Grand Junction, where he cofounded Jones Enstrom Ice Cream Company. The siren song of candy remained strong, and on nights and weekends, Enstrom began experimenting to create the perfect toffee. Almond toffee proved to be the winner. Finally, in 1960, the Enstroms opened a mom-and-pop candy kitchen. Five years later, with production that had swelled to 10,000 pounds a year, their son and daughter-in-law, Emil and Mary Enstrom, joined the business. By 1979, Enstrom's was producing 65,000 pounds of toffee, and Chet and Vernie's granddaughter, Jamee, and her husband, Doug Simons, joined the business, which they now run.

The toffee, based on Grandpa Chet's recipe, is justifiably famous. *The Washington Post* wrote, "There's toffee. Then there's the rich, buttery, crushed-almond coated coffee that the Enstrom family has been making for more than 60 years." Toffee accounts for 70 percent of Enstrom's business, but their hand-rolled or hand-dipped candies— truffles and nut-filled or other centers bathed in milk, dark, or pastel-colored chocolate—are top-drawer too.

Enstrom Candies, 200 South Seventh Street, Grand Junction; (800) 367-8766, (970) 242-1655, or www.enstrom.com. Denver area retail stores are at 201 University Boulevard, Cherry Creek North, Denver; (303) 322-1005, and 14415 West Colfax, Lakewood; (303) 215-9905.

Lil' Ole Winemaker

If your travels around the Grand Valley's wine country inspire you to try your hand at winemaking, stop at this half-store on Grand Junction's Main Street. You'll find everything you need to start fermenting, perhaps a vintner's kit to get you going and a selection of books to tell you what to do. If you aren't pressing grapes, you can buy juice concentrates for Cabernet Sauvignon, Pinot Noir, Merlot, Ruby Cabernet, Pinot Noir, and others. When you get your wine in bottles, the Lil' Ole Winemaker will sell you corks, wine bottle tags, and customizable labels; when you're ready to drink it, you can select from an assortment of corkscrews, drip rings, and wine racks. If brewing beer is more your style, the Lil' Ole Winemaker has home-brewing supplies too.

The Lil' Ole Winemaker, 516 Main Street, Grand Junction; (970) 242-3754.

Palisade Pride

Palisade Pride shares a large store in Palisade's small downtown with a gift shop and a florist. In addition to retail, it is also packages dried local fruit—plain or dipped in white, milk, or dark chocolate as well as vanilla cream, caramel, or a combination. Snow Cherries, dried cherries dipped in white chocolate, and Peaches 'n Crème, dried peaches dipped in vanilla cream, are the line's signatures. Palisade Pride glazed local walnuts with milk and white satin or with cinnamon. The Fruit and Chocolate Fondue set includes dried pears, apples, and tart cherries, as well as dark chocolate, a melting glass, and even skewers.

These specialty foods are available elsewhere in the state, and by mail order, but this is where they are made. Other local products that take advantage of Palisade's abundant crops are cranberry-apple pie filling, Amaretto peach cake, spiced peaches, and cherry apple jelly. The store also carries other Western Slope gourmet foods.

Palisade Pride, 119 West Third Street, Palisade; (800) 777-4330, (970) 464-0719, or www.palisadepride.com.

Quality Meat Company

In 1946, John Emerson founded a meat wholesale business in Grand Junction. In 2000, his son, Phil, dipped tentatively into retailing, and in late 2002, he expanded the operation to give retail customers access to top-quality meat, game, and poultry, mostly from the Western Slope. The shop, a former meat locker, was redone in a simple "convenience store style," with refrigeration coils remaining on the ceiling as a reminder of what the space once was. Emerson and his crew cut meat and game the old-fashioned way, aging it for at least 21 days. Quality Meat carries a premium brand called Sterling Silver Beef, natural beef from Hotchkiss, elk from Paonia, natural pork from Cedaredge, local organic Rocky Mountain lamb, sausage from Craig, yak from Montrose, and organic, free-range poultry "all the way from Denver," says Emerson.

Additionally, the store is a year-round source for some 50 brands of Colorado-made jams, jellies, preserves, and other mom-and-pop products generally available only from seasonal farmstands. It also carries shade-grown Toucan Coffee, roasted in Palisade by a grower who owns a plantation in Colombia and roasts in Colorado.

Quality Meat Company, 340 North Avenue, Grand Junction; (970) 242-1872.

Sundrop Grocery

If a store like Sundrop were in Boulder, no one would blink an eye, but the existence of a thriving natural food market in downtown Grand Junction is remarkable. In fact, the store's ads even say, "Food like this in Grand Junction? You betcha!" It started as a classic granola-head kind of store. The health-conscious and home cooks looking to enhance their food by using ingredients made with minimal processing and minimal preservatives shop there, for the store's organic inventory passes the taste test too. Sundrop has a fantastic bulk food room for pasta, rice, vegetarian chili mix, beans, sea salt, various whole-grain flours, blue cornmeal, whole rye, and herbs and spices from agar-agar to yarrow flowers. Other lines of interest to cooks include such packaged products as seasonings from Spice Hunter and dried mushrooms under the Melissa's label. The store carries artisan breads from Main Street Bagels and traditional ones from Slice O' Life. The huge selection of oils and vinegars includes such gourmet exotica as truffle oil and Chianti vinegar. Pear Blossom Farms pickles and Palisade Gardens salsas and jams are lines that you don't see everywhere either.

The enterprise was established in 1978, but it took until 2001 to expand into prepared foods. In what Sundrop calls the Garden Deli, all dishes are vegetarian, and many are ethnic—and interesting. Tangy sesame noodles, chili rellenos, vegetarian lasagna, enchilada pie, Chilean empanadas, Vietnamese spring rolls, Hot Caribbean Cakes, Moroccan phyllo pockets, sun-dried tomato polenta, spanakopita, curry samosas, and a vegetable medley whimsically called "soycatash" are examples of the healthy prepared foods. Desserts can be delicious and nutritious, as demonstrated by Slice O' Life sweets and such interesting high-nutrition spins on ethnic foods as Soynut Spelt Baklava.

Sundrop Grocery, 321 Rood Avenue, Grand Junction; (970) 243-1175.

Talbott Farms and The Mine Shack

At first glance, Talbott's sprawling hilltop packing house looks like a fruit factory—and in a way, it is. The production line washes, sorts, packs, and ships truckloads of the Grand Valley's peaches, apples, pears, and other produce to markets near and far. It seems so impersonal—until you meet the Talbotts and see what four generations of knowledge about and passion for the fruit business mean. For visitors, it's also gratifying that the family saves some of the best produce to sell in their own on-site farmstore, called The Mine Shack, which seems to be an odd name for a produce store—until you remember that the Talbotts call their peaches "mountain gold."

The current operation is a straight-line descendent from a modest family farm. Joseph Yager came from Iowa to the Grand Valley in 1905 to grow peaches, one of numerous farmers to leave the corn and wheat fields of the Midwest for high, dry Colorado. Fourteen years later, Joseph's son Charlie, his wife, and three daughters, moved to Palisade, becoming the second generation of Yagers in the Colorado peach business.

One daughter, Margaret, took a shine to Harry A. Talbott, a young cowboy from Eckert who had signed on with a summer picking crew. They married, and Harry A. and sons established the foundation for what is now the Grand Valley's biggest grower and packer. One of those sons, Harry C. Talbott, *his* four sons, and assorted daughters-in-law and grandkids now operate the massive enterprise, which is really the 800-pound gorilla of Western Slope peach growers. At this writing, they operate some 40 orchards and vineyards on owned and leased land, pack and ship for themselves

---

Fabulous Farmstands

A ride through the Grand Valley or other Western Slope growing areas—on a bike or in a car—is a soul-satisfying Colorado experience. As long as the tentacles of housing development and suburban sprawl can be kept at bay, these vistas of authentic orchards, vineyards, and farms will remain.

Top chefs and dedicated home cooks all attribute the use of the freshest ingredients for the success of their best dishes, and you can't get much fresher than to buy from the growers. Some Grand Valley growers are certified organic, and all sell fresh-picked and tree- or vine-ripened produce. To buy directly from the growers, visit farmstands in the Grand Valley and elsewhere in the Grand Junction area. Some are located right at the orchard or farm; others are along a nearby main road.

Talbott Farms is unquestionably the region's big kahuna, but smaller local growers' family farmstands are truly worth a stop too. In addition to their own crops, some also carry outstanding jams, syrups, and other condiments, either their own or other mostly local brands. Most are open seasonally, but a very few are open year-round. Below are some growers to visit. Chat with them, learn about the Western Slope's bounty—and remember to buy some produce.

Alida's Fruits, 3402 C½ Road, Palisade; (970) 434-8769 or (877) 434-8769
Antelope Hill Fruit Farm, 3328 L-70 Drive, Eckert; (970) 835-3111
AppleShed, 250 Grand Mesa Drive, Cedaredge; (970) 856-7007
B2 Orchards, 3916 Hickman Road, Palisade; (970) 464-9441
Ball Fruit, 3806 G Road, Palisade; (970) 464-7370
Bikki Ranch of Liberty, 3848 G¼ Road, Palisade; (970) 464-7524
C&R Farms, 3620 F Road, Palisade; (970) 464-7544
Clark Family Orchards, 3901 G¼ Road, Palisade; (970) 464-5065 or (970) 464-7780
DeVries Farm Market, 3198 C Road, Grand Junction; (970) 434-4870
Excelsior Orchards, 1390 4280th Drive, Paonia; (970) 527-6860

---

and others, and produce up to 10,000 gallons a day of some of Colorado's finest blended cider.

The overwhelming majority of peaches grown in Colorado come from within 10 miles of Talbott's Orchard Mesa headquarters. They themselves grow 20 kinds of peaches, all timed to ripen sequentially between mid-July and early fall. The best are sold at The Mine Shack, a large store located in what was once Talbott's cider mill open from mid-July through mid-December. In addition to fresh-from-trees seasonal fruits and fresh-from-the-press cider, it sells such local and regional products as Ruth's Toffee from Bedrock, beans from Dove Creek, Palisade Gardens jams, and Vorhees Dried Fruit from down the street in Palisade. As an example of growers who complete a loop, a Gypsum beekeeper who brings his hives to Talbott's to pollinate the trees retrieves them and makes honey, which The Mine Shack then sells.

Fitzsimmons Red Barn Farm & Garden (known locally as Fitz's),
   3419 U.S. Highway 6, Clifton; (970) 434-1555
Fruit Basket, 253 32½Road, Grand Junction; (970) 434-5309
Gobbo 7 Produce, 1156 22½ Road, Grand Junction; (970) 243-2446
Helmer's Fresh Produce, 384½ Road, Palisade; (970) 434-1636
Herman Produce, 753 Elberta Street, Palisade; (970) 464-0420
La Ceiba Orchards, 311 34 Road, Palisade; (970) 434-6896
McLean Farms, 727 37 3/10 Road, Palisade; (970) 464-5391
Mesa View Produce, 271 22 Road, Palisade; (970) 434-4040
Mt. Garfield Fruit & Vegetable Stand, 3371 Front Street, Clifton; (970) 434-7906
Morton Orchards, 3651 E½ Road, Palisade; (970) 464-7854
   or (303) 421-8977 (Denver area line)
Neal Fruit Company, 5915 5800 Road, Olathe; (970) 323-5991
Noland Orchards, 3654 F Road, Palisade; (970) 464-7158
Pfaffly Greenhouse and Vegetable Market, 3669 G Road, Palisade:
   (970) 464-7460 or (970) 464-7895
Pope's Orchard, 3685 G 4/10 Road, Palisade; (970) 464-7974
Ranch Fruita Country Store, 3415 C½ Road, Palisade; (970) 434-5867
Red Mountain Ranches, 1948 Highway 65, Cedaredge; (970) 856-3808
Rettig Farms, 265 32nd Road, Grand Junction; (970) 434-8470
Rice's Colo-Color Orchards, Palisade, 621 37¼ Road, Palisade; (970) 464-7175
Robertson Fruit, 3611 F Road, Palisade; (303) 87-PEACH (Denver area line)
Ron Crist Orchards, 3236 C Road, Grand Junction; (970) 434-6667
St. Francis Farm, 732 35 6/10 Road, Palisade; (970) 464-1257
Sunset Orchards, 3644 G 4/10 Road, Palisade; (970) 464-7575
Thunder Mountain Fruit Company, 3548 E½ Road, Palisade; (970) 464-5241
Valley Fruit Stand, 757 Elberta Avenue, Palisade; (970) 464-0578
Walcher Orchards, 710 35 Road, Palisade; (970) 250-5907

Talbott's books tours for groups from school kids to seniors, but if you stop by for some cider, a basket of fruit, or a jar of honey, ask for a behind-the-scenes look. If at all possible, the Talbotts will happily oblige.
   Talbott Farms and The Mine Shack, 3782 F¹/₄ Road, Palisade; (877) 834-6686, (970) 464-5943, (970) 464-5656 (sales), or www.talbottfarms.com.

Vorhees Dried Fruit

While most Grand Valley farmstands sell fresh fruit, Vorhees dries it. Harold Vorhees started the business, which is now run by son Jim and daughter-in-law Pam. They process half-a-ton of local peaches, apples, apricots, nectarines, plums, pears, and cherries a day, with peak drying season from mid-June through mid-December.

Harvest Times

When those of us who live on the Front Range often hear springtime news and weather reports about late-season cold and snow, it's either an inconvenience or a providential extension of the ski season. To Grand Valley growers, it's a recipe for crop failure. When we buy western Colorado fruit from summer farmers' markets or at farmstands, we can't appreciate the lengths growers have gone through to protect their crops. Below is when fruits are generally harvested. For more specific dates, which vary from season to season, visit the website of the Palisade Chamber of Commerce at www.palisadecoc.com.

Apples
Late July through late October (typical harvest times for popular varieties follow):
    Gala—Beginning in late July
    Jonathan—Beginning in early September
    Golden Delicious—Beginning in mid-September
    Red Delicious—Beginning in early October
    Granny Smith—Beginning in early October
    Fuji—Beginning in late October
Apricots
    Late June through mid-July
Cherries
    Bing and Lambert (sweet, for eating)—Late June through mid-July
    Montmorency (sour or pie cherries, for cooking and baking)—
        Last three weeks of July
Grapes
    Mid-September
Peaches
Late June through early September (typical harvest times for popular varieties follow):
    Red Haven—Mid-July
    Glohaven—Late July
    Red Globe—Early August
    Cresthaven—Mid-August
    J. H. Hale—Late August
    Elberta—Early September
Pears
    Mid-August through mid-September
Plums
Early August to mid-September (typical harvest times for popular varieties follow):
    Santa Rose—early to mid-August
    Prune—late August to mid-September

If you've ever tasted Palisade Pride dipped dried fruit or Slice O' Life fruitcakes, know that Vorhees supplied the operative ingredients. All fruit is washed, peeled, hand-cut, and put on trays to dry. Apples and pears are dried plain or sprinkled with sugar and cinnamon.

Certified organic fruit and some conventionally grown fruit is dried using solar power and without preservatives. Jim Vorhees points out that "solar isn't sun-dried." Solar energy powers fans that pull air out of a top-floor room, which gets as hot as 140 degrees. Apples take 10 hours to dry, peaches 40 hours, and cherries almost three days. Think about that the next time quality dried fruit seems expensive. The other drying method, used for the remainder of the conventional produce, is light smoking. The fruit is put into the smoker with a small amount of sulphur as a preservative. Really ripe fruit is puréed and set on a floured tray to be made into fruit leather.

Whether for snacking, cooking, or reconstituted for baking, Vorhees dried fruit is a big cut above the mass-produced supermarket stuff. It starts closer to the growers, is dried fresher, and finishes drier, with about 10 percent water content remaining rather than the 15 to 18 percent water content found in the fruit of the big producers. Vorhees sells from the stand and also by mail order.

Vorhees Dried Fruit, 3702 G 7/10 Road, Palisade; (970) 464-7220 or e-mail voorfam@gjct.net.

Other

Colorado Wine Country

I promised that this would not be a winery guide, and it isn't. I again refer you to *The Guide to Colorado Wineries* by Alta and Brad Smith if this topic interests you as much as it does me. However, I'd be negligent if I didn't emphasize that Colorado's fruit-growing country largely overlaps with Colorado wine country. Of the 40-odd wineries operating at this writing, 13 are in the Grand Valley and seven fall within a loose area defined by Delta, Montrose, Cedaredge, and Paonia, with more grapes being planted and wines made every year. Most, but not all, have tasting rooms.

For more information on Colorado wineries, contact the Colorado Wine Industry Development Board, 4550 Sioux Drive, Boulder, CO 80303; (720) 304-3406 or www.coloradowine.com.

Recipes

Jim and Pam Vorhees, who run Vorhees Dried Fruit, have found uses for dried fruit beyond trail mix. Prepare the other ingredients in the following recipe while the rice is cooking. This turkey stuffing recipe is equally suitable for duck or goose.

Cherry Wild Rice Stuffing

9 cups chicken broth
1 cup wild rice, rinsed and drained
2 cups long-grain white rice
2 tablespoons butter
1 cup diced onion
1 cup diced celery
1 cup dried cherries
1 teaspoon ground cinnamon
grated zest of 2 oranges
2 tablespoons fresh chopped thyme (or 2 teaspoons dried)
2 teaspoons dried marjoram
1 tablespoon fresh sage leaves, chopped (or 1 teaspoon rubbed sage)
salt and freshly ground pepper to taste
1 cup shelled pecan halves
1 cup pitted prunes, quartered

In a saucepan, bring 4½ cups broth to a boil. Reduce heat to medium low, add wild rice, lower heat if necessary, and cook, uncovered, at a gentle simmer for 45 minutes or until rice is tender. Strain and place in a large bowl.

Meanwhile, in another saucepan, bring remaining 4½ cups broth to a boil. Stir in white rice, return to boil, then reduce heat and simmer, covered, for 25 minutes or until rice is just tender. Fluff with a fork and add to wild rice. In a saucepan or chef's pan, melt butter over medium-low heat. Add onion, celery, and cherries. Sprinkle with cinnamon. Cook, stirring occasionally, until vegetables are wilted (about 5 minutes). Toss with rice mixture. Add orange zest, herbs, salt, and pepper. Fold in pecans and prunes. Allow to cool to room temperature before stuffing turkey. Yield: 12 cups or enough to stuff a 9- to 12-pound turkey.

Note: To heat stuffing outside turkey, place in an ovenproof, lightly buttered pan and bake, covered, at 350 degrees for 20 to 25 minutes.

Much of the Grand Valley's appeal to Tom Favor (a.k.a the Country Cook) is the region's abundant fresh produce. Here is his version of the versatile cold soup from Spain that doesn't use the valley's famous stone fruit but blends so many of summer's most flavorful vegetables.

Grand Valley Gazpacho

3 cloves garlic, chopped
3 cups chopped tomatoes, seeded
½ cup beef stock
3 tablespoons extra-virgin olive oil
3 tablespoons fresh lime juice
3 tablespoons cider vinegar
½ tablespoon paprika
2 teaspoons salt
1 teaspoon freshly ground black pepper
1 teaspoon ground cumin
pinch cayenne or a splash of bottled hot sauce
1 cup chopped, peeled, and seeded cucumbers
½ cup chopped green bell pepper
1 cup chopped white onion
sour cream as a garnish

Place garlic in blender and pulse to distribute. Add tomatoes and next 9 ingredients; purée thoroughly. Taste and adjust seasonings. Chill (this can be done hours ahead). To serve, place reserved chopped veggies (or variations) in a soup bowl and pour in chilled soup to cover. Garnish with dollop of sour cream and or any of the variations below. Serves 4 to 6.

Variations on the Theme of Grand Valley Gazpacho

Some of the garnishes below will underscore the soup's Spanish roots while others provide a cultural contrast. Add modest amounts to begin with, for some of these ingredients are potent. Try adding chopped anchovy; cooked and crumbled bacon; crumbled blue cheese; peeled and chopped hard-boiled egg; cooked and chopped calamari; peeled, blanched, and chopped carrots; caviar; chopped celery; cooked and chopped chorizo; Dijon mustard; dill pesto; crumbled feta cheese; flavored vinegar (balsamic, black raspberry, sherry, etc.); fresh chopped herbs (dill, basil, chives, etc.), chopped ginger; seeded and chopped green chilies; freshly grated or bottled and drained horseradish; peeled and chopped jicama; pitted and chopped olives; chopped radish; red wine; cooked and chopped scallops; cooked, peeled, and chopped shrimp; chopped smoked salmon; splash of vodka, or cooked white beans, cooked (drained and rinsed if canned).

The Southern Mountains

Crested Butte

Crested Butte arguably has the highest ratio of culinary attractions per capita of any town in Colorado. This small community of about 1,500 people boasts a cooking school, a cookware shop, a gourmet take-out store, a wine bar, special events revolving around food, and a number of good restaurants, all the more remarkable because Crested Butte is practically dead-center in the Colorado Rockies, almost at the head of a long valley, and surrounded on three sides by designated wilderness. In summer, there are two vehicular roads into town, one paved and the other not. In winter, the unpaved road over Kebler Pass is not plowed, so the only access is from Gunnison to the south. Denver is a five-hour drive, give or take.

People who live there, and people who visit, treasure Crested Butte's end-of-the-road isolation, scenic splendor, and year-round sports opportunities, which are extensive even by Colorado standards. Although best known for its great skiing on an uncrowded mountain, fantastic hiking and mountain biking, and some of Colorado's finest wildflower fields, Crested Butte has strong aesthetic and lifestyle sides too. The community supports the performing and visual arts with passion, and clearly, part of the valued lifestyle is eating well.

There are two residential pods, the old mining town of Crested Butte with its wonderful false-front Victorians and charming miners' cottages and the more recent base-of-the-lifts development called Mt. Crested Butte. The former, a national historic district, is immaculately maintained, while the latter is still a hodgepodge of private residences, lodging properties, and limited commercial and retail space. They are connected via the umbilical cord of a twisty road traveled summer and winter by free buses. Mt. Crested Butte, still a simple resort development as such things go, is struggling with harmonious and attractive expansion and development, so for the present, most of the best food finds are downtown.

Cooking School

Now You're Cookin'

Now You're Cookin' offers hands-on, and homey cooking classes. They are intimate because Kristina St. George Patten limits them to a minimum of five and a maximum of eight participants, which fits comfortably into her home kitchen. The sessions are hands-on, because that's the way she and her guest chefs like to teach— and what most of her regular students prefer. The gorgeous kitchen boasts mountain views two directions, custom pine cabinets, granite countertops, a humongous refrigerator/freezer, a Dacor rangetop set into a large center island, two ovens, an overhead rack laden with pots and pans, and a pantry shelf stocked with all manner of dried ingredients. A collection of (mostly) blue-and-white pottery shows through glass cabinet doors, and baskets are displayed above. Patten might eventually seek larger space and develop a more extensive curriculum.

Now You're Cookin' offers mostly midweek day and evening classes, and many participants are repeat students from the local community. The classes are scheduled for three hours, but in a town as small as Crested Butte, everyone knows everyone, and in such a congenial and effervescent atmosphere, they often run over. No one minds. Year-round residents, second-home owners, and vacationers seem to bond immediately. No one feels like a stranger. No one feels left out of the banter.

Patten pampers her students by setting up the class beautifully. Prep work is done on the center island where, for each student, she puts out a plastic cutting board on a nonslip mat, two sharp knives (a chef's knife and a paring knife), measuring spoons, a chef's apron, a couple of towels, and a glass of ice water. Cooking is done on the side counter, where each student has his or her own Bunsen burner, the appropriate pots and pans for the day's class, and a jar equipped with a spatula, spoons, a skimmer, tongs, a ladle, and the like—also set up in advance. Patten even prepares some of the ingredients—perhaps roasting tomatoes or peppers or measuring out some ingredients before the class. Sometimes she'll prepare a sample of a sauce, soup, or other dish, so that students can sample it to find out what it's supposed to taste like before cooking their own. In many classes students take on different prep tasks, but each one assembles and cooks his or her own finished dish. Afterwards, everyone sits down to eat together.

"Kitchen Basics" is perfect for real novices who want to learn the fundamentals in order to follow recipes and get them right. Probably the most popular offerings at Now You're Cookin' are sushi classes, both at beginner and advanced levels. Other classes are themed by main ingredient, technique, or region. Topics include Tofu, Tuscan, Steaming, Soups and Stocks, Tamales, Thai Cuisine, Finger Foods, Canning, Fat Free, Fish and Shellfish, Edible Flours, Southwestern, and Mushrooms. Pastry and baking classes include Bread, Basic Cakes, and Plated Desserts, and even such occasional exotica as Peruvian Desserts. During the Wildflower Festival, there might be classes on Delicious Herbs or Cooking with Edible Flowers, and during the Mushroom Festival, one on Wild Mushrooms.

Patten teaches some of the classes herself. Others are taught by such leading local chefs and bakers as Chris Coady, Michael Marchitelli, Dana Mulitz, Stacee Schultz, Candace Targos, and Jean-Marc Ventimiglia, and occasionally by guest chefs from out of the area. Students get a card good for a 15 percent discount at Cookworks in downtown Crested Butte. Patten's career reflects her involvement with food and cooking. She started Cookworks (see page 369) in 1984, sold it in 1986, and moved to Connecticut with her family for several years. When the Pattens returned to Crested

Butte, she had several cooking jobs before deciding to start a private chef business and cooking school.

Now You're Cookin', 505 Slate River Drive, Crested Butte; (970) 349-0501 or www.nowyourecookin.com.

Dining

Bacchanale

The wine-red walls, gleaming wood floors, natural woodwork, and a quasi-New Orleans–style wrought-iron balcony over the main-floor bar and dining area present an inviting backdrop to good Italian food and a commendable wine list. Bacchanale often is described as a Northern Italian restaurant, and indeed, some of the dishes are from that region of Italy, but there's more on the menu from the pasta belt farther south. In fact, an off-hand slogan at the restaurant is "Eat Pasta, Ski Fasta." Maybe, for the sake of accuracy, the owners should simply drop the "northern." Or, more likely, they are less interested in accuracy than in providing hearty and well-priced food from somewhere along the boot.

No one complains about the geographical fuzziness, because Bacchanale's pasta is good—and perhaps people are skiing faster too. Fettucini a la Bacchanale (which some purists would say should read Fettuccine alla Bacchanale on the menu) is a house specialty. Filled pastas include cannelloni, ravioli, and lasagna (meat and vegetarian varieties). Linguini comes with a saucy choice of Bolognese, garlic butter, vegetarian, Fra Diavolo, marinara, white clam, or pesto sauces. Other featured entrées include various veal and chicken preparations (Parmesan, *piccata*, Marsala), plus the ever-popular eggplant Parmesan.

In addition to tried-and-true appetizers, *caprese* salad, too rarely offered in mountain-town restaurants, prime the appetite's pump, and house-made desserts cap off the meal. On the progressive wine list, each varietal is ranked by weight and richness, starting with the lightest.

Bacchanale, 209 Elk Avenue, Crested Butte; (970) 349-5257 or www.visitcrestedbutte.com/link.cfm?who=bacchanale.

Le Bosquet

Candace and Victor Shepard established Le Bosquet in 1976, and it has served some of the resort's most consistently good food ever since. Though it originally was located on the town's main street, it now resides in a small shopping center on the outskirts of downtown. The windows, curtained halfway up in lace, allow views of Mt. Crested Butte and other summits over the curtain tops. The tables are attractively set with pink overcloths on top of white tablecloths. A large wine rack dominates one wall, a gleaming wooden bar another.

Many dishes are Le Bosquet's variations on French bistro classics, but others have crept onto the menu even as they have inserted themselves into the lives of American diners. Baked Onion Soup is served with a crouton topped with melted Gruyère and Parmesan cheeses. The cheese and pâté platter includes the expected French Brie, but also English Stilton and Spanish Manchego, as well as duck mousse pâté, crackers, and fruit. Escargots are served in mushroom caps rather than in snail shells, but the rich and aromatic garlic butter is traditional. Crab cakes with three sauces—corn–red bell pepper relish, basil pesto mayonnaise, and aïoli—are a signature starter. Americans don't typically think of a heap of fries as an appetizer, but perfect *pommes frites*, crisp and golden on the outside and silky, starchy, and soft on the inside, are a bistro classic. Le Bosquet serves them with three similar dipping sauces—aïoli, basil mayonnaise, and *sauce rouge*. Portobello fries come with a rich Gorgonzola cream sauce.

Many dishes change seasonally, but some classics endure on the menu season after season. You can always expect to find Steak Frites, a true bistro standard of New York strip and hefty fries. Tenderloin comes in a rich Cabernet–black peppercorn sauce, and Steak au Poivre bathes a New York strip with a spicy black peppercorn sauce. Expect to find Rack of Lamb, four chops with Cabernet and garlic butter sauce; Hazelnut Chicken, "breaded" with chopped nuts, sautéed, and finished with an orange-thyme cream sauce; and Ginger-Glazed Filet of Salmon with a wild rice blend. There will also be a poultry dish, a couple of seafood entrées, game, and several vegetarian options, including Tofu Piccata, firm tofu that has been breaded, sautéed, and served with lemon butter and capers, an ingenious meatless adaptation of an Italian classic.

In true bistro fashion, Le Bosquet doesn't overdo it in the side-dish department by preparing different ones for each entrée. At this writing, you'll get either roasted Yukon Gold potatoes or horseradish mashed potatoes and seasonal vegetables on almost every plate. House-made desserts, including at least one chocolate item (mousse and another) and something with fruit, are palate-pleasers.

The reasonably priced Twilight Menu, available from 5:00 to 6:30 P.M., is a prix fixe dinner with a choice of soup (that wonderful French onion or the soup of the day) or house salad, a choice of four entrées (meat, seafood, poultry, and vegetarian options), and a choice of vanilla ice cream or chocolate mousse.

The much-lauded wine list, which has held a *Wine Spectator* award since 1992, concentrates on quality affordable wines, mostly from California and France and mostly in the $20 to $30 range. A dozen are available by the glass.

Le Bosquet, Majestic Plaza, Sixth and Belleview, Crested Butte; (970) 349-5808 or www.visitcrestedbutte.com/link.cfm?who=lebosquet.

Buffalo Grille & Saloon

The Clark family has operated a guest ranch in Bigfork, Montana, since 1945. After Jimmy, the oldest of the seven brothers (no sisters), left to become a rodeo rider and to work for Levi Strauss, one of the brothers who stayed to run the ranch started raising buffalo. When Jimmy retired from the company (but not from the rodeo—at least at this writing, he still rides bulls on the senior circuit), he started buying small hotels in several resort towns and eventually ended up in Crested Butte. He bought into a commercial building at the entrance to town, where The Backcountry Gourmet had closed, leaving a prominent space vacant. Jimmy told his partner, "If that space isn't leased by November, I'll take it."

The space wasn't leased, and Jimmy kept his word. The Buffalo Grille & Saloon was born. Directly to the right of the entrance door is the wine bin, a small, locked cabinet, where regular customers—of which there are many—store their bottles. Just beyond is the mahogany and brass bar, sitting on a foundation of backlit glass blocks. Order a beer, and it will come in a frosted glass shaped like a cowboy boot.

The dining room features huge windows with a drop-dead view of Mt. Crested Butte—a view shared by warm-weather diners who do, however, have to look at the peak through a veil of trees surrounding the patio. Martha Stewart's scouts have been around to study the gold-glazed walls with diaphanous black swirling patterns. Perhaps by the time you read this, she will have spilled the secret of the technique— or you can ask Jimmy how it was done. In any event, against those free-form yet fairly formal walls hang paintings of buffaloes, Indians, and other appealing Western scenes. Napkin rings and menu covers are made of thick, tooled leather—perfectly setting the stage for the specialty of the house: buffalo. Jimmy gets delivery of buffalo from the family ranch every two weeks.

Time to segue to the Clark family ranch, located in the Flathead Valley. A thousand head of bison roam on open range, feeding on natural grass that is subjected to no pesticides and no chemicals. The animals are not given growth hormones, nor subjected to other market-readying so prevalent in the cattle industry. The meat is delicious and, if you are concerned about such things, nutritious and proportionally lower in fat and calories than beef.

Back to the restaurant, which does wonderful things with buffalo, offering it as New York strip, rib eye, tenderloin tips, filet mignon, and stew. The tenderloin tips are braised with peppercorns and finished with a sun-dried cherry *démi-glace*; the filet mignon comes with either a rosemary-portobello *démi-glace* or an aromatic olive oil, caper, and parsley compote. If you don't want the buffalo—perhaps because a stuffed bison head is staring down at the dining room from over the bar—you can also order beef or New Zealand red deer, similarly cut and also perfectly sauced, or seafood, poultry, or pasta.

Appetizers, salads, soups, desserts, and wine by the glass or by the bottle match the entrées in terms of quality and flavor combinations. Crab cakes, made from blue-crab meat blue crabs, are sensational, as is the portobello mushroom cap stuffed with chèvre, Monterey Jack, and sun-dried tomatoes, grilled and accompanied by grilled zucchini, roasted garlic, and sliced tomatoes. The Greek, house, and Caesar salads are equally fresh and well prepared

Buffalo Grille & Saloon, 435 Sixth Street, Crested Butte; (970) 349-9699.

Dinner @ 10,000 Feet and Ice Bar and Restaurant

The 2002–2003 ski season a new on-mountain eating spot, Andiamo Restaurant in the Paradise Warming House the venue for Dinner @ 10,000 Feet. Guests arrive by snowcat-pulled sleigh ride to a four-course, prix fixe northern Italian dinner. It starts with a lavish antipasto display, followed by a choice of the soup of the day or a salad, a choice of entrées, and an Italian dessert. Available entrées consist of Osso Bucco Milanese, Shrimp and Spinach Canelloni, Portobello and Eggplant Parmesan, Tenderloin of Pork Madeira, and Chicken Marsala Youngsters have the option of a junior-size portion of a regular entrée or an item from the children's menu. Andiamo serves domestic and imported wines.

Additionally, the Ice Bar and Restaurant, located in the revamped Twister Warming House at mid-mountain, also provides culinary adventure. Start with a martini or other specialty drink and move on to a full meal. A sophisticated lunch menu and great desserts are this restaurant's hallmarks. Twice a week, guests for the Last Tracks Dinner board the Keystone Lift at 4:30 and ski, snowboard, or snowshoe to the Ice Bar & Restaurant for a gourmet meal that ends with chocolate "hot rock" fondue dessert and an easy torchlight procession back to the base area.

Dinner @ 10,000 Feet, Ice Bar and Restaurant, and Last Tracks Dinner, Crested Butte Mountain Resort; (970) 349-2211 or www.crestedbutteresort.com.

Lil's Land & Sea

Notched into an alcove off Elk Avenue is Lil's Land & Sea, Crested Butte's only sushi bar but also offering commendable dishes from other traditions. Sushi-level confidence in the freshness of its seafood spills over to the rest of the menu, which offers reliable fish and shellfish. Other dishes include good New England Clam Chowder, succulent Oysters Rockefeller, grilled mahi-mahi, elk tenderloin, roasted duck, a Thai-inspired curried shrimp and scallop combination, a fine lobster manicotti, and *cioppino*, an assortment of house-made desserts.

The décor is sushi-bar simple, which gives it that magic feeling of intimacy and simplicity at the same time. It is open for dinner only, not surprisingly, for presenting that complexity and variety in a small restaurant twice a day is difficult—perhaps impossible.

Lil's Land & Sea, 321 Elk Avenue, Crested Butte; (970) 349-5457 or www.visitcrestedbutte.com/link.cfm?who=lils.

Marchitelli's Gourmet Noodle

When I first heard raves about a downtown restaurant that everyone called "The Gourmet Noodle," I thought it probably featured some spaghetti and linguine dishes, some *udon*, some *lo mein*, some kind of long noodles with peanut sauce, and perhaps, for nostalgic patrons, the house version of mac and cheese. When I approached the restaurant and saw that it was, in fact, called Marchitelli's Gourmet Noodle, I rightly figured that Italian specialties are its forte.

Michael Marchitelli, an ebullient, extroverted, and personable local chef, runs friendly, informal restaurant with his wife, Jennifer. It specializes in well-done versions of Italian standbys, many passed down from Marchitelli's grandmother. Expect to find stuffed mushrooms, mozzarella sticks, and fried calamari on the appetizer menu. The most popular sauces—Alfredo, hearty red, regular marinara, Italian hot sausage, and clam—bathe quality pasta of your choice. Similarly, Chicken Florentine, Veal Marsala, and Lasagna lead the entrée roster, with elk medallions the main departure from the standard Italian repertoire. The wine list is heavy on California and Italian wines, and the desserts are homemade.

Families and budget-watchers make dinner pilgrimages half-a-block from the main street for the early-bird special, which at this writing included four salads, two loaves of bread, and four orders of spaghetti and meatballs for under $20. Not gourmet Italian, but good Italian and a value that's hard to beat. You couldn't fill four stomachs at a fast-food chain place—if Crested Butte were cursed with the syndrome—for so little.

When Marchitelli competed in Crested Butte's first Iron Chef competition (see pages 367–8), he didn't win—but he was a crowd-pleaser as well as a worthy contender. When he teaches a Tuscan cuisine class at Now You're Cookin' (see page 360), it always fills up. People love to learn from him—and they love his quick sense of humor and lively interaction with students. Showmanship and spaghetti notwithstanding, he is a talented and creative chef. If you can rustle up a group, rent the private Wine Room and let him really show off with one of his excellent tasting menus. The room presents a more sophisticated option to the casual, friendly, and often family-filled main dining area.

Marchitelli's Gourmet Noodle, 411 Third Street, Crested Butte; (970) 349-7401 or www.visitcrestedbutte.com/businesspage.cfm?businessid=28.

Soupçon

Super-charming Soupçon is a tiny jewel located in an achingly quaint log cabin tucked into a Crested Butte alley. How typically quirky of Crested Butte to find one of its most *au courant* and creative restaurants in one of its oldest buildings. The quality of the food matches the uniqueness of the surroundings—and I'm not the only one who thinks so. *Zagat* has graced Soupçon with 28 out of a possible 30 points for food, one of only seven restaurants in Colorado to be so highly honored—and certainly the smallest. When you dine there, you wonder how so modestly sized a place can turn out such fine cuisine—and you also wonder where they manage to store their wine selection.

Two important elements come in twos at Soupçon. When you walk through the small doorway for one of the two nightly seatings (at 6:00 and 8:15 P.M.), you will be led into one of the two rooms that comprise the dining area. Both are exquisite and romantic, and neither is "better" than the other. You'll sit either on a wooden bench, resembling those found in old railroad stations set against the walls, or on a bentwood chair. The ceiling is low, the windows tiny, and the atmosphere intimate. The simple décor, with discreetly patterned wallpaper, crisp white table linens, fresh flowers, and flickering oil lamps, forms an excellent stage on which the food stars.

Scott Greene has run this Crested Butte classic since 2000. He is both the general manager, which superficially doesn't matter much to patrons, and the chef, which matters a great deal, because he is masterful in the kitchen. A Johnson & Wales graduate (see page 24), he worked in top restaurants in New York and France. Since Soupçon is open only during the ski season and in summer, he often spends autumn in France, cooking with such Michelin-starred chefs as Georges Blanc and Michel Rostaing. Greene won the first Crested Butte Iron Chef battle in 2002 (see page 367) against two other talented and creative local chefs.

Greene cooks with a strong French accent, offering just six appetizers, seven entrées, and six or seven desserts every evening. Everything is house-made from scratch, including the breads and pastries. The menu almost always features lamb, fish, elk, beef, duck, and a vegetarian entrée. If anything can be called a signature dish in a menu that is tweaked almost daily, it is the Crispy Wasabi Petite Filet Mignon. The summer version is served with Blistered Asparagus, Gratin Potatoes, and Wasabi/Spinach Cream, but when asparagus is not in season, there might well be another accompaniment. Greene also does a Roast Crisp Duck, with an Asian-inspired sweet orange lacquer and a hash of fingerling potatoes and lobster—or perhaps another perfectly matched accompaniment.

On one recent early-summer menu, starters included Chilled Garden Gazpacho and Lump Crab Soup; Sashimi Tuna and Avocado Tartare with Wonton Chips, Caviar and Ginger Dressing; and Seared Hudson Valley Foie Gras with Pan-Roasted Figs and 12-Year-Old Balsamic Vinegar. During that same visit, the lamb *du jour* was Double-Grilled Lamb Chops with Pearl Couscous/Spinach Sauté, Lamb *Jus*, and White Truffle Oil. There were two fish, one of which was a Pistachio-Crusted Atlantic Salmon with Jalapeño/Sweet Potato Mash, Vanilla Rum Butter, and Frizzled Leeks. Sublime.

On any given evening, the dessert selection might include house-made ice cream (the hazelnut is particularly yummy) with suitable accompaniments, Chocolate Bourbon Cake, Berry Cobbler, Marble Cheesecake, and Greene's version of crème brulée. This silky custard topped with caramelized sugar gently rests upon a *tuille,* a feather-light French sugar cookie baked in the shape of a spoon, and on that perches a perfect fresh raspberry garnished with a sprig of mint. Such simple yet lovely presentations befit this jewel of a restaurant that enduringly makes it one of the best in the Butte.

Soupçon, 127 Elk Avenue, Crested Butte; (970) 349-5448.

Swiss Chalet

Of the several Swiss restaurants in the Rockies named Swiss Chalet, this one, at Crested Butte Mountain Resort has the most authentic location. Even though it is decades old rather than centuries old, the location recalls the Swiss Alps—if only loosely—perhaps because the commanding 12,162-foot stand-alone peak of Mt. Crested Butte dominates the landscape of the valley much as the Matterhorn dominates the landscape around Zermat.

Red-checked tablecloths, dirndl-clad waitresses, and a touch of chalet-style décor set the stage for fondue and raclette dinners, as well veal, pork, beef, chicken, and trout dinner specialties. This was one of the Crested Butte resort's first smoke-free restaurants, so that the Swiss–German cuisine could be inhaled in unpolluted air.

Downstairs in the Swiss Pub, after-ski sets in early. Six Paulaner beers are on tap, and there's also a bar menu that includes so-called appetizer-size cheese fondue, gnocchi (Italy, after all, is just south of Switzerland), and a "Swiss Reuben" sandwich that might make you swear off the American deli version. When you buy into the "Mug Club," you get a genuine half-liter German beer stein with a custom-engraved medallion mounted and $1.00 off a Paulaner beer every time you come in. The Swiss Pub will hang your stein at the bar or pub with other club members' mugs, or you may take it home. The Swiss Chalet is not a retail store as such, but if you want to special-order authentic fondue or raclette cheeses or equipment, they'll do it for you with advance notice.

Swiss Chalet, 621 Gothic Road, Mt. Crested Butte; (970) 349-5917 or www.visitcrestedbutte.com/navigate.cfm?nav=businesspage.cfm_BusinessID=1679.

Events

Tour de Forks

Summer—In 2002, the Crested Butte Center for the Arts launched an ambitious, summer-long food-oriented fund-raising campaign called the Tour de Forks. A different event was scheduled at least once a week, and at this writing, no one knows yet if this complex format will be continued in future years. I certainly hope so, because it enables locals, second-home owners, and vacationers to sample some of the best Crested Butte cooking in some truly enticing settings.

The tour launched with the first annual Crested Butte Iron Chef contest, which was energetic, instructive, and simply a whole lot of fun. Chefs Scott Greene of Soupçon, Josephine Kellett of the Club at Crested Butte, and Michael Marchitelli of Marchitelli's Gourmet Noodle took to the stage at the arts center and performed an hour's worth of power cooking on makeshift folding tables and Bunsen burners.

Following the format of the made-in-Japan cult cooking show, *Iron Chef,* Crested Butte's own top toques were presented with a "secret ingredient." They had to incorporate fresh peppers in their various forms and hues—red, green, yellow, poblano, and so on into as many dishes as possible. Greene, who went on to win the closely contested competition, even managed to make pepper ice cream.

Post-2002 events are not yet firm, but I can't resist sharing other varied, fun, and delicious events of that inaugural year, which included the Dueling Diva Dinner with Elizabeth "Dueling Diva" Bond; Wine Tasting Tour with Kristina Patten of Now You're Cookin'; Lunch Among the Wildflowers with Mary Whitson and Sally Johnson of Cucina; Cards in the Clouds with John-Marc Ventimiglia, former chef at Soupçon;

Double Top Dining with Andy Floyd of Boulder's Cooking School of the Rockies; Skyland Ranch Sunday Brunch with Mike Byrd, general manager of the Club at Crested Butte; Sunset at Skyland with Josephine Kellet, chef at the Club at Crested Butte; Fashionable Tea Time with Scott Greene of Soupçon; the Art of Grilling with Jennifer Bushman, an award-winning chef, traveling instructor for Weber Grill, and culinary ambassador of *Fine Cooking* magazine; Table for Twelve with Tim Egelhoff of Timberline Restaurant; Flavors of Italy with Michael Marchitelli of Marchitelli's Gourmet Noodle; and A Vita for Venison with Martha Hunt of the Swiss Chalet Restaurant.

Most included fine wines too—and many featured music or other entertainment. They were held in a variety of venues, including fabulous private homes. Seating was understandably limited for all these events and will be as long is the format continues, so check with the arts center and make your reservations early for upcoming years. It's worth it.

> Center for the Arts, P.O. Box 1819, Crested Butte, CO 81224; (970) 349-7487
> or e-mail cftarts@rmi.net.

Crested Butte Wild Mushroom Festival

August—The Crested Butte Wild Mushroom Festival, which takes place annually over a weekend in mid-August, includes lessons in mushroom identification, guided forays to find 'shrooms in the forest, and cooking classes to teach you how to use what you picked. You can sign up for the entire weekend or separately for a single workshop, lecture, or the cooking session. The whole program and its constituent parts are both very reasonably priced.

> Crested Butte Wild Mushroom Festival, c/o Crested Butte Chamber of
> Commerce, 601 Elk Avenue, Crested Butte; (800) 545-4505, (970) 349-6438,
> or www.crestedbuttechamber.com.

Fall Festival

September—In Crested Butte, a Sunday in early September can mean blazing sun or falling snow—but for sure, it's Fall Festival time. The multicomponent annual event features entertainment, sports, and a chili cook-off with professional and amateur categories. A microbrew tasting accompanies the cook-off, as heavenly a match as salt and pepper, Laurel and Hardy, Click and Clack. Admission to the Festival of Beers is modest ($15 in 2002), with chili sampling only $5 more, with proceeds benefiting the Crested Butte/Mt. Crested Butte Chamber of Commerce.

> Crested Butte Chamber of Commerce, 601 Elk Avenue, Crested Butte;
> (800) 545-4505, (970) 349-6438, or www.crestedbuttechamber.com.

Retail

Cookworks

An adorable house on Elk Avenue draws Crested Butte cooks like a magnet draws sewing needles. It's the yellow one with a white picket fence in front and red, white, pink, and green trim. It's Cookworks. You can't miss it. You shouldn't miss it. Kristina Patten, who runs Now You're Cookin' (see page 359), started the store, and Holly Hicks is the current owner. She has stocked Cookworks with "anything to do with the kitchen that's fun and beautiful," as one of the saleswomen put it. Cookworks' style is breezy, informal, and charming.

Step onto the front porch where, in warm weather, there might be a baker's rack filled with sale items. Inside, your eyes will light on a lovely table set with something from the store's inventory, perhaps graceful linens, Vietri tableware, and gorgeous wineglasses. Shelves around the room are stacked with colorful pottery, table linens, glassware, and Emile Henry oven-to-table-ware in green, red, blue, and gold.

In the former front parlor you'll find Joyce Chen sauces and accessories (sushi mats, sushi kits, vegetable knives, scissors, and such) displayed in and atop an antique bureau. The room also holds gorgeous teak salad bowls and beautifully shaped spoons, pasta lifters, salad servers, and spatulas from Good Woods, which come in one style but two colors, lighter ones carved in France from beech and darker ones carved in Italy from olive wood, as well as all of the cookbooks and most of the gourmet foods. Cookworks carries Spice Library four-packs of themed seasonings, single bottles of Spice Hunter herbs and spices, Epic Valley salsa made in Crested Butte, and various good lines of condiments, pasta, tea, oil, vinegar, and more. They include such homey products as Plentiful Pantry's chicken and dumpling mix and sophisticated and even exotic products like Robert Rothschild Farm condiments. Who would ever have thought that you'd be able to pick up a jar of Lemon Wasabi Sauce in the old mining town of Crested Butte?

The back room—perhaps the original location of the kitchen when the house was a home—showcases pots, pans, gadgets, and utensils. Among the lines are Emerilware, Cuisinart, Kitchen Aid, Wüsthof, and Gourmac, the latter a little-known gadget brand. There are lots of bakers' toys, from pie-weight chains to bakeware, including cookie sheets, pie tins, tart forms, and springform pans.

Cookworks, 321 Elk Avenue, Crested Butte; (970) 349-7398, (800) 765-9511 or www.cookworks.com.

Why Cook?

Right next door to Le Bosquet (see page 361), sharing the same kitchen and under the same ownership, is Crested Butte's best reason to eat at home and yet enjoy a restaurant-caliber meal. When the restaurant moved from its previous site at the other end of downtown to its current location in 1997, Candace and Victor Shepard turned the adjacent space into a gourmet take-out market, with interesting food prepared by a real chef. Why Cook? always has such perennial favorites as lasagna, meatloaf, roast chicken, and tuna, chicken, and pasta salads. Le Bosquet's signature crab cakes are also available to take home. Other offerings might include duck quesadillas, Cajun chicken, spicy frog legs with *rémoulade*, calamari with red peppers and soy, and probably a couple of interesting pasta entrées. Breads include small baguettes, rosemary focaccia, and French white and honey wheat. Chocolate cake, apple *galette*, cannoli, and chocolate mousse are normally there for dessert lovers.

Why Cook?, Majestic Plaza, Sixth and Belleview, Crested Butte; (970) 349-5858 or www.visitcrestedbutte.com/link.cfm?who=lebosquet.

Recipes

Students at the hands-on classes at Now You're Cookin' come away with recipes for delicious dishes that are interesting but legitimately do-able at home. The school's owner, Kristina St. George Patten, tinkers with recipes to perfect them technically before passing them on to her students. But she is outspoken in her belief that every cook needs to adjust seasonings to his or her taste rather than slavishly following recipes. Her tamale classes include both classic and adapted recipes of this Mexican delicacy.

Chicken Tamales with BBQ Masa and Red Chili Crema

15–20 dried cornhusks, soaked in warm water for 30 minutes
BBQ *masa* dough (see below)
Chicken Filling (see below)
Red Chili *Crema* (see below)

Set a deep pot fitted with a steamer and a tight-fitting lid on the stove, fill with water to just below the steamer, and heat to boiling while you prepare the *masa* dough and *crema*.

BBQ Masa Dough

1½ cups *masa harina* (available in Latino markets and most supermarkets)
1 teaspoon salt
1 teaspoon baking powder
½ cup shortening or lard at room temperature
½ cup barbecue sauce, homemade or prepared
1 cup warm water

Place *masa harina,* salt, and baking powder in the bowl of an electric mixer fitted with the paddle attachment. Add the shortening and beat on medium speed for 2 minutes. Add shortening or lard, barbecue sauce, and water, and beat for 2 minutes, scraping down the sides of the bowl as necessary. The dough should reach a very soft consistency, rather like your earlobe. Remove *masa* from the bowl, wrap in plastic wrap and let rest at room temperature for 30 minutes. The dough will thicken as it rests.

Chicken Filling

1 pound boneless, skinless chicken breast, poached in chicken broth
    and cooled in the broth
salt and freshly ground pepper to taste
2 tablespoons barbecue sauce, homemade or prepared
    (more if you prefer a moist filling)

Shred chicken; mix with salt, pepper, and barbecue sauce. Set aside.

Red Chili *Crema*

1 cup heavy cream
1 clove roasted garlic, peeled
1 tablespoon canned chipotle chilies (smoked jalapeños in roasted
    tomato sauce, available in Latino markets and some supermarkets)

While the tamales are steaming (see below), make the *crema*. Place all ingredients in a blender and blend on medium-high speed until thoroughly combined. Place in a small bowl, cover, and refrigerate until ready to use.

To assemble, lay the cornhusks on a flat surface. Use one large husk or two over-lapping smaller ones for each tamale. Depending on how you like to shape your tamales, you can have the pointed or wide side toward you. Divide the dough into 16 pieces and form each one into a rectangle. Place each rectangle on a corn husk (if using two husks, place the rectangle on the seam). Place 1/16 of the chicken filling lengthwise on each rectangle. Using the husk rather than your hands, nudge the dough to fold over itself, *masa* to *masa,* folding the husk loosely around the dough (the dough needs room to expand), and folding the bottom up by one turn. (You can tear a narrow lengthwise strip off the cornhusk to tie your tamale if you wish.) Repeat until you have 16 tamales.

Add more water to the pot if you need to and carefully place the assembled tamales in the steamer, standing them vertically or on a slant with the open end on top. Cover the pot and steam for 30 to 25 minutes. The tamales are done when the dough is firm to the touch and pulls away from the husk. Let rest for 5 minutes before opening.

To serve, place two tamales on each plate, with *crema* underneath, on top, or on the side. Serves 8.

Telluride

Colorado is blessed with myriad marvelous mountain communities, but not one is more spectacularly situated than Telluride. In addition to its charmed location in the magnificent San Juan Range, the town of Telluride also comprises a noteworthy historic district. The big boom years, when the mines were producing millions, lasted only from the town's establishment in 1878 until the rocky years following the 1893 silver panic. Even the railroad cut way back, maintaining only a tenuous link from the remote box canyon where Telluride is located. The last mine and the last bordello both closed in 1959. The town hung on, probably because it was the county seat, and fortunately for Telluride's historical heritage, no one had the money or the inclination to fix up anything much. When an Aspen developer named Joe Zoline arrived with visions of ski resorts dancing in his head, the old town was remarkably intact, and it remained so until big-time skiing started and money started trickling in at first and then rolling in. The community, which had exported its wealth a century earlier, began importing it.

Then in the 1990s, construction began on a golf course and the nucleus of a luxurious development called Telluride Mountain Village, and the beautiful people discovered Telluride. Austrian Olympic ski champ Franz Klammer lent his name and his presence to the Franz Klammer Lodge in Mountain Village. Oprah Winfrey, Susan St. James, Ralph Lauren, and Oliver Stone have or had houses in or near Telluride. Geraldo Rivera, Darryl Hannah, Dustin Hoffman, Sting, James Taylor, and Clint Eastwood came to ski, snowboard, or just be. Christie Brinkley and Richard Taubman, and Tom Cruise and Nicole Kidman were married there. Neither marriage lasted, but it wasn't the town's fault, and eyebrows certainly were raised when Cruise showed up some years later with Penelope Cruz.

The two Tellurides made transportation history with an up-and-over transportation gondola in 1996 to link Telluride and Mountain Village. It runs from early morning until the wee hours, providing an efficient and free way for people to shuttle between the old town and the new development. A by-product of all the wealth, the glamour, the lofty real estate prices, and the abundant upscale accommodations has been outstanding dining. Telluride is an eating-out or call-the-caterer kind of town, with a tremendous assortment of fine restaurants run by immensely gifted chefs. A handful of food-oriented festivals provide reasons to come to town and—what else?—eat.

Bakeries

Baked In Telluride

Telluride isn't the same place it was in 1977, when Jerry Greene started baking for a restaurant at the Ice House and opened a retail bakery and deli on a nearby side street. Sure, the town still has its legendary "free box," where those who need clothing can root around and pick up donated items, but practically everything else has been cleaned up, spruced up, fixed up, or replaced with something grandiose—except Baked In Telluride. To walk into the well-worn, barn-red building is to turn back the calendar. This funky bakery retains an ambience common in Telluride more than a quarter of a century ago. In a town where maître d's, sommeliers, and star chefs now romp, some of Telluride's consistently best-baked goods come from such a time-less place.

This casual bakery and deli is as much a meeting place as a feeding trough. Everyone seems to know everyone. Go in, and you might feel the same way. Breathe in the aromas of baking and cooking—nothing sanitized or hidden away at B-I-T. Just look around. Baked goods are at one counter, sandwiches at another, and hot foods elsewhere. Cast an eye over the displays, read the posted menus, and then belly up to the counter and order. Eat inside or on the covered front porch furnished with mix-and-unmatched furniture—or order it to go.

Still, B-I-T is first and foremost a bakery. I've known people to travel far for the éclairs, croissants, and Napoleons. Good fresh bagels, bialys, rolls, doughnuts, croissants, breakfast pastries, cookies, and cakes are made from scratch—every day. Check out the racks of bread. You'll find them laden with a choice of "Almost White," raisin wheat, challah, 7-Grain, Jewish rye, baguette, wheat, French, pumpernickel, Tuscan, sourdough wheat, and some other crusty sourdough each day. Have the B-I-T build you a sandwich between a couple of slices, or buy a whole loaf. Rugelach and potato knishes from the Jewish dairy tradition compete for customers' attention with calzones, pizza, and pasta from the southern Italian kitchen.

Not only will the atmosphere and the largely local clientele take you back to a time when Telluride was a simpler place, but the moderate prices will seem to come from another era too. Good soups and salads, nightly specials, and a short list of wine and local beers complete B-I-T's simple formula. This hearty, freshly made food won't cost a mint, which is novel in Telluride today.

Baked In Telluride, 127 South Fir Street, Telluride; (970) 728-4775 or www.bakedintel.com.

Wildflour Cooking Company

When you see someone in the gondola line at Station Telluride balancing a cup of java, a fabulous pastry, and perhaps skis or a snowboard, there's a good chance that the baked goods came from Wildflour Cooking Company. French-trained Monica Callard, whose love of pastries was inborn thanks to a Viennese great-grandmother and nurtured by her own mother, prepares artisan breads and other quality goods in this spacious bakery across the plaza from the gondola entrance. Her baguettes and olive breads are tops.

Morning offerings include eat-in hot breakfasts. Some people—skiers or not—return at lunch for a deli sandwich, from-scratch soup, or crisp salad. The Wildflour also sells fine cheeses and pâtés, and it is an enormously popular après-ski option too, serving wine, half-a-dozen draft beers, and hot chocolate for children of any age.

Wildflour Cooking Company, 250 West San Juan Avenue, Telluride; (970) 728-8887.

Dining

Allred's

Telluride's unique over-the-top gondola connecting the old town of Telluride and Telluride Mountain Village makes it possible for Allred's to exist. The restaurant is perched at the gondola's high point at 10,500 feet, which is called Station San Sophia. By day during ski season, it operates as Club San Sophia, a private luncheon club. At dinnertime in summer and winter, it morphs into Allred's, literally and figuratively Telluride's culinary high spot. Have a fast, easy, and comfortable ride from either lodging base. Dinner is more egalitarian than lunch. You don't need to be a member to dine there; just bring a wad of cash or a credit card. The restaurant was named for the Telluride ski company's long-time (and now former) owner, Ron Allred. He conceived of Telluride Mountain Village, a super-luxe community nestled deep in the valley called Goronno Basin—and made it happen. It is fitting that one of the most ambitious and upscale restaurants in Colorado honors a man who had the vision to create an ambitious and upscale resort development.

The high-altitude restaurant boasts a creative menu, attentive service, and drop-dead views. The décor is striking and the fireplace inviting, and the food as rarified as the elevation. Chef de Cuisine Bob Scherner has built a powerful menu in a distinctive contemporary American style. Everything is meticulously prepared and artfully presented in a creative and refined manner. The combinations sizzle, and I think of the venue as being Station San Sophistication rather than Station San Sophia.

Scherner has wide-ranging experience across the contemporary culinary spectrum. Raised in Boulder, the graduate of Oregon's Western Culinary Institute and returned to his hometown to cook at the Flagstaff House (see page 110), before becoming a sous-chef under Charlie Trotter and working with other name chefs. He moved to Telluride in 1991 to open 221 South Oak (see 381) and then went up the mountain to Allred's.

Allred's starters include such complex and beautifully arranged dishes as Wild Mushroom and Potato Soup with truffle oil and sage crème fraîche; Sake-Steamed Puget Sound Mussels with lemongrass, lime leaves, ginger, and cilantro; and Chilled Diver Sea Scallops with *somen* noodle salad, pickled cucumber, and spicy *phim* sauce. The Mediterranean Bread Salad with Seranno ham is based on an Italian country classic, but with Salade Niçoise–style green beans, olives, and red wine vinaigrette

The wild and wonderful mix of entrées often add a twist to conventional (and easily obtainable) main ingredients. You'll find beef, fish, lamb, duck, and even venison on many a Colorado menu, but not the way Scherner presents them. The rib eye is grilled and served with four types of peppercorns, smoked-bacon mashed potatoes, sautéed spinach, and a finish of red wine butter. There's not a steakhouse in the state that does rib eye with such sophistication. The New Zealand venison is basted with tamari, served with dried-fruit bread pudding and caramelized onions, and finished with a flavorful red plum reduction. Sesame-Crusted Japanese Yellowtail is complemented with warm Asian greens, macadamia nuts, coconut, a tropical fruit mélange, and curried coconut broth. Even the local standby, Rocky Mountain trout, gets the treatment, accompanied by pearl couscous, shiitake mushrooms, Napa cabbage, and saffron-champagne crème fraîche.

Spiced Carrot Cake comes with mascarpone cream and apple sorbet. The Bittersweet Chocolate Cake's lily is a gilded with Chocolate Ricotta Cheesecake and passion fruit sorbet—three desserts in one. Cranberry and Chèvre Dumplings sided with cranberry sorbet is a sweet and yet slightly tangy dish.

If you can't decide on what to order, consider the Chef's Menu, a medley of nightly specials paired with wines from Allred's well-filled 8,000-bottle wine cellar in the sky. You can also book a Chef's Table, where a beyond-dazzling dinner will be presented, again with paired wines if you like.

Allred's, Station San Sophia, Telluride; (970) 728-7474 for dinner reservations and (970) 728-7302 for information on wintertime club membership. The ski resort website is www.tellurideskiresort.com.

The Bluepoint Grill

The Bluepoint Grill, a sleek, chic, and oh-so-trendy spot opened in 2001 as a mostly seafood-and-steak restaurant upstairs and a hip nightspot called the Noir Bar in the basement. An upmarket urban style, combining simple yet expensive decorative elements, prevails on both levels. Finding fresh seafood at Telluride's lofty elevation and remote location is a treat. The Bluepoint Grill express-ships its signature shellfish, including oysters served raw on the half-shell, and mussels and clams lightly cooked in a choice of interesting broths and brews. Or start dinner with New England Clam Chowder, a wedge of iceberg lettuce with Maytag blue cheese dressing from Iowa, or go exotic, with Thai Chili Glazed BBQ Prawns, "New Style" Ahi Sashimi with warm ginger *ponzu,* or Chipotle-Lime Calamari Nachos with tomato *salsa fresca.* The metaphors may be mixed, but the presentation and taste are memorable.

The menu features salmon, mahi mahi, rock cod, tilapia, ruby red trout, grouper, halibut, and catfish that can be grilled, broiled, blackened, or steamed. Steaks, chops and such Bluepoint Blueplate Specials as fried chicken, meatloaf, scampi, and fish and chips address the comfort food issue.

Rich and swank desserts include great pies made with seasonal fruit, a warm brownie with Ben & Jerry's ice cream, and a calorie bomb called Grievous Angel's Chocolate Chip Cookie Dough Pie. I have no idea who or what the Grievous Angel reference is, but the dessert is over the top. The wine list is extensive.

The Noir Bar serves the restaurant dinner menu and can be considered overflow space, but it is known for martinis, other cocktails, and wine served in a swanky and decadent atmosphere. Booths upholstered in velvet, leather couches, a fireplace, and live music and dancing on some nights attract Telluride sophisticates until the wee hours—especially the ones who don't mind if they miss first tracks on a powder morning.

The Bluepoint Grill, 123 South Oak Street, Telluride; (970) 728-8862.

Campagna

The quaint frame house on West Pacific Avenue is Victorian on the outside and Tuscan on the inside. Impeccable cuisine is served, in the straightforward and simple manner of that charmed region of Italy. Campagna appears to be the destiny as well as the fulfillment of the dreams of owners Vincent and Joline Esposito.

Brooklyn-born Vincent's immigrant grandparents founded the first family restaurant, where the little boy, then only age five and probably called Vinnie, used to stand on a milk can to help his father assemble lasagna. Vincent studied art history in college, but a trip to Florence reignited his culinary flame. Joline, a marketing executive for whom Manhattan had lost its appeal, married into the Esposito restaurant family, and developed a passion for Tuscany and a talent for wine. The couple moved to Colorado, found the building, and personally devoted a year to stripping, refinishing, repainting, and otherwise turning a tired house into a cozy restaurant. Think of it as the prep work necessary before they began serving some of Telluride's best and priciest food. The restaurant opened in 1990 and has been a hit ever since.

Enter through a side door into a small foyer and past a compact open kitchen, with copper pots hanging overhead. The air is perfumed with fresh herbs, simmering soups, fulsome risotto in the pot, and meats or poultry being grilled. Talk about an appetizer. Campagna's aromatic and visual appetizers attack your senses even before the first sip of an apéritif or bite of bread—even before you sit down.

The small and intimate dining rooms are tied together visually with lemon-yellow walls, natural woodwork, and tiles here and there. Ladderback chairs with rush seats are set around polished-wood tables. Placemats enhance the feeling of a small inn or country home. To keep things flowing in so small a place (Campagna only accommodates 32 diners at a time), there are two seatings: between 6:00 and 6:30 and again between 8:00 and 8:45.

Vincent Esposito takes fresh ingredients—not only what's seasonally best but what he finds best that very day—and prepares simple, authentic food known for true flavors, rather than complex preparation. If you find *panzanella* on the menu, order it. There's a story that *Gourmet* magazine wanted the recipe for this classic Tuscan bread salad, but Vincent refused because he couldn't guarantee the quality of the bread a reader might use. He bakes his own bread daily and mixes dried crumbles with super-ripe tomatoes, fresh basil, and quality olive oil to create this distinctive version.

Whatever is on the menu on any given day, know that Esposito lavishly uses such cheeses as Pecorino Romano, Reggiano Rocca Parmesano, ricotta, and goat cheese, plus fresh seafood, and such vegetables as summer or winter squash, eggplant, mushrooms, fennel, broccoli rabe, string beans, beets, cardoon, leeks, and anything else fresh and seasonal. He favors green extra-virgin olive oil, fresh rosemary and sage, and truffles in season.

Italian Arborio rice is formulated into some of the finest risotto this side of the Tiber, and Campagna also offers outstanding pasta creations. Pasta and risotto can be ordered in half-portions in appetizer or entrée portions. Primary ingredients for main courses might include veal, Black Angus beef, New Zealand lamb, Colorado veal, rabbit, quail, wild boar, venison, and seafood. You'll find tuna and scallops on many a menu, but how many Colorado chefs offer eel, salt cod, and other true Italian specialties, in particular, for the Christmas holidays?

If soups, appetizers, salads, and entrées are simple, the house-made desserts are simpler still. In the true Tuscan manner, they tend to be straightforward, such as marmalade tart, tìramisu, *sorbeti,* and *gelati.* Joline Esposito assembles the mostly Italian wine list, including older and harder-to-find vintages, as well as a goodly number of wines by the glass. Log onto the restaurant's website, send Joline an e-mail, and she'll answer with a current wine list—and have your selection waiting when you arrive at the restaurant.

Campagna, 435 West Pacific Avenue, Telluride; (970) 728-6190 or www.campagnarestaurant.com.

Cosmopolitan

Many of Telluride's historic buildings now house fine restaurants, But Cosmopolitan is an anomaly. This bright and stylish eatery is located on the main floor of the Hotel Columbia, built in 1996. The main dining room resembles a greenhouse, with lots of glass surfaces to let in the light and enable diners to look up at the steep mountain just across the street. The tables, set with immaculate white linens and simple but hefty tableware and flatware, don't try to compete with the views—or the food.

Concurrent with the hotel's opening, Chad Scothorn launched the Cosmopolitan. Before coming to Telluride, he opened at Beano's Cabin and then was the creator of Chadwicks, both in Beaver Creek (see page 265).

Because Cosmopolitan is a hotel restaurant, it serves breakfast, lunch, and dinner—all with panache and style. The daytime meals are all very good, but dinners are unabashedly great, with a menu that changes weekly and takes particular advantage of seasonal produce. In late summer, local tomatoes (which doesn't necessarily mean from Telluride but does mean from Montrose, just an hour away) might appear on the Rare Tuna Bruschetta on toasted *ciabatta,* with fresh mozzarella in the Local Tomato Salad, or in the Local Tomato Pizza. And that's just the appetizer course. Scothorn also digs deep into Thai, Japanese, Italian, and French flavors and techniques for inspiration, but he avoids mixing cuisines on one plate. Flavor contrasts? Yes. Texture contrasts? Yes. Visual artistry? Of course. But he keeps his culinary lines untangled.

Within his self-imposed constraints, Scothorn does a particularly refined job of matching the main ingredient in his entrées with interesting accompaniments that exhibit a perfect interplay of flavors, textures, and colors—Barbequed Salmon with crispy corn-potato ravioli, green bean and bacon salad, and corn broth. Grilled Pork Tenderloin with celeriac-potato hash, pumpkin seed–crusted asparagus, and mustard sauce. Seared Duck Breast and Seared Sea Scallops with lemon potatoes, arugula-orange salad, and ginger sauce. Seared Tuna with barbecued eggplant, vanilla rice, chive vinaigrette, and calamari.

Leave room for Cosmo's Molten Chocolate Cake, crème brulée, strawberry short-cake built on a poppy seed biscuit foundation, Chocolate Pistachio Bread Pudding with pistachio ice cream and bittersweet chocolate ice cream—or a simple house-made ice cream or sorbet.

Wineries of California, Australia, France, and Italy are represented in on the 200-selection wine list. Cosmo's ultimate wine experience is a dinner in the Tasting Cellar, adjacent to the restaurant. For the six-course prix fixe dinner available here, Scothorn focuses on modern French cuisine, and sommelier Keith Rainville pairs five selected wines with it. Dinner in the Tasting Cellar is available for groups of ten or more—and it's worth inviting, dredging up, or making nine friends so that you can experience it.

Cosmopolitan, Hotel Columbia, 300 West San Juan Avenue, Telluride; (970) 728-1292 or www.cosmotelluride.com.

Harmon's at the Depot

Telluride's solid, squat Queen Anne–style railroad depot opened in 1890, just in time for Thanksgiving turkeys and plum pudding from the wife of the Ridgway stationmaster to be unloaded. Regular trains operated to Telluride for only a few years before the Silver Panic of 1893 turned the town's first mineral boom into a bust. The Galloping Goose, an oddball hybrid of a truck body and engine that ran on the rails, carried passengers, mail, and some freight, then provided a link between Telluride and the world until 1951, after which the town no longer needed a railroad depot. For a while, San Miguel County used the station to store heavy equipment, and then it was rehabilitated into a brewpub.

The original interior space had been gutted, but at least the building still stood at the foot of South Townsend. In 1996, Harmon's at the Depot opened, with both the interior and exterior carefully restored. Beyond the preservation of this historically significant building, Telluride gained an elegant new restaurant, with a beautiful deck overlooking the San Miguel River for an idyllic summer spot.

One of the two main dining rooms is a little more woody and casual, the other a little more formal with pastel walls and fancier furnishings. The banquettes and chairs are covered with classic striped upholstery. On each table are a crisp white cloth, a starched fanned-out napkin, and a single white taper. Elegant simplicity—or simple elegance—on the tabletop.

The first executive chef, David Denman, and his successor, James Ackard, gave Harmon's its rep as a place for food that is variously described as New American, Rocky Mountain, or contemporary Colorado. Specific preparations and combinations have varied from year to year, season to season, and chef to chef. Foie gras, for instance, has been seared and served with butternut squash au gratin and cranberry syrup, grilled and served with a corn cake and huckleberry syrup, or pan-seared and served with caramelized pears and balsamic syrup. Similarly, the menu has, at various times, featured different species of trout, with crab cream and parsley piñon pilaf, finished with currant-Cabernet almandine, or New Mexican–style with Napole ragout. And so it goes through the menu. You can always expect a balance of meats, seafood, poultry, and vegetarian dishes, made with fresh ingredients and beautifully served.

Harmon's at the Depot, 300 South Townsend, Telluride; (970) 728-3773 or www.harmonsrestaurant.com.

La Marmotte

La Marmotte was the first fine French restaurant that I ate at in Telluride. Perhaps that's because it was then the only fine French restaurant in Telluride. Bertrand and Noelle Lepel-Coointet have maintained this super-French aura, immune to the growth and modernization in Telluride, since they opened the doors in 1987. He was born in Cognac—the region, not in a snifter of brandy—and grew up in Paris and the Pyrenees; she was born and raised in Lorraine. Over the years, a succession of French and American chefs have worked in their small kitchen, each one bringing another insight, another instinct, another aspect of culinary experience to La Marmotte.

Located in a century-old brick and weathered-wood building that was once the town's old ice storage house, La Marmotte is a cozy and inviting place, with low beamed ceilings, lots of warm wood, and intimate tables set with white linens, fresh flowers, and candles. It offers a seasonally changing menu that keeps the flavors refreshed and the kitchen *au courant*.

The menu retains its strong French accent, with all the dishes named in French, even if they are derivative. Therefore, you'll find Le Potage Vichyssoise à la Truffe for the classic chilled potato-leek soup with crème fraîche and truffle oil, but the Southwestern-style appetizer of shrimp marinated in garlic, lime, and smoked chilies appears on the menu as Les Gambas Grillées Marinées au Piment. La Marmotte builds many of its dishes on such mainstream ingredients as beef tenderloin, rack of lamb, chicken breast, salmon, tuna, and shrimp, and some familiars on French menus such as escargots, rabbit, and veal sweetbreads, as well as venison or other game. Another authentic *auberge* touch is *Le Menu Grand-Mère d'Aujourd'hui*— a four-course, prix fixe meal of the day—just like many a small inn in France. Bertrand himself presides over the extensive wine cellar, which holds French wines plus some from elsewhere around the world. The restaurant closes in spring and fall.

La Marmotte, 150 San Juan Avenue, Telluride; (970) 728-6232 or www.lamarmotte.com.

9545

Some restaurants, like 221 South Oak in downtown Telluride, call themselves by their street addresses, but 9545 in Mountain Village identifies itself just by its elevation. This attractive restaurant, located in The Inn at Lost Creek, combines

Scandinavian simplicity with lots of natural wood, stylish and subdued lighting, and San Juan Mountain views. Only the floor-to-ceiling wine rack in one corner can compete visually, at least in oenophiles' eyes.

Executive Chef Aaron Woo, who grew up in San Francisco and is a high honors graduate of the California Culinary Academy, cooked his way up the ladder in some of California's best-known restaurants. He worked at Absinthe, a San Francisco brasserie known for recreating French food from the Belle Époque era, at Stars Restaurant in the city's theater district, at the four-star La Folie under Chef Roland Passot, and at the Plumpjack Café with Keith Luce, named by the James Beard Foundation as a "Rising Star." Woo kept climbing the ladder to 9,545 feet, where he is the top toque.

His modern American cuisine, with some French and pan-Mediterranean accents, creates beguiling combinations for breakfast, ski-in ski-out lunches, and the best après-ski nibbles at the mountain resort, as well as gourmet dinners trendy as they come. The menu changes seasonally, but Woo draws from a culinary bag of tricks at dinner. He always sears something—Alaskan halibut served with Moroccan herb butter and barley *coulis,* or Atlantic salmon served with roasted beets, fresh herb salad, and red wine sauce. He might grill a pork tenderloin and present it with watercress and dried cherry port sauce. He might present grilled Black Angus rib eye with grilled red onions, watercress *marchand de vin* butter, and kohlrabi gratin He might braise beef shortribs and serve them with roasted beets, fennel, and chèvre potatoes.

A commendable wine list, Telluride's best selection of single-malt scotches, and a dessert list that changes as often as the dinner menu—and matches it in quality and creativity—complete the pretty picture at 9545.

9545, The Inn at Lost Creek, Telluride Mountain Village; (970) 728-5678, (970) 728-6293 or www.innatlostcreek.com.

221 South Oak

This charming restaurant, which was also named after its street address, is an American bistro encased in a quaint downtown Victorian. Within the old house, the delightful contemporary eatery sports buttery sponged walls, white table linens, and a spotlight on the food's beauty. Bob Scherner, who now heads the kitchen at Allred's (see 375) established the restaurant and set the culinary bar high. Current owner, Chef Eliza H. S. Goodall, spent her career refining her skills, knowledge, and food philosophy into what you will now find at 221 South Oak.

Goodall commanded her first kitchen while still a student at Tennessee's University of the South. She moved to New Orleans to immerse herself in Creole cuisine, cooking at Galatoire's and then at Mr. B's, a bistro managed by the Brennans, another New Orleans restaurant family. She attended the Culinary Institute of America at Greystone in Napa Valley; cooked at nearby Brix, an Asian-influenced fusion restaurant that was a James Beard nominee for the best new restaurant of 1997; and then moved to Paris to study at Le Cordon Bleu under some of France's best chefs. She cooked at 221 for a winter and bought the restaurant in the fall of 2000.

She made her mark quickly, but the dishes are moving targets, for the menu changes nightly. Goodall shines with her sizzling combos of super-fresh seafoods, vegetables, and a lesser selection of meats. With the playful and provocative combinations of ingredients that characterize New American cuisine, there's sophistication of preparation and presentation to Goodall's creations, and sometimes there's just plain wit—a quality in short supply in serious restaurants. Example? A recent appetizer called Menage à Foie, composed of foie gras, duck liver-Port pâté with caramelized shallots, and pecan-crusted foie gras baked in bread, all on one plate.

Having learned to love crawfish in New Orleans, Goodall uses it occasionally but effectively in such dishes as Crawfish Tails and Scallions, artfully arranged with pea shoots in a phyllo cup. She ranges far and wide in her choice of ingredients, centering dishes on such varied items as diver scallops, Muscovy duck breast, ahi tuna, rabbit, Peekytoe crab, and pheasant pastrami, some of which are positively exotic and others more common. She augments her dishes with sauces, vegetables, compotes, and other essences that are innovative to the max. The wines of California and France comprise the majority of 221 South Oak's wine cellar. On the list, the wines are categorized by varietal for American wines and by region for French wines.

221 South Oak, 221 South Oak Street, Telluride; (970) 728-9507 or www.221southoak.com.

Events

Chocolate Lover's Fling

February—The annual Chocolate Lover's Fling, held around Valentine's Day, showcases some of Telluride's finest pastry chefs to benefit the San Miguel Resource Center's domestic violence and sexual assault services. Guests are encouraged to assault the chocolate creations with forks, spoons, whatever it takes. Most people try to taste as many different kinds of chocolate dishes as possible, but chefs compete in a serious culinary contest for honors in the categories of Most Decadent, Most Original, Most Artistic, Most Whimsical, and Fruit Forward (for the rare chocophobes in the crowd). Chocolate quesadillas, a chocolate dragon, and a stunning assemblage of cakes, tortes, pastries, mousses, and more have appeared on, and been snatched from, the tasting tables at past Flings.

For a relatively modest outlay ($45 in 2002) guests work off some of the immodest caloric intake by dancing to music matched to that year's theme. Recently, it has been Cuban–Latino, with "tropical black tie" the recommended dress to recall the decadent ambience of pre-Castro Cuba. The venue is the Wyndham Peaks in Mountain Village.

For information, call (970) 749-5842.

Telluride Wine Festival

June—Telluride established its groundbreaking Telluride Wine Festival in 1981, long before there was a wine industry in the Rocky Mountain Region—and, some would say, before there were many true wine drinkers. One of the event's philosophical underpinnings was to provide a comfortable forum in which consumers with all levels of wine experience could sample fine wines from around the world. In the first year, the festival attracted 200 guests and 28 wineries from the United States, France, Portugal, and Germany, which is pretty remarkable when you think about it.

By 1989 there were 50 wineries, and 1,200 consumers. That led to the Toast of Telluride, in which attendees stroll through town tasting wine at various locations, followed by a gala Sunday brunch, featuring local chefs and regional cuisine. In 1991, the festival finally grew large enough to require a tent village set up in Town Park, a beautiful location with spectacular views of Bear Creek and the surrounding 13,000-foot peaks with 70 wineries from more than 11 countries represented.

Since the early 1990s, wine-maker luncheons have been held each day of the event. Great chefs prepare fabulous midday feasts matched with three or four wines for each course. A featured sommelier hosts each luncheon, guiding guests course by course. Wine makers and civilians dine together at luncheon tables, providing an opportunity to learn about the featured wines.

Cooking demonstrations were added in 1995, the number of seminars was increased and expanded, and a fine-wine tasting was added on Saturday afternoon. The Culinary School of Denver's Colorado Institute of Art (see page 20), which began partnering with the festival in 1997, now sends 20 to 30 students to work with such stellar guest chefs as John Ash, Christopher Gross, Ann Rosenzweig, Bobby Flay, Doug Rodriguez, Chris Schlesinger, and Joyce Goldstein.

The Telluride Wine Festival is a nonprofit corporation operated exclusively for the benefit of the community. Net proceeds are given to different local charitable, cultural, or educational organizations each year. The festival, which now is divided between events in Telluride and Mountain Village, has grown to four days in late June.

Among the notable sommeliers, chefs, and restaurateurs who have recently lent their palates and expertise are Wayne Belding and Sally Mohr of the Boulder Wine Merchant (see page 141). From New York's Blue Ribbon Restaurant came Bruce Bromberg and Morgan Grove.

Brian Julyan, the author of three books to the trade, is a master sommelier and creator of the Court of Master Sommeliers worldwide (see page 142). Mark Krasic, a former chef at the Peaks Resort, now is a Telluride caterer. Neither Julyan nor Chad Scothorn, owner/chef of Telluride's Cosmopolitan, have to travel to share their expertise with festival-goers, and the Telluride Wine Festival is fortunate to have them so close at hand.

Joshua Wesson, another 2002 speaker, is one of the country's wine celebs. He won the first competition as the United States' best sommelier when he was only 28 and has since managed to sip and spit his way into the highest ranks of the wine world. Wesson also coauthored *Red Wine with Fish: The New Art of Matching Wine with Food* and is a popular speaker on the wine festival circuit.

For information on the Telluride Wine Festival, call (970) 728-4773 or log onto www.telluridewinefestival.com.

Telluride Mushroom Festival

August—The Telluride Mushroom Festival attracts both experienced and wannabe mycologists. People are drawn there for a variety of reasons; they include aging hippies interested mainly in the hallucinatory properties of psilocybin mushrooms, health-conscious folks who want to learn about mushrooms' nutritional and medicinal qualities, ecologists who want to learn how various fungi can decontaminate toxic areas, growers who want to learn how to cultivate mushrooms, and, of course, culinary connoisseurs who love to eat mushrooms and often want to learn how to forage for them.

Some people cruise into Telluride in gleaming SUVs and dine on mushroom dinners put on by some of the town's top restaurants. They wear stylish sportswear and exude a sense of "today." Others rattle into town in pickups and psychedelic VW buses. They wear tie-dyed shirts, granny skirts, long hair, and Birkenstocks or Tevas and radiate an aura of "yesteryear." It's the oddest, and in many ways most satisfying, of Colorado's many food festivals because it remains aggressively noncommercial with no high-profile official anything. The old hippies feel right at home, and the well-off gourmands feel as if they've gone local.

Kick-off is a wacky parade down Colorado Avenue, Telluride's wide main street. Participants wear costumes, hats, masks, or umbrellas resembling their favorite fungi and thump on drums or some other percussion instrument. Art Goodtimes, one of the festival's originators, drives a red pickup with white dots resembling a four-wheeled, motorized fly mushroom (*amanita muscaria*, beautiful but poisonous). Mushroom dishes are encouraged for the first-night potluck picnic in Elks Park, but in truth, many people seem to bring store-bought. The back-to-the-land, make-it-from-scratch ethos that characterized Telluride's real hippie years certainly has eroded. On the two following days, the tent that had housed the potluck becomes a temporary mushroom museum for specimens collected on forays into the nearby mountains. Scores of examples are displayed, labeled, and described—and similar-looking mushrooms, one species edible and the other not, are paired with the subtle differences explained in writing. People spend a lot of time in the tent, picking up and sniffing the mushrooms and comparing the real ones with the posted pictures and information. Mushroom identification lectures appeal to everyone from beginning to experienced wild mushroom collectors.

Sessions bounce back and forth between venues, from the high school—where acoustics are excellent—to Elks Park, where even with amplification, speakers are sometimes hard to hear. One message that comes through loud and clear is that most Americans are afraid of mushrooms unless under cellophane in a supermarket. One recent speaker called Brits and Americans "mycophobic," pointing out that mushrooms are part of the tradition of other cultures. Germans, French, and Asians love and trust mushrooms. They go into the woods to pick them, taking their children along so that they too grow up loving and trusting mushrooms. They know the difference between those they can eat and those they can't. "To mycologists, knowing the difference between poisonous and safe mushrooms is like knowing the difference between a carrot and a tomato," the speaker commented.

Experts guide daily forays—some very early in the morning—to find wild mushrooms in the nearby mountains and woods, an unsurpassed opportunity go out with an experienced mycologist who will help identify what you put into your basket. Boletes and chanterelles, both fairly easy to identify, are among the more common edibles in the San Juans—and they are very tasty too. Experienced fungophiles are properly equipped for their mushroom safaris with flat-bottomed collecting baskets. After being identified, prized specimens are wrapped in wax paper and taken home or to a condo kitchen for a mushroom-centered meal. The annual Mushroom Taste and Feast takes place on the last night, followed by Mushroom Music and Poetry.

If the festival's eclectic nature leaves you doubting that it belongs in a food book, consider the menu for a recent final feast: Tempura Chanterelles with Arugula and Maytag Blue Cheese paired with a 1999 Mirassou Pinot Blanc; Seared Tuna with Shrimp Russula Mushroom Crostini with 1999 Domaine Côtes de Gascogne; Shiitake Egg Drop Soup with 1999 Drouhin Beaujolais-Villages; Pan-Roasted Alaskan Halibut with Purple Sticky Rice and Oyster Mushroom Broth with 1998 Hunter Ashby Chardonnay; an intermezzo of Lemon Sorbet; a fifth course of New Zealand Cervena Venison with Porcini Green Peppercorn Sauce and Wehani Rice Roll with 1999 Ellen Landing Petit Verdot; and finally Bittersweet Chocolate Soufflé with Truffle Honey Ice Cream.

To warm up for the big feast and escape from the festival's funkier aspects to Telluride's fancier side, visit one of several top local restaurants that usually offer special Mushroom Festival menus such as Campagna, Cosmopolitan, La Marmotte, and 221 South Oak. During the classes, you can glean more mushroom knowledge than you ever thought existed, and any of these divine chef-prepared dinners remind you why well-selected, well-prepared mushrooms are true delicacies.

Telluride Mushroom Festival, c/o Fungophile, Inc., P.O. Box 480503, Denver, CO 80248-0503; (970) 296-9359 or www.telluride.com/mushroom.html.

Retail

At Home in Telluride

On the east end of Colorado Avenue, where Telluride's main street tapers off is At Home in Telluride, which supplies cooking utensils and tableware to local cooks and visitors alike. An indication of the temptations that lie within is seating designated as the "spouse chair" for husbands waiting while their wives shop.

Those temptations include kitchen essentials and "wanna-haves." Cookware and gadgets by Progressive and NorPro and additional gadgets by OXO entice the cooking enthusiast. But Telluride is as much about entertaining as cooking, so festive table-ware and glassware get big play. Among the most popular themes are stoneware pieces on natural mountain themes. "If it's got an elk or a moose, we probably carry it," one saleswoman says. At Home in Telluride also specializes in such decorative accessories as candles, frames, ceramics, linens, and bed and bath products. The store also stocks craft items by Colorado artisans and gourmet foods such as soup mixes, spreads, seasonings, and cheese from Colorado and elsewhere.

At Home in Telluride, 137 East Colorado Avenue, Telluride; (970) 728-6865.

Rose Victorian Food Mart

Behind the red awning is Telluride's town supermarket, located in the gray visitors center building at the entrance to town. In addition to providing all the staples required by locals and visitors from pasta to Pampers, dairy products to baked goods, canned soups to condiments, it is also the leading source for deli and gourmet products, fresh produce, meats, and perhaps most significantly, a good assortment of fish flown in on Tuesdays and Fridays. That, of course, is when locals line up for salmon, ahi tuna, red trout, halibut, swordfish, shrimp, scallops, crab, and whatever else might be seasonal and good. Such a store wouldn't be worth an eyeblink in a big city, but for the small and rather remote town of Telluride, it's worth a long stare. Geared for locals and visitors, it is open every day of the year. Prices are high, but it beats a 65-mile drive to Montrose for just a few items—and even fresh fish from there won't improve during the 65-mile drive back.

Rose Victorian Food Mart, 700 West Colorado Avenue, Telluride; (970) 728-3124.

Wines

Fine Wine at Mountain Village

Old-town Telluride has the lion's share of the resort's good restaurants with the most ambitious wine lists, but Fine Wine at Mountain Village caters to the resort's oenophiles—and even downtown Telluridians hop onto the gondola to shop for wine there too. The store, located in the Franz Klammer Lodge, offers more than 100 domestic and imported wines. With seven-figure condos and stratospherically priced vacation homes nearby, the shop stocks wines priced up to $300 a bottle.

In addition, it sells spirits, beer, cigars, what it calls "wine-friendly food," snacks for kids, and wine accessories. Manager and buyer Mike Florence, who passed the first-level master sommelier exam not long before this book was written, is knowledgeable about the store's selections and fills special orders for varieties not in stock.

Member benefits of the store's wine club include a 10 percent discount on all purchases, first invitations to and discounts on wine tastings and wine dinners at local restaurants, e-mail specials, first notice of the arrival of hard-to-find wines, access to local restaurant wine lists, a wine and cheese party before a Sunset Concert Series show, and wine classes. Also, members who come to Telluride as visitors or homeowners who are only in Telluride part-time can pre-order their wines before arrival. Just to show how high-toned Telluride Mountain Village has become, the store offers free delivery in Telluride and Mountain Village for purchases over $150 and free delivery in the surrounding area for purchases over $250.

Fine Wine at Mountain Village, Franz Klammer Lodge, Mountain Village; (970) 728-2311.

Recipes

Bob Scherner who presides over the kitchen at Allred's, Telluride's mountaintop culinary temple, is a master of complex, exquisite dishes that combine artistic presentation and sublime taste. His simpler creations are equally wonderful. For a smaller group, this recipe can be halved, or you can make the entire quantity of soup and refrigerate or freeze some for later use.

Celery and Apple Soup with Spicy Pecans

¼ pound (1 stick) unsalted butter
1 yellow onion, peeled and medium diced
3 medium heads of celery root, peeled, washed, and medium diced
2 gala apples, peeled, cored, and medium diced
2 quarts chicken stock
salt and pepper to taste
Spicy Pecans (recipe below)
peeled, diced, and blanched celery for garnish
diced apple for garnish
fresh thyme leaves for garnish

In a soup pot over medium heat, melt butter and gently cook onions until clear. Add celery root and apples, lower heat, and continue cooking 15 minutes, stirring occasionally. Add chicken stock, bring to a boil, then lower heat and simmer 20 minutes, or until all vegetables are tender. Pour mixture, in batches, into blender, and blend on high until smooth. Strain, season with salt and pepper to taste, reheat in a clean pot, and serve with Spicy Pecans and garnishes of celery, apple, and thyme. Serves 12.

Spicy Pecans
2 tablespoons grapeseed or canola oil
1 cup pecan halves and pieces
1 teaspoon cayenne pepper
½ teaspoon ground cumin
½ teaspoon ground coriander
salt and pepper to taste

In a sauté pan over medium heat, heat oil. Add pecans and spices, and cook until toasted. Cool.

Cosmopolitan puts on mushroom feasts to coincide with the annual Telluride Mushroom Festival. Festival time or not, Chef Chad Scothorn likes this versatile ragout with chicken, various meats, or by itself. He especially recommends serving it with grilled chicken breast and garlic mashed potatoes. The ragout can be held warm for up to an hour, or chilled and reheated. King bolete mushrooms are also known in this country by their Italian name (*porcini*), their French name (*cèpes*), and occasionally even by their German name (*Steinpilze*). They are found growing wild in Colorado, are sometimes available in select gourmet grocery stores and ethnic markets, and can be purchased dried year-round.

King Bolete (Porcini) Ragout

1 large king bolete (approximately 1 pound)
1 tablespoon unsalted butter
1 leek, sliced and well washed
2 cloves garlic, peeled and chopped
2 tablespoons brandy
¼ cup white wine
½ cup chicken stock
½ cup tomato, peeled, seeded, and diced
4 tablespoons unsalted butter
salt and pepper to taste
chopped chives to garnish

If you are using wild king bolete, inspect it for pine needles and remove. Rinse mushroom very quickly, pat dry, and slice. In a sauté pan, melt 1 tablespoon butter and, over high heat, sauté the bolete and leeks, stirring occasionally, until cooked thoroughly. Add the garlic and continue cooking for 20 seconds. Add brandy and white wine, and ignite carefully. Flambé to burn off the alcohol. Add chicken stock and diced tomato. Lower heat and simmer for 5 minutes. Season to taste with salt and pepper. Just before serving, stir in 3 tablespoons of cold butter. Garnish with chopped chives. Serves 4.

Durango

Durango feels like part of Colorado yet detached from it. It is the "capital" of south-western Colorado, the region's largest community, and the fulcrum between the southwestern desert of the Four Corners area and the Alp-like peaks of the San Juan Range. It is a recreational mecca for skiers, mountain bikers, fly-fishermen, and rafters, the home of Fort Lewis College (which sits on a mesa just east of downtown), and offers a base for excursions to nearby Mesa Verde National Park and rides on the Durango & Silverton Narrow Gauge Railroad, which depart from the downtown depot.

Nestled in a broad valley where the mountains taper off into mesaland, Durango is separated from other significantly sized communities by the natural mountain barriers and open spaces typical of the Western landscape. Coal Bank Pass, Molas Pass, and the scenic but formidable Red Mountain Pass lie to the north; to the east, Wolf Creek Pass; to the west, the Four Corners' arid mesa and canyon country, akin to the landscapes of adjacent New Mexico, Arizona, and Utah. Farmington, New Mexico, is to the south, and beyond lies Albuquerque, which is actually much closer to Durango than is Denver.

This gives Durango a feeling of uniqueness and independence—not in an introverted, isolated sense but in a way that has allowed the small city to develop its own character. The traditional downtown center, full of Western history and home-town charm, is also the epicenter of Durango's culinary scene. Most of the top restaurants, bakeries, and brewpubs are located within a few blocks of each other, as are shops, galleries, a couple of historic hotels, and a few landmark bed-and-breakfast inns. Locals, tourists, and college kids alike do appreciate the abundance of good, varied, and often reasonably priced restaurant food. Gourmet food products and quality cooking apparatus are becoming ever easier to find, and local food and wine events keep foodies' taste buds sharp.

Bakeries

Bread

The best bread in Durango is made by Bread. In fact, some of the best bread in Colorado is made by Bread. This friendly, family-oriented bakery turns out quality, natural breads handcrafted from organic ingredients and made with skill and love. Owner Rob Kaberry has been baking breads since 1980, both in the United States and France—as well as for good causes in developing countries.

Before settling in Durango, he also baked on Nantucket, in Boston, and Atlanta; owned Bigwood Bread in Sun Valley, Idaho; and worked briefly at Daily Bread in Boulder. You've got to admire anyone who can turn out first-rate breads in climates as different as hot and humid Atlanta, cool and coastal Nantucket, and high and dry Durango at more than 6,500 feet above sea level, as well as someone who has taken his useful craft to countries where his skills have been needed.

Bread's substantial, handcrafted loaves taste as delicious as they look. Kaberry bakes only with organic flour, sea salt, water, and whatever flavors or add-ins a particular recipe requires. The long Italian loaf and the oblong semolina are encrusted with sesame seeds. The ciabatta has a rich yet subtle goodness. The raisin-pecan is a double-ended torpedo full of texture and flavor, as is the round potato-sage. The Pain de Olive is Bread's own thick, crusted calamata-filled olive bread. The multigrain, as healthy as they come, looks and tastes like a provincial artisan bread. Bread's slogan is "Fresh Fuel . . . Hand Crafted and Baked Daily." Under Kaberry's guidance, reality matches the slogan.

In addition to outstanding artisan bread and related baked goods, Bread also turns out excellent croissants, Danish, and scones. Locals stop by for excellent breakfast pastry, coffee, sandwiches, and such, either to take out or to eat at the store or on the small patio right by the parking lot. There's even a swing for kids to play on while parents relax, and if youngsters root around amid the newspapers and magazines that adults enjoy browsing, they might unearth a treasured copy of photojournalist Ken Heyman's classic children's book *Bread, Bread, Bread*, about the role of breads in the lives of children around the world.

Kaberry says that he might eventually expand into the dessert category—or perhaps even open a bakery or two elsewhere—but for the moment, there is but one location where his breads are baked and sold oven-fresh. His life is all about baking and selling a tight selection of first-rate products, including excellent cheeses and natural juices and soft drinks. Bread doesn't advertise, and Kaberry doesn't promote. He just bakes—and welcomes locals and visitors who appreciate his efforts. And they do.

Bread, Florida & County Road 250, Durango; (970) 247-1000.

Jean Pierre Bakery of North America

The Jean Pierre behind Jean Pierre Bakery of North America has been baking original breads, pastries, and cookies since 1969. He was born virtually in the center of France but moved to Paris as a young teen to train formally at the baking academy called Le Grand Moulin de Paris—the Great Mill of Paris. He eventually left the City of Lights to bake in coastal Houston, where he met his wife, Rebecca. In 1992, they opened the Durango bakery that bears his name.

He began producing the baked goods that he knows best and shipping them all over the country. In addition to the sensational French sourdough called Pain au Levain, specialty breads include baguettes, French rolls, and a po'boy sandwich bread from New Orleans with French roots. His sinful butter cookies called *galettes* are absolutely addictive, and plain or filled croissants are another specialty.

Though primarily a wholesale and mail-order bakery located in a no-nonsense building, Jean Pierre Bakery will sell to anyone who comes in the door during business hours. "We always bake extra baguettes," says Rebecca, "because people always want them." If you want them too, follow Old Main Highway (more properly Eighth Avenue) on the southeast corner of town, turn right half-a-block north of the Sonic Drive-In, and there you are.

Jean Pierre Bakery of North America, 873 East Third Street, Durango; (800) 742-4863, (970) 247-7700, or www.jeanpierrebakery.com.

Le Rendezvous Swiss Bakery

Another Pierre bakes at Durango's little corner of Switzerland, Le Rendezvous Swiss Bakery, which is considerably easier find. Pierre Rochat's Le Rendezvous is in the heart of downtown. Pastry cases display a scrumptious assortment of authentic European pastries, plus popular American varieties. In fact, several Durango area cafés get their pastries from Le Rendezvous, so you might have sampled its goods without even knowing it.

Baked goods are made with Continental panache. The croissants are excellent alone or fashioned into sandwiches. The Four Corners Croissant—sliced in half, filled with scrambled eggs, cheese, avocado, tomatoes, and sprouts, and served with potatoes or cheese—is a locals' favorite. There's usually a daily special too, perhaps crêpes or another treat, and you can also get light meals, either to eat in or take out. A couple of tables at each window for people-watching and more in the back accommodate eat-in patrons.

Le Rendezvous Swiss Bakery, 750 Main Avenue, Durango; (970) 385-5685.

Cooking Classes

Guido's Favorite Foods

In addition to offering fine prepared foods and gourmet groceries (see page 402) all with an Italian flair, Guido's owner Sean Devereaux, a trained chef, conducts week-night cooking and baking classes in the commercial kitchen behind the store. Not surprisingly, his focus is on Italian cuisine, which is his personal passion and his store's retail specialty. Several levels of participation classes are offered, from a very basic introduction to those focusing on more complex and time-consuming techniques such as making from-scratch pasta and desserts.

Guido's Favorite Foods, 3000 Main Avenue, Durango; (970) 259-5028.

Dining

Ariano's

Vincent Ferraro, Ariano's owner-chef, has been preparing northern Italian cuisine since 1984, quite an impressive run for a fine dining restaurant in a tourist and college community. Soothing peach-colored walls and subdued decorative touches create a tranquil and pleasing atmosphere. Rather than exploring new culinary territory, Ferraro's dishes are really well-done classics, with pasta made in-house of semolina and egg, fresh mozzarella and seafood, and quality meats and poultry.

Chances are that the menu will show several ways favorites can be prepared. Calamari comes deep-fried or in a salad. Fettuccini comes with choice of Alfredo sauce, Napolitano (light tomato sauce with herbs, crushed red pepper, and shrimp), prosciutto, and two versions of primavera sauce (one with cheese, butter, and cream, the second with tomatoes instead of cream). Same idea with the linguine, offered with a choice of three sauces. Chicken is done either with Marsala sauce, baked in parchment with prosciutto and herbs, with tomato sauce and mozzarella, and with olives. Chicken Vincent, a house specialty, is chicken breast sautéed in olive oil and finished with bell peppers, scallions, and mushrooms.

Veal is served in six versions: Veal Michael (despite the name, actually an Alfredo sauce), Pizziola (with tomato sauce and mozzarella), Piccata with oil and garlic, Marsala with sage and garlic, or Zingara (sautéed with prosciutto, mushrooms, and red bell peppers). The signature beef entrée is a sautéed tenderloin on toast and topped with herb sauce. Clams are key ingredients in several of the linguine dishes, and other seafood dishes center on shrimp and trout. Ferraro does Rocky Mountain and rainbow trout stuffed and baked, sautéed, and also left whole (rolled in cornmeal, sautéed in olive oil and deboned at the table).

Silky zabaglione, rich Chocolate Kahlua Cheesecake, and a restaurant classic, three-flavor spumoni ice cream roll, are standards on Ariano's dessert menu, but you will also be offered daily specials. The full wine list features domestic and Italian wines, of course.

Ariano's, 190 East College Drive, Durango; (970) 247-8146 or www.durango.com/dp/arianos/.

Chez Grand-mère

If you still wonder, as I long did, what happened to Chez Grand-mère, wonder no more. This classic French and Belgian restaurant, established in Snowmass in 1982, was reborn in Durango in 1996, garnering much less attention than the original location in glamorous Aspen's outlier received.

Owner-chef Michel Poumay reestablished the restaurant's charming setting and again began to serve full-on, multicourse feasts and à la carte dinner selections. Located in a quaint false-front Victorian building behind the Ralph Lauren Polo outlet in downtown Durango, this intimate restaurant is romantically furnished with pressed-back chairs, white napery, antique accents, floral displays, and lace curtains. Attentive service is as much a hallmark as the atmosphere and the carefully prepared and artfully presented food.

Chez Grand-mère is all about leisurely dining, especially if you go for the sumptuous six-course dinner, Poumay's specialty. Chez-mère's prix fixe menu consists of an hors d'oeuvre selection, a choice of appetizer, salad with the restaurant's own fresh bread, a choice of entrée with suitable vegetable accompaniment, a choice of desserts from the pastry cart, and coffee or tea. The dishes do change, but among the appetizers you are likely to find something like Pâté Garni Maison, Coquille of Fruits de Mer, Tartellette of Salmon-Shallot Beurre Blanc, Sea Scallops with Honey and Ginger, and Escargot Ravioli with Goat Cheese and Vodka. Typical of the entrée list are Striped Bass with Avocado and Shrimp, Rack of Lamb with Fines Herbes, Roast Duck with Raspberries and Port-Stuffed Quail Forestière, Red Snapper with Mussels and Saffron, Filet Mignon with Green Peppercorn Sauce, and Medallion of Deer with Lingonberry Sauce. The extensive wine list of imported and domestic vintages complements the menu, and the entire Chez Grand-mère experience is a compliment to Durango.

Chez Grand-mère, 3 Depot Place, Durango; (970) 247-7979 or www.frontier.net/chezgrand-mere.

Cyprus Café

A converted Victorian house in historic downtown Durango serves excellent and interesting Mediterranean dishes in a romantic and charming setting. In the warm months, the patio is one of Durango's most evocative places to dine. Owner chef Alison Dance combines a little bit of Greek, a little bit of Middle Eastern, and a little bit of Italian for her dishes. She spent 18 years in San Francisco, eating and cooking her way through wonderful restaurants in the City by the Bay before opening her own Greek restaurant there. In 1996, she launched Cyprus Café, satisfying Durango's tastes for the slightly exotic.

The menu changes quarterly, and Dance and sous-chef David Steward use it to play a Mediterranean medley. With commonality of some key ingredients but totally different realizations, the approach works on the café's Colorado lamb and other meat, seafood, pasta, and vegetarian selections.

Two combo appetizers are offered, an Italian antipasto platter and the Combo Mezze, featuring such eastern Mediterranean favorites as hummus, baba ghanoush, tzatziki, olives, feta, and spanakopita with grilled pita. The entrées always include a Colorado lamb dish. The cuts vary—shank, chops, or whatever. So do the preparations—marinated, chargrilled, and so on. Lamb Souvlakia on pita bread comes with a cool, yogurt, cucumber, garlic, and mint sauce, and there's generally at least one other lamb dish. Kota Salata, grilled free-range chicken breast served on a bed of greens with feta cheese and toasted walnuts, is a house specialty. The signature seafood entrée is Salmon sto Fourna, fresh fish baked in a parchment packet with goat cheese, grape leaves, and olive–caper tapenade.

Rich house-made desserts include baklava, traditional or updated with cashews and chocolate. Chocolate *pots de crèmes* are another Cyprus signature. Dance dismisses them as being "nothing unusual—just a bucket of chocolate," but regulars would mount a rebellion if she ever removed them from the menu.

Order some wine—domestic or imported, with Greece's powerfully flavored *retsina* strictly optional—and transport yourself from Durango to sunny (or moonlit) Greece and other parts of the Mediterranean.

Cyprus Café, 725 East Second Avenue, Durango; (970) 385-6884.

Henry's Chop House

Henry's is a hotel restaurant at the landmark Strater, built in 1887 of brick and sandstone. This jewel probably looks better, and definitely looks more romantic, than it did more than 125 years ago, with hand-screened wallpapers, one of the world's largest collections of antique furniture from that era, one of America's few remaining authentic vaudeville melodramas, a listing on the National Register of Historic Places, and a heart-of-downtown location. The Strater belongs to the prestigious Historic Hotels of America group and the Historic Hotels of the Rockies group. When the engineer toots the whistle as the Durango & Silverton train passes behind it, you'll feel as if you've traveled back in time and are living back in the hotel's early history. Louis L'Amour loved the place and penned some of his Sackett novels there—and you'll love it too.

The opulently decorated hotel restaurant, Henry's Chop House—or more properly, Henry's Chop House & Italian Bistro—recalls the atmosphere that the famous author experienced. A pianist plays ragtime tunes to entertain diners, as was customary before the age of canned music and a TV over the bar. Within the context of back-in-time ambience and in-your-face haute-Victorian décor, the kitchen turns out hearty meat dishes and Italian specialties. aimed squarely at the hordes of tourists who eat there.

The meant-to-share starter is Warm Spinach, Crab, & Artichoke Dip with toasted French bread and tortilla. Aimed at the sophisticated palate? No, but tasty? Yes. Same with the Special Recipe Deep Dish Lasagna, with Italian sausage, mozzarella, ricotta, and Bolognese sauce layered between sheets of fresh pasta. People love the Gorgonzola Salad, made of mixed greens, red grapes, and toasted walnuts with crumbled blue cheese and raspberry vinaigrette, an unusual meld of tart and sweet.

The menu category of "House Classics" offers the big meat dishes and many of the Italian entrées, such as grilled New York steak with a Texas dry rub or "New York pesto rub," buffalo rib eye, center-cut pork chops, and the tongue-tingling, tummy-filling house specialty pepper steak. Henry's surf and turf couples filet mignon Oscar with crayfish. Italian entrées under "House Classics" include chicken Parmigiana and eggplant Parmigiana served with linguine veal Florentine-style scaloppini, with porcini mushrooms, or as Marsala-braised *osso bucco*.

Desserts are as rich as the 19th-century entrepreneurs who once stepped through the Strater's doors. Tìramisu with vanilla bean *crème anglais*, White Chocolate Cheesecake in a pistachio nut crust, Blackberry Crème Brulée, Chocolate Torte with hazelnut ice cream from the Durango Creamery, and the unique Chocolate-Covered Banana Eggroll lead the dessert parade. Wines? Of course. Breakfast? Yes, as a hotel restaurant, Henry's sets out a full buffet breakfast. Sunday brunch? Sensational.

Henry's Chop House, Strater Hotel, 699 Main Avenue, Durango; (970) 247-4433, (907) 247-4431 (hotel number) or www.strater.com.

Ken & Sue's

Ken and Sue Fusco—he a Culinary Institute of America graduate—moved to Durango from south Florida in 1998 and established a cutting-edge restaurant at 937 Main Street. With its bistro style and innovative mixture of upscale comfort food, contemporary Southwestern dishes, and a few that touched on Asian and Italian cuisine, it gained a reputation as one of the best new restaurants, not only in Durango, but also in the entire Four Corners Region.

So successful was that restaurant that the couple opened a second, larger establishment a few blocks to the east at 636 Main Avenue. To avoid confusion, or perhaps create it, the restaurants were respectively called 937 Main Ken & Sue's Place and 636 Main Ken & Sue's East. The new one had a more sophisticated look and a slightly more Asian influence on the menu than the original. Still, running two excellent restaurants with similar names and similar approaches became a little too schitzy, and in late 2002, the Fuscos consolidated them into the stylish space at 636 Main. The merged restaurant, simply called Ken & Sue's, serves lunch and dinner seven days a week.

The interior is noteworthy for the generous use of mahogany—bar, back bar, and wall trim—contrasted against white walls to create a sophisticated setting. Add to that subtly lighted artwork on the walls, a sculpture tucked into a corner of the bar, small red-shaded lights suspended over the bar, and shining wood floors, and you have ambience galore. The restaurant is divided almost 50/50 between dining and bar areas, but when you add the tables in the glass-enclosed patio in back, dining wins over drinking.

Ken presides over what is arguably Durango's most creative kitchen. The menu, which changes periodically but not frantically, is a symphony of Italian, Thai, Chinese, Japanese, Asian, and North American influences—sometimes two or more in one dish. There are no more than a dozen entrées, but fusion reigns. Prince Edward Island Mussels are served in a fiery Green Curry Broth that harkens to Southeast Asia. Grilled Sirloin Satay comes with spicy slaw and a tamari-sake dipping sauce. Ancho-Dusted Gulf Shrimp with Arugula, Mangoes, Avocado, Tomatoes, and Cilantro–Lime Vinaigrette combines flavors from the Caribbean/Gulf of Mexico region, Mexico, and Italy. And that's just for starters.

A recent summer special was Lobster–Mascarpone-Stuffed House-Made Spinach Ravioli in Brown Butter Sauce, four large—and rich—ravioli pillows artfully arranged on the plate. Cilantro-Crusted Halibut with Sticky Rice, Baby Bok Choy, and Sake–Tamari Sauce and Grilled Tuna with Basmati Rice, Peanut–Lime Sauce, and Mango Salsa are examples of taking two popular American fish, preparing them perfectly, and complementing them with Asian flavors.

Creative side dishes are a hallmark, and I love making an entrée of the Sampler Platter—a choice of four of eight side dishes. That same summer menu presented Giant Onion Rings, Blistered Asparagus, Crispy Spinach, Sticky Rice, Red and Blue Smashers, Lobster-Yukon Smashers, Marinated Plum Tomatoes, and Baby Bok Choy. Any four will comprise a satisfying meal and make for a fine vegetarian option. Smashers is Ken and Sue's name for the restaurant's signature beautifully flavored mashed potatoes, intentionally left chunky for texture. The restaurant's popular nightly pasta special is so large that doggie bags are the order of the day. On the small dessert list, the house specialty is a rich Molten Chocolate Cake with Durango Creamery Home-Made Coconut Ice Cream. Made to order, it should be requested while the meal is in progress. Michael's Bananas Foster with Crème Caramel combines two popular dessert flavors. The wine list, strong on both California and imported vintages, is selected to work well with this eclectic menu.

Sunday brunch is a standout. If you're in the mood for the breakfast part of the spectrum, try one of the omelettes (some locals declare the cream-cheese version to be winner). If lunch is more to your liking, you can get anything from the likes of a hearty spicy Korean noodle soup to American-style chicken potpie—with exotic touches, of course. The specific offerings change, but the range is always there.

Ken & Sue's, 636 Main Avenue, Durango; (970) 385-1810.

Meritage Café

The "Meritage" sign on the side of the building near the Durango & Silverton Narrow Gauge Railroad depot marks an upscale sandwicheria that offers an economical alternative to the ubiquitous fast-food joints and Tex-Mex places for lunch or early dinner.

Deep red-and-yellow walls accented with tiles, basketry, and nostalgic and collectible memorabilia are easy on the eyes. Meritage plays several roles from such a small stage: deli, kitchen specialty boutique, restaurant, bistro/café by day, and low-key dinner spot in the evening. It serves quality soups, chowders, salads, and excellent sandwiches. Good versions of ham, roast beef, turkey, and other standards are made mostly with imported meats and cheeses, with pasta or potato salad on the side. Meritage also offers exotics like Thai pork, surprisingly good between two slices of bread. Whether standard or special, sandwiches packed to go are great for a ride on the Durango & Silverton. In addition, Meritage serves a selection of appetizers, a good match for the wines by the glass or bottle that inspired its name.

Meritage Café, 558 Main Avenue, Durango; (970) 259-3148.

The Red Snapper

The Red Snapper has been offering good seafood since the late 1980s—in many ways creating a regional demand for it. To contrast with the nearby desert environment, the restaurant has established an aquatic atmosphere, including acrylic saltwater aquariums scattered about. Owners Rick and Karen Langhart instituted "First Catch" early-bird special dinners and also an oyster hour with oysters on the half-shell, Oysters Rockefeller, Oysters Creole, Oysters Durango, and Oysters Parmesan. If mollusks are not your thing, consider one of the mushroom appetizers. Another option is to jump straight to the salad bar, included with all entrées, which some locals swear is the best in town.

The restaurant gets its fish and shellfish fresh, and the kitchen treats them right. Take your choice of species and preparation, some traditional, some adapted, and others invented. Of course, the Red Snapper serves red snapper, presented as Red Snapper Monterey, Louisiana, or Parmesan. Other options include shrimp scampi, ahi tuna from Hawaii, Australian lobster tails, Scallops Dijonaise or Santa Cruz, New Orleans Shrimp, Blackened Salmon, Cajun Mahi-Mahi, and king crab legs. Rocky Mountain trout also is available, served amandine or Parmesan.

In addition to finding the town's most extensive selection of seafood, guests snap up fine prime rib, poultry, and pasta entrées, which The Red Snapper calls "landfood." Daily specials, both "by land or by sea," are also available. The wine list is extensive, and among the house-made desserts, Death by Chocolate, Turtle Cheesecake, and Mint Alaska are house specialties with major, medium, and minor hits of chocolate.

The Red Snapper, 144 East Ninth Street, Durango; (970) 259-3417 or www.durango.com/redsnapper/.

Seasons Rotisserie & Grill

This stylish contemporary restaurant sets out to dazzle with lots of wood, lots of wine, a show kitchen with counter seating, and a powerful oak-fired rotisserie and grill. Bright-white linens, oversized plates, and hefty flatware are part of the look, and according to the dictum handed down from the restaurant's Albuquerque headquarters, service must be efficient and knowledgeable.

Executive Chef Dennis Morrisroe grills spit-roasted herbed chicken, Black Angus bone-in rib eye portioned for one or two, double-cut pork chops, Atlantic salmon, rack of Colorado lamb, and even portobello mushrooms, but he has other techniques up his chef's coat sleeve too. On Seasons' hip and seasonally changing menu, many dishes show strong Italian inspiration. Start with Four Cheese Bruschetta (chèvre, fontina, Parmesan, and fresh mozzarella, plus basil pesto), a seasonally changing antipasto, or house-made soups. Side dishes, whether standard with an entrée or offered à la carte, are made with verve and imagination. Roasted garlic mashed potatoes and roasted Yukon Golds are on many menus these days, but the likes of Grilled Vegetable Skewer, Pan-Roasted Baby Vegetables, braised chard, and Fried Onion Strings are unique to the Seasons style.

If Seasons seems familiar, that is because Durango is one of three locations (Scottsdale, Arizona, is the second) for this Albuquerque-based mini-chain run by veteran restaurateur Roger Roessler, who also owns Roessler Cellars in Sonoma County, California. It would seem to be a win–win situation when it comes to food and wine pairings. (If you owned the winery, wouldn't you have your wine maker try to formulate your wines to match the cuisine, and if you ran restaurants, wouldn't you ask your chefs to devise recipes that go well with your wines?) The restaurant has a wine room, and tasting events are held periodically.

Roger's nephews, Keith and Kevin Roessler, have joined him in the business, and it is conceivable—even likely—that there will eventually be more than the current three locations. If and when that happens, this restaurant might find itself in "The Chain Gang" chapter of any future editions of this book. But for the moment, there is but one in Colorado, so it belongs here.

Seasons Rotisserie & Grill, 764 Main Avenue, Durango; (970) 382-9790 or www.seasonsonthegrill.com.

Events

Durango Wine Festival

April—This fundraiser for the Durango chapter of the Volunteers of America takes place over four evenings in April. Thursday, Saturday, and Sunday feature wine-maker dinners, each at a different Durango restaurant. Chez Grand-mère has been dinner venue since the inception of the event in 1996. For the Friday night Ultimate Tasting, the Bank of Colorado is turned into a food mecca with tasting stations set up by 15 or more wineries and wine distributors and a similar number of local restaurants, bakeries, and caterers. Recent participants include Alpine Pastries, Restaurant Kody, Scoop's BBQ, The Chocolate Moose Catering Company, Stefano's, Masterpiece Cake Shop, The Local Grind, Thuy Hoa Restaurant, and Tuscany Tavern.

Tickets are available for each event, with a discount available for three or more events. Advance reservations are required for wine-maker dinners. Ultimate Tasting tickets can be purchased at the door. Tickets and further details are available from Volunteers of America; (970) 259-7462.

Taste of Durango

May—During the Taste of Durango, held for four intense hours on a Sunday in mid- to late May, the heart of town becomes street-food central. Three Main Avenue blocks between Seventh and Tenth are closed to traffic and lined with tasting booths, vendors' stands, and sponsors' exhibits. A sound stage at Ninth Street is entertainment central, but foodies flock to the cooking exhibition area at Eighth Street.

The local chefs who presented flash-fast 20-minute cooking demonstrations at the 2002 Shamrock Foods Exhibition Cooking Stage were Alison Dance of the Cyprus Café, Sergio Verduzco of East by Southwest, Ken Fusco of Ken and Sue's, Dennis Morrisroe of Seasons Rotisserie & Grill, Mary Badgley of the Cascade Grill, Joey

Hughes of Joey's Italian Bistro, and Dean Sprague of Antlers Grille at Tamarron. Other restaurants, bakeries, and caterers represented with tasting tables (and cowinners in the festival's culinary competition) included Dolci dalla Montegna, Durango Mountain Resort, Hamilton Chop House, Mountain Market and Deli, Norton's to Go and Catering, Señor Pepper's, Randy's Restaurant and Bar, Le Rendezvous Café, and Swiss Bakery.

The Taste of Durango includes a culinary competition, and 2002 categories in which the chefs and bakers were judged were Most Creative Cuisine, Most Creative Presentation, Definitely Durango, Most Tantalizing Taste, Most Miraculous Mouthful (that's the dessert category, in case you're wondering), Taste of Durango Spirit Award (for staff enthusiasm in addition to culinary excellence), and Best of the Year. Tom Hamilton of Hamilton's Chop House and Chuck Norton of Norton's to Go and Catering shared 2002 Definitely Durango honors. Aaron Riggert of Randy's Restaurant and Bar, and Dean Sprague of Antlers Grille at Tamarron were the honorees in the Best of 2002 category.

Festival admission is free. Proceeds of tickets for tastes go to the Durango Foundation for Educational Excellence. In addition to aiding a good local cause and tasting some divine food, an incentive to attend are drawings for $500 in restaurant gift certificates, so that you can eat still more fine food.

Taste of Durango is organized by the Durango Chapter of the Colorado Restaurant Association. In 2002, the event coordinator was John Carpenter, 1970 West Second Avenue, Durango, CO 81303; (970) 267-4686, (970) 759-5422, or e-mail jcm@gobrainstorm.net. Event headquarters was Ken and Sue's (see page 396). But these responsibilities could change, so the best information source is the festival's website, www.tasteofdurango.com.

Will Fjerstad Wine Tasting and Art Festival

Late August—The Annual Will Fjerstad Wine Tasting and Art Festival takes place over several days in town and at Purgatory Village at Durango Mountain Resort. It honors the late owner of the Needles General Store and the north La Plata County children's charity he supported. Fjerstad was highly respected locally for his generosity and good works, and people continue to turn out to honor his spirit and commitment. In the process, they get to eat and drink very well too, raising a glass to the spirit of the man many still miss.

Three nights of wine-maker dinners at three local restaurants are a prelude to two weekend days of eating, drinking, music, and art at Durango Mountain Resort. The festival gets serious with a Saturday champagne brunch at Durango Mountain Resort's events tent, followed by a modestly priced grand tasting to the mellow sounds of live jazz. Scores of Colorado, other domestic, and imported wines are poured, and gourmet fare prepared by local restaurants is sold à la carte. An art show, a silent auction, and live entertainment are part of the fun.

Will Fjerstad Wine Tasting and Art Festival, c/o Durango Mountain Resort, #1 Skier Place (off U.S. Highway 550), Durango; (970) 385-2149 or www.durangomountain.org.

San Juan Brewfest and Purgatory Chili Cookoff

September—More than 20 breweries from the Front Range to the Four Corners descend on Purgatory Village at Durango Mountain Resort for brews, food (mainly chili), and music in the resort's big festival tent. It is perfect for the person who likes to drink beer and the person who wants to make his or her own. Home-brew kits are available for purchase, and purveyors are gold mines of advice on how best to use them.

Local establishments sell food, but the big food component is the Purgatory Chili Cookoff. It debuted in 2002 with the intention of making it an annual event. This contest, organized on an International Chili Society format, was looking for gifted amateurs. Who knows who can move from Purgatory to the celestial reaches of national and world competition?

San Juan Brewfest and Purgatory Chili Cookoff, Durango Mountain Resort, #1 Skier Place (off U.S. Highway 550), Durango; (970) 385-2149 or www.durangomountain.org.

Cinders, Song, & Sauvignon

Late September—This annual three-day event, which usually takes place in conjunction with Fort Lewis College's Parents' Weekend, features the Wine Charter on the Durango & Silverton Narrow Gauge Railroad. The train's coal-fired engine is the reason for the first word of this event's title, which takes place midday on Saturday. The excursion includes a sampling of domestic and imported wines from half-a-dozen distributors. Norton's Catering provides lunch, which is served at the Cascade Canyon turnaround.

Sunday is the weekend's culinary highlight with a three-course gourmet brunch accompanied by wine, sparkling and otherwise. The Palace Restaurant hosted a recent brunch and served lobster ravioli, grilled duck breast, and fresh strawberry Napoleon, and Gruet champagnes were poured. Whether or not the wines are Sauvignons, organizers don't like to lose the alliteration and therefore keep it as part of the festival name. The "song" in Cinders, Song, & Sauvignon is a Friday-evening concert in the Fort Lewis College Community Concert Hall.

Tickets and details are available from Fort Lewis College Concerts, (970) 247-7657 or www.durangoconcerts.com.

DURANGO

Retail

Durango Coffee Company

This big corner store purveys latte, cappuccino, and bracing espresso, perhaps accompanied by a pastry from one of Durango's top bakeries. In the back is a retail area where you can buy your own home version of the Rancilio espresso *macchina* that the Durango Coffee Company's baristas use behind the counter. In addition to espresso makers, the store carries such espresso enhancers as Oscar's Syrups, plus teapots and teas to go in them. This café's retail department sells Durango's most complete selection of quality cookware, utensils, and tableware. Gourmet Standard's sets of heavy stainless cookware are perfect for anyone setting up a household from scratch, or wanting a wholesale replacement for the cheap stuff that no longer suffices. Calphalon cookware comes by the piece for the à la carte pot or pan purchaser. Eucalyptus Stoneware from California is an attractive oven-to-table line. You'll find lots of gadgets by NorPro, OXO, and Zyliss, Wüsthoff Trident knives, Cuisinart small appliances, and several lines of attractive and functional pasta sets, including bowls, servers, and colanders.

Decorative items for kitchen or dining room include a beautiful line of Polish pottery, lots of mugs (one line with reproductions of Old Masters' paintings), and Luigi Bormioli glassware from Italy. Linens by DII, Tag, and Mango brighten any kitchen or dining room, and to tie it all together from the kitchen to the table is a good selection of cookbooks.

Durango Coffee Company, 730 Main Avenue, Durango; (970) 259-2059, (800) 748-2275, or www.durangocoffee.com.

Guido's Favorite Foods

On the north end of Durango, near the edge of town just before U.S. 550 begins its climb into the mountains, is a delightful Italian deli and gourmet food market known locally simply as Guido's. Owner Sean Devereaux has an Irish first name and a French surname, but his culinary heart is Italian, and he has stocked the store with some of that country's tasty products. His store is painted in cheery Mediterranean colors, with track lighting showcasing the wares. Shelves are laden with excellent products, most of which are found nowhere else in the Four Corners area and some of which are not widely available elsewhere in Colorado.

Guido's offers excellent cheeses, meats, sausages, cold cuts, house-made to-go meals, good sandwiches, and a commendable selection of imported canned and packaged products for the home cook. The small selection of cookware comprises mostly hefty pots and pans, quality kitchen knives, gadgets, woodenware, stainless colanders, and spaghetti portion gauges. And, oh yes, you can even buy a Swiss raclette grill.

Dried pastas include beautiful Castellana shapes, plus Spaghetti di Martelli, La Pasta, and Barilla and Lidia's pasta sauces are available too. One shelf is full of olive oils from Italy (specifically including Umbria), Crete, and Spain, plus Spanish and French vinegars, including unusual balsamic fig vinegar. Extras include the roasted peppers Mancini, Cucina Aromatica, and Divina roasted peppers, a sizable selection of mustards, olive and artichoke pastes, capers, preserved peppercorns, and more. You'll also find Stonewall Kitchen condiments, Lavazza coffee, those Pomi Parmalat boxed tomatoes favored by chefs, and good canned bouillabaisse concentrate. The refrigerated cases include Fontina Val d'Aosta, Fior di Sardinia, Pecorino-Romano, *locotelli*, Tomme de Savoie, Ossau Istara, cambozola, Port Salut, Manchego, and Brinata sheep cheeses. Adjacent are the olives, sun-dried tomato and basil pesto, prepared salads, and imported and domestic cold cuts to take out as they are or as sandwich ingredients.

Guido's offers house-made take-out food, including one and often two soups, made with from-scratch stocks. Regular side dishes are *caprese* salad, Italian potato salad, farfalle pasta salad, Italian red potato salad, Parmesan green beans, truffle oil and garlic mashed potatoes, marinated artichokes, and veggie dolmas. There are always six or seven entrées, which might include poached salmon filets with sour cream dill sauce; stuffed pork chops with prosciutto, porcini mushrooms, bread crumbs, and sweet balsamic-mushroom sauce; farfalle pasta with asparagus, tomatoes, basil, and light cream sauce; eggplant Parmesan; spinach and ricotta shells; and Italian meatballs, the latter three blanketed with house-made marinara. Cheesecake in various flavors is the top dessert. In addition to a brisk take-out business, Guido's has installed high tables and stools in the front of the store for patrons who prefer to eat right then and right there.

Guido's Favorite Foods, 3000 Main Avenue, Durango; (970) 259-5028.

Honeyville

Honeyville, on the west side of U.S. Highway 550 north of Durango, looks like a typical tourist establishment, but Honeyville is, in fact, a long-standing local business selling various related food products. Its origins go back to Duarte, California, where a beekeeper named Albert Meyer opened the business in 1918. His son, Joe, moved to Durango in 1954, taking Honeyville with him and selling honey from his house.

Meanwhile, a young man named Vernon Culhane took up beekeeping as a hobby in 1926 and hauled his first few buckets of wildflower honey 12 miles into town—perhaps in a Model T that his family knows he owned at one time. Residents soon began anticipating his visits and would wait for him when they needed more honey. With his demand growing, he added more and more beehives to the meadows and valleys surrounding Durango. Today, the bees continue to make honey from flowers growing in those same fields.

The two businesses were combined in 1982, when Vernon took on Albert's

Honeyville and opened the present retail store. Vernon's son, Danny, and Danny's wife, Sheree, now run the business.

The company's signature Colorado Wildflower Honey has gained a reputation as some of the state's best. Honeyville has blossomed forth with other products too. You'll find whipped honey, a rainbow of excellent jams and jellies (wild chokecherry, baked apple, jalapeño, black cherry, strawberry–rhubarb, cherry–rhubarb, apricot, black raspberry, and the cleverly named BlackBeary), apple butter, syrups, and a sublime dessert topping called Chocolate Buzz, along with sauces and salad dressings. The syrups deserve a word, because other than pure Vermont maple, about the best thing you can do to doctor up plain pancakes, waffles, or French toast is to pour on some of Honeyville's strawberry–rhubarb, wild chokecherry, apple–cinnamon, or butter pecan. The store now offers such Honey Mountain Home Bakery premium mixes as honey buttermilk hot rolls and bread, old-fashioned country biscuits, pancakes and waffles, country cobbler, and Southwest sopaipillas and tortillas.

Honeyville sells other quality lines, mainly such regional products as pinto beans from the Four Corners, Religious Experience salsa, Apocalypse Hot Sauce, Colorado Popcorn from Dove Creek, Cliff Dweller Soup Mix, and the Durango Diner's green chili sauce. There's also Durango Coffee Company coffee and log rolls, and popcorn from New Mexico's Stahmann's Farms. The bottom line is that Honeyville may look like a typical tourist haunt, but, in fact, lovers of good honey and other condiments are drawn to it like, well, bees are to honey.

Honeyville, 33633 U.S. Highway 550 North, Durango; (800) 676-7690, (970) 247-2474, or www.honeyvillecolorado.com.

Norton's To Go

An unpretentious adobe-style building on Durango's north end holds the take-out component of a multifaceted business that also includes catering, coffee shop, and sampling and sales of its own condiments under the Durango Red label. Owner–chef Chuck Norton's menu of popular and innovative Southwestern, Mexican, Italian, and Cajun dishes to eat on site or take home includes appealing appetizers, entrées, salads, pasta, and such casual fare as burrito wraps, all freshly made in excellent combinations. Some dishes are ready to eat; others are ready to heat.

Durango Red makes hot sauce, steak sauce, steak rub, and something called "steak shake," a pre-mixed blackening mixture. The café is called the Community Coffeehouse, named to honor a New Orleans institution called Community Coffee, and is open from early morning until mid-afternoon for coffee, pastries, and a friendly atmosphere.

Norton's To Go, 3600 North Main Avenue, Durango; (970) 247-4702 or www.nortonscatering.com.

Wines

The Wine Merchant

In October 2002, Durango's first wine specialty retail shop opened in a strip shopping center—next door to an organic food store, a bonus for cooks who prefer natural ingredients. The small store carries wines in a broad price range but really specializes in those selling for $7 to $17 per bottle. Wines are displayed on custom-built racks, with five or six bottles—one wine in each category—lined up on an eye-level shelf and the rest in bins just below. Wines are organized by style—with reds and whites divided into lighter, medium, and fuller body categories. The left end of each display shelf shows wines selling for under $10, progressing up the price scale from left to right. When you get to the end of one row of bins, the next group of wines on display again starts with the least expensive. The Wine Merchant offers a good selection of Colorado vintages, as well as organic wines that go so well with food from the store next door.

Partners Eric Allen and Ron Greene display both knowledge of and passion for wine, and Allen, conducts a popular World of Wines course at Durango Arts Center. The Wine Merchant also posts food-pairing suggestions, issues a newsletter, organizes tastings, and has a very flexible wine club. Members can select a case, half-case, or even bottle of the month. The store also carries a limited selection of spirits, many of them specialty items, and a selection of popular and obscure beers.

The Wine Merchant, 1119 Camino del Rio, Durango; (970) 375-0076.

Recipes

This recipe originated at a restaurant called di Guido in Costigliole d'Asti in Italy's Piemonte (Piedmont) region. Sean Devereaux, owner of Guido's, learned it in culinary school in Italy. He loves the coincidental connection between di Guido there and his own Guido's here. The store's advanced Italian cooking class prepares this uniquely shaped, filled spinach pasta that Devereaux calls "beyond normal ravioli" and serve with a simple tomato-mushroom sauce.

Cappelletti di Patate e Porri con Porcini

(Cappelletti with Potato and Leeks with Mushroom Sauce)

Cappelletti (see below)
Mushroom–Tomato Sauce (see below)
grated Parmesan cheese to taste

Assembly

In a pot large enough to cook pasta, bring lightly salted water to a boil. Stir in *cappelletti* and cook *al dente* (about 3 minutes if freshly made, up to 6 minutes if drier). Drain the pasta. Add the cooked pasta into the saucepan and coat with the Mushroom-Tomato Sauce. Serve with additional grated Parmesan cheese. Serves 8.

Cappelletti

Make the filling in advance and set aside while preparing the pasta dough.

Filling:

2 tablespoons unsalted butter
1 leek (mostly white part), rinsed well and finely chopped
pinch of nutmeg
1 whole egg
1 egg yolk
½ pound potato, boiled, cooled, skinned, and coarsely mashed
½ cup grated Parmesan cheese
salt and pepper to taste

In a medium pan over medium heat, melt butter. Sauté finely chopped leeks until soft, not browned. Add nutmeg to taste (remember, this isn't a dessert). Beat whole egg and egg yolk lightly with a fork to mix. Add leeks and remaining ingredients to the potatoes, stirring until smooth. Add salt and pepper to taste.

Pasta:

1¾ cups flour, preferably unbleached all-purpose flour or semolina
3 eggs
pinch of salt
⅓ pound fresh spinach, washed, stemmed, boiled, cooled, and squeezed dry
   (or ⅓ cup of frozen spinach, cooked according to directions and squeezed
   hard to minimize the water content), chopped extremely fine

If making pasta dough by hand, mound flour on a pastry board or clean kitchen counter. Make a deep hole or "crater" in the top of the flour all the way down to the work surface. In a small bowl, lightly beat eggs with a fork and add salt. Pour the eggs into the crater. With a fork in one hand, stir the eggs to allow flour slowly to fall into the crater, while "reinforcing" the crater wall with the other hand to contain the eggs. Some of the flour will begin falling into the egg mixture. In the early stages of this mixing process, add the spinach. When the mixture becomes too difficult to stir with the fork, begin working the sticky dough with your fingers until flour and egg/spinach mixture are amalgamated and the dough is smooth. Flour your hands and begin kneading the dough until the flour cannot absorb any more of the eggs. (In Colorado's dry climate, it may be necessary to add a few drops of water to use all the flour.) Clean the work surface, dust with flour, and begin kneading the dough into an oblong, folding it over on itself, and continuing to work it for 10 or 15 minutes until it is smooth and elastic.

You can also mix the pasta dough in a food processor fitted with a steel blade. Add all ingredients into the food processor bowl and mix until the dough is amalgamated and rides around on the blade.

On a clean, lightly floured work surface, begin rolling the dough, about a tennis-ball piece at a time. Rolling and turning it 90 degrees as you go, roll to an even thickness and dust the surface with flour as needed. When the dough is the desired thickness, set aside on a dry towel while you work the other portions of dough. You can also roll out the dough using a manual or electric pasta machine, following the manufacturer's instructions.

When you have prepared the sheet pasta, cut out 4-inch circles (an empty and cleaned 10-ounce tunafish can works well for this), and place a small teaspoon of filling in center of each. Fold over, pressing edges firmly to seal filling inside. Pull the resulting outer corners to overlap in back, pressing to seal. The resulting lip should flip up if pulled tight enough, forming the *cappelletti*, or "little hats." You can store prepared *cappelletti*, uncovered, in the refrigerator for up to a day.

Mushroom–Tomato Sauce
3 tablespoons unsalted butter
⅓ cup olive oil
2 large portobello mushrooms, cleaned and coarsely chopped
2 large tomatoes, seeded and chopped (or canned tomatoes,
    but some of the recipe's texture will be lost)

In a large saucepan, heat butter and oil. Add chopped mushrooms and cook, stirring occasionally, until softened but not overcooked. Add tomatoes and heat thoroughly. The desired results are a firm tomato and mushroom sauce with sufficient butter and oil to cover pasta.

The Chain Gang

In the introduction to this book, I confessed to a personal preference (some would justifiably call it a prejudice) for locally owned business over invasive chains. My own strong feelings were key in deciding what this book would include, and I admit a particular antipathy to chain restaurants. In such chains, the personal touch of a creative chef is often lost and even the waitstaffs' interaction with customers is scripted, for each location is mandated to meet a marketer's "concept" and to turn the profits that chains demand.

It stands to reason that imaginative or well-prepared food usually is the last thing you can expect from a corporate-controlled establishment. Still, a few chains manage to put out well-above-average fare—and the atmosphere isn't offensively contrived. This chapter contains those chains that, to my personal, prejudiced way of thinking, are worth considering. For the most part, they either maintain a spiritual and culinary link with the individual entrepreneur or founding family—or have knowledgeable and particular chefs on a key management team that insists on foods elevated beyond the factory-made.

This chapter also includes such retail operations as Whole Foods and Wild Oats markets, which are distinguished by their commitment to fresh food, their support of local artisan purveyors, staff training, and service. I have also included a couple of well-regarded national cookware and kitchenware chains with well-earned reputations for quality products and service, plus a few chain bakeries that consistently bake good breads and pastries. What's not here? Local businesses that have expanded to a few outlets are included in the location-appropriate chapters.

Bakeries

Atlanta Bread Company

Since its founding in 1993 (or more accurately, since it began franchising in 1995), the Atlanta Bread Company has grown to more than 200 locations. The doughs are prepared in the central commissary in Smyrna, Georgia, and delivered to each store ready to be proofed and baked. The company is especially proud of its scones, European sourdough, Asiago bread, and other breads. It boasts that its food is made from fresh ingredients.

The chain emulates the traditional neighborhood café. Its pleasant stores combine a relaxed and attractively designed setting (hardwood floors, brick fireplace, and classical music in the background) with the zippy service. In addition to breakfast, there's a lunch and dinner menu of soups (the company issues a "weekly soup schedule" so that you can predict which soups will be available at all locations any day of the week), salads, and made-to-order sandwiches, including six on *panini*. Beverages include fruit smoothies and Cafechillos, the company's name for their chilled coffee drinks.

Atlanta Bread Company, 321 South McCaslin Boulevard, Louisville,
(303) 664-5222; 2209 West Wildcat Reserve Parkway, Highlands Ranch,
(303) 471-5595; and 351 West 104th Avenue, Northglenn, (303) 452-8222.

Breadsmith

Breadsmith, a Milwaukee-based chain, boasts low-fat breads made from scratch every day and baked in an imported, six-ton bread oven with stone hearth, radiant heat, and steam injection to produce a crisp-crusted hearty loaf. It was established in 1993, and franchising began the following year. One of its loaves soon medaled at the International Culinary Salon. At this writing, there are 38 stores in 10 states, Colorado being the westernmost.

Each location bakes about a dozen fairly hard-crusted Continental-style breads every day, though none bakes every bread every day. Breads include Austrian pumpernickel, cheddar sourdough, cheddar-jalapeño sourdough, ciabatta, dark rye, focaccia, French baguette, French *boule*, Greek olive, Norwegian rye, onion rye, pumpernickel brick, Russian rye, rustic Italian, semolina, sourdough, sourdough rye, Swedish limpa rye, and Tuscan *rustica*. The repertoire further includes soft-crusted challah for the Friday start of the Jewish Sabbath, sandwich and tea breads, such breakfast breads as cinnamon spice, and oil-free, fat-free cornbread. Breadsmith also makes dessert breads, holiday breads, muffins, and whole grain and multigrain loaves. Preserves, coffees, and other "go-withs" are available as well.

Breadsmith, 8290 South Holly, Centennial; (303) 850-7699 or
www.breadsmith.com.

The Corner Bakery

This large bakery is located in the Denver Pavilions, adjoining Maggiano's Little Italy (see page 415), and is related by ownership to that chain. The Corner Bakery's breads, rolls, muffins, and pastries are mostly Italian, and it makes dynamite sandwich breads too. Still, the bakery is best known as a stop for a quick breakfast or lunch.

The Corner Bakery, Denver Pavilions, 500 16th Street, Denver; (303) 572-0166.

Great Harvest Bread Company

The Great Harvest Bread Company story is a 1960s classic, in the manner of Ben

& Jerry's Ice Cream or Mo Siegel's Celestial Seasonings Tea. When he was seven or eight, Pete Wakeman and his Aunt Polly started baking bread together. In the late 1960s, the teenager from Connecticut attended a boarding school in the California desert. He and his classmates ordered *The Tassajara Bread Book*, and Pete became the resident baker.

Fast-forward to college. Pete and his girlfriend, Laura, enrolled in Cornell University—she to study nutrition; he, agriculture. During their second summer, Pete began baking fresh-ground whole-wheat bread in his mother's oven and selling it from a roadside card table adorned with a big hand-painted sign that said "Homemade Bread." The bread sold amazingly well, and the following summer, Laura joined Pete. They commandeered four kitchen ovens and repainted their sign to read "The Happy Oven." Business boomed, and the young couple refined the recipe, combining what they learned from books with their own experiments.

It was also their personal summer of love. They fell in love with the magic of hot whole-wheat bread and with the baking business. They married that September. They dreamed of buying a dairy farm in Wisconsin but decided to have one last fling before settling into the life of 4:00 A.M. milkings. They hiked from Yellowstone to Glacier National Park, and by summer's end, they had found a new love: Montana.

They got jobs in Great Falls, and when Pete learned about a little bakery for sale in the "bad" part of town, with an adult bookstore on one side and a halfway house on the other, he smelled a deal. An auction of used equipment and $200 worth of paint later, the Great Harvest Bakery was theirs. On the first day in February 1976, he baked 12 loaves and sold out. Three months later, Laura quit her job, and soon they were producing up to 144 loaves a day. Along came people interested in opening similar bread shops. They began to teach others how to run great whole-wheat bakeries and began franchising. The couple sold the original Great Falls bakery and haven't looked back.

The whole-wheat bread, perfected in Connecticut so many summers ago, remains the core of the Great Harvest line-up. There are now more than 140 stores, with some similarities but also some differences. The company has tried to find a middle ground between traditional franchises, with brand identification and business and marketing savvy from the corporation, with the fun people get from a let's-do-it-all-ourselves start-up. They call it a "freedom-based franchise"; owners can run their stores within the context of their own community and a Great Harvest community of like-minded and like-talented and like-spirited owners.

Great Harvest Bread Company, 7745 Wadsworth Boulevard, Arvada,
(303) 420-0500; 2525 Arapahoe, Boulder, (303) 442-3062;
6942 North Academy, Colorado Springs, (719) 528-6442;
101 North Tejon, Colorado Springs, (719) 635-7379; Belcaro Shopping Center,
765 South Colorado Boulevard, Denver, (303) 778-8877;
Scotch Pines Village, 2601 South Lemay, Fort Collins, (970) 223-8311;
3600 South College Avenue, Fort Collins, (970) 225-0353;
5910 South University Boulevard, Littleton, (303) 347-8767.
The corporate website is www.greatharvest.com.

Il Fornaio

This Italian restaurant chain with three metro Denver locations actually began as a California bakery in 1981, and even though customers tend to think of it as a full-service restaurant first and bakery second, baked goods are still important in the Il Fornaio repertoire. Il Fornaio (Italian for "the baker") mixes its dough with machines and bakes with modern ovens and other mechanized equipment suitable for large batches. Still, the company believes that there is no substitute for doing some things by hand. Handcrafted, traditional breads are made daily using the simple basics of flour, water, yeast, and salt.

The company traces its bread recipes back to Il Fornaio Baking School, founded in Barlassina, near Milan, to serve as a repository for authentic regional recipes and also to teach traditional Italian baking methods. America's Il Fornaio similarly operates a *panificio* (or production bakery), a 12,000-square-foot facility in Burlingame, California, where new bakers are trained in age-old artisan baking techniques. Il Fornaio serves and sells about 50 kinds of breads and 20 kinds of pastries, all still shaped by hand.

Michael Mindel, the Il Fornaio exec who turned the bakery brand into a restaurant chain, brought Jan Schat aboard as the firm's head baker. This gifted bake master headed the three-member Baking Team USA that took the Gold Medal in the artisan breads category at the 1999 Coupe du Monde de la Boulangerie (literally, world cup of bread baking) in Paris. Previously, American teams had never finished higher than fifth place. Prior to joining Il Fornaio, Schat completed a three-year professional baking apprenticeship in Europe, where he learned Old World baking methods.

For Colorado locations, see page 415.

Panera Bakery

Panera—more than 260 across the country at this writing and ambitious plans to mushroom to nearly 650—has institutionalized the concept of the neighborhood bakery-café. Panera cranks out preservative-free breads all day, every day. Sourdough, made from dough aged for three days, is Panera's signature bread. The company's founder, Ken Rosenthal, brought the "mother" (i.e., sourdough starter) to St. Louis from San Francisco in 1987 and opened the Saint Louis Bread Company, which he sold six years later to Au Bon Pain. In 1995 the company developed Panera breads and the bakery-cafés that sell them, and three years later an investor corporation bought the whole shebang and further tightened the concept.

Dough is prepared in central facilities and shipped to individual locations. In addition to the sourdough, Panera also bakes whole-grain breads, focaccia, bagels, croissants, muffins, and some sweets. *Panini* became the first hot item, other than soups, on the menu. Panera issues a soup schedule daily. In addition to Broccoli Cheddar and Low Fat Chicken offered every day, Panera serves soups on a regular rotation and also schedules "seasonal soups."

Panera Bakery, Iliff Commons, 12293 East Iliff Avenue, Aurora, (303) 755-6800;
Pearl Street Mall, 1207 Pearl Street, Boulder, (303) 545-2253;
Capitol Heights, 1330 Grant Street, Denver, (303) 830-7101;

240 Milwaukee Street, Denver, (303) 316-8181;
4955 South Ulster Street, Denver, (303) 741-3770;
5910 South Holly Street, Greenwood Village, (720) 482-1455;
9579 South University Boulevard, Highlands Ranch, (720) 348-1112;
8501 West Bowles Avenue, Littleton, (303) 978-0200; Aspen Grove,
7301 South Santa Fe Drive, Littleton, (303) 795-2121; Colony Square,
1132 West Dillon Road, Louisville, (303) 604-9292.

Paradise Bakery

The first Paradise Bakery & Café, created in Long Beach, California, earned a quick reputation for freshly baked muffins and cookies. By 1987 there were 14 company-owned and two franchised bakery-cafés in operation. There are now more than 30 locations in seven Western and Southwestern states. All items are still prepared daily, using fine ingredients. It remains a hands-on operation, making everything on-site and from scratch every day. Its specialty baked goods include Big Paradise Cookies, Paradise Muffins, Chippers, Double Fudge Brownies, 24 Carrot Cake, butter and filled croissants (fruit, spinach and cheese croissants, and ham and cheese), bagels, and cinnamon rolls. Paradise Bakery & Café is now headquartered in Aspen.

Paradise Bakery & Café, 320 South Galena Street, Aspen, (970) 925-7585;
FlatIron Crossing Mall, 1 West Flatiron Circle, Broomfield, (720) 887-1434;
Southglenn Mall, 6911 South University Boulevard, Centennial, (303) 738-0918;
1001 16th Street Mall, Denver, (303) 436-1192;
Park Meadows Mall, 8515 Park Meadows Center Drive, Littleton, (303) 706-4712;
and 74 Snowmass Village Mall, Snowmass Village, (970) 923-4712.
The website for all locations is www.paradisebakery.com.

Dining

Del Frisco's Double Eagle Steak House

The restaurant is part of the Del Frisco Double Eagle Steak House group, which comprises a small cog in the larger wheel of a corporation called Lone Star Steakhouse & Saloon Inc. The company's namesake chain vaulted from 23 locations in 1992 to something approaching 300 restaurants at this writing. These full-service, midprice, and very casual eateries specialize in mesquite-grilled steaks, ribs, chicken, and fish, all served in a tidied-up Texas roadhouse atmosphere and concentrated on the fringes of major metropolitan areas across the country.

The company also operates Sullivan's Steakhouse, but Del Frisco's Double Eagle Steak House is the crown jewel on the Lone Star corporate diadem. Only a handful are in operation, including one in Greenwood Village, south of Denver. All are clubby in feeling, hard on the wallet, and satisfying to the palate. Like many steakhouses, Del Frisco's feels like a guys' place, specializing in man-sized, beautifully aged, and well marbled meats. The house specialty is a bone-in Double Eagle Strip, but other smaller prime cuts have their fans. If you like beef but not that much, consider something from the menu's "Lagniappe" section, including 10-ounce rib eye, six-ounce filet, or filet tips over angel-hair pasta.

The appetizer portion of oysters (on the half-shell or fried) is large enough to be an entrée, and the huge lobster tail, spicy crab cakes, and other poultry and seafood offerings also satisfy appetites of non–beef-eaters. Shrimp cocktail, salads, sides (try the skillet-fried chip-like potatoes and onions), and desserts aren't what will make you return, but if you're a meat-lover, the massive hunks of perfectly cooked beef will. The wine list is good and hearty and extensive enough to justify a sommelier, and underscoring the masculine nature of the place, there's a cigar room and plenty of Port and other after-dinner drinks.

Del Frisco's Double Eagle Steak House, 8100 East Orchard Road, Greenwood Village; (303) 796-0100.

Il Fornaio

This California-based Italian restaurant and bakery chain has three metro Denver locations: the original in Lower Downtown and one each to the north and south. The restaurants look somewhat different from one another (the downtown Denver location being very LoDo, with white columns supporting the high ceilings, wood floors, and track lighting), but all set their tables with brilliant white linens, and all take their food and baked goods as seriously as does any chain restaurant—and far more seriously than most.

In each location, the front of the house is run by someone who is titled the "managing partner," while the back of the house is under the direction of the "chef partner." The company's two-dozen chef-partners, many of whom are Italian-born and -trained, developed a menu based on authentic recipes, with an emphasis on simple, fresh ingredients and Italian cooking methods. Every Il Fornaio restaurant serves this core lunch and dinner, which always includes a selection of antipasti, soups, salads, pizzas, pastas, grilled and rotisserie-roasted meats, and a good selection of desserts. Each location bakes its popular pizzas in a wood-fired oven and makes some fresh pasta in-house daily, supplemented with dried pastas imported from Italy. All meals are accompanied by Il Fornaio's excellent breads and mostly Italian wines, often from small, regional wineries. Il Fornaio attempts to continue the tradition of Italy's wonderful neighborhood trattorias, where mornings begin with fresh, crisp-crusted breads and freshly brewed espresso. Of the three Denver-area restaurants, only the LoDo location does breakfast; the other two are open just for lunch and dinner.

Compared with most chains, the company boasts of the high level of autonomy each chef has in the kitchen. Chefs are mandated to carry on the mission of teaching Italian culinary traditions, preparations, and presentations to the entire staff, and are also supposed to cultivate European-style relationships with growers in the local market and offer daily special menus and regional menus. Each year, Il Fornaio sends a group of chef-partners to Italy to reestablish personal relationships, often with the chefs who trained them, and to gain menu inspiration.

Fiesta Regionale, a company-wide promotion, celebrates Italy's culinary diversity. During the first two weeks of each month, Il Fornaio locations supplement the core menu with an original menu from a different region of Italy, usually created by a chef-partner who hails from there. Food and wine from the highlighted region are served at all Il Fornaio restaurants, taking the place of the daily specials. During the second half of the month, the core menu is supplemented with each chef's own daily lunch and dinner specials that utilize available fresh local ingredients and cater to popular community tastes.

Some Il Fornaio locations also include retail operations, where you can buy a wine from an 11th-century Tuscan vineyard or a far newer one in California, olive oil, balsamic vinegar, pasta, coffee, and, of course, those excellent baked goods.

Il Fornaio, 1631 Wazee Street, Denver, (303) 573-5050;
FlatIron Crossing Village, 1 West Flatiron Circle, Broomfield, (720) 887-1400;
and Belleview Promenade, 8000 East Belleview Avenue, Greenwood Village,
(303) 221-8400. The website for all Il Fornaio restaurants is www.ilfornaio.com.

Maggiano's Little Italy

Maggiano's is not about haute cuisine. Maggiano's is about eating a lot of good, soul-satisfying, and well-prepared southern Italian fare in an appealing faux-1930s setting. Denver's first Maggiano is a sprawling 20,000-square-foot downtown restaurant in Denver Pavilions, and the second is a chateau-style edifice near the Denver Tech Center. Each serves slightly, and only slightly, updated versions of the fine, filling food that emerged from *nonna*'s kitchen, Sunday after Sunday. Like so many traditional Italian grandmothers, Maggiano's chefs turn out multicourse meals

Despite a corporate headquarters in so un-Italian a city as Dallas, Maggiano's has pulled off the trick of creating the mood and food of southern Italy, as interpreted by immigrant restaurateurs half a century ago and half a continent away. The décor harkens back to the restaurants of New York's Little Italy around World War II—tile floors, dark paneling, sturdy wooden chairs, and crisp table linens—when it wasn't "décor" but simply the way neighborhood Italian restaurants looked. To maintain that long-ago, lower Manhattan ambience, these pig-out palaces are parceled into warm cozy room after warm cozy room in a crazy quilt, and vintage photographs of men in fedoras, women in cocktail dresses, and families gathered to celebrate weddings decades ago. Sinatra and other crooner tunes are piped in—and they sound right.

Individuals can order off the extensive lunch and dinner menu, and two can share a special multicourse meal for a very modest sum (under $20 at this writing), but groups are immersed in the real *famiglia* experience. The restaurant serves large bowls of freshly tossed salads, heaping platters of meat or chicken or seafood, mountains of pasta, and killer desserts, which everyone always seems to have room for. Maggiano's periodically puts on a special-event dinner—for example, a seven-course Valentine's Day dinner that strays considerably from the restaurant's southern Italian roots and features wines paired to each course.

Adjacent to the downtown restaurant is The Corner Bakery (see page 410), best known for its variety of freshly baked breads, most of Italian or French derivation. This annex to Maggiano's also proffers eat-in or take-out breakfasts, sandwiches, soups, salads, personal pizzas, and pastries. (Hint: The lemon cookies have been such a hit that The Corner Bakery packs them in a holiday gift tin.)

To enter Maggiano's annual Best Italian Cook Contest, submit a favorite Italian recipe, along with a story about the recipe or its origins. Six finalists are invited to prepare their dish for a panel of judges, and the winning recipe appears as a special at the restaurant for one month. Every time someone orders the dish, Maggiano's donates $2 to a selected charity.

The contest gave rise to another fundraiser for a good cause, with Maggiano's cosponsoring *Recipes for a Cure*, a cookbook whose proceeds go directly to breast cancer research. The book features recipes from the restaurant, the Denver Broncos and other local celebrities, *5280* magazine, and the Best Italian Cook contestants.

Maggiano's Little Italy, 600 16th Street, Denver, (303) 260-7707;
and 7401 South Clinton Street, Englewood, (303) 858-1405.
The website for both (and the entire chain) is www.maggiano.com.

McCormick's Fish House

This attractive restaurant in the historic Oxford Hotel has the look of a vintage fish house—hexagonal-tile floors, dark wood, old-style lighting fixtures, pale walls above high wainscoting, and simple, old-fashioned chairs. But despite its unchain-like ambience, it's actually one of literally dozens of related seafood restaurants across the country. Some, like Denver's, are called McCormick's Fish House. Others operate under the trade names of McCormick & Schmick's Seafood Restaurant, Jake's Grill, Jake's Famous Crawfish, M & S Grill, McCormick & Kuleto's, Spenger's Fresh Fish Grotto, and McCormick & Schmick's Harborside Restaurant and Pilsner Room. Half, like Denver's, are located in buildings on the National Register of Historic Places, and the company works hard to retain the historic feeling in the décor of even the newest locations.

With 30 to 40 varieties of fresh seafood, plus meat, poultry, and vegetarian selections, you can expect 85 or more items on the menu every day. Regional tastes are accommodated, and each chef is given considerable latitude in menu planning and recipe development.

Not only does McCormick's totally reflect the style of the Historic Oxford Hotel, which was built in 1891, but its companion bar is a historic landmark in its own right. The Cruise Room first opened on December 5, 1933, the day Prohibition was repealed. This long, narrow bar was inspired by a lounge aboard the *Queen Mary*, a fabled ocean liner. Its Art Deco style features red neon lighting setting off the bar's black lacquer finish. The Cruise Room, which has its own listing in the National Register of Historic Places, won the prestigious Miami Art Deco Society's Annual Award in 1984. Be sure to stop in for a drink before or after dining at McCormick's.

McCormick's Fish House, 1659 Wazee Street, Denver; (303) 825-1107.
The website for the entire chain is www.mccormickandschmick.com.

Morton's of Chicago

The Long Island, New York–based Morton's Restaurant Group is proud of running what it describes as "the nation's premier steakhouse group." Denver's two Morton's of Chicago, like every other Morton's of Chicago, feature various sizes and cuts of USDA prime aged beef (the 14-ounce porterhouse is the house specialty, with a 20-ounce New York sirloin and a 24-ounce double-cut filet for the famished).

There's sizzle to the steak too, with what Morton's calls its "famous animated signature tableside menu presentation." That means a loaded cart is rolled to your table, where you can select your steak, or whole Maine lobsters and other seafood, additional meat and poultry options, plus fresh vegetables. The server, presumably hired as much for his or her sales presentation as for serving skills, displays and describes each item. It's a rolling road show. Some people love it; others find it hokey and intrusive, especially because you will be subjected to the same presentation at nearby tables as well as your own. If you want to see what it's like before committing yourself to an expensive dinner, and if you have a video player in your computer, log onto the company's website and click on "Morton's Menu Presentation #1" and on "Morton's Menu Presentation #2."

Something on the order of 65 Morton's of Chicago restaurants spread across the map, mostly in the United States but also in Canada and Hong Kong. Morton's Restaurant Group also operates a chain of Italian restaurants called Bertolini's Authentic Trattoria.

Morton's of Chicago, 1710 Wynkoop Street, Denver, (303) 825-3353; and Denver Crescent Town Center, 8480 East Belleview Avenue, Englewood, (303) 409-1177. The website for all of the group's restaurants is www.mortons.com.

The Palm

Though a relative newcomer to Denver, The Palm has the longest history of any of the chains covered in this book. Pio Bozzi and John Ganzi, who intended to bring the food of their native Parma, Italy, to New York's East Side, founded the original in New York in 1926. According to legend, they originally wanted to call it Parma, but when they went for their business license, the bureaucrat thought they said "Palm." So their strong Italian accents were responsible for a name that has become legendary.

The Palm was located just half-a-block from the old *New York Daily Mirror,* so it became a hangout for newspapermen. The *Mirror's* illustrators and cartoonists festooned the walls with original and spontaneous caricatures of prominent New Yorkers, a tradition present in locations across the country now. When customers wanted to order a steak that was not part of the original Italian menu, owner John Ganzi would run up Second Avenue to a nearby butcher shop, buy a steak, and cook it to order. The Palm soon became known for great steaks.

The restaurant earned its reputation for seafood under the third generation of owners, Wally Ganzi and Bruce Bozzi, who began serving gargantuan four- to eight-pound lobsters in the 1970s, disproving the notion that large lobsters are tough. Almost overnight The Palm went from selling 150 pounds of lobster per week to

25,000 pounds. It remains a steakhouse in the public image—albeit a steakhouse with great seafood too—and some of John Ganzi's original Italian dishes are on the menu to this day.

When Wally and Bruce took over from their fathers in the early 1960s, there was still only one Palm. Now there are two dozen. The original space is now a neighborhood convenience store, and The Palms that stretch from glamorous East Hampton to trend-setting Los Angeles are a far cry from the original, which sported sawdust on the floor, newspapermen knocking back boilermakers, and John Ganzi running up the street to buy one steak at a time. Denver's Palm opened in 1996 on the ground level of the Westin at Tabor Center.

Bruce, Wally, and Bruce's son-in-law Alfred Thimm Jr. run the operation, but many people—from cooks and waiters on up—have been with The Palm for so long that they are like family. Executive Chef Tony Tammero, who oversees quality control, develops The Palm's menu, and trains all Palm chefs and kitchen staff, has been with The Palm since the early 1970s. He is a true heir to the tradition established by John Ganzi and his sprints to the butcher shop. In the 1970s, Tammero had a regular New York Palm customer who would order steak that was raw on the outside and well-done on the inside. His trick was to sear the steak briefly, split it down the middle, fold it over, and literally serve it inside-out.

The Palm in Denver, as elsewhere, is a power-lunch kind of place. Meals often launch with a drink made by one of the skilled bartenders. If you go for the salad list, you'll be hard-pressed to find one that's vegetables only, as most come with chicken. The Blackened New York Strip Salad is a staple, and the Caesar is a classic. Enormous sandwiches, pasta (some traditional, and some—like the Jalapeño Linguine with Chicken—more Southwestern trendy), generous entrées (steaks, of course, but also excellent crab cakes and other seafood and poultry items), and side orders of potatoes and vegetables portioned for two people to share are standard.

The dinner menu shows more starters, more salads, no sandwiches, veal added to the entrée list, more steaks, a different mix of pastas, and the same assortment of side dishes, again designed for two. House specialties include a 36-ounce New York Strip Steak for two and Jumbo Maine Lobster, promised at three pounds or larger and priced by weight. The wines are mostly from California, partly from Italy and France, and sparingly from other wine regions. There's even a section on the wine list for "large bottles"—not jug wines, certainly, but jug-size from one-and-a-half to three liters.

Named in honor of the original Palm's street number, the 837 Club is like a frequent-eater club for regular customers. Eat, earn points, and trade them in for meals, wine, special events, members-only dinners, and other benefits.

The Palm, Westin at Tabor Center, 1672 Lawrence Street, Denver; (303) 825-7256 or www.thepalm.com.

Palomino Restaurant Rotisseria Bar

This huge and stylish 16th Street Mall restaurant is a study in contrasts—the image of the palomino, a horse breed associated with the West, and food that derives, albeit loosely, from European fare, mostly Italian. The restaurant is part of a Seattle-based group with a dozen locations.

Inspired by the bistros of France, Spain, and Italy, designer and restaurateur Don Adams sought what the company calls "a romantic recreation of those classic gathering places on a grand scale: dramatic spaces, exhibition cooking from the spit-rotisserie and wood oven, Italian marble, polished wood, and fresh local products prepared using old-world techniques." That became Palomino Restaurant Rotisseria Bar, characterized by urban style and simply prepared dishes made from fresh ingredients. Denver's Palomino occupies a large space on the first floor of a downtown office tower, brought down to scale with clever design. A big bar, several dining areas, and interesting lighting all make the large restaurant seem smaller, more human in scale. Being downtown, the Palomino gallops in with a popular lunch menu. House-made soups, a good selection of salads, burgers, bistro sandwiches, pizza, and roasted and grilled meats and poultry comprise the list of starters, light lunches, and entrées. The menu is designed to appeal to the most mismatched taste buds of coworkers lunching together. Dinner is offered in the categories of "Small Plates," "Spit Roasting," "Pasta," "Plates of the House," "Hardwood Fired Oven and Grill," and "Roma Style Pizza." A relatively small dessert list and relatively modest list of primarily West Coast and French wines offer quality rather than knock-'em-dead quantity.

Whether eclectic or European, everything is freshly prepared and served with alacrity. The food is so good, in fact, that Denver's Charlie Stauter joined colleagues from other locations to cook at the James Beard House in New York. Stauter prepared a show-stopping lavender ice cream, literally and figuratively la crème de la crème of an all-Palomino feast.

Palomino Restaurant Rotisseria Bar, 1515 16th Street, Denver; (303) 534-7800 or www.palominodenver.com.

Ruth's Chris Steak House

You can think of this nationwide chain as "The House that Ruth Built"—and not in the context of baseball. For behind Ruth's Chris Steak House is a real Ruth: Ruth Fertel. Born in 1927 and raised in the Mississippi Delta backwater of Happy Jack, she was definitely a woman ahead of her time. Wanting to become a pediatrician, she enrolled in Louisiana State University. Soon she changed majors and was only 19 when she earned a degree in chemistry with a minor in physics. This chemist and physicist by education, teacher in passing, single mother by circumstance, and entrepreneur by necessity opened a modest restaurant in her beloved New Orleans to help send her two sons to college.

In 1965, as she was setting off on that entrepreneurial path, she found a classified ad listing Chris Steak House for sale for $22,000. She mortgaged her house to buy it from founder Chris Matulich, who said she could keep the name as long as she stayed in the original location. Fertel, then age 38, had no background in food service, but her instincts were sound. She envisioned a comfortable oasis serving excellent food and treating customers as honored guests. On May 24, 1965, her opening day, Ruth sold 35 steaks at $5 each.

Business quickly grew, but the restaurant business was not without its setbacks. When Hurricane Betsy dealt all of New Orleans a savage blow later that year, there was no electricity for a week. Rather than let the steaks that filled her cooler spoil, she cooked them all up and served them to the emergency workers. Good karma there. It lasted for a decade, until the original Chris Steak House burned down. Forced to relocate and therefore free of the name restriction, she reestablished her restaurant by prefixing her name to the original—and though the tongue-twisting name Ruth's Chris Steak House is a marketing expert's nightmare, it remains so to this day.

Meanwhile, Ruth's had become a popular gathering spot with the city's media personalities, political leaders, sports figures, and businesspeople, who appreciated its quality, service, and fine steaks. It still is. Ruth opened two more restaurants in Louisiana and in 1977, at the urging of a regular customer, granted the first franchise for a Ruth's Chris Steak House.

Over the years, and with each new restaurant opening, Ruth imbued her staff with the values of hard, honest work and a passion for quality and service. With more than 80 locations in the United States and abroad, Ruth's Chris Steak House Inc., a privately held corporation, is now said to be the world's largest fine-dining restaurant group, a far greater success and with wider reach than its enthusiastic and determined founder ever anticipated. Ruth Fertel died in April 2002 at the age of 75, leaving a legacy for steak-lovers.

In keeping with Ruth Fertel's long-time senses about the link between food and community, portions are big enough to share. Ruth's Chris does steaks as well as, if not better than, anyone in the business. Many dishes that orbit around the beef core have a decided New Orleans flavor. The appetizers include what are listed as Barbecue Shrimp but in fact are sautéed in a white wine reduction with garlic, butter, garlic, and regional seasonings. Creole seasonings also enhance the rémoulade served with the Gulf shrimp cocktail. Louisiana Seafood Gumbo is rich, flavorful, singing of the sea, and sizzling with the pungency of New Orleans's fabled cuisine. The Chop Salad is another regionally inspired house specialty. Several cuts of veal, several varieties of seafood, poultry, and even a portobello steak for vegetarians are available at Ruth's Chris. If you have room for dessert, you can't go wrong with any of them, but the bread pudding, served with whiskey sauce, is a true New Orleans version.

Located in LoDo space as prime as the steak it serves, Denver's Ruth's Chris Steak House is the only one for hundreds of miles around, the closest others being one in Kansas City, five in the southern quadrant of Texas, one in Las Vegas, and two in Arizona.

Ruth's Chris Steak House, 1445 Market Street, Denver; (303) 446-2233 or (800) 544-0808, followed by 46. The website for all Ruth's Chris Steak Houses is www.ruthschris.com

Wolfgang Puck Café

Wolfgang Puck, the Austrian-born, self-described "chef to the stars," has pumped up a single glamorous Hollywood restaurant called Spago into a culinary conglomerate and into a personal high profile for himself. He stars in a Food Network television show. He writes cookbooks. His name is emblazoned on some of the most prestigious awards in the culinary world. He appears at important food festivals, sometimes including Aspen's *Food & Wine* Magazine Classic and A Taste of Colorado. His name is on gourmet supermarket foods including soups and frozen pizza. He has launched a signature wine label in cooperation with Kendall–Jackson and a line of cookware with his name on every pot and pan. And restaurants—has he got restaurants!

Puck started his culinary apprenticeship at the age of 14 and worked his way up to the kitchens of some notable Michelin three-star restaurants in France before coming to the United States in 1973. As chef and part-owner of Los Angeles's Ma Maison, he hit the pinnacle of classic French cuisine in America. Still, what captivated him was the bright and brash California culture, and Spago was born. Puck's former wife and still (at this writing) business partner, Barbara Lazaroff, designed a sprightly restaurant with a trend-setting open kitchen. The original Spago Hollywood is gone, but there are now Spagos in Beverly Hills, Chicago, Las Vegas, and Palo Alto.

The pair opened other noteworthy up-market restaurants on the West Coast (Chinois on Main in Santa Monica, Postrio in San Francisco, Granita in Malibu, and another Postrio and Trattoria del Lupo in Las Vegas casino-resorts), but Puck also was interested in offering the same verve and style at more moderate prices and in more casual surroundings. Wolfgang Puck Cafés and Grand Cafés bring his peppy interpretation of California cuisine to select locations in California, Florida, Seattle, Chicago, Las Vegas—and Denver, where Puck's restaurant occupies big space at The Denver Pavilions. The big, bustling restaurant with the signature open kitchen is distinctive and dramatic, befitting a Hollywood-based eatery. It opened in 1999, becoming one of 68 Wolfgang Puck Grand Cafés around the country.

Wolfgang Puck may have his name on hundreds of doors and millions of cans, bottles, and frozen-food boxes, but the man did start out as a chef, with open-mindedness and creativity coursing through his veins. He was a culinary pioneer, topping pizza with goat cheese, duck sausage, sun-dried tomatoes and baking them in an old-fashioned brick oven. This departure from red sauce and pepperoni pizza made him the culinary toast of Hollywood. Wood-fired pizzas with such trendy toppings remain signature at all Puck's locations. You can also expect abundant Pacific Rim, Mediterranean, and Southwestern influences: spring rolls of various sorts, potstickers, calamari, quesadillas, bruschetta, pastas, salads, barbecued chicken, complex sandwiches, grilled meats, and other offerings from currently hot cuisines. Desserts are a big part of the Puck pitch too.

Denver International Airport is one of three cities (Los Angeles and Chicago being the others) with Wolfgang Puck Airport Express locations, and another opened in a Black Hawk casino. The menu is a scaled-down version of that served at the cafés, and the atmosphere hints of the style set in the larger establishments.

Wolfgang Puck Café, Denver Pavilions, 500 16th Street, Denver; (303) 595-5693.
Wolfgang Puck Express, Denver International Airport, Concourse B,
(303) 342-7611; and Black Hawk Casino by Hyatt, 111 Richman Street,
Black Hawk, (303) 467-1234. The website for all Wolfgang Puck restaurants,
from one-of-a-kind West Coast culinary temples to grab-a-bite express stations,
is www.wolfgangpuck.com.

Retail

Rocky Mountain Chocolate Factory

On Memorial Day weekend, 1981, Frank Crail opened a small candy store on Main Street in downtown Durango. The seductive smell of chocolate wafted onto the sidewalk, luring passersby. As they peered into the window, they could see an energetic young man pouring a huge mass of rich fudge on a massive marble slab and mixing it on the spot. The store is still there—as are more than 225 other company-owned and franchised Rocky Mountain Chocolate Factory shops all across the United States and some in Canada and Asia too.

The famous fudge is made on the spot in each location, as is the caramel for the candied apples and other treats. Watch as a skewered apple is spun into a copper pot of caramel or witness the spreading out of a fresh batch of fudge, and I'll wager you'll find it hard to walk out without buying some.

The stores also carry a dazzling assortment of premium chocolates and other candies made on-site or in the company's 53,000-square-foot factory and office in Durango. A master chocolatier has developed recipes for some 300 items made year-round, with another hundred or so made for such chocolate-y holidays as Valentine's Day, Easter, Mother's Day, and Christmas.

If you think Rocky Mountain Chocolate Factory's chocolates are bigger than most, you're right. In the early days, Crail and his friends were not very competent candy-makers, so they didn't consider the addition of the chocolate coating in calculating size or shape and therefore they made the candy centers bigger than they should have. That meant the pieces weren't always even enough or pretty enough to sell, so they would dip them again until they looked good. Customers loved these heavyweight chocolates. These days, the Rocky Mountain Chocolate Factory is very good at the art and craft of making premium chocolates, but each piece is still large.

Rocky Mountain Chocolate Factory's signature chocolate is a patty called The Bear. Paw-sized and paw-shaped, it is a concoction of chewy caramel, roasted nuts, and a heavy coating of milk or dark chocolate. Other favorites include nut clusters, butter creams, exotic-flavored truffles, toffee, and a king-sized peanut butter cup dubbed "The Bucket." The company also makes sugar-free and no-sugar-added candies, so that people with special dietary requirements can still satisfy their sweet tooths with some of the best candy around. If you want to see it being made, take a factory tour offered daily from Memorial Day through Labor Day.

Rocky Mountain Chocolate Factory, 265 Turner Drive, Durango
(factory and head office); the corporate toll-free number is (888) 525-2462,
and the company website is www.rmcf.com. Colorado stores are located in the

following places (usually downtown, unless indicated otherwise):
523 East Cooper Street, Aspen, (970) 925-5112; 1300 Pearl Street, Boulder,
(303) 444-8455; 222 Main Street, Breckenridge (970) 453-2094;
Flatlron Crossing, 1 West Flatiron Circle, Broomfield, (303) 635-1037;
5050 Factory Shops Boulevard, Castle Rock Factory Shops, Castle Rock, (303)
660-1320; Citadel Mall, 750 Citadel Drive, Colorado Springs, (719) 591-2254;
2431 West Colorado Avenue, Old Colorado City, Colorado Springs, (719) 635-4131;
1710 Briargate Boulevard, Chapel Hills Mall, Colorado Springs, (719) 590-7623;
Village Square, Copper Mountain, (970) 968-2354; 314 Elk Avenue, Crested
Butte, (970) 349-0933; Denver International Airport, Concourse B, #1
(303) 342-7860, DIA #2 (303) 342-3472; 1512 Larimer Square (Writer Square),
Denver, (303) 623-1887; Durango, (970) 259-1408; Stanley Village, 517 Big
Thompson Avenue, Estes Park, (970) 586-6601; Foothills Mall, Fort Collins,
(970) 226-5550; 172 North College Avenue, Old Town, Fort Collins;
(970) 226-5550; Mesa Mall, Grand Junction, (970) 243-3833; 1117 Grand Avenue,
Grand Lake, (970) 627-3840; Keystone Village, Keystone, (970) 262-1267;
River Run, Keystone, (970) 262-9184; Southwest Plaza, Littleton, (303) 773-0615;
Manufacturer's Marketplace, 5669 McWhinney Boulevard, Loveland,
(970) 593-0106; Prime Outlets, Silverthorne, (970) 468-9168;
Snowmass Village, Snowmass, (970) 923-2875; 845 Village Avenue, Steamboat
Springs, (970) 879-6194; Ski Time Square, Steamboat Springs, (970) 879-5098;
304 Bridge Street, Vail, (970) 476-7623; Cooper Creek Square, Winter Park,
(970) 726-8361.

Sur La Table

Sur La Table, across from Seattle's historic Pike Place Market, has been a
landmark for more than 30 years. Established to satisfy the demands of culinary
professionals, the store quickly became a mecca for home cooks who wanted
quality wares. Especially after it became the first West Coast retailer to carry the
Cuisinart food processor, for which it garnered a cutting-edge reputation for the latest and greatest products.

In 1995 an investment group purchased Sur La Table and expanded it across the
country. Colorado's Sur La Table is in Cherry Creek. President Renée Behnke and a
buying team travel the world to seek out products. In recent years, the team has gone
to France, Italy, England, Portugal, Germany, Morocco, Croatia, Mexico, and Vietnam.
Behnke herself spends an extended time in a single foreign location, attending
cooking schools and immersing herself in learning the techniques, seasonings,
ingredients, and traditions of the cuisine.

Sur La Table's 12,000-item inventory features cookware, bakeware, small
appliances, cutlery, kitchen tools, cookbooks, table linens, tableware, both common
and hard-to-find gadgets, and seasonal and specialty foods. You can get brands like
All Clad, Bunzlauer Stoneware, Calphalon, Capresso, Le Creuset, Cuisinart,
Emerilware, Henckels, Krups, Messermeister, OXO, Waring, Wüsthoff, and many
more. The store is also renowned for a line of French copper cookware, a direct

import from a sixth-generation family of artisans and a Sur La Table specialty. If the local store doesn't have what you need or crave, it can be quickly ordered, because, in addition to its multiple locations, Sur La Table has a successful mail-order business and catalog.

Sur La Table, Cherry Creek Shopping Center, 3000 East First Avenue, Denver; (303) 780-7800 or www.surlatable.com.

The Cutting Edge

The sign above the door of this small store in the Colorado Mills shopping mall says "The Cutting Edge," but it is the first Colorado location for California-based Merlo's Cutlery, a name more familiar elsewhere. It carries such excellent kitchen knives as Henckels Four Star products, sold either open stock or in sets with a wooden storage block and perhaps even an instructional video on proper knife skills, carving knives and sets, steak knives, scissors, and a small assortment of spatulas and other cooking accessories. The store also offers knife-sharpening services.

The Cutting Edge, Colorado Mills, Store # 362, 14500 West Colfax Avenue, Lakewood; (303) 216-0893.

Whole Foods Markets

The three Colorado outposts of this Dallas-based natural foods supermarket chain put the fun and the flavor back into grocery shopping in a supermarket. Colorado gourmet cooks who want quality ingredients, health-foodies, vegetarians and vegans, and a cadre of fussy but time-pressed eaters who want great take-out food flock to Whole Foods' 103 stores (at this writing) across the nation and Canada. Customers are willing to pay a premium for the highest-quality, least-processed, most-flavorful naturally preserved foods, unadulterated by artificial additives, sweeteners, colorings, and preservatives. These standards meet the criteria both of meticulous cooks and of consumers who believe that, indeed, we are what we eat.

The markets combine the service and quality that remain the hallmarks of small specialty retailers with the variety and scope of products of a mainstream super-market, but without the socks, sewing notions, motor oil, folding chairs, Colorado sports team memorabilia, school supplies, and other nonfood miscellany that fills so many big stores' aisles. Whole Foods concentrates on providing an array of first-quality and ultra-fresh meats, seafood, and produce—as much as possible locally sourced; plus bulk dried foods, nuts, grains, herbs and spices; a fantastic selection of imported and domestic artisan cheeses; an on-site bakery, pizzeria, and juice bar; and quality prepared foods to eat in or take home. Many foods are offered in sampling stands so that you can taste the organic chips, the whole-grain cereal, the grapes or pineapple or oranges, fresh-baked breads, salsas, dips, beverages, and other products. You can also request samples of cheeses, cured meats and charcuterie, olives, and prepared foods.

Service is a true hallmark of the Whole Foods approach. Even the newest hire is thoroughly introduced to the products before being unleashed on the sales floor, and training is ongoing. Ask a staffer where something is, and he or she won't just point vaguely and mumble "Aisle 7" but will lead you directly to the item you are seeking. It's old-time grocery service with a smile—that's rare in a big business.

Whole Foods Market was founded in Austin, Texas, a university town that has been compared to Boulder in terms of ambience, social conscience, and lifestyle. John Mackey, owner of Safer Way Natural Foods, and Craig Weller and Mark Skiles, owners of Clarksville Natural Grocery, decided that there was a place for super-market-style sourcing, merchandising, and selling of quality natural foods. The first Whole Foods Market opened in 1980, when there were fewer than half-a-dozen natural food supermarkets in the United States.

Whole Foods has grown both by launching its own new stores and through mergers and acquisitions with other regional natural-foods retailers with similar product lines and philosophies. Whole Foods sees itself as a citizen of each community in which it operates, the nation, and the world and so offers both locally produced products and ones from all over the globe, often from small, uniquely dedicated food artisans. Whole Foods also believes that companies, like individuals, have an obligation to assume responsibility "as tenants of Planet Earth." On a global basis, the chain actively supports organic farming, acknowledged as the best method for promoting sustainable agriculture while protecting both the environment and farm workers. Each store is actively involved in its community by supporting food banks, sponsoring neighborhood events, compensating team members for community service work, and contributing at least 5 percent of total net profits to not-for-profit organizations. This admirable corporation is a good global citizen, a wonderful asset to each Colorado neighborhood where it has put down roots, and a place to buy darned good food as well.

Whole Foods Market, Crossroads Common Shopping Center, 2905 Pearl Street, Boulder, (303) 545-6611; Cherry Creek, 2375 East First Avenue, Denver, (720) 941-4100; 9366 South Colorado Boulevard, Highlands Ranch, (303) 470-6003. The website for all locations is www.wholefoodsmarket.com.

Wild Oats Markets

From a modest beginning with the 1987 purchase of Crystal Market, a small vegetarian food store in Boulder, Wild Oats has grown into a mainstream market chain with a dozen stores on Colorado's Front Range and more than a hundred in the United States and Canada. Some stores were acquired (like Alfalfa's Market and Ideal Market in Boulder, the latter still operating under its original name), and some opened initially under the Wild Oats name. The emphasis of this Boulder-based company is to sell products that "promote health and well-being," to use the corporation's phrase. For cooks, this means an availability of excellent ingredients in a supermarket-sized setting, and for the time-pressed, it means quality prepared foods.

Wild Oats maintains a commitment to selling natural products, both fresh and packaged. Products offered with the store's private label are—like most brands it carries—free of artificial colors, flavors, or preservatives, with environmentally conscious manufacturing and packaging and organic ingredients used whenever possible. The initial commitment to vegetarianism that characterized the old Crystal Market has long gone, and the stores carry quality and hormone-free meats, seafood, and poultry, as well as preservative-free dairy products. The prepared foods are largely made by Wild Oats, and the stores also carry breads and desserts from excellent bakeries.

Wild Oats Markets, 12131 Iliff Avenue, Aurora, (303) 695-8801;
2584 Baseline Road, Boulder, (303) 499-7636; 1651 Broadway Street (formerly
Alfalfa's), Boulder, (303) 442-0909; 5075 North Academy Boulevard, Colorado
Springs, (719) 548-1667; 1111 South Washington Street, Denver,
(303) 733-6201; 200 West Foothills Parkway, Fort Collins, (970) 225-1400;
14357 West Colfax Avenue, Lakewood, (303) 277-1339;
and 9229 North Sheridan Boulevard, Westminster; (303) 650-2333.
Ideal Market, 1275 Alpine Avenue, Boulder, (303) 443-1354. Wild Oats' general
information number is (800) 494-WILD and website is www.wildoats.com.

Williams–Sonoma

In 1947, a contractor named Chuck Williams arrived in Sonoma, California, to build homes in what has since become one of the nation's leading wine-growing regions. To service home-buyers, he opened a hardware store and expanded into cookware. By 1958, the store had moved to San Francisco, offered a bridal registry, and later issued a mail-order catalog. The company was incorporated in 1972, allowing for rapid expansion to other California locations. In 1978, when Howard Lester and Jay McMahan purchased Williams–Sonoma Inc., the first out-of-state store was opened in Dallas.

Chuck Williams's little hardware store has ballooned into a multi-billion-dollar corporation—a lifestyle conglomerate that now includes Pottery Barn, Hold Everything, Chambers, and Pottery Barn Kids. They all have retail outlets—more than 300 at last count—and publish catalogs. Williams–Sonoma also got into the cookbook and food-book publishing business, with more than 10 million copies in print. Meanwhile, Chuck Williams was honored with a Lifetime Achievement Award from the James Beard Foundation and published an authoritative history of American food.

Williams–Sonoma initially made its reputation as a purveyor of high-quality cookware and knives imported from France, which were hard to come by when Williams was starting out. Today, each store, and the catalog as well, offers a dazzling array of stylish and practical products for the kitchen and home. Williams–Sonoma carries such varied and perennially popular products as a full line of gorgeous Mauviel copper pots and pans made in Normandy since 1830, simple and functional brasserie tableware from France, Dualit toasters from England (which carry Rolls-Royce–type heft and durability), and, oh yes, the ceramic chickens that Chuck Williams found in France many years ago.

Of course, those popular exotics do not begin to cover a vast inventory that includes other types of cookware (the kinds that don't require polishing), both more formal and funkier tableware, great-looking flatware and glasses, kitchen and table linens, bakeware, appliances, and even the endearing and useful little objects that Chuck Williams dismissed in the early days by saying, "I don't do gadgets."

Williams–Sonoma, Cherry Creek, 3000 East First Avenue, Cherry Creek, Denver, (303) 394-2226; 7301 South Santa Fe Drive, Aspen Grove, Littleton, (303) 794-4744; 8405 Park Meadows Center Drive, Littleton, (303) 790-2565; FlatIron Crossing, 1 West Flatiron Circle, Broomfield, (720) 887-2900. The website for all locations is www.williams-sonoma.com.

RETAIL

Other Tastes and Treats

Colorado's culinary attractions in the main section of this book are concentrated in and near the Front Range cities and in the state's major ski and summer resort communities. There you will find the most fine dining, the most food events, and also the greatest array of resources for the home cook. Still, some real gems are scattered elsewhere throughout the state—a wonderful restaurant here, a terrific cookware store there, a fabulous bakery somewhere else, an interesting food festival in yet another community. They're worth a detour, or at least a stop.

Food festivals are found all over too, in small communities where they might just be the biggest event of the year. These are not normally blowout gourmet feasts, but rather endearing hometown celebrations of a major local crop or showcases for favorite ways to prepare chili, buffalo burgers, and the like. These events might not, by any stretch, qualify as haute cuisine, but they are usually great fun, especially for families who love to explore and eat. And don't forget the state's abundant farmers' markets (see page 463–469 for a list) when you're roaming around the state in search of good food.

Bakeries

Absolute Bakery & Cafe (Mancos)

This congenial bakery and café offers exceptional baked goods and finely wrought informal breakfasts and lunches. Owners Carla Borelli and Sean McCall, both Culinary Institute of America graduates, prepare from-scratch foods that are both environmentally and often nutritionally responsible, but of the highest quality as well. Borelli majored in pastry arts at the CIA and does the breads and other baked goods, while McCall, a culinary arts major, prepares everything else. They use what McCall describes as "the cleanest products available," such as organic flour, dairy products, and eggs from free-range chickens fed a vegetarian diet. "Even our table ketchup is organic," he says.

Borelli, a full-on pastry chef, turns out everything from ethereal pastries and elaborate wedding cakes to hearty bread, including five signature breads and three wheat-free, spelt-based specialty breads, basic breakfast items, and popular cookies.

People come from miles around for her coconut macaroons. She also bakes "alternative pastries" for those who cannot tolerate or prefer not to eat wheat, sugar, nuts, or dairy products, and, of course, she can also make low-fat baked goods.

McCall's specials include soups that change almost daily, outstanding quiches, sandwiches built on those wonderful breads, salads, and entrée specials. Some regulars come in just for the Tamari Ginger Wrap with Cashew Sauce, a happy melding of Southwestern and Asian flavors.

The café, located in the historic and lovingly restored Bauer Bank Building built in downtown Mancos in 1905, features wood floors, high pressed-tin ceilings, and art-filled walls. Used books, for sale or just for browsing, fill shelves around the café as well. Locals hang out in this friendly, casual, and even homey place—and so, increasingly, do visitors.

Absolute Bakery & Café, 110 South Main Street, Mancos; (970) 533-1200.

Kate's Cakes (Gunnison)

Kate's Cakes is a self-described "cakery within an art gallery," which in turn is located in an old Gunnison landmark. Delectable house specialties are cheesecakes, beautiful tortes, coffee cakes, bundt cakes, and the loveliest special-occasion cakes in the valley. In addition to these scratch-baked cakes from quality ingredients, the bakery offers cookies, brownies, cream puffs and éclairs of comparable quality. Kate's Holiday Fruitcake is a seasonal specialty made with naturally dried fruits, honey, fresh butter, and nuts, wrapped in brandy-soaked cheesecloth as a natural preservative that keeps it fresh for up to three months—though in truth, most people eat it long before that.

Kate's Cakes, Johnson Building, 124 North Main Street, Gunnison; (970) 641-1189 or www.gunnison.com/Business/katecoleman.

Harsh Haus (Eaton)

One of the great joys of the table is really good bread—bread with flavor, texture, crustiness, and aesthetic beauty. Alas, people with wheat or gluten allergies are generally only able to enjoy the looks of a loaf of fine bread—and cakes and other baked goods as well. Tasting is *verboten* to them. Baker Pam Harsh, who lives on a 75-acre farm on the eastern plains, has developed a line of gluten-free products to fill that need to taste as well as to look. She had been supplying bread to small food stores in such places as Eaton, Greeley, and Windsor that do not usually carry out-of-the-ordinary breads. One day, a woman with a strong wheat allergy requested a birthday cake—her first in two decades. Harsh fulfilled the request by using an alternative flour, and another specialty was born.

Amaranth, certain beans, corn, potatoes, rice, soy, tapioca, an Ethiopian staple called *sef,* and tapioca all can be made into flour—and using these products by themselves or in combination, Harsh can turn out breads, cakes, bagels, and pizza—not exotic treats for most of us, but a fabulous find for those with wheat allergies.

Harsh Haus, 600 Oak Avenue, Eaton; (970) 454-2291 or www.harshhaus.com.

Ingrid's Cup & Saucer (Glenwood Springs)

This charming bakery and café is located on a narrow sliver of street just above the railroad tracks. Hop off Amtrak, hop out of Glenwood Springs' Hot Springs Pool, or hop off Interstate 70 and make your way to this small bright bakery overlooking, yes, the tracks, the pool, and I-70—as well as the landmark towers and façade of the Hotel Colorado. Ingrid Jacobsen, who had baked for the previous owners, purchased the popular Wild Rose Bakery in late 2002, changed the name to her own, and now offers a combination of the excellent breads and pastries from the Wild Rose era but with the addition of more sandwiches and homemade soups.

It is a warm and pleasantly low-key place. An antique brass scale perches atop the baked-goods display, joined by a collection of antique silver trays, photographs from Jacobsen's travels to Italy and elsewhere, and old cabinets rescued from remodeled Aspen homes.

Ingrid's quality breads are all baked fresh daily from organic flours. The seeded multi-grain, the signature bread, tastes fabulous and also is nutritious. Excellent sandwiches with a choice of breads, deli meats, and heaps of veggies (or just veggies) make this an excellent lunch stop. For breakfast or midmorning or afternoon coffee, the bakers hand-roll the Danishes, fruit turnovers, seasonal fruit pastries, and killer cinnamon rolls. The cheesecake and éclairs are sensational, and people come for miles around for specialty birthday cakes and wedding cakes made by Ingrid's—or by referral to previous Wild Rose owner Avtar Perrault, with whom Jacobsen maintains a mutually supportive relationship.

Ingrid's Cup & Saucer, 310 Seventh Street, Glenwood Springs; (970) 928-8973.

La Papillon (Ouray)

The Big Easy comes to the big mountains in this small bakery and cafe, which really feels like a corner of New Orleans transplanted to the Rockies. The décor runs to ceiling fans and New Orleans Jazz Festival posters on the walls. The patio is heavenly in summer. From-scratch baked goods include French bread, tasty pastries, and of course, *beignets*—New Orleans–speak for donuts. La Papillon's all-day breakfasts features a huge breakfast sandwich (sausage, bacon, or ham) on a house-made sandwich bun (move over, McMuffins). At lunch, La Papillon offers sandwiches on their signature buns.

La Papillon, 219 Seventh Avenue, Ouray; (970) 325-0644.

Cooking Classes

Cottonwood Inn & Gallery (Alamosa)

The Cottonwood Inn is a charming country-style B&B on the outskirts of old Alamosa. It is an art gallery. It is a catering service. And it is a place to go for cooking classes, held in what might just be Alamosa's best-appointed kitchen. The spacious room, featuring ample counterspace and a commodious range, accommodates up to 15 people in the full hands-on classes. Students prepare and enjoy a five- to-seven-course meal, typically Italian, Provençal, Chinese, or Mexican, with a suitable wine. Sometimes, a special theme class, such as soups or another particular course, is scheduled. Monthly classes are held on Saturdays except in summer, beginning no later than 10:00 A.M.

Cottonwood Inn owner Deborah Donaldson teaches most of the classes, but guest chefs conduct some. For those who want to make a weekend of it, the inn offers a lodging discount for students on the Friday night before or the Saturday night of the class.

Cottonwood Inn, 123 San Juan Avenue, Alamosa; (800) 955-2623, (719) 589-3882 or www.cottonwoodinn.com.

West Pawnee Ranch B&B Cooking Classes (Grover)

You can't take cooking classes at the West Pawnee Ranch Bed & Breakfast any old time, but one March weekend a year, the working ranch/B&B inn offers hands-on classes on Western Hemisphere foods taught by Beverly Cox, an authority on Latin American foods. Learn to prepare and enjoy the food, and take time to explore the expansive Pawnee National Grassland and Pawnee Buttes, both nearby.

West Pawnee Ranch Bed & Breakfast, 29451 Weld County Road 130, Grover; (970) 895-2482 or www.bbonline.com/co/pawnee.

Vegan Cooks (Evergreen)

Vicki Johnston, who grew up as a meat-and-potatoes kid and shifted first to vegetarianism and then veganism as an adult, has messianic zeal. Her vegan cooking classes, held in her Evergreen home and elsewhere, help people make that transition. She believes that meatless recipes can turn out fine-tasting food, and she teaches the techniques that make that happen.

Her two- to three-hour classes, usually midday on Saturday, are mostly demonstration, with limited participation. The Introduction to Vegetarian Ingredients is the cornerstone to vegetarian cooking. Other ingredient-based and specialty classes focus on one topic at a time, including Whole Grains, Soups, Seitan, Beans, Asian Noodles, Soy Foods, Vegetables, Sushi and Spring Rolls, Pies and Tarts, and Cookies and Brownies. Johnston also hands out a wealth of printed material on general vegan cooking, specific ingredient information, and, of course, recipes.

Vegan Cooks, 33001 Alpine Lane, Evergreen; (303) 674-0955 or www.vegancooks.com.

Dining

Grandmaison's Chalet Room (Estes Park)

The Marys Lake Lodge was built in 1913 as a boarding house for vacationers and expanded to become a posh haven for visitors to the then newly designated Rocky Mountain National Park. In the late 1920s, the hotel was known as The Estes Park Chalet, a prime example of a distinctive regional style known as Rocky Mountain Stick architecture design. It was one of three stops along a multi-day circle tour of this section of the Colorado Rockies—the others being the Grand Lake Lodge near Grand Lake Village and the Hot Springs Hotel near Idaho Springs.

Despite this pedigree, the structure had fallen on hard times before it was purchased in 1999 by Don DeBey, Ron Noble, and Frank Theis, who promised to restore the venerable building. Fortunately for the project, Theis is a trained architect, capable of discerning what needed to be restored and saved and what needed to be modernized and upgraded. Part of the lodge's renaissance involved the establishment of a restaurant experience worthy of the historic structure. Marc Grandmaison, a Massachusetts native, learned the fundamentals of cooking from his mother and followed it with wide-ranging New England restaurant experience. In Colorado, he became executive chef at The Historic Stanley Hotel in Estes Park and joined Marys Lake Lodge which, when renovated, became a suitable venue for his skills. Together with chef Scott Anderson, he is responsible for Grandmaison's Chalet Room and the less formal Tavern Restaurant.

The kitchen expands its offerings by preparing a few key ingredients in several ways. For instance, little neck clams can be ordered casino-style (peppers, butter, and lemon), *catalpana* (chorizo, wine, and peppers), or simply on the half-shell (with horseradish sauce and lemon). The filet mignon entrée is available *au poivre* (black pepper, Cognac, shiitake mushrooms, and shallots), Prince des Galles (shrimp, Cognac, and crème fraîche), or Au Diane (Amaretto, shiitake mushrooms, and shallots). Of the nearly a dozen additional entrées, half are seafood, the rest meat or chicken, plus a daily pasta special.

Grandmaison's offers two special dinner menus. The first is a "European Culinary Tour." From Lisbon comes *Proco con Ameijoas a Alentejana* (mildly spiced baby clams, shrimp, Portuguese sausage, and fava beans in a rich tomato broth), from Barcelona a *Zarzuela* (shrimp, octopus, squid, mussels, and whitefish with red chilies and fresh herbs), and from Athens Macedonia-Style Lamb Shank (roasted with rosemary, marjoram, wine, garlic, and balsamic vinegar and served with bulgur wheat, spinach, and pine nuts). Being an equal-opportunity chef, Grandmaison's second special menu displays well-prepared vegetarian and vegan entrées.

The wine list is heavily canted to California selections, grouped by varietal, plus imports from France, Italy, and South Africa. Inexplicably, a handful of domestic wines are listed under "World Whites" and "World Reds." Fifteen or more wines are also available by the glass.

Grandmaison's Chalet Room, Marys Lake Lodge, 2625 Marys Lake Road, Estes Park; (970) 586-5958, (970) 586-5308, (877) 442-6279 or www.maryslakelodge.com.

Metate Room (Mesa Verde National Park)

The Metate Room, the fine-dining room of the Far View Lodge, faces west and is bathed in the glorious glow of the setting sun. But after dark, diners' attention turns inward. The beamed-ceiling restaurant boasts a dazzling display of antique Navajo rugs and Native American pottery. The furnishings are in a classically elegant Santa Fe style, and the table settings are simple, with black-and-white dinnerware that allows the beautifully presented dishes to star.

The hotel and the restaurant are open between mid-April and mid-October, but Chef Brandon Shubert manages to pack a year's worth of great meals into that seven-month period. The honors graduate from the Western Culinary Institute in Portland, Oregon, has developed what he calls "native Southwest fusion cuisine," combining the heritage foods of ancestral pueblo peoples and the chilies and spices characteristic of Southwestern cuisine done with contemporary flair.

The dinner menu perfectly targets both conservative and adventurous diners, with an emphasis on game, beans, and every course reflecting Shubert's own form of fusion cuisine. A Grilled Ear of Sweet Corn comes with chili–lime oil. Tricolor tortilla chips accompany the Spinach Artichoke Dip. Buffalo quesadillas accompanied by roasted red pepper–cilantro sour cream, Venison Stuffed Mushrooms topped with melted cheese, and Smoked Duck Tamales use meats known to Native Americans in centuries past. The white Bean Chili Soup, made of Great Northern beans, chicken, fresh smoked jalapeños, and Southwestern spices, is one of the finest soups you'll ever eat.

More mainstream entrées include broiled baby back pork ribs, New York strip steak, and chicken, but with Shubert's deft touch. The ribs, for instance, are basted with a chipotle barbecue sauce, and the chicken strips are sautéed with tomatoes, black olives, and cilantro pesto and served with pasta, a rare Mediterranean concept among such intense Southwestern entrées.

Epicures gravitate to dishes listed on the menu under "Chef's Specialties." Blue Adobe Trout consists of fresh trout dusted in blue cornmeal and sautéed in fresh lemon and brown butter. Elk tenderloin is bathed with chokecherry *démi-glace*. Marinated quail is broiled and topped with fire-roasted tomato salsa. Salmon is baked on a cedar plank, brushed with a tangy barbecue butter. The Metate Room's prime rib is prime rib of buffalo, herb-rubbed, served with rosemary *jus*, and offered in eight- or 12-ounce cuts.

Desserts tend toward the whimsical. The Cliff Palace Cinnamon Crisp is a crisp flour tortilla filled with sweet mascarpone mousse, rolled in cinnamon and sugar, and presented with vanilla ice cream and chocolate sauce. Decadence indeed. Deep Dish S'Mores consist of a heap of graham crackers, toasted marshmallows, chocolate, and ice cream. Decadence again. The White Chocolate Raspberry Blitz is a brownie in a seriously altered state. It is stuffed with raspberries, dipped in white chocolate, and bathed in chocolate and fresh raspberry sauce. The Bourbon Pecan Pie served with chocolate sauce and even the apple pie à la mode are simpler but no less decadent.

The wine list is about 70 percent domestic, with California, Oregon, and Colorado wineries well represented. The rest are imports, primarily from Europe. The by-the-glass selection is worthy, and local wineries and microbreweries from the Four Corners areas are also well represented.

Seasonal restaurants don't normally shine culinarily, but the Metate Room certainly does. The *Denver Post* selected it as one of Colorado's top 10 restaurants, rare recognition from a newspaper published more than 400 miles away, and during the off-season, Brandon Shubert has been as one of the few chefs in an international chef exchange program.

Metate Room, Far View Lodge, Mesa Verde National Park, Mancos;
(800) 449-2288, (970) 529-4421, or www.visitmesaverde.com.

Romantic RiverSong Inn (Estes Park)

This isn't "private dining" as in the small dining room that a hotel or restaurant makes available to groups. It's private dining in the sense that Chef Carol Graham prepares a meal for just you and a companion. This special meal is available to guests of Estes Park's Romantic RiverSong Inn, who can add a private dinner to their overnight stay. It is difficult to find a more lovey-dovey dining experience

You have to decide on your entrée from the limited menu when you make your reservation. You can afford to drink the very best wine or champagne with your dinner. The Romantic RiverSong Inn has no liquor license, but guests are welcome to bring their own. A bottle of fine bubbly or vintage wine from a liquor store costs far less than it would at a conventional restaurant.

Graham's food preparation is a bit retro—first-quality food, careful preparation, and attractive presentation, but she doesn't go over the top in ultra-hip ingredients or fussy food constructions on the plate. And, for the male half of the typical couple, the portions are generous. The usual entrée choice is between a beef and a chicken dish, though vegetarians can be accommodated on request. The four-course dinner—soup, salad, sorbet as an intermezzo, choice of entrées, and dessert—proceeds at an unhurried pace, but when you've sighed your last sigh over the final forkful of dessert, your room is close by.

You will be seated at a table for two or perhaps, on a busy weekend, at one end of the long table that is this B&B's center for breakfast congeniality. In any case, the room is not overcrowded because dinner is available for a maximum of five couples per night, and low lights, candles, flowers, and pretty place settings set the tone of togetherness even if others are together nearby.

Valentine's Day evening and most weekends, especially on such big anniversary months as June, are booked well in advance. And so they should be, for this distinctive dining experience is just that—equal parts "dining" and "experience."

Romantic RiverSong Inn, P.O. Box 1910, Estes Park, CO 80517; (970) 586-4666 or www.romanticriversong.com.

Tennessee Pass Cookhouse (Leadville area)

Nomadic herdsmen on the steppes of Mongolia never had it as good as guests at the Tennessee Pass Cookhouse, an authentic yurt set up just a mile from the Piney Creek Nordic Center and Ski Cooper, atop Tennessee Pass northwest of Leadville. The restaurant is open for winter weekend lunches and also summer dinners, but dinner in winter is the best way to experience the yurt's warmth and coziness. This round canvas structure is furnished with antique chairs, gleaming tables, and scatter rugs on the wood floor. A fire in the fireplace, oil lamps, candles, and tiny dried-flower arrangements on each table and subtle background music, make for a romantic scene.

Cookhouse operator Ryor Triesenburg schedules one dinner seating per evening. Guests meet at the Nordic center to pick up headlamps and cross-country skis or snow-shoes for the guided one-mile trip in. Those who are unwilling or unable to ski or hike that distance up to 10,800 feet above sea level can be ferried back and forth by snow-mobile. For everyone else, the short trek through the backcountry is the best part of the experience, especially when the moon is high or snow drifts softly through the trees.

Because of the logistics of getting food to the yurt, reservations and an advance choice of entrée on the limited menu are required. The selection may be modest, but the quality is as high as the elevation. The carefully prepared prix fixe dinner consists of an elegant appetizer platter, soup or salad, a choice of entrées (elk tenderloin, rack of lamb, trout, chicken, or a vegetarian option), and dessert. Wine and microbrewed beers are available. Fortunately, it's downhill on the return to the Nordic center.

Tennessee Pass Cookhouse, Piney Creek Nordic Center/Ski Cooper, Leadville; (719) 486-1750 or www.tennesseepass.com.

The Wyman Hotel & Inn (Silverton)

The Wyman Hotel & Inn has been a Silverton landmark through the gutsy old mining town's boom times and bust times. Now operated by Lorraine and Tom Lewis—she a lapsed attorney, he a former engineer—the inn began staying open through the winter only in 2002–2003. For such nearly year-round operation, the Lewises upgraded the kitchen to provide restaurant service to outsiders as well as hotel guests. Tom—who had been cooking breakfast and whipping up evening desserts—turned his attention also to dinner. And believe me, Silverton really has needed a good place to dine.

Tom grew up in Fort Worth, but his mother was a Louisiana girl who was cooking Cajun when Cajun wasn't cool. He learned in his mother's kitchen but eventually gravitated to engineering, a profession that took him to places as diverse as Asia, the Middle East, and the Caribbean, and he learned about the culture and cuisine every place he went.

Dinner, a four-course meal, with choices at each course, consists of appetizers, either a soup or a salad, two or three entrées from a particular cuisine each night

(Thai, French, Italian, German, Mediterranean, or an Asian combination such as Thai-Chinese or Chinese-Japanese), and dessert (specialties being crème brulée and chocolate *pots de crème)* including two glasses of wine. The modest price was just $50 during opening season of dinner at the Wyman. At this writing the Lewises aren't sure how the concept will play out, but Tom's skill in the kitchen and ability to draw from the foods of many places around the globe, plus favorable customer response, will hopefully assure continuation of dinner service.

The Wyman Hotel's dining room is picture pretty, with high ceilings, large windows, solid oak antique furniture, and historic photographs and local artwork on the walls. The hotel was built in 1902, and it took a century for the availability of food to match the atmosphere.

The Wyman Hotel & Inn, 1371 Greenle Street, Silverton; (800) 609-7845, (970) 387-5372, or www.thewyman.com.

Events

Chocolate Lovers' Extravaganza (Salida)

February—The annual Chocolate Lovers Extravaganza, held on a weekend evening in February, typically around Valentine's Day, is a fundraiser to help end domestic abuse. The event takes place in a spacious auditorium and features the unlimited sampling of savory and sweet treats—that is to say, both appetizers and chocolates. Local restaurants such as Bongo Billie's, Country Bounty, Dakota's Bistro, and Laughing Ladies provide the food. Additionally, it includes a silent auction, entertainment, and a cash bar.

For more information or tickets, call the Alliance Against Domestic Abuse; (719) 539-7347. Tickets can also be purchased at Moonlight Pizza, 242 F Street, Salida. Do not call the Alliance's emergency numbers.

Estes Park Festival of Wines

May—Since the Estes Park Festival of Wines was launched in 2001, connoisseurs have had a reason to visit for a weekend in early May, one of the most quiet times of year. With so new an event (only two had been held at this writing), the format and venues could change, but currently it includes open seminars and wine tastings on Friday and Saturday at The Historic Stanley Hotel, followed by wine-pairing dinners at half-a-dozen local restaurants.

Organizers don't call them wine-pairings, however, but use the far more romantic name of Wine Marriage Dinners. In 2002 they took place on Friday at the Stanley Hotel (an optional black-tie event at the atmospheric hotel where Eric

Skokan, formerly of Alice's Restaurant at Gold Lake Resort, had started cooking), the Aspen Lodge, and The View Restaurant. Saturday's dinners were at the Twin Owls Steakhouse, Lake Shore Lodge, and Timberline Steakhouse. Additionally, the Lake Shore and the Stanley hosted champagne brunch on Sunday. The restaurant mix could, of course, change in the future.

If you attend this à la carte festival, you can mix and match seminars, tastings, and dinners, buying tickets for each. Packages were also available; they include all seminars and tastings and a choice of the Stanley Hotel Black Tie Marriage Dinner or the Marriage Dinner at the Lake Shore Lodge. If you decide to make a weekend of it, local lodging rates are at their off-season lowest. The festival benefits the Children's Hospital in Denver and Quota Club International.

Estes Park Festival of Wines; (970) 577-7772 or www.estesparkfestivalofwines.com.

Strawberry Days (Glenwood Springs)

June—Here's a quick quiz. Question: What is Colorado's oldest civic celebration? Answer: Strawberry Days. Q: What is the oldest continuously held festival west of the Mississippi? A: Strawberry Days. The first Strawberry Days were organized in 1897, and the event has survived two world wars, one depression, and countless other larger and small crises. This enduring Western Slope tradition, established on the theme of one of early summer's sweetest fruits, is held the second or third weekend of June, when Sayre Park becomes Strawberry Park. It starts with a hometown parade and culminates with free strawberry and ice cream, food booths, children's activities, entertainment, and a juried art show, all in the park.

Details are available from the Glenwood Springs Chamber Resort Association; (970) 945-6589 or www.strawberrydaysfestival.com.

Buffalo Barbecue (Grand Lake)

July—This village on the west side of Rocky Mountain National Park has been nurturing its Old West flavor with an annual Buffalo Barbecue since 1947. There's a parade, of course, followed by a midday barbecue that takes place in the Town Pavilion on a weekend in mid- to late July. Barbecued buffalo is sided by such fixin's as potato salad, biscuits, and cookies. The price is low, the event authentic, and the smells and tastes genuine.

The Grand Lake Chamber can provide details at (970) 627-3402 or www.grandlakechamber.com.

Paonia Cherry Days

July—This three-day festival held around the Fourth of July centers on cherry-harvest time, but it really is a small-town event that goes way beyond the fruit. Started in 1947, it includes a parade with local school bands, the Lions' Club Clown Band, Shriners, antique cars, floats, horseback riders, and the Cherry Days Queen and her retinue. Other diverse activities include a pancake breakfast, a barbecue lunch, a library book sale, crafts and food booths, a carnival, and such entertainment as live music, dance performances, and a melodrama—or at least it did in 2002. The local farmers' market also coincides with Cherry Days. Cherries enter the picture with a cherry pie-eating contest and an evening wine and hors d'oeuvres event at Paonia Historical Park.

Details on Paonia Cherry Days are available from the Paonia Chamber of Commerce; (970) 527-3886 or www.paoniachamber.com.

King Boletus Mushroom Festival (Buena Vista)

August—Under the right circumstances, some boletus species can grow up to eight inches across—dinner-plate size by many measures. Edible varieties of this and other families of mushrooms were the inspiration for the annual King Boletus Mushroom Festival, over a weekend in late August in Buena Vista. A Friday evening wine and cheese party sponsored by the Buena Vista Heritage Society starts the festival. Saturday morning follows with a mushroom identification seminar. Mushroom-finding forays are scheduled for both Saturday afternoon and Sunday morning. The festival, which wraps up on Sunday, traditionally closed with a class in mushroom cookery, but alas, the instructor passed away, and until a replacement is found, it ends with a mushroom pizza party. The festival severely limits attendance, so contact organizers early.

Information on the Buena Vista Mushroom Festival is available from the Buena Vista Chamber of Commerce; (719) 395-6612 or www.buenavistachamber.org.

Olathe Sweet Corn Festival

August—Olathe, north of Delta in western Colorado, is the center of the state's sweet corn belt. Elephant-eye-high stalks grow so dense and tall that the scene could be in Iowa. "Corn-oisseurs" have long treasured Olathe corn's toothsome tenderness, but it has recently gone big-time. Area farmers have started branding their corn crops to give it an identity, so if you see the name Olathe Sweet, you'll know that it comes from 1,650 acres around this Western Slope town. Most of the corn is now shipped to King Soopers grocers, but a handful of local farmstands sell it—and it's worth a stop.

The corn is also the reason behind the annual Olathe Sweet Corn Festival, a one-day gala held early each August since 1991. The folksy festival starts with a pancake breakfast, features cob upon cob of corn, and winds up with a gala fireworks display. In recent years, some 20,000 people have attended—and each of them has nibbled down an average of three to four ears of corn. Slather on some sunscreen, bring your appetite, and join the fun.

For festival details, call (970) 323-6006.

Best of the West

September—The annual Best of the West showcases the food, art, and culture of Western Colorado. Held all afternoon during the first Saturday of September, it features culinary demonstrations and tastings with local and visiting chefs from throughout the state. The common thread is the lavish use of Western Slope foods, including meat, game, poultry, and of course, the region's outstanding produce. Chefs prepare dishes from apple bread pudding to yak tenderloin (yes, there's a yak ranch near Montrose, and if there were a zebra farm, someone would doubtless develop a recipe for that too). Local growers (many organic), ranchers, food purveyors, cooking schools, and others in the Western Slope culinary community set up booths for information and tastings for an end-of-summer celebration of the region's bounty.

> The event is held at the Montrose Pavilion. Tickets are reasonably priced ($17 in advance at area City Market stores or the Montrose Chamber of Commerce, and $22 at the door in 2003). Best of the West, P.O. Box 662, Montrose, CO 81402; (970) 249-1465 or e-mail to jmo@rmmc.biz.

Big Chili Cook-Off (Evergreen)

September—There were hot times in Evergreen in late September 2002, when the first (hopefully) annual Big Chili Cook-Off took place to benefit the Mountain Area Fire Departments. The first-year format was the classic chili cook-off contest, with tastes of all available for attendees after the judging was done. The event took place at the Evergreen Elks Club, convenient for chili-lovers from greater Denver as well as from the mountain communities.

> Ticket information is available from (303) 291-7911 or by e-mailing highelev@aol.com. Request contest entry forms from (303) 763-3335 or by e-mailing steven_huckaby@kindermorgan.com.

Potato Day (Greeley)

September—Careful readers of James Michener's *Centennial,* or viewers of the mini-series made from the novel, might remember Potato Brumbaugh, an unforgettable German immigrant character who grew tubers in the dry, stubborn soil of north-eastern Colorado. Michener described a genuine part of Colorado's agricultural history, which Greeley still celebrates with a one-day festival in early September. In addition to all the usual entertainment and carnival goings-on for adults and youngsters, free baked potatoes are offered, and other food items are sold as well.

> For information on the Potato Day Festival, (970) 330-8008 or www.ci.greeley.co.us.

Taste of Creede

September—Labor Day Weekend, the traditional kick-off for the summer travel season, also provides a reason to explore this picturesque town deep in the San Juan Mountains for the annual Taste of Creede. The three-day event showcases the efforts of local restaurants and food purveyors, both year-round and seasonal enterprises.

> Details are available from Creede/Mineral County Chamber of Commerce; (800) 327-2102, 719-658-2374, or www.creede.com.

Taste of Salida

September—The Taste of Salida was inaugurated in 1988 to showcase the growing number of interesting restaurants in this lively community along the Arkansas River. The event was canceled in 2002, and there is some question as to whether it will be re-established. If it is, know that it offers fun eating in a fun town. In the past, it has taken place on a Saturday afternoon early in September, with large tents set up in Riverside Park, the town park in this charming and historic community. Twenty of the area's best restaurants prepare the food, and domestic and imported wine and beer from local producers are available.

Information on the Taste of Salida is available from the Salida Convention & Visitors Bureau; (877) 772-5432 or (719) 539-2068.

Taste of Italy (Salida)

September—Salida's Sons of Italy cook up a storm for the Taste of Italy to feed up to 500 hungry Italian food aficionados. The annual event held around Labor Day weekend in St. Joseph Great Hall is the kind of old-fashioned feast well known in Italian neighborhoods in northeastern cities, but a novelty in Colorado. Members of this fraternal organization do the cooking, always producing several kinds of pasta—"everything but spaghetti," according to one organizer. The Sons also fired up their stoves for the 2002 Ride the Rockies, and the buzz was that the Salida stop dished up the best food of the entire bicycle tour.

If you plan to go, expect something on the order of lasagna, rigatoni, or stuffed shells with sausage and/or meatballs, and at least one other dish. Italian garlic bread, often homemade, and abundant heaps of salad accompany the pasta pig-out, and the Knights of Columbus sell wine. The dessert, which is usually spumoni or similar, tends to be anticlimactic but totally suited to the menu. In three short hours, eager and hungry attendees pick the place clean.

Ticket prices are modest, and it is wise to buy them in advance. Information for the 2002 was available from (877) 287-7645 or (719) 539-3535, but event chairs do change, so you can also contact the Salida Convention & Visitors Bureau at (877) 772-5432 or (719) 539-2068, which can refer you to the phone number.

Wine & Music Festival (Lake City)

September—This historic town deep in the San Juan Mountains holds an infamous place in Colorado history because there, in the extreme winter of 1874, a prospector named Alferd Packer allegedly ate his companions after they became stranded by deep snows. He certainly had no wine to accompany his grisly feast! Late September 2001 marked a more civilized era with the first Annual Wine & Music Festival to benefit the Lake City Prostate Cancer Awareness Fund. Features included food and wine samplings and musical performances of various genres, plus the golden glow of fall foliage along the tree-lined town streets and in the aspen groves blanketing the surrounding mountains.

For information on the Wine & Music Festival, call (970) 944-2527.

Annual Applefest (Cedaredge)

October—Around apple harvest time each October, Applefest fills downtown Cedaredge with craft and art booths, food venues, and entertainment. Tractors are still big; there's a display of antique tractors and also a tractor pull. Other big draws are food booths and music in and around the park, and other booths laden with apple crisps, bags of apples, heaps of apples, apple pies and other apple foods, apple dolls, and other apple items. Concurrent with Applefest, which began in 1977, is the Apples, Aspen, & Art Show and Sale, which premiered in 1992 and features juried artworks in three categories: apple-related subjects, aspen-related subjects, and "other" subjects.

Information on Applefest is available from the Cedaredge Area
Chamber of Commerce; (970) 856-6961 or www.cedaredgecolorado.com.

Arts, Wine, and Microbrew Festival (Glenwood Springs)

October—The Glenwood Springs Arts Council and the Center for the Arts host an annual Arts, Wine, & Microbrew Festival from mid-afternoon through early evening on a Saturday in mid-October. Currently held at the historic Hotel Colorado, this fundraiser features demonstrations by three gourmet chefs, a grand tasting of fine wines, gourmet foods, an ice sculpture demonstration, and the opportunity to taste some of the region's finest microbrews.

More information is available from the Center for the Arts; (970) 945-2414.

Chateau Shavano Wine Tasting (Salida)

November—This annual festival event, held in early November since 1998, features three hours of wine tasting and food to benefit the local chamber of commerce. The venue changes (it's often held in a bank), and includes tastings from six or seven wine distributors' lines, as well as the Mountain Spirits Winery, located a few miles west of town. A different restaurant caters the event each year. In the past, Laughing Ladies and Dakota's Bistro, two well-regarded local eateries, have provided the food. Live music, on the mellow side, adds to the atmosphere.

Information is available from the Salida Convention & Visitors Bureau,
406 West U.S. Highway 50, Salida; (877) 772-5432, (719) 539-2068, or
www.salidachamber.org.

Chocolate Tasting Festival (Creede)

November—In 1989, a fund-raiser for the Creede/Mineral County Chamber of Commerce was organized to lure off-season visitors to the picturesque town deep in the San Juan Mountains to shop, sightsee, and spend. The Chocolate Tasting Festival takes place on the Friday and Saturday afternoon of the long Thanksgiving weekend. For a modest fee ($7 at this writing), you can stroll through downtown and sample a variety of chocolate treats put out in shops and restaurants. But reserve in advance, because the 250 tickets sell out fast.

For information or reservations, contact the Creede/Mineral County Chamber of Commerce; (800) 327-2102, 719-658-2374, or www.creede.com.

Wine in The Pines (Genesee)

November—The local Rotary Club puts on an annual food and wine tasting in early November at The Pines at Genesee, located in the foothills west of Denver. Begun in 2001, the black tie-optional festival grew quickly and by the second year attracted nearly 600 attendees, 17 food purveyors, and a like number of wine distributors and wineries that poured 250 different wines. The three-hour festival fills two floors, with food and wine stations interspersed with tables displaying live and silent auction items. The layout invites strolling, eating, sipping, and socializing.

Information is available from the event chair at (303) 674-9142.

Retail

Abbot's Pantry (Estes Park)

Gourmet food products galore fill the shelves at Abbot's Pantry, but of all the categories the store carries, none has given it more of a rep than its hot sauces and salsas. Forty to fifty varieties are on hand, and the store sets up a tasting bar so that you can compare them—as long as your palate can handle it. Actually, some—like Abbot's Pantry's private label Champagne Artichoke Salsa, which rates just a 2 on the 1 to 10 hotness index—are mild and flavorful rather than fiery. Several of Southwest Spirit's sauces, by contrast, rate a 9.5 on that same scale, and Abbot's carries everything in between.

Other categories of foodstuffs include spreads and dipping sauces; cooking oils; soup mixes; pasta and pasta sauces; jellies, jams, and spreads; vinegars, chutneys, pickles, olives, and other condiments; and dessert syrups, toppings, and sprinkles. You can fill your pantry with good staples from Abbot's Pantry. Colorado-made products include such brands as Colorado Hotlips, Denver Salsa Company, Honeyville, Lydia's Garden, Mary Anne's Beans, Mountain Gold, Prairie Thyme, and Pueblo Chili Company. One of my favorite items is Rocky Mountain National Park Animal Crackers. How can you resist those for a child you know—or for the child in you?

Abbot's Pantry, Old Church Shops, 175 West Elkhorn Avenue, Estes Park; (888) 372-6879, (970) 577-1857, or www.abbotspantry.com.

A la Carte (Estes Park)

Tucked into a small complex of shops and restaurants and behind a chocolate kiosk along Elkhorn Avenue is an unobtrusive shop that carries kitchen and table treasures for year-round residents and visitors alike. If you need a special pot, pan, baking implement, wok, gadget, placemats, mugs, woodenware, glassware, cookbook, recipe box, or cutting board, you'll probably find it and more at A la Carte. In addition to the usual gadgetry that cooks so treasure, the crammed-full shop carries such unusual and irresistible objects as a set of disk-like plate-warmers, a tubular garlic peeler, and a "foolproof" combination cake cutter and server. A la Carte has a good selection of Bortner's practical and attractive glazed terracotta casseroles, lasagna pans, chip-and-dip servers, and salsa bowls. One section sells all sorts of kettles, teapots, tea cozies, and even a special kettle brush—and of course a great variety of herbal and black teas.

Whether you're at home in Estes, a short-time visitor who has rented a kitchen unit during your vacation and want some fancy condiments to perk up a meal, or just stopping by for a hostess gift, A la Carte's roster of gourmet goodies will most likely meet your requirements. Good brands of herbs, spices, mustards, crackers, and other products fill A la Carte's shelves, including The Fresh Herb Company's seasoned vinegars, Joy's Pepper Jellies, Melina's Seasoned Olive Oils, and a variety of quality mixes for fondue, scones, and other specialties. A la Carte also sells fine pasta—and a big pot to cook it in.

A la Carte, 336 East Elkhorn Avenue, Estes Park; (970) 586-5518 or www.alacarte-estes.com.

Belvedere Belgian Chocolate Shop (Castle Rock and Other Locations)

Master *chocolatiers* Han De Kesel and Johan Devriese left their native Bruges, Belgium, for Colorado, where they planned to establish an import company. The cou ple selected Castle Rock in Denver's fast-growing southern suburbs as a good place to raise their children, but decided to make rather than import authentic Belgian-style chocolates. They distribute to wholesale accounts but also established an on-site retail sales outlet at their busy chocolate factory. Move over, Willy Wonka.

Authentic Belgian recipes are used for the from-scratch chocolate shells and centers, and all chocolates are natural, without preservatives, artificial colorings, or other additives. Belvedere is especially known for its silky truffles and also for themed holiday chocolates for Valentine's Day, Mother's Day, Thanksgiving, Christmas, and even St. Patrick's Day, and special wedding chocolates are available. Signature items include Bonbons, decadent signature ice-cream-filled chocolates, and a line of liqueur-filled chocolate confections. The most recent additions are sweet, crunchy almond toffee and Belvedere Butter Cookies. In addition to the sweet treats, Belvedere sells Belgian antique furniture and Belgian lace.

Belvedere Chocolate Shop, 350A Perry Street, Castle Rock, (303) 663-2364. Franchised retail outlets are at 1634 Walnut Street, Boulder, (303) 447-0336; 238 E. Harmony Road, Suite D-10, Fort Collins, (970) 226-3774; and

231 Milwaukee Street, Denver, (720) 298-4209. The website for all is
www.belvederechocolates.com.

Corner Cupboard (Gunnison)

The Corner Cupboard, located in the heart of Gunnison, has a gift large section with adjoining space devoted to things culinary. The store is simple but stocks an array of kitchen and table items that are practical, attractive, and often both. Chantal enamel cookware is prominently shown. Shelves are heaped with lots of stainless steel—mixing bowls, pots, pans, covered and open roasters, colanders, chafing dishes, and numerous small utensils. You'll find an assortment of GripEZ and NorPro gadgetry, including peelers, knives, graters, gravy separators, onion keepers, tortilla warmers, metal and plastic spoons, spatulas, stirrers, and whisks, suitable for both nonstick and metal pots and pans. Salt and pepper shakers come in wood, metal, and Lucite in a variety of shapes and sizes, and GoodWoods woodenware fulfills a variety of functions.

Canisters in as many sizes as Russian nesting dolls, enormous spoon rests, teakettles, grilling accessories, fondue sets, coffee pots, and French presses are displayed too. Small kitchen appliances include coffee and espresso machines, blenders, toasters, food processors, mixers, and hand blenders. The extensive baking inventory includes rolling pins, cake pans, tart pans, loaf pans, springform pans, pie tins in regular and pie-for-one sizes, ramekins, and such to outfit any household for numerous baking tasks. The store also helps customers set a pretty table with a selection of colorful table linens, bright dinnerware, and glassware, including a cute hand-painted glass pitcher, and cruet sets.

The assortment of gourmet foods, many from Colorado, includes condiments by Joy's, Honeyville, Kokopelli, Epic Valley, Alida's, and GigiAnn's, such Mountain House Kitchens mixes as cornbread, tortillas, and various soups, edible seeds from Seedsations, and Villa Pasta Company pastas and seasoning mixes.

Corner Cupboard, 101 North Main Street, Gunnison; (970) 641-0313.

House of Smoke (Fort Lupton)

If you love game, are thrilled to find it on more and more restaurant menus, and are interested in preparing it at home, make a safari to the House of Smoke in Fort Lupton. This wholesale supplier of game, poultry, and fish to many restaurants also welcomes retail customers. Most of the products are farm- or ranch-raised, and a U.S. Department of Agriculture inspector is on site for quality control and food safety.

You can get such run-of-the-mill products as free-range chicken, duck, lamb, veal, salmon, and trout, but most customers make the trip to pick up exotica and near-exotica for a special dinner or to stock their freezers. Various cuts are available, and in many cases, customers have a choice of fresh and smoked versions. House of Smoke also has alligator, antelope, black buck, buffalo (bison), caribou, Cornish game hen, elk, goat, goose, Guinea hen, Kobe beef, musk ox, ostrich, pheasant, rattlesnake, snapping turtle, squab, venison, wild boar from Texas, and yak from the Himalayas. If you are a card-carrying member of the World Wildlife Federation or have made it this far but with trepidation, don't think about reading the next list: They also sometimes sell African lion, American black bear, beaver, kangaroo, and chuckar partridge.

Bratwurst is made of virtually every meat, game, and poultry; summer sausage and jerky are made of some; and a few meats also come as pâtés. Dried morels, truffle peelings for flavoring, truffle oil, porcini, and frozen wild huckleberries are also for sale.

House of Smoke, 825 Denver Avenue, Fort Lupton; (800) 738-2750, (303) 857-2750 or www.houseofwildgame.com.

Mountain Meat and Gourmet Sausage (Craig)

This Western Slope sausage company makes more than 50 types of sausage, all from its own recipes. In addition to versions of common hot dogs and sausages of various sorts (including several award-winners), what sets this place apart is its line of gourmet sausages, developed by and made under the supervision of master sausage maker Josef Brunner. This Austrian native began apprenticing at the age of 15. In true European fashion, his training was deemed complete 11 years later. The Colorado mountains lured him from the Alpine nation of his birth, and he teamed up with Mountain Meat owners Gary and Carolyn Baysinger.

Brunner's fabulous gourmet sausages are all nitrite-free, and most are fully cooked in natural casings. The Epicurean Chicken Sausage and Pheasant Epicurean Sausage both contain the named poultry meat, plus fresh spinach, mushrooms, and Parmesan. The Chicken Cilantro Sausage is seasoned with that distinctive herb and a special mix of spices. The Spicy Chicken with Sweet Pepper Bratwurst combines the texture of this classic German sausage with sweet red peppers and a little spicy zing. Mediterranean-Style Turkey Sausage contains premium turkey, cream cheese, fresh basil, and black olives. Game specialties include Smoked Buffalo Cheddar Bratwurst, Smoked Elk Cheddar Bratwurst, and Yak with Red Wine and Black Pepper Sausage. Traditional sausages from various cultures includes buffalo hot dogs, country-style breakfast link sausages, frankfurters, both German-style and American-style, white bratwurst, sweet and hot Italian sausage, *andouille*, and *chorizo*. Would you expect less from a master sausage maker?

In addition to more than 20 recent awards from the Colorado/Wyoming chapter of the American Association of Meat Producers' Cured Meat Championships, Brunner's Chicken Supremo was named grand champion in the Cooked Poultry Sausage category, and the Pheasant Epicurean Sausage received that same honor in the 2002 national competition. Mountain Meat's retail store carries them all.

Mountain Meat and Gourmet Sausage, 291 Lincoln Street, Craig; (877) 451-4749, (970) 824-4878, or www.mountainmeat.com.

RSVP (Cañon City)

Cañon City cooks can go to Colorado Springs or even Denver for kitchenware and other culinary needs, but they don't need to, because this downtown Cañon City shop stocks cookware, bakeware, cooking accessories, tableware, home and kitchen decorative items, and gourmet food products. Suzanne Wilson runs the store that she and her late mother started in 1979. Initially, the store carried mostly cookware and kitchen items, but it has morphed into a kitchen and home-décor shop.

You won't find much in the way of pots and pans anymore, but RSVP still carries ovenware, casseroles, mixing bowls, hand-thrown pottery, such specialty cookware as waffle irons and *pizzelle* irons, salt and pepper shakers, and gadgets galore. In addition to Copco, NorPro, and Villaware, one of the top brands is R.S.V.P. International—no relation, just coincidence.

In a small space, Wilson also manages to stock an impressive inventory of cookbooks, organic coffee, a small selection of gourmet food products, and a great array of formal and casual dinnerware, flatware, glasses, mugs, salad bowls, canisters, and more. The store is small, the inventory is huge, and RSVP remains the best place in town for your own kitchen or for a gift for a food lover.

RSVP, 515 Main Street, Cañon City; (719) 275-0294.

Village Gourmet (Evergreen)

Denver's far western exurbs stretch to the mountain town of Evergreen. Its population has swelled since its early days as a ranching community, but residents still think of their community as a village. Those interested in food and cooking frequent the Village Gourmet, a friendly and incredibly busy shop whose floor-to-ceiling shelves are crammed with everything for the cook and the epicure. In fact, things culinary are hanging from the ceiling, piled on the floor, and heaped on country-style tables and other furniture too. The Village Gourmet inventory of kitchenware, cookware, gadgets, tableware, cookbooks, and specialty food items—many from Colorado—is profound.

Laurie Ward, a number-crunching CPA by training but with the epicurean flame burning within her, established the store in 1982, mainly to sell gourmet coffees. In the two decades that followed, the store nearly doubled in size, and its stock has grown geometrically. Yet Ward still runs it with knowledge and passion. She still loves good coffee. She loves good chocolate. She loves tasty condiments. And she loves quality cookware and kitchen accessories so that home cooks can make great meals—and she loves great dishes, glasses, flatware, and table linens so that every meal can be presented beautifully as well.

Village Gourmet, The Market Place at Bergen Park, 1193 Bergen Parkway, Evergreen; (303) 670-0717.

Other

La Boheme (Mancos)

Nick Keefer and Daniela Marinache brought a touch of Bay Area élan to the Four Corners when they opened this wine bar, art gallery, and limited-menu restaurant in Mancos in 2002. In an old building that had originally housed a carriage maker and later an auto dealership and assorted other enterprises they added a few tables, laid in a stock of wine, hung contemporary art on the walls on the walls, and opened the doors.

The furnishings are an eclectic mix of antiques and handmade pieces, the art is for sale, and the wines are South American and Australian selections, with a smattering of Italian and French imports and California wines as well. La Boheme always has at least ten reds, five whites (more in summer), four or five rosés, and three or four each in the dessert wine and Champagne/sparking wine categories, all available by the glass or bottle.

The couple began serving "foods that go with wines," which meant fine imported meats and cheeses. They now also offer a limited selection of from-scratch food. Keefer is the cook, who prepares a daily special soup, pasta, and entrée or two. His artistic nature demands that his food look as good as it tastes—and it does. Art exhibitions (and their attendant openings) and Wednesday movie nights (sometimes with food paired not only to the wines but also to the film) quickly made La Boheme an interesting social center for the Four Corners area.

La Boheme, 128 West Grand Avenue, Mancos; (970) 533-9837.

Appendices

Appendix A

Organizations

Lovers of food and wine can join other connoisseurs and oenophiles in organizations that celebrate the pleasures of the table. Conviviality reigns at the events put on by these gastronomic associations, which have Colorado chapters.

American Food and Wine Lovers

The American Institute of Wine and Food (AIWF) is a not-for-profit organization established in 1981 by Julia Child, Robert Mondavi, the late Richard Graff, and other culinary luminaries by and for people who love gastronomy in all its aspects. The stated mission of this educational organization is to understand and celebrate the pleasures, health and social benefits, and traditions of the table—and to share that joy with one another. There are thirty chapters in the United States and one in France. Members are food educators, nutritionists, chefs, food and wine professionals, and amateur connoisseurs of fine wine and fine food.

Individual chapters' activities feature special dinners—and more. AIWF programs have included such specials as a barrel tasting in a private wine cellar, a behind-the-scenes tour of an organic farm, a symposium on taste and healthy eating, wine component tastings, and an ethnic pantry-tasting series. The Colorado Chapter organizes many events in cooperation with the Cook Street School of Fine Cooking in Denver (see page 21).

The organization's Day of Taste is a unique nationwide program undertaken by local chapters in schools to introduce fourth- and fifth-graders to the basics of taste. Day of Taste activities include farm visits, hands-on cooking classes with a local chef, and a visit to that chef's restaurant. AIWF offers scholarships, fellowships, and research grants to men and women working in fields related to the institute's mission. In addition to invitations to all chapter and national AIWF events, membership benefits include a subscription to *American Wine & Food*, a bimonthly newsletter, and discounts on a variety of other food and wine publications.

Membership information is available from the American Institute of Wine & Food, 304 West Liberty Street, Suite 201, Louisville, KY 40101; (800) 274-AIWF (274-2493), (502) 992-1022 or www.aifw.org. The reservation line for Colorado chapter activities is (303) 333-2378.

Chaîne des Rôtisseurs—International Gastronomic Society

Long before there was a Colorado, the foundation for the Chaîne des Rôtisseurs was laid in France. What is now an international gastronomic society traces its traditions back to the ancient guild of royal goose roasters, whose authority eventually expanded to the roasting of other poultry, and eventually meat and game. In 1610 the king granted a royal charter to the guild, whose coat of arms consists of crossed turning spits, flames, and a chain representing the mechanism used to turn the spit.

The modern Chaîne des Rôtisseurs was founded in Paris in 1950 to promote fine dining and preserve the camaraderie and pleasures of the table. Today, the society has members in more than 100 countries. The United States has nearly 150 chapters or *bailliages* (a French word related to the English *bailiwick*), each headed by a *bailli* (think "bailiff"). The U.S. *confrérie* (society) by and large follows the programs and policies set forth by the international society headquartered in Paris, with both professional members and gastronomes who appreciate the finest food but are not in the culinary business.

The Chaîne proudly points out that this interaction between professional and amateur members is a feature that distinguishes it from other culinary organizations. Members share a common interest in fine dining and good fellowship, and chefs and restaurateurs gain the opportunity to demonstrate their exceptional skills and creativity to a particularly discerning, appreciative audience and receive a plaque recognizing their Chaîne stature. Membership benefits include a subscription to *Gastronome*, a full-color magazine that provides a calendar of forthcoming events around the country and reports on those that have occurred, and an annual guide to Chaîne-affiliated restaurants and hotels. All members are invited to attend events around the world. If your interests also lie in the wine and spirits area, the Chaîne des Rôtisseurs has a society within the society, L'Ordre Mondial des Dégusteurs, which organizes wine-related events and trips to the world's wine-producing regions.

Information on the Chaîne des Rôtisseurs is available from the national office, 444 Park Avenue South, Suite 301, New York, NY 10016; www.chaineus.org. There are three Colorado *bailliages*. Contact phone numbers for the *baillis* are (303) 639-9935 for the Denver Mile High Chapter, (970) 728-9406 in Telluride, and (970) 476-1192 in Vail.

Slow Food

The Slow Food movement exists for one simple purpose: the protection of the right to taste. Assaulted by fast food, factory-made food, and overall bland food that defies the aesthetic and gustatory pleasures, a group of Italian gourmands established Slow Food in Piemonte in 1986. The organization's birthplace is Barolo in the Langhe District of the province of Cuneo, and the movement went international in 1989 when a branch was founded in Paris.

Slow Food has grown to more than 60,000 members on five continents. About half are in Italy, and the association's main offices are in Bra, also in Cuneo, the hub of a close-knit network of chapters in Italy and abroad. These are called *convivia*, which stage local events, debates, and other initiatives.

Slow Food's U.S. membership is about 7,000, second only to Italy. Slow Food USA is now a nonprofit organization whose core aim is to support, celebrate, and safeguard the food traditions and heritage of North America. How wonderful that in the country that invented fast food and fast living, Slow Food helps people rediscover pleasure and quality in everyday life.

While the organization specifically aims to encourage people to learn to appreciate what Slow Food calls "the convivial traditions of the table," it is really the culinary manifestation of the pop-slogan "Stop and smell the roses." Of the 60 *convivia* in the United States, four are in Colorado. Like chapters around the world, they organize gastronomic, educational, and cultural events.

Slow Food U.S.A., 434 Broadway, 7th Floor, New York, NY 10013; (212) 965-5640 or www.slowfood.com. Colorado *convivia* contacts are: in Boulder, Peggy Markel, peggy@foodinitaly.com; in Colorado Springs, Melinda Murphy, (719) 475-1444, mmurphy@csfineartscenter.org, or Jan Webster, (719) 684-9207; in Denver, Sally Kennedy, sallykennedy@aol.com; and in Fort Collins, Kristi Johnson, Kristi@binghamhill.com.

Wine Brats

Wine Brats is a national not-for-profit organization of people—mostly young on the calendar and all young at heart—who want to share their appreciation and enhance their knowledge of wine in a demystifying, nonintimidating way. Anyone of legal drinking age may join. The Denver chapter was established to raise the level of acceptance of wine, especially in the 25 to 35 age group, more or less. Membership is free, but there are fees for specific events.

Denver Wine Brats events sell out fast. Recent ones, at this writing, included a sit-down dinner at the Rialto with a fixed menu accompanied by King Estate Wines, a brilliant evening at the now-shuttered Nicois with tapas paired with wines from Organic Vintners, and an exploration of the relationship between wines and cheeses held at Gumbo's on Denver's 16th Street Mall and sponsored by the Robert Mondavi Family of Wines and www.ilovecheese.com.

For more information or to join, contact Wine Brats, P.O. Box 5432, Santa Rosa, CA 95402; (877) 545-4699, or e-mail info@winebrats.org. To contact the Denver chapter directly, log onto www.denver.winebrats.org/contact_us.htm and click the site's e-mail link.

Appendix B

Culinary Awards

In France and elsewhere in Europe, restaurants vie for stars from Michelin. One star is a reason for the chef to break out the best bottle of champagne. Two stars are cause for local celebration. Three stars result in nationwide—even international—recognition. The United States has no honors of such magnitude, but there are numerous other ways restaurants are recognized for their exceptional cuisine and/or wine programs and individual chefs are honored for their high culinary standards and lofty achievements.

DiRoNA Awards

Distinguished Restaurants of North America (DiRoNA), a not-for-profit organization was formed in 1990 to preserve and promote fine dining throughout Canada, Mexico, and the United States. Two years later, the DiRoNA Award Program was created to honor restaurants exhibiting the highest standards in food and the entire dining experience. Independent and anonymous inspectors, who are "trained industry professionals," evaluate the restaurants—the only North American program with such independent judges. To be considered, a restaurant must be in business under the same ownership for three years and pass an evaluation on 75 points. Restaurants retain their awards for three years by maintaining their high standards and are then re-inspected. For more information on the organization and the awards, log onto www.DiRoNA.com.

R.I.P.

Major awards and recognition do not guarantee a restaurant's continuity. Not only do chefs move around with dizzying regularity, but restaurants close—sometimes abruptly—or change names, ownership, and/or style. Among the award recipients permanently gone from the Colorado dining scene are Boulder's Dandelion, Denver's Micole, Colorado Springs' Primitivo, and Telluride's Campagna. Nicois in Denver was not open long enough to appear on these lists, but Kevin Taylor, who developed it, has been recognized with numerous other awards. They appear on the award lists here, but alas, you won't be able to dine there anymore. The highly honored Restaurant at the Little Nell, in Aspen's Little Nell Hotel, has reemerged as Montagna, nearby Renaissance has been turned into Range, and Mel's Bar & Grill in Denver is now Mel's Restaurant & Bar.

The following Colorado restaurants were 2002 DiRoNA Award holders:

221 South Oak, Telluride
Alfredo's Restaurant, Vail
Alice's Restaurant, Gold Lake Resort, Ward
Alpenglow Stube, Keystone
Antares Restaurant, Steamboat Springs
Antica Roma, Boulder
Aspen Meadows Restaurant, Aspen
Barolo Grill, Denver
Beano's Cabin, Beaver Creek
The Blue Star, Colorado Springs
Bon Ton Restaurant, Ouray
Boulder Cork, Boulder
Bravo! Ristorante, Denver
Briarhurst Manor, Manitou Springs
The Bristol, Arrowhead, Edwards
The Broker, Denver
Brooks Steakhouse, Englewood
Café Alpine, Breckenridge
California Café, Littleton
Campagna, Telluride
Century Room, Hotel Jerome, Aspen
Charles Court, The Broadmoor, Colorado Springs
The Cliff House, Manitou Springs
Cosmopolitan, Hotel Columbia, Telluride
Cucina Colore, Denver
Dandelion, Boulder
Del Frisco's Double Eagle Steak House, Greenwood Village
Deno's Mountain Bistro, Winter Park
Dolan's Restaurant, Boulder
Excelsior Café, Telluride
The Flagstaff House Restaurant, Boulder
Fourth Story Restaurant, Tattered Cover Bookstore (Cherry Creek), Denver
Gabriel's Restaurant, Sedalia
Giovanni's Ristorante, Steamboat Springs
Great Northern Tavern, Keystone
The Greenbriar, Boulder
Grouse Mountain Grille, Beaver Creek
Harmon's of Telluride, Telluride
Hearthstone Restaurant, Breckenridge
Jack's, Sardy House, Aspen
Keystone Ranch, Keystone
L'Apogee, Steamboat Springs
La Papillon, Denver

La Tour, Vail
Larkspur, Vail
Laudisio, Boulder
Le Bousquet, Crested Butte
The Left Bank, Vail
Little Nell Restaurant, Little Nell Hotel, Aspen
Ludwig's, Vail
Marlowe's, Denver
Matsuhisa, Aspen
Mel's Bar and Grill, Denver
Mirabelle, Beaver Creek
Nico's Catacombs, Fort Collins
Olives Aspen, St. Regis Aspen, Aspen
Pacifica Seafood Brasserie, Aspen
The Palace Arms, Brown Palace Hotel, Denver
Palm Restaurant, Denver
The Penrose Room, The Broadmoor, Colorado Springs
Piñons, Aspen
Primitivo, Colorado Springs
Pulcinella Ristorante, Fort Collins
Q's Restaurant, Boulder
Renaissance and R Bistro, Aspen
Restaurant Conundrum, Aspen
Restaurant Kevin Taylor, Hotel Teatro, Denver
Restaurant Picasso, The Lodge at Cordillera, Edwards
Rustico Restaurant, Telluride
Ruth's Chris Steak House, Denver
Sam's No. 3 Restaurant, Aurora
Splendido at the Chateau, Beaver Creek
St. Bernard Inn, Breckenridge
Strings, Denver
Sweet Basil, Vail
Syzygy, Aspen
Tante Louise, Denver
Terra Bistro, Vail
Toscanini, Beaver Creek
tra'Monti, Beaver Creek
Trios Grille and Wine Bar, Boulder
Trios Enoteca, Denver
The Tyrolean, Vail
Wellington's, Breckenridge
The Wildflower, The Lodge at Vail, Vail

Wine Spectator Awards

Wine Spectator, a glossy tabloid-size publication, is the bible for wine-lovers and food-lovers as well. Restaurants apply for the coveted annual Awards of Excellence by submitting the current wine list and dinner menu, along with a brief letter describing the wine program and an entry fee. Then, the publication sends out another form for the restaurant to fill out, and judging is based on these materials. Of the 848 new restaurants that applied in 2002, 670 won an award.

Three levels of awards are granted. The highest is the Grand Award, earned in 2002 by just 95 of the 2,886 award winners that in *Wine Spectator*'s judgment offer an "unparalleled wine experience" with comprehensive wine lists and cellars that include older vintages from top producers. The Best Award of Excellence, earned by 365 establishments, recognizes "restaurants that take their wine programs a step above the norm." The largest category of recipients is the 2,406 holders of the 2002 Award of Excellence, recognizing "restaurants that provide a sound wine program—whether it's a modest 80-selection list or a list with a few hundred selections." The awards list is published in the issue that comes out in late August.

The following Colorado restaurants were honored by *Wine Spectator* in 2002:

Grand Award of Excellence

Flagstaff House, Boulder
The Restaurant at the Little Nell, Little Nell Hotel, Aspen

Best Award of Excellence

L'Apogee, Steamboat Springs
Charles Court, The Broadmoor, Colorado Springs
Del Frisco's Double Eagle Steak House, Greenwood Village
Deno's Mountain Bistro, Winter Park
The Greenbriar Inn, Boulder
Nico's Catacombs, Fort Collins
The Palace Arms Brown Palace Hotel, Denver
Piñons, Aspen
Primitivo, Colorado Springs
Pulcinella Ristorante, Fort Collins
Renaissance, Aspen
Restaurant Kevin Taylor, Hotel Teatro, Denver

Award of Excellence

Ajax Tavern, Aspen
Alice's Restaurant, Gold Lake Resort, Ward
Allred's, Telluride
Antica Roma, Boulder
Barolo Grill, Denver
Beano's Cabin, Beaver Creek

Bloom, Broomfield
The Blue Star, Colorado Springs
Blue Point Grill & Noir Bar, Telluride
Le Bosquet, Crested Butte
Bravo! Ristorante, Adams Mark Hotel, Denver
The Bristol at Arrowhead, Edwards
Brook's Steakhouse and Cellar, Greenwood Village
The Cabin, Steamboat Grand Resort Hotel, Steamboat Springs
Café Alpine, Breckenridge
California Café Bar & Grill, Littleton
Campagna, Telluride
The Century Room, Hotel Jerome, Aspen
Chefs', Grand Junction
Ciao Vino, Fort Collins
The Cliff House, Manitou Springs
Cosmopolitan Restaurant, Hotel Columbia, Telluride
Cucina Colore, Denver
Diamond Cabaret & Steakhouse, Denver
Excelsior Café, Telluride
1515, Denver
Fourth Story Restaurant, Tattered Cover Bookstore (Cherry Creek), Denver
Full Moon Grill, Boulder
Game Creek Club, Vail
Great Northern Tavern, Keystone
Grouse Mountain Grill, Beaver Creek
Harmon's at the Depot, Telluride
The Hearthstone Restaurant, Breckenridge
Jack's, Sardy House, Aspen
Jake & Telly's Greek Cuisine, Colorado Springs
Keystone Ranch, Keystone
La Papillon Café, Denver
Larkspur, Vail
Laudisio, Boulder
Ludwig's, Sonnenalp Resort of Vail, Vail
Mel's Restaurant & Bar, Denver
Micole, Denver
Mirabelle Restaurant, Beaver Creek
Montauk Seafood Grill, Vail
Morton's of Chicago, Englewood
Olives, St. Regis Aspen, Aspen
The Palm, Westin Hotel at Tabor Center, Denver
Patina, Hyatt Regency Beaver Creek (now Park Hyatt Beaver Creek),
    Beaver Creek
The Penrose Room, The Broadmoor, Colorado Springs
Restaurant Picasso, Lodge at Cordillera, Edwards

Rustico Ristorante, Telluride
Ruth's Chris Steak House, Denver
Salt Creek Restaurant & Saloon, Breckenridge
SIX89 Restaurant & Winebar, Carbondale
Splendido at the Chateau, Beaver Creek
Sullivan's Steakhouse, Denver
Sweet Basil, Vail
Tante Louise, Denver
Terra Bistro, Vail Mountain Lodge, Vail
Toscanini, Beaver Creek
La Tour, Vail
Tra'Monti, The Charter, Beaver Creek
Trattoria Toscana, Aspen
Trios Enoteca, Denver
Trios Grille & Wine Bar, Boulder
The Tyrolean, Vail
Village Tavern, The Village at FlatIron Crossing, Broomfield
Vista, Avon
The Wildflower, The Lodge at Vail, Vail
Zino Ristorante, Edwards

Doubly Honored Restaurants

If you're equally enamored of fine food and fine wine, the following restaurants earned both DiRoNA and *Wine Spectator* honors in 2002. Chefs from those marked with an asterisk have, at one time or another, also cooked at the James Beard House:

Beano's Cabin, Beaver Creek
*Charles Court, The Broadmoor, Colorado Springs
Flagstaff House, Boulder
Keystone Ranch, Keystone
Ludwig's, Sonnenalp Resort of Vail, Vail
*Mirabelle Restaurant, Beaver Creek
*The Palace Arms Brown Palace Hotel, Denver
Piñons, Aspen
*Primitivo, Colorado Springs
*Renaissance, Aspen
*The Restaurant at the Little Nell, Little Nell Hotel, Aspen
Restaurant Picasso, The Lodge at Cordillera, Edwards
*Sweet Basil, Vail
Tante Louise, Denver
Terra Bistro, Vail Mountain Lodge, Vail
The Tyrolean, Vail
*The Wildflower, The Lodge at Vail, Vail

James Beard House Honors

The late James Beard has been called the father of American gastronomy, and his Greenwich Village brownstone has been turned into nothing less than a culinary temple. The James Beard House is known as a place where members—dedicated foodies all—can sample the culinary creativity of some of the country's most talented chefs, who apply for an invitation to cook there. A bonus for Colorado foodies is that invited chefs frequently rehearse their James Beard House menus before going to New York or reprise them afterwards. Keep an eye on the local papers or your ear to the culinary gossip ground to join in one of these extraordinary meals.

The James Beard House presents chefs with an honor and a logistical challenge. Though large for an urban townhouse, by restaurant standards the Beard House kitchen is tiny. Guests enter through the kitchen, gawking, sniffing, and occasionally snitching hors d'oeuvres as they pass. It is common for guest chefs to bring members of their own kitchen staffs to help—and Colorado chefs frequently tote to New York such from-home specialties as lamb, trout, wild mushrooms, or Palisade peaches. They prepare a multicourse feast accompanied by the finest wines for a hundred or so James Beard House members and a few guests. When this group of fussy foodies gives a standing ovation, it's something to be proud of.

The honor goes to the chef, not the restaurant. The Colorado chefs below have thus far cooked there (their restaurants at that time are listed). For more information on the James Beard House, log onto www.jamesbeard.org.

James Beard House Guest Chefs

Chris Adrian, La Petite Maison, Colorado Springs
Mark Black, Brown Palace Hotel, Denver
John Broening, Primitivo, Colorado Springs
Charles Dale, Renaissance and Range, Aspen
Siegfried "Sigi" Eisenberger, The Broadmoor, Colorado Springs
Paul Ferzaca, Game Creek Club, Vail
Mark Fischer, SIX89, Carbondale
Tom Gay, The Wildflower, The Lodge at Vail, Vail
Marcus Guilano, Walter's Bistro, Colorado Springs
Bradford Heap, Full Moon Grill, Boulder
Craig Hartman, The Cliff House, Manitou Springs
Daniel Joly, Mirabelle, Beaver Creek
Rick Kangas, Grouse Mountain Grill, Beaver Creek
Ian Kleinmann, Hilltop Café, Golden
Stephen Kleinmann, Gasthaus Eichler, Winter Park, and Ian Kleinmann,
    Hilltop Café, Golden
Sean Kelly, Aubergine, Denver
Jesse Llapitan, Vail Cascade Resort and Spa, Vail
George Mahaffey, The Restaurant at the Little Nell, Little Nell Hotel, Aspen
James Oetting and Kim Heideman, Yia Yia's Eurocafé, Denver
Richard Sandoval, Tamayo, Denver

Robert Scherner, Allred's, Telluride, and Chad Scothorn, Cosmopolitan, Hotel
    Columbia, Telluride
Michael Shiell, Michael's, Cherry Creek, Denver
Charlie Stauter, Palomino Restaurant Rotisseria Bar, Denver
Kevin Taylor, Zenith American Grill, Denver
David Walford, Splendido at the Chateau, Beaver Creek
Tyler Wiard and Frank Bonanno, Mel's Bar and Grill, Denver
Bruce Yim, Sweet Basil, Vail
Matthew Zubrod, Willow Creek Bistro, Ritz-Carlton Club, Aspen

Out-of-House Events in Colorado

In conjunction with the 2000 *Food & Wine* Magazine Classic at Aspen, the James
Beard Foundation held what it calls an "out-of-house event" at SIX89 in Carbondale,
an all-Colorado event, starring:

Mark Fischer, SIX89, Carbondale
Thomas Colosi, Blue Maize, Aspen
Charles Dale, Renaissance and Rustique, Aspen
George Mahaffey, Conundrum, Aspen
Jason Rogers, Olives Aspen, St. Regis Aspen, Aspen

Another out-of-house event was held in August 2002 when SIX89 again hosted a
group of distinguished Colorado chefs (plus one from next-door New Mexico):

Mark Fischer, SIX89, Carbondale
Frank Bonanno, Mizuna, Denver
D. Barkley Dodge, Mogador, Aspen
Ryan Hardy, Coyote Café, Santa Fe, New Mexico
Chad Scothorn, Cosmopolitan, Hotel Columbia, Telluride
Glenn Smith, Cooking School of Aspen and G. H. Smith Catering, Aspen
Paul Wade, Montagna, The Little Nell Hotel, Aspen

Colorado Springs area chefs presided over an out-of-house event there in July 2000:

John Broening, Primitivo Wine Bar
Chris Adrian, La Petite Maison
Brent Beavers, Sencha
Marcus Giuliano, Walter's Bistro
Craig Hartman, The Cliff House, Manitou Springs
Ketil Larsen, The Phantom Canyon Brewing Company
Giovanni Russo, Cafe Giovanna
Nicholas Sonveau, Garden of the Gods

Food & Wine Best New Chefs in America

Since 1986, a group of young chefs has annually been named the Best New Chefs at the *Food & Wine* Magazine Classic in Aspen (see page 326). The Colorado honorees to date have been Charles Dale, Renaissance, Aspen, in 1995, James Mazzio, 15 Degrees, Boulder, in 1999, and Bryan Moscatello, Adega, in 2003. Owner-chef Dale has changed Renaissance to Range and owns its sister restaurant, Rustique. Mazzio went on to launch Triana, also in Boulder, and later opened ChefJam in Broomfield.

AAA Diamonds

The American Automobile Association (AAA) grants from one to five diamonds to restaurants, hotels, and resorts evaluated by full-time professional field representatives. They conduct annual unannounced visits and evaluate restaurants and accommodations throughout North America. The Five Diamond Award, a rare honor, is given to only an estimated 5 percent of the more than 10,000 AAA-approved restaurants and 5 percent of the nearly 24,000 hotels and resorts. For a restaurant, the rare Five Diamond award signifies "the ultimate in adult dining." Even a Four Diamond rating means extremely high quality in the opinion of the evaluators. Three Diamonds indicate an upscale, professional, and very commendable establishment that is suitable for both adult and family dining. A Two Diamond restaurant prepares food with standard ingredients and serves it attentively but far more informally in a comfortable setting that also may be trendy, casual, or upbeat. A One Star restaurant is a good, reliable place to eat in clean, pleasant surroundings. Though the ambience in the latter category is simple, it usually is awarded to a family or ethnic restaurant that serves basic, wholesome food.

To be considered for diamond awards, a restaurant must fill out an application and meet 12 specific criteria before evaluators visit. If you are interested in the fine points of the process and criteria, log onto www.aaabiz.com:8001/AdSales/production/diamond.html and www.aaabiz.com:8001/AdSales/production/dia_criteria.html. You can pick up a Colorado AAA *TourBook* with current ratings.

Mobil Stars

The *Mobil Travel Guides* award one to five stars to lodging properties and dining establishments. The criteria are defined in great detail, and I find them fascinating, because they provide insight into the persnickety process used to separate the outstanding from the ethereal.

The quality and preparation of the food and the fundamentals of fine service are only part of what Mobil looks for in awarding its treasured stars. There are only 38 Five Star lodging establishments in the country—3 in Colorado (The Broadmoor in Colorado Springs, the Little Nell Hotel in Aspen, and Tall Timbers near Durango). There are no Five Star restaurants in the state. Wonder why? Here is what Mobil requires of a Five Star restaurant:

Restaurant provides consistently superlative service to make it one of the best in the country. Guests at a Five-Star restaurant can expect all of the characteristics for a

Four-Star restaurant (below), plus:

Cocktails are carried from bar to table and check transferred automatically without request;

The guest's name is used effectively as a signal of recognition, but discreetly;

A sommelier is present and extremely helpful;

Mixed drinks are served with club service;

Wines ordered by the glass will be presented in the bottle and poured at the table;

Food is flawless, and a delightful and interesting experience;

Service is flawless; it is seamless from the first phone call to the departure following dinner;

A cheese course is offered;

Only solid cubes of ice are used (no hollow cubes);

Mignardise or petits fours are served at the conclusion of the meal;

Excellent quality and varying patterns of china ;

If a public phonebook is present, it is displayed in an attractive cover;

Public washrooms feature well-maintained cloth towels and fresh plants or flowers ;

Coats checked are anticipated and retrieved ahead of the guest ;

Upon departure, guests are escorted to the doorway and the door is opened for them.

A Four Star rating signifies an outstanding establishment with exceptional service and cuisine, but a notch lower in terms of formality. You can find the criteria for all Mobil star ratings at www.exxonmobiltravel.com/rating_criteria/index.cfm?act= RestaurantCriteria.

The Colorado restaurants currently holding Four Stars by Mobil are:

Conundrum, Aspen
Flagstaff House, Boulder
Restaurant Kevin Taylor, Hotel Teatro, Denver
Mirabelle, Beaver Creek
Montagna, Aspen
The Palace Arms Brown Palace Hotel, Denver
The Penrose Room, The Broadmoor, Colorado Springs
Piñons, Aspen
Q's, Hotel Boulderado, Boulder
Renaissance, Aspen
Splendido at The Chateau, Beaver Creek
Tante Louise, Denver
The Wildflower, The Lodge at Vail, Vail

Gabby Gourmet's "To Die For" Restaurants

Denver food writer and broadcaster Pat Miller (a.k.a. the Gabby Gourmet) publishes an annual called, of course, *The Gabby Gourmet Restaurant Guide.* She and her contributors describe and rate literally hundreds of Colorado restaurants, most of them along the Front Range and most of those in Denver. Although this is not a nationwide or international honor roll, a high ranking from the Gabby Gourmet is coveted by restaurateurs and chefs, and followed closely by her legions of fans. You can get more information on Gabby and her book at www.gabbygourmet.com, but if all you want to know is which eateries she feels are "to die for," this was her 2002 list:

240 Union, Denver
Aix, Denver
Barolo Grill, Denver
Carmine's on Penn, Denver
The Cliff House, Manitou Springs
Del Frisco's Double Eagle Steakhouse, Greenwood Village
Fourth Story Restaurant, Tattered Cover, Cherry Creek, Denver
Full Moon Grill, Boulder
Hilltop Café, Golden
India's, Denver
La Papillon, Denver
Little Ollie's, Denver
Marigold Café and Bakery, Colorado Springs
The Market on Larimer, Denver
Restaurant Kevin Taylor, Hotel Teatro, Denver
Mizuna, Denver
Morton's of Chicago, Denver
The Palm, Westin at Tabor Center, Denver
Panzano, Hotel Monaco, Denver
Primitivo, Colorado Springs
The Savoy, Berthoud
Strings, Denver
Tamayo, Denver
Tante Louise, Denver
Thai Bistro, Littleton
Vesta Dipping Grill, Denver

Appendix C

Colorado Farmers' Markets

Culinarians love Colorado's seasonal outdoor farmers' markets, which start with early-season herbs and bedding plants and end with fall's bounty of apples. Whenever and whatever farmers are harvesting, markets sell an abundance of newly picked produce. Farm-fresh produce abounds in the hot months of summer, as do the opportunities to meet growers, as well as cheese makers, bakers, and other purveyors of fresh foods. Some markets focus on certified organic products, while others offer conventionally grown produce or a mix from different growers. You can also expect to find honey, homemade jams and preserves, herbs, herbal teas, mustards and other condiments, artisan cheeses, fresh mushrooms, artisan breads, and other treats. Some markets also offer crafts, cut flowers, and/or a food court or food stands.

In addition, many farmers sell their products from roadside stands right at the farm, in town, or along a nearby highway. I've included several growers in the "Grand Junction and the Grand Valley" chapter (see page 352–353) and wish there were room for all. The Colorado Department of Agriculture, Colorado State University Cooperative Extension, and Colorado Proud, a promotional organization for locally produced foods, issues an annual "Colorado Farm Fresh" booklet. It lists farmers' markets, roadside and farm stands, and pick-your-own farms by region and is often inserted into local newspapers. Or you can request it by calling (303) 239-4114.

You can get general information on some farmers' markets by logging onto www.coloradofarmersmarket.com/locations.htm and on others from the state by contacting Jim Rubingh, Colorado Dept. of Agriculture, Markets Division, 700 Kipling Street, Suite 4000, Lakewood, CO 80215; (303) 239-4114 or e-mail jim.rubingh@ag.state.co.us. Days of operation, hours of operation, and length of season do change from year to year. Here are Colorado's seasonal farmers' markets, including phone or on-line contact information where available (otherwise, call the local Chamber of Commerce or visitors' information office):

Aspen Park/Conifer Farmers' Market

RTD Park & Ride lot (U.S. Highway 287 east of Conifer), Aspen Park
(303) 421-2076
Open Sundays, 10:00 A.M. to 2:00 P.M., late June to mid-September

Arvada Farmers' Market

5590 Olde Wadsworth Boulevard, Arvada
Open Thursdays, 9:00 A.M. to 2:00 P.M., from mid-June to late September

Aurora South Farmers' Market I (also called Denver Farmers' Market)

Buckingham Square Shopping Center (South Havana and Mississippi), Aurora
(303) 361-6169; e-mail: Daurorabus@aol.com
Open Tuesdays, 11:00 A.M. to sell-out, from late June to late October; Saturdays
from 7:00 A.M. to sell-out

Aurora Farmers' Market II

9750 East Colfax Avenue, Aurora
(303) 361-6169; e-mail: Daurorabus@aol.com
Open Tuesdays, 11:00 A.M. to sell-out, from late June to late October; Saturdays
from 7:00 A.M. to sell-out

Aurora South Farmers' Market II

15324 East Hampden Circle, Aurora
(303) 361-6169; e-mail: Daurorabus@aol.com
Open Wednesdays, 7:00 A.M. to sell-out, June through October

Boulder County Farmers' Market

13th Street between Arapahoe Avenue and Canyon Boulevard, Boulder
(303) 910-2236; e-mail: info@boulderfarmers.org; www.boulderfarmers.org
Open Saturdays, 8:00 A.M. to 2:00 P.M., early April through early November;
Wednesdays 4:00 to 8:00 P.M., mid-May through early October

Cañon City/Fremont County Farmers' Market

Holy Cross Abbey, U.S. Highway 50, Cañon City
(719) 275-1514; e-mail: fremont@coop.ext.colostate.edu or
stultzranch@earthlink.net
Open Wednesdays, 7:30 A.M. to 1:00 P.M., early June through early October

Centennial Farmers' Market

6911 University Boulevard, north end of Southglenn Mall (near Wells Fargo
Bank), Centennial
Open Tuesdays, 10:00 A.M. to 4:00 P.M., June through October

Cherry Creek Fresh Market

Bed, Bath, & Beyond parking lot, 1st Avenue and University, Denver (Cherry Creek)
(303) 449-1982
Open Saturdays, 7:30 A.M. to 12:30 P.M., early May through late October;
Wednesdays, 9:00 A.M. to 1:00 P.M., early June through late September

Collbran Farmers' Market

202 Main Street, Collbran
Open Saturdays, 9:00 A.M. to 12:00 noon, May through September

Colorado Springs Farmers' Market I (also called Pikes Peak Farmers' Market)

Acacia Park on Bijou and Nevada Streets, Colorado Springs
(719) 598-4215
Open Mondays, 7:00 A.M. to 1:30 P.M., mid-June through mid-October

Colorado Springs Farmers' Market II

24th Street and West Colorado Avenue, Colorado Springs
(719) 598-4215
Open Saturdays, 7:00 A.M. to 1:30 P.M., mid-June to mid-October

Colorado Springs Farmers' Market III

Memorial Park, East Pikes Peak Avenue and Union Boulevard, Colorado Springs
(719) 598-4215
Open Thursdays, 7:00 A.M. to 1:30 P.M., July to early October

Colorado Springs Farmers' Market IV

5225 East Platte Avenue, Colorado Springs
(719) 598-4215
Open Fridays, 7:00 A.M. to 1:00 P.M., June to September

Colorado Springs Farmers' Market V

4515 Barnes Road, Colorado Springs
Open Saturdays, 7:00 A.M. to 1:30 P.M., mid-June through mid-October

Cortez Farmers' Market I (also called Farmers' Market on Market Street)

25 North Market Street, Cortez
(970) 565-1151; e-mail: cultural@fone.net
Open Saturdays, 8:00 A.M. to 12:00 noon, mid-June through late October

Cortez Farmers' Market II (also called Montezuma County Farmers' Market)

Montezuma County Courthouse, 109 West Main Street, Cortez
(970) 565-3123; e-mail: ksmith@coop.ext.colostate.edu
Open Saturdays, 6:00 A.M. to sell-out, late July through November

Denver Farmers' Market

Main number: (303) 887-FARM; www.farmersmarket.com
City Park Esplanade, between 17th and Colfax, Denver
(303) 254-8451
Open Saturdays, 7:00 A.M. to sell-out, late June through late October; Sundays, 9:00 A.M. to 1:00 P.M., early June through late September

Buckingham Square (Havana and Mississippi), Denver
Open Tuesdays, 11:00 A.M. to sell-out, last week of June through late October

Broadway and Ridge Road, Littleton
Open Wednesdays, 11:00 A.M. to sell-out, last week of June through October

Villa Italia (Alameda and Wadsworth), Denver
Open Thursdays, 11:00 A.M. to sell-out, last week of June through October

Southwest Plaza (West Bowles and South Wadsworth), Denver
Open 8:00 A.M. to sell-out, first weekend of May through October

Marketplace at Northglenn (104th Street and Interstate 25), Northglenn
Open 8:00 A.M. to sell-out, last week of June through October

Larimer Square, 14th and Larimer Streets, downtown Denver
Open 8:00 A.M. to sell-out, last week of June through October

Dillon Farmers' Market

Marina Park parking lot, Lake Dillon Drive, Dillon
(970) 262-3402; e-mail: dillonpr@ci.dillon.co.us
Open Fridays, 9:00 A.M. to 1:00 P.M., late June through late September

Durango Farmers' Market

1st National Bank parking lot, 259 West Ninth Street, Durango
(970) 259-9339
Open Saturdays, 8:00 A.M. to 1:00 P.M., late June to late October

El Rancho Farmers' Market

Home Depot parking lot (I-70 and Evergreen Parkway), Evergreen
(303) 421-2076
Open Tuesdays, 10:00 A.M. to 2:00 P.M., early June through late October

Englewood Civic Center Farmers' Market

(303) 421-2076
Open Saturdays, 10:00 A.M. to 2:00 P.M., early June through late October

Estes Park Farmers' Market

2200 Mall Road, Estes Park
Open Thursdays, 8:00 A.M. to 1:00 P.M., early June through late September

Farm and Art Market

120 West First Street, Salida
(719) 539-1219; e-mail: farm_artmarket@bwn.net
Open Wednesdays, noon to 6:00 P.M., year-round (greenhouse produce is
available off-season)

FlatIron Crossing Fresh Market

FlatIron Crossing Village (U.S. 36 and Storage Tech Drive), Broomfield
Open Thursdays, 3:00 to 8:00 P.M., and Saturdays, 10:00 A.M. to 4:00 P.M.,
   June through October

Farmers' Market at Union Station

Wynkoop and 18th Streets (LoDo), Denver
(303) 628-5424
Open Sundays, 8:00 A.M. to 1:00 P.M. (noon on Colorado Rockies
   home game days), late June through October

Fort Collins Farmers' Market I

Larimer County Courthouse parking lot, Mountain and Mason Streets, Fort Collins
(970) 493-1427
Open Saturdays, 8:00 A.M. to 12:00 noon, early July through late September

Fort Collins Farmers' Market II

Market Centre (Steele's Market parking lot), 802 West Drake, Fort Collins
(970) 493-1427
Open Sundays, 9:00 A.M. to 1:00 P.M., early June through late September;
   Wednesdays, 2:00 to 6:00 P.M., early June through late September

Glenwood Springs Farmers' Market
(also called Farm Fresh Market of Glenwood Springs)

TruValue/Van Rand Shopping Center parking lot, 1605 Grand Avenue,
   Glenwood Springs
(970) 876-2850
Open Saturdays, 8:00 A.M. to 3:30 P.M., July through October

Grand Junction Farmers' Market I (also called F.A.R.M.,
for Farm and Ranch Market)

Teller Arms Shopping Center, 2401 North Avenue, Grand Junction
(970) 243-2446
Open Wednesdays and Saturdays, 7:00 A.M. to 12:00 noon, from mid-April
   through mid- to late November

Grand Junction Farmers' Market II

First and Colorado, Grand Junction
(970) 243-2446
Open Mondays and Fridays, 7:00 A.M. to 12:00 noon, early July through October

Greeley Farmers' Market at the Depot

902 Seventh Avenue, Greeley
(970) 350-9783
Open Saturdays, 7:30 A.M. to 11:00 A.M. and Wednesdays, 4:00 P.M. to 6:00 P.M.,
late June through late October

Lakewood Farmers' Markets

Villa Italia Mall parking lot, West Alameda and Wadsworth, and Southwest
Plaza Shopping Center I, South Wadsworth and West Bowles, Lakewood
Open Thursdays, 11:00 A.M. to sell-out, late June through late October

Larimer County Master Gardeners' Farmers' Market

1525 Blue Spruce Drive, Old Town Fort Collins
(970) 498-6000
Open Saturdays, 8:00 A.M. to noon, early July through late September

Littleton Farmers' Market

Littleton, Square Plaza Shopping Center II, Broadridge Plaza Shopping Center
(Broadway and Ridge Road), Littleton
Open Wednesdays, 11:00 A.M. to sell-out, late June to late October; Thursdays,
9:00 A.M. to 1:00 P.M., early June to late September

Longmont Farmers' Market

Boulder County Fairgrounds (northwest corner), Hover Road and Boston
Avenue, Longmont
www.longmontfarmers.com
Open Saturdays, 8:00 A.M. to 1:00 P.M., early June through late October;
Mondays and Tuesdays, 3:00 to 6:00 P.M., mid-July 11 to mid-September

Louisville Downtown Farmers' Market

908 Main Street, Louisville
Open Saturdays, 9:00 A.M. to 2:00 P.M., late June or early July through late
September

Loveland Farmers' Market

Lincoln & 5th Streets, Loveland
Open Tuesdays, 2:00 to 6:00 P.M., July through late October

Market at Sloan's Lake

Sloan's Lake parking lot (25th and Sheridan), Denver
Open Thursdays, 9:00 A.M. to 2:00 P.M., mid-June through late September

Montrose/Uncompahgre Farmers' Market

Stough Street, two blocks north of Main Street, Montrose
(970) 249-9725
Open Saturdays, 8:30 A.M. to 1:00 P.M., late April through late October, and
  Wednesdays, 8:30 A.M. to 1:00 P.M., mid-July through late September

Northglenn Farmers' Market

Northglenn Market Place (104th Street and I-25, north end of Melody Drive
  near Marshalls), Northglenn
Open Fridays, 7:00 A.M. to sell-out, late June through late October

Old South Pearl Street Farmers' Market

Old South Pearl Street (between Buchtel and Evans), Denver
Open Sundays, 10:00 A.M. to 2:00 P.M., mid-June through late September

Parker Farmers' Market

Mainstreet Center, Parker
Open Sundays, 8:30 A.M. to 11:00 A.M., mid-May through October

Pikes Peak Farmers' Market

Acacia Park, Nevada and Bijou Streets, Colorado Springs
(719) 574-1283
Open Mondays, 7:00 A.M. to 1:30 P.M., mid-June through mid-October

Plum Creek Valley Farmers' Market

Human Services Building parking lot (100 Third Street), Castle Rock
(303) 660-7312; e-mail: douglas@coop.ext.colostate.edu
Open Sundays, 8:00 A.M. to 12:00 noon, mid-July through late September

Pueblo Farmers' Market

Midtown Shopping Center (West Sixth Street), Pueblo
(719) 583-6566
Open Fridays, 7:00 A.M. to 1:00 P.M., early to mid-July to early to mid-October

Ridgway Farmers' Market

Ouray County Fairgrounds (U.S. Highway. 550 and Colorado 62), Ridgway
(970) 626-9775; e-mail: jbennett@co.ouray.co.us
Open Sundays, 8:00 A.M. to 1:00 P.M., June through September

Teller County Farmers' Market

Kavanaugh Parking Area (turn from U.S. 24 at Vectra Bank onto West Street),
  Woodland Park
(719) 689-2503 or (719) 689-3133
Open Fridays, 7:00 A.M. to 1:00 P.M., late June through early September

Vail Farmers' Market

Village Park, Meadow Drive, Vail
Open Sundays, 10:00 A.M. to 4:00 P.M., June through September

Westminster Farmers' Market

City Park, 105th and Sheridan, Westminster
Open Sundays, 10:00 A.M. to 4:00 P.M., June through October

Windsor Farmers' Market

Pioneer Village Museum, 116 North Fifth Street, Windsor
(970) 686-6404; e-mail: generalstore@earthlink.net
Open Thursdays 4:00 to 7:00 P.M., mid-July through September

Winter Park Farmers' Market

King's Crossing, U.S. Highway 50, downtown Winter Park
(303) 421-2076
Suspended for 2003; call for day and time in 2004 and beyond.

Index